The Law Relating to Receivers, Managers and Administrators

*This edition is dedicated to the memory of
two Avocats à la Cour d'Appel de Paris*

My father

Pierre Adrien Picarda (1897–1985)

Docteur en Droit
Barrister of the Middle Temple
Chevalier de la Légion d'Honneur
Croix de Guerre, Médaille Militaire

and

My grandfather

Emile Picarda (1873–1942)

Docteur en Droit
Professeur de Législations Commerciales
Étrangères à l'Institut Commercial
Author of *Précis de Législations
Commerciales Étrangères* (Paris, 1903)

The Law Relating to
Receivers, Managers and Administrators

Third edition

Hubert Picarda BCL, MA(Oxon)
One of Her Majesty's Counsel
of the Inner Temple, Lincoln's Inn and Gray's Inn
Profumo Scholar of the Inner Temple

Butterworths
London, Edinburgh, Dublin
2000

United Kingdom	Butterworths, a Division of Reed Elsevier (UK) Ltd, Halsbury House, 35 Chancery Lane, LONDON WC2A 1EL and 4 Hill Street, EDINBURGH EH2 3JZ
Australia	Butterworths, a Division of Reed International Books Australia Pty Ltd, CHATSWOOD, New South Wales
Canada	Butterworths Canada Ltd, MARKHAM, Ontario
Hong Kong	Butterworths Asia (Hong Kong), HONG KONG
India	Butterworths India, NEW DELHI
Ireland	Butterworth (Ireland) Ltd, DUBLIN
Malaysia	Malayan Law Journal Sdn Bhd, KUALA LUMPUR
New Zealand	Butterworths of New Zealand Ltd, WELLINGTON
Singapore	Butterworths Asia, SINGAPORE
South Africa	Butterworths Publishers (Pty) Ltd, DURBAN
USA	Lexis Law Publishing, CHARLOTTESVILLE, Virginia

 A member of the Reed Elsevier plc group

A CIP Catalogue record for this book is available from the British Library.

First edition   1984
Second edition   1990

ISBN 0 406 91346 3

Typeset by Phoenix Photosetting, Chatham, Kent
Printed by Redwood Books, Trowbridge, Wiltshire

Visit Butterworths LEXIS *direct* at: http://www.butterworths.com

Coventry University

Preface

The last edition of this book appeared some three years after the enactment of the Insolvency Act 1986 and hard on the heels of the arrival on the statute book of the Companies Act 1989. Ten years of case law and some significant statutory changes have now had to be accommodated in what was already a bulky, indeed overweight, book. With reluctance I have had to jettison the Appendices of Statutes, Rules and Company Forms. Insolvency practitioners will almost inevitably have to hand the English insolvency legislation and rules and I can take comfort from the fact that the Far Eastern materials are to be reproduced in my forthcoming *Receivers and Managers in the Far East* (Butterworths Asia). I have in consequence had more space to cover the substantive law, a significant *quid pro quo*.

Much of interest happened during the last decade of the twentieth century. The collapse of Paramount Airways, the Maxwell empire, BCCI, and Polly Peck have all generated considerable litigation. Important jurisprudential points have engaged the attention of the appellate courts. The duties of mortgagees and receivers in relation to sale and management, and the much criticised decision in *Downsview Nominees v First City Corpn* [1993] AC 295, have been subjected to scrutiny by the Court of Appeal in *Medforth v Blake* [2000] Ch 86. The controversial appellate decision in *Re New Bullas Trading* [1994] 1 BCLC and its rejection by the New Zealand Court of Appeal in *Re Brumark Investments* [2000] 1 BCLC 353 have revived lively discussion of the criteria for distinguishing fixed from floating charges. I have added my voice to the chorus in a recent article 'Labels: a Voyage Round Fixed and Floating Charges'[1] written after the copy of this edition had been delivered to the publishers. *Brumark* is going to the Privy Council and the article was able to explore the most recent authorities in more depth than was possible in a textbook and to rehearse the opposing arguments anew, and in advance of what it is devoutly hoped will be a much needed clarification of the law by the Privy Council.

It has also been necessary to make substantial revisions in the chapters which discuss employees' rights and the adoption of contracts, following the various decisions in the *Paramount Airways* case and the ensuing urgent legislative reforms introduced by the Insolvency Act (No 2) 1994. Account has been taken of the court procedural reforms and the changes in terminology associated with them.

Following the practice in previous editions interesting new cases from the Commonwealth have been incorporated into this edition in an effort to increase its usefulness. Among many others there are from Australia, *Fire Nymph Products Ltd v*

1 [2000] 4 RALQ 109–136.

Heating Centre Pty Ltd [1992] 7ACSR 365 from New Zealand, *Supercool and Refrigeration and Airconditioning v Hovard Industries Ltd* [1994] 3 NZLR 300 and *Re Brumark Investments Ltd* [2000] 1 BCLC 353, and from Singapore *Dresdner Bank AG v Ho Mun Tuke Don* [1993] 1 SLR 114 and *Chase Manhattan Bank NA v Wong Tui San* [1993] 11 ACLC3, 112. I have also continued to pay just due to articles in the legal journals and, where appropriate, to other text writers.

Court-appointed receivers have attracted their due share of space in the law reports with a leading decision on remuneration of such receivers in *Mirror Group Newspapers v Maxwell (No 2)* [1998] 1 BCLC 638.

The case law in the field of administration has mirrored the growth of this part of the corporate rescue culture and I have done my best to compress into digestible portions of prose all that has happened here. Some of the cases have been of primarily procedural effect but others explore substantive issues within the procedure.

I was the first textbook writer to address conflict of laws problems in relation to receivers and administrators and since the last edition there has been much comment on and movement in this area too. All this has necessitated substantial revision of Chapter 40 and reconsideration of the vexed problem of whether there is an original jurisdiction to appoint an administrator over a foreign company.

Pleasurable though the business of research has been, I have, nevertheless, at times felt like Sisyphus pushing a huge boulder uphill, only to see it relentlessly roll back. But my task has been lightened by the cheerful efficiency of the editorial staff at Butterworth Tolley to whom I am most grateful, as I am to those who have prepared the Tables of Cases and Statutes and Index. Separate and several thanks are also due to the librarians and staff of the libraries of the three Inns of Court to which I belong, of the Squire Law Library at Cambridge, of the Bodleian Law Library at Oxford and of the National University of Singapore.

I should also thank first, all those solicitors and accountants whose instructions and reports respectively have, over the last 10 years, yielded me so much quarried material. Secondly, I must, with no less warmth, thank successive professional audiences in the Far East, particularly in Singapore, for providing me with stimulating questions that have, I hope, provoked fresh insights on my part. All these contributions have been of the greatest assistance to me in the process of revising this book.

Lastly, and chiefly, I owe an enormous debt of gratitude to my wife Sarah for her enduring patience and encouragement. Sisyphus had no such touchline supporter. It is for all these reasons that I hope it will be possible to say of this latest edition, as the Roman poet Martial said of one of his books, that the labour bestowed on it was not wasted:

'securus erit nec inquieta lassi marmora Sisyphi videbit'[2]

As always, suggestions for improvement will be genially entertained.

The text reflects my best efforts to track down as many relevant cases as possible up to 1 September 2000.

Hubert Picarda QC
3 New Square
Lincoln's Inn
London WC2A 3RS

---

2 'It will be free from anxiety and will not be looking at the restless marble block of weary Sisyphus.' Mart 5.80.11. For the Sisyphus tale, see Ovid *Metamorphoses* 4. 460.

Contents

Table of Statutes

PAGE

Foreign Legislation

Table of Cases

C

H

Q

R

CHAPTER 1

Introduction

DEFINITION

The law relating to receivers and managers[1] encompasses an important and flexible equitable remedy invented by the Court of Chancery and a more modern extra-curial remedy usually operating pursuant to an agreement made between lender and borrower. For this reason it is difficult to distil in one or two sentences the meaning of the terms 'receiver' and 'receiver and manager'. The functions of a court receiver and a 'private' or extra-curial (or out of court) receiver resemble each other in many respects but in others they differ.

Nevertheless it may be considered helpful to consider first the terminology used in the courts where the equitable remedy is being invoked, before turning to the task of defining the equivalent terms in relation to the 'contractual' remedy, in which we must distinguish administrative receivers (as creatures of the Insolvency Act 1986 (IA 1986)) from other private receivers.

Equitable remedy

In Viner's *Abridgement of Law and Equity*[2] the term 'receiver' is defined as follows:

> 'A receiver is an indifferent person between the parties, appointed by the Court to receive the rents, issues or profits of land or other thing in question in this Court, pending the suit, where it does not seem reasonable to the Court that either party should do it; and he is to account for such his receipt when the Court shall require him. And to secure his doing so, he is commonly ordered to enter into a recognizance with such sureties in such sum as the Court directs.'

Perhaps the classic definition of the terms is that of Sir George Jessel MR in *Re Manchester and Milford Rly Co*:[3]

---

1 As opposed at the law relating to administrators under the Insolvency Act 1986.
2 (1793) Vol 18 *Abridgement of Law and Equity* 160.
3 (1880) 14 Ch D 645 at 653, CA.

'A "receiver" is a term which was well known in the Court of Chancery, as meaning a person who receives rents or other income paying ascertained out-goings, but who does not, if I may say so, manage the property in the sense of buying or selling or anything of that kind. We were most familiar with the distinction in the case of a partnership. If a receiver was appointed of partner-ship assets, the trade stopped immediately. He collected debts, sold the stock-in-trade and other assets, and then under the order of the court the debts of the concern were liquidated and the balance divided. If it was desired to continue the trade at all it was necessary to appoint a manager, or a receiver and manager as it was generally called. He could buy and sell and carry on the trade.'

There is, therefore a well-drawn distinction between the two terms 'receiver' and 'manager'. The receiver merely takes the income, and pays necessary outgoings, and the manager carries on the trade or business.[4] The same distinction was well known also in the working of mines. If a receiver only was appointed the working of the mine was stopped,[5] but if it was desired to continue the working of the mine, a receiver and manager was necessary.[6]

Despite the careful distinction drawn by Sir George Jessel MR between a receiver and a receiver and manager, it has become commonplace to refer to the latter as a receiver *simpliciter*.[7] A debenture holder's 'receiver' is almost invariably a receiver and manager. Moreover this legal shorthand is reflected in the section in the Supreme Court Act 1981 (SCA 1981) dealing with the court's jurisdiction to appoint a receiver: there is no specific reference to the power to appoint a manager.[8] It should also be noted that the receiver by way of equitable execution is a very special kind of receiver. In the exercise of equitable execution a receiver would be given the power to sell the personalty and distribute the proceeds of such sale and the rents and profits of real estate, subject to his receivership, to the judgment creditors.

A similar blurring of terminology occurs in the case of extra-curial or privately appointed receivers. It has always been the case that a statutory receiver, that is, one appointed under what is now the Law of Property Act 1925 (LPA 1925), has power only to receive income.[9] Such a receiver is a receiver pure and simple, and in no way a manager. But debentures usually contain a power for the receiver to carry on business.[10] A receiver so empowered is usually termed a receiver although he is in effect a 'receiver and manager'.[11] Sometimes, of course, he is specifically constituted as a receiver and manager. If the debenture provides that

---

4 (1880) 14 Ch D 645 at 653.
5 *Gloucester County Bank v Rudry Merthyr Steam and House Coal Colliery Co* [1895] 1 Ch 629, 64 LJ Ch 451, CA.
6 [1895] 1 Ch 629, 64 LJ Ch 451, CA.
7 For example the relevant title of *Halsbury's Laws of England* 4th edn is entitled 'Receivers' and many text books 'telescope' the term; see *Kerr on Receivers* (17th edn); Hooper *Receivers for Debenture Holders* (1933); *Snell's Principles of Equity* (30th edn 2000); Meagher Gummow and Lehane *Equity: Doctrines and Remedies* (3rd edn) (1984).
8 SCA 1981, s 37.
9 See LPA 1925, s 101(1)(iii).
10 See eg, *Bompas v King* (1886) 33 Ch D 279, CA (mortgagee given power to manage).
11 Hooper *Receivers for Debenture Holders* (1933) p 19.

a receiver and manager may be appointed, the debenture holder may not appoint a non-managing receiver.[12] Conversely, where the debenture authorises the appointment of a receiver it is not open to the lender to appoint a receiver and manager,[13] unless of course the debenture clearly authorises him to carry on the business of the company.[14]

HISTORY

Court-appointed receiver

The history of the equitable remedy of appointing a receiver has, surprisingly, attracted little attention, and could usefully engage the diligence of legal historians.[15] The remedy appears to have surfaced in the Court of Chancery in the second half of the sixteenth century as a supplement to common law and statutory remedies which were proving inadequate. The first bill that is to be met with for restraining a party from receiving rents and profits is in the reign of Edward VI.[16] The appointment of sequestrators and receivers of rents and profits, which became very common in the reign of Elizabeth I, would naturally have started about the same time. In *Jordan v Armes*[17] property was sequestered into the hands of the Chamberlain of London and one of the aldermen pending the trial of the right at law and later a sequestrator or receiver of land and personal estate was appointed. Echoes of the remedy's antiquity are to be found in random references by later judges. Thus Giffard V-C in *Hopkins v Worcester and Birmingham Canal (Proprietors)*[18] described it as 'one of the oldest remedies in this court'.

The appointment by the court of a receiver and manager is also an equitable remedy albeit 'a far more modern one'.[19] It emerged as a remedy in connection with partnership disputes where the subject matter in dispute was a business which would need to be run until sale or other resolution of the dispute. But its application was directed to other situations as the law of companies expanded and new forms of security were devised covering business as well as properties.

The equitable remedy granted by the Court of Chancery to alleviate the harshness of the common law was, ex hypothesi, not available in the courts of common law. This rigid separation of common law and equity came to an end with the enactment of the Supreme Court of Judicature Act 1873. Section 16 of that Act vested all the jurisdiction of the Court of Chancery in the High Court of Justice. And s 25(8) of the 1873 Act provided that a receiver might be appointed

---

12 *Harold Meggitt Ltd v Discount Finance Ltd* (1938) 56 WNNSW 23.
13 (1938) 56 WNNSW 23.
14 *Re Odessa Promotions Pty Ltd (in liquidation)* (1979) ACLC 32 at 103.
15 The remedy is barely touched upon in Holdsworth *History of English Law*. For an American summary, see 9 St Louis L Rev 111–117.
16 *Savell v Ramsden* Cal i cxxxi.
17 20 May 1588: Reg Lib 5 P & M fol 48.
18 (1868) LR 6 Eq 437, 37 LJ Ch 729.
19 *Re Newdigate Colliery Ltd* [1912] 1 Ch 468 at 472, CA by Cozens Hardy MR.

by interlocutory order in all cases where it appears to the court to be just and convenient that such an order be made and it might be made either unconditionally or upon such terms and conditions as the court thinks fit. The modern formulation of the jurisdiction is to be found now in s 37 of the Supreme Court Act 1981.

The history of the rather special receivership by way of equitable execution shows it to be a remedy which developed later than the equitable relief by way of sequestration but which, once emergent, quickly supplanted sequestration in importance as an equitable remedy. The growth of the remedy in the nineteenth century is touched upon elsewhere in this book.[20]

Privately appointed receiver

The emergence of the privately appointed receiver was a nineteenth century phenomenon. It dawned on conveyancers in that period that time and expense could be saved by incorporating into agreements, particularly agreements made between borrowers and lenders, provisions enabling the lender, without reference to the court, to appoint a receiver to protect his interest in the security given for the loan. The most obvious circumstance was in the contract of mortgage of land. It soon became common practice for conveyancers to write into the mortgage document provisions enabling the mortgagee of land upon default by the mortgagor to appoint a receiver, to receive the rents and profits of the land. Where the mortgage included a business the security document went further and provided for the appointment of a manager of the business or a receiver and manager. Then, what conveyancers were wont to express was made the subject of express statutory implication, where the mortgage was by deed.[1]

Latterly the private receiver and manager has been most commonly encountered in company charges. In an era of inflation, high interest rates and expensive litigation, the debenture holder's application for the appointment of a receiver and manager has, in this country, become virtually obsolete. Modern business requirements necessitate quick decisions which cannot be achieved by successive applications, at no small cost, to the court. The private receiver and manager, not shackled by constant answerability to the court, is therefore, from the lender's point of view, an attractive intermediary.

While, therefore, court receiverships still have a role to play, especially where assets of an income bearing nature are in jeopardy, the private receiver is a far more common creature. It is for that reason that, after some preliminary general observations about the two species, the private receiver will be given pride of place and preliminary treatment in this work.

---

20 See at p 376 below. For more detailed discussion of the development of equitable execution in England see Huston *The Enforcement of Decrees in Equity* (1915) pp 71–86; Millar *Civil Procedure of the Trial Court in Historical Perspective* (1952) pp 422–426, 437–442; CRB Dunlop *Creditor Debtor Law in Canada* (1981) pp 278–291 which also, of course, deals with its development in Canada at pp 292–306.

1 See Conveyancing Act 1881, s 19(1), (iii) and LPA 1925, s 101.

It would, however, be a mistake to treat court receiverships as a dead letter. In partnership disputes receivership is often ordered.[2] There are other areas, too, where receivership, under the aegis of the court, has a part to play: disputes between directors[3] or shareholders,[4] actions for specific performance,[5] and actions to enforce a vendor's lien[6] are perhaps the most obvious cases. There has even been a recent reminder that a court-appointed receiver may be appointed over the property of a charity.[7]

PURPOSE

Court-appointed receiver

The purpose and function of a court-appointed receiver depend very much upon the particular context in which he is appointed. In most cases such a receiver has been appointed because assets which are in dispute are also in jeopardy. The purpose and function of a receiver or receiver and manager are to act as a caretaker pending the resolution of the dispute. But the receiver's function may be different if the appointment is sought to enforce a judgment debt or a security. In such cases sale is the ultimate object and receivership a means to that end.

Privately appointed receiver

An extra-curial receiver is, as has already been remarked, most commonly appointed under the express or statutorily implied[8] powers in a mortgage, or other form of fixed or floating charge.[9] Apart from the case where statute confers the power to appoint a receiver because the parties have agreed to use a deed as the method of constituting a mortgage or charge, there are certain other cases where statutes give powers which can lead to the appointment of a receiver. The statutes in question include the Public Health Act 1936, the Housing Act 1985 and the Highways Act 1980. These last-mentioned statutes confer powers on

2 See ch 21 at p 326.
3 *Stansfield v Gibbon* [1925] WN 11; *Featherstone v Cooke* (1873) LR 16 Eq 298; and see *Trade Auxiliary Co v Vickers* (1873) LR 16 Eq 303.
4 See (1980) 1 Co Law 7 noting an unreported decision of Templeman J; *Duffy v Super Centre Development Corpn Ltd* [1967] 1 NSWR 382.
5 *Stilwell v Wilkins* (1821) Jac 280.
6 *Poole v Downes* (1897) 76 LT 110; and see *A-G v Wright* (1841) 3 Beav 447.
7 *A-G v Schonfeld* [1980] 3 All ER 1, [1980] 1 WLR 1182; an earlier example not cited to Sir Robert Megarry V-C was *A-G v St Cross Hospital* (1856) 8 De GM & G 38 at 41–42 (receiver and manager). The order appointing a receiver and manager was made by Walton J. For a description, see [1979] Ch Com Rep 19, paras 46–51. See further at 339 below. The Charity Commissioners are now empowered to appoint a receiver and manager whose functions and powers are very much sui generis: see the Charities Act 1993, ss 18 and 19 and the Charities (Receiver and Manager) Regulations 1992, SI 1992/2355.
8 See LPA 1925, s 101.
9 Debentures are conventionally secured by a floating (or fixed and floating) charge. See the discussion at p 13 below.

local authorities to enforce statutory provisions relating to real property.[10] A receiver appointed under one of these statutes is a rare bird.

In the New South Wales case of *Duffy v Super Centre Development Corpn Ltd*[11] Street J (as he then was) in discussing the role of the privately appointed receiver of a company said that such a receiver to some extent makes an effort to restore the financial prosperity of the company. The view, as one commentator has observed,[12] is a rosy picture. The publicity usually attaching to what the press refers to as 'calling in the receiver' is inevitably damaging. Far from being the company doctor he is probably thought of more as the undertaker or financial priest coming to administer last rites.

In fact none of the colourful similes is entirely satisfactory. Receivership commonly is, in the case of a company, the prelude to liquidation. The receiver salvages what he can of the undertaking of which he is appointed receiver and manager. His salvage may be total, in which case the company survives and the debenture holder is satisfied. Or the debenture holder is satisfied, and the company survives in attenuated form. Or, finally, the company may go under.

Differences

Some of the more important legal differences need emphasis at this stage. A receiver appointed by the court is an officer of the court; his acts are the acts of the court. He does not act as agent for anyone and is not a trustee. Any interference with his possession and the conduct of his receivership is a contempt of court. In contrast, a receiver appointed out of court is, ex hypothesi, *not* an officer of the court. Interference with his possession can ground a civil action but not, of course, any committal application. He is either agent for his appointor or, where provision is made to that effect, deemed agent for the borrower. For reasons which will be explained later an express provision is often inserted in debentures specifying that the receiver shall be the agent of the company.

RECEIVERS AND MANAGERS IN THE COMPANIES ACTS

The Companies Acts distinguished between the following types of receiver and manager:

(a)   a receiver of the property of a company;[13]

(b)   a receiver or manager of the property of a company;[14]

---

10 See at p 314, below.
11 [1967] 1 NSWR 382.
12 JH Farrar 'Recent Developments in the Law of Receivers' (1975) JBL 23 at 24.
13 Companies Act 1985 (CA 1985), s 489 (repealed) re-enacting the Companies Act 1948 (CA 1948), s 366 (repealed) (disqualification of body corporate as receiver).
14 See, eg, CA 1985, ss 493 and 499 (repealed) re-enacting CA 1948, ss 370 and 375 as amended (repealed).

(c)   a receiver or manager of the whole, or substantially the whole, of the property of a company;[15]
(d)   a receiver or manager of the property of a company appointed under the powers contained in any instrument.[16]

Each of the foregoing except (d) could be either court, or privately appointed. A receiver or manager in category (d) will ex hypothesi be a private receiver or manager. It is pertinent also to note that under the Companies Acts, except where the context otherwise required, (i) any reference to a receiver or manager of the property of a company, or to a receiver thereof included a reference to a receiver or manager, or as the case might be to a receiver of *part* only of the property and to a receiver only of the income arising from that property, or from part thereof; and (ii) any reference to the appointment of a receiver or manager under powers contained in any instrument included a reference to an appointment made under powers which by virtue of any enactment are implied in and take effect as if contained in an instrument.[17]

The new insolvency legislation attributes a similar meaning to the terms 'receiver or manager' of a company and to 'receiver' of it where these terms appear in the Companies Act 1985 or the Insolvency Act 1986.[18] (IA 1986). Accordingly, 'receiver and manager', or 'receiver', is defined and includes partial receiverships. However, the major innovation is the distinction drawn between administrative receivers and other receivers or managers.

ADMINISTRATIVE RECEIVER

The term 'administrative receiver' was introduced by the insolvency legislation following the Cork Report. It is defined in a statutory provision which comprise two limbs. According to s 29 of the Insolvency Act 1986 an administrative receiver is:

> '(a) a receiver or manager of the whole[19] (or substantially the whole) of a company's property appointed by or on behalf of the holders of any debentures of the company secured by a charge which, as created, was a floating charge, or by such a charge and one or more other securities;[20] or
> (b) a person who would be such a receiver or manager but for the appointment of some other person as the receiver of part of the company's property.'[1]

---

15 See, eg, CA 1985, ss 495–498 (repealed) re-enacting CA 1948, ss 372–374 as amended (repealed).
16 See, eg, CA 1985, ss 492, 494 and 498 (repealed) re-enacting CA 1948, ss 369, 371 and 374(1) as amended (repealed).
17 CA 1985, s 500 (repealed) re-enacting CA 1948, s 376 (repealed).
18 IA 1986, s 29(1) repeating substantially the language of CA 1985, s 500 set out above.
19 As determined at the date of appointment.
20 IA 1986, s 29(1). Bank charges usually charge *all* the property to secure administrative receivership.
1 IA 1986, s 29(2).

The first limb of this definition reflects the language of provisions[2] in the Companies Act 1985 prescribing a quantitative test by reference (it is thought) primarily to the value of each part to the company. The second limb enables a subsequent chargee to appoint an administrative receiver.

The Insolvency Act 1986 contains some provisions applicable only to administrative receivers and some which apply to receivers and managers of the property of a company generally. Provisions of the latter kind apply both to administrative receivers, and to receivers and managers of part only of the assets of the company ('non-administrative receivers').

There is some debate as to whether the statutory definition of administrative receiver is apt to include a court-appointed receiver. A court-appointed receiver is strictly appointed by the court. The expression 'appointed by or on behalf of the holders of any debentures of the company' is appropriate to cover appointments out of court by the debenture holders themselves or by trustees on their behalf. It is not appropriate to cover an appointment by the court since the court does not appoint on behalf of debenture holders, and a court-appointed receiver is not the agent of the debenture holders. Accordingly one must conclude that a court-appointed receiver cannot fall within the definition of administrative receiver.

SEQUESTRATOR

The position of a court-appointed receiver should be compared with that of a sequestrator[3] appointed by the court.

The writ of sequestration is frequently classified as a writ of execution.[4] But as Chitty J observed in *Pratt v Inman*,[5] sequestration 'unquestionably was and is a process of contempt'. In earlier times it was used to enforce appearance in the courts but it is now used to coerce a contemnor to comply with orders of the court. The proceedings on a writ of sequestration are in rem not in personam.[6] The writ is effective from the date of its issue and not its execution, and binds real and personal property as soon as it is issued.[7] But the res must be within the jurisdiction or in a jurisdiction which will recognise the writ and authorise the sequestrators to seize the property in question.

The effect of the writ is well described by Windeyer J in *Australian Consolidated Press Ltd v Morgan*:[8]

---

2 CA 1985, ss 495–498 (repealed) re-enacting CA 1948, ss 372–374 (repealed).
3 See Sir Jack Jacob 'Sequestration for Contempt of Court' (1986) Current Legal Problems 221; Gavin Lightman QC 'A Trade Union in Chains: Scargill Unbound – The Legal Constraints of Receivership and Sequestration' (1987) Current Legal Problems 25–54.
4 See 17 *Halsbury's Laws* (4th edn) 309, para 5.
5 (1889) 43 Ch D 175 at 179. It is founded on an existing contempt only: *Hulbert and Crowe v Cathcart* [1894] 1 QB 244. See also *Burne v Robinson* (1844) 7 I Eq R 188 and *Meyers v Meyers* (1874) 21 Gr 214 (Can).
6 *Re Suarez* [1918] 1 Ch 176 at 181, CA per Swinfen Eady LJ and *Tatham v Parker* (1855) 22 LJ Ch 903 at 904 per Stuart V-C.
7 *Burdett v Rockley* (1682) 1 Vern 58; *Dixon v Rowe* (1876) 35 LT 548.
8 (1965) 39 ALJR 32 at 40.

'When the property of a contemnor is actually sequestered and held under sequestration it is not confiscated. The contemnor is deprived of the enjoyment of his rents and profits for the duration of the sequestration; but he does not forfeit his property in them. When whatever is considered necessary to purge the contempt has been done, the sequestrator is discharged by the order of the court: and the sequestrator must then give up possession as having those costs and expenses.'

In other words, the writ does not effect a change of title but simply a change of possession. The sequestrated property remains the property of the contemnor: the writ vests in the sequestrators the right to possession of all the contemnor's assets except for those assets vested in the contemnor as trustee.[9] The writ of sequestration does not, it should be added, give the person issuing the writ any charge over the property seized.[10]

A party whose property is subjected to a receivership order does have a voice to object to the identity of a receiver if for example the receiver does not measure up to the rule of practice that 'some indifferent person ought to be appointed'.[11] The contemnor faced with a sequestrator has no voice in the matter:

'the sequestrators are named by the Plaintiff, or the party who applies for the sequestrations; the court hath no concern in the perpetuity of the nomination; and they do not give security for what they receive'.[12]

A receiver appointed by the court usually does give security.[13]

On the other hand, both sequestrators and receivers may be liable for negligence.[14]

The sequestrator has priority over the receiver and if there is a receiver appointed and a sequestrator is still in office the receiver must account to the sequestration.[15] Since sequestration is a penal order this may have repercussions if a parallel receivership is attempted to be enforced in another jurisdiction, which recognises and enforces foreign receivership orders. In such circumstances the enforcement of the receivership order might be said indirectly to be an enforcement of a foreign penal order.[16]

COMMONWEALTH LAW

The equitable remedy of receivership is no parochial remedy. It has travelled to and settled in many jurisdictions in the common law world. Thus it flourishes

---

9 *Con-Mech (Engineers) Ltd v Amalgamated Union of Engineering Workers* [1973] ICR 620 at 627.
10 *Re Pollard, ex p Pollard* [1903] 2 KB 41 at 47, CA.
11 *Fripp v Chard Rly Co* (1853) 11 Hare 241 at 261.
12 *Rowley v Ridley* (1784) 2 Dick 622 at 630.
13 See below.
14 *IRC v Hoogstraten* [1985] QB 1077, [1984] 3 All ER 25, CA.
15 So held in the receivership ordered in *Clarke v Heathfield* [1985] ICR 203, CA.
16 Cf *Larkins v National Union of Mineworkers* [1985] IR 671; and see p 622 below.

with statutory encouragement in Canada,[17] Australia,[18] New Zealand[19] and many other parts of the Commonwealth. The same applies to the contractual remedy or private receiver. All the jurisdictions just mentioned are familiar with the use of a private receiver to enforce securities: mortgages, mortgage debentures and statutory charges. Caution is nonetheless necessary in dealing with Commonwealth authorities in some contexts. For example in the field of company law the exact wording of the relevant company law statute must be referred to. In this connection it is germane to point out that although the company law statutes of Singapore and Malaysia closely follow the now repealed Australian Uniform Companies Act,[20] the Companies Ordinance in Hong Kong is based on the English Companies Act 1929 with some amendments. In Canada the private type of receivership has attracted some legislative control over the last decade or so,[1] These legislative interventions are beyond the scope of this work. Indeed, with the exception of some provisions of particular comparative interest references to overseas statutes will largely be eschewed. For the convenience of practitioners in Hong Kong, Malaysia and Singapore, however, some attempt has been made to make this book more helpful by the citation of the more important case law decisions in these jurisdictions.

Despite these formal caveats it remains to be said that Commonwealth experience particularly in the field of private receivers and especially in Australia and New Zealand provides very considerable assistance to the solution of problems in this country. It is significant that the Cork Committee,[2] for example, turned to antipodean experience; and now not only commentators in legal journals and periodicals, but also judges look to the Southern hemisphere and Canada for illumination and debate.

---

17 See Judicature Act (Rev 1980), s 19 (Ontario).
18 Supreme Court Act 1970, s 67 (NSW); Supreme Court Act 1958, s 62(2) (Vic); Supreme Court Civil Procedure Act 1932, s 11(12) (Tas); Judicature Act 1876, s 5(8) (Qld); Supreme Court Act 1935, s 25(9) (WA); Supreme Court Act 1935, s 29(1) (SA). The leading work on the Australian law is O'Donovan *Company Receivers and Managers* (2nd edn, 1992) with looseleaf updates; and see also Blanchard and Gedye *The Law of Company Receiverships in Australia and New Zealand* (2nd edn, 1994).
19 See *Blanchard and Gedye*.
20 See the Australian Companies Act 1981 (ACA). See also Malaysia and Singapore.
 1 See Ronald B Moldaver 'Abuse of Power by Receivers and Appointment of Receivers as a Remedy' Law Society of Upper Canada Special Lectures (1979) Abuse of Power 209, 211–212 and 253–260. Frank Bennett 'The Administration of a Corporate Receivership' 27 CBR (NS) 113, and Frank Bennett *Receiverships* (1985).
 2 Insolvency Law and Practice Report of the Review Committee (June 1982) (Cmnd 8558).

Part 1

Private receivers

CHAPTER 2

Fixed and floating charges

The charges under which receivers are appointed out of court may be (i) fixed charges or (ii) floating charges or (iii) a combination of both, ie a fixed and floating charge. The fixed charge in its most classic form is the legal mortgage over land although fixed charges may be given over future book debts and fixed plant and machinery. But the commonest type of charge under which today a privately appointed receiver is appointed is the floating charge,[1] constituted almost invariably by a debenture created by a company to secure loans made to it.

This chapter discusses first the nature of the fixed charge, then that of the floating charge and, lastly, the process known as crystallisation, by which a floating charge becomes converted into a fixed charge.

FIXED CHARGE

General

A fixed or specific charge is one that without more fastens on ascertained and definite property or property capable of being ascertained and defined.[2] Under a fixed charge the asset is appropriated to satisfaction of the debt immediately or upon the debtor acquiring an interest in it.[3] A fixed charge can therefore be

---

1 Often in an instrument containing both a fixed and floating charge. See generally WJ Gough *Company Charges* (2nd edn, 1996). For other studies, see Pennington 'The Genesis of the Floating Charge' (1960) 23 MLR 630; JH Farrar 'World Economic Stagnation puts the Floating Charge on Trial' (1980) 1 Co Law 83–91; GC Thorpe 'Floating Charges, Crystallisation and After-Acquired Property' Auckland Law Faculty Seminar Series 1981, Legal Research Foundation Inc (available at the Institute of Advanced Legal Studies); RJ Calnan 'Priorities between Execution Creditors and Floating Chargees' (1982) 10 NZ ULR 111 especially at 120–124. Eilis Ferran 'Floating Charges The Nature of the Security' [1988] CLJ 213; Hubert Picarda QC 'Labels: A Voyage round Fixed and Floating Charges' (2000), 4 RALQ 109–136.

2 *Illingworth v Houldsworth* [1904] AC 355 at 358, per Lord Macnaghten.

3 Goode *Legal Problems of Credit and Security* (2nd edn) p 15. One problem is distinguishing between a charge and a contract of sale: see *Re Curtain Dream plc* [1990] BCLC 925 (contract of sale and resale with retention of title as part of resale constituted as a charge); *Welsh Development Agency v Export Finance Co Ltd* [1992] BCC 270, CA; and see *Re Hamlet International plc* [1999] 2 BCLC 506, CA.

granted over existing defined property or over future property.[4] An important incident of such a charge is that the creditor gets immediate real rights over the charged asset, and these rights can only be defeated by a disposition to a bona fide purchaser of the legal estate or title for value without notice. This is in sharp contrast with the position under a *floating* charge where, as appears from the discussion below, the charge hovers over assets which are subject to the ordinary course of the company's business.

A mortgage of future or after-acquired property[5] creates an immediate equitable charge upon the property coming into existence independently of the contract to execute some future charge.[6] It 'binds the property itself directly it is acquired – automatically on the happening of the event and without any further act of the borrower'.[7]

A fixed charge is a direct charge on specific assets particularised in the instrument of charge. Unlike a floating charge it prevents the chargor from dealing with the charged asset or assets except with the consent of the chargee.

Where the debenture charges specific assets, the words often found in a floating charge to the effect that the company is not to be at liberty to create any mortgage or charge in priority to the debenture do not convert the specific fixed charge into a floating charge.[8] The subject matter of the charge is usually a fixed asset. Examples are land, buildings, plant, machinery, ships, aircraft and other chattels, as well as shares and equitable interests. A fixed charge over fixed plant and machinery is a charge over fixed plant and fixed machinery: the latter term means machinery which is firmly attached to the premises and heavy free-standing woodwork machinery does not answer that description and is not therefore fixed machinery.[9] Insurance money may be the subject of a fixed charge, and assignment of the charge will not convert a fixed charge into a floating one.[10] The Court of Appeal in *Re Atlantic Computer Systems plc*[11] held that a company which had charged to the bank all of the terms of each of the subleases of computer equipment let by the bank to the company for subletting on to the company's customers had effected a fixed and not a floating charge because the property charged 'was confined to rights to which the company was entitled under specific existing contracts'.[12]

FUTURE BOOK DEBTS

Assets which at first sight appear to be (as it were) 'floating' assets can, it has been held, nevertheless, be subjected to a fixed charge. Thus a debenture may on its true

---

4 *Holroyd v Marshall* (1862) 10 HL Cas 191, HL.

5 First upheld in equity in *Holroyd v Marshall* (1862) 10 HL Cas 191, HL.

6 *Re Lind* [1915] 2 Ch 345 at 358, CA per Swinfen Eady LJ.

7 [1915] 2 Ch 345 at 360.

8 *Grigson v Taplin & Co* (1915) 85 LJ Ch 75.

9 *Re Hi Fi Equipment (Cabinets) Ltd* [1988] BCLC 65.

10 *Re CCG International Enterprise Ltd* [1993] BCLC 1428 (the money in question was to be paid to the bank pursuant to the fixed charge).

11 [1990] BCC 859; criticised by Professor R M Goode in (1994) 110 LQR 592. *Cf Re Atlantic Medical Ltd* [1992] BCC 653 (security extended to *future* leases: held to be floating).

12 [1990] BCC 859 at 873. And see *State Bank of India v Lisbellow Ltd* [1989] 2 HKLR 604 (fixed charge on quotas).

construction confer on the chargee a specific charge on all future book debts so that the right of the specific chargee attaches in equity to the proceeds of those debts as soon as they are paid. That was in fact the true construction of the debenture given to the bank in *Siebe Gorman & Co Ltd v Barclays Bank Ltd*[13] where the proceeds of the future book debts were actually paid into an account with the bank, thus giving the bank control over any dealings with the cash proceeds.

In *Hart v Barnes*,[14] a debenture purported to grant a fixed and specific charge over a company's future book debts. The debenture further recited that it was the intention that as to each and all future book debts they be specifically charged and that the legal title should vest in the debenture holder upon the same coming into existence. Anderson J doubted that such an intention could be given effect to 'for that intention is repugnant to the nature of a charge over a future asset, the disposition of which is still at the will of the company'. He then continued:[15]

'It cannot sensibly be said that in respect of each present and future book debt of the company the debenture holder obtains a legal title when the fact is that such "title" is defeasible and capable of being destroyed by the company which is able to use the proceeds of such book debt in its business without any way being accountable to the debenture holder for such proceeds. Notwithstanding the brave attempts to define the charge given over book debts of the company as a fixed and specific charge and to purport to transfer the legal title in future book debts to the debenture holder, I am of the opinion that these objectives cannot be achieved, and that, at most, all that can be given is a floating charge which cannot crystallise until a specific event occurs, namely the default by the company and the appointment of a receiver, and it is only then that the floating charge settles, so to speak, and the rights of the debenture holder can be enforced against such book debts as are then in existence.'

Notwithstanding this criticism and other doubts which have been expressed, the efficacy of a fixed charge on future book debts was accepted by the Supreme Court in Eire in *Re Keenan Bros Ltd*.[16] There the company had executed in favour of two banks two charges over its present and future book debts, both charges being expressed to be fixed. The charges required the company to pay all money it received with respect to the book debts secured by the charges into designated bank accounts, withdrawals from which could be made only with the consent of the relevant bank. The charges also precluded the company from disposing of its book debts or of creating any other charges over them without the consent of the relevant bank. The question before the court was whether the charges created over the book debts were fixed or floating, the decision of the court below having been that the charges were floating charges.

---

13 [1979] 2 Lloyd's Rep 142 (following *Evans, Coleman & Evans Ltd v RA Nelson Construction Ltd* (1958) 16 DLR (2d) 123); and see *Re Permanent Houses (Holdings) Ltd* [1988] BCLC 563.

14 (1982) 7 ACLR 310. See also *Supercool Refrigerator and Air Conditioning v Herard Industries Ltd* [1994] 3 NZLR 300.

15 (1982) 7 ACLR 310 at 315.

16 [1986] BCLC 242; and see *Re Permanent Houses (Holdings) Ltd* [1988] BCLC 563. Cf *Rhodes v Allied Dunbar Pension Services Ltd* [1989] 1 All ER 1161, [1989] 1 WLR 800, CA reversing [1988] 1 All ER 524, [1987] 1 WLR 1703 (legal charge over land held to include rents from subtenants which did not therefore rank as a book debt subject to a separate fixed charge or as a debt caught by a further floating charge on crystallisation).

The Supreme Court allowed the appeal, holding that as a matter of principle it was possible to create a fixed charge over present or future book debts. In determining whether a charge was fixed or floating the court had to examine not only the declared intention of the parties but also the effect of various instruments by which the charge was created. There were significant restrictions which the charges placed on the company's ability to deal with the book debts in the normal course of its business, in particular the requirement that it pay all money received in respect of the book debts into a designated account from which withdrawals could be made only with the bank's consent and that it could not without the bank's written consent diminish or dispose of its book debts other than by collecting them. In the light of these restrictions, it was held that the charges created in favour of the banks were fixed and not floating charges.[17]

CRITERIA FOR CLASSIFICATION AS FIXED OR FLOATING[18]

It remains to be added that in the matter of the classification of a charge as fixed or floating the label put on the charge is not conclusive.[19] The classification will depend on what provisions, if any, there are in the charge document preventing the debtor from disposing of the unencumbered title to the subject matter of the charge.[20] A common provision, as has clearly been indicated, is that the proceeds of sale or collections be accounted for with the debtor being required to hold them on trust for the creditor in a separate account. Where the debenture holder fails to 'police' such a provision, the question arises as to whether plain words intended to set up a fixed charge will in effect be displaced by subsequent conduct of the debenture holder. It has been suggested that such conduct would characterise the charge as a floating charge and there is Australian authority to that effect.[1]

Again, the changing content of the charged property does not necessarily dictate the essence of the charge. Partnership assets may be changing all the time but it does not follow that a charge by a partner of his partnership share is a floating charge. The charge is over 'ascertained and definite property', namely the chose in action; it is a fixed charge.[2]

---

17 See also *William Gaskell Group Ltd v Highley* [1993] BCC 200 (fixed charge discerned because of restrictions on dealing); cf *Re Holidair Ltd* [1994] 1 IRLM 481, SC.

18 Gabriel Moss QC 'Fixed Charges on Book Debts – Puzzles and Perils' (1995) Insolv Int 25–28; Doyle 'Fixed or Floating Charge' (1998) 142 SJ 1052; 1088; 1110. Picarda 'Labels: A Voyage round Fixed and Floating Charges' (2000) 4 RALQ 109–136.

19 See *Re Armagh Shoes Ltd* [1982] NI 59, [1984] BCLC 405; *Re Lakeglen Construction Ltd* [1980] IR 347; *Re Keenan Bros Ltd* [1986] BCLC 242. These cases are considered in Pennington (1985) 7 Co Law 9. *Re G E Tunbridge Ltd* [1994] BCC 563. See also *Taxation Comr v Lai Corpn Pty Ltd* (1986) 83 FLR 63, FCWA and Pearce [1987] JBL 18. Letters of hypothecation have been held to be charges of a floating nature: *Re Lin Securities Pte* [1988] 2 MLJ 137, Sing HC; *Re City Securities Pte* [1990] 2 MLJ 257, Sing HC.

20 For a useful analysis of control techniques to ensure fixed charge status see Goode *Legal Problems of Credit and Security* (2nd edn) pp 55–59.

1 *Goode* 58–59; *Waters v Widdows* [1984] VR 503. And see *Re E G Tan & Co Pte* [1991] 3 MLJ 301 (company had access to safe in which charged shares kept: floating charge; upheld sub nom *Chase Manhattan Bank NA v Wong Tui San* (1993) 11 ACLC 3, 112.

2 *United Builders Pty Ltd v Mutual Acceptance Ltd* (1980) 144 CLR 673, 33 ALR 1.

If the charge contemplates that the debtor shall have freedom to manage the assets comprising the security the charge will be a floating charge even though there is no express reference to that freedom in the charge instrument.[3] Again, in *Re Brightlife Ltd*[4] the liberty afforded to the company was inconsistent with a fixed charge. The significant feature was that the company was free to collect its debts and pay the proceeds into its bank account. Once in the account, they would be outside the charge over debts and at the free disposal of the company. A right to deal in this way with the charged assets for its own account is a badge of a floating charge and is inconsistent with a fixed charge.[5] An unfettered freedom to deal with an asset in the ordinary course of business is inconsistent with a fixed charge.[6]

However some degree of freedom is not inconsistent with a fixed charge:[7] and a restriction on disposal of part of the charged property does not preclude characterisation of the charge as floating.[8]

In any event such control as is relied upon in support of a claim that the relevant charge is a fixed charge must be control exercised by the debenture holder in his capacity of debenture holder.[9]

RE NEW BULLAS TRADING LTD

One question which may legitimately be posed is the weight to be attributed to the Court of Appeal decision in *Re New Bullas Trading Ltd*[10] in relation to the fixed and floating charge debate.

In the court below

The central question which arose in the case was whether the charge over a particular company's book debts created by cl 3 of a particular debenture described as a fixed charge was a fixed or floating charge. The charge was in favour of 3 i plc (3i). Knox J said there were two ways of discarding a plain description given by parties to their agreed transaction. The first was to classify the arrangement as a sham, a cloak or a device. The second was by a finding that the

3 *Re Armagh Shoes Ltd* [1982] NI 59, [1984] BCLC 405.
4 [1987] Ch 200, [1986] 3 All ER 673. The credit bank balance was also held not to fall within the term 'book debts or other debts' as that term was used in the debenture. See also on this latter point *Re Permanent Houses (Holdings) Ltd* [1988] BCLC 563 at 566H–567C.
5 [1987] Ch 200 at 209G–H per Hoffmann J.
6 *Cosslett (Contractors) Ltd v Mid Glamorgan County Council* [1997] 4 All ER 46; revsd sub nom *Re Cosslett (Contractors) Ltd* [1959] 1 BCLC 205, CA without affecting this point; *Re Pearl Maintenance* [1995] 1 BCLC 449 (no restriction: floating charge).
7 *Re Cimex Tissues Ltd* [1994] BCC 626 (power to replace machinery from time to time).
8 *Re G E Tunbridge Ltd* [1994] BCC 563.
9 *Re Double S Printers Ltd* [1999] 1 BCLC 220; and see *Re ASRS Establishment* [2000] 1 BCLC 727 and Picarda (2000) 4 RALQ 109–136 for further comment.
10 [1994] 1 BCLC 485. For a most illuminating appraisal see Naccarata and Street '*Re New Bullas Trading Ltd: Fixed Charge over Book Debts – Two into One Won't Go*' (1994) JIB & FL 109–115. And see *Re Brumark Investments Ltd* [2000] 1 BCLC 353, NZCA.

transaction entered into by the parties was, on analysis, of a different nature from the description that they had given to it. He put the argument very graphically:[11]

> 'If the transaction is a cow and has cloven hooves, the parties cannot turn it into a horse by using equine terminology or saying that it is a horse'.

There was however no question of a sham in the case. So one had to look at the characteristics, in particular as defined by cl 12 of the debenture. In the touch-stone for whether the terms of the charge were susceptible of creating a fixed charge was the extent to which the chargee was left free to deal with the book debts and the proceeds if and when collected. His freedom to do so is the 'badge of the floating charge'.[12]

Clause 12 required that the company should pay into a current account or separate designated account (as 3i might require) of the company with the bank all money received in respect of the book debts and, on its property construction gave 3i the right, until payment in, to give directions on how to deal with such money. After payment in, cl 12 expressly released that money from the fixed charge and made them subject to a floating charge, although this was subject, inter alia, to any such directions given prior to payment in.

Such a power to give directions was well capable of producing a fixed as opposed to a floating charge if directions were given in a particular way. However, in the absence of such direction there was a freedom of action conferred upon the company which was, in the judgment of the court, inconsistent with the existence of a fixed charge at the creation of the charge and s 40 of the Insolvency Act 1986 pointed the court to the position at the creation of the charge.

This conclusion was not affected by the existence of the provision preventing assigning factoring or discounting, designed to limit the company's rights to deal with the debts to merely getting them in and not permitting parting with any interest in them. What there was not, but which would no doubt (had it been there) have been adequate, was a restriction on the way in which the money could be dealt with, absent a direction by 3i, and on that basis the charge was necessarily a floating charge.

In the Court of Appeal

In the Court of Appeal Nourse LJ (the only Chancery member of the court) fixed on a novel and ingenious point and the argument took a different tack. This resulted in a different conclusion, namely that the charge was part fixed and part floating.

The argument ran as follows:[13]

(a)   Prior to collection, a debt is a natural subject matter of a fixed charge. Once collected, the proceeds, being required for use in the business, are a natural subject matter for a floating charge.

---

11 [1994] BCLC 485 at 1394H.
12 *Re Brightlife Ltd* [1987] Ch 200.
13 For this succinct summary see Professor Roger Gregory in (1994) 1 RALQ 98–99.

(b) In *New Bullas*, unlike previous reported cases, the draftsman had 'deliberately and conscientiously' set out to subject uncollected debts to a fixed charge and the proceeds to a floating charge.

(c) There are no public policy grounds to prevent the parties from making any contract they chose (his Lordship later cited Lord Macnaghten's dictum to the same effect in *Tailby v Official Receiver*.[14]

(d) The answer to the preference creditors' argument, that any distinction between the debt and its proceeds is artificial and that a security cannot be specific if the chargor can unilaterally cause it to cease as a security, resides in the fact that here the chargor alone could not cause it to cease, rather both parties by agreement had caused it to cease.

(e) It was open to the parties to make the agreement over book debt charges which they had in fact made and freedom of contract prevailed.

Implications of the decision of the Court of Appeal

The Court of Appeal decision caused, at the time, some concerns in the banking and receivership world, chiefly because book debts and their proceeds had been held indivisible and the fate of the proceeds was treated as determining the nature of the charge.

It was thought that the judgment of Nourse LJ would encourage subsequent chargees to redraft their book debt charge clauses and side-step the 'control of the bank account' test which was so central to previous thinking. However, particularly in the light of the dicta of Millett J in *Royal Trust Bank v National Westminster Bank plc*[15] about the indivisibility of a debt and its proceeds, it seems most likely that the action will be treated as a one-off turning on its own facts and that book debts and their proceeds will continue to be treated as indivisible.

FLOATING CHARGE

Definition, description and theory

The floating charge is a species of security in practice peculiar to company borrowers.[16] The meaning of the term is best conveyed by description rather than by definition. Indeed, in *Re Yorkshire Woolcombers' Association Ltd*[17] Vaughan

14 (1888) 13 App Cas 523 at 545.
15 [1996] 2 BCLC 682 at 704 f. h. See also the criticism of the case in Lightman and Moss *Law of Company Receivers* (2nd edn 1994) 35–37; and see Picarda (2000) 4 RALQ 109 at 124.
16 Theoretically an individual could grant a floating charge to a lender but the effect of several statutes in combination deprives the floating charge of any practical effectiveness: see Gough *Company Charges* (2nd edn, 1996). For the theory: see GF Curtis 'The Theory of the Floating Charge' (1941–1942) 4 Univ Tor LJ 131; E Ferran [1988] CLJ 213–237. K J Naser 'The Judicial Nature of the Floating Charge' (1994) 15 Co Law 11–18.
17 [1903] 2 Ch 284, CA.

Williams LJ while considering the nature of a floating charge said, rather plaintively:[18] 'Unfortunately the words "floating charge" although they have been frequently used in legal documents and in judgments of the Courts, have never been defined with any great degree of accuracy.' That comment was made at a point in time when one classic description had already been formulated by Lord Macnaghten who described the term 'floating security' in the following way:[19]

'A floating security is an equitable charge on the assets for the time being of a going concern. It attaches to the subject charged in the varying condition in which it happens to be from time to time. It is of the essence of such a charge that it remains dormant until the undertaking charged ceases to be a going concern, or person in whose favour the charge is created intervenes. His right to intervene may of course be suspended by agreement. But if there is no agreement for suspension, he may exercise his right whenever he pleases after default.'

Seven years later Lord Macnaghten in *Illingworth v Houldsworth*,[20] an appeal in the very case from which the dictum of Vaughan Williams LJ already cited comes, approached the task of definition with little doubt:

'I should have thought there was not much difficulty in defining what a floating charge is in contrast to what is called a specific charge. A specific charge, I think, is one that without more fastens on ascertained and definite property or property capable of being ascertained and defined; a floating charge, on the other hand is ambulatory and shifting in its nature, hovering over and so to speak floating with the property which it is intended to affect until some event occurs or some act is done which causes it to settle and fasten on the subject of the charge within its reach and grasp.'

Kay LJ in *Driver v Broad*[1] had expressed himself with similar confidence in relation to the term 'floating security':

'That term only expresses what is more fully expressed in the conditions endorsed in the debentures, viz, that the company shall notwithstanding the debentures be at liberty to carry on its business, and in the ordinary course of such business to dispose of the property as if the debentures did not exist. That is the ordinary meaning of the term "floating security". It does not mean that there is not to be a charge, and an immediate charge, on the property, but merely that, notwithstanding the existence of the charge on all the property, including the real property, of the company, power is reserved to dispose of the property if in the ordinary course of carrying on the company's business it becomes necessary to do so.'

18 [1903] 2 CJ 284 at 291.
19 *Governments Stock and Other Securities Investment Co v Manila Rly Co* [1897] AC 81 at 86, HL.
20 [1904] AC 355 at 358.
 1 [1893] 1 QB 744 at 748–749, CA; and see *Hoare v British Columbia Development Association* (1912) 107 LT 602; *Re Dawson* [1915] 1 Ch 626, CA; *National Provincial Bank of England Ltd v United Electric Theatres Ltd* [1916] 1 Ch 132, 85 LJ Ch 106.

This notion of a floating charge giving the borrower a licence to deal is supported by a number of cases.[2] But the notion gives rise to difficulties. If a floating charge is treated as a present charge subject to a licence to deal with property in the ordinary course of business this would appear to preclude execution by judgment creditors; but as will be seen that is not in fact the case.[3] Another analysis describes a floating charge as a *present* security or mortgage of future assets. For example in *Evans v Rival Granite Quarries Ltd*[4] Buckley LJ approached the point in the following way:

'A floating security is not a future security; it is a present security, which presently affects other assets of the company expressed to be included in it. On the other hand, it is not a specific security; the holder cannot affirm that the assets are specifically mortgaged to him. The assets are mortgaged in such a way that the mortgagor can deal with them without the concurrence of the mortgagee. A floating security is not a specific mortgage of the assets, plus a licence to the mortgagor to dispose of them in the course of his business, but it is a floating mortgage applying to every item comprised in the security but not specifically affecting any item until some event occurs or some act on the part of the mortgagee is done which causes it to crystallise into a fixed security.'

Yet another variant is to be found in the analysis by Speight J who in *Re Manurewa Transport Ltd*[5] steered a middle course, emphasising that a floating charge covers the assets. He said that although a floating security 'does not attach specifically (for to do so would defeat its purpose) it covers the assets but with power of automatic relinquishment provided they are dealt with in a way authorised by the debenture i.e. in ordinary course of business'.

Yet again, in Ireland in the case of *Re Old Bushmills Distillery Co*,[6] floating debenture charges were described by Fitzgibbon LJ[7] as being 'always subject to the continued ebbing and flowing under them of the working capital of the undertaking – the conversion of money into goods and goods into money and back again'. And in the same case Walker LJ[8] describing a charge covering all the assets of the company said that 'the floating security follows the concern, reduced or added to through every form of its trading existence, which existence continues as if the debentures were not there until the floating charge becomes a fixed one.'

Perhaps the most helpful (and certainly the most quoted) of all descriptions of a floating charge was given by Romer LJ in a case in 1903 namely *Re Yorkshire Woolcombers' Association Ltd*:[9]

2 *Re Florence Land and Public Works Co* (1878) 10 Ch D 530 at 541, CA; *Davey & Co v Williamson & Sons Ltd* [1898] 2 QB 194 at 200; *George Barker (Transport) Ltd v Eynon* [1974] 1 WLR 462 at 467, CA per Edmund Davies LJ.
3 See the discussion at p 193 et seq.
4 [1910] 2 KB 979 at 999, CA. See also *Cretanor Maritime Co Ltd v Irish Marine Management Ltd* [1978] 3 All ER 164, [1978] 1 WLR 966, CA.
5 [1971] NZLR 909 at 916.
6 [1897] 1 IR 488, CA.
7 [1897] 1 IR 488 at 504.
8 [1897] 1 IR 488.
9 [1903] 2 Ch 284 at 295, CA.

'I certainly do not intend to attempt to give an exact definition of the term "float-ing charge" nor am I prepared to say that there will not be a floating charge within the meaning of the Act which does not contain all three characteristics that I am about to mention, but I certainly think that if a charge has the three characteristics that I am about to mention, it is a floating charge.

(1)   If it is a charge on a class of assets of a company present and future;
(2)   If that class is one which, in the ordinary course of business of the company, would be changing from time to time
(3)   If you find that by the charge it is contemplated that, until some future step is taken by or on behalf of those interested in the charge, the company may carry on its business in the ordinary way as far as concerns the particular class of assets I am dealing with.'

In *Re Bond Worth Ltd*[10] Slade J stressed that in this passage Romer LJ had not classified each of the characteristics as pre-conditions. Thus a floating charge could cover a 'closed' fund which cannot increase by additions but can only reduce.

A further theory of the nature of a floating charge is that the charge creates a charge on the particular assets from time to time of the debtor company, but the company retains its power to deal with its assets and by that means to overreach the floating charge in any manner whatsoever until crystallisation. Wickham J in *Landall Holdings Ltd v Caratti*[11] in the Western Australian Supreme Court identified in such a charge an equitable proprietary interest, adding the comment that since a floating charge floats:

'it follows that the equitable proprietary interest originated by the charge is also relatively floating. It may spring up when the thing comes within the ambit of the charge eg is acquired by the chargor and it may float away from under the charge eg when an equitable interest in another is conferred by the chargor and this is so even although the thing itself may remain in the possession of the chargor and even although the level of proprietary interest in the thing may remain in the chargor.
When a third party acquires the equitable interest in the asset the matter is sometimes discussed in the language of priorities, but it may also I think be correctly said that, if a third party acquires the equity in the asset before the chargee gathers in his equity, then when the chargee comes to gather it he finds that it has gone – in the language of the metaphor it has floated away – or, if it is a matter of priorities has submerged.'

The theory that a floating charge transfers a species of equitable interest which is defeasible finds support in a number of other cases[12] and appeals to at least two commentators.[13] But whether the interest is a defeasible

---

10   [1980] Ch 228, [1979] 3 All ER 919.
11   [1979] WAR 97 at 108–109.
12   *Driver v Broad* [1893] 1 QB 744, 63 LJQB 12, CA; *Wallace v Evershed* [1899] 1 Ch 891, 68 LJ Ch 415; *Re Dawson* [1915] 1 Ch 626, 84 LJ Ch 476, CA; *Dempsey v Traders' Finance Corpn Ltd* [1933] NZLR 1258 at 1286; *Re Manurewa Transport Ltd* [1971] NZLR 909 at 915.
13   See especially JH Farrar 'World Economic Stagnation puts the Floating Charge on Trial' (1980) 1 Co Law 83; GC Thorpe 'Floating Charges, Crystallisation and After-Acquired Property' Legal Research Foundation Inc (Auckland) Occasional Paper (1981) p 4.

equitable interest or as another writer asserts a mere equity which does not vest or become fixed until crystallisation,[14] while academically not without interest, is a question which in practice does not matter. The practical result of applying either theory to the interests of the third party in, for example *Landall Holdings Ltd v Caratti*[15] was the same. Until crystallisation the subject matter can still be alienated as was the land in the *Landall Holdings* case.

Ordinary course of business

It is implicit in the grant of a normal floating charge, that is to say one which is not subjected to some special expressed restriction, that the company granting the charge reserves the right, or is at liberty, to carry on its business in what is known as its ordinary course. That involves in turn the sale of any assets which have not been subjected to a fixed charge.

This point was well stressed by Walker LJ in *Re Old Bushmills Distillery Co*:[16]

> 'It is involved in such a charge that the company shall continue a going concern and the debenture holder has no power to interfere till his charge becomes payable. He can claim no account of mesne profits or challenge any authorised dealing by the company with its property or business. The directors, as masters, carry on meantime the business for which the company was incorporated according to its constitution and remain clothed with the power of doing all things necessary for carrying on that business, including the meeting of special emergencies. Assets may be withdrawn by sale and the proceeds from them take their place, or other assets may be substituted or additional assets added by trading.'

What then, it may properly be asked, is envisaged by the ordinary course of business? The phrase is not to be confined to the straitjacket of mundane every-day trade dealings. Certainly in the absence of prohibitions the creation of further mortgages or charges[17] will be allowed as being in the ordinary course of business.

Examples

Other examples of trading in the ordinary course of business include: making payments to secured or unsecured creditors[18] even where the company is insolvent[19] or sales of stocks to a syndicate of creditors.[20] The sale of part of the

14 Gough *Company Charges* (2nd edn, 1996) pp 332–348.
15 [1979] WAR 97. See also *Wily v St George Banking Partnership Ltd* [1999] BPIR 1030, FCA.
16 [1897] 1 IR 488 at 507, CA.
17 *Cox Moore v Peruvian Corpn Ltd* [1908] 1 Ch 604; *Re Hamilton's Windsor Ironworks* (1879) 12 Ch D 707; *Reynolds Bros (Motor) Pty Ltd v Esanda Ltd* (1984) 8 ACLR 422.
18 *Hamer v London City and Midland Bank Ltd* (1918) 87 LJKB 973, 118 LT 571.
19 *Willmott v London Celluloid Co* (1886) 34 Ch D 147, 56 LJ Ch 89, CA.
20 *Re Old Bushmills Distillery Co* [1897] 1 IR 488, CA.

stock of the company with a lease back and option to purchase arrangement[1] or a sale of part of the business itself may be in the ordinary course of business.[2] Where a company sells goods to its customers on hire purchase terms, that too is in the ordinary course of business.[3]

Sometimes even the sale of almost all the assets of a company (including its goodwill) in exchange for debentures and shares in the purchaser company may constitute a dealing in the ordinary course of business. Thus in *Re Borax Co.*[4] such a stage piece was enacted but it was nevertheless held that the undertaking had not ceased to be a going concern.

Sale not in ordinary course

A case in which sale of part of a business was held *not* to be in the ordinary course of business is *Torzillu Pty Ltd v Brynac Pty Ltd*.[5] There the debenture expressly provided that the charge would not prevent the company from dealing with its assets 'in the ordinary course of business'. The company was carrying on business as wholesaler of various goods. It had two main areas of activity, one dealing with camping and leisure goods, the other involving the disposal of motor cycle accessories. The debenture holder appointed receivers and managers of the defendant company. Only six days before their appointment the defendant company had executed a hurriedly prepared agreement with the plaintiff company whereby the plaintiff company was to acquire the wholesale camping and leisure goods division of the defendant company's business. The purchase price was to be paid over six years. The plaintiff company was owned by a former employee of the defendant with his wife. Prior to the sale agreement there had been no separate 'wholesale camping and leisure goods division' but this aspect of the company's business had been the most profitable. Both the directors of the defendant and plaintiff companies knew that the defendant company was in financial difficulties. The ex-employee had been involved in a reconstruction plan while employed by the defendant company and was a friend of the proprietor of the defendant company. The receivers and managers took possession of the entire business and business premises and excluded the plaintiff company and its officers. The plaintiff company sought an injunction to restrain the receivers and managers from interfering with the plaintiff's rights under the agreement.

The court refused to grant the relief sought. After setting out material parts of the transcript of evidence Helsham CJ in Eq continued:

> 'I can imagine circumstances in which the severance of the part of the business might be considered necessary for the orderly conduct of a business for its reconstruction, for its survival. Such may, in particular facts, amount to a

---

1 *Yorkshire Railway Wagon Co v Maclure* (1882) 21 Ch D 309, 51 LJ Ch 857, CA.
2 *Re HH Vivian & Co Ltd* [1900] 2 Ch 654 (sale of one of three separate businesses); cf *Torzillu Pty Ltd v Brynac Pty Ltd* (1983) 8 ACLR 52.
3 *Dempsey v Traders' Finance Corpn Ltd* [1933] NZLR 1258.
4 [1901] 1 Ch 326, 70 LJ Ch 162, CA.
5 (1983) 8 ACLR 52.

dispersal of assets which could be said to be in the ordinary course of business. It may be that even a transmogrification of the owner of the business into a new entity may involve dealing with the assets of a business in a way that could be regarded as not affecting the operations carried on otherwise than in the ordinary course of business. But I cannot see that a plan made between the proprietor and one other interested party to dissemble the various aspects that go to make up the entity of a business in order to bring it to an end in a way best calculated to serve those who have an interest in its assets can be labelled in its execution as dealing with those aspects in the ordinary course of business. It was put that the dealing with assets in the ordinary course of bringing a business to an end can be characterised as being in the ordinary course of business. I am not persuaded that this could be so but it is not necessary to decide that here. In the case of a company facing liquidation, the recipient of a s 364 notice,[6] unable to meet its commitments to one of its secured creditors and insolvent (even using that word only in accordance with the definition of the company's legislation) then dispersal of its assets would have to be according to some plan involving creditors before it could be suggested that the procedure was ordinary. To have a close associate of the proprietor acquire the viable portion of its business in haste without notice upon terms of payment over many years is so peculiar as to be properly labelled as "extraordinary"; that is what I think this transaction was.'

Interestingly none of the English cases appears to have been cited to the court. Certainly there is no mention of them in the judgment.

Restrictive, prohibition or negative pledge clauses

The ample opportunity left to a company to carry on dealing despite the existence of a floating charge is not always acceptable to lenders. Hence one now commonly finds in instruments which create a floating charge a clause with words to the effect that the floating charge is not to authorise the company to create any mortgage or charge ranking in priority to or pari passu with the debentures. These clauses have attracted a variety of nomenclature. Some refer to them as 'restrictive' clauses, others dub them 'prohibition' clauses while a third appellation is 'negative pledge'[7] clauses. Prohibition and negative pledge suggest a purely contractual effect. The words 'restriction' or 'restrictive' carry the hint that the clause sets up some kind of equitable incumbrance capable, in appropriate circumstances, of binding third parties.

'Prohibition' or 'restrictive' clauses, are construed strictly.[8] So a restrictive term in a debenture under which a specific charge on certain assets is given will not by implication raise a floating charge on the remaining assets.[9] Neither will it prevent a lender without notice from acquiring a charge upon specific property

---

6 The equivalent of a notice under IA 1986, s 123.
7 See generally Philip Wood *Law and Practice of International Finance* (1980); Grant Gilmore *Security Interests in Personal Property* (1965).
8 *Robson v Smith* [1895] 2 Ch 118 at 126.
9 *Grigson v Taplin & Co* (1915) 85 LJ Ch 75, 112 LT 985.

taking priority over the debenture[10] nor the creation of liens.[11] Further, such a term will not permit the granting of specific charges over property subsequently acquired, such charge being created contemporaneously with, or in pursuance of such acquisition. Thus the restriction does not preclude a vendor who leaves the purchase price of property acquired from him by the company from obtaining priority for that mortgage,[12] or a lender who provides the purchase price of property acquired by the company in consideration of a first mortgage from obtaining priority for that mortgage.[13]

The subsequent specific charge granted over *goods* to secure part of the purchase price owing in respect of them is likewise no breach of a restrictive provision in an antecedent debenture.[14] If a specific charge is made expressly subject to a floating charge, the specific charge is postponed when the floating charge crystallises by the appointment of a receiver.[15]

A crucial question in relation to such clauses is whether they do achieve priority for the charge in question subject of course to the question of notice.

There has been surprisingly little case law on the point since the turn of the century. The landmark case is the decision of the Court of Appeal in *English and Scottish Mercantile Investment Co v Brunton*.[16] In that case a legal mortgagee with knowledge of the existence of an earlier floating charge, but not of its terms, was held not to have inferred knowledge or constructive notice of a restrictive clause in the floating charge. The mortgagee's solicitor pursuing inquiries as to the effect of the earlier charge was put off the scent by a misrepresentation by the managing director of the company. All three members of the Court of Appeal laid emphasis on this point:[17] things might have turned out differently if the mortgagee or his solicitor had failed to make, or deliberately refrained from making proper inquiries.

In his perceptive analysis of the history of restriction clauses Professor Farrar[18] observes that *Brunton's* case was, of course, decided before the introduction of a statutory scheme for registration of company charges[19] and also at a

---

10 *English and Scottish Mercantile Investment Co v Brunton* [1892] 2 QB 700, 62 LJQB 136, CA (mortgage of an insurance policy); *Re Castell and Brown Ltd* [1898] 1 Ch 315, 67 LJ Ch 169 (deposit of title deeds).

11 *Brunton v Electrical Engineering Corpn* [1892] 1 Ch 434, 61 LJ Ch 256 (solicitor's lien); *Dales Freightways Ltd v New Zealand Forest Products Ltd* [1970] NZLR 150 (sub-contractor's statutory lien); *Waitomo Wools (NZ) Ltd v Nelsons (NZ) Ltd* [1974] 1 NZLR 484, CA; *George Barker (Transport) Ltd v Eynon* [1974] 1 All ER 900, [1974] 1 WLR 462, CA (general lien under contract). A Mareva injunction is not in the nature of a lien and so may be defeated by a debenture holder's charge which has crystallised: *Cretanor Maritime Co Ltd v Irish Marine Management Ltd* [1978] 3 All ER 164, [1978] 1 WLR 966, CA.

12 *Wilson v Kelland* [1910] 2 Ch 306, 79 LJ Ch 580.

13 *Re Connolly Bros Ltd (No 2)* [1912] 2 Ch 25, 81 LJ Ch 517, CA.

14 *Mathiesen v Wahlen* (1928) 29 SRNSW 189 where the subsequent charge is wrongly described as a floating charge.

15 *Re Camden Brewery Ltd* (1911) 106 LT 598n, CA; *Re Robert Stephenson & Co Ltd* [1913] 2 Ch 201, CA.

16 [1892] 2 QB 700.

17 [1892] 2 QB 700 at 711 per Lord Esher MR; at 712 per Bowen LJ and at 717 per Kay LJ.

18 JH Farrar 'Floating Charges and Priorities' (1974) 38 Conv NS 315.

19 See Companies Act 1900, s 141.

point of time when restrictive clauses were not the commonplace they are today. A line of first instance authorities establishes that knowledge of the existence of an earlier floating charge does not give *constructive* notice of the terms of the charge or of a commonplace restrictive clause.[20] The most recent of these English authorities is the decision of Slade J in *Siebe Gorman & Co v Barclays Bank Ltd.*[1]

However, Professor Farrar's argument that 'constructive knowledge of the charge itself, the common practice of inserting such clauses and the entitlement of an existing creditor under s 408 of the Companies Act 1985 to inspect a copy of the charge at the company's registered office may possibly give rise to an inference of *actual* knowledge on the basis of wilful blindness' has now been incorporated into one leading practitioners' tome.[2] The argument is criticised by one author[3] as having been 'impliedly rejected' in *Re Standard Rotary Machine Co:*[4] certainly in that case it was not expressly *accepted*, no doubt because of the uncommon occurrence of such clauses at that time. Other writers express themselves sympathetic to *judicial* revision of the law on this point.[5] The Irish Supreme Court rejected the occasion to carry out such a revision in *Welch v Bowmaker (Ireland) Ltd.*[6] The effect of that decision was to perpetuate the vulnerability of prohibition clauses by denying that actual notice of such a clause can be inferred from the fact that a mortgagee knows of the existence of an earlier floating charge and knows that prohibition clauses are commonly (if not invariably) attached to such a charge. The case involved a priority dispute between a debenture holder holding a somewhat confusing fixed and floating charge and a subsequent equitable mortgagee who had taken a deposit of title deeds over a piece of land not mentioned in the schedule of fixed charge properties in the earlier debenture. The argument that a particular provision in the debenture had the effect of *mortgaging* the piece of land in question was rejected by the majority of the Irish Supreme Court. The equitable mortgagee of the piece of land was aware of the debenture but not of its terms which included a prohibition clause. Despite the fact that prohibition clauses are invariably attached to such charges the court was unwilling to extend the doctrine of constructive or implied notice to such a situation. According to Parke J, difficult policy questions were involved and any change in the state of the law should be left to the legislature. He added:[7]

'The doctrine of constructive or implied notice like that of public policy, may be an unruly horse and it should be ridden with a firm hand.'

---

20 *Re Castell and Brown Ltd* [1898] 1 Ch 315; *Re Valletort Sanitary Steam Laundry Co* [1903] 2 Ch 654; *Re Standard Rotary Machines Co* (1906) 95 LT 829; *Wilson v Kelland* [1910] 2 Ch 306; *G & T Earle Ltd v Hemsworth Rural District Council* (1928) 44 TLR 605.

1 [1979] 2 Lloyd's Rep 142.

2 *Palmer's Company Law* (24th edn) p 714, para 45–08 (emphasis added).

3 WJ Gough *Company Charges* (2nd edn, 1996) pp 844–846.

4 (1906) 95 LT 829.

5 See Diane M Hare and David Milman 'Floating Charges, Prohibition Clauses and Problems of Notice' (1982) 126 Sol Jo 74–77.

6 [1980] IR 251.

7 [1980] IR 251 at 262.

Until legislative reform is forthcoming (and none is in prospect) it seems likely that an English court would follow *Welch v Bowmaker* with the result that only those with *actual* notice of the restriction will be bound by it.[8]

JUDICIAL RECOGNITION

Judicial recognition of the concept of the floating charge came in 1870.[9] Previously, in 1862, the House of Lords had in *Holroyd v Marshall*[10] accepted that an equitable mortgage with suitably drafted provisions could extend to after acquired machinery. In the case itself this enabled the mortgagee to prevail over an execution creditor. In the years immediately following the decision in *Holroyd v Marshall* courts of equity had baulked at the prospect of accepting the notion of a floating charge in three reported cases.[11] The turning point was *Re Panama, New Zealand and Australian Royal Mail Co*[12] where a shipping company had issued debentures each of which was expressed to 'charge the . . . undertaking, and all sums of money arising therefrom, and all the estate, right, title, and interest of the company therein'. Counsel for the liquidator submitted that the word 'undertaking' referred to the 'enterprise' of the company but did not refer to any property to be charged. The argument was rejected; and it was held that the word 'undertaking' meant all the property, present and future, of the company and that the charge thereon was valid and effective. Giffard LJ[13] put the matter thus:

> 'I take the object and meaning of the debenture to be this, that the word "under-taking" necessarily infers that the company will go on, and that the debenture holder could not interfere until either the interest which was due was unpaid, or until the period had arrived for the payment of his principal, and that principal was unpaid. I think the meaning and object of the security was this, that the company might go on during that interval, and, furthermore, that during the interval the debenture holder would not be entitled to any account of mesne profits, or of any dealing with the property of the company in the ordinary course of carrying on their business . . . I see no difficulty or inconvenience in giving that effect to this instrument. But the moment the company comes to be wound up, and the property has to be realised, that moment the rights of those parties, beyond all question, attach. My opinion is, that even if the company had not stopped, the debenture holders might have filed a bill to realise their security. I hold that under these debentures they have a charge upon all property of the company, past and future, by the term "undertaking" and that they stand in a position superior to that of the general creditors, who can touch nothing until they are paid.'

8 *Cox v Dublin City Distillery* [1906] 1 IR 446. See also Goode *Legal Problems of Credit and Security* (2nd edn) pp 41–45; *Fire Nymph Products v Heating Centre Pty Ltd* (1992) 7 ACSR 365.
9 For the history of the floating charge, see RR Pennington 'The Genesis of the Floating Charge' (1960) 23 MLR 630; Gough *Company Charges* (2nd edn, 1996) pp 102–108.
10 (1862) 10 HL Cas 191.
11 *King v Marshall* (1864) 33 Beav 565, 4 New Rep 258; *Re Marine Mansions Co* (1867) LR 4 Eq 601, 37 LJ Ch 113; *Re New Clydach Sheet and Bar Iron Co* (1868) LR 6 Eq 514.
12 (1870) 5 Ch App 318.
13 (1870) 5 Ch App 318 at 322–323.

Whether a particular instrument constitutes a floating charge or floating security is a question of construction. The instrument must evince a contractual intention on the part of the parties to create a valid floating charge.

Following the decision in *Re Panama, New Zealand and Australian Royal Mail Co* that a charge on the 'undertaking' created a charge on all present and future property draftsmen have commonly employed the following form of words:

> 'the company charges its undertaking and all its (real and personal) property present and future, including its uncalled capital'.

For good measure, and as confirming the relevant contractual intentions, the words 'by way of floating charge' or 'by way of floating security' are often added.[14] But, as has already been pointed out,[15] the label which the parties themselves put upon the transaction is not, necessarily decisive.[16]

EFFECT OF A FLOATING CHARGE

Since a floating charge is only an equitable charge on the assets for the time being until it becomes fixed or crystallised, the company may in the ordinary course of business[17] and subject to the terms of the debenture sell,[18] mortgage or otherwise deal with its assets and pay dividends out of profits[19] as though the floating charge had not been created.[20] Any mortgage so effected while the charge is still floating will take priority over the debenture,[1] unless the company purports to give a charge over all its assets in priority to or pari passu with the existing floating charge.[2] It is however possible to give a floating charge over some assets in priority to the general floating charge.[3]

---

14 Gough *Company Charges* (2nd edn, 1996), 63 cites many examples.
15 See at p 16 above.
16 See in addition to the cases cited above: *Re Wallyn Industries Pty Ltd* (1983) 7 ACLR 661; *Waters v Widdows* [1984] VR 503.
17 As to what acts or payments come within 'the ordinary course of business', see *Willmott v London Celluloid Co* (1886) 34 Ch D 147, 56 LJ Ch 89, CA; *Hamer v London City and Midland Bank Ltd* (1918) 87 LJKB 973, 118 LT 571; *Re Hubbard & Co Ltd* (1898) 68 LJ Ch 54, 79 LT 665; *Re HH Vivian & Co Ltd* [1900] 2 Ch 654, 69 LJ Ch 659; *Cox Moore v Peruvian Corpn Ltd* [1908] 1 Ch 604, 77 LJ Ch 387. See also the discussion at pp 23–25.
18 *Hamer v London City and Midland Bank Ltd* (1918) 87 LJKB 973, 118 LT 571 (sale of fixtures which were not removed before crystallisation); *Re HH Vivian & Co Ltd* [1900] 2 Ch 654, 69 LJ Ch 659 (sale of business); *Caratti v Grant* (1978) 3 ACLR 322 (sale of land: transfers not registered before crystallisation). A sale of stock-in-trade for the purpose of paying trade debts and other pressing liabilities is still within the ordinary course of business: *Re Old Bushmills Distillery Co* [1897] 1 IR 488, CA.
19 *Bosanquet v St John D'El Rey Mining Co Ltd* (1897) 77 LT 206 (interest paid in previous years need not be made up); *Lawrence v West Somerset Mineral Rly Co* [1918] 2 Ch 250, 87 LJ Ch 513.
20 *Robson v Smith* [1895] 2 Ch 118 at 124 per Romer J; *Biggerstaff v Rowatt's Wharf Ltd* [1896] 2 Ch 93 at 103, CA per Lopes LJ.
1 *Ward v Royal Exchange Shipping Co, ex p Harrison* (1887) 58 LT 174 (equitable mortgage only); *Cox Moore v Peruvian Corpn Ltd* [1908] 1 Ch 604, 77 LJ Ch 387.
2 *Re Benjamin Cope & Sons Ltd* [1914] 1 Ch 800; *Re Automatic Bottle Makers* [1926] Ch 412, CA.
3 *Re Automatic Bottle Makers Ltd* [1926] Ch 412, CA (power to do so specifically reserved).

Until a crystallising event occurs[4] debenture holders are not entitled to intervene except in accordance with the terms of their contract[5] unless the company does some act which is ultra vires the memorandum or jeopardises the debenture holders' security[6] or the company has ceased to be a going concern.[7] But obviously the court will not interfere merely because a sale of part of the concern has altered not the nature of the undertaking but the extent of it.[8]

After the security becomes a fixed charge the company cannot therefore sell or mortgage any part of the property affected by that fixed charge, except subject to the fixed charge.[9] Goods subject to a floating charge on crystallisation by the appointment of a receiver are assigned to the debenture holder: they are no longer goods of the company and a local authority is thereby precluded from denying distress on those goods for non-payment of rates.[10] But it should be noted that where the security merely provides that the company is to be at liberty to deal with the property charged until the happening of a specified event, the security continues to 'float' until a receiver is appointed or the company goes into liquidation.[11] The mere issue of a writ asking for a receiver is not sufficient to affect the company's powers of disposition.[12]

CRYSTALLISATION

Crystallisation[13] is simply the metaphorical term for the conversion of a floating into a fixed security. A security must be either floating or fixed. The terms are mutually exclusive; the existence of one by definition excludes the other.[14] A receiver appointed under a floating charge will be concerned to know the precise point of time at which the conversion took place since crystallisation has certain important consequences.

The term 'crystallisation' was described in 1897 by Kekewich J in *Re Victoria Steamboats Ltd*[15] as a 'newly adopted term'. The adoption has been a happy one in the sense that the metaphor is now conventionally applied to the process of conversion. However not all the mooted occasions for crystallisation are accepted as having that effect, or as being appropriate to have that effect. Mixed metaphors bear witness to the uncertainties, and learning has been deployed

4 See the discussion under the head 'Crystallisation' below.
5 *R Jaffe Ltd (in liquidation) v Jaffe* [1932] NZLR 168.
6 *Thorn v Nine Reefs Ltd* (1892) 67 LT 93, CA; *Re Borax Co* [1901] 1 Ch 326, CA.
7 *Hubbuck v Helms* (1887) 56 LJ Ch 536, 56 LT 232.
8 *Re HH Vivian & Co Ltd* [1900] 2 Ch 654.
9 *Governments Stock and Other Securities Investment Co Ltd v Manila Rly Co Ltd* [1897] AC 81, HL.
10 *Re ELS Ltd* [1994] 1 BCLC 743.
11 [1897] AC 81, HL.
12 *Re Hubbard & Co Ltd* (1898) 68 LJ Ch 54, 79 LT 665.
13 For an admirably clear and detailed discussion, see JH Farrar 'The Crystallisation of a Floating Charge' (1976) 40 Conv NS 397–415; and see also Gough *Company Charges* (2nd edn) pp 135–178; Report of Cork Committee, Insolvency Law and Practice (Cmnd 8558) 355–358; RL Dean 'Crystallisation of a Floating Charge' (1983) Companies and Securities Law Jo 185–203.
14 *Evans v Rival Granite Quarries Ltd* [1910] 2 KB 979 at 997, CA per Fletcher Moulton J.
15 [1897] 1 Ch 158 at 161.

upon the efficacy or legal validity of automatic or semi-automatic crystallisation clauses in debentures. The permissibility of partial crystallisation is also a point of interest. So too is decrystallisation or reflotation.

Established crystallising events

It is now well settled that a floating security crystallises in the following circumstances: (i) on the company going into liquidation[16] even if only for the purpose of reconstruction;[17] (ii) on the intervention of the debenture holder by taking possession[18] or by the appointment under the relevant charge[19] of, or the obtaining of the appointment of, a receiver[20] (but not at any stage preliminary to such an appointment[1]); and (iii) on cessation of the company's business.

Liquidation

When a company goes into liquidation, whether by resolution of the members or by order of the court, that very event causes a floating charge to crystallise.[2] The reason for this is that on liquidation a company must cease to carry on its business

---

16 *Re Colonial Trust Corpn* (1879) 15 Ch D 465 at 472 per Jessel MR (members' voluntary winding up); *Evans v Rival Granite Quarries Ltd* [1910] 2 KB 979 at 1001, CA.

17 *Re Crompton & Co Ltd* [1914] 1 Ch 954, 83 LJ Ch 666.

18 *Re General South American Co* (1876) 2 Ch D 337 at 342 per Malins V-C; *Re Hamilton's Windsor Ironworks Co* (1879) 12 Ch D 707 at 710 per Malins V-C; *Biggerstaff v Rowatt's Wharf Ltd* [1896] 2 Ch 93 at 105–106 per Kay LJ; *Geoghegan v Greymouth-Point Elizabeth Rly and Coal Co Ltd* (1898) 16 NZLR 749; *Dempsey and National Bank of New Zealand Ltd v Traders' Finance Corpn Ltd* [1933] NZLR 1258 at 1301–1302 per Smith J; *Mercantile Bank of India Ltd v Chartered Bank of India Australia and China and Strauss & Co Ltd* [1937] 1 All ER 231.

19 See the discussion at p 32, below.

20 *Re Florence Land and Public Works Co* (1878) 10 Ch D 530 at 541 per Jessel MR; *Re Colonial Trusts Corpn* (1879) 15 Ch D 465 at 472 per Jessel MR; *Taunton v Sheriff of Warwickshire* [1895] 2 Ch 319, 64 LJ Ch 497; *Re Carshalton Park Estate* [1908] 2 Ch 62 at 66 per Warrington J; *Re Tilt Cove Copper Co Ltd* [1913] 2 Ch 588, 82 LJ Ch 545; *Re New Vogue Ltd* [1932] NZLR 1633 at 1643 per Myers CJ; *Re Otway Coal Co Ltd* [1953] VLR 557 at 571 per O'Bryan J; *MG Charley Pty Ltd v FH Wells Pty Ltd* [1963] NSWR 22 at 26 per Jacobs J; *Re Quality Camera Co Pty Ltd* [1965] NSWR 1330 at 1332 per McLelland CJ in Eq; *Stein v Saywell* [1969] ALR 481; *Rother Iron Works Ltd v Canterbury Precision Engineers Ltd* [1974] QB 1, [1973] 1 All ER 394; *George Barker (Transport) Ltd v Eynon* [1974] 1 All ER 900, [1974] 1 WLR 462, CA; and see Gough *Company Charges* (2nd edn, 1996) pp 160–167.

 1 *Re Colonial Trusts Corpn* (1879) 15 Ch D 465 at 472; *Governments Stock and Other Securities Investment Co v Manila Rly Co* [1895] 2 Ch 551; *Re Roundwood Colliery Co* [1897] 1 Ch 373, CA; *Re Hubbard & Co Ltd* (1898) 68 LJ Ch 54, 79 LT 665 (commencement of debenture holders' action: no crystallisation). The issue of a writ in a debenture holders' action was held to be a crystallisation event in a Canadian case; see *Industrial Development Bank v Valley Dairy Ltd and McDonald* [1953] OR 70 at 73–74 per Judson J.

 2 *Re Panama, New Zealand and Australian Royal Mail Co* (1870) 5 Ch App 318 at 322–323; *Re Colonial Trusts Corpn, ex p Bradshaw* (1879) 15 Ch D 465 at 472–473 per Jessel MR; *Hodson v Tea Co* (1880) 14 Ch D 859, *Wheatley v Silkstone and Haigh Moor Coal Co* (1885) 29 Ch D 715 at 718; *Wallace v Universal Automatic Machines Co* [1894] 2 Ch 547, CA; *Re Westmoreland Box Co* [1968] NZLR 826 at 845; *Re Asiatic Electric Co Pty Ltd* [1970] 2 NSWR 612 at 612–613. For a voluntary liquidation as a crystallising event, see *Re Colonial Trusts Corpn* (1879) 15 Ch D 465 at 472 per Jessel MR (members' voluntary winding up).

except so far as may be required for its beneficial winding up. The liquidation need not be an insolvent liquidation: a voluntary winding up for the purpose of reconstruction will still cause a floating charge over the company's assets to crystallise because the old company ceases to carry on its business. In the case of a voluntary winding up, the crucial date will be the date of the resolution for winding up. In the case of a compulsory winding up, crystallisation takes place on the date of the winding up order and is not retrospective to the date on which the winding up petition was presented. The mere presentation of a winding up petition does not cause the floating charge to crystallise, nor indeed does the appointment of a provisional liquidator. The presentation of a petition for an administration order is equally *not* a crystallising event, unless it is specified in the debenture to be such.[3]

Intervention of debenture holder

If a debenture holder wishes to cause a floating charge to crystallise he must do some act which (i) is done with the intention of converting the floating charge into a fixed charge, (ii) is authorised by the express or implied terms of the debenture, and (iii) divests the company of legal control of the assets.

Taking possession

The most obvious, but now rare, form of 'crystallising' intervention is by the debenture holder taking possession lawfully under the charge.[4] The relevant act may be symbolic, for example taking possession of part in the name of the whole.[5] An order for possession in favour of the debenture holder would have the same effect.[6]

Sale

Because of its divesting effect an order for sale should be regarded as a crystallising event. Sale itself is a fortiori a crystallising event since it deprives the company of legal control of the assets sold.

Appointment of receiver by debenture holder

The most frequent intervention by the debenture holder which has the effect of crystallising the relevant charge is the appointment out of court of a receiver and manager.[7] Such a receiver does not need to take possession of the assets subject to the charge,[8] it is sufficient if the office of receiver and manager is accepted by

---

3 Such a provision is deemed to be included in any floating charge created before the commencement of the Act: see the IA 1986, s 437, Sch 11, para 1.

4 *Evans v Rival Granite Quarries Ltd* [1910] 2 KB 979 at 997, CA per Fletcher Moulton LJ. The accountability of a chargee in possession is unattractively strict.

5 Pollock and Wright *Possession in the Common Law* (1888) pp 60–61, 70, 78–79.

6 *Re St John's Heritage Foundation and Garnet Kindervater Ltd* (1984) 28 ACWS (2d) 271 (Nfld TD).

7 *Evans v Rival Granite Quarries Ltd* [1910] 2 KB 979, CA.

8 Hence a sheriff who has levied execution against goods but has not sold them is displaced by the appointment of a receiver: *Re Standard Manufacturing Co Ltd* [1891] 1 Ch 627, CA; *Re Opera Ltd* [1891] 3 Ch 260, CA.

the appointee.[9] Possession is unnecessary because in giving the debenture holder the power to appoint a receiver the company accepts that its powers of management will be terminated by his appointment.[10] Notice of the appointment of a receiver and manager need not be given to the company, or to anyone other than the receiver, to achieve crystallisation.

Appointment of receiver by court

A debenture holder may apply to the court for the appointment of a receiver and manager in a debenture holders' action. While such applications have in recent times been rare, the possibility that foreign courts will give greater weight to the status of a court-appointed receiver may increase their frequency. A floating charge will crystallise only when a court appointment takes effect, since until that point of time the company is legally in control of the charged assets. The mere initiation of proceedings is, in England, not enough to crystallise the floating charge.[11] There are, however, in Canada some decisions which treat the initiation of proceedings as a crystallising event so long as the debenture holder's right to enforce his security is not in issue.[12] In the absence of some express provision making such an event one of crystallisation[13] such a result is decidedly odd; the starting of proceedings does not divest the company of its control of its assets, and so the distinction made between proceedings where the right of enforcement is in issue and those where it is not appears irrelevant.

Cessation of business

It has long been assumed that a floating charge will crystallise automatically, without any express provision to that effect, on the company's ceasing to carry on business, or ceasing to be a going concern, or disposing of the whole of its undertaking with a view to the cessation of trading. Even before the decision of Nourse J in *Re Woodroffes (Musical Instruments) Ltd*[14] the assumption was made by some text books,[15] and underpinned various obiter dicta.[16]

---

9 As to acceptance of office, see at p 77; and see IA 1986, s 33(1) and IR 1986, r 3.1.

10 *Alberta Paper Co Ltd v Metropolitan Graphics Ltd* (1983) 49 CBR (2d) 63.

11 *Re Hubbard & Co Ltd* (1898) 68 LJ Ch 54; *Re Roundwood Colliery Co* [1897] 1 Ch 373, CA; *Norton v Yates* [1906] 1 KB 112. Cf *Evans v Rival Granite Quarries Ltd* [1910] 2 KB 979 at 986, CA per Vaughan Williams LJ.

12 *Great Lakes Petroleum Co v Border Cities Oil Co* [1934] OR 244, CA; *Industrial Development Bank v Valley Dairy Ltd* [1953] OR 70 at 73–74, per Judson J; *Gatsby Enterprises (Kelowna) Ltd v Gatsby Kelowna (1976) Ltd* (1978) 30 CBRNS 1; *Armstrong Contracting Canada Ltd v Public Cold Storage Brandon Ltd* (1969) 6 DLR (3d) 622; *Mercantile Bank of Canada v Nelco Corpn* (1982) 47 CBRNS 165.

13 *General Brake and Clutch Service Ltd v WA Scott & Sons Ltd* (1975) 59 DLR (3d) 741 (no such provision in the debenture: *held* no crystallisation).

14 [1986] Ch 366, [1985] 2 All ER 908.

15 See JH Farrar 'The Crystallisation of a Floating Charge' (1976) 40 Conv NS 397 at 399.

16 See *Hubbuck v Helms* (1887) 56 LJ Ch 536 at 538; *Robson v Smith* [1895] 2 Ch 118 especially at 124–125; *Governments Stock and Other Securities Investment Co Ltd v Manila Rly Co Ltd* [1897] AC 81 at 86, HL; *Edward Nelson & Co v Faber & Co* [1903] 2 KB 367 at 376–377; *Evans v Rival Granite Quarries Ltd* [1910] 2 KB 979 at 990, 993 and 997, CA.

In *Hubbuck v Helms*[17] a debenture holders' action sought a declaration that a particular transaction was void and an injunction to restrain the person who had affected to purchase the undertaking and assets from dealing therewith. Stirling J granted an interlocutory injunction and gave leave to amend the writ to claim the appointment of a receiver and realisation of the security. In analysing the effect of a floating charge he said that its effect was that so long as the company was a going concern there was no right to interfere with the dealings of the directors and then continued:[18]

> 'but the moment that the principal or interest falls in arrear, or the company comes to be wound up, or, as it appears to me ceases to be a going concern, then the right of the debenture-holders arises to ask the court to interfere by appointing a receiver of the assets of the company for the time being, and to realise them for the benefit of the debenture-holders.'

The company in question was at the date of the writ already in liquidation and the dicta recited above related to an application to the court. Four years later a leading precedent book[19] referred to a floating charge which ceases to float and becomes specific when the company ceases to be a going concern. That textbook proposition was relied on in *Robson v Smith*[20] by counsel for the debenture holder. Romer J accepted that a floating security allows the company 'to deal with its assets in the ordinary course of business until the company is wound up or *stops business*, or a receiver is appointed at the instance of the debenture-holders'.[1] But he found on the facts that the company had not 'in fact, even stopped business, and still less had the defendants notice of any stoppage'.[2] Then in *Re Victoria Steamboats Ltd*[3] there arose a situation in which a winding up petition had been presented against a company but no order had been made. Kekewich J was not prepared to assume that in those circumstances the company must have stopped trading. In the absence of evidence that the company had closed its doors he was not prepared to assume that the business was not being carried on or that the charge had (in what was then a neologism) 'crystallised'. Nevertheless in the event, because of jeopardy, a receiver was appointed. Lord Macnaghten said in relation to a floating charge in *Governments Stock and Other Securities Investment Co Ltd v Manila Rly Co Ltd*[4] that:

> 'It is of the essence of such a charge that it remains dormant until the undertaking charged *ceases to be a going concern* or until the person in whose favour the charge is created intervenes.'

Joyce J in *Edward Nelson & Co v Faber & Co*[5] itemised a number of cases where a floating security would cease to be a floating security and become what he

17 (1887) 56 LJ Ch 536.
18 (1887) 56 LJ Ch 536 at 538.
19 Palmer *Company Precedents* (5th edn) p 476.
20 [1895] 2 Ch 118 at 124.
 1 [1895] 2 Ch 118 at 124.
 2 [1895] 2 Ch 118 at 125.
 3 [1897] 1 Ch 158, 66 LJ Ch 21.
 4 [1897] AC 81 at 86.
 5 [1903] 2 KB 367 at 376–377.

dubbed an 'active' security: one of those was when the company *stops business*. In *Evans v Rival Granite Quarries Ltd*[6] both Vaughan Williams LJ and Fletcher Moulton LJ[7] cited with approval Lord Macnaghten's dicta about ceasing to be a going concern being an occasion of crystallisation; and Fletcher Moulton LJ paraphrased the wording used by Lord Macnaghten as showing 'that that which changes the character of a floating security to that of a fixed charge is either *the cessation of the carrying on of business* by the company or the actual intervention of the debenture-holder'.

The differing phraseology of the judges raises an obvious question. Is there any distinction between 'ceasing to carry on business' or 'stopping business (or trading)' on the one hand and 'ceasing to be a going concern' on the other? As has been just mentioned Fletcher Moulton LJ treated the phrases as synonymous.[8] The concept of cesser of business perhaps allows for more objective assessment than 'ceasing to be a going concern': a company could cease to be a going concern without actually ceasing to carry on business. But even if the phrases are not being used interchangeably in the authorities, it is clear that the material event to cause crystallisation is a cessation of the business and not, if that is something different, ceasing to be a going concern.[9]

The uniform assumption that cessation of business causes a crystallisation of a floating charge was specifically considered in the case of *Re Woodroffes (Musical Instruments) Ltd*.[10] There one of the questions which arose was whether cessation of business automatically caused a floating charge to crystallise. Nourse J referred to many of the cases cited in the previous paragraphs[11] and summarised their effect as being that they all, to a greater or lesser extent, assume that crystallisation takes place on a cessation of business. Perhaps the assumption appeared most authoritatively in the judgment of Fletcher Moulton LJ in *Evans v Rival Granite Quarries Ltd*,[12] one of the latest of the cases to which he was referred. He concluded that by the time of that decision the assumption had become well established; and he noted that he had not been referred to any case in which the assumption in favour of automatic crystallisation on cessation of business had been questioned.[13] Then he continued as follows:[14]

> 'On that state of the authorities it would be very difficult for me to question it, even if I could see a good ground for doing so. On the contrary, it seems to me that it is in accordance with the essential nature of a floating charge. The thinking behind the creation of such charges has always been a recognition that a fixed charge on the whole undertaking and assets of the company would paralyse it and prevent it from carrying on its business: see, eg *In re Florence Land and Public*

6 [1910] 2 KB 979, 79 LJKB 970, CA.
7 See [1910] 2 KB at 990 and 993.
8 So too did Nourse J in *Re Woodroffes (Musical Instruments) Ltd* [1986] Ch 366 at 376H–377A (citing this passage from the first edition of this book).
9 See [1986] Ch 366 at 376H–377A.
10 [1986] Ch 366, [1985] 2 All ER 908.
11 He referred to the discussion of the authorities in the first edition of this book: see [1986] Ch 366 at 376F–G, and to the authorities at [1986] Ch 366 at 377A–E.
12 [1910] 2 KB 979 at 993, CA.
13 [1986] Ch 366 at 377E–F.
14 [1986] Ch 366 at 377G–378B, citing also with approval Goode *Legal Problems of Credit and Security* (2nd edn).

Works Co, ex p Moor.[15] On the other hand it is a mistake to think that the chargee has no remedy while the charge is still floating. He can always intervene and obtain an injunction to prevent the company from dealing with its assets otherwise than in the ordinary course of its business. That no doubt is one reason why it is preferable to describe the charge as "hovering", a word which can bear an undertone of menace, rather than as "dormant". A cessation of business necessarily puts an end to the company's dealings with its assets. That which kept the charge hovering has now been released and the force of gravity causes it to settle and fasten on the subject of the charge within its reach and grasp. The paralysis, while it may still be unwelcome, can no longer be resisted.'

However, in the result the judge found on the evidence that at the relevant date there had been no relevant cesser of business.

Express automatic crystallisation

There has also in the past been some debate as to whether crystallisation may occur on the happening of an event specified in the instrument constituting the floating charge. This contingency is sometimes referred to as 'automatic' or 'self-generating' crystallisation in contrast to the crystallisation which may occur as a result of the debenture holder's intervention. The Cork Committee denied that there was any conceptual difficulty in the automatic crystallisation of a floating charge in a specified event, although accepting that the practical consequences are extremely inconvenient.[16] Prior to the decision of Hoffmann J in *Re Brightlife Ltd* it was suggested that there was no direct English authority on the point.[17] The concept had been embraced by a New Zealand court,[18] though strongly criticised in a Canadian case.[19] In fact as Professor Farrar had in 1976 rightly asserted,[20] there was at least one English case which clearly recognised the validity of automatic crystallisation clauses.[1] One may add in parentheses that in *Re Bond Worth Ltd*[2] Slade J referred in an obiter dictum to crystallisation taking place on a winding up, on the appointment of a receiver 'or the happening of some other agreed event'. One purpose of such a clause was to convert the floating charge into a fixed charge so as to secure the position of the debenture holder against the claims of preferential creditors.[3]

Commonwealth cases

In the New Zealand case of *Re Manurewa Transport Ltd*[4] the debtor company operated a carrying business and the debenture in question stated that the float-

---

15 (1878) 10 Ch D 530 at 541, CA per Sir George Jessel MR.
16 Cork Report (Cmnd 8558) 355, para 1572.
17 *Gore Browne on* Companies (43rd edn) para 18–5; Cork Report (Cmnd 8558) para 1572.
18 *Re Manurewa Transport Ltd* [1971] NZLR 909.
19 *R v Consolidated Churchill Copper Corpn Ltd* [1978] 5 WWR 652.
20 (1976) 40 Conv NS 397 at 400–403.
 1 *Re Horne and Hellard* (1885) 29 Ch D 736.
 2 [1980] Ch 228 at 266.
 3 But see now pp 262–264.
 4 [1971] NZLR 909; and see DW McLauchlan 'Automatic Crystallisation of a Floating Charge' (1972) New Zealand LJ 330. Cf *Covacich v Riordan* [1994] 2 NZLR 502 (effect of continued trading after automatic crystallisation).

ing charge should 'attach and become affixed' inter alia if the company should mortgage charge or encumber or attempt to mortgage charge or encumber any of its property or assets without the prior written consent of the lender. Subsequently the company, under pressure from another creditor, executed a chattel mortgage, by way of security, in other words it created a specific charge over chattels already subject to the floating security. Speight J held that the floating charge took priority over the chattel mortgage. The mere attempt to execute the chattel mortgage caused the floating charge, according to its terms, to crystallise at a point of time prior to the coming into force of the chattel mortgage. Speight J said:[5]

> 'After all a floating charge is not a word of art, it is a description for a type of
> security contained in a document which may provide a variety of circumstances
> whereupon crystallisation takes place. In this case, to mortgage or attempt to
> mortgage it is one of them.'

In other words the court held that the intervention of the debenture holder was *not* a prerequisite of crystallisation: crystallisation 'may be self-generated or at least debtor-generated'.[6] The decision was based on an analysis of earlier dicta and decisions[7] which has itself been criticised.[8] But the decision does not stand alone. It can be supported by reference to the decision of the New Zealand Court of Appeal in *Geoghegan v Greymouth-Point Elizabeth Rly & Coal Co Ltd*[9] and the High Court of Australia had provisionally recognised the validity of automatic crystallisation clauses in *Stein v Saywell*.[10]

An example of a debtor generated automatic crystallisation was envisaged in the clause at issue in *Fire Nymph Products Ltd v Heating Centre Pty Ltd*[11] where it was provided that crystallisation should take place at the moment immediately prior to any dealing with the charged property. The efficacy of such a clause was upheld not as a retrospective crystallisation but one which operated contemporaneously so that the assets passed to the disponee subject to a fixed charge.

English cases

In England the decision of Pearson J in *Re Horne and Hellard*[12] is clear authority for the recognition of automatic crystallisation clauses. He held that a purchaser was entitled to reasonable evidence that there had been no default occasioning a crystallisation, there being in the charge a clause providing that the charge should 'until default in the payment of the principal and interest ... be a floating

---

5   [1971] NZLR 909 at 917.
6   [1971] NZLR 909 at 916.
7   *Davey & Co v Williamson & Sons* [1898] 2 QB 194, 67 LJQB 699; *Evans v Rival Granite Quarries Ltd* [1910] 2 KB 979 at 1000, CA, *Paintin & Nottingham Ltd v Miller, Gale and Winter* [1971] NZLR 164.
8   See JH Farrar (1976) 40 Conv NS 397 at 400–404; Gough *Company Charges* (2nd edn, 1996) pp 247–252 which does not refer to Farrar's discussion.
9   (1898) 16 NZLR 749 at 768 and 771 which was not cited to Speight J.
10 [1969] ALR 481.
11 (1992) 7 ACSR 365.
12 (1885) 29 Ch D 736, 54 LJ Ch 919.

security'. It is true that the case was criticised by Kekewich J in *Brunton v Electrical Engineering Corpn*[13] who said that in such a case the security should continue to be regarded as floating until the appointment of a receiver, and that it is classified as anomalous by one writer.[14] But whatever policy objections[15] there may be to automatic crystallisation clauses, in the absence of legislation to the contrary, it is likely that an English court would rely on *Re Horne and Hellard* and the antipodean cases, and uphold the validity of an automatic crystallisation clause. Certainly it is common practice to include in debentures an automatic crystallisation clause along the lines of that upheld in *Re Manurewa Transport Ltd*.[16]

The question of automatic crystallisation was in 1986 subjected to rigorous analysis by Hoffmann J in *Re Brightlife Ltd*.[17] What was actually in issue was the validity of notices served by the debenture holder. The charge contained a provision in favour of Norandex Inc in the following terms:[18]

> 'Norandex may at any time by notice to Brightlife convert the floating charge into a specific charge as regards any assets specified in the notice which Norandex shall consider to be in danger of being seized or sold under any form of distress or execution levied or threatened or to be otherwise in jeopardy and may appoint a receiver thereof.'

Before the company went into voluntary liquidation the debenture holder had served notices under this provision and it was important to establish whether such service had the effect of causing the floating charge to crystallise so that the debenture holder had priority over the company's preferential creditors. Counsel for the Customs and Excise Commissioners argued that the events of crystallisation were fixed by law and not by the agreement of the parties: the only relevant events were winding up, appointment of a receiver and ceasing to carry on business.[19] Hoffmann J rejected this submission. He held that the authorities did not justify such a restrictive approach. The events on which a floating charge is to crystallise are purely a matter of contract. His decision was, it is true, to the effect that the notices constituted an intervention by the debenture holder which was considered effective. But he made it clear that his reasoning on the authorities and by reference to the considered nature of a floating charge was not only applicable to crystallisation by notice (sometimes called semi-automatic crystallisation): it was equally applicable to automatic crystallisation independent of any notice by the creditor.[20]

---

13 [1892] 1 Ch 434 at 440.
14 Gough *Company Charges* (2nd edn, 1996) pp 249–250.
15 See Farrar (1976) 40 Conv NS 397 at 400–404.
16 [1971] NZLR 909. For one common form clause, see GC Thorpe 'Floating Charges, Crystallisation and After-acquired Property' Legal Research Foundation Inc (Auckland) Occassional Paper (1981) pp 23–24.
17 [1987] Ch 200, [1986] 3 All ER 673.
18 [1987] Ch 200 at 207H–208A.
19 [1987] Ch 200 at 205–206.
20 [1987] Ch 200 at 212–214. See also Goode *Legal Problems of Credit and Security* (2nd edn) pp 70–74.

So far as the authorities were concerned, Hoffmann J pointed out that crystallisation on notice was implicitly recognised in *Re Griffin Hotel Co Ltd*,[1] and that apart from crystallisation being a matter of contract between lender and borrower the imposition of restrictions on automatic crystallisation in the interests of public policy was a matter for Parliament and not the courts. The validity and efficacy of an automatic crystallisation clause had been upheld by the New Zealand Supreme Court in *Re Manurewa Transport Ltd*[2] and Hoffmann J preferred the views expressed in that case to criticisms of the concept elsewhere. As indicated above, there are other overseas cases which uphold the concept of automatic crystallisation. Additionally, Nourse J treated cesser of business as a form of automatic crystallisation in *Re Woodroffes (Musical Instruments) Ltd*.[3] If the concept was to be challenged in an appellate court the challenge would be likely to fail both on conceptual grounds and by reason of the weight of authority in favour of automatic crystallisation. This weight has been increased by a further decision of Hoffmann J in *Re Permanent Houses (Holdings) Ltd*[4] that the making of a demand for all money due under the debenture was an event of default as defined in the debenture, which in accordance with a cognate provision caused the floating charge forthwith to crystallise. The judge referred to his earlier decision in *Re Woodroffes (Musical Instruments) Ltd*,[5] that, provided the language of the debenture was sufficiently clear, there was no conceptual reason why the parties should not agree that any specified event should cause the charge to crystallise. In the case before him the language, he held, 'could hardly be clearer'.[6]

It is pertinent to note here that where a right to appoint an administrator receiver was granted before 29 December 1986, the presentation of a petition for the appointment of an administrator will be deemed to be a condition precedent to the exercise of the right to appoint an administrator receiver.[7] Accordingly the prudent lender will specify as a crystallising event enabling the appointment of a receiver the presentation of a petition for an administrator; and on the happening of that event he will equally appoint a receiver before it is too late.[8]

Effect on third parties

Automatic crystallisation puts at risk anyone who deals with a company which has given a floating charge. Crystallisation can occur without the knowledge of the floating charge holder and the company might contrive to trade when, strictly speaking its trading power had ceased. This could happen, for example, where a complicated borrowing limit had been exceeded and the charge specifies that such an event shall occasion a crystallisation. Again it is absurd that a floating charge should automatically crystallise against the wishes of both parties as for

1 [1941] Ch 129, [1940] 4 All ER 324.
2 [1971] NZLR 909.
3 [1986] Ch 366, [1985] 2 All ER 908.
4 [1988] BCLC 563.
5 [1986] Ch 366, [1985] 2 All ER 908.
6 [1988] BCLC 563 at 567C–E.
7 IA 1986, Sch 11, para 1.
8 Once the administrator is in office it is too late: IA 1986, s 11(3)(b).

example where there is a technical default which the debenture holder is happy to overlook. In such a case there may be room for the operation of the doctrine of estoppel.[9] So far as third parties are concerned it is also arguable, in the absence of any authority directly in point, that automatic crystallisation does not necessarily give the holder of the crystallised charge priority over subsequent claimants. Depending on the circumstances a subsequent purchaser or mortgagee may be entitled to rely on the company's continued apparent authority to dispose of its assets free from the floating charge and so obtain priority over the holder of the floating charge.[10]

The Canadian courts have, as has already been mentioned, been resistant to the acceptance of automatic crystallisation. Thus Berger J in *R v Consolidated Churchill Copper Corpn Ltd*[11] concluded that the English cases did not support a general concept of automatic crystallisation and in particular did not admit of such a concept where the causative event was a simple default in payment. He also found the whole concept objectionable on policy grounds:[12]

> 'The company would not know where it stood; neither would the company's creditors. How is anyone to know the true state of affairs between the debenture holder and the company unless there is an unequivocal act of intervention?'

But on careful scrutiny the case appears less decisive.[13] The wording of the relevant clause did not in fact specify *automatic* attachment on the occurrence of the specified event.

It is true that various commentators have also drawn attention to what they perceive to be practical and conceptual disadvantages of automatic crystallisation.[14] The necessity for an intervention by the debenture holder has been emphasised in two subsequent Canadian decisions,[15] but in neither was there any close analysis of the wording of the relevant automatic crystallisation clause. Moreover, *Re Brightlife Ltd* is of persuasive authority to the contrary, suggesting as it does that English law accepts the concept and does not require intervention by the debenture holder.

Necessity for clear words

The extent to which some courts will go to avoid a construction in favour of automatic crystallisation is demonstrated in another Canadian case, namely *Re*

---

9 Goode *Legal Problems of Credit and Security* (2nd edn) p 73.
10 *Goode* at pp 59 and 90.
11 [1978] 5 WWR 652.
12 [1978] 5 WWR 652 at 665.
13 For such a scrutiny, see David Milman and Diane Hare. 'Automatic Crystallisation Controversy is Revived' (1980) 1 Co Law 110.
14 Farrar (1976) 40 Conv NS 397 at 404–406; Gough *Company Charges* (2nd edn, 1996) pp 241–242; and see GC Thorpe 'Floating Charges, Crystallisation and After-Acquired Property' Legal Research Foundations Inc (Auckland) Occasional Paper (1981); RL Dean 'Crystallisation of a Floating Charge' (1983) Company and Securities Law Jo 185 at 196–198.
15 *Bank of Montreal v Woodtown Developments Ltd* (1979) 99 DLR (3d) 739 at 744 per Osler J; *Federal Business Development Bank v Red Lion Restaurant Ltd* (1979) 101 DLR (3d) 480 at cf 484 per Moore J.

Caroma Enterprises Ltd.[16] A company had assigned its future book debts to a bank in such a way as to confer on the bank a floating charge over the debts. The agreement provided that the company should be free to deal with the book debts in the ordinary course of business 'until default *or*[17] until notice by the bank'. The question was whether there could be crystallisation without the intervention of the bank. Despite the use of the word 'or' in the provision just quoted Macdonald J held that it was the clear intention of the parties that the charge should only crystallise on the bank giving notice to the company:[18]

> 'If simple failure of the debtor to make promised payments to the bank were sufficient to crystallise the floating debenture such an event would not necessarily indicate any intention on the part of the bank to convert the floating charge into a specific charge. In fact financial arrangements and the conduct of business would become well nigh impossible if a floating charge became automatically crystallised on any default of payment no matter how minor.'

As the learned judge articulated it, 'the act or event relied upon to crystallise the charge must clearly show that it is capable only of the interpretation that crystallisation took place'.

The dictum just cited from *Re Caroma Enterprises Ltd* underlines the need for explicit language to effectuate an automatic crystallisation. A court would obviously lean against construing a temporary exceeding of a borrowing limit or technical irregularities of payment (both of which might be unknown to the parties) as crystallisation events.[19] Such cases are far removed from a case where the relevant event is the levying of execution against the company's assets[20] or the attempt to create an unauthorised charge,[1] as indeed was suggested by Berger J in *R v Consolidated Churchill Copper Corpn Ltd.*[2] So there must be words so clear that third parties should be able, easily, to discover whether particular events have occurred, and to be satisfied that the intervention of the debenture holder is to be triggered by the event in question. It is not therefore sufficient to provide that the security shall become 'enforceable'[3] or that on default the lender 'may collect, deal or otherwise deal' with the assets.[4] It must be made plain beyond peradventure that on a clearly identifiable event there will be no place for optional intervention by the debenture holder. A provision that on the relevant event the charge will 'crystallise automatically' can leave no room for doubt on this score: nor indeed does a provision that the charge shall 'attach immediately'.[5]

---

16 (1979) 108 DLR (3d) 412. For an appraisal of this decision, see David Milman and Diane Hare 'Company Charges: Recent Developments in Canada' (1981) 125 Sol Jo 549–550.
17 Emphasis added.
18 (1979) 108 DLR (3d) 412 at 418.
19 See Farrar (1976) 40 Conv 397 at 405.
20 *Davey & Co v Williamson & Sons* [1898] 2 QB 194.
1 *Re Manurewa Transport Ltd* [1971] NZLR 909.
2 (1979) 90 DLR (3d) 357.
3 *R v Consolidated Churchill Copper Corpn Ltd* (1979) 90 DLR (3d) 357; cf *Davey & Co v Williamson & Sons* [1898] 2 QB 194.
4 *Re Caroma Enterprises Ltd* (1979) 108 DLR (3d) 412.
5 *Re Manurewa Transport Ltd* [1971] NZLR 909.

The debenture in *Re Bismarck Australia Pty Ltd*[6] provided that the money secured 'shall at the option of the mortgagee immediately become due and payable without necessity for any demand or notice (notwithstanding any delay or previous waiver of the provisions of this clause by the mortgagee) and this security shall become enforceable and the right of the company to deal for any purpose with the mortgaged property shall forthwith cease' on a number of specified events. It was held by Jenkinson J in the Supreme Court of Victoria that the introductory words just quoted did not cause the floating charge to become fixed upon the happening of any one or more of the events specified in the numbered sub-clauses. The provisions of the clause *postponed* the 'crystallisation' of the charge until the debenture holder exercised an option, which the occurrence of one of the specified events conferred on him, to bring about that result. So in the event the floating charge did not become fixed in relation to the assets over which it had been given until the receivers were in fact appointed.

Position of prior debenture holder if receiver appointed under later charge

One problem which has prompted considerable speculation among practitioners in England is what is the position of a first debenture holder where a receiver is appointed under a subsequent debenture. In *Stein v Saywell*[7] it was assumed that a *subsequent* floating charge crystallised automatically on the appointment of a receiver under an *earlier* floating charge. If this assumption be correct then a fortiori the converse must be true. However, the point was not actually argued in *Stein v Saywell*: it appears to have been agreed by counsel.[8] Moreover there is no statement in any reported English case or in any textbook to the effect that where there are two successive floating charges on the same property the appointment of a receiver under the later debenture automatically crystallises the earlier.

If the appointment has this effect it must be either (i) because the appointment of a receiver is analogous to a winding up or (ii) because, on the appointment of a receiver the company ceases to carry on business as a going concern (this being a crystallising event) or (iii) because the crystallisation of the later security is inconsistent with the continued floating of the earlier. But each of these suggested explanations fails to persuade.

First, there is no sufficiently convincing analogy between the appointment of a receiver under a floating charge and the liquidation of a company. Once a company is in course of winding up, it no longer has any power to carry on business except for the purposes of a beneficial winding up. The assets of a company in a winding up are treated as a distributable fund; and they are distributable to unsecured proving creditors ordinary as well as preferred and subject thereto *to the shareholders*. They are not (unless the liquidation is stayed) returnable *to the company*. There cannot sensibly be a floating charge on a distributable fund; and the scheme of distribution which puts non-preferential

6 [1981] VR 527.
7 (1969) 121 CLR 529.
8 (1969) 121 CLR 529 at 542, 553 and 558.

creditors and shareholders before the debenture holder who does not prove as an unsecured creditor is inconsistent with the existence of a security on the assets of *the company.*

On the other hand, in the case of a receivership the position is completely different. The receiver may and often does carry on the business at a profit, realise sufficient to pay preferential claims and discharge the debenture, and hand the business back to the company as a going concern. In other words the company never ceases to carry on business, albeit through the medium of the receiver; its assets never become a distributable fund; and they never become payable to ordinary non-preferential creditors or shareholders intended to rank behind the earlier debenture; they are returnable to the company and remain subject to the earlier debenture.

Next, as to the suggestion that on the appointment of a receiver the company ceases to carry on business it must be reiterated that the appointment of a receiver does not, necessarily, constitute cessation of business. It may, but need not, have that consequence.

There are dicta in *Re Crompton & Co Ltd*[9] which appear to support the contention that the business necessarily ceases on the appointment of a receiver, but a closer examination shows that they do not: the case was in fact one concerned with a liquidation, not a receivership; and the question before the court was, strictly, not whether the security had crystallised, but whether the debt was payable and whether a receiver should be appointed.

Again it is true that in *MG Charley Pty Ltd v FH Wells Pty Ltd*[10] Jacobs J stated that 'the appointment of the receiver had the effect that the company would cease to carry on business on its own account and would cause the charge to crystallise'. Here however the learned judge was speaking of the appointment of a receiver under the debenture in question; it is not a general statement of principle. Certainly it is a curiously roundabout and unnecessary proposition to say that the appointment of a receiver by the debenture holder himself crystallises the charge because it involves the cessation of trade by the company.

Thirdly, the argument that the crystallisation of the later security is inconsistent with the continued floating of the earlier security is fallacious. The argument probably derives from the supposition that, by causing his security to crystallise, the second debenture holder thereby obtains priority over the first, as if the two securities ranked in the order in which the receivers were appointed. But this is not the case. The appointment of the receiver under the second charge converts it into a fixed charge, but does not affect its priority. It continues to rank subject to the earlier floating charge.

The first debenture holder, then, remains entitled, at any time, to appoint a receiver, cause his charge to crystallise and demand possession of any assets not yet applied in payment of the company's debts, whether secured or unsecured. Just so long as the first debenture holder acts in time, that is, before the receiver under the later charge has actually paid the preferential claims or his own debenture holder, he retains his own priority. It is also not without significance

9 [1914] 1 Ch 954.
10 [1963] NSWR 22.

that in the Companies (Floating Charges and Receivers) (Scotland) Act 1972, which introduced the floating charge into Scotland, and provided for crystallisation upon the commencement of the winding up of the company or upon the appointment of a receiver the only floating charge to crystallise in the latter event is the charge 'by virtue of which he was appointed'. So in Scotland the appointment of a receiver under a later charge did *not* crystallise the earlier charge. It would be odd if the position were any different in England.

In Canada it has been held that where two floating charges are executed by a company, both duly registered, the earlier in execution and registration takes priority notwithstanding that the later charge is first crystallised by the appointment of a receiver.[11] Although by the presumed intention of the parties to the earlier debenture a charge on specific property would take priority over the debenture,[12] it would be contrary to that intention to contemplate its subordination to a subsequent floating charge in the absence of express words.[13] The act of crystallisation does not alter the nature of the interest held by a subsequent debenture holder so as to give it priority over a predecessor, where the interest in both cases is bestowed by a floating charge. Crystallisation, in a word, does not change priorities.

Priorities between mortgage and floating charge

An interesting question of priorities between a *mortgage* and a floating charge occurred in *Security Trust Co v Royal Bank of Canada*[14] in the Privy Council on appeal from the Court of Appeal of the Bahama Islands. The appellant entered into a contract to sell certain land in the Bahamas, the contract providing that the purchaser should grant a mortgage of the property to the appellant to secure the balance of the purchase price. When, after several extensions of time, a conveyance was executed by the appellant and a mortgage was executed by the purchaser both were held by the appellant in escrow until the balance of the purchase price was paid. The purchaser then executed a floating charge in favour of the respondent bank. The appellant mortgagee was held to have priority over the debenture holder, who had appointed a receiver, and had paid off the balance of the purchase price. In these circumstances the charge under the debenture only bites on property which is already fettered by the agreement to give the other charge.[15] Had the mortgage been created out of an interest unfettered by any such agreement the charge would have had an unencumbered fee simple upon which to bite, and the priority would have been different.[16]

---

11 *Re Household Products Co Ltd and Federal Business Development Bank* (1981) 124 DLR (3d) 325 following *Harvey Dodds Ltd v Royal Bank of Canada* (1979) 105 DLR (3d) 650 at 653–654, 34 CBRNS 163 at 167.
12 *Re Benjamin Cope & Sons Ltd* [1914] 1 Ch 800 at 806–807.
13 *Re Automatic Bottle Makers Ltd* [1926] Ch 412, CA.
14 [1976] AC 503, [1976] 1 All ER 381.
15 [1976] AC 503 at 520.
16 On the analogy of *Church of England Building Society v Piskor* [1954] Ch 553, [1954] 2 All ER 85, CA.

DECRYSTALLISATION OR REFLOTATION

There is as yet no case which establishes whether a floating charge which has crystallised is a changeling capable of being reconverted into a floating charge, in other words whether the crystallised fixed charge can be, so to speak, de-crystallised, or refloated.

The answer to the question, it is thought, is that 'it all depends'. The crucial point is whether the debenture holder is still in direct control. If he is, he can always agree with the chargor that the charge shall float again. Equally, if a subsequent floating charge has automatically crystallised the prior charge could refloat with the consent of the subsequent debenture holder. Indeed, such contingencies may be covered by express provision in the debenture itself. No re-registration would seem to be necessary under the provisions of s 395 of the Companies Act 1985: the charge is the same but is just detached from that to which it was attached.

The position is otherwise if a receiver has been appointed or the company is in liquidation. If a receiver has been appointed it is the receiver and not the debenture holder who is in control of the company's assets. And failing some express provision in the debenture the debenture holder cannot direct the receiver to hand back the management of the assets to the company. Moreover the receiver is bound by a statutory obligation to pay preferential debts out of the assets that are subject to the charge.[17] But the debenture holder may be entitled to remove the receiver without replacing him. If that happens then indeed subject to payment of the receiver's remuneration and expenses and of the preferential creditors the debenture holder will be in a position to restore control to the directors. Naturally, if the receiver completes his task, and the debenture holder and preferential creditors are satisfied, control of the remaining assets can again be transferred back to the directors. But that cannot be done when the company is in liquidation: control will then be transferred to the liquidator.

Once a liquidator is appointed de-crystallisation is no longer a possibility. But that case apart there seems no good reason why a debenture should not contain a provision enabling the charge to refloat.[18]

PARTIAL CRYSTALLISATION

In the absence of some express provision in the debenture a floating charge cannot be made to crystallise as to a part only of the assets so as to enable a debenture holder to seize a particular asset, while leaving the charge floating over the rest of the assets.[19] But if there is such an express provision the charge

---

17 IA 1986, s 40.
18 See O'Donovan 'Termination of Receivership' (1979) Chartered Accountant of Australia (Sept) 47; RL Dean 'Crystallisation of a Floating Charge' (1983) Companies and Securities Law Journal 185 at 200–201; Low Chee Keong 'Automatic Crystallisation and Reflotation Clauses: The Advent of a New Pouncing Security [1995] 3 MLJ xcvii–cxxiv.
19 *Evans v Rival Granite Quarries Ltd* [1910] 2 KB 979, 79 LJKB 970, CA.

will of course continue to float over the assets not subject to the appointment of a receiver.[20]

Presumably it would be open to a lender to devise a clause providing for automatic partial crystallisation so as to attach to any particular asset if that asset should be put in jeopardy, for example by threatened execution.[1]

It is true that Fletcher Moulton LJ in *Evans v Rival Granite Quarries*[2] asserted that:

> 'It is inconsistent with the nature of a floating security that the holder should be able to pounce down on particular assets and to interfere with the company's business while still keeping his security a floating security; he cannot at once give freedom and insist on servitude.'

But this statement is directed to a floating charge which lacks any express wording that can override the generally accepted nature of a floating charge.

Partial crystallisation actually occurred in *Re Griffin Hotel Co Ltd*,[3] a case of a court-appointed receiver. In the light of the actual wording of the order appointing the receiver and manager, only partial crystallisation took place and the creditors had no relief against that part of the property on which the floating charge had fixed. Bennett J commented:[4]

> 'On December 9 1938, that charge ceased to float on the property and assets of which Mr Veale was appointed receiver. The charge on that day crystallised and became fixed on that property . . . It remained a floating charge on any other assets of the borrowers.'

Thus the notion of partial crystallisation has been held feasible so long as the wording is right.

20 *R v Consolidated Churchill Copper Corpn Ltd* [1978] 5 WWR 652.
 1 For this possibility, see Gough *Company Charges* (2nd edn, 1996), pp 401–403.
 2 [1910] 2 KB 979 at 998, CA.
 3 [1941] Ch 129, [1940] 4 All ER 324.
 4 [1941] Ch 129 at 135.

CHAPTER 3

Grounds for appointment

Apart from any statutory power of appointment arising out of a deed of charge the circumstances in which an appointment may be made are invariably defined in the instrument creating the charge. Naturally institutional lenders, debenture holders or trustees for debenture holders will be anxious to make sure that the relevant document sets out all the relevant circumstances which are to trigger the option to appoint a receiver and manager of the company's business.

In its simplest form a debenture will provide that the debenture holder may appoint a receiver and manager of the charged property where the company so requests or at any time after the principal monies secured by the debenture has become immediately payable, and will define the circumstances when the principal monies and all unpaid interest accrued thereon shall become immediately payable and the security enforceable.[1] The events which are usually made the occasion of an immediate obligation to pay are:[2]

(a) if the company makes default for a stipulated period in the payment of any interest thereby secured and the debenture holder before such interest is paid by notice in writing calls in the principal moneys;

(b) if a distress or execution is levied or issued against any of the property of the company and is not paid within a stipulated period;

(c) if an order is made or an effective resolution is passed for the winding up of the company;

(d) if the company ceases or threatens to cease to carry on its business or substantially the whole of its business;

(e) if an incumbrancer takes possession or a receiver is appointed of any part of the assets of the company;

(f) if the company is unable to pay its debts within the meaning of s 123 of the Insolvency Act 1986 or any statutory modification or re-enactment thereof;

(g) if a prior debenture becomes enforceable;

---

1 6 *Forms and Precedents* (4th edn) 1184, and see 10 *Forms and Precedents* (5th edn) 758–759.
2 6 *Forms and Precedents* (4th edn) at 1183–1184.

(h)   if the company makes default in observing or fulfilling any of its obligations under the debenture (other than its obligation in respect of interest) and the debenture holder by notice in writing calls in the principal monies secured by the debenture;

Other additional events singled out by another common form debenture[3] include:

(i)   if any execution or other process of any court or authority is issued out against the mortgaged premises or any part thereof for any sum whatever;

(j)   if the balance sheet of the company should not be duly made out in accordance with the company's articles of association and the provisions of the Companies Act 1985 and certified by the auditors of the company;

(k)   if at any time it appears from the balance sheet of the company that the liabilities of the company exceed its assets, including uncalled capital, or that the company is carrying on business at a loss or that the company's book debts, stock-in-trade and cash are together less than a stipulated amount or that further prosecution by the company of its business will endanger the security of the debenture holder;

(l)   if the company shall without the consent of the debenture holder make or attempt to make any alteration in the provisions of its memorandum or articles of association which might in the opinion of the debenture holder detrimentally affect the security;

(m)   if the company, without the written consent of the debenture holder, shall create or purport or attempt to create any charge or mortgage ranking or which by any means may be made to rank on the mortgage premises, other than the general assets pari passu with or in priority to the security constituted by the debenture;

A further precedent[4] yields yet another event:

(n)   if in the opinion of the debenture holder the security shall be in jeopardy.

Other specific events could be chosen: the reduction of capital; the passing of a resolution that uncalled capital should not be capable of being called up save in a liquidation; and detrimental dissension at board level. Lenders and their advisers should keep abreast of precautions taken by other lenders and should scrutinise, in particular, common forms used by the banks and other institutional lenders. No doubt the last listed event (jeopardy) will cover comprehensively many of the situations where a debenture holder would be justified in getting worried enough to appoint a receiver.

   It should, however, be noted that in the absence of an express provision covering the point, the debenture holder is not entitled to appoint a receiver out

---

3 See Palmer's *Company Precedents* Part 3 (16th edn) pp 279–280 (a trust deed whose contents are adopted in the list which follows).
4 6 *Forms and Precedents* (4th edn) 1315 (a trust deed).

of court where the security is, or is thought to be, in jeopardy.[5] That could only constitute a basis for having a receiver appointed by the court.[6] In *Cryne v Barclays Bank plc*,[7] where the Court of Appeal held that the absence of an express 'jeopardy' provision meant that the debenture holder could not itself appoint a receiver, it was argued that there was an implied term that the debenture holder was entitled to appoint a receiver if it, on reasonable grounds, considered that the security was in jeopardy. Such a term could be implied only where it was necessary to give business efficacy to the contract.[8] But since the agreement between the parties contained a number of express provisions designed to protect the debenture holder's security there was no justification for implying any further terms to deal with 'jeopardy'.[9] If the debenture holder wanted any such right it should have inserted an express term, or made the loan repayable on demand.[10]

---

5 *Cryne v Barclays Bank plc* [1987] BCLC 548, CA. See especially at 554 F–G referring to head (n) above in the first edition of this book.
6 *Re London Pressed Hinge Co Ltd* [1905] 1 Ch 576.
7 [1987] BCLC 548, CA (Kerr LJ and May LJ).
8 See *Liverpool City Council v Irwin* [1977] AC 239 at 252, HL et seq.
9 [1987] BCLC 548 at 556F–557A.
10 [1987] BCLC 548 at 557A.

CHAPTER 4

Choice of receiver

INTRODUCTION

Prior to the insolvency law reforms now contained in the Insolvency Act 1986 the only positive qualification required of a receiver and manager of a company was that he should be an individual of full age. Negatively, a person was disqualified from being a receiver if a body corporate[1] or an undischarged bankrupt.[2] In particular there was no requirement of professional or practical qualification, though of course the appointor owed a duty to the debtor company to take reasonable care not to appoint a person who was incompetent.[3] Beyond this, in England at least, there was no other bar.

The law remains undisturbed so far as receivers who are *not* administrative receivers are concerned. But as regards administrative receivers of a company only individuals who are qualified to act as insolvency practitioners can now be appointed.

It will be convenient therefore to discuss first administrative receivers before turning to non-administrative receivers and to the qualifications and disqualifications which obtain in other jurisdictions. The appointment of joint receivers and managers is discussed in the last section of this chapter.

ADMINISTRATIVE RECEIVER

In England and Wales a person who acts as an administrative receiver of a company is acting in relation to it as an insolvency practitioner.[4] An 'administrative receiver' means:

(a) a receiver or manager of the whole (or substantially the whole) of a company's property appointed by or on behalf of the holders of any debentures of the company secured by a charge which, as created, was a floating charge, or by such a charge and one or more securities;

1 See CA 1985, s 489 (repealed) and CA 1948, s 366 (repealed).
2 See CA 1985, s 490 (repealed) and CA 1948, s 367 (repealed).
3 *Shamji v Johnson Matthey Bankers Ltd* [1986] BCLC 278.
4 IA 1986, s 388(1).

(b)   a person who would be such a receiver or manager but for the appointment of some other person as the receiver of part of the company's property.[5]

A receiver who is not an administrative receiver (ie a receiver of less than a 'substantial' part of the company's property[6]) is not required to be qualified to act.

Disqualification and professional qualification

The scheme of the new law is to continue the pre-existing disqualifications while at the same time ensuring that administrative receivers are of a suitably high standard of competence and integrity. This latter aim is secured by requiring administrative receivers to be qualified insolvency practitioners.

The pre-existing (and rather curious) bar on corporate receivers[7] is therefore continued. A body corporate is not qualified for appointment as receiver of the property of a company, and any body corporate which acts as such a receiver is liable to a fine.[8] Corporations are also barred from being qualified to act as insolvency practitioners.[9] The appointment of a corporate body as a receiver has been held to be a complete nullity.[10] As Wynn Parry J explained in *Portman Building Society v Gallwey*:[11]

> 'In my view, the language is perfectly clear and it is intended to prevent, and has the effect of preventing, a body corporate from being the receiver of the property of a company. It has, in my view, the effect of making it ultra vires anybody corporate to act as receiver, and it follows, in my judgment, that any attempt to appoint a body corporate as receiver of the property of a company must be a nullity and must fail to create any contractual relations between the body corporate in question and the company over whose property it purports to be appointed receiver.'

A further effect of the appointment being a complete nullity is that it will or may be inoperative to cause crystallisation of the floating charge.

Again, the previous bar on an undischarged bankrupt acting as a receiver[12] is also continued. It is provided that if a person being an undischarged bankrupt acts as receiver or manager of the property of a company on behalf of debenture holders, he is liable to imprisonment or a fine, or both.[13] This last-mentioned provision does not apply to a court-appointed receiver but it is almost inconceivable that the court would appoint an undischarged bankrupt to be a receiver.

---

5   IA 1986, s 29.
6   IA 1986, ss 29(2), 251.
7   See CA 1985, s 489 (repealed) and CA 1948, s 366 (repealed).
8   IA 1986, s 30. For penalties, see s 430 and Sch 10.
9   IA 1986, s 390(1).
10 *Portman Building Society v Gallwey* [1955] 1 All ER 227, [1955] 1 WLR 96.
11 [1955] 1 WLR 96 at 100.
12 See the CA 1985, s 490 (repealed) and CA 1948, s 367 (repealed).
13 IA 1986, s 31.

Undischarged bankrupts are also disqualified from acting as insolvency practitioners,[14] as are persons subject to a disqualification order.[15]

The method by which statute has provided that an administrative receiver shall be properly qualified in order to act is by defining specifically the phrase 'act as an insolvency practitioner' in relation to a company[16] by acting as its administrative receiver. So where the Insolvency Act 1986 lays down provisions for persons acting as insolvency practitioners it is, among other things, laying down those provisions in respect of administrative receivers.[17] For example, a person who acts as an insolvency practitioner in relation to a company when he is not qualified to do so is liable to imprisonment or a fine, or both.[18] In other words it is an offence for a person to act, inter alia, as an administrative receiver if he lacks the requisite qualifications of an insolvency practitioner.

Independently of any statutory disqualification, a person may be precluded by contract from being a receiver as happened in a case where investigating accountants had contracturally agreed not to act as receivers.[19]

Qualifications of an insolvency practitioner

Definition of 'insolvency practitioner'

In order to qualify[20] as an insolvency practitioner a person must either (i) be a member of (or a person bound by the rules of) a recognised professional body,[1] or (ii) obtain authorisation to act from a competent authority as prescribed by statute,[2] but (iii) must in either case, as a condition of his holding office, have given the required security.[3]

Clearly the majority of qualified individuals will be members of a recognised professional body but some will be directly licensed by the competent authority. These terms 'recognised professional body' and 'competent authority' require explanation, as does the security required.

The Act also specifically lists other persons who are not qualified to act as insolvency practitioners. These are persons who are not individuals (in other words corporate bodies), undischarged bankrupts, persons subject to a

---

14 IA 1986, s 390(4)(a).

15 Company Directors Disqualification Act 1986, ss 1(1), 2–12.

16 As to what is a company for this purpose, see IA 1986, s 388(4) incorporating the definitions of 'company' in CA 1985, s 735.

17 Both professionally and in respect of his special eligibility to act in relation to a particular company.

18 IA 1986, s 389(1). For penalties, see IA 1986, s 430 and Sch 10.

19 *Sheppard & Cooper Ltd v TSB Bank plc* [1997] 2 BCLC 222, CA.

20 Both professionally and under the subordinate legislation.

 1 IA 1986, s 390(2)(a). The body must be recognised under IA 1986, s 391.

 2 IA 1986, ss 390(2)(b) and 393.

 3 IA 1986, s 390(3). The adequacy of the security is subject to review: IR 1986, r 12(2). And see Insolvency Practitioners Regulations 1990, SI 1990/439 Part III (as amended by SI 1993/221).

disqualification order made under the Company Directors Disqualification Act 1986[4] (CDDA 1986) and patients within the meaning of Pt VII of the Mental Health Act 1983.[4] Persons falling within these categories are automatically debarred from acting as insolvency practitioners: their disqualification or disqualification undertaking[5] does not depend upon the withdrawal[6] of any relevant authorisation. Acts done by such a disqualified person may, however, be valid.[7]

Authorisation by virtue of membership of a recognised professional body

A person is qualified to act as an insolvency practitioner subject to the condition of providing security if he is authorised to act by virtue of membership of a professional body whose rules allow him so to act.[8]

The Secretary of State is empowered to declare by order which bodies seem to him to fall within the statutory criteria.[9] So far the following bodies have been recognised by such an order: (i) the Chartered Association of Certified Accountants, (ii) the Institute of Chartered Accountants in England and Wales, (iii) the Institute of Chartered Accountants in Scotland, (iv) the Institute of Chartered Accountants in Ireland, (v) the Insolvency Practitioners Association, (vi) the Law Society of Scotland and (vii) the Law Society.[10]

Membership of any of the foregoing 'recognised' bodies is not in itself enough, nor in some cases even necessary.[11] The recognised professional body must regulate the practice of a profession and enforce rules for securing that such of its members as are permitted by or under the rules to act as insolvency practitioners (a) are fit and proper persons to act in that capacity, and (b) meet acceptable requirements as to education and practice, training and experience.[12] The Secretary of State can withdraw recognition from the professional body concerned.[13] This power of revocation will be a sanction to keep up standards. Revocation is effected by an order revoking the previous order granting recognition and any such order revoking a previous order may make provision whereby members of the body in question continue to be treated as authorised to act as insolvency practitioners for a specified period after the revocation takes effect.[14]

---

4 IA 1986, s 390(4). For disqualification orders see CDDA 1986, s 1 as amended by Insolvency Bill 2000, cl 5 and for grounds, see cll 2–5 (general misconduct in connection with companies), 6–9 (unfitness), 10–12 (other costs).
5 CDDA 1986, s 1(1A) added by Insolvency Bill 2000, cl 6.
6 Under IA 1986, s 393.
7 See IA 1986, s 232. The protection afforded is confined to acts done by an *individual*: IA 1986, s 232. Presumably an act done by a corporate appointee would be wholly void.
8 IA 1986, s 390(2).
9 IA 1986, s 391(1).
10 See the Insolvency Practitioners (Recognised Professional Bodies) Order 1986, SI 1986/1764.
11 IA 1986, s 391(3).
12 IA 1986, s 391(2).
13 IA 1986, s 391(4).
14 IA 1986, s 391(5).

Definition of competent authority

Most insolvency practitioners will qualify by virtue of their membership of a recognised professional body satisfying the criteria just discussed. But a person who is unable to get a licence from that body may make an application to a competent authority, for authorisation to act as an insolvency practitioner.[15]

The 'competent authority' to whom an application for authorisation must be made will be either a person or body designated by the Secretary of State in relation to specified types of case or, where no such designation has been made, the Secretary of State himself.[16] No competent authority has been specified in directions given under this provision. Accordingly, for the time being, the only competent authority is the Secretary of State.

Authorisation by competent authorities

A competent authority may, on an application duly made in accordance with the statutory procedure and after being furnished with all such information as it may require under that procedure, grant or refuse the application.[17] The authority must, it is provided, grant the application if it appears to the authority, from the information furnished by the applicant, and having regard to such other information as it may have, that the applicant (i) is a fit and proper person to act as an insolvency practitioner, and (ii) meets the prescribed requirements with respect to education and practical training and experience.[18] Regulations detail the matters which are to be taken into account in determining whether an applicant is a fit and proper person.[19] In theory there is a power to require from the applicant details of the required educational qualifications and practical experience.[20] This avenue for access to qualification is unlikely to represent an easy alternative to membership of, and qualification through, a recognised professional body.

The application must be made in such form as the competent authority may direct, and must contain or be accompanied by such information as that authority may reasonably require for the purpose of determining the application.[1] The prescribed fee must accompany the application,[2] and the authority may direct that notice of the making of the application shall be published in such manner as may be specified in the direction.[3] The 'competent authority' may also, at any time after receiving the application and determining it, require the applicant to furnish additional information.[4] Directions and requirements given or imposed in

---

15 IA 1986, s 392(1).
16 IA 1986, s 392(2).
17 IA 1986, s 393(1).
18 IA 1986, s 393(2).
19 *Royal Trust Bank v Buchler* [1989] BCLC 130 (proper case for leave must be shown).
20 Insolvency Practitioners Regulations 1990, SI 1990/439, regs 4, 5 and 6.
 1 IA 1986, s 392(3).
 2 IA 1986. At present the fee is £200: see Insolvency Practitioners Regulations 1990 (IPR 1990), SI 1990/439, reg 9.
 3 IA 1986, s 392(3).
 4 IA 1986, s 392(4).

relation to the application or any further information in connection with such application may differ as between different applications.[5] Any information to be furnished to the competent authority under s 392 must, if the competent authority requires, be in such form or verified in such manner as the competent authority may specify.[6] An application may be withdrawn before it is granted or refused.[7]

The Secretary of State is charged to pay any application fees received by him into the Consolidated Fund.[8] Other competent authorities may restrict the sums paid to them and will thereby be enabled to be wholly or partly self-funded.[9]

Grant, refusal and withdrawal of authorisation

An authorisation granted by a competent authority, if not previously withdrawn, continues in force for such period (not exceeding the prescribed maximum) as may be specified in the authorisation.[10] The prescribed maximum is at present three years from the date on which the authorisation was granted.[11] A duly granted authorisation may be withdrawn if it appears to that authority: (i) that the holder is no longer a fit and proper person; or (ii) that the holder has failed to comply with any of the provisions of Pt XIII of the Insolvency Act 1986 or any regulations or under the Rules; or (iii) the holder has, in purported compliance with any such provision, furnished a competent authority with false, misleading or inaccurate information.[12] A duly granted authorisation may also be withdrawn by the competent authority at the request, or with the consent, of the holder of the authorisation.[13]

If a competent authority grants an authorisation it must give written notice of that fact to the applicant, specifying the date on which the authorisation takes effect.[14] Likewise where an authority proposes to refuse or withdraw an authorisation it must give the applicant or holder written notice of its intention to do so, setting out the grounds on which it proposes to act.[15] In the case of a proposed withdrawal, the notice must state the date on which it is proposed that the withdrawal should take effect.[16] A notice of proposed refusal or withdrawal must give particulars of the statutory rights of making representations thereon and of having the matter referred to the Insolvency Practitioners Tribunal.[17] It would appear to follow that in order to be consistent with the scheme of the Act as a whole, the date when any withdrawal is to take effect should be fixed at least

---

5 IA 1986, s 392(5).
6 IA 1986, s 392(6).
7 IA 1986, s 392(7).
8 IA 1986, s 392(8).
9 IA 1986, s 392(8).
10 IA 1986, s 393(3).
11 IPR 1990, SI 1990/439, reg 10 .
12 IA 1986, s 393(4). The procedure for appeal from the withdrawal of the refusal of an authorisation is set out in ss 394–398.
13 IA 1986, s 393(5).
14 IA 1986, s 394(1).
15 IA 1986, s 394(2).
16 IA 1986, s 394(3).
17 IA 1986, s 394(4).

28 days ahead,[18] and the notice should probably state in addition 'or such later date as the authority may subsequently fix, if steps are taken by the holder to have the case reconsidered or reviewed'.[19]

A person on whom a notice of refusal or withdrawal is served may within 14 days after the date of service make written representations to the competent authority.[20] The competent authority is required to have regard to any representations so made in determining whether to refuse the application or withdraw the authorisation as the case may be.[1]

Reference to Tribunal

On 1 July 1986 there came into being a tribunal known as the Insolvency Practitioners Tribunal.[2] This Tribunal was confirmed in its position under the Insolvency Act 1986 and the provisions of Sch 7 to that Act regulate its constitution and operation.[3]

Reference procedure

A person who has been notified of a purported refusal or withdrawal of his authorisation may invoke the jurisdiction of the Tribunal. He can take this course on receipt of notification of the implied decision[4] or after confirmation of that decision following reconsideration of the matter.[5] In either case he must give written notice to the authority requiring the case to be referred to the Tribunal and the written notice must be given within 28 days of service of the relevant notice upon him.[6] He can also interrupt any process of reconsideration by asking the authority to refer the matter to the Tribunal forthwith.

On receipt of the notice requiring the case to be referred to the Tribunal the authority has seven days to alter its decision and notify the person accordingly. Unless it does revise its decision, it *must* refer the matter to the Tribunal though the relevant reference does not have to be within the seven-day period.[7]

Action of Tribunal

Following a reference to it, the Tribunal must investigate the case and make a *report* to the competent authority.[8] The report is not a decision. It is simply a statement of what in the opinion of the Tribunal would be the appropriate

---

18 See Sealy and Milman *Annotated Guide to the 1986 Insolvency Legislation* (2nd edn, 1989) p 418.
19 *Sealy and Milman* 418. See IA 1986, ss 395 and 396.
20 IA 1986, s 395(1).
1 IA 1986, s 395(2).
2 It was established under IA 1985, s 8(6) (repealed).
3 IA 1986, s 396(1).
4 IA 1986, s 396(2)(a).
5 IA 1986, s 396(2)(b).
6 IA 1986, s 396(2).
7 IA 1986, s 396(3).
8 IA 1986, s 397(1).

decision in the matter, and of the reasons for that opinion.[9] The competent authority is then duty bound to decide the matter accordingly. The Tribunal is required to send a copy of the report to the applicant or, as the case may be, the holder of the authorisation and the competent authority must serve him with a written notice of the decision made by it in accordance with the report.[10] The competent authority may, if it thinks fit, publish the report of the Tribunal.[11]

Membership and procedure of Tribunal

The membership and other constitutional arrangement of the Tribunal and the provisions applicable to its procedure are set out in Sch 7 to the Insolvency Act 1986.

Constitution

Schedule 7 provides for the Secretary of State to draw up and from time to time to revise (i) a panel of persons who are barristers, advocates or solicitors in each case of not less than seven years' standing and are nominated for the purpose by the Lord Chancellor, and (ii) a panel of persons who are experienced in insolvency matters. The members of the Tribunal are to be selected from these panels in accordance with the provisions of Sch 7.[12]

The Secretary of State is entitled out of money provided by Parliament to pay to members of the Tribunal such remuneration as may be approved by the Treasury and such expenses as may be approved by the Secretary of State and the Treasury.[13]

The Tribunal may sit either as a single tribunal or in two or more divisions[14] and its functions require to be exercised in relation to any case referred to it by three members consisting of a legal chair and two other members experienced in insolvency matters.[15]

Procedure

Any investigation by the Tribunal requires to be so conducted as to afford a reasonable opportunity for representations to be made to the Tribunal by or on behalf of the person whose case is the subject of the investigation.[16] For the purposes of any such investigation, the Tribunal may require any person to attend by notice in writing, to give evidence or produce any books, papers and other records in his possession or under his control which the Tribunal considers it necessary to examine for the purpose of its investigation and may take evidence on

---

9 IA 1986, s 397(1)(b). The requirement of a statement of reasons obviously envisages the possibility of a dissatisfied applicant applying for judicial review.
10 IA 1986, s 397(2).
11 IA 1986, s 397(3).
12 IA 1986, Sch 7, para 1(1).
13 IA 1986, Sch 7, para 2.
14 IA 1986, Sch 7, para 3(1).
15 IA 1986, Sch 7, para 3(2).
16 IA 1986, Sch 7, para 4(1).

oath and for that purpose administer oaths.[17] No person is required to go more than ten miles from his place of residence unless the necessary expenses of his attendance are paid or tendered to him.[18] Every person who fails to attend a Tribunal without reasonable excuse or who suppresses or refuses to produce any document which the Tribunal may require shall be liable to a fine on summary conviction.[19]

NON-ADMINISTRATIVE RECEIVERS

Receivers who are not administrative receivers, in other words non-administrative receivers, are not required to be insolvency practitioners. The only mandatory qualification required of them is that they should not be disqualified under any relevant statutory provision.

Three statutory disqualifications are capable of applying to receivers who are not administrative receivers. First, a body corporate is not qualified for appointment as receiver of the property of a company and any body corporate which acts as such a receiver is liable to a fine.[20] The appointment is also a nullity, so it would presumably not operate so as to cause a crystallisation of the floating charge. This general prohibition applies (as has been seen) to administrative receivers as well; but it will apply to a receiver or manager who is *not* appointed over the whole or substantially the whole of a company's property by or on behalf of debenture holders but only over part of such property. Secondly, an undischarged bankrupt who acts as receiver or manager of the property of a company is liable to a fine.[1] Such a person is disqualified but the appointment may not be a complete nullity.[2] Thirdly, a disqualification order may operate.

Neither of these provisions applies to a receiver appointed over property which is not the property of a company. Accordingly it would theoretically be possible for a mortgagee to appoint as a receiver over the property of an individual, a person who would be disqualified from acting as a receiver of corporate property. But a mortgagee would not willingly select an undischarged bankrupt as a receiver and would be unlikely to select a body corporate to act as a receiver.

APPOINTMENT OF A MULTIPLICITY OF RECEIVERS AND MANAGERS

Introduction

It is by no means uncommon for more than one receiver or more than one receiver and manager to be appointed. There are special provisions in the

---

17 IA 1986, Sch 7, para 4(2).
18 IA 1986, Sch 7, para 4(2).
19 IA 1986, Sch 7, para 4(3).
20 IA 1986, s 30. On penalties, see the IA 1986, s 430 and Sch 10.
 1 IA 1986, s 31. The penalty on indictment is two years' imprisonment or a fine or both; on summary prosecution, six months' imprisonment or the statutory maximum fine or both: IA 1986, s 430 and Sch 10.
 2 Cf IA 1986, s 30 and *Portman Building Society v Gallwey* [1955] 1 All ER 227, [1955] 1 WLR 96.

Insolvency Act 1986 and under the Insolvency Rules for the acceptance and confirmation of acceptance of appointment by joint administrative receivers, and rules governing what must be stated in the appointment.[3] But such 'multiple' appointments have given rise to difficulties.

The first question is whether the relevant power authorises a multiple appointment. This is a matter of construction. The second question is whether, assuming there is such a power, it remains open to the debenture holder exercising the power to specify that the appointees shall act jointly, severally or jointly and severally. A further question is what the status is of appointees where the appointment itself fails to specify the nature of the appointment. Lastly, to what extent can an appointment be valid *pro tanto* if the appointment goes beyond the limits laid down by the power conferred by the debenture?

More than one receiver

Where it is envisaged that more than one receiver (or receiver and manager) may be appointed, the debenture usually spells this out. Either the substantive clause specifically states that in certain events the debenture holder may appoint a receiver and manager or a plurality of receivers and managers,[4] or the relevant power, expressed to be one under which the debenture holder may appoint a receiver (or receiver and manager), is to be read as enabling a multiple appointment either because of a statutory presumption as to deeds and contracts and other instruments that the singular includes the plural or because of an interpretation clause specifying that unless the context otherwise requires the singular shall include the plural.[5]

In some jurisdictions there is a statutory presumption that in an instrument a singular word shall be presumed to include the plural, as for example in England and Wales.[6] However, in Malaysia, Singapore and Hong Kong there is no relevant statutory presumption or equivalent of s 61(c) of the Law of Property Act 1925. Accordingly, in all of these three jurisdictions in a case where there is no express provision, and no implication can be discovered in the language used, that more than one receiver and manager can be appointed, no multiple appointment will be possible. The manifest inconvenience of such a result makes it all the more important that the draftsman should cover the matter expressly in a substantive provision in the debenture.

3 See O'Donovan *Company Receivers and Managers* (2nd edn, 1992) para 3.100–3.220; David Marks and Dominic Emmet 'Administrative Receivers: Questions of Identity and Double Identity (1994) JBL 1–7. IA 1986, s 33; IR 1986, r 3.1 (acceptance); IA 1986, s 231 (declaration as to which acts are to be done by one or more).

4 *DFC Financial Services Ltd v Samuel* [1990] 3 NZLR 156, NZCA; *NEC Information Systems Australia Pty Ltd v Lockhart* (1991) 9 ACLC 658.

5 For the statutory presumption, see LPA 1925, s 61(c). For express clauses, see *R J Wood Pty Ltd v Sherlock* (18 March 1988, unreported); *Wright's Hardware Pty Ltd v Evans* (1988) 13 ACLR 631; *Kerry Lowe Management Pty Ltd v Isherwood* (1989) 15 ACLR 615; *Melsom v Velcrete Pty Ltd* (1996) 14 ACLC 778.

6 LPA 1925 s 61(c).

Ambit of the power of appointment: joint, joint and several, several

It is again a question of construction whether the debenture authorises, in the case of an appointment of more than one receiver (or receiver and manager), the appointment of joint receivers and managers or several receivers and managers or joint and several receivers and managers. Sometimes the debenture will put the matter beyond doubt by express words, but this is not invariably so.

If the debenture gives express power to appoint a multiplicity (or plurality) of receivers and managers but is otherwise silent, the position is that such receivers and managers may be appointed jointly and severally, unless upon the true construction of the empowering document it can be seen that such an appointment was not authorised. That was the conclusion reached by the New Zealand Court of Appeal in *DFC Financial Services Ltd v Samuel*[7] where the debenture enabled the debenture holder on default to 'appoint any person or persons . . . to be a receiver'. Somers J rejected the approach adopted in earlier Australian cases[8] which indicated that an appointment of two or more receivers severally would only be justified if the terms of the document empowering appointment expressly or by necessary implication so provide. Bisson J agreed:[9]

> 'If a company gives a debenture to secure funds provided by a lender, and authorises the appointment by the debenture holder of more than one receiver without specifying that the receivers should act jointly, then the company has left the debenture holder free to make its own decision, as a matter of choice, whether the receivers should act, as in this case, jointly and severally.'

To like effect was the opinion of Hardie Boys J:

> 'There are sound practical reasons for the appointment of more than one receiver and equally so for the appointment to be joint and several. I am not persuaded that there is any reason to assume that the less practical joint appointment must be intended unless the contrary is specifically indicated.'

The court of Appeal in New South Wales came to a similar decision in *NEC Information Systems Australia Pty Ltd v Lockhart* where again there was an express provision contemplating the appointment of 'any person or persons to a Receiver or Receiver and Manager or Receivers and Managers'. The issue for decision before Giles J, who heard the case at first instance, was whether the debenture empowered the appointment of the appointees jointly and severally as distinct from strictly jointly. If the appointment of them jointly and severally went beyond the power, the question then arising was whether their appointment as joint receivers was valid and severable from their appointment as 'several receivers'. Giles J was of the opinion that 'multiplicity does not mean

---

7 [1990] 3 NZLR 156, NZCA (Somers, Bisson and Hardie Boys JJ).

8 *R J Wood Pty Ltd v Sherlock* (18 March 1988, unreported), Davies J (FCA); *Wright's Hardware Pty Ltd v Evans* (1988) 13 ACLR 631, Franklyn J (WA SC) *Kerry Lowe Management Pty Ltd v Isherwood* (1989) 15 ACLR 615.

9 [1990] 3 NZLR 156 at 163.

severalty'.[10] He therefore construed the appointment of two receivers and managers with no words pointing to severalty as constituting them only as joint, and not joint *and several*, receivers and managers. The appellate court held that he had fallen into error in construing the charge as not authorising a joint and several appointment and followed the New Zealand appellate decision.

As already mentioned, debentures often contain an interpretation clause specifying that unless the context otherwise requires words importing the singular includes the plural. Such a clause will apply to a provision providing for the appointment of a 'receiver' or a 'receiver and manager' so as to authorise a 'multiple' appointment. Here again, in the absence of express words or some other textual pointer indicating a restrictive ambit of the power, the presumption is that a joint and several appointment is permissible. This very point arose in *Melsom v Velcrete Pty Ltd*.[11] A mortgage given by a company gave the mortgagee the power to appoint a receiver. The term receiver was defined so as to include a receiver and manager. An interpretation clause in the mortgage provided that 'words importing the singular number … shall include the plural number'. Acting under the mortgage the mortgagee appointed two receivers and managers[12] of the company's property and undertaking in a joint and several appointment. The company claimed that the appointment was invalid because the mortgage did not allow for joint and several appointments. This argument succeeded at first instance but failed before the appellate court in Western Australia.

In a closely reasoned judgment Malcolm CJ (with whom Owen and Wallworth JJ agreed) concluded that once the stage is reached where more than one receiver or receiver and manager may be appointed it is open to the appointor to appoint them on the basis that they may act jointly, severally, or jointly and severally.[13] Despite an earlier suggestion to the contrary,[14] there was no distinction between an express power to appoint a receiver and manager or more than one receiver and manager and the case where there is an interpretation clause saying that the singular would include the plural and there is a simple power to appoint 'a receiver or receiver and manager'. An interpretation clause which provides that words in the singular include the plural does not lead to an 'inference' or 'implication' of the plural case if the singular case only is mentioned in a substantive provision in the body of the instrument.[15] By virtue of the interpretation clause the substantive clause not only *expressly* contemplates the appointment of a receiver and manager but also *expressly* contemplates the appointment of more than one receiver and manager.[16] It followed that the reasoning of the Court of Appeal in New Zealand in *DFC Financial Services Ltd v Samuel*[17] should be followed. In other words, a power to appoint one or more receivers empowered

---

10   [1990] 3 NZLR 156 at 167.
11   (1996) 14 ACLC 778.
12   (1990) 8 ACLC 969–972 per Giles J at first instance. See *NEC Information Systems Australia Pty Ltd v Lockhart*.
13   (1996) 14 ACLC 778.
14   (1996) 14 ACLC 778 at 794.
15   (1996) 14 ACLC 778–794.
16   (1996) 14 ACLC 778.
17   [1990] 3 NZLR 156.

a joint and several appointment unless upon the true construction of the document under which the appointment was made it can be seen that such an appointment is not authorised.[18] There was, in truth, no presumption that, in the absence of express words, contemplating a joint and several appointment, receivers had to act jointly.[19] Accordingly, the appointment made was perfectly valid.

In reaching this conclusion Malcolm CJ refused to follow the earlier Australian decisions in *R J Wood Pty Ltd v Sherlock*[20], *Wright's Hardware Pty Ltd v Evans*[1] and *Kerry Lowe Management Pty Ltd v Isherwood*.[2] The first of these, in his view, wrongly equated the position of a receiver or receiver and manager with that of a trustee and so wrongly applied to the appointment of more than one receiver the rule of general law stated with respect to trustees by Gibbs J in *Re Gudgeon ex p Pegler*.[3] The second case wrongly followed the erroneous decision in the first case and, to the extent that it is also based on strict agency principles, wrongly imports a rule which applies to an appointment[4] into the construction of the power itself. The *Kerry Lowe* case was distinguished by the New South Wales Court of Appeal in *NEC Information Systems Australia Pty Ltd v Lockhart*[5] on two spurious grounds. One ground was that in the *NEC* case the clause obviously contemplated the appointment of more than one person. But it did likewise in *Kerry Lowe*. The only 'distinction' seems to have been that in *Kerry Lowe* the right to appoint multiple receivers was found in the definition of receiver whereas in the *NEC* case it was in the substantive clause. Yet that distinction too is without merit and was treated as unpersuasive in *DFS Financial Services Ltd v Samuel*,[6] the decision in which was followed in the *NEC* case. The distinction, if it ever was one, was laid to rest in *Melsom v Velcrete Pty Ltd*.[7] It is, in effect, a distinction without a difference, and the fact that it was still perceived as a distinction in the *NEC* case was stigmatised in the *Melsom* case.

Failure in deed of appointment to specify exact role of multiple receivers

Normally, as one would expect, every properly drawn instrument appointing multiple receivers will specify that the appointees are to act as joint and several receivers. If, contrary to good practice, no such specification is made, the appointees may nevertheless be able to argue that it should be assumed that the amplest power which the appointors could give was given by the instrument of appointment. If the original power was expressly confined to the appointment of

18   (1996) 14 ACLC 778 at 801.
19   (1996) 14 ACLC 778 at 786–787.
20   (18 March 1988, unreported) FCA per Davis J.
 1   [1988] 13 ACLR 631.
 2   [1989] 15 ACLR 615.
 3   (1969) 13 FLR 350.
 4   [1989] 15 ACLR 615.
 5   [1990] 3 NZLR 156.
 6   [1990] 3 NZLR 156.
 7   (1996) 14 ACLC 778.

joint receivers and managers then the instrument of appointment will be similarly confined. But if it can be assumed that the appointor may choose between joint, several, and joint and several roles for his appointees[8] he should be presumed to have conferred the amplest role (to act jointly and severally) on his appointees.

Appointment exceeding limits of power of appointment

There have been cases where at the end of the day the power itself has been construed as enabling only a multiple appointment of *joint* receivers who can only act jointly but not severally. If in such a case the instrument of appointment goes beyond what the appointor is empowered to do and appoints appointees who are to act jointly *and severally* instead of just jointly, the appointment will usually be treated as valid *pro tanto*. The appointees will still have the requisite authority to act jointly, except where the appointment can be construed as showing that the appointment was to be of persons to act jointly and severally or not at all.[9]

8 *Melsom Velcrete Pty Ltd* (1996) 14 ACLC 778.
9 *Kerry Lowe Management Pty Ltd v Isherwood* (1989) 15 ACLR 615 at 618 per Priestley JA.

CHAPTER 5

Over what property

INTRODUCTION

In order to see what property falls within the scope of the privately appointed receiver and manager's powers it is necessary to go back to the instrument under which he is appointed. One looks at the instrument as a whole to see what can fairly be construed as forming the subject matter of the relevant charge; both recitals and operative parts may be relevant.[1] For example, the equitable charge under scrutiny in *Re Data Technology Pty Ltd*[2] was one securing 'advances made by the creditor'. The recitals referred to the creditor having 'advanced certain moneys'. Though the operative part did not specifically tie the advances charged to the advances referred to in the recitals the advances were tied to the description in the recitals in other ways. Having regard to the recitals, 'advances' was therefore construed as restricted to cash advances.

In general debenture charges over the assets of a company are partly specific and partly floating, in other words the charge will be a 'fixed and floating charge'. Here again it is a question of the intention of the parties and the language used to establish that intention, and the nature of the assets. Assets which are expected to be dealt with in the course of trading by the company will usually be subject to a floating charge. Fixed assets are normally subjected to a fixed charge. Fixed assets are the assets of a company which are normally expected to the available to a company and remain 'permanently' with the company for the purpose of carrying out the business of the undertaking. They are those assets which are basic to the operation of that particular business. Land and buildings and plant and machinery are the most common fixed assets of a business.[3]

It is in all cases a matter for interpretation of the document of charge whether

---

1 *Re Data Technology Pty Ltd (in liquidation)* (1976) 2 ACLR 120.
2 (1976) 2 ACLR 120.
3 See *Tudor Heights Ltd (in liquidation) v United Dominions Corpn Finance Ltd* [1977] 1 NZLR 532 at 534. For fixed charges, see further ch 2. Fixed plant and machinery that are firmly attached will be covered by a fixed charge over fixed plant and machinery: *Re High-Fi Equipment (Cabinets) Ltd* [1988] BCLC 65. Such affixation will displace retention of title rights: *Gebrueder Buehler AG v Kwang* [1988] 2 MLJ 69, Sing CA.

particular charged assets fall within the fixed charge or floating charge component of an 'all assets' fixed and floating charge.[4]

Assets may or may not cover movables depending on the context.[5] Land will normally carry the rents arising from it and be subject to the fixed charge affecting the land[6] and a specific charge over specific land may leave unspecified land subject to a floating charge.[7] However a fixed charge over 'all policies of assurance' does not cover insurance against adventitious events like fire or death before a certain age.[8]

PROPERTY SUBJECT TO FLOATING CHARGE

While the usual way of constituting a floating charge is by charging the 'undertaking' of the company[9] there is no particular incantation required to constitute a floating charge. A general charge may be construed as a floating security even though the instrument does not expressly so describe it. The rationale of this approach is that the charge envisages the continuance of the company as a going concern and that state of affairs is inconsistent with a fixed (as opposed to a floating) charge. So a charge on all property both present and future of a company will create a floating security.[10] Likewise debentures given to bind a company and all its estate property and effects,[11] or its real and personal estate[12] will operate as a floating security.

It is not a prerequisite of a floating charge that it should 'float' over the whole of the undertaking or all the present and future assets of a company.[13] A floating charge may be given merely over part of the property of a company or over a particular class of assets.[14] Thus it may be expressed to operate on all the present and future book and other debts of a company with the benefit of the securities for those debts;[15] or 'the furniture and effects which now are or may from time to

---

4 See Gough *Company Charges* (2nd edn, 1996) 121–122; cf *National Bank of New Zealand Ltd v IRC* [1992] 1 NZLR 250 (fixed plant and machinery does not include computer software).

5 *Re Shoe Lace Ltd* [1993] BCC 609 at 622–623 per Sir Christopher Slade (furniture and stock in trade of a trading company not subject to a fixed charge where charge contained mortgage covenants relevant to mortgaged *land*).

6 *Rhodes v Allied Dunbar Pension Services Ltd* [1989] 1 WLR 800 at 808, CA per Nicholls LJ.

7 *Welch v Bowmaker (Ireland) Ltd* [1980] IR 251 at 254–255 per Hinchey J and at 261 per Parke J; and see *Composite Buyas Ltd v State Bank of New South Wales* (1990) 3 ACSR 196 at 198–199 per Hodgson J (future land not specified in fixed charge falls under floating charge over 'present and future *assets*').

8 *Re C C G International Enterprises Ltd* [1993] BCC 580 at 583–584, per Lindsay J.

9 *Re Panama, New Zealand and Australian Royal Mail Co* (1870) 5 Ch App 318, 39 LJ Ch 482; *Marshall v Rogers & Co* (1898) 14 TLR 217.

10 *Wheatley v Silkstone and Haigh Moor Coal Co* (1885) 29 Ch D 715, 54 LJ Ch 778.

11 *Re Florence Land and Public Works Co* (1878) 10 Ch D 530, CA.

12 *Re Colonial Trusts Corpn* (1879) 15 Ch D 465.

13 *Rother Iron Works Ltd v Canterbury Precision Engineers Ltd* [1974] QB 1, [1973] 1 All ER 394.

14 See *Re Yorkshire Woolcombers' Association Ltd* [1903] 2 Ch 284 at 295 per Romer LJ. In the same case Cozens Hardy LJ at 298 expressly rejected an argument to the contrary.

15 *Re Yorkshire Woolcombers' Association Ltd*, above; affd as *Illingworth v Houldsworth* [1904] AC 355.

time be placed' on certain specified premises[16] or on the whole or a fraction of the profits of a business.[17]

Foreign assets

A company owning land or other property in a country whose laws do not recognise the creation of a floating charge can grant such a charge on the relevant property in a manner valid under its own domestic law.[18] Thus in *Re Anchor Line (Henderson Bros) Ltd*[19] Luxmoore J said:

> 'When an English company possesses land abroad and purports to charge it by way of floating charge, the charge, putting it at its lowest, amounts to an agreement to charge that land, and is a valid equitable security according to English law.'

The position is otherwise with a legal mortgage which must comply with the *lex situs*.[20]

In enforcing the English equitable right over the foreign asset the court will only do so *in personam* and subject to any rights which may in the meantime have been acquired under the relevant foreign local law.

Claims

The proceeds of a successful misfeasance claim[1] against the company directors or officers represent another example of an intangible asset which can fall within the province of a floating charge.[2] The company acquires the intangible asset on commission of the relevant misfeasance although the right of action does not accrue until the company goes into liquidation or receivership.[3]

The proceeds of a successful challenge to a disposition as being a preference stand on a different footing. They form no part of the charge and the claim never forms part of the general assets of the company.[4] The claim is made by the

16 *National Provincial Bank of England Ltd v United Electric Theatres Ltd* [1916] 1 Ch 132.
17 *Hoare v British Columbia Development Association Ltd* [1912] WN 235, 107 LT 602; *Dempsey and the National Bank of New Zealand Ltd v Traders' Finance Corpn Ltd* [1933] NZLR 1258 at 1286.
18 *Coote v Jecks* (1872) LR 13 Eq 597; *Hicks v Powell* (1869) 4 Ch App 741; *Re Scheibler, ex p Holthausen* (1874) 9 Ch App 722.
19 [1937] Ch 483 at 487.
20 See Dicey and Morris *Conflict of Laws* (13th edn) Vol 2, p 929 para 22-035.
 1 Under the IA 1986, s 212. Such a claim may be actionable: *Wood v Woodhouse and Rawson United* [1896] WN 4 per Vaughan Williams J.
 2 *Re Anglo-Austrian Printing and Publishing Union* [1895] 2 Ch 891; *Re Standstill Development Finance Ltd* [1966] VR 499; *Re Buick Sales Ltd* [1926] NZLR 24; *Re Asiatic Electric Co Pty Ltd* [1970] 2 NSWR 612, 92 WNNSW 361.
 3 *Re Park Gate Waggon Works Co* (1881) 17 Ch D 234 at 239, CA.
 4 *Bayley v National Australia Bank Ltd* (1995) 16 ACSR 38; *Campbell v Michael Mount PPB* (1995) 16 ACSR 296; and see *Re Quality Camera Co Pty Ltd* [1965] NSWR 1330, 83 WN (Pt 1) NSW 226.

liquidator for the general creditors or by the administrator and the proceeds of the claim, even if obtained under a compromise rather than by a court order,[5] are held on trust for the unsecured creditors who would otherwise have been postponed.[6]

In *NA Kratzmann Pty Ltd v Tucker (No 2)*,[7] a decision of the High Court of Australia, it was held that money paid by the insolvent company as a preference was at the time of that payment subject to the charge and that it mattered not whether the charge had previously crystallised. However, any money *recovered* by the liquidator was not the same money and did not become the property of the company subject to the charge. The recovered money was impressed in the hands of the liquidator with a trust for the creditors amongst whom he had had a duty to distribute the assets.[8]

ASSETS ACQUIRED BY THE COMPANY BEFORE CRYSTALLISATION

The very nature of the floating security is that it is a charge on the assets of the company for the time being. Assets come and assets go and in the meanwhile the charge hovers over them. It follows that items of property acquired by the company *after* the creation of a floating charge, but prior to its crystallisation, may be subject to the charge.[9] The other side of this coin is, of course, that the company can dispose of such subsequently acquired property in the ordinary course of business[10] before crystallisation. Thus unless it is otherwise agreed and until the security becomes fixed the company can, in the ordinary course of business, sell,[11] let, mortgage[12] or otherwise deal with any of its assets, and pay dividends out of profits just as if the floating charge had not been created.[13] This is the case even if the charge is described as a first charge.[14]

The floating charge, it should be underlined, will only fix upon assets of which the company is, at the time of crystallisation, absolute owner. So if the company obtains possession of goods held subject to a 'Romalpa' (or title retention) clause[15] that property will not be bound by the security unless the title has in fact

---

5 *Re Masureik and Allan Pty Ltd* (1981) 6 ACLR 39.

6 *Re Yagerphone Ltd* [1935] Ch 392.

7 (1968) 123 CLR 295.

8 See *Re Yagerphone Ltd* [1935] 1 Ch 392 at 396.

9 *Re Panama, New Zealand, Australian and Royal Mail Co* (1870) 5 Ch App 318; *Re McKenzie Grant & Co* (1899) 1 WALR 116; and see David Milman 'The Floating Charge and After-Acquired Assets' [1979] Conv 138–147.

10 As to what acts or payments are in the ordinary course of business, see *Willmott v London Celluloid Co* (1886) 34 Ch D 147, 56 LJ Ch 89, CA; *Hamer v London City and Midland Bank Ltd* (1918) 87 LJKB 973; *Re Hubbard & Co Ltd* (1898) 68 LJ Ch 54, 79 LT 665; *Re HH Vivian & Co Ltd* [1900] 2 Ch 654; *Cox Moore v Peruvian Corpn Ltd* [1908] 1 Ch 604; cf *Williams v Quebrada Railway Land and Copper Co* [1895] 2 Ch 751; and see the discussion at pp 23–25.

11 *Re HH Vivian & Co Ltd* [1900] 2 Ch 654; *Caratti v Grant* (1978) 3 ACLR 322 at 330–331; affd sub nom *Landall Holdings Ltd v Caratti* [1979] WAR 97.

12 *Re Florence Land and Public Works Co* (1878) 10 Ch D 530, CA. The mortgage may be by deposit of the deeds: *Wheatley v Silkstone and Haigh Moor Coal Co* (1885) 29 Ch D 715.

13 *Robson v Smith* [1895] 2 Ch 118 at 124.

14 *Cox Moore v Peruvian Corpn Ltd* [1908] 1 Ch 604.

15 For title retention clauses pp 204–218.

passed to the company before the crystallisation occurs. Again, assets held by the company merely as trustee for a third party[16] will not fall within the scope of the charge.

Uncalled capital, that is to say the sums of money due from the company's shareholders in respect of shares which have not been fully paid up, may fall within the scope of a floating charge. Certainly uncalled capital represents a *right* of the company.[17] But it is only 'property' potentially: that is to say when the call is made and collected.[18] The question is: can the debenture holders claim these sums of uncalled capital if the calls are made *after* crystallisation?

The answer to this question depends upon whether the company had authority to charge its uncalled capital[19] and whether indeed the uncalled capital was included in the security. In the context of the creation of a charge it has been held that the word 'property' does not include uncalled capital. This was decided in the old case of *Re British Provident Life and Fire Assurance Society, Stanley's Case*[20] and apparently rests on the technicality that uncalled capital does not become a debt due to the company until the call is actually made.[1] The judge in *Stanley's* case had difficulty in understanding how such 'future' property could validly be the subject of a charge. But some six years later that point was established in the *Panama*[2] case. There is, in fact, a later case, *Re Colonial and General Gas Co Ltd, Lishman's Claim*,[3] where both *Stanley's* case and the *Panama* case were drawn to the attention of Stuart V-C who held that a general charge over the company's property could take in amounts representing uncalled capital.

The conclusion reached in *Re Colonial and General Gas Co* seems the preferable one. For while uncalled capital is not 'owed until a call is made' it is close to reach. Unfortunately, subsequent decisions[4] have confirmed *Stanley's* case in preference to *Re Colonial General Gas Co Ltd*. The result is that while a charge over a company's 'property both present and future' apparently does *not* include uncalled capital,[5] a charge over a company's 'property or any other security'[6] or over a company's 'assets'[7] will include uncalled capital. Niceties of this kind present a most unattractive mien to lawyer[8] and layman alike. It is submitted that the courts should follow the line that because 'future' property can be caught by a

---

16 *Re Kayford Ltd* [1975] 1 All ER 604, [1975] 1 WLR 279; cf *Re Bond Worth Ltd* [1980] Ch 228, [1979] 3 All ER 919. See the discussion of 'Trust Creditors' at p 218 et seq.

17 *Howard v Patent Ivory Co* (1888) 38 Ch D 156.

18 *Irvine v Union Bank of Australia* (1877) 2 App Cas 366.

19 A power to borrow includes, unless the contrary appears, a power to charge uncalled capital: *Re Pyle Works* (1890) 44 Ch D 534, CA.

20 (1864) 4 De GJ & Sm 407.

1 *Re China Steamship and Labuan Coal Co* (1869) 38 LJ Ch 512; *Re Phoenix Bessemer Steel Co* (1875) 44 LJ Ch 683, 32 LT 854.

2 (1870) 5 Ch App 318, discussed at p 28, above.

3 (1870) 23 LT 759.

4 *Bank of South Australia v Abrahams* (1875) LR 6 PC 265, and cases in n 7, below.

5 *Re Streatham and General Estates Co* [1897] 1 Ch 15; *Re Russian Spratts Patent Ltd* [1898] 2 Ch 149, CA.

6 *Re Phoenix Bessemer Steel Co* (1875) 44 LJ Ch 683, 32 LT 854.

7 *Page v International Agency and Industrial Trust Ltd* [1893] WN 32; *Re Andrew Handyside & Co Ltd* (1911) 131 LT Jo 125.

8 David Milman [1979] Conv 138 at 141 describes it as doing 'little credit to the law'.

floating charge the decision in *Re Colonial and General Gas Co Ltd* should likewise be followed. The draftsman can of course avoid all hazards in the choice of terminology by making the position quite explicit and in modern floating charges 'uncalled capital' is usually expressly specified as included in the charge.[9]

ASSETS ACQUIRED AFTER CRYSTALLISATION

There is at least one confident statement to the effect that a 'crystallised floating charge extends not merely to assets owned by the company at the date of crystallisation but also to all future classes of assets subject to the security subsequently acquired by the company'.[10] Elsewhere the matter is put more tentatively.[11]

The better view is that it all depends on the charge itself, and the genesis of the asset. The earliest guidance on this point is to be found in a New Zealand case, *Wellington Woollen Manufacturing Co Ltd v Patrick*.[12] In that case a receiver and manager went on trading after crystallisation of the floating charge. Ostler J held that goods ordered by the receiver on credit after the moment of crystallisation would be covered by the charge as soon as the goods in question became the property of the company. The English Court of Appeal in *NW Robbie & Co Ltd v Witney Warehouse Co Ltd*[13] has also confirmed that crystallisation still enables the charge to attach to debts which become due to the company after the date of crystallisation. Russell LJ observed that the floating quality of a floating charge 'only means that its full operation is so to speak, in suspense until certain events occur, and when such an event occurs the charge (or agreement to charge) loses that suspended quality.'[14] He then continued:

> 'That in no way justifies the conclusion that the field of the charge is in any way restricted: it only means that after this particular quality disappears equity will fasten the charge directly upon all assets thereafter.'[15]

Further confirmation of the principle that assets coming in to the company after crystallisation of a charge binding its assets is provided by the case of *Ferrier v Bottomer*,[16] a decision of the High Court of Australia. In that case a floating charge was expressed to affect present and future property in Queensland and

---

9 *Newton v Debenture Holders etc of the Anglo-Australian Investment Finance & Land Co* [1895] AC 244 ('security of any description'); *South Australian Barytes Ltd v Wood* (1975) 12 SASR 527.

10 See Gough *Company Charges* (2nd edn, 1996) p 123.

11 See David Milman 'The Floating Charge and After-Acquired Assets' [1979] Conv 138 at 144–146; see also GC Thorpe 'Floating Charges, Crystallisation and After-Acquired Property' 42–49.

12 [1935] NZLR 23.

13 [1963] 3 All ER 613, [1963] 1 WLR 1324, CA (Donovan LJ dissenting).

14 [1963] 1 WLR 1324 at 1337.

15 [1963] 1 WLR 1324 at 1337.

16 (1972) 126 CLR 597; and see *Mineral & Chemical Traders Pty Ltd v T Tymczyszyn Pty Ltd (in liquidation)* (1994) 15 ACSR 398 at 412–414 per Santow J; cf *Re Rex Developments Pty Ltd (in liquidation)* (1994) 13 ACSR 485, criticised in Gough *Company Charges* (2nd edn) 127–128.

New South Wales. A receiver was appointed and this, of course, crystallised the charge. The company was owed debts in Victoria and the Australian Capital Territory. Various sums of money were paid to the receiver by those debtors, in other words the money came in *after* the receivership started. It was contended that the charge having crystallised before the money was received in Queensland could not and did not attach to that money. The High Court of Australia rejected that argument. It held that those sums of money paid to the receiver were caught by the crystallised charge. In the view of Barwick CJ:[17]

> 'Upon the charge being a fixed charge it spoke for the future according to its terms. Thus after-acquired property became charged as it came into existence in Queensland or came within Queensland.'

Of course the money received by the receiver was property of the company in Queensland and the charge was expressed to cover all property of the company present and future. Moreover there was no reason to suppose that because the charge had lost its floating quality it had therefore lost its capacity to affect after-acquired property.

A fixed charge just as much as a floating charge is capable of attaching to after-acquired property.[18] So the result of the case was inevitable on the wording of the charge itself, which must naturally in such cases be carefully scrutinised.

As noted in greater detail earlier in this book[19] there has been an increasing tendency over the last two decades for lenders at the outset to seek to take fixed charges over species of assets previously not considered as eligible for a fixed (rather than floating) charge. A striking example is *Siebe Gorman & Co Ltd v Barclays Bank Ltd*[20] where Slade J held that there was no reason in principle why a fixed charge could not be taken over book debts, so long as the terms of the relevant instrument of charge make it clear that the debtor company was not free to deal with those book debts in the ordinary course of business. Although the decision in the *Siebe Gorman* case met with some criticism[1] it reflects, in fact, a principle which is well established in Canada,[2] and the decision itself was followed by the Supreme Court in Ireland in *Re Keenan Bros Ltd*,[3] and by Morritt J in *William Gaskell Group Ltd v Highley (Nos 1, 2, 3)*.[4]

17 (1972) 126 CLR 597 at 603. The earlier unreported decision of McLelland CJ in *Permanent Nominees Ltd v Australian Factors Ltd* (1966) was rejected.
18 *Holroyd v Marshall* (1862) 10 HL Cas 191, 33 LJ Ch 193: 'All machinery, implements, and things, which, during the continuance of this security shall be placed in or about the said mill'; *Tailby v Official Receiver* (1888) 13 App Cas 523: 'All the book debts due and owing or which may during the continuance of this security become owing'; and see Kebler 'Some Reflections on *Holroyd v Marshall*' (1969) 3 Adel L Rev 360.
19 See at pp 13–16.
20 [1979] 2 Lloyd's Rep 142; cf *Hart v Barnes* (1982) 7 ACLR 310 (where the *Siebe Gorman* case was not cited).
1 Report of the Cork Committee 'Insolvency Law and Practice' (Cmnd 8558); and see Lingard *Bank Security Documents* (2nd edn, 1988) paras 8.32–8.45.
2 *Evans, Coleman & Evans Ltd v RA Nelson Construction Ltd* (1958) 16 DLR (2d) 123; and see further authorities at pp 13–16.
3 [1986] BCLC 242; followed in *Re Masser Ltd* (1987) 5 ILT 43; *Re Wogan's (Drogheda) Ltd* [1993] 1 IR 157 (charge sufficiently restricted).
4 [1994] 1 BCLC 197.

One of many[5] examples of an ineptly drafted charge over book debts which failed to qualify as a *fixed* charge is to be found in the Irish case of *Kelly v James McMahon Ltd.*[6] This was a case involving a company which was admittedly insolvent at the date of the creation of a charge whose validity was being impeached under the Irish equivalent of what was s 322 of the Companies Act 1948.[7] The charge had been created within the relevant objectionable period. After a specific charge over goodwill, uncalled capital and certain shareholdings and a general floating charge over its undertaking the instrument of charge purported to charge the company's book debts in the following terms:

> 'The company and the holding company as beneficial owners hereby charge in favour of the major creditors all their respective book debts and all other rights and powers of recovery in respect thereof to hold the same unto the major creditors absolutely.'

Naturally the decision of Costello J turned on the particular wording of this clause which he subjected to rigorous analysis. There was little help to be derived from the form of the sub-clause itself. The word 'charge' is one of chameleon-like quality. There was no expression in the sub-clause itself which suggested any solution. However the common intention of the parties, to be deduced from the instrument as a whole, was that the company was to continue to trade.[8] While not repudiating the legal possibility of a fixed charge over book debts[9] Costello J concluded that 'when permission to trade is given in a debenture, permission to recover book debts is more readily to be inferred than in an arrangement by which the company is required to hand them over to a debenture holder.'[10] Here the characteristics of a *floating* charge as identified by Romer LJ in *Re Yorkshire Woolcombers' Association Ltd*[11] were present. A factor which the learned judge might have taken into account was the existence of a general floating charge which might tend to indicate, as might the position of the sub-clause between an assignment and a fixed charge, that a fixed charge was intended. But the distinctions drawn between the case before him and the *Siebe Gorman* case are convincing.

After-acquired property ought obviously always to be properly described so as to identify it, although general descriptive words will suffice.[12] Problems can nevertheless arise in connection with the drafting of a satisfactory instrument intended to charge stock-in-trade which, of its very nature, is intended to be disposed of in the ordinary course of business. There appears to be no reason in principle why a company should not be able to grant a specific charge over such

---

5 *Re G E Tunbridge Ltd* [1994] BCC 563; *Re Pearl Maintenance Services Ltd* [1995] BCC 657.
6 [1980] IR 347. See also *Hart v Barnes* (1982) 7 ACLR 310.
7 Floating charges in England are in this respect now governed by IA 1986, s 245 (replacing CA 1985 s 617).
8 [1980] IR 347 at 354.
9 See *Siebe Gorman & Co Ltd v Barclays Bank Ltd* [1979] 2 Lloyd's Rep 142 which he distinguished as being a clear case going the other way.
10 [1980] IR 347 at 353–354.
11 [1903] 2 Ch 284. These characteristics are set out at p 22, above.
12 *Tailby v Official Receiver* (1888) 13 App Cas 523, HL.

stock and probably over the proceeds of sale of such stock,[13] but such cases are of their very nature rare.[14] The instrument in question will need strictly to curtail the rights of the company to deal with the stock in trade in the ordinary course of business.[15]

13 See DW McLaughlan (1976) 7 NZULR 83.
14 *R in Right of British Columbia v Federal Business Development Bank* (1987) 17 BCLR (2d) 273, BCCA.
15 *Siebe Gorman & Co Ltd v Barclays Bank Ltd* [1979] 2 Lloyd's Rep 142.

CHAPTER 6

Mode of appointment

This chapter is concerned with three matters. First, what precautions should be taken by an eligible, suitable and willing person to whom a corporate receivership is offered? Then, what formalities attach to the appointment itself? Finally, what procedure should be followed immediately after the receiver and manager is appointed? The answers to these questions involve both matters of law and matters of practice.

PRECAUTIONS BEFORE ACCEPTANCE

A would-be receiver needs to know where he stands in relation to his appointment. His main anxiety will be to ensure that if appointed he will be validly appointed. But there are other important matters which will be of concern to him. He will want to have a fair idea of the scale of the task that faces him and to take every possible step to protect himself against all possible disadvantageous consequences of taking on the corporate receivership.

The first step the would-be receiver is likely to take, even before checking the validity of the charge under which he would be appointed, is to assess whether the particular receivership is one which he has the personal capacity[1] and available competent staff to take on board. For this purpose he must get, at the earliest possible stage, a rough idea of the size, nature, turnover and management needs of the business in question. Only then can he sensibly proceed to take all the precautions which it is necessary for him to take.

The charge is the fount or source of the receiver's appointment and so if it is contaminated by invalidity any purported appointment of a receiver pursuant to the charge will likewise inevitably be invalid. Since anyone who acts under an invalid appointment is accounted in law a trespasser in respect of any property with which he interferes[2] a would-be receiver will check, with the help of his legal advisers if necessary, the validity of the legal charge itself. The question of

---

1 Ie the requisite professional capacity and experience. If he is to act as an *administrative* receiver he must be an 'insolvency practitioner' (as defined).
2 *Ford & Carter Ltd v Midland Bank Ltd* (1979) 129 NLJ 543, HL.

validity is dealt with in the next chapter in some detail. But in summary form the matters which the receiver should investigate are as follows.

First, he should obtain a copy of the debenture and debenture trust deed if any and ensure that it has been validly drawn and executed.[3] If a seal is affixed it should have been done in accordance with any formalities prescribed by the article of association.[4] It should be added that it is still at common law the rule[5] that an agent may not execute a deed unless his authority to do so has been granted under seal. If a debenture is granted by a company under seal and contains a clause irrevocably appointing any receiver who might be appointed by the mortgagee as attorneys for the company with power to execute deeds, that is enough under the common law rule, and receivers who were subsequently appointed only in writing can validly execute a deed.[6] Then he should search the file of the Companies Registry to see that the charge was validly registered by delivery of particulars of the charge within the prescribed period after its creation or within such further period as may have been allowed under the statute.[7] While searching the file he should take note of any further charges which may be registered and which rank in priority to, or pari passu with, the charge under which he is to be appointed. At the same time he will note the details of the officers and shareholders of the company and any other available information.

His next steps will be to take such measures as he can to see that the debenture does not fall foul of any invalidating statutory provisions.

If any floating charge comprised in the debenture is created within 12 months of the commencement of the winding up of the company it will be invalid 'except to the extent of the value of so much of the consideration for the creation of the charge as consists of money paid, or goods or services supplied, to the company and so much of that consideration as consists of the discharge or reduction of any debt of the company and in trust thereon at the same time as or after the creation of the charge'.[8] If the charge is more than 12 months old there is no problem under the last-mentioned provision unless the chargee is a connected person, in which case the transaction may be invalid if entered into at any time within two years ending with the onset of insolvency.[9] But if it is less than 12 months old the receiver should check (i) whether the borrower was solvent at the time[10] and (ii) whether the charge was given for a relevant consideration as defined at the time of or subsequent to the charge. In the light of this information the receiver may need to get an indemnity from the debenture holder, and to wait for expiry of the 12-month period or longer.

---

3 Ie sealed. But a document issued under the hand of two directors can be a valid debenture: *British Indian Steam Navigation Co v IRC* (1881) 7 QBD 165. See also CA 1985, s 36A (no need to affix common seal: document expressed as a deed and signed by two directors or the secretary suffices).

4 See LPA 1925, s 74 (for protection of purchasers).

5 Despite the Law of Property (Miscellaneous Provisions) Act 1989, s 1(1)(c).

6 *Phoenix Properties Ltd v Wimpole Street Nominees Ltd* [1992] BCLC 737.

7 See CA 1985, s 398 (as amended by CA 1989).

8 IA 1986, s 245, which is discussed at p 248, below.

9 IA 1986, s 245(3)(a).

10 IA 1986, s 245(3)(b).

Again the charge may be vulnerable to invalidation if the charge forms part of an extortionate credit bargain,[11] or a transaction at an undervalue.[12]

The proposed receiver should also try to establish whether the charge, when executed, was executed in the desire to produce in relation to the chargee the effect of putting the chargee in a better position than would otherwise have obtained.[13]

He should also investigate whether there has been any contravention of the statutory prohibition of the giving of financial assistance by the company for the purpose of acquiring its own shares, or those of its holding company.[14]

FORMALITIES OF APPOINTMENT

There is no set statutory form for the appointment of a receiver and manager out of court. On the other hand any formalities laid down by the relevant debentures or trust deed must be followed. If the debenture requires the appointment to be made in writing or under hand an oral appointment is not sufficient. Again if the appointment is required to be by deed that formality must be observed. A deed is required not only where the appointment provision expressly states that the appointment shall be by deed, but also where the receiver and manager is given the power to execute deeds in the name of the debenture holders. Sometimes the debenture in question requires the consent of a certain number of debenture holders. Where that is so the relevant consents must be obtained and it is a sensible precaution to recite in the relevant appointment that the relevant consents have been obtained.

The form of appointment usually sets out the names and addresses of those making the appointment and ought also to state the event or ground giving rise to the appointment. Often, too, it will include a provision expressly authorising the appointor to exercise all the powers conferred by the debenture on the receiver and declaring that all his receipts shall be applied in the manner laid down in the debenture.

Preparation, communication and acceptance

A form of appointment may quite validly be prepared in anticipation of an occasion giving rise to the need for a receiver. In other words a form of appointment can be prepared signed and even dated without any intent that the document should have any present effect and merely in preparation for a day which might or might not arrive. The appointment will only take effect when the document is given to the receiver and manager by the debenture holder or by his duly authorised agent and the receiver and manager accepts the appointment.[15] In

11   IA 1986, s 244 discussed at p 252 below.
12   IA 1986, s 238(4) discussed at p 246, below.
13   IA 1986, s 239 discussed at p 241, below.
14   CA 1985, s 151 discussed at p 94, below.
15   *Windsor Refrigerator Co Ltd v Branch Nominees Ltd* [1961] Ch 375, [1961] 1 All ER 277, CA; *Cripps (Pharmaceuticals) Ltd v Wickenden* [1973] 2 All ER 606, [1973] 1 WLR 944.

Windsor Refrigerator Co Ltd v Branch Nominees Ltd,[16] counsel for the plaintiff was treated as having argued that a valid appointment could only be prepared after a demand for payment had been made.[17] Harman LJ stigmatised the argument as 'an absolute novelty and not convenient in practice, or right in law'.[18] He continued:

> 'I can see no reason why you should not write down certain words on a piece of paper and keep them in your bosom pocket book, and produce them at the right moment. Nor do I see why, if you so produce them, they should not have effect at the moment when you do produce them to the proper person, here to the receiver.'

Clearly the contents of this document must be communicated at least to the receiver before his appointment can be valid. This can be illustrated by the converse case of removal. If communication of the appointment were not necessary the same would apply to removal. This would have the effect that the receiver would go on managing the company's business, acting in the company's name and receiving the company's property perhaps for weeks before he became aware of the fact that he had ceased to be receiver, and had been removed.[19] An argument which proceeds on the assumption that a receiver might be removed by a writing of which he need know nothing is patently absurd.[20]

The document of appointment must not only be communicated but also be accepted. Acceptance can, however, be implied from a tacit acknowledgement of the document of appointment.[1] The document constitutes an offer which the receiver is free to reject at any time prior to his acceptance.[2]

Necessity for formal demand?

A moot point is whether a formal demand for payment of money due is a vital step in the procedure to be followed prior to the appointment of a receiver. Certainly there are dicta in *Windsor Refrigerator Co Ltd v Branch Nominees Ltd*[3] which suggest that before an appointment can be made there must be a demand, even though no such requirement was in fact specified in that case. And the Court of Appeal seems to have been prepared to import such a requirement. But no persuasive reason has been suggested for *importing* a demand as a prerequisite to the validity of an appointment. Of course express words may make a demand a crucial element in the appointment of a receiver. But in the absence of express

---

16 [1961] Ch 375, CA.
17 See [1961] Ch 375 at 397 per Harman LJ. Counsel's argument at 385 does not go quite that far. He argued that initialling after demand was necessary.
18 [1961] Ch 375 at 397.
19 See [1961] Ch 375 at 398–399 per Donovan LJ.
20 [1961] Ch 375 where Donovan LJ uses the word 'fallacy'.
 1 *Cripps (Pharmaceuticals) Ltd v Wickenden* [1973] 1 WLR 944 at 953 per Goff J.
 2 Cf *Re Lister* [1926] Ch 149 at 166, CA (non-acceptance or renunciation of office of trustee or executor).
 3 [1961] Ch 375 at 394, per Lord Evershed MR; and see the observations of Harman LJ at 396 and Donovan LJ at 399.

words requiring a demand to be made the necessity of demand should not be implied.

An example of a case where express words made it clear that a demand was *de rigueur* before a receiver could be appointed was *Cripps (Pharmaceuticals) Ltd v Wickenden.*[4] There the debenture contained a clause making the money repayable on demand. Goff J held that a demand was essential before the right to appoint a receiver arose.

Amount stated in demand

Normally a demand will be valid notwithstanding that the sum mentioned in the demand exceeds the true debt or that the demand is otherwise incorrect as to the amount of the debt. There is authority to this effect not only in England[5] but also in Australia[6] and Canada.[7] The mechanics of payment test would obviously allow the debtor time to sort out the true position, while the wider test, which has found favour in some Commonwealth cases, would also allow the debtor time to establish the correct sum.[8] Even a demand for 'the sum due', without any other mention of the amount in the demand, has been held to be effective.[9] Nor would a demand in these terms be sabotaged by a simultaneous offer to accept payment by instalments and not to appoint a receiver if those instalments are duly paid.[10]

Time to meet demand

English cases

One question (raised in a number of other cases) which also fell to be considered in *Cripps (Pharmaceuticals) Ltd v Wickenden* was whether an 'on demand' debtor must be allowed a reasonable time to meet the demand before the security is enforced. In fact, Goff J answered the question by stating that where money is payable on demand 'all the creditor has to do is to give the debtor time to get it from some convenient place not to negotiate a deal which he hopes will produce

---

4 [1973] 1 WLR 944; see also Hubert Picarda 'Receivers and On Demand Debentures' (1984) 5 Bus L Rev 105–107.
5 *Bank of Baroda v Panessar* [1987] Ch 335, [1986] 3 All ER 751.
6 *Bunbury Foods Pty Ltd v National Bank of Australasia Ltd* (1984) 153 CLR 491, 51 ALR 609 (no sum specified). Even a notice given to the mortgagor by the mortgagee as a condition precedent of a power of sale is valid though the sum demanded is excessive: *Clyde Properties Ltd v Tasker* [1970] NZLR 754 at 757–758; *MIR Bros Projects Pty Ltd v 1924 Pty Ltd* [1980] 2 NSWLR 907 at 924.
7 *Four-K Western Equipment Ltd v CIBA* (1983) 46 CBRNS 146; *Holiday Ford Sales (1977) Inc v Ford Credit Canada Ltd* (1982) 17 ACWS (2d) 236.
8 As to these two tests, see the discussion under 'Time to meet demand' below.
9 *Bank of Baroda v Panessar* [1987] Ch 335, [1986] 3 All ER 751; *NRG Vision Ltd v Churchfield Leasing Ltd* [1988] BCLC 624 at 637H–I per Knox J; and see *Bunbury Foods Pty Ltd v National Bank of Australasia Ltd* (1984) 153 CLR 491, 51 ALR 609.
10 *NRG Vision Ltd v Churchfield Leasing Ltd* [1988] BCLC 624 at 638A.

the money'.[11] This test is sometimes referred to as the 'mechanics of payment' test.

The relevant period of time in that case between the actual demand and the appointment of a receiver was one hour or so.[12] It was argued by the debtor company that even where money is payable on demand, still a reasonable time must be given to enable the payment to be made.[13] On the facts, even an hour was reasonable because the debtor company had not got the money and had no convenient place to which to go to get it.[14] The earlier authorities referring to a reasonable time to get the money from a convenient place were referred to and applied. Walton J has twice expounded the rationale in *Cripps (Pharmaceuticals) Ltd v Wickenden*. In *Hawtin & Partners Ltd v Pugh*[15] he said of a debtor faced with a demand for payment:

> 'The debtor is therefore not in default in making the payment demanded unless and until he has had a reasonable opportunity of implementing whatever reasonable mechanics of payment he may need to employ to discharge the debt. Of course this is limited to the time necessary for the mechanics of payment. It does not extend to any time to raise the money if it is not there to be paid.'

The relevant period of time between demand and the appointment of a receiver in *Bank of Baroda Ltd v Panessar*[16] was also about an hour. Walton J held that English law had definitely adopted the 'mechanics of payment' test.[17] This was in contrast, he observed, to some Commonwealth courts which formulated the test in terms of a 'reasonable time in all the circumstances of the case',[18] a test which he found 'wholly imprecise' and 'wholly unfair' because the creditor might very well not know and have no means of knowing all such circumstances.[19]

Commonwealth cases

In two Canadian cases a more liberal view was taken. In *West City Motors Ltd v Delta Acceptance Corpn Ltd*[20] it was held that where money is payable on demand, the debtor is entitled to a reasonable time to meet the demand, the question of what is reasonable being a question of fact to be determined in the circumstances of the particular case.[1] This approach was followed by Rutherford J at first instance in *Ronald Elwyn Lister Ltd v Dunlop Canada Ltd*[2]

---

11 [1973] 1 WLR 944 at 955. See however the discussion in Blanchard and Gedye *Law of Company Receiverships in Australia and New Zealand* (2nd edn, 1994) pp 72–76, para 4.09.
12 [1973] 1 WLR 944 at 955F–G.
13 [1973] 1 WLR 944 at 954H.
14 [1973] 1 WLR 944 at 955F.
15 (25 June 1975, unreported) but noted at [1987] Ch 348A–E.
16 [1987] Ch 335 at 343–344.
17 [1987] Ch 335 at 348F. He cited in particular *Toms v Wilson* (1862) 4 B & S 442 at 453, per Lord Cockburn CJ; *Moore v Shelley* (1883) 8 App Cas 285 at 293, PC per Sir Barnes Peacock and *Cripps (Pharmaceuticals) Ltd v Wickenden* above.
18 [1987] Ch 335 at 349C.
19 [1987] Ch 335.
20 [1963] 2 OR 683, 40 DLR (2d) 818.
 1 40 DLR (2d) 818 at 825 citing *Massey v Sladen* (1868) LR 4 Exch 13, 38 LJ Ex 34.
 2 (1978) 85 DLR (3d) 321.

who found Goff J's formulation to be too restrictive and held that 'a demand for payment must be reasonable and a reasonable time given to meet it'. Demand and the appointment were almost simultaneous so that no time at all was given. For that reason Rutherford J held that the seizure of stock by the receiver was wrongful. On appeal the Ontario Court of Appeal held that the term of a security document by which money is payable on demand is to be construed so that a reasonable time is allowed to the debtor to meet the demand.[3] Weatherston JA cited with approval the dictum of Pigott B in *Massey v Sladen*[4] that the question of what is a reasonable time for compliance 'must be a question of the circumstances and relations of the parties, and it would be difficult, perhaps impossible to lay down any rule of law on the subject, except that the interval must be a reasonable one'. In the particular circumstances of the case the Ontario Court of Appeal held that the debenture holder was not required to give time to the debtor to borrow money with which to pay up the indebtedness, unless time had been asked for, and no such indulgence had been requested. The Supreme Court of Canada allowed an appeal from the Ontario Court of Appeal, and restored the judgment at trial.[5] This was on the ground that, contrary to what had been held by the Ontario Court of Appeal there had been no waiver of the right to reasonable notice. Absence of any request for time is not determinative. But the Supreme Court of Canada affirmed the principle that reasonable notice should be given.[6]

An unsuccessful claim for damages based on the alleged failure of a creditor to give reasonable time for repayment of a demand loan occurred in *Mister Broadloom Corpn (1968) Ltd v Bank of Montreal*.[7] This was a case where the court at first instance held that the bank had been guilty of no impropriety. But the bank's conduct according to Linden J, could not be characterised as considerate or thoughtful to its long-standing customer. It was not such that it would make its borrowers feel comfortable in their future dealings with the bank or attract new customers. The time which elapsed between demand and the appointment of a receiver was about 40 minutes.

Linden J posed the question what was meant by money being payable on demand. Did it mean that the money must be paid immediately or did it mean that it must be paid a reasonable time thereafter? He acknowledged that the debtor did not have the right in every case to get as much time as he needs to see if he can raise the money.[8] If he did a demand note would be useless. But neither can he expect the debtor to have the money ready in his pocket to hand over

---

3 (1979) 105 DLR (3d) 684.

4 (1868) LR 4 Exch 13, 38 LJ Ex 34.

5 (1982) 135 DLR (3d) 1. For strong criticism, see (1982) 60 Can Bar Rev 733 especially at 739–740 (MH Ogilvie).

6 For other modern Canadian illustrations of this principle see *Royal Bank of Canada v Cal Glass Ltd* (1979) 9 BLR 1, BC Sup Ct; *Mister Broadloom Corpn (1968) Ltd v Bank of Montreal* (1984) 4 DLR (4th) 74. In both cases *Cripps (Pharmaceutical) Ltd v Wickenden* [1973] 2 All ER 606, [1973] 1 WLR 944 was cited. See also *Pullman Trailmobile Canada Ltd v Hamilton Transport Refrigeration Ltd* (1979) 96 DLR (3d) 322, Ontario High Court (same result whichever test is applied).

7 (1984) 4 DLR (4th) 74.

8 (1979) 101 DLR (3d) 713. At 721 citing *Cripps (Pharmaceuticals) Ltd v Wickenden*, above.

instantly. Even the strictest of the old cases allows the debtor enough time to go and get the money from his desk or from his bank.[9] Yet Linden J held that a reasonable time had been given.

The hearing of the appeal was long delayed awaiting the decision of the Supreme Court of Canada in *Ronald Elwyn Lister v Dunlop Canada Ltd.*[10] The appellate court held that a period of 40 to 50 minutes could not be a reasonable time to meet an unexpected demand for immediate payment of a large sum unless there plainly were no resources available to meet the debt or unless it were certain that the debtor would abscond with their assets. As in the *Lister* case it was stressed that the debtor did not have to request time to pay as a condition for an extension of time for payment.[11] The bank did not really dispute that the company could have paid off the debts within three or four days. The long-standing relationship between the parties and the absence of risk in granting an appropriate delay in all the circumstances were also relevant factors in assessing the question whether reasonable time had given.[12] No reasonable time had been given and an inquiry as to damages was therefore ordered.

The procedural context in which the dispute in *Lowes Chrysler Dodge Ltd v Bank of Montreal and Price Waterhouse Ltd*[13] arose was that a company, in default under a debenture security agreement and presented with an immediate demand and with the appointment of a receiver, obtained an injunction restraining the bank and the receiver. There were then presented to the court two motions, one to continue the injunction: the other to discharge it. In the Ontario Supreme Court Steele J discharged the injunction. A previous letter from the bank evidencing its dissatisfaction and evidencing a desire on the part of the bank to organise reasonable alternative financing had preceded the relevant disputed receivership by some six months. The notice given both made an immediate demand and appointed Price Waterhouse as a receiver. Even though that notice may not have been reasonable there was no evidence that the company made any attempt to pay the bank or to do anything to avoid the default that was admitted. Steele J refused to continue the injunction and discharged it. Here again was a case of a debtor with no prospects of refinance trying to pray in aid 'the reasonable time' argument in a situation where even with reasonable time things could have gone no differently.

It is indeed questionable whether there is any real distinction between English and Canadian authorities. Under English law it has always been the case that where money is repayable on demand a reasonable time must be allowed to pass before any enforcement procedure is appropriate.[14] The debtor is not, in the graphic words of Lord Cockburn J in *Toms v Wilson:*[15]

---

9   *Toms v Wilson* (1863) 4 B & S 442; *Moore v Shelley* (1883) 8 App Cas 285.

10   (1982) 135 DLR (3d) 1.

11   (1984) 4 DLR (4th) 74 at 80 per Blair JA.

12   (1984) 4 DLR (4th) 74 at 81 per Lacourciere JA.

13   (1979) 31 CBRNS 71.

14   *Brighty v Norton* (1862) 3 B & S 305.

15   (1863) 4 B & S 442 at 453 cited with approval by the Privy Council in *Moore v Shelley* (1883) 8 App Cas 285 at 293, per Sir Barnes Peacock.

'bound to pay in the very next instant of time after the demand, but he must have a reasonable time to get it from some convenient place. For instance he might require time to get it from his desk or to go across the street or to his bankers for it.'

It is arguable that the mid-Victorian 'instance' given is only an example of a broader principle which needs to be interpreted by reference to modern mobility, modern conditions and modern business practices. But however it is interpreted the creditor is not obliged to give the debtor time to negotiate a deal which *might* produce the money, particularly where the debtor had no immediate source for the money. It was for this reason that in *Cripps (Pharmaceuticals) Ltd v Wickenden*[16] the time for compliance with the demand, namely one hour, was in the circumstances not inadequate. But it does all depend on the circumstances. So again where a debtor company has through its controllers indicated that there is no likelihood of the demand being satisfied an immediate appointment of a receiver is permissible.[17] In less exceptional cases the counsel of caution must be to let a reasonable time elapse between the demand for payment and initiation of the receivership procedure.

The conduct on the part of the bank in *Skyrotors Ltd v Bank of Montreal*[18] was held to have been reasonable. Skyrotors claimed that certain steps taken by the defendant bank in exercising its security rights were unreasonable. A challenge was made to the conduct of the bank and the way in which it took steps to enforce its security. Osborne J remarked that it was not the demand to pay as such that is significant. What is significant is the time extended to the debtor before action is taken to enforce the security. And he continued:[19]

'The security becomes enforceable when default occurs. The right to appoint a receiver is triggered by default. The appointment of a receiver is one of the first steps in the process of enforcement. The creditor's right to regard the security as enforceable is not to be equated to a right to actually enforce the security.'

The learned judge paid considerable attention to what Weatherston JA had had to say in *Ronald Elwyn Lister Ltd v Dunlop Canada Ltd*[20] concerning the reasonableness of the demand having to be judged as it appeared at the time of the seizure. The learned judge pointed out that the reasonableness of the creditor's position is a question of fact.

The *Lister* case as reported in the Ontario Court of Appeal was cited in the New Zealand case of *ANZ Banking Group (NZ) Ltd v Gibson*.[1] The last-mentioned case involved an action by a debenture holder against three guarantors of two companies' debts. A demand was made on both companies by leaving a written demand at their registered office between 10 am and 10.30 am

16 [1973] 2 All ER 606, [1973] 1 WLR 944; and see *Williams & Glyn's Bank v Barnes* [1981] Com LR 205.
17 *Skyrotors Ltd v Bank of Montreal* (1980) 34 CBRNS 238.
18 (1980) 34 CBRNS 238.
19 (1980) 34 CBRNS 238 at 242.
20 (1979) 32 CBRNS 4.
 1 [1981] 2 NZLR 513.

in the morning. The secretary was out of town but the chairman knew of the impending 'fall of the axe'. Formal notice of appointment of receivers was served at the registered office at 12.15 pm and on the guarantors half an hour later. The receivership proceeded to its conclusion: there was a deficit. The guarantors challenged the demand. The compelling factors which persuaded Holland J that reasonable time had in fact been given to meet the demand were that there was no indication at any stage ever given to the bank that the demand could or would be met; that it was a commercial transaction between two trading corporations who had skilled competent advice; and that the demand was not precipitate but followed several months of expressed concern.

Any debate or uncertainty about the requirement of a formal demand can of course be avoided by making a formal demand and giving the debtor a reasonable time[2] to comply with it before appointing a receiver. And even this inconvenience can be forestalled by including in the debenture express words rendering a demand unnecessary and giving the debenture holder the right to appoint a receiver as soon as a particular situation arises.

PROCEDURE FOLLOWING APPOINTMENT

As regards appointment itself

On appointment there are first some steps which every receiver must take in relation to the appointment itself. He should obtain the original of the deed of appointment and confirmation from his lawyers of its validity. Then he should ensure that notice of the appointment is filed at the Companies Registry within seven days (a duty in fact of the debenture holder[3]). This he can do by asking for a copy of the relevant notification. Next he should establish what precisely is due to the debenture holder on fixed and floating charges by way of principal and interest (as the case may be). And finally, by way of formality, he should arrange for all documents issued by the company to contain a statement that a receiver has been appointed,[4] preferably with the date from which the appointment was operative.

Immediate steps following appointment

Many of the steps which a receiver should, as a matter of practice, take immediately following his appointment are not matters of legal obligation but are rather matters of commercial common sense and have a place in practice

2   In Malaysia too the reasonable time test has found favour. The Federal Court of Malaysia approved that test (in preference to the mechanics of payment test) in *Emar Sdn Bhd v Aidigi Sdn Bhd* [1992] 2 MLJ 734 and *Bank Bumiputra Malaysia Bhd Kuala Terengganu v Mae Perkayuan Sdn Bhd* [1993] 2 MLJ 76.
3   CA 1985, s 405.
4   IA 1986, s 39 which refers to every invoice order for goods or business letter issued by or on behalf of the company or the receiver or manager.

manuals[5] rather than in a work such as the present. Plainly the company's insurers shold be notified, as should its bankers and all bailiffs, sheriffs, execution officers, garnishors and other creditors. So far as the bank account is concerned the receiver should cancel all existing authorities and transfer the company's assets into new bank accounts in the name of the receiver. Notification to the local offices and branch offices of the company, to the directors, secretary and managers of the company and to employees generally and the unions involved and suppliers (particularly suppliers of essential services or facilities) should follow. The receiver should take control of the assets for which he is responsible and make sure that everything that needs to be under lock and key is so safeguarded. This applies not merely to physical assets but also to books and records. He will then review the affairs of the company generally.

Statutory duties and liabilities following appointment

There are various specified statutory duties for receivers and administrative receivers to fulfil following their appointment. These are discussed elsewhere.[6]

---

5 See Samwell *Corporate Receiverships – a practical approach* (2nd edn) pp 67–102; Chilvers and Shewell *Receivership Manual* (2nd edn) ch 4.
6 See at pp 127–128 (receivers) and 128 and 149–156 (administrative receivers).

CHAPTER 7

Validity of appointment

INTRODUCTION

The need for the receiver to check the validity of his appointment at the outset has already been touched on in the last chapter. The discussion which follows is addressed to the particular flaws in an appointment which are not closely bound up with the possibility of liquidation or the making of an administration order. There are, for example, particular statutory provisions which avoid wholly or in part floating charges granted within a certain period prior to liquidation or the making of an administration order. These can more conveniently be dealt with when considering the impact of a winding up on a receivership already in train. But the point deserves emphasis here as elsewhere that a conscientious liquidator will be on the look out for chinks in the receiver's armour. He will be astute to discover any possibility there may be of successfully impugning the receiver's standing. This may be either by reference to the validity of the charge under which the receiver was appointed or by reference to some defect in the form or manner of the appointment. A court-appointed administrator will also be concerned to challenge the receiver's position.

The most common attack then on the validity of a receiver's appointment comes from a subsequently appointed liquidator.[1] He will, in the interests of the general body of creditors, carefully scrutinise all aspects surrounding the appointment of the receiver to see if there is any vulnerable point in the receiver's title. The liquidator is not however the invariable protagonist. He may be unwilling to mount the attack while another interested party may be willing. And in the absence of a winding up there is no liquidator and the field is clear for other combatants in any event.

Certainly the company can challenge the appointment[2] and others with an

---

1 But not, it seems, the *provisional* liquidator whose only function is to preserve the status quo: *Re Chateau Hotels Ltd* [1977] 1 NZLR 381.

2 *Re Jaffe Ltd (in liquidation) v Jaffe (No 2)* [1932] NZLR 195; *Hawkesbury Development Co Ltd v Landmark Finance Pty Ltd* [1969] 2 NSWR 782. But it may be estopped from doing so: *Village Cay Marina LA v Acland (Barclays Bank plc third party)* [1998] 2 BCLC 327, BC.

interest and locus standi to do so include other debenture holders,[3] a judgment creditor[4] an execution creditor[5] or an administrator.

The burden of proof is on the debenture holder to show that an event has occurred justifying the appointment of a receiver.[6] But the debenture holder owes no duty of care to the company or its creditors when making the appointment: the decision to exercise the power cannot be challenged except perhaps on grounds of bad faith.[7]

The question whether and in what circumstances debenture holders can be stopped from declaring debentures valid has been raised but not resolved.[8]

CONDITIONS PRECEDENT

Clearly any expressed conditions precedent to the appointment of a receiver must be faithfully satisfied if the appointment is to be valid. In *R Jaffe Ltd (in liquidation) v Jaffe (No 2)*[9] a debenture provided that after the occurrence of a certain event the debenture holder might appoint by writing a receiver and manager of the property charged and might from time to time remove any receiver and manager so appointed and appoint another in his stead. The day before the relevant event occurred the debenture holder purported to appoint a receiver and manager by an appointment in writing. No subsequent appointment in writing was made. It was not argued that the premature appointment was valid, but it was argued that writing was evidentiary only, and a matter of form rather than substance. The court rejected the argument, and held that written appointment was essential and that the receiver and manager, not having been properly appointed, was a trespasser, although acting bona fide. The importance of the strict observance of the due requirements of the debenture is underlined by two further considerations. Such a receiver is not an officer of the court, but, if he is duly appointed, his title is superior to that of a person interfering with the assets under his control and the court will then grant an injunction.[10] If a receiver were unable to prove his title according to the terms of his contract, it is doubtful whether he would be entitled to an injunction. Furthermore, while the company is a going concern, a receiver, if the conditions of the debenture so provide, may be the agent of the company, and the company will then be responsible for his contracts. This is particularly important if the debenture holder has power to

---

3 *Re Maskelyne British Typewriter Ltd* [1898] 1 Ch 133, CA (court-appointed receiver); *Re Metropolitan Amalgamated Estates Ltd* [1912] 2 Ch 497; *Re Slogger Automatic Feeder Co Ltd* [1915] 1 Ch 478 at 485.

4 *Harris v Beauchamp Bros* [1894] 1 QB 801 at 810, CA.

5 *Kasofsky v Kreegers* [1937] 4 All ER 374.

6 [1937] 4 All ER 374.

7 *Shamji v Johnson Matthey Bankers Ltd* [1986] BCLC 278 at 284 per Hoffmann J; approved in [1991] BCLC 36, CA.

8 *Re Torvale Group Ltd* [1999] 2 BCLC 605.

9 [1932] NZLR 195. A company no longer needs to have a seal, and a document intended to operate as a deed will operate as such notwithstanding that it has not been sealed: see CA 1985, s 36A.

10 [1932] NZLR 195 at 199–200.

appoint not merely a receiver, but a receiver and manager. In such a case it seems only right and proper that the debtor company should be entitled to insist upon the fulfilment of the terms of the debenture as regards appointment as a condition of its liability.[11] Contractual terms as to the form and method of appointment are to be strictly observed.[12]

If a power to appoint a receiver is on its true construction one which was exercisable by each of several lenders there is no reason to interpret the power as being exhausted once an appointment was made by one of them.[13] The validity of the appointment can also be attacked on the basis that the appointor lacked the necessary authority or was not the person designated by the debenture to effectuate the appointment.[14] The necessary authority may be lacking at the relevant time and this too is fatal to the validity of the appointment.

LACK OF AUTHORITY

The validity of an appointment can also be attacked on the ground that the appointor lacked the necessary authority at the relevant time. Such authority is an implicit condition precedent to the validity. An attack was mounted successfully in *Harris & Lewin (in liquidation) v Harris & Lewin (Agents)*[15] against two appointors who had purported to appoint one Luckins as receiver and manager. The debenture had originally been issued in favour of the company's bank to secure the company's overdraft. The appointors claimed to be entitled to appoint a receiver and manager as assignees of the debenture. But at the relevant time, namely the time of the appointment, the assignment had not been completed. Gillard J held that they therefore lacked the necessary authority: only a debenture holder could appoint and they were not debenture holders until the assignment was completed.

The other assault made upon the appointment was unsuccessful. It was contended that the appointment was conditional on the provision of an indemnity by the appointors and that at all material times no such indemnity had been given. The evidence, it was held, did not support that contention. Gillard J reached the conclusion that the receiver and manager had accepted the appointment unconditionally. He relied on the fact that Luckins himself had acted on the assumption that his appointment was valid by asking for a statement of affairs from the company immediately after his appointment. That showed that he had accepted the appointment unconditionally and that his demand for an indemnity was a separate and distinct matter. Of course a person who is offered an appointment as receiver and manager can simply put his foot down and refuse to take up

11 [1932] NZLR 195 at 200.
12 *Wright's Hardware v Evans* (1987) 13 ACLR 631.
13 *Gwembe Valley Development Co Ltd v Koshy* (1998) 2 BCLC 613.
14 See *Pan Asia Shipyard Engineering Co Pte Ltd v Lim Kuy Bak* (1950–1985) MSCLC 459: *Marka Industrial Sdn Bhd v Elgi Marka Sdn Bhd* [1989] 1 MLJ 243, (1989) MSCLC, 90, 247.
15 (1975) ACLC 28, 279.

the appointment until he is given an indemnity. In that case his appointment remains inchoate until his demand is met.

DEFECT IN POWER OF ATTORNEY UNDER WHICH DEBENTURE WAS EXECUTED

Some apparent defects do not enable a borrower to subvert the receiver's title over the borrower's assets. Thus it was held in a Malaysian case that where an attorney has executed a debenture pursuant to some power of attorney it is not open to the borrower to challenge the validity of the charge on the basis that the bank's power of attorney pursuant to which the attorney executed the charge was valid or ineffective.[16]

LACK OF CAPACITY

A company incorporated under the Companies Acts only has the capacity to do those acts which fall within its objects as set out in its memorandum of association or are reasonably incidental to the attainment or pursuit of those objects.[17] Usually an express power to borrow is included in the company's memorandum of association, although it is not always essential that powers should be expressly given, and a power of borrowing may be *implied* from the objects of the company.[18] Thus an ordinary trading or commercial company may, unless positively prohibited,[19] borrow money for its commercial purposes. Even where no express power to do so appears in the memorandum,[20] it may validly secure repayment of such a loan by mortgage. On the other hand, no implication is possible with a non-trading company. Such a company can only borrow if and when it is specifically authorised to do so.[1] In *Rosemary Simmons Memorial Housing Association Ltd v United Dominions Trust Ltd*,[2] a charitable housing association guaranteed the debt of a non-charitable housing association (with which it was not associated in any legal sense) and secured that debt with a mortgage. Mervyn Davies J held that a charity had no business to be guaranteeing the debts of a non-charitable body, no matter how near to its own corporate heart the proposed housing project was.[3] The guarantee was 'gratuitous' in the sense that the charity received no right or benefit at law and was therefore ultra vires, and the mortgage was equally tainted and void.

---

16 *Scotch Leasing Sdn Bhd v Permira Habib Bank* [1987] 2 MLJ 458, HC (VC George J).
17 *Rolled Steel Products (Holdings) Ltd v British Steel Corpn* [1986] Ch 246, [1985] 3 All ER 52, CA.
18 [1986] Ch 246 at 287.
19 *General Auction Estate and Monetary Co v Smith* [1891] 3 Ch 432.
20 *Howard v Patent Ivory Manufacturing Co* (1888) 38 Ch D 156.
 1 *Re Badger* [1905] 1 Ch 568.
 2 [1987] 1 All ER 281, [1986] 1 WLR 1440.
 3 The project would in fact have promoted the object of the charity but the non-charitable housing association would not have been bound to run the project as a charitable one.

A receiver appointed under a debenture which was ultra vires because the company had no borrowing power, may be able to claim the benefit of the protection afforded to the debenture holder under ss 35 and 35A of the Companies Act 1985, as amended. The doctrine of ultra vires can no longer be relied upon by the company as against the lender if two cumulative conditions are satisfied, namely (i) the lender acted in good faith, and (ii) the transaction in question was decided upon by the directors.[4] Formerly a person was treated as having acted in good faith if he acted genuinely and honestly in the circumstances[5] but not if he actually knew the transaction was ultra vires.[6] A decision of the directors requires a duly convened board meeting with a quorum present and a valid resolution passed by the meeting.[7]

A party to a transaction decided upon by the directors is not bound to inquire as to the capacity of the company to enter into it, or as to any limitation on the powers of the directors under the memorandum or articles of association, and must be presumed to have acted in good faith unless the contrary is proved.[8] The doctrine of constructive notice of a company's memorandum and articles is in effect abolished.[9]

ABSENCE OF REGISTRATION

Another way in which the ground may be cut from under the receiver's feet is where the charge under which he was appointed was not registered. In that event the liquidator may attack his appointment on the ground that the charge itself is void for want of registration.[10] That is not to say that for the period between the date of his appointment and the date of the company going into liquidation he is not fully justified in any actions which he took as receiver.[11] As against the company the charge remains valid and effective. But as against the liquidator and creditors non-registration of the charge on which his appointment depends is a fatal flaw.[12] The receiver will have to account for all the assets in his hands to the liquidator and he cannot properly act after the winding up has started. Even before liquidation any assets subject to a valid subsequent charge will be taken out of the receivership.

---

4 CA 1985, s 35A(1).
5 *Barclays Bank Ltd v TOSG Trust Fund Ltd* [1984] AC 626, [1984] 1 All ER 1060, HL.
6 *International Sales and Agencies Ltd v Marcus* [1982] 3 All ER 551. But see now CA 1989 which inserts new ss 35A and 35B into the CA 1985.
7 Lingard *Bank Security Documents* (1985) p 14.
8 CA 1985, s 35B (as amended by CA 1989).
9 *TCB Ltd v Gray* [1986] Ch 621, [1986] 1 All ER 587; but see *International Sales and Agencies Ltd v Marcus* [1982] 3 All ER 551.
10 CA 1985, s 396. New sections intended to replace the existing sections 395–409 of the Companies Act 1985 are not now to come into force.
11 *Burston Finance Ltd v Speirway Ltd (in liquidation)* [1974] 1 WLR 1648 at 1657E per Walton J.
12 Cf *Re Destone Fabrics Ltd* [1941] Ch 319 (a case under the predecessor of s 396 in its unamended form).

Charges registrable under Companies Act 1985

The charges created[13] by the company[14] which under the Companies Act 1985[15] are required to be registered at the Companies Registry within 21 days of creation[16] are:

(a)   a charge for the purpose of securing any issue of debentures;[17]

(b)   a charge on uncalled share capital of the company;[18]

(c)   a charge created or evidenced by an instrument which, if executed by an individual, would require registration as a bill of sale;

(d)   a charge on land wherever situate, or any interest therein, but not including a charge for any rent or other periodical sum issuing out of the land;[19]

(e)   a charge on book debts of the company;

(f)   a floating charge on the undertaking or property of the company;

(g)   a charge on calls made but not paid;

(h)   a charge on a ship or aircraft or any share in a ship;

(i)   a charge on goodwill, on a patent on a licence under a patent;

(j)   on a trade mark or on a copyright or a licence under a copyright.

Two of these categories merit supplementary consideration.

Corporate bill of sale

Category (c) was brought into the system of registration because companies were not otherwise subject to the Bills of Sale Acts 1878 and 1882. A bill of sale as defined by s 4 of the Bills of Sale Act 1878 includes all assurances of personal chattels with certain exceptions. But a pledge effected by physical change of possession and which can be proved without reference to any written document

---

13 The creation of the charge and not the advance of the money is the basis of the requirement to register.

14 Charges arising by operation of law are not registrable: *London and Cheshire Insurance Co Ltd v Laplagrene Property Co* [1971] Ch 499, [1971] 1 All ER 766.

15 CA 1989.

16 CA 1985, s 396. The court may extend the time in some circumstances: CA 1985, s 404 (unamended). For the basis on which the court will exercise its discretion to extend time for registration, see *Re Braemar Investment Ltd* [1989] Ch 54.

17 Ie an issue of an aggregate number and not just one debenture: *Automobile Association (Canterbury) Inc v Australasian Secured Deposits Ltd* [1973] 1 NZLR 417, NZCA. Otherwise this category would overlap all others.

18 Not of another company: see Jenkins Report (Cmnd 1749) paras 301 and 30(f) recommending otherwise.

19 This category includes equitable charges created by simple deposit of title deeds: *Re Wallis & Simmonds (Builders) Ltd* [1974] 1 All ER 561; *Re Molton Finance Ltd* [1968] Ch 325, [1967] 3 All ER 843, CA.

is not caught by the Bills of Sale Act 1878.[20] The Acts are aimed at documents not at transactions, and the pledgee's rights do not derive from the document. A sale and hiring agreement is not normally a bill of sale[1] but it may be a bill of sale if the court concludes that the real purpose of the transaction was to secure a loan.[2] Section 4 of the Bills of Sale Act 1878 excludes: (i) transfers of goods in the ordinary way of business of any trade or calling, as well as the transfer of documents used in the ordinary course of business as proof of the possession or control of goods; and (ii) a charge of goods situated outside England and Wales. Later statutory provisions exclude letters of lien or hypothecation on imported goods, whether they are executed before the goods are warehoused, purchased stored or re-shipped or delivered to a purchaser.[3]

Book debts

There is no definition in the Companies Act 1985 of the term 'book debts'. The language of judicial definition of the term predictably varies but the verbal differences are small.[4] Four members of the Common Pleas Divisional Court gave judgment in *Shipley v Marshall*[5] as to the meaning of the term 'book debts'. Erle CJ defined a 'book debt' as a debt connected with and growing out of the business regardless of whether or not it was entered in the relevant books.[6] Williams J defined the term as meaning debts in respect of which entries could or would in the ordinary course of business be made in the relevant books.[7] Willes J agreed with him.[8] Byles J also said that he agreed with Williams J[9] that they must be such as are commonly entered in books.[10]

Lord Esher MR defined the term as meaning 'debts arising in a business in which it is the proper and usual course to keep books and which ought to be entered in the books'.[11] Another formulation describes book debts as debts of which in the ordinary course of business there would be 'such entries in the books that the owner of the business or his accountant can tell from them what moneys are to become payable, when they should be paid, and what of them are paid'.[12] The most recent descriptive statement of the nature of book debts is that

---

20 *Re Hardwick, ex p Hubbard* (1886) 17 QBD 690, CA; *Charlesworth v Mills* [1892] AC 231, HL; *Wilkinson v Girard Frères* (1891) 7 TLR 266; *Re Cunningham & Co Ltd, Attenborough's Case* (1884) 28 Ch D 682; *Re Hall, ex p Close* (1884) 14 QBD 386. Cf *Re David Allester Ltd* [1922] 2 Ch 211; *Wrightson v McArthur and Hutchisons (1919) Ltd* [1921] 2 KB 807.

1 *North Central Wagon Co v Manchester, Sheffield and Lincolnshire Rly Co* (1887) 35 Ch D 191, CA; *Stoneleigh Finance Ltd v Phillips* [1965] 2 QB 537, [1965] 1 All ER 513, CA.

2 *Yorkshire Railway Wagon Co v Maclure* (1882) 21 Ch D 309, CA.

3 Bills of Sale Act 1890, s 1 (as amended by Bills of Sale Act 1891).

4 *Paul & Frank Ltd v Discount Bank (Overseas) Ltd* [1967] Ch 348 at 360–361 per Pennycuick J.

5 (1863) 14 CBNS 566; and see *Dawson v Isle* [1906] 1 Ch 633; *Independent Automatic Sales Ltd v Knowles & Foster Ltd* [1962] 3 All ER 27, [1962] 1 WLR 974.

6 (1863) 14 CBNS 566 at 570.

7 (1863) 14 CBNS 566 at 571.

8 (1863) 14 CBNS 566 at 571–572.

9 (1863) 14 CBNS 566 at 571 and 572.

10 (1863) 14 CBNS 566 at 573.

11 *Tailby v Official Receiver* (1888) 13 App Cas 523, HL.

12 *Re WF Le Cornu Ltd Liquidator v Federal Traders Ltd* [1931] SASR 425 at 440 per Piper J.

'they would normally be entered in well-kept books of a company carrying on the business [in question] when they became due and payable'.[13]

A charge in this context included a mortgage and a lien or equitable charge[14] created by the company in any recognised way.[15] If a retention of title clause was construed as a bill of sale or floating charge it was registrable as such.[16] So too was an agreement constituting a present equitable interest,[17] though not an agreement to give a security at some future time or to some further extent.[18]

DEBENTURE SECURING ACQUISITION OF COMPANY'S OWN SHARES

Yet another situation in which the receiver's position can be set at naught is where it can be shown that the security under which he was appointed infringes the statutory provision forbidding a company, except in certain circumstances, to give financial assistance in the acquisition of its own shares.[19] In *Victor Battery Co Ltd v Curry's Ltd*[20] the statutory prohibition was held to have only penal consequences and a second debenture issued by a company to assist in financing the purchase of its own shares was held valid. That decision attracted much criticism and has been rejected by most Commonwealth courts which hold the infringing transactions invalid.[1]

13 *Contemporary Cottages (NZ) Ltd v Margin Traders Ltd* [1981] 2 NZLR 114 (surveying the English and Antipodean cases). See further the cases referred to under the head 'Future book debts' in ch 2, at pp 14–19. For recent cases, see *E Pfeiffer Weinkellerei-Weineinkauf GmbH & Co v Arbuthnot Factors Ltd* [1988] 1 WLR 150, [1987] BCLC 522 (sale proceeds of goods supplied subject to retention of title clause); *Re Welsh Irish Ferries Ltd* [1986] Ch 471 [1985] 3 WLR 610 (lien on sub-freights created by a company under a time charter in favour of shipowner); cf *Annangel Glory Cia SA v Coldetz Ltd Middle East Marketing Corpn (UK) Ltd* [1988] 1 Lloyds Rep 45. As to liens on sub-freights, see Fidelis Oditah 'The juridical nature of a lien on sub-freights' [1989] LMCLQ 191–197. Such liens are no longer required to be registered: see CA 1985, s 396.
14 CA 1985, s 396.
15 By deed, writing or deposit of title deeds.
16 *Re Bond Worth* [1980] Ch 228, [1979] 3 All ER 919; *Borden (UK) Ltd v Scottish Timber Products Ltd* [1981] Ch 25, [1979] 3 All ER 961, CA.
17 *Re Jackson & Bassford* [1906] 2 Ch 467, 75 LJ Ch 697.
18 *Re Gregory Love & Co* [1916] 1 Ch 203, 85 LJ Ch 281. But the later charge pursuant to the agreement will be registrable: *Re Eric Holmes (Property) Ltd* [1965] Ch 1052, [1965] 2 All ER 333.
19 CA 1985, s 151 (superseding CA 1948, s 54). The actual wording of CA 1985, s 151 renders the giving of financial assistance unlawful and creates a criminal offence, but like s 54 of the 1948 Act; says nothing of the consequences of the breach. The 'old' case law on this topic is therefore still relevant. The restrictions of s 151 are relaxed for private companies: CA 1985, s 155. 'Financial assistance' is defined in CA 1985, s 152(1). For transactions not prohibited by s 151, see CA 1985. Express reference to the timing of the financial assistance is now included. The prohibition now applies to the *acquisition* of shares rather than their purchase or subscription, so it clearly includes subscriptions and transfers of shares when payment is not in cash.
20 [1946] Ch 242, [1946] 1 All ER 519; and see *Spink (Bournemouth) Ltd v Spink* [1936] Ch 544, [1936] 1 All ER 597.
 1 For a detailed review of the Commonwealth cases up to 1974, see Reginald Barrett 'Financial Assistance and Share Acquisitions' (1974) 48 ALJ 6 at 8–10. See also the 2nd edn of this book at pp 79–80.

One Jaina was a director of and principal shareholder in two battery manufacturing companies, British Lion, and Princely. He agreed to buy from certain vendors the entire issued share capital in Victor Battery Co for £15,000. He paid £6,000 down and obtained transfers of 40% of the issued capital. To pay the balance, which under the contract was payable by instalments, he needed financial assistance. Currys Ltd wanted torch batteries which the two battery companies already controlled by Jaina could supply. Currys Ltd advanced £6,000 to British Lion, £2,000 to Princely and £2,000 to Victor Battery Ltd, making £10,000 in all. By using the £2,000 advanced to Victor Battery as a security Jaina procured Princely to advance to him the sum of £3,000 and British Lion lent him £6,000. Thus he was able to complete the purchase, following which he arranged for Victor Battery to issue to Currys Ltd a debenture securing payment of the total amount advanced. Currys Ltd knew the facts but it was neither pleaded nor proved that they knew that the transaction, as carried out, contravened the section. Later a receiver was appointed by the debenture holder. Then Victor Battery Co challenged the validity of the debenture and thus the very authority of the receiver to act, claiming in the action a declaration that the debenture was void and of no effect.

Roxburgh J refused to hold the debenture invalid. He accepted that the debenture had been issued by the company 'in connection with a purchase'[2] of its own shares. In effect there were two grounds for his decision. First, he construed the section as one which provided merely for the punishment of the offending company and its officers but which did not invalidate a security given in contravention of it. Second, he held that even if the issue of the debenture were illegal both parties were in pari delicto: the plaintiff company was not a person for whose protection the illegality had been created by statute so that there could be no relief from the rule expressed in the maxim 'in pari delicto potior est conditio defendentis'.

The decision of Roxburgh J in the *Victor Battery* case has found very few friends indeed. In Australia it is settled law that transactions which contravene the provisions of the section which classifies as unlawful the provision by a company of finance to purchase its own shares are themselves invalid.[3] Such transactions (the Australian courts have ruled) are invalid whether they are merely loans and the claim is for repayment of money lent[4] or are debentures executed by the company.[5]

---

2 The prohibition now applies only to the provision of financial assistance 'for the purpose of' the acquisition and *not* in connection with 'an acquisition'.

3 See the cases in the next two footnotes. For New Zealand, see *Skelton v South Auckland Blue Motels Ltd* [1969] NZLR 955. In Malaysia the same conclusion was reached by the Supreme Court in *Chuang Khiaw Bank Ltd v Hotel Rasa Soyang Sdn Bhd* [1990] 1 MLJ 356, criticised in Suhendram S, Lim TH & Chew E *Corporate Receivership: The Law and Practice in Malaysia and Singapore* (1997) 66–68.

4 *Dressy Frocks Pty Ltd v Bock* (1951) 51 SRNSW 390; *Shearer Transport Co Pty Ltd v McGrath* [1956] VLR 316; *Re Toowoomba Welding Works Pty Ltd (No 2)* [1969] Qd R 337; *Vam Ltd v McDonald Industries Ltd* [1970] 3 NSWR 3.

5 *Re J & H Pinkster & Co Pty Ltd* [1968] Tas SR 77.

The prohibition is not confined to financial assistance to the purchaser: it is directed to financial assistance to whomsoever given, provided that it be for the purchase of shares or in connection with a purchase of shares.[6]

It is curious that there is no reported case other than the *Victor Battery* case in which the validity of a security taken by an outsider lender from a company to finance the purchase by that company of its own shares has been in issue. In *Dressy Frocks Pty Ltd v Bock*[7] Owen J said:

> 'I refrain from expressing any opinion as to the rights of the parties, if, for
> example, a question arose between a company which had given assistance to a
> purchaser of its shares in contravention of the section, and an innocent third party
> such as a bank, which had advanced money for the purchase of the shares on the
> faith, for instance, of a guarantee of the borrower's overdraft given by the
> offending company.'

Of course the mortgagee in the *Victor Battery* case was not the vendor but a third party. And in that case as was pointed out in *Shearer Transport Co Pty Ltd v McGrath*[8] it had been neither pleaded nor proved that the mortgagee was aware that the giving of the loan was illegal.

The tendency of the Commonwealth courts to treat debentures which contravene the statutory provision as invalid has now been mirrored by a decision (rather than mere obiter dicta) in this country. Fisher J in *Heald v O'Connor*[9] declined to follow the *Victor Battery* case and struck down a debenture given by a company to the vendor of its shares to secure a loan made available to the purchaser to enable him to pay the price. The purchaser had guaranteed the company's obligations under the charge. For reasons into which it is unnecessary to go the charge was said to have been issued ultra vires. The learned judge held that as the charge was illegal under the section the guarantee given in support of it was void and unenforceable. Whether the same result would have ensued had the guarantee been framed as an indemnity was a matter which he left open. While one commentator[10] had mixed feelings about the judgment, it is now clearly the preponderant view that a debenture which infringes s 151 of the 1985 Act, or any of its equivalents elsewhere, is void.[11] Accordingly, a receiver appointed under a power contained in such a debenture cannot assert his title once the charge has been successfully attacked.

---

6 *EH Dey Pty Ltd (in liq) v Dey* [1966] VR 464 at 474 per McTierney J.
7 (1951) 51 SRNSW 390 at 396.
8 [1956] VLR 316.
9 [1971] 2 All ER 1105, [1971] 1 WLR 497.
10 See [1971] ASCL 458 at 467–468 (LS Sealy).
11 Where there is an agreement to execute a debenture *restitutio in integrum* may be possible: see
South Western Mineral Water Co Ltd v Ashmore [1967] 2 All ER 953, [1967] 1 WLR 1110
(Cross J) noted with approval in [1967] ASCL 461–475 (PS Atiyah). But this decision is difficult
to reconcile with the earlier decision of Cross J in *Curtis's Furnishing Stores Ltd (in liquidation)
v Freedman* [1966] 2 All ER 955, [1966] 1 WLR 1219 where the learned judge followed the
Victor Battery case. In *Lawlor v Gray* (1980) 130 NLJ 317, CA the purchaser was able to
enforce the agreement.

APPLICATION TO COURT FOR DIRECTIONS

A receiver or manager of the property of a company appointed under the powers contained in any instrument may apply to the court[12] for directions in relation to any particular matter arising in connection with the performance of his functions and on any such application the court may give such directions as it thinks fit.[13]

It is to be noted that the directions sought must relate to some 'matter arising in connection with the performance of his functions'. The latter phrase would not, on the face of it, allow an application by a person acting as receiver and manager, but whose title is disputed, to seek the guidance of the court as to the validity of his appointment.[14] The statutory provision envisages directions being sought by an unimpeached receiver as to the performance of his functions as a receiver: it does not envisage his raising a question as to whether he is a receiver.

INDEMNITY

Following a recommendation of the Cork Committee[15] there is now a statutory provision giving the court a discretion to order that the appointor of a receiver does indemnify the receiver against any liability which arises solely by reason of the invalidity of the appointment.[16] It has also been established independently of any statutory provision that the appointor may be liable to indemnify the receiver in respect of any liability to the company or a third party incurred by the receiver acting pursuant to the instructions of his appointor.[17]

---

12 By originating application. For a form 10(1) see *Court Forms* (1999 Issue) 109, Form 62.
13 IA 1986, s 35.
14 There is, perhaps, a parallel in the position of a de facto liquidator applying under CA 1985, s 651; that section is only available to a duly appointed liquidator: *Re Wood and Martin Ltd* [1971] 1 All ER 732, [1971] 1 WLR 293.
15 (1982) (Cmnd 8558) para 830.
16 See 10(1) Court Forms (1999 Issue) 105–108, Forms 59–60. IA 1986, s 34.
17 *Re B Johnson & Co (Builders) Ltd* [1955] Ch 634 at 647–648 per Sir Raymond Evershed MR.

CHAPTER 8

Position of privately appointed receiver

The position of a receiver and manager appointed out of court is always to be determined by reference to the floating charge or instrument under which he was appointed.[1] A crucial question is that of agency. Is he agent of the debenture holder who appointed him? Or is he agent of the company whose assets his function is to call in and get into possession? There are other aspects of his position which also deserve attention.

Modern debentures almost invariably provide that any receiver appointed shall be the agent of the company. Moreover, statute deems an administrative receiver to be the agent of the company unless and until the company goes into liquidation. In the rare cases where there is no such specification of 'deemed agency' the receiver and manager will indeed be the agent of the debenture holder.[2] It is convenient to deal with this (exceptional) agency relationship first before considering the more usual deemed agency for the company and the statutory agency which applies in the case of a receiver appointed by a mortgagee under s 109 of the Law of Property Act 1925 and in the case of an administrative receiver.

AGENT FOR DEBENTURE HOLDER

Where the receiver and manager is agent for the debenture holder he goes into possession of the company's assets and operates the business on behalf of the debenture holder. The debenture holder is accordingly in the unattractive position of being virtually a mortgagee in possession through his agent. The debenture holder will be liable for the acts and defaults of the receiver.[3] He will be answerable for the commitments entered into by his receiver in the carrying on of the business and the debenture holder must fulfil those commitments whether or not there are charged assets to which the debenture holder can look for ultimate recoupment. There is at least one judicial statement by Warrington J in *Robinson Printing Co Ltd v Chic Ltd* to the effect that for some purposes a

---

1 *Central London Electricity Ltd v Berners* [1945] 1 All ER 160.
2 *Re Vimbos Ltd* [1900] 1 Ch 470.
3 *Robinson Printing Co Ltd v Chic Ltd* [1905] 2 Ch 123.

receiver and manager acting as agent for the debenture holder must be regarded as agent of the company at least 'to such an extent as may be necessary to enable him to exercise the powers conferred upon him by the debenture'. The precise ambit of this extent, however, remains to be solved by cases yet to be decided.

A further drawback for the debenture holder is his liability for his agent's remuneration[4] in the absence of some express bargain to the contrary subsisting between them. Ultimately he may be able to recoup these expenses from the company but meanwhile he faces the primary responsibility.

AGENT FOR THE COMPANY

Express deemed agency

As has already been mentioned, the debenture normally constitutes the receiver and manager agent of the company. That agency represents an agreed feature of the contract between the company and the debenture holder. The company will accordingly be bound by acts performed by the receiver and manager within his authority. He can therefore enter into contracts on behalf of the company and dispose of its property, validly conferring title on the disponee.

The company will be liable for breaches of pre-existing contracts by the receiver;[5] for debts contracted by him as receiver,[6] and for torts committed by him in the course of his performance of his duties.[7] Moreover, depending on the circumstances,[8] the company may even be held responsible for criminal offences arising out of his performance of his duties.[9]

Statutory deemed agency

A receiver appointed under the powers conferred by the Law of Property Act 1925 is by s 109(2) of that Act deemed to be the agent of the mortgagor and the mortgagor is solely responsible for the receiver's acts or defaults unless the mortgage deed otherwise provides.[10]

By virtue of s 44 of the Insolvency Act 1986 an administrative receiver is deemed to be the company's agent unless and until the company goes into liquidation.[11] The power of a receiver other than an administrative receiver to act as deemed agent of the company must cease in the case of a compulsory winding up on the

4 *Deyes v Wood* [1911] 1 KB 806, CA.
5 *George Barker (Transport) Ltd v Eynon* [1974] 1 WLR 462 at 471, CA per Stamp LJ.
6 *Cully v Parsons* [1923] 2 Ch 512.
7 Cf *Re Simms* [1934] Ch 1, CA.
8 See *Meigh v Wickenden* [1942] 2 KB 160, [1942] 2 All ER 68 (receiver held liable for breach of Factories Acts).
9 *Re John Willment (Ashford) Ltd* [1979] 2 All ER 615, [1980] 1 WLR 73 (breaches of VAT regulations).
10 See the discussion at pp 305 and 308.
11 IA 1986, s 44(1)(a).

date of the winding-up order[12] and in the case of a voluntary winding up on the date of the resolution to wind up.[13] In the case of the statutory deemed agency it is expressly provided that it is to last only until the company goes into liquidation.[14] Presumably after the liquidation the liquidator may authorise an administrative receiver to act as agent for the company.[15]

The deemed agency of an administrative receiver differs from a normal agency in a number of significant respects. Firstly, unlike most agents, he will be personally liable on contracts entered into by him unless he expressly excludes such personal liability under the relevant contract;[16] he will also be personally liable on any contracts of employment 'adopted' by him in carrying out his functions as receiver.[17] Secondly, his deemed principal, the company, is unable to dismiss him. In the third place, although nominally the agent of the company, his primary duty is to realise the assets in the interests of the debenture holder and his powers of management are really ancillary to that duty.[18] This has an impact on the company's right to get information from the receiver as Hoffmann J pointed out in *Gomba Holdings UK Ltd v Homan*.[19] So in the absence of express contrary provision made by statute or the terms of a debenture, any right which the company may have to be supplied with information must be qualified by the receiver's primary duty to the debenture holder:[20]

> 'If the receiver considers that disclosure of information would be contrary to the interests of the debenture-holder in realising the security, I think he must be entitled to withhold it and probably owes a duty to the debenture-holder to do so. The company may be able to challenge the receiver's decision on the grounds of bad faith or possibly that it was a decision which no reasonable receiver could have made, but otherwise I think that the receiver is the best judge of the commercial consequences of disclosing information about his activities.'

The interplay between the respective duties owed by a receiver as agent for the company and as agent for the debenture holder was further considered by the Court of Appeal in *Gomba Holdings UK Ltd v Minories Finance Ltd*.[1] Two receivers on the discharge of their receiverships and pursuant to a court order handed over various documents, which belonged to the plaintiff companies, to those companies. But they withheld other categories of documents on the ground that they did not belong to the plaintiffs. The plaintiffs sought delivery up of the withheld documents on the basis that they owned them, contending that during the receivership the receivers had been agents of the companies and, as between

---

12 *Gosling v Gaskell* [1897] AC 575 at 581, HL.
13 *Thomas v Todd* [1926] 2 KB 511.
14 IA 1986, s 44(1)(a).
15 Cf *Re Northern Garage Ltd* [1946] Ch 188, [1946] 1 All ER 566 (debenture provided receiver to be agent of company; liquidator *impliedly* authorised receiver to act as agent).
16 See at p 161, above.
17 IA 1986, s 44(1).
18 *Gomba Holdings UK Ltd v Homan* [1986] BCLC 331 at 334G; and see *Re B Johnson & Co (Builders) Ltd* [1955] Ch 634 at 644–645, CA.
19 [1986] BCLC 331.
20 [1986] BCLC 331 at 336 and 337.
 1 [1989] 1 All ER 261, CA.

principal and agent, documents concerning the principal's offices which had been prepared or received by the agent belonged to the principal. Hoffmann J rejected this proprietary claim[2] and so too did the Court of Appeal. Fox LJ who delivered the leading judgment[3] accepted the general principle that as between principal and agent all documents concerning the principal's affairs which had been prepared or received by the agent belonged to the principal, but said that it could not be applied mechanically to the somewhat complex position of a receivership. The agency of a receiver was not an ordinary agency. Striking a balance between the duties owed by a mortgagor, Fox LJ held[4] that the ownership of documents in the context of a receivership depended on whether the documents were brought into existence in discharge of the receivers' duties to the mortgagor, or the debenture holder, or to enable the receiver to carry out his professional duties. It was only documents in the first category to which the plaintiffs could lay a proprietary claim. The fact that a document relates to the mortgagor's affairs cannot be determinative.

One important consequence of a receiver being deemed to be the agent of the company is that in normal circumstances the receiver cannot be regarded as being in rateable occupation of the property charged. This is well illustrated in *Ratford v Northavon District Council*[5] where joint receivers were appointed under a debenture (i) which contained the usual agency provision deeming them to be the company's agents (which gave rise to a true agency relationship as between the receivers and the company), and (ii) which merely empowered the receivers to take possession of the property charged and did not effect a transfer of possession to them or oblige them to dispossess the company. The receivers could not, the Court of Appeal held, be regarded as being in rateable occupation of the property charged unless it was proved that they had dispossessed the company and taken possession of the property in an independent capacity as principal, and thus otherwise than in their capacity as the company's agents. The question, to paraphrase a dictum of Dixon J in *Australian Mutual Provident Society v Geo Myers & Co Ltd*[6] is whether the receiver is in control of the company's premises in the exercise of an *independent* possession or is merely in charge of the company's undertaking on its behalf so that the company continues in occupation. Possession held by a person in his capacity as agent is in law the possession of his principal.[7]

More recently it has been held by Arden J that a receiver is not, by reason only of his appointment as such, liable for unoccupied property rates where he is appointed on terms that he is agent of the company. Such agency did not constitute the receiver as a person entitled to possession of the premises or owner for the purposes of rateable liability.[8]

---

2 [1988] BCLC 60.
3 Stocker LJ and Butler-Sloss LJ agreed with his judgment: [1989] BCLC 115 at 121D.
4 [1989] BCLC 115 at 117A–H.
5 [1986] BCLC 397, CA.
6 (1932) 47 CLR 65 (mortgagee's right of distraint under Queensland statute still exercisable against company's goods and chattels because company remains in occupation despite receivership).
7 [1986] BCLC 397 at 416F.
8 *Brown v City of London Corpn* [1996] 1 WLR 1070.

FIDUCIARY ELEMENT

The 'very special and . . . limited' agency of the receiver has been described as 'perhaps the only genuinely non-fiduciary agency'.[9] At the other end of the scale a privately appointed receiver has been described as a fiduciary.[10] The truth is possibly somewhere in between these two statements. Perception of the receiver's role as genuinely non-fiduciary bases itself on the alleged inability of the company to complain of anything except ultra vires acts, breaches of expressed terms, mala fides or fraud.[11] Yet one recent tendency of the courts in England has been to analyse the duties of a receiver and manager in the language of tort and of using reasonable care[12] rather than as being fiduciary. That tendency was temporarily halted by the persuasive but by no means universally lauded authority of the decision of the Privy Council in *Downsview Nominees Ltd v First City Corpn Ltd*,[13] discussed later.[14] The ambit of that decision has however been reviewed by the Court of Appeal in *Yorkshire Bank plc v Hall*[15] and in *Medforth v Blake*.[16] The middle way is to concede a fiduciary element in *some* of the duties, but to reject any all-pervading fiduciary element.

Although he may be an agent of the company the receiver is not a trustee of its assets for the company or, for that matter, for the debenture holder or the preferential creditors,[17] although of course he owes some fiduciary duties to all of them.[18] Upon a liquidation any agency will cease and only fiduciary duties can remain. However, once he has reached the stage of paying all the debts for which he has personal liability and has paid off the debenture holder it may be said that he holds any surplus money in trust for subsequent incumbrancers and the company.[19]

The receiver is not an agent for the creditors even when in opposition to the debenture holder's wishes, he acts in accordance with a creditor's resolution.[20] Nor ex hypothesi is he a debtor of the company: money received by him for the company is already the property of the company and cannot be owed to it. Thus until his job is done money in his hands cannot be reached by garnishee proceedings.[1] He is under no obligation to carry on the company's business at the expense of the debenture holders.[2]

---

9 Meagher Gummow and Lehane *Equity: Doctrine and Remedies* (2nd edn, 1986) p 669, para 2841 (not repeated in 3rd edn).

10 *Visbord v Federal Comr of Taxation* (1943) 68 CLR 354 at 383 per Williams J (appointment under statutory power).

11 *Re B Johnson & Co (Builders) Ltd* [1955] Ch 634 at 662, CA per Jenkins LJ.

12 *Cuckmere Brick Co Ltd v Mutual Finance Ltd* [1971] Ch 949, CA; *Standard Chartered Bank Ltd v Walker* [1982] 1 WLR 1410, CA. Contrast the attitude of the Australian courts discussed at p 139, below.

13 [1993] AC 295, PC.

14 See at p 136, below.

15 See at p 137, below.

16 [1999] 2 BCLC 221, CA.

17 *Visbord v Taxation Comr* [1943] ALR 153, 68 CLR 354.

18 See at pp 141–143.

19 *Expo International Pty Ltd v Chant* [1979] 2 NSWLR 820.

20 *Rendell v Doors and Doors Ltd* [1975] 2 NZLR 191.

1 *Seabrook Estate Co Ltd v Ford* [1949] 2 All ER 94.

2 *Re B Johnson & Co (Builders) Ltd* [1955] Ch 634 at 662, CA.

RELATIONSHIP WITH DIRECTORS AND THE COMPANY

In considering the effect of a receivership on the powers of the board of directors it is important to bear in mind the distinction between a receiver on the one hand, and a receiver and manager on the other.

A receiver appointed under the statutory power does not enjoy any powers of management of the company's business. His receivership cannot therefore interfere with the managerial powers exercised by the board of directors.

The position of a receiver and manager appointed under the terms of a debenture is different. Such a person ex hypothesi enjoys powers of management. A man cannot serve two masters; and it would be intolerable if the board of directors and the receiver-manager were to vie with each other to manage the company's business, for the company would not know whose directions to follow. At one time it was supposed, on the basis of the decision in *Moss Steamship Co Ltd v Whinney*,[3] that the appointment of a receiver and manager resulted in the suspension or paralysis for all practical purposes of the directors' powers.

Residual status of the directors

Indeed it is now clear that the receiver and manager does not usurp all the functions of the company's board of directors. The directors have continuing powers and duties. Their statutory duties in relation to the preparation of annual accounts,[4] the auditing of those accounts, calling the statutory meetings of shareholders, maintaining the share register and lodging returns remain.

The existence of residual powers in the board of directors was recognised by Street J (as he then was) in *Hawkesbury Development Co Ltd v Landmark Finance Pty Ltd*.[5] The point at issue in that case was whether directors could start proceedings in the name of the company challenging the security under which the receiver was appointed and hence his appointment and his subsequent acts. Street J held that they could and had this to say on the subject:[6]

> 'There are directors of Landmark Finance currently in office. Indeed, it was the managing director, RJ Blackburn, who gave instructions for the submitting appearance to be filed on behalf of Landmark Finance. Receivership and management may well dominate exclusively a company's affairs and dealings and relations with the outside world. But it does not permeate the company's internal domestic structure. That structure continues to exist notwithstanding that the directors no longer have authority to exercise their ordinary business management functions. A valid receivership and management will ordinarily supersede, but not destroy, the company's own organs through which it conducts its affairs. The capacity of those organs to function bears an inverse relationship to the validity and scope of the receivership and management.'

---

3 [1912] AC 254. But Lord Atkinson at 263 does not in fact say that *all* the parts are in suspension.
4 The receiver is also under a duty to keep and produce on request full account of his dealings with the company's assets: *Smiths Ltd v Middleton* [1979] 3 All ER 842.
5 [1969] 2 NSWR 782.
6 [1969] 2 NSWR 782 at 790.

This decision is not inconsistent with the view that a receiver and manager supplants the board of directors in the control, management and disposition of the assets over which the security exists. And the judgment of Street J pays due tribute to the general principle that the extent to which the powers of the directors are supplanted will vary with the scope of the receivership and management vested in the appointee. Thus if a receiver is given power to manage the company's business that must be to the exclusion of the directors; and equally if a receiver is given power to make title to a particular asset or to particular assets of the company that must be to the exclusion of the directors' power to make such title. On the other hand, on the logic of Street J's decision, directors of a company in receivership would presumably also have the right to bring proceedings in the name of the company to challenge acts of a *validly* appointed receiver on the grounds of excess of authority or misfeasance on his part. Within its scope the receiver's agency is exclusive: to the extent to which the receiver has power to bind the company and deal with its property the powers of the directors are excluded.[7] Moreover, it has been held by the Court of Appeal that directors of a company in receivership might bring an action in the name of the company, without the receiver's consent, against a subsidiary of the debenture holder for breach of contract.

The facts in *Newhart Developments Ltd v Co-operative Commercial Bank Ltd*[8] were unusual. The plaintiffs were property developers who in January 1973 issued a debenture in favour of Cooperative Bank Ltd. In October 1973 they entered into an arrangement with the defendant bank which was a subsidiary of the debenture holder. Under the arrangement (i) the plaintiffs were to find properties for development particularly in North Wales and deal with all matters relating to such development, (ii) the plaintiffs and the defendant bank were to set up a new company each holding 50% of the share capital, and (iii) the defendant bank was to provide the entire finance. By April 1974 the defendant bank had become disillusioned with the project and the plaintiffs were heavily indebted to it. The bank called for the plaintiffs to transfer their holding in the new company to the bank and withdrew its financial support. Subsequently, a receiver and manager was appointed by the debenture holder. In the usual way the receiver was deemed expressly to be the agent of the company, ie the plaintiffs, and had the usual power 'to take possession of collect and get in the property charged by [the] debenture and for that purpose to take any proceedings in the name of the company or otherwise'. After a couple of months it appeared to the plaintiffs that the conduct of the bank in April 1974 was a breach of contract. They sent a letter before action which went unanswered. Then they issued a writ in the Queen's Bench Division. The defendant bank applied to set aside the writ on the ground that it had been issued without the knowledge or consent of the receiver 'who is alone entitled to the proceeds of [the] action'.

The registrar dismissed the application and there was an appeal to the judge. Chapman J allowed the appeal and set the writ aside on the basis that it was inherent in the power conferred on the receiver to bring proceedings that no action could be brought without his consent and also on the ground that 'an

---

7 See *Re Scottish Properties Pty Ltd* (1977) 2 ACLR 264 at 272–273 per Needham J.
8 [1978] QB 814, [1978] 2 All ER 896, CA.

action by the ... company which would stultify or frustrate the receiver's activities must be contrary to the terms of [the] debenture'.[9] The judge commented that it was 'curious that there is no authority', and added: 'Any action which would interfere with the receiver must be something which should not be allowed.'[10]

The plaintiff developers appealed to the Court of Appeal and the appeal came before a court consisting of Stephenson LJ and Shaw LJ. The appeal was successful and the writ and action were reinstated. It was held that the power given to the receiver to bring proceedings was an enabling provision so that he could realise the company's assets and carry on business for the benefit of the debenture holders. The provision did not divest the directors of the company of *their* power to pursue a right of action if it was in the company's interest and did not in any way impinge prejudicially on the position of the debenture holders by threatening or imperilling the assets which were the subject of the charge.[11] Shaw LJ accepted that directors could not dispose of assets within the debenture charge without the consent of the receiver. It is the function of the receiver to deal with the assets in the first place so as to provide the means of paying off the debenture holders' claims. But that said, it was in his view only within the scope of the assets covered by the debenture and only in so far as it is necessary to apply those assets in the best possible way that the receiver had a real function. If, in the exercise of his discretion, he chooses to ignore some asset such as a right of action, or decides that it would be unprofitable from the point of view of the debenture holders to pursue it, there is nothing in the authorities which suggests that it is not then open to the directors of the company to pursue that right of action if they think that it would be in the interests of the company.

In the eyes of Shaw LJ, while a receiver might be entitled to ignore the claims of anybody outside the debenture holders, the company and its directors stand in a different position. Accordingly, he concluded, if there is a asset which appears to be of value, although the directors cannot deal with it in the sense of disposing of it, they are under a duty to exploit it so as to bring it to realisation which may be fruitful for all concerned. Obviously the rights or functions of the receiver are not affected if the company is indemnified against any liability for costs. That was the position in the *Newhart Developments Ltd* case: the directors had agreed to indemnify the company against any costs incurred in the action. The decision of the court may also have been affected by the fact that the receiver would have been placed in an unenviable position, faced with a very great conflict of interest, had his consent to proceedings been mandatory. But the absence of prejudice to the debenture holders was the crucial factor. Indeed Shaw LJ went so far as to say that there was no principle of law or expediency which precluded a duly constituted board of directors from seeking to enforce a claim, however ill-founded it may be, provided only, of course, that nothing in the course of the proceedings which they institute is going in any way to threaten the interests of the debenture holders.[12] As one commentator has pointed out the decision could

9 [1978] QB 814 at 818–819.
10 [1978] QB 814.
11 [1978] QB 814 at 819F.
12 [1978] QB 814 at 821.

give rise to considerable difficulties for receivers if directors attempt to exercise powers upon the basis of their view that their actions are not prejudicial to the debenture holders. If their view appears to the receiver to be palpably wrong he would have to move for injunctive relief. But issues are not always clear cut, and then comes the unenviable occasion for a decision on the issue.

The *Newhart* case was followed in the New Zealand Court of Appeal case *Paramount Acceptance Co v Souster*[13] in which directors sought an order invalidating the debenture under which the receiver had been appointed. On the other hand in *Tudor Grange Holdings Ltd v Citibank NA*,[14] where the plaintiff companies started an action against a bank for misrepresentation without the receiver's consent, Sir Nicolas Browne-Wilkinson V-C indicated that he had substantial doubts about the correctness of the *Newhart* decision, suggesting that the case might have to be looked at on a future occasion.[15]

While treating the *Newhart* case as undoubtedly binding on him in a case where it exactly covered the point in issue he nevertheless distinguished it from the case before him:

> 'Unlike the position in the *Newhart* case, when the directors of the plaintiff companies decided to start proceedings in the name of the company they were starting proceedings which could directly impinge on the property subject to the receiver's powers in that they held no indemnity against the liability of the companies' assets to satisfy a hostile order for costs made against the companies.'

The directors had no power to start proceedings because the receiver's position was prejudiced by the decision.

It is, in truth, as was pointed out in *Re Geneva Finance Ltd*,[16] a question of fact in each case whether the purported exercise of power by the directors is detrimental to the function of the receiver. Where it is, the directors must bow to the right of the receiver. If there is no prejudice to the receiver's functions it does not offend the principle which *Newhart* articulates:[17]

> 'The real question is whether the directors, wishing to exercise a power which they would otherwise have, can do so without prejudicing the legitimate interests of the receiver and the secured creditor in the realisation of the assets.'

Thus directors can choose solicitors to represent the company in litigation which had no legal connection to the chargee's rights, even though it might have an impact upon the mortagagee's recovery.[18] Equally, directors of a company in receivership must have power to exercise the company's right of redemption on its behalf so long as that may be done in a way which does not prejudice the debenture holder or the receiver.[19]

13 [1981] 2 NZLR 38.
14 [1992] Ch 53.
15 [1992] Ch 53 at 63.
16 (1992) 7 WAR 496.
17 (1992) 7 WAR 496 at 511.
18 *Sun-Life Properties Pty Ltd v Chellaston Pty Ltd* (1993) 10 ACSR 476 (in which the *Re Geneva Finance* approach is approved at 481).
19 *Brooklands Motor Co Ltd (in receivership) v Bridge Wholesale Acceptance Corpn (Australia) Ltd* (1994) 7 NZCLC 260,449 especially at 260,458.

A company must also be able to sue its receiver for the improper discharge of his duties, though a derivative action by the shareholders directed to that end would not be proper.[20] The company, at the instigation of the directors, can challenge the validity of the receiver's appointment[1] or oppose a winding-up petition even one launched by the debenture holder.[2] And pending any actual exercise of the relevant power by the receiver the directors can defend a winding-up application brought in respect of the company.[3] However, should there be any difference of opinion between the directors and the receiver as to whether a winding-up petition should be supported or resisted the views of the receiver should prevail.[4]

Finally, it should be observed that challenges to the debenture and to the appointment of a receiver under it can be mounted by the company acting by its directors[5] but not by the directors and shareholders acting in their own right.[6]

ADMINISTRATIVE RECEIVER AS OFFICE HOLDER

Under the Insolvency Act 1986, an administrative receiver is classified for certain purposes as an 'office-holder', and by virtue of being an office holder is given certain powers and responsibilities.[7]

Supplies by public utilities

Where a request is made by or with the concurrence of an administrative receiver for the giving, after the date of his appointment,[8] or, in the case of an administrative receiver who replaces an earlier administrative receiver, the date of the appointment of the first administrative receiver, of supplies of gas, electricity, water or telecommunication services,[9] the relevant supplier (a) may make it a condition of the giving of the supply that the administrative receiver personally guarantees the payment of a charge in respect of the supply, but (b) shall not make it a condition of the giving of the supply or do anything which has the

---

20 *Watts v Midland Bank plc* [1986] BCLC 15.

 1 *Bunbury Foods Pty Ltd v National Bank of Australasia Ltd* (1984) 153 CLR 491.

 2 *Re Reprographic Exports (Euromart) Ltd* (1978) 122 Sol Jo 400.

 3 *Bank of New Zealand v Essington Developments Pty Ltd* (1990) 5 ACSR 86.

 4 *Bank of New Zealand v Essington Developments Pty Ltd* (1990) 5 ACSR 86.

 5 *Re Jaffe Ltd v Jaffe* [1932] NZLR 195; *Watts v Midland Bank plc* [1986] BCLC 15; *Emar Sdn Bhd v Aidiqi Sdn Bhd* [1992] 2 MLJ 734, SC.

 6 *Malaysian Ropes v Malaysian Prestressed Concrete Strand Manufacturing Sdn Bhd* (6 March 1992, unreported); notes in Suhendram S, Lim TH & Chew E *Corporate Receivership The Law and Practice in Malaysia and Singapore* (1997) 73; *Watts v Midland Bank plc*, above.

 7 IA 1986, ss 233–236.

 8 IA 1986, s 233(4)(b).

 9 IA 1986, s 233(3) defines the relevant supplies. Telecommunication services means services by a public telecommunications operator as defined in the Telecommunications Act 1984; s 233(3)(d).

effect of making it a condition of the giving of the supply that any outstanding charges in respect of a supply given to the company before the receivership are paid.[10] The latter restriction prevents a statutory undertaker or similar body from threatening to cut off supplies to compel preferential payment of outstanding arrears, a practice which prior to the Insolvency Act 1986 had been upheld as permissible.[11]

Getting in the company's property

Where any person has in his possession or control any property, books, papers or records to which the company appears to be entitled, the court may require that person forthwith (or within such period as the court may direct) to pay, deliver, convey, surrender or transfer the property, books, papers or records to the administrative receiver.[12] Immunity is given to an administrative receiver (and a lien for his expenses) where he mistakenly but bona fide[13] seizes or disposes of property which does not belong to the company.[14] The protection is given whether or not he has acted in pursuance of a court order,[15] though no doubt such an order would buttress his claim to have acted in good faith. The immunity is in respect of any loss or damage resulting from a seizure or sale, except insofar as that loss or damage is caused by the administrative receiver's own negligence.[16] He will have a lien on the property, or the proceeds of its sale, for such expenses as have been incurred in connection with the seizure or disposal.[17]

Co-operation with administrative receiver

Former officers and employees of the company as well as other designated persons are under a statutory duty to co-operate with an administrative receiver. The persons bound by this duty are:

(a)   those who are, or have at any time been, officers[18] of the company;

(b)   those who have taken part in the formation of the company at any time within one year before the effective date;

---

10 IA 1986, s 233(2).
11 *Wellworth Cash and Carry (North Shields) Ltd v North Eastern Electricity Board* (1986) 2 BCC 99, 265.
12 IA 1986, s 234(1).
13 IA 1986, s 234(3).
14 IA 1986, s 234(4).
15 IA 1986, s 234(3)(a).
16 IA 1986, s 234(4)(a). The owner could still sue for recovery of the property or the proceeds of the sale.
17 IA 1986, s 234(4)(b).
18 As to who is an officer, see the IA 1986, s 251, which incorporates the definition in the CA 1985, s 744.

(c)   those who are in the employment of the company, or have been in its employment (including employment under a contract for services) within that year, and are in the administrative receiver's opinion capable of giving information which he requires;

(d)   those who are, or have within that year been, officers of, or in the employment (including employment under a contract for services) of, another company which is, or within that year was, an officer of the company in question; and

(e)   in the case of a company being wound up by the court, any person who has acted as administrator, administrative receiver or liquidator of the company.[19]

The obligation on each such person is: (i) to give to the administrative receiver such information concerning the company and its promotion, formation, business dealings, officers or property as the administrative receiver may at any time after his appointment (or that of his earliest predecessor) reasonably require, and (ii) attend on the administrative receiver at such times as the latter may reasonably require.[20] Failure without reasonable excuse to comply with this obligation will render the guilty person liable to a fine and, for continued contravention, a daily default fine.[1] The court may, on application by the administrative receiver, make such orders as it thinks necessary for the enforcement of this statutory duty[2] and such an order of the court may provide that all costs of and incidental to the application for it shall be borne by the person against whom the order is made.[3]

Inquiry into company's dealings

The court is now empowered, on the application of an administrative receiver, to summon to appear before it: (i) any officer of the company; (ii) any person known or suspected to have in his possession any property of the company or supposed to be indebted to the company; or (iii) any person whom the court thinks is capable of giving information concerning the promotion, formation, business dealings, affairs or property of the company.[4] The court may require any of these persons to submit an affidavit to the court containing an account of his dealings with the company or to produce any books, papers or other records in his possession or under his control relating to the company or any matters concerning the promotion, formation, business dealings, affairs or property of the company.[5]

---

19 IA 1986, s 235(3).
20 IA 1986, s 235(2).
 1 IA 1986, s 235(5). For penalties, see s 430 and Sch 10.
 2 IR 1986, r 7.20(1)(a) and (2).
 3 IR 1986, r 7.20(3).
 4 IA 1986, s 236(2).
 5 IA 1986, s 236(3).

Arrest and seizure

The court is also given suitably strong powers of enforcement where a person without reasonable excuse fails to appear before the court when he has been summoned for that purpose, or where there are reasonable grounds for believing that a person has absconded, or is about to abscond, with a view to avoiding his appearance before the court pursuant to a summons.[6] In such a case the court may, for the purpose of bringing that person and anything in his possession before the court, cause a warrant to be issued to a constable or prescribed officer of the court (i) for the arrest of that person or (ii) for the seizure of any books, papers, records, money or goods in that person's possession.[7] The person may be kept in custody and anything seized may be held, in accordance with the rules, until that person is brought before the court or until such other time as the court may order.[8]

Other enforcement powers

If it appears to the court, on consideration of any evidence obtained under the foregoing procedure or any exercise of its enforcement powers, that any person has in his possession any property of the company, the court may, on the application of the administrative receiver, order that person to deliver the whole or any part of the property to the administrative receiver at such time, in such manner and on such terms as the court thinks fit.[9] Then if it appears to the court, on consideration of any evidence so obtained, that any person is indebted to the company, the court may, on the application of the administrative receiver, order that person to pay the administrative receiver at such time and in such manner as the court may direct the whole or any part of the amount due, whether in full discharge of the debt or otherwise as the court thinks fit.[10]

There are also supplemental provisions about the examination of persons. Firstly, the court may, if it thinks fit, order that any person, who if within the jurisdiction of the court would be liable to be summoned to appear before it under this procedure, shall be examined in any part of the United Kingdom where he may be for the time being, or in a place outside the United Kingdom.[11] Secondly, any person who appears or is brought before the court under this procedure may be examined on oath or (except in Scotland) by interrogatories, concerning the company or its promotion, formation, business dealings, affairs or property.[12]

6   IA 1986, s 236(4).
7   IA 1986, s 236(5).
8   IA 1986, s 236(6). For rules and forms, see IR 1986, rr 7.23 and 7.24 and Forms 7.8 and 7.9.
9   IA 1986, s 237(1).
10 IA 1986, s 237(2).
11 IA 1986, s 237(3).
12 IA 1986, s 237(4).

CHAPTER 9

Powers

INTRODUCTION

The powers of a privately appointed receiver and manager depend upon the terms of the debenture under which he is appointed, subject always to any statutory provisions affecting those powers. The source of his authority is the debenture under which he is appointed. From that source all his powers flow or are derived. Many of his powers are *express* powers set out in the debenture. Indeed, a debenture will usually bestow upon any receiver and manager wide powers to enable him to fulfil his primary duty of realising such of the company's assets as are charged under the debenture so as to pay off the money due to the debenture holders. Other powers though not expressed are *implicit*. Where a person is given express authority to pursue a course of action he has implied authority to do whatever is necessary for or incidental to the effective execution of his express authority in the usual way.[1] The grant of the power carries with it the grant of all proper means not expressly prohibited to effectuate the power itself.[2]

TO TAKE POSSESSION

The first power which falls to be considered is that which entitles him to take possession of the company's assets. In the standard debenture it is common form to have a power:

> 'To take possession of, collect, and get in the property charged by the debenture, and for that purpose to take any proceedings in the name of the company or otherwise [as may seem expedient].'[3]

---

1 *Pole v Leask* (1860) 28 Beav 562.
2 *Merchant Service Guild of Australasia v Commonwealth Steamship Owners' Association* (1913) 16 CLR 664 at 688 per Jacobs J.
3 See Hooper *Receivers for Debenture Holders* (1933) 15; *Sowman v David Samuel Trust Ltd* [1978] 1 WLR 22 at 25; Palmer's *Company Precedents* Vol 3 at p 239; *Re Emmadart Ltd* [1979] Ch 540 at 542 ('as he shall think fit').

The first part of the power, which authorises the receiver and manager to take possession of, collect and get in the property charged expresses in terms of power what is in fact a duty of the receiver and manager. It is indeed one of the main duties of a receiver to get in the assets charged. If anyone prevents him from obtaining possession or interferes with his possession when obtained, proceedings can be taken to obtain possession or prevent such interference.[4] A receiver and manager appointed out of court under a debenture is not ex hypothesi an officer of the court, so that interference with his possession is not a contempt of court, as it is in the case of a receiver appointed by the court. There is of course no 'interference' when the receiver's possession is challenged by someone who has in fact a prior right to the property concerned. A receiver cannot retain possession as against such a person, who can exercise his rights without any leave of the court.

As a general rule a receiver, as such, is not entitled to being an action in his own name as receiver.[5] This is because no property is automatically vested in him by his appointment.[6] But he may acquire a right to sue in his own name arising out of his receivership, but not in consequence of it alone. Thus a receiver who is holder of a bill of exchange or payee of a cheque which has been made payable to him personally may sue in his own name.[7] Likewise if he is the assignee in his own name of a judgment debt he will, after getting leave to issue execution, be entitled to serve a bankruptcy notice and present a petition based on that notice in his own name.[8]

On the other hand a receiver can sue in the company's name even without its consent.[9] He does not have to go hat in hand to get the leave of the company. As it is one of his main duties to get in the company's assets, he has the right for this purpose to sue in the company's name to recover those assets.[10] An *express* power to that effect is often inserted in a debenture. But even in the absence of an express power a power to sue in the company's name had been implied. This point arose in *M Wheeler & Co Ltd v Warren*[11] in the context of a general power to get in the property charged. Lawrence J referring to such a power said:[12]

> 'That power, in my judgment, implies a power to do all things necessary or proper for the purpose of getting in the property and in particular a power for the purpose of collecting debts and other moneys of the plaintiffs in the hands of third parties to take all proper legal proceedings in that name. It is true that in many debentures there is found express authority to bring proceedings in the company's name, but

---

4 *Bayly v Went* (1884) 51 LT 764.
5 *Re Sacker* (1888) 22 QBD 179, 58 LJQB 4, CA (bankruptcy petition based on debt due to the company).
6 *Re Sartoris* [1892] 1 Ch 11 at 14; *Bolton v Darling Downs Building Society* [1935] SR Qd 237 at 243 per Henchman J (a case involving a liquidator); *Re Scottish Properties Pty Ltd* (1977) ACLC 29,271 at 29,277. The note applies not only to actions to recover goods or money but also to an action for a declaration: *Bolton v Darling Downs Building Society*, above.
7 *Re Sacker* (1888) 22 QBD 179 at 183 per Lord Esher.
8 *Re Macoun* [1904] 2 KB 700, 73 LJKB 892, CA; cf *Re Sacker*, above.
9 *M Wheeler & Co Ltd v Warren* [1928] Ch 840 at 846, CA.
10 [1928] Ch 840.
11 [1928] Ch 840.
12 [1928] Ch 840 at 845–846.

in my judgment there is no real necessity for the insertion of such a provision which in a case like the present is clearly implied. If no such authority were implied, the power conferred on the receiver for the greater security of the debenture holder of getting in the property of the plaintiffs would be illusory.'

The factual situation in *M Wheeler & Co Ltd v Warren*[13] was that a debenture of a company empowered the holder to appoint a receiver and manager and provided: 'A receiver and manager so appointed shall be the agent of the company and shall have power to take possession of and get in the property charged.'[14] The company had entered into a contract with the defendant to sell a house in the course of construction to the defendant. Not long afterwards the debenture holder appointed a receiver and manager. Difficulty arose in enforcing the contract against the defendant. The receiver and manager brought an action in the name of the company claiming rescission of the contract and forfeiture of the deposit or alternatively specific performance. The Court of Appeal, reversing the decision at first instance,[15] held that the express power included an implied power to bring legal proceedings without the company's consent. It was argued that to make a claim for rescission of a contract was not to 'get in' the property of the company. But the specific performance claim, if sustained, clearly would have the effect of getting in property of the company – namely the purchase money. And the alternative claim for rescission was classified as 'a lawyer's mode of getting all questions of substance decided between the parties':[16] in that sense the proceedings were brought to 'get in' the property charged. A power to gather in the company's assets and to take proceedings for that purpose has been held to include the power to sue for conversion and trespass claiming injunctive relief and punitive damages.[17] Whether the receiver's power to bring actions includes the power to bring actions against the debenture holder who appointed him is an open question.[18]

The power to get in the property charged does not enable a receiver to make a call for unpaid share premiums.[19]

Where a receiver and manager is empowered to sue in the company's name the defendant may be able to make out a case for security for costs. This is a course of action made possible by a statutory provision which empowers the court 'if it appears by credible testimony that there is reason to believe that the company will be unable to pay the costs of the defendant if successful [to] require sufficient security to be given for those costs and stay all proceedings until the security is given'.[20] In an Australian case[1] the fact that the company was in

---

13 [1928] Ch 840, CA.
14 [1928] Ch 840 at 841, CA.
15 Of the Vice Chancellor of the then Lancaster Palatine Court.
16 [1928] Ch 840 at 845, CA per Lord Hanworth MR.
17 *Inglis Electrix Pty Ltd v Healing (Sales) Pty Ltd* [1965] NSWR 1652.
18 *Newhart Developments Ltd v Co-operative Commercial Bank Ltd* [1978] QB 814 at 821–822, CA, per Stephenson LJ. The case is discussed at pp 105–107.
19 *South Australian Barytes Ltd v Wood* (1975) 12 SASR 527.
20 CA 1985, s 726; Hong Kong Companies Ordinance (HKCO), s 357; Malaysian Companies Act (MCA), s 351; Singapore Companies Act (Sing CA), s 388.
 1 *HG Palmer Pty Ltd v Hill* (1917) 1 DCRNSW 250 (NSW Dist Ct).

receivership which appeared in the title of the action was held enough to justify an order for security for costs, and a stay until such security was given.

There is a suggestion in a dictum of Cotton LJ in *Re Henry Pound Son & Hutchins*[2] that once the company has gone into liquidation the receiver cannot bring proceedings in the company's name. But this is highly questionable. His right to bring an action, it is submitted, is merely an incident of his more general power to get in the security. There is some discussion of this point in *Gough's Garages Ltd v Pugsley* where Romer LJ says:[3]

> 'When the company was ordered to be wound up by the Court . . . that right which had been given by contract to the debenture holders of, among other things, taking proceedings to obtain this new lease in the name of the company was in nowise affected. It is perfectly true (and it has been laid down over and over again) that where, as happened in this case, the debenture or trust deed securing the debentures contains the usual clause, that the receiver appointed under the deed shall be deemed to be the agent of the company, that this winding up of the company or the compulsory liquidation of the company puts an end to the agency. But it does not put an end in anyway to the powers of the receiver. In my opinion, when this liquidation order was made, the right of the receiver to proceed in the name of the company in the county court was in nowise affected.'

The statement that winding up 'does not put an end *in anyway* to the powers of the receiver' is too sweeping if intended to be a general proposition. But so long as it is confined, as it was no doubt intended to be confined, to the context of starting and carrying on litigation in the name of the company (upon which no limitation is placed) it is unexceptionable.

If the receiver brings or defends proceedings it should be borne in mind that the court may, where the justice of the case requires it, order the receiver to pay the costs personally.[4]

TO COMPROMISE

The appointment of a receiver and manager is a mark of the debenture holder's lack of confidence in the financial stability of the company which granted the debenture. The financial problems leading to such an appointment tend to produce two other consequences. The company will be anxious to pursue its debtors; and its creditors will be concerned to apply pressure to the company. Disputes about both those matters are likely to result in litigation. And so it is that a receiver and manager will often inherit litigation based on disputes which arose prior to his appointment. Clearly a receiver and manager needs to be equipped to deal with litigation, whether in being or threatened. For this reason debentures

---

2 (1889) 42 Ch D 402 at 421, CA; see also *Newman Bros Ltd v Allum* [1934] NZLR 694.
3 [1930] 1 KB 615 at 626.
4 *Anderson v Hyde* [1996] 2 BCLC 144; *Forest Pty Ltd (Receivers and Managers Appointed) v Keen Bay Pty Ltd* (1991) 9 ACLC 460 and *Johns Perry Industries Pty Ltd v Triosi Steel Fabrications Pty Ltd (Receiver and Manager appointed)* [1993] ACL Rep 325, summarised in Konrad de Kerloy 'The Personal Liability of a Liquidator and Administrative Receiver for the Costs of an Unsuccessful Action' (2000) 4 RALQ 13–33.

almost invariably give an express power to a receiver and manager to make compromises or arrangements in the interests of the debenture holders. The classic formulation of the power enables the receiver and manager 'to make any arrangement or compromise which he shall think expedient in the interests of the debenture holders'. A power in those terms was conferred on the receiver and manager in *Robinson Printing Co Ltd v Chic Ltd*,[5] and the debenture did not provide that the receiver was to be the agent of the mortgagors. Warrington J held that the receiver was therefore the agent of the debenture holders, and that the power enabled the receiver to pledge the company's assets in priority to the debenture holders' charge if he thought it desirable to do so to ensure the effectual carrying on of the business.

TO CARRY ON BUSINESS

Unless the debenture expressly authorises him to carry on business a receiver appointed out of court cannot carry on business. For that reason debentures almost invariably confer an express power on any receiver who may be appointed to carry on business of the company. Where there is such an express provision then although the person appointed is termed a 'receiver' only, he is in effect, also a receiver *and manager*.[6]

The power to manage has been said, in essence, to be really ancillary to the primary duty to realise the assets in the interests of the debenture holder.[7] But more recently it has been classified as independent of the power to sell. A receiver can manage a business for the purpose of generating profits from which the secured debt can be discharged. The management of the business does not have to be ancillary to an intended eventual sale.[8]

An express power to carry on business is often amalgamated with an express power to borrow, and may also be amplified by a plethora of incidental powers which are tacked on the main powers. One typical formulation of the power to carry on business gives the receiver power:

> 'To carry on or concur in carrying on the business of the company and for that purpose to raise money on the premises charged in priority to the debentures or otherwise.'[9]

That very power was contained in the debenture in *Caines v JE Austin & Sons Ltd*.[10] The power to carry on business may also expressly authorise the receiver

5 [1905] 2 Ch 123, 74 LJ Ch 399.
6 A power to 'manage' gives sufficient authority if the subject matter of the charge includes 'profits' of a business: *Bompes v King* (1886) 33 Ch D 279, 56 LJ Ch 202, CA.
7 *Gomba Holdings UK Ltd v Homan* [1986] 1 WLR 1301 at 1305.
8 *Medforth v Blake* [1999] 2 BCLC 221 at 237d–e, CA.
9 Hooper *Receivers for Debenture Holders* (1933) p 15; Palmer's *Company Law Precedents* (16th edn) p 239; 6 *Forms and Precedents* (4th edn) 1185 (where the borrowing power reads 'and for this purpose to borrow money on the security of the property hereby charged in priority to this debenture or otherwise').
10 (1958) 75 WNNSW 267.

to do all acts which may be done in the ordinary conduct of the business for the protection of the assets used or employed therein and for obtaining a return from such assets. In *Inglis Electrix Pty Ltd v Healing (Sales) Pty Ltd*[11] a decision of the Supreme Court of New South Wales, Asprey J held that such a power enabled a receiver to claim damages for any wrong done to the business.

TO INSURE AND REPAIR

A receiver and manager 'can only insure or do necessary or proper repairs to the mortgaged property to the extent to which he is directed to insure or to do such repairs by the mortgagee in writing'.[12] For this reason it is desirable, and in many cases no doubt essential, to confer on the receiver and manager a broad power to repair and insure. One well-known precedent book[13] contains a broad power framed in the following terms:

> 'To make and effect all such repairs improvements and insurances as he shall think fit and renew such of the plant machinery and other effects of the company whatsoever as shall be worn out lost or otherwise become unserviceable.'

Many debentures incorporate the statutory provision[14] which stipulates, inter alia, that the receiver may apply money received by him in paying:

> 'the premiums on fire, life and other insurances, if any, properly payable under the mortgage deed or under this Act and the cost of executing necessary or proper repairs directed in writing by the mortgagee.'

Where this statutory provision is incorporated the receiver should be careful about expending money for such purposes unless he does so with the written directions of the debenture holders, otherwise he may find himself unable to recoup his expenditure at the expense either of the debenture holders or of subsequent incumbrancers.[15]

TO BORROW

It has already been seen that a power to borrow is frequently annexed to the power to carry on the business. Apart from the example already quoted from *Caines v JE Austin & Sons Ltd*,[16] there is the closely similar power in the debenture in *Sowman v David Samuel Trust Ltd*[17] which was a power:

---

11 [1965] NSWR 1652.
12 *Visbord v Federal Taxation Comr* (1943) 68 CLR 354 at 382 per Williams J.
13 6 *Forms and Precedents* (4th edn) 1190.
14 LPA 1925, s 109(8)(iii).
15 *White v Metcalf* [1903] 2 Ch 567, 72 LJ Ch 712.
16 (1958) 75 WNNSW 267.
17 [1978] 1 All ER 616, [1978] 1 WLR 22.

'to manage or carry on or concur in carrying on the business of the company as he may think fit and for that purpose to raise or borrow money to rank for payment in priority to this security and with or without a charge on the property hereby charged or any part of it.'

On the other hand a power to borrow is sometimes set out in an entirely separate power. Thus one of the leading precedent books[18] provides the following power as an alternative:

'Subject as hereinafter provided [a receiver] may for the purpose of carrying on the business of the company and of defraying any costs charges losses or expenses (including his remuneration) which shall be incurred by him in the exercise of the power authorities and discretions vested in him and for all other purposes thereof or any of them raise and borrow money on the security of the mortgaged premises or any part thereof either in priority to the stock and security hereby constituted or otherwise and at such rate or rates of interest and generally on such terms and conditions as he may think fit and no person lending any such money shall be concerned to inquire as to the propriety or purpose of the exercise of this power or to see to the application of any monies so raised or borrowed provided that [the receiver] shall not exercise this present power without obtaining the prior written consent of the [debenture holder] but the [debenture holder] shall incur no responsibility or liability to the lender or otherwise by reason of [his] giving or refusing such consent whether absolutely or subject to any limitation or condition.'

At first sight this power might appear prolix. But in fact few, if any, words are wasted. It has the virtue of being comprehensive as well as explicit. It is also, of course, a wider power not limited simply to the carrying on of the business. It is therefore a matter for commercial decision whether the debenture should confer on any receiver to be appointed a wide power or a narrower power.

In the absence of an express borrowing power the question may arise whether a power to borrow can be implied. Of course that question does not even arise if a power to borrow is expressly prohibited. But assuming that there is no such express prohibition what then? There is no authority expressly in point. It is well established that a trading or commercial company has, prima facie, an implied power to borrow, even if the memorandum is entirely silent on the matter.[19] The implied power encompasses borrowing a reasonable amount for the purposes of the business. This implication follows from the doctrine that a person with a particular express authority has in addition an implied authority to do whatever is necessary for or incidental to the effective execution of the express authority.

In turn, a necessary incident to the power to borrow is the (implicit) power to mortgage or charge property to secure the borrowing. It seems to be assumed that these powers, implied for the benefit of trading and commercial undertakings, are implied powers of a receiver and manager of such undertakings. In *Robinson Printing Co Ltd v Chic Ltd*,[20] the receiver appointed by debenture holders had

---

18 6 *Forms and Precedents* (4th edn) 1316.
19 *General Auction Estate and Monetary Co v Smith* [1891] 3 Ch 432, 60 LJ Ch 723; *Re Patent File Co* (1870) 6 Ch App 83 at 86 and 88.
20 [1905] 2 Ch 123, 74 LJ Ch 399.

power under the debentures '(1) to take possession of the property charged by the debentures (2) to carry on or concur in carrying on the business of the company (3) to sell or concur in selling any of the property charged by the debentures and (4) to make any arrangement or compromise which he shall think expedient in the interests of the debenture holders'. He was not, however, expressed to be the agent of the company. After his appointment he agreed with the plaintiffs to assign to them book debts of the company in consideration of their doing certain printing work. It was argued by the plaintiffs that the powers to carry on the business and to make such arrangements as he might think expedient in the interests of the debenture holders each authorised him to pledge the assets of the company in priority to the debenture holders' charge. Warrington J held that the receiver was in pledging the assets an agent for the debenture holders and that in that capacity and by virtue of the power to do whatever he might think expedient in the debenture holders' interests he had the necessary authority to pledge the company's assets in priority to the debenture holders' charge. Had the receiver been, as is more usually the case, agent for the company only, the position might have been different. The propriety of a receiver who is the agent of the company raising money on the property charged by the debentures in priority to the debentures without the express consent of the debenture holders has been doubted. Presumably if his appointment clearly authorised him to take such a course there should be no difficulty. But in the absence of some clear authorisation to that effect a prudent receiver will either secure the express consent of the debenture holders to their being postponed or will apply to the court. The receiver might in fact be driven to one of those courses or to giving his own personal covenant to repay by the reluctance of a prudent lender to advance money without some such protection.

Such a charge creates merely an equitable interest, so that when the charge crystallises the whole legal estate remains vested in the company. As a result the consent of the company as evidenced by the affixation of its common seal is normally a prerequisite to conveyance or assignment to a purchaser.

TO EMPLOY AGENTS OR EMPLOYEES

There are certain situations in which the appointment of a receiver and manager by the debenture holders will terminate the contracts of service of company employees. A receiver and manager intending to carry on the business will need to enter into fresh contracts of service with the same or new employees. His entry into such contracts would appear to be fairly incidental to his power to carry on the business so that he would in any case have an *implied* power to employ agents or employees for the purposes of carrying on the business. In fact most well drawn debentures avoid all argument on the point by incorporating an *express* power for the receiver to employ agents and other persons.

A typical express provision empowers the receiver:

> 'To appoint managers accountants servants workmen and agents for the aforesaid purposes upon such terms as to remuneration or otherwise as the receiver may determine.'

The particular precedent in which this expressed power occurs places the express power at the end of all the other powers conferred on the receiver, save the residual incidental power. In *Inglis Electrix Pty Ltd (Receiver Appointed) v Healing (Sales) Pty Ltd*,[1] the placement of a very similar power to employ agents was inept. The debenture after conferring on the receiver and manager the usual powers of sale and power to carry on the business also gave the receiver power 'to employ managers solicitors officers and agents . . . and servants for all or any of the purposes *aforesaid* on such salaries and remuneration' as he thought fit. There then followed a number of other specific powers.

The question was whether the express power to delegate was restricted by the words 'for all or any of the purposes aforesaid' to the situations envisaged by the preceding clauses in the deed. Asprey J rejected such a construction as absurd and construed the words as tantamount to 'herein contained'. Use of the latter phrase would have avoided any debate and is to be preferred.

TO MAKE CALLS

It has been held that a receiver and manager's general powers to get in the charged property, and to enforce contracts, and to do anything else necessary in the interests of the debenture holder do not cover the making of a call of uncalled premiums. Such general powers do not extend to the creation of property as distinct from exercising a mortgagee's security over property.[2] On the other hand it is now well established that a company may charge its uncalled capital. It has been stated that where uncalled capital is made a security for debentures, the receiver cannot make calls unless the articles give power to the directors to delegate to a receiver their power of making calls.[3] That proposition was accepted in general terms by Sangster J in *South Australian Barytes Ltd v Wood*.[4] But he qualified it by saying that it was not necessary for the articles to give such powers in express terms. For example, a power to mortgage uncalled capital would readily lend itself to an interpretation which includes power to delegate to the mortgagee or to a receiver and manager appointed by the mortgagee, the directors' power to make calls of uncalled capital. One of the debentures in *South Australian Barytes Ltd v Wood* authorised:

> 'any Receiver appointed hereunder in trust for the Mortgagor at any time after the moneys hereby secured become payable to make calls on its members in respect of the uncalled capital hereby charged and to sue in the name or otherwise for the recovery of moneys becoming due in respect of calls so made and to give valid receipts for such moneys and the provision contained in its Articles of Association in regard to calls shall mutatis mutandis apply to calls made under this authority and this authority shall subsist during the continuance of this security notwithstanding any change of its Directors shall be exercisable to the exclusion of the powers of its Directors and shall be assignable.'

1 [1965] NSWR 1652.
2 *South Australian Barytes Ltd v Wood* (1975) 12 SASR 527 especially at 548 per Sangster J.
3 Palmer's *Company Precedents* Pt 3 (4th edn) p 611.
4 (1975) 12 SASR 527.

The company's borrowing powers and the directors' powers in that behalf were wide enough to authorise the inclusion of that clause in the debenture. But although the receiver and manager had power to make calls of uncalled capital he had no power to make calls of uncalled instalments of premiums on share issues. The call in *South Australian Barytes Ltd v Wood*[5] was a composite one (partly capital and partly premiums) and could not be severed. The receiver therefore had to apply to the court to be appointed receiver and manager by the court and for the relevant power.[6] These additional court proceedings could have been avoided had the original powers been sufficiently wide.

The powers of the receiver to make calls are no greater than those of the directors and are governed by any restrictions or procedures binding the latter.[7]

TO SELL

One of the commonest standard form express powers conferred on a receiver and manager by a debenture is a power of sale. It is found in various forms. One formulation gives the receiver power:

> 'To sell or concur in selling any of the property charged by the debentures after giving the company at least seven days' notice of his intention to sell and to carry any such sale into effect by conveying in the name and on behalf of the company or otherwise.'

An alternative formulation gives the receiver power:

> 'To sell or concur in selling any of the property hereby charged or otherwise deal therewith on such terms in the interests of the debenture holder as he shall think fit PROVIDED ALWAYS that section 103 of the Law of Property Act 1925 shall not apply.'

The latter power, it will be noted, does not include a power to convey the legal estate. A well prepared debenture will be in such form as to include a power for the receiver to convey in the name of or as attorney for the company. The need for such a conveyancing power is a consequence of the nature of a floating charge.

TO INCORPORATE A SUBSIDIARY AND SELL ASSETS TO IT

Modern floating charges usually empower the receiver and manager to incorporate a subsidiary company and to sell assets to it. The inclusion of such an

---

5 (1975) 12 SASR 527.

6 *Re South Australian Barytes Ltd (No 2)* (1977) ACLC 29, 578, 3 ACLR 52.

7 A resolution is required by the general law: *Re Cawley & Co* (1889) 42 Ch D 209. See *Chocolate Box Confections Ltd v Wonnacott* [1984] 2 NZLR 755 (absence of resolution); *Kepler Developments Ltd (in receivership) v Stonway* (1988) 4 NZCLC 64, 690 (letter of demand mentioning powers sufficed where signed by both receivers).

express power is designed to preclude any possible objection to a proposal to hive down a viable part of the business into a subsidiary company. This practice, which is very common, is discussed elsewhere.[8]

ANCILLARY POWERS

One neat device for spelling out the ancillary powers of a receiver is the formulation of a separate power enlarging the scope of *all* the powers conferred upon the receiver.[9] Such a power really does no more than express what is implicit anyway. For, as has been said already, the grant of a power carries with it the grant of all proper means not expressly prohibited to effectuate the power itself.[10] So where a power to carry on business is conferred by a debenture it is implicit that a receiver may do what is reasonably necessary for carrying on that business, including the buying and selling of goods and the employment of servants. In *Lawson (Inspector of Taxes) v Hosemaster Machine Co Ltd*[11] the Court of Appeal held that power to carry on a business carried with it a duty to enter into transactions clearly advantageous to the company and its debenture holders. The particular transaction in question in that case was part of a tax-saving scheme which involved 'dividend stripping'. The transaction added some £240,000, in the form of repayment of tax, to the taxpayer company's funds available for (among others) the debenture holders.

STATUTORY POWERS OF AN ADMINISTRATIVE RECEIVER

The Cork Committee recommended that receivers' powers should be amended with a view to facilitating rescues. The idea of setting out the general powers of a receiver in a statute was so that it would not be necessary for a person dealing with him to refer to the particular debenture to find out what powers the receiver can exercise in a particular case. That was at the time already the case in Scotland.

These recommendations have been implemented so far as *administrative* receivers are concerned. It is provided that the powers conferred on the administrative receiver of a company by the debenture by virtue of which he was appointed are *deemed* to include (except in so far as they are inconsistent with any of the provisions of the relevant debenture) the powers specified in Sch 1 to the Insolvency Act 1986.[12] These deemed powers are treated as written into the

---

8 See at p 174, above.
9 See at p 125 below.
10 See at p 113.
11 [1966] 2 All ER 944, [1966] 1 WLR 1300, CA.
12 IA 1986, s 42(1). For the property to which the powers apply and the effect of an appointment of a receiver by a prior chargee, see s 42(2)(b). Most receivers are administrative receivers: see p 7 note 20.

debenture, in contrast to the identical powers conferred on an administrator as a matter of statute.[13]

The powers set out in Sch 1 are as follows:

(1) power to take possession of, collect and get in the property of the company and, for that purpose, to take such proceedings as may seem to him expedient;

(2) power to sell or otherwise dispose of the property of the company by public auction or private contract or, in Scotland, to sell, feu, hire out or otherwise dispose of the property of the company by public roup or private bargain;

(3) power to raise or borrow money and grant security therefor over the property of the company;

(4) power to appoint a solicitor or accountant or other professionally qualified person to assist him in the performance of his functions;

(5) power to bring or defend any action or other legal proceedings in the name and on behalf of the company;

(6) power to refer to arbitration any question affecting the company;

(7) power to effect and maintain insurance in respect of the business and property of the company;

(8) power to use the company's seal;

(9) power to do all acts to execute in the name, and on behalf, of the company any deed, receipt or other document;

(10) power to draw, accept, make and endorse any bill of exchange or promissory note in the name, and on behalf, of the company;

(11) power to appoint any agent to do any business which he is unable to do himself or which can more conveniently be done by an agent and power to employ and dismiss employees;

(12) power to do all such things (including the carrying out of works) as may be necessary for the realisation of the property of the company;

(13) power to make any payment which is necessary or incidental to the performance of his functions;

(14) power to carry on the business of the company;

(15) power to establish subsidiaries of the company;

(16) power to transfer to subsidiaries of the company the whole or any part of the business and property of the company;

---

13 IA 1986, s 14(1). An administrator has additionally the general statutory powers set out in the IA 1986, s 14(1), and the specific powers given by ss 14(2) and 15.

(17) power to grant or accept a surrender of a lease or tenancy of any property required or convenient for the business of the company;

(18) power to make any arrangement or compromise on behalf of the company;

(19) power to call up any uncalled capital of the company;

(20) power to rank and claim in the bankruptcy, insolvency, sequestration or liquidation of any person indebted to the company and to receive dividends; and to accede to trust deeds for the creditors of any such person;

(21) power to present or defend a petition for the winding up of the company;

(22) power to change the situation of the company's registered office;

(23) power to do all other things incidental to the exercise of the foregoing powers.

Administrative receivers have express statutory power to effect and maintain insurances in respect of the business and property of the company.[14] Non-administrative receivers have only such power as is conferred by the debenture. Because the necessary information about the extent and adequacy of existing or required cover takes time to collect, receivers tend to resort to schemes of blanket cover from the moment of appointment for all standard risks up to fairly large amounts.[15]

A person dealing with the administrative receiver in good faith and for value is not concerned to inquire whether the receiver is acting within his powers.[16]

POWER TO DISPOSE OF CHARGED PROPERTY

In addition to the above listed 'Schedule' powers, a novel and most convenient power has been conferred on administrative receivers by the Insolvency Act 1986. The relevant power enables an administrative receiver to apply to the court for authority to dispose of charged property as if it were not subject to the security. The new power is based on recommendations in the Cork Report[17] designed to promote rescue schemes by receivers. The existence of a prior security may represent an undue fetter on a sensible realisation of the business and property of a company. Accordingly, an administrative receiver is empowered to apply to the court for authority to dispose of the property as if it were not subject to the security, in other words free from the prior charge.[18] But the court must first be satisfied that the disposal (with or without other assets) of a relevant property which is subject to a security would be likely to promote a more advantageous realisation of the company's assets than would otherwise be

14 IA 1986, Sch 1, para 7.
15 See Samwell *Corporate Receiverships* (2nd edn) p 69.
16 IA 1986, s 42(3).
17 Cork Report (Cmnd 6659) paras 1510–1513.
18 IA 1986, s 43(1).

effected.[19] 'Relevant property' in relation to the administrative receiver means the property of which he is or, but for the appointment of some other person as receiver of part of the company's property, would be a receiver or manager.[20]

An application cannot, however, be made in the case of any security held by the person on whose behalf the administrative receiver was appointed, or of any security to which a security so held has priority.[1]

Conditions of order itself

It must be a condition of an order made on any application under the new power that (i) the net proceeds of the disposal, and (ii) where those proceeds are less than such amount as may be determined by the court to be the new amount which would be realised on the sale of the property in the open market by a willing vendor, such sums as may be required to make good the deficiency shall be applied towards discharging the sums secured by the security.[2] Where a condition imposed in this way relates to two or more securities, that condition shall require the net proceeds of the disposal and, where paragraph (ii) of that subsection applies, the sums mentioned in that paragraph to be applied towards discharging the sums secured by those securities in the order of their priorities.[3]

Transmission of order

An office copy of an order made under this procedure must, within 14 days of the making of the order, be sent by the administrative receiver to the registrar of companies.[4] If the administrative receiver without reasonable excuse fails to comply with the obligation to send the copy of the order to the registrar, he is liable to a fine and, for continued contravention, to a daily default fine.[5]

Procedure

The court must fix a venue for the hearing of the application, and the receiver must forthwith give notice of the venue to the person who is the holder of the security.[6] If an order is made the receiver shall forthwith give notice of it to that person.[7] The court shall send two sealed copies of the order to the receiver, who shall send one of them to that person.[8]

19 IA 1986, s 43(1).
20 IA 1986, s 43(7).
 1 IA 1986, s 43(2).
 2 IA 1986, s 43(3).
 3 IA 1986, s 43(4).
 4 IA 1986, s 43(5).
 5 IA 1986, s 43(6). For penalties, see IA 1986, s 430 and Sch 10.
 6 IR 1986, r 3.31(2).
 7 IR 1986, r 3.31(3).
 8 IR 1986, r 3.31(4).

CHAPTER 10

Duties and liabilities

INTRODUCTION

The duties of a receiver and manager appointed under a debenture[1] consist of duties imposed by statute, duties imposed expressly upon him by his appointment and duties that arise out of his peculiar status as (usually) deemed agent of the company,[2] while being primarily answerable to the debenture holders who appointed him.

After some general observations it is convenient to deal in turn with what may be termed the threshold duties of a receiver and manager, then his duties in respect of carrying on the business before turning to his duties in connection with sale and his accounting duties. His duties on termination of the receivership are discussed in the chapter dealing with termination.

The foremost duties of a receiver and manager appointed out of court mirror his very function. He is there to get in the assets covered by the charge pursuant to which he is appointed and to manage and realise those assets with a view to discharging the debt owed to the debenture holders.[3] In a sense he appears to wear two hats, for though appointed by the debenture holders he is usually expressed to be the agent of the company. Yet it must be remembered that his agency is a very special and limited one.[4] And within its ambit he is primarily responsible to those to whom he owes his appointment, the debenture holders.[5]

THRESHOLD STATUTORY DUTIES AND LIABILITIES

Notification by appointor

Before turning to the duties and liabilities of the receiver and manager attending upon his appointment, one particular 'notification' duty calls for mention. A

---

1 For a discussion from the Australian viewpoint, see James O'Donovan 'The Duties and Liabilities of a Receiver Appointed out of Court' (1979) 12 MULR 52–78.
2 See David Milman 'Receivers as Agents' (1981) 44 MLR 658.
3 *Re B Johnson & Co Builders Ltd* [1955] Ch 634, [1955] 2 All ER 755, CA; *Gosling v Gaskell* [1897] AC 575, HL.
4 *R v Board of Trade, ex p St Martin Preserving Co Ltd* [1965] 1 QB 603 at 617 per Winn J.
5 *Gomba Holdings Ltd v Homan* [1986] 3 All ER 94, [1986] 1 WLR 1301.

person appointing a receiver and manager of the property of a company under any powers contained in any instrument[6] must, within seven days from the date of the appointment, give notice[7] of the fact of appointment to the registrar[8], who must enter the fact in the registry of charges.[9]

Notification by administrative receiver

Independently of any obligation of his appointor, an administrative receiver must himself on appointment forthwith send to the company and publish in the prescribed manner a notice of his appointment.[10] The notice must set out certain prescribed matters. These are:

(a)   the registered name of the company as at the date of the appointment, and its registered number;

(b)   any other name with which the company has been registered in the 12 months preceding that date;

(c)   any name under which the company has traded at any time in those 12 months, if substantially different from its registered name;

(d)   the name and address of the administrative receiver, and the date of his appointment;

(e)   the name of the person by whom the appointment was made;

(f)   the date of the instrument conferring the power under which the appointment was made, and a brief description of the instrument; and

(g)   a brief description of the assets of the company (if any) in respect of which the person appointed is not made the receiver.[11]

Publication of his apppointment in the prescribed manner involves advertisement in accordance with the rules in the London Gazette, and one other newspaper. The administrative receiver must cause notice of his appointment to be advertised in the London Gazette, and once in such other newspaper as he thinks most appropriate for ensuring that it comes to the notice of the company's creditors.[12] The notice must, in either case, state all the matters specified in (a) to (g) above.[13]

---

6 Including statutorily implied powers in an instrument: see CA 1985, s 405(1).
7 For the form of notice see *Butterworths Corporate Law Service (I)* Receivership Precedent 8.
8 CA 1985, s 405(1). For the register see the CA 1985, s 401.
9 CA 1985, s 405(1).
10 IA 1986, s 46(1)(a).
11 IR 1986, r 3.2(2).
12 IR 1986, r 3.2(3).
13 IR 1986, r 3.2(4).

An administrative receiver must also, within 28 days after his appointment, unless the court otherwise directs, send a similar notice to all creditors of the company (so far as he is aware of their addresses).[14]

These notification duties apply if the company is being wound up even though the administrative receiver and liquidator are the same person, but with any necessary modifications.[15]

This provision does not apply in relation to the appointment of a receiver or manager to act with an existing receiver or manager or in place of a receiver or manager dying or ceasing to act, except that where it applies to a receiver or manager who dies or ceases to act before it has been fully complied with his successor or any continuing receiver or manager will be the person to whom the statement must be supplied and who must be responsible for its onward transmission.[16] If a receiver makes default in complying with any of these provisions he is liable to a fine not exceeding one-fifth of the statutory maximum, or on conviction after continued contravention to a default fine not exceeding one-fiftieth of the statutory maximum.[17]

Notice of the appointment must also be given on every invoice, order or business letter issued by or on behalf of a receiver or manager in which the name of the company appears.[18] Default in complying with this provision renders every receiver knowingly and wilfully authorising or permitting the default liable to a fine of not exceeding one-fifth of the statutory maximum.[19]

DUTY TO ACT

A mortgagee has no duty to exercise his power of sale[20] but if unfair prejudice to the mortgagor may result from his inaction the court may exercise its discretionary power to order a sale,[1] despite the objections of the mortgagee.[2] A receiver's duties have been equated to those of a mortgagee[3] and while he has no duty to make a decision to sell[4] he owes a duty to act so as to protect and preserve the security, for example in the case of a lease by inspecting the lease and triggering a rent review.[5]

---

14 IR 1986, r 3.2.
15 IA 1986, s 46(3).
16 IA 1986, s 46(2).
17 IA 1986, s 46(4) and Sch 10.
18 IA 1986, s 39.
19 IA 1986, Sch 10.
20 *China Sea Bank Ltd v Tan Soon Gin* [1990] 1 AC 536, PC; *Routestone Ltd v Minories Finance Ltd* [1997] BCC 180.
 1 Under the LPA 1925, s 91(2) where applicable.
 2 *Palk v Mortgage Services Funding plc* [1993] Ch 330, CA.
 3 *RA Price Securities v Henderson* [1989] 2 NZLR 257 at 262, NZCA; *Medforth v Blake* [1999] 2 BCLC 221, CA at 233c.
 4 *Routestone Ltd v Minories Finance Ltd* [1997] BCC 180.
 5 *Knight v Lawrence* [1991] BCC 411.

DUTIES IN CARRYING ON THE BUSINESS

Primary responsibility

In carrying on the business the receiver and manager has to bear in mind his primary responsibilities to his appointors. His agency for the company does not place him under the usual duties of compliance with his principal's requirements. Indeed the very reverse applies. A receiver is appointed 'not to receive directions from the directors but to give directions'.[6] Those directions need not necessarily be followed if such non-compliance does not interfere with the realisation of the security.[7] A relatively recent recognition of the inability of the company to control the receiver was the refusal of a Scottish court in *Macleod v Alexander Sutherland Ltd*[8] to compel a company in receivership to carry out its existing contracts because that would expose the company to contempt proceedings should the receiver over whom the company had no control fail to follow its requests.

Clearly in relation to management the receiver and manager must at every stage have close regard to the purpose for which he has been appointed, and must not exercise his powers of management for a collateral purpose or one alien to the purpose for which he was appointed.[9]

In *Expo International Pty Ltd v Chant*[10] the decision by receivers and managers to grant substantial discounts to agents who were threatening to return unsold stock was held by Needham J not, on the facts, to be in the interests of the debenture holders or of the company. Leaving aside for the moment the relevant *standard* of duty which the learned judge applied, the case is notable because it confirmed by the liability imposed on the receiver to the company that duties are owed not merely to the debenture holders but also to the company. Needham J accepted that a receiver was not obliged to carry on the business of the company at the expense of the debenture holders to whom he owes his primary responsibility. But his identification of *good faith* as the yardstick by which a sale or other administrative decision is to be tested,[11] even where there has been negligence, probably does not represent the law in England.[12]

In relation to trading, as in other respects, an administrative or other out of court receiver owes a primary duty to his appointor, the debenture holder. As Hoffmann J pointed out in *Gomba Holdings Ltd v Homan*,[13] 'his primary duty is to realise the assets in the interests of the debenture holder, and his powers of management are really ancillary to that duty'. It follows that his duty to the

---

6   See *Meigh v Wickenden* [1942] 2 KB 160 at 166 per Viscount Caldecote CJ.
7   *Newhart Developments Ltd v Co-operative Commercial Bank Ltd* [1978] QB 814, [1978] 2 All ER 896, CA.
8   1977 SLT (Notes) 44.
9   Cf *McKendrick Glass Manufacturing Co Ltd v Wilkinson* [1965] NZLR 717 (where a *third party* was liable for wrongfully inducing a receiver to abuse his powers).
10   [1979] 2 NSWLR 820.
11   [1979] 2 NSWLR 820 at 841–842.
12   Cf *Cuckmere Brick Co v Mutual Finance Ltd* [1971] Ch 949, [1971] 2 All ER 633, CA; *Standard Chartered Bank Ltd v Walker* [1982] 3 All ER 938, [1982] 1 WLR 1410, CA.
13   [1986] 1 WLR 1301 at 1305.

company itself is merely secondary, being subordinated to his primary duty. He must (it is conceived) take care not to cause avoidable loss to the company, but only so far as that is consistent with his primary duty. The decision whether or not to continue to trade is necessarily reached after a careful reconciliation of the two duties. Where the company has the necessary funds and continuance of trading is presumably likely to result in a beneficial realisation whereas immediate sale would result in a disadvantageous sale, the decision to trade may satisfy both duties and a decision not to continue may constitute a breach of the duty of care owed to the company itself. The assertion by Sir Raymond Evershed MR in *Re B Johnson & Co (Builders) Ltd*[14] that 'a receiver appointed for the purpose of receiving the debenture holders' security was under no obligation to the company or its contributories to continue its business' was combined with the assertion that the only duty owed to the company in any respect was one of good faith.[15] The latter proposition has been repudiated by the Court of Appeal[16] and by the Privy Council[17].

Content of the duty

According to Robert Walker LJ in the *Yorkshire Bank plc v Hall*[18] case the general duty (owed both to subsequent encumbrances and to the mortgagor) is for the mortgagee and his receiver to use his powers only for proper purposes and to act in good faith. The specific duties arise if the mortgagee exercises his express or statutory powers. If he exercises his power to take possession, he becomes liable to account on a strict basis (which is why mortgagees and debenture holders operate by appointing receivers whenever they can). If he exercises his power of sale he must take reasonable care to obtain a proper price.

The content of the receivers duty to some persons in equity in relation to managing a mortgaged property was reviewed by Sir Richard Scott V-C in the case of *Medforth v Blake*.[19] He drew a distinction between the duty in relation to the decision whether to continue or stop trading and the duty which applies where he decides to trade and manages the mortgaged property.

Where a receiver manages mortgaged property, his duties to the mortgagor and anyone else interested in the equity of redemption were not necessarily confined to a duty of good faith. Rather, in exercising his powers of management, the receiver owes a duty to manage the property with due diligence, subject to his primary duty of attempting to create a situation where the interest on the secured debt can be paid and the debt itself repaid. Thus, although due diligence did not oblige the receiver to continue business of the mortgaged property, it did require

14 [1955] Ch 634 at 651–652, CA.
15 [1955] Ch 634 at 662.
16 *Cuckmere Brick Co Ltd v Mutual Finance Ltd* [1971] Ch 949, [1971] 2 All ER 633, CA; cf *Standard Chartered Bank Ltd v Walker* [1982] 3 All ER 938, [1982] 1 WLR 1410, CA; and see *American Express International Banking Corpn v Hurley* [1985] 3 All ER 564.
17 *Tse Kwong Lam v Wong Chit Sen* [1983] 3 All ER 54, [1983] 1 WLR 1349, PC.
18 [1999] 1 All ER 879 at 893, CA.
19 [1999] 2 BCLC 221, CA.

him to take reasonable steps to manage it profitably if he did choose to continue that business. Such a duty, like the duties owed by a mortgagee to a mortgagor was imposed by equity. All of this has been recently clarified in the case of *Medforth v Blake*.[20]

DUTIES IN CONNECTION WITH SALE

In those cases in which a power of sale is expressly conferred upon a receiver and manager his duties in connection with the exercise of the power have been equated to those of a mortgagee exercising his power of sale. So, for example, in *Re B Johnson & Co (Builders) Ltd*[1] referring to a receiver's power of sale it was said 'his power of sale is, in effect, that of a mortgagee'. In other words the same standards are expected of a receiver exercising his power of sale as are expected of a mortgagee exercising his power of sale. What, then, is the duty owed by the mortgagee? The question appears to have received different answers in two contrasting strands of authority. According to the first the *only* duty is to act bona fide in the conduct of the sale. This means that he must not act fraudulently, dishonestly or recklessly; and he must not disregard the interests of the mortgagor or, in the case of a debenture, the company which issued it.

According to the second strand of authority a mortgagee is under an additional duty to take reasonable care to obtain 'the true market value'[2] at the date of the sale or 'a proper price'[3] for the realisation of the security.

These two strands followed the rejection of an earlier analysis of the mortgagee's position in regard to sale in terms of trusteeship.

Rejection of trust concept

It is now well settled that a mortgagee is not a trustee for the mortgagor in relation to the exercise of the power of sale. This was not always so. In the first half of the nineteenth century the preponderant view seems to have been that the mortgagee was trustee of his power of sale. Lord Eldon LC in *Downes v Grazebrook*[4] setting aside a sale where an agent for the mortagee was the only bidder said this:

> 'But the great question is on the sale itself, and, as to that, I am of opinion that Grazebrook cannot be considered otherwise than as a trustee under the conveyance to him by the deed of the 16th September 1815.'

The deed referred to expressly constituted the mortgagee as trustee. The mortgagee held the mortgaged property on trust for the mortgagor until default

20 [1999] 2 BCLC 221 at 237, CA a–d, discussed below in connection with sale.
 1 [1955] Ch 634, [1955] 2 All ER 755, CA.
 2 *Cuckmere Brick Co Ltd v Mutual Finance Ltd* [1971] Ch 949 at 966, CA per Salmon LJ.
 3 [1971] Ch 949 at 978 per Cairns LJ.
 4 (1817) 3 Mer 200 at 207.

and then on trust to sell by public auction or private sale. Accordingly when Lord Eldon used the language of trusteeship in relation to the exercise of the power of sale it is arguable that he was merely dealing with the position of a mortgagee expressly constituted as a trustee. However, in some of the later cases and commentaries it has been assumed that Lord Eldon was laying down a general rule covering sales by mortgagees whether or not they were constituted express trustees. That certainly appears to have been the considered view of Lord Cottenham in *Re Bloye's Trust*.[5] Despite other statements analysing the mortgagee's position as a vendor in terms of trust, there was no unanimity on the point. The last case in which the concept of trusteeship of the power of sale was accepted was the subsequently discredited decision of Stuart V-C in *Robertson v Norris*.[6] He referred to Lord Eldon as having said that the mortgagee was a trustee for the benefit of the mortgagor in the exercise of the power of sale and added this gloss:[7]

'That expression is to be understood in this sense, that in construing the power given to enable him to recover the mortgage money this Court requires that he shall exercise the power of sale in a provident way, with a due regard to the rights and interests of the mortgagor in the surplus money to be produced by the sale.'

The proposition that a mortgagee was trustee of his power of sale was rejected outright by the Court of Appeal in 1880. In the case in point, *Nash v Eads*,[8] Sir George Jessel MR said that the mortgagee was not a trustee of the power of sale for the mortgagor. He cited no authority in support of his robust dismissal of the trust concept in this context. And he denied that Lord Eldon had ever said anything of the kind which Stuart V-C in *Robertson v Norris*[9] had supposed him to have said. The Vice-Chancellor, he said, must have been citing the judgments to which he referred without looking at the reports. The final nail in the coffin of the trust concept was hammered in by Kay J in his much cited judgment in *Warner v Jacob*.[10] After reviewing most of the authorities he concluded that the 'result seems to be that a mortgagee is strictly speaking not a trustee for sale'. And he said of *Robertson v Norris* 'that case only decided that where the mortgage was in the form of a trust for sale, the mortgagee could not buy'. Whether or not *Robertson v Norris* can be so confined, in *Martinson v Clowes*[11] North J said that the opinion of Kay J in *Warner v Jacob* was 'correctly laid down and that *Robertson v Norris* no doubt goes considerably beyond anything to be found in the cases relied upon as authoritative for it, as was pointed out by the Court of Appeal in the recent case of *Nash v Eads*'.

After the rejection of the trust concept a confusion developed in the law. This confusion has however been clarified following the decision of the Privy Council

---

5 (1849) 1 Mac & G 488, 19 LJ Ch 89, affd sub nom *Lewis v Hillman* (1852) 3 HL Cas 607, 19 LTOS 329.
6 (1857) 1 Giff 421, 30 LTOS 253.
7 (1857) 1 Giff 421 at 424.
8 (1880) 25 Sol Jo 95, CA.
9 (1857) 1 Giff 421, 30 LTOS 253, affd (1858) 52 LT 706, CA.
10 (1882) 20 Ch D 220.
11 (1882) 21 Ch D 857, affd (1885) 52 LT 706, CA.

in *Downsview Nominees Ltd v First City Corpn Ltd*[12] and the decisions of the Court of Appeal in *Yorkshire Bank plc v Hall*[13] and in *Medforth v Blake*,[14] which related the duty to act in good faith and the duty to take reasonable precautions and to exercise due diligence to each other.

Duty to act in good faith

Many of the cases suggested that the *only* duty of a mortgagee exercising his power of sale was to act in good faith.

The doctrine that the only duty of a mortgage engaged in selling the mortgaged property is to act bona fide was enunciated with great clarity by Kay J in *Warner v Jacob*.[15] According to him the power of sale is given to the mortgagee 'for his own benefit, to enable him better to realise his debt. If he exercises it bona fide for that purpose, without corruption or collusion with the purchaser, the court will not interfere even though the sale be very disadvantageous, unless indeed the price is so low as in itself to be evidence of fraud'.[16] This statement of principle was cited, with apparent approval, by the Privy Council in *Haddington Island Quarry Co Ltd v Huson*.[17] However, it is the decision of the House of Lords in *Kennedy v De Trafford*[18] which is most frequently cited for the proposition that the only duty of a mortgagee in the process of sale is to act in good faith. Certainly the headnote to that case lends support to a narrow view of the mortgagee's duty for it states un-equivocally:

> 'The only obligation incumbent on a mortgagee selling under and in pursuance of a power of sale in his mortgage is that he should act in good faith.'

Yet reference to the speeches of their Lordships does not wholly justify this dogmatic statement in the headnote. True it is that Lord Herschell LC puts good faith to the forefront of the mortgagee's duty:[19]

> 'My Lords, I am myself disposed to think that if a mortgagee in exercising his power of sale exercises it in good faith, without any intention of dealing unfairly by his mortgagor, it would be very difficult indeed, if not impossible, to establish that he had been guilty of any breach of duty to the mortgagor.'

After referring to the dictum of Lindley LJ in the court below that 'it is not right or proper or legal for him either fraudulently or wilfully or recklessly to sacrifice the property of the mortgagor,' Lord Herschell continued:[20]

12 [1993] AC 295.
13 [1999] 1 All ER 879, CA.
14 [1999] 2 BCLC 221, CA.
15 (1882) 20 Ch D 220.
16 (1882) 20 Ch D 220 at 224.
17 [1911] AC 727 at 729.
18 [1897] AC 180, HL.
19 [1897] AC 180 at 185.
20 [1897] AC 180 at 185.

'Well, I think that is all covered really by his exercising the power committed to him in good faith. It is very difficult to define exhaustively all that would be included in the words "good faith" but I think it would be unreasonable to require the mortgagee to do more than exercise his power of sale in that fashion. Of course, if he wilfully and recklessly deals with the property in such a manner that the interests of the mortgagor are sacrificed, I should say that he had not been exercising his power of sale in good faith.'

But it is questionable whether his judgment can be interpreted as a ruling that the mortgagee's *only* duty is to act bona fide. The cautious 'I am disposed to think' is to be read with the following often overlooked passage in Lord Herschell's judgment, which immediately follows the passage just quoted:[1]

'My Lords, it is not necessary in this case to give an exhaustive definition of the duties of a mortgagee to a mortgagor, because it appears to me that, if you were to accept the definition of them for which the appellant contends, namely, that the mortgagee is bound to take reasonable precautions in the exercise of his power of sale, as well as to act in good faith, still in this case he did take reasonable precautions. Of course, all the circumstances of the case must be looked at.'

This seems to leave the door ajar for the application of the 'reasonable precautions' test. Lord Macnaghten on the other hand plumped for the bona fide test saying:[2] 'If a mortgagee selling under a power of sale in his mortgage takes pains to comply with the provisions of that power and acts in good faith, I do not think his conduct in regard to the sale can be impeached.'

Duty of care imposed by equity

Other cases suggested that in addition to the duty of good faith a mortgagee also owed a duty of care in the conduct of the sale. One can single out in particular dicta of Cotton LJ in *Tomlin v Luce*[3] with whom Bowen and Fry LJJ concurred. But there were even earlier examples.[4] None of these authorities was cited in *Kennedy v De Trafford*.[5] On the other hand, *Kennedy v De Trafford* escaped the diligence of counsel in the Privy Council case of *McHugh v Union Bank of Canada*,[6] where Lord Moulton in giving the opinion of an exceptionally strong Board said:[7]

'It is well settled law that it is the duty of a mortgagee when realising the mortgaged property by sale to behave in conducting such realisation as a reasonable man would behave in the realisation of his own property, so that the mortgagor may receive credit for the fair value of the property sold.'

1 [1897] AC 180 at 185.
2 [1897] AC 180 at 192.
3 (1889) 43 Ch D 191 at 194, CA.
4 *Wolff v Vanderzee* (1869) 20 LT 350; *National Bank of Australasia v United Hand in Hand and Band of Hope Co* (1879) 4 App Cas 391, PC; *Farrar v Farrars Ltd* (1888) 40 Ch D 395 at 411.
5 [1897] AC 180, HL.
6 [1913] AC 299, PC.
7 [1913] AC 299 at 311.

This view of the law, though expressed in relation to a chattel mortgage, found favour with the Court of Appeal in *Cuckmere Brick Co Ltd v Mutual Finance Ltd*;[8] and since that decision has been followed in a number of subsequent English decisions[9] it can now be taken that English law is wedded to the principle that a mortgagee exercising his power of sale (and by justifiable extension a receiver exercising a power of sale vested in him) owes a duty of care in the conduct of the sale.

That duty of care, however, is not the common law tortious duty of care[10] but one imposed by equity arising out of the mortgage relationship;[11] it is accordingly owed only to those with an interest in the equity of redemption, including any guarantor of the secured indebtedness,[12] but not of the company's indebtedness.[13]

The receiver is not obliged to carry on the business. He can decide not to do so. He can decide to close it down. In taking these decisions he is entitled, and perhaps bound, to have regard to the interests of the mortgagee in obtaining repayment of the secured debt. Provided he acts in good faith, he is entitled to sacrifice the interest of the mortgagor in pursuit of that end.[14]

The impact of Downsview Nominees Limited v First City Corpn

The tendency discussed by many commentators to analyse a receiver's duties in sale as attributable to concepts of tortious liability had already been attacked in *Parker-Tweedale v Dunbar Bank plc*[15] which characterised these duties as those of a mortgager as arising in equity only. The Privy Council in *Downsview Nominees Ltd v First City Corpn*[16] confirmed that categorisation as correct. Lord Templeman delivering the opinion of the Board pointed out that the general duty of care said to be owed by a mortgagee to subsequent encumbrances and the mortgagor in negligence was inconsistent with the right of the mortgagee and the duties which the courts applying equitable principles have imposed on the mortgagee. The ambit of the *Cuckmere* decision in the Court of Appeal had to be

---

8 [1971] Ch 949, [1971] 2 All ER 633, CA.

9 *Palmer v Barclays Bank Ltd* (1971) 23 P & CR 30, 220 Estates Gazette 1871; *Waltham Forest London Borough v Webb* (1974) 232 Estates Gazette 461; *Johnson v Ribbins* (1975) 235 Estates Gazette 757; *Bank of Cyprus (London) Ltd v Gill* [1979] 2 Lloyd's Rep 508; *Standard Chartered Bank v Walker* [1982] 1 WLR 1410, CA (receiver owes duty of care to guarantor); *American Express International Banking Corpn v Hurley* [1985] 3 All ER 564. But a receiver does not have to disclose information about the proposed purchase price to the guarantor or creditors: *McGowan v Gannon* (1983) 3 ILRM 516.

10 Statements to that effect in *Cuckmere Brick Co Ltd v Mutual Finance Ltd* [1971] Ch 949 at 966 and 977, are therefore to be disregarded.

11 *Downsview Nominees Ltd v First City Corpn Ltd* [1993] AC 295 (sale); *Yorkshire Bank plc v Hall* [1999] 1 All ER 879, CA; *Medforth v Blake* [1999] 2 BCLC 221, CA.

12 See in addition to the authorities in the immediately preceding footnote, *Burgess v Augur*; *Burgess v Vanstock* [1998] 2 BCLC 478, Lightman J.

13 [1998] 2 BCLC 478.

14 *Medforth v Blake* [1999] 2 BCLC 221, CA.

15 [1991] Ch 12, CA.

16 [1993] AC 295.

restricted in the light of that consideration. *Cuckmere* has simply Court of Appeal authority for the proposition that, if the mortgagee decides to sell, he must take reasonable care to obtain a proper price, but is no authority for any wider proposition. A receiver exercising his power of sale also owes the same specific duties as a mortgagee. But that apart, the general duty of a receiver and manager appointed by a debenture holder left no room, in their Lordships view, for the imposition of a general duty to use reasonable care in dealing with the assets of the mortgagor company.[17]

Nature of duty: common law or equity

The most recent analysis of the nature of the mortgagee's duties (and by extension the nature of the receiver's duties) is to be found in two recent decisions in the Court of Appeal. In *Yorkshire Bank plc v Hall*[18] Robert Walker LJ stated that recent cases of high authority[19] together established or re-affirmed that a mortgagee's duty to the mortgagor or to a surety depend partly on the express terms on which the transaction was agreed and partly on duties (some general and some particular) which equity imposes for the protection of the mortgagor and the surety. The mortgagee's duty is not a duty imposed under the tort of negligence, nor are contractual duties to be implied.[20] In other words the duty is an equitable and not a common law duty.

Acceptance of the reasonable precautions test elsewhere

The 'reasonable precautions' test has been accepted in Ireland,[1] Hong Kong[2] and the Cayman Islands.[3] In New Zealand before legislation the position was indeterminate. The suggestion[4] that the principle in *Cuckmere Brick Co Ltd v Mutual Finance Ltd*[5] had been accepted in New Zealand perhaps overstated the case. In *Nelson Bros Ltd v Nagle*,[6] the attack mounted on the receiver's conduct of a sale challenged his action in selling on the wholesale market and not on the retail market. The court considered that the receiver had acted unwisely but refused to find him liable for any breach of duty. Myers CJ,

---

17 [1993] AC 295 at 315.
18 [1999] 1 All ER 879.
19 *China and South Sea Bank Ltd v Tan* [1990] 1 AC 53; *National Bank of Greece SA v Pinios Shipping Case, The Maira* [1990] 1 AC 637 and *Downsview Nominees Ltd v First City Corpn* [1994] 1 BCLC 49.
20 [1999] 1 All ER 879 at 893.
 1 *Holohan v Friends Provident and Century Life Office* [1966] IR 1.
 2 *New Territories Housing Development Co Ltd v Hong Kong and Shanghai Banking Corpn* (1978) summarised in (1979) 9 HKLJ 78–80 (H Bramwell).
 3 *Becker v Bank of Nova Scotia* [1986] LRC (Comm) 638, CA.
 4 Peter Bates 'The Mortgagee's Duty on Sale' (1979) 53 ALJ 172 at 180.
 5 [1971] Ch 949, [1971] 2 All ER 633, CA.
 6 (1940) GLR 507, SC.

basing his conclusions on the ordinary principles of agency, was of the view that the receiver owed a duty to the company to exercise due care, skill and judgment in selling the company's goods and getting the best results reasonably possible in the circumstances. Had the receiver failed to use reasonable diligence, he would have been liable to the company in negligence for any loss which it had suffered.[7] But in the circumstances there had been no breach of duty. The decision of the New Zealand Court of Appeal in *Alexandre v New Zealand Breweries Ltd*[8] was, for a similar reason, not a decisive support for the *Cuckmere* principle. The correctness of the decision in *Cuckmere* was not fully canvassed in argument because it was a member of the court who drew the case to the attention of counsel and not counsel who cited the case to the court. The Court of Appeal was prepared to assume that *Cuckmere* had been correctly decided for the limited purpose of deciding whether the mortgagee had fallen short of the duty of care prescribed in the *Cuckmere* case. This assumption went further than the judge below would go. To him 'the mortgagee is not a trustee for the mortgagor and his duty is only to act bona fide'.[9] In the event, however, the decision of the appellate court was that there had been no breach of the assumed duty. Legislation has now defined the duty of a receiver or manager on the sale of assets. A receiver or manager of the property of a company who sells any of that property must exercise all reasonable care to obtain the best price reasonably obtainable for the property as at the time of sale.[10]

In Canada there was at one time pretty consistent support for the principle that the mortgagee's *only* duty is to act bona fide. Thus in *British Columbia Land and Investment Agency v Ishitaka*[11] the Canadian Supreme Court endorsed the test laid down by Lord Herschell in *Kennedy v De Trafford*[12] which had already been applied in *Finkelstein v Locke*.[13] A whole string of subsequent authorities followed the same line[14] and in the British Columbia Court of Appeal in *J & W Investments Ltd v Black*[15] Tysoe JA, after referring to the 'reasonable precautions' test, continued:

> 'To say that a mortgagee must take reasonable steps and precautions to obtain a proper price is somewhat misleading for the mortgagor will have recourse against the mortgagee only if the failure to take reasonable steps and precautions can be described as fraudulent wilful or reckless and has resulted in the property being sacrificed.'

---

7   (1940) GLR 507 at 508.
8   [1974] 1 NZLR 497.
9   [1972] NZLR 867 at 874.
10 New Zealand Companies Act 1955, s 345B(1) which applies to all receivers' acts after 1 April 1981.
11 (1911) 45 SCR 302, 1 WWR 549.
12 [1897] AC 180 at 185.
13 (1907) 6 WLR 173.
14 *Fern's v Nowitskey and Wilkin* (1951) 3 WWRNS 49 at 61–62; *Murchison v Bank of Nova Scotia* (1958) 43 MPR 383 at 386–387; *Canadian Imperial Bank of Commerce v Heppner* (1965) 52 WWR NS 295 at 302.
15 (1963) 38 DLR (2d) 251 at 273.

Many of the decisions which followed *Black's* case either hark back[16] to the decision of the Canadian Supreme Court in *British Columbia Land and Investment Agency v Ishitaka*[17] or rehearse the judgments in *Black's* case.[18]

However, the test enunciated in *Cuckmere Brick* has more recently been applied in Ontario,[19] Alberta[20] and New Brunswick,[1] and treated in Newfoundland as part of the test of good faith.[2]

On the other hand, the *Cuckmere Brick* test has not yet been accepted in Australia,[3] although the door would still appear to be open to its admission.[4] In some states[5] legislation has imposed a duty to take reasonable care.

Sale to himself

A mortgagee 'cannot sell to himself either alone or with others, or to a trustee for himself nor to any one employed by him to conduct the sale',[6] save where the sale is made by the court and he has obtained leave to bid.[7] The reason assigned for this rule is that 'a sale by a person to himself is no sale at all, and a power of sale does not authorise the donee of the power to take the property subject to it at a price fixed by himself, even though such price be the full value.' The same rule applies to any officer of the mortgagee or the solicitor or other agent who is acting for the mortgagee in the matter of sale.[8] Thus a receiver, whether acting as agent for the debenture holder or as agent for the company, cannot sell to himself. In exercising

---

16 *British Columbia Packers Ltd v Cape Trawlers Ltd* (1970) 7 NSR (2d) 85 at 101; *Flying 'L' Ranching Co Ltd v Toronto-Dominion Bank* (1976) 9 N & PEIR 209 at 219.

17 (1911) 45 SCR 302.

18 *Miller v Davis Lumber Co Ltd* (1969) 69 WWRNS 161 at 169–170; *Massey-Ferguson Industries Ltd v Tafer* [1971] 2 WWR 358 at 364–365; *Gulf and Fraser Fishermen's Credit Union v Calm C Fish Ltd* [1975] 3 WWR 474 at 478–479, sub nom *The Calm C* [1975] 1 Lloyd's Rep 188; cf *Wilson & Hayes v Unicorn Management Inc* [1978] 3 WWR 301 at 303.

19 *Siskind v Bank of Nova Scotia* (1984) 46 OR (2d) 575, Ont HC; *Sterne v Victoria & Grey Trust Co* (1984) 49 OR (2d) 6, Ont HC. See also *Wood v Bank of Nova Scotia* (1979) 10 RPR 156; affd (1980) 29 OR (2d) 35, CA; *Bank of Nova Scotia v Barnard* (1984) 46 OR (2d) 409.

20 *Bank of Montreal v Petronech* (1984) 52 CBRNS 17, Alta QB.

1 *Canadian Imperial Bank of Commerce v Haley* (1979) 100 DLR (3d) 470, NBSC; *Nova Scotia Savings and Loan Co v Mackenzie* (1979) 29 NBR (2d) 78, NBQB; *Hansen v Canadian Imperial Bank of Commerce* (1980) 29 NBR (2d) 195.

2 *Frost Ltd v Ralph* (1980) 115 DLR (3d) 612 at 622, affd (1982) 140 DLR (3d) 572, Nfld CA.

3 See, in particular, *Australian and New Zealand Banking Group Ltd v Bangadilly Pastoral Co Pty Ltd* (1978) 139 CLR 195, HC of A, discussed with earlier cases in (1979) 53 ALJ 172 (Peter Butt) and see *Commercial and General Acceptance Ltd v Nixon* (1983) 152 CLR 491; *Goldcel Nominees Pty Ltd v Network Finance Ltd* [1983] 2 VR 257; *Citicorp Australia Ltd v McLoughney* (1984) 35 SASR 375; *Cachot Nominees Pty Ltd v Prime Nominees Pty Ltd* [1984] WAR 380.

4 *Pollnow v Garden Mentor – St Leonards Pty Ltd* (1985) 9 ACLR 82; and see *Australia and New Zealand Banking Group Ltd v Tacoma Nominees Pty Ltd* (1983) 1 ACLC 1081.

5 Eg Queensland: Property Law Act 1974–1982 (Qld), s 85(1).

6 *Farrar v Farrars Ltd* (1888) 40 Ch D 395 at 409, CA; *Hodson v Deans* [1903] 2 Ch 647.

7 *National Bank of Australasia v United Hand in Hand and Band of Hope Co* (1879) 4 App Cas 391, PC; *Farrar v Farrars Ltd* (1888) 40 Ch D 395, CA.

8 *Martinson v Clowes* (1882) 21 Ch D 857, on appeal (1885) 52 LT 706, CA; *Hodson v Deans* [1903] 2 Ch 647.

the power of sale as deemed agent of the company he also owes fiduciary duties to the debenture holder and a sale to himself would equally breach those duties.

Sale to his company

'There is both on authority and on principle no hard and fast rule that a mortgagee may not sell to a company in which he is interested'.[9] The interest of the mortgagee in the corporate purchaser of the mortgaged premises in *Tse Kwong Lam v Wong Chit Sen*[10] was, to put it mildly, heavy: he held a large beneficial interest in its shares, was a director of it and was entirely responsible for financing it, and the other shareholders were his wife and children. Counsel for the borrower did not attempt to argue in favour of a rule absolutely prohibiting such a sale; indeed he admitted that there could not be such a general rule. But he argued that the company could only purchase where the sale was negotiated at arm's length and where it was clear that the mortgagee had no influence on the decision of the company to purchase or on the implementation of that decision. The view of the Board of the Privy Council was that the mortgagee and the company seeking to uphold such a transaction must show that the sale was in good faith and that the mortgagee took reasonable precautions to obtain the best price reasonably obtainable at the time.

In view of the close relationship between the company and the mortgagee in the case, the sale had to be closely examined. A heavy burden lay on the mortgagee to show that in all respects he acted fairly to the borrower and used his best endeavours to obtain the best price reasonably obtainable for the mortgaged property. On the facts the Board concluded that reasonable steps had not been taken but in view of the inexcusable delay of the borrower in prosecuting his counterclaim the Board refused to set aside the transaction, leaving the borrower to his remedy in damages.

In the course of delivering the judgment of the Board, Lord Templeman analysed what currently may be considered reasonable precautions:

> 'A mortgagee who wishes to secure the mortgaged property for a company in which he is interested ought to show that he protected the interests of the borrower by taking expert advice as to the method of sale, as to the steps which ought reasonably to be taken to make the sale a success and as to the amount of the reserve.'[11]

The mortgagee is not, however, under an obligation to postpone the sale in the hope of obtaining a better price or to adopt a piecemeal method of sale which could only be carried out over a substantial period or at some risk of loss.[12] Moreover, sale by auction does not necessarily prove the validity of a transaction. The price obtained at any particular auction may be less than the

---

9   *Tse Kwong Lam v Wong Chit Sen* [1983] 3 All ER 54 at 59B. [1983] 1 WLR 1349 at 1355A–B. The previous leading authority was *Farrar v Farrars Ltd* (1888) 40 Ch D 395 at 415, CA.
10   [1983] 3 All ER 54, [1983] 1 WLR 1349, PC on appeal from the Hong Kong Court of Appeal.
11   [1983] 1 WLR 1349 at 1359G.
12   [1983] 1 WLR 1349 at 1355B.

price obtainable by private treaty and may depend on the steps taken to encourage bidders to attend.[13]

PERSONS TO WHOM DUTY IS OWED

Debenture holder

A receiver plainly owes duties to the debenture holder who appointed him. And he owes those duties to his appointor both in contract and in tort. His appointment on acceptance becomes a contract between his appointor and himself giving rise to contractual and tortious duties. He will also owe fiduciary duties to his appointor in respect of the realisation of charged assets.

Company

It is also further established that a receiver owes duties to the company over whose assets he is appointed receiver.[14] Accordingly, a mortgagor company in receivership may sue the receiver appointed by the mortgagee if the receiver acts improperly and to the detriment of the company.[15] This means that as the company can maintain any relevant action for breach of duty[16] there is no justification for allowing a derivative action by directors and majority shareholders, because those persons could have procured the company to bring the action on its own behalf.[17]

Other secured creditors

It is now also perfectly clear that a receiver owes a duty of care in equity to any other mortgagee.[18]

Guarantor

A receiver also owes a duty of care in equity to a guarantor of the company's secured debt. This was at one stage denied, but the two cases which denied any

13 [1983] 1 WLR 1349 at 1356–1357.
14 *Gomba Holdings Ltd v Homan* [1986] 3 All ER 94, [1986] 1 WLR 1301.
15 *Watts v Midland Bank plc* [1986] BCLC 15. He must provide the company with full accounts: *Smiths Ltd v Middleton* [1979] 3 All ER 842; cf *Gomba Holdings Ltd v Homan* [1986] 3 All ER 94, [1986] 1 WLR 1301 (no duty to disclose to the company information prejudicial to the interests of debenture holders).
16 See [1986] BCLC 15 at 22A–B. Aliter if the receiver acts properly.
17 [1986] BCLC 15.
18 *Midland Bank Ltd v Joliman Finance Ltd* (1967) 203 Estates Gazette 1039 (second mortgagee); *Alliance Acceptance Co Ltd v Graham* [1974–75] 10 SASR 220 (third mortgagee). See also the cases cited at 131.

such duty have been repudiated. A line of cases now underpins the proposition that a receiver owes a duty of care to a guarantor of the debtor company's debt.[19] But a guarantor of unsecured indebtedness has no duty owed to him.[20]

Ordinary creditors

The question is whether the duty of care is owed to anyone else, and in particular to ordinary unsecured creditors of the company. On this point the position had been stated thus by Sir Neil Lawson in *Lathia v Dronsfield Bros Ltd*:[1]

> 'On authority, we must look at the context to determine to whom the duties are owed. Primarily [receivers] owe a duty to their debenture holders, and also, as agents, to the company. In my judgment, they do not owe a duty to the general creditors, to contributors, to officers of the company and members. They also owe a duty to guarantors. But that is a secondary liability. It is clear on the authorities, and no authority has been cited to the contrary, that the receivers do not owe a duty to the creditors of the company or to contributors.'

The authority for the proposition that receivers owe no duty of care to unsecured creditors of the company is *Northern Development (Holdings) Ltd v UDT Securities*[2] where the Court of Appeal indicated that the receiver owed no duty to protect the interests of the creditors at the expense of the debenture holders. Certainly in *Latchford v Beirne*[3] Milmo J equated a guarantor with an ordinary unsecured creditor who, he held, had no duty owed to him. The basis on which an unsecured creditor was excluded from the ambit of any duty of care owed by the receiver was stated by him to be twofold: (i) because the learned authors of a textbook[4] had referred only to a duty owed to the company and not to its creditors, and (ii) because if each of the individual creditors as distinct from the company itself, has a cause of action in negligence against the defendant, the assessment of damage suffered by each individual would present problems of very considerable, if not insoluble, complexity. Lord Denning MR in *Standard Chartered Bank Ltd v Walker*[5] expressly refrained from commenting on the position of an unsecured creditor. In Australia,[6] the duty has been expressed as one owed to the creditors of the mortgagor generally and since the discrediting of the decision in *Latchford v Beirne*[7] the point seems still open to argument in

---

19 *Standard Chartered Bank Ltd v Walker* [1982] 3 All ER 938, [1982] 1 WLR 1410, CA; *American Express International Banking Corpn v Hurley* [1985] 3 All ER 564; and see *Canadian Imperial Bank of Commerce v Haley* (1979) 100 DLR (3d) 470.
20 *Burgess v Augur; Burgess v Vanstock* [1998] 2 BCLC 478, Lightman J. But see the discussion at 143 below.
1 [1987] BCLC 321 at 324.
2 [1977] 1 All ER 747, [1976] 1 WLR 1230.
3 [1981] 3 All ER 705 at 709.
4 *Palmer's Company Law* (22 edn, 1976) Vol I, p 443.
5 [1982] 3 All ER 938, [1982] 1 WLR 1410 at 1416A.
6 *Expo International Pty Ltd v Chant* [1979] 2 NSWLR 820.
7 [1981] 3 All ER 705, disapproved in *American Express International Banking Corpn v Hurley* [1985] 3 All ER 564 and *Standard Chartered Bank Ltd v Walker* [1982] 3 All ER 938, [1982] 1 WLR 1410, CA.

this country. If a mortgagee when exercising his power of sale owes a duty of care to other *secured* creditors[8] and to guarantors of the mortgagor it appears to be eminently arguable that a duty of care is owed by the lender's receiver to ordinary unsecured creditors of the company. The ordinary creditors of the company are, it is suggested, in such proximity to the receiver that it must be in his reasonable contemplation that lack of care on his part would be likely to cause damage to them.

The cases which limit the equitable duty of care as one owed simply to those interested in the equity of redemption including guarantors of the secured indebtedness might be thought to preclude claims by unsecured creditors, just as guarantors of unsecured indebtedness of the company were precluded in *Burgess v Auger*[9] At the end of the road unsecured creditors do have an interest in all the property and equity of the company.[10] Moreover, the equitable duties imposed are designed to take into account the interests of the mortgagor and others interested in the mortgaged property and these duties are not inflexible. They could in the future be fashioned to accommodate a case where a surplus after satisfying several creditors was reduced by the negligence of the receiver.[11]

TORTIOUS LIABILITIES

It is well established that a receiver and manager may in that capacity[12] be liable in tort to a third party. Thus in *Re Goldburg (No 2)*[13] a receiver and manager was held liable in trespass. Debenture holders appointed a receiver and manager of the business of a one man company. The business (a milliner's business in London's Oxford Street) had been transferred to the company by an individual who went bankrupt. The transfer was set aside as an act of bankruptcy to which the title of the trustee in bankruptcy related back. Meanwhile the receiver and manager had been running the business. It was held that the receiver was liable as a trespasser to account to the trustee for the assets (if any) of the debtor which may have come to his hands or for the value of them. Phillimore J commented[14] as follows:

> 'That which the receiver takes possession of, as a trespasser he must account for, and he cannot set up any claim for anything that he has usefully done. On the other hand, he cannot be charged with any profits that he has made out of the bankrupt's goods. He is merely accountable for those assets . . . which are traced to his hands, and he has either to deliver them up or to pay damages for their conversion.'

---

8 See cases cited in n 18, p 141, above.
9 [1998] 2 BCLC 478.
10 [1998] 2 BCLC 478 at 236C–D.
11 [1998] 2 BCLC 478 particular facts of the case must be borne in mind as regards the discharge of the duty.
12 The receiver and manager in *Fenton Textile Association Ltd v Lodge* [1928] 1 KB 1, 96 LJKB 1016, CA was being sued in tort for a pre-receivership matter.
13 [1912] 1 KB 606.
14 [1912] 1 KB 606 at 611.

However Phillimore J's dicta have been criticised.

In *Re Simms*,[15] Lord Hanworth MR joined issue with the statement that a receiver cannot set up any claim for anything that he has usefully done. The statement went 'beyond what was intended by the learned judge or what was needed for the judgment'. It ran counter, inter alia, to the decision in *Re Riddeough, ex p Vaughan*,[16] a decision of the Divisional Court and therefore of higher authority than the decision of Phillimore J. Nor can the rightful owner approbate and reprobate, in other words eat his cake and have it. Once he has elected to treat the receiver as a tortfeasor he cannot treat the receiver as his agent and liable to account for the profit realised as money had and received to the true owner's use or as special damages for conversion. But he can of course elect, if he wishes, to treat the receiver as his agent for the purpose of receiving such profits.

It has already been observed in the preceding chapter, that a receiver will be preoccupied with keeping his flanks protected. Should his appointment turn out to have been invalid he will then have been only a purported receiver. Such purported receivers and the debenture holders who appointed (or purported to appoint) them may be held to have been trespassers in relation to their conduct towards the assets of the company, even though they may have been acting bona fide.[17] The debenture holder's guilt is that of a principal, since he will have appointed the 'receiver'.

The gravity of the interference of debenture holder and receiver alike stems from the stigma which, commercially, attaches to receivership. That is the very point being made by two incisive comments of Owen J in *Harold Meggitt Ltd v Discount and Finance Ltd*.[18] In the first he says:[19]

> 'it is a most serious invasion of a person's rights if possession of his assets and the management and control of his business is taken out of his hands, even if for a short period without legal justification. If that invasion is made under a claim that the person trespassing is a receiver, the matter becomes even more serious, and the most far-reaching damage may be done to the person injured.'

Secondly, as he graphically puts it:[20] 'Even a limited liability company is, I think entitled to claim that there is no place like home.'

The question whether a receiver might be liable in tort where he deliberately causes a company to repudiate a contract with a third party was left open in *Re Botibol*[1] where Evershed J said:[2] 'There is a further ground that, even if the receiver could not be sued ex contractu, it would not follow that he could not be sued in tort if he had taken steps which effectively prohibited the completion of the contract.' The possible tortious liability mooted in *Re Botibol* was mentioned

15 [1934] Ch 1 at 15, CA.
16 (1884) 14 QBD 25.
17 *Re Jaffe Ltd (in liquidation) v Jaffe (No 2)* [1932] NZLR 195.
18 (1938) 56 WNNSW 23.
19 (1938) 56 WNNSW 23 at 24.
20 (1938) 56 WNNSW 23 at 25.
 1 [1947] 1 All ER 26.
 2 [1947] 1 All ER 26 at 28.

in *Airlines Airspares Ltd v Handley Page Ltd*[3] where an ex parte injunction to restrain a sale of shares by a receiver and manager was discharged on the inter partes interlocutory hearing. However, Graham J did not find it necessary to comment on the point. Presumably in most cases a receiver and manager could pray in aid as a defence legal justification for the inducement. Most attempts to give a complete and satisfactory definition of 'justification' in this context would probably be mischievous and it has been said that it must be left to the good sense of the tribunal to analyse the circumstances of the particular case.[4] In analysing the circumstances regard might be had to the nature of the contract broken; the position of the parties to the contract; the grounds for the breach; the means employed to procure the breach; the relation of the person procuring the breach to the person who breaks the contract; and the object of the person in procuring the breach.[5]

A receiver may also be liable in tort where he threatens to deal with property in a manner inconsistent with the equitable rights of another and for *that reason* may properly be joined as a party to proceedings against the company, and if the claim against them succeeds, be ordered to pay the costs.[6]

The liability of a receiver and manager to guarantors of the company and possibly even to ordinary creditors for negligent mishandling of a sale of the company's property is a further possible illustration of the tortious liability of the receiver-manager.[7]

To the extent that he is the agent of the company or of the debenture holders the relevant principal will be liable for any torts committed by the receiver within the scope of the receiver's authority or for any torts subsequently ratified or adopted by the principal. In *MacManus v Royal Bank of Canada*,[8] the court found on the evidence that both the defendant bank and the receiver had been guilty of negligence in disposing of the goods of the company in receivership without calling for bids from the two parties who had expressed an interest to purchase them. In consequence the plaintiff or guarantor of the corporation suffered damages. The bank in its defence relied on certain clauses of the debenture and in particular on one which provided that 'any such receiver shall so far as concerns responsibility for his acts be deemed the agent of the Company and in no event the agent of the holder, and the holder shall not be in any way be responsible for any misconduct, negligence or non-feasance on the part of any such receiver'. Leger J held that although the maker of the debenture might be bound by the provisions of its contract, the plaintiff as guarantor and in his own right was not so bound.[9]

---

3 [1970] Ch 193 at 197.
4 *Glamorgan Coal Co Ltd v South Wales Miners' Federation* [1903] 2 KB 545 at 574–575 per Romer LJ. For a helpful review of the cases see *Posluns v Toronto Stock Exchange* [1964] 2 OR 547, 46 DLR (2d) 210.
5 *Dirassar v Kelly Douglas & Co Ltd* (1966) 59 DLR (2d) 452 at 481–482.
6 *Telemetrix plc v Modern Engineers of Bristol (Holdings) plc* [1985] BCLC 213.
7 *Standard Chartered Bank Ltd v Walker* [1982] 3 All ER 938, [1982] 1 WLR 1410, CA.
8 (1983) 47 CBRNS 252, NBQB (following *Canadian Imperial Bank of Commerce v Haley* (1979) 25 NBR (2d) 304, NBCA).
9 (1984) 47 CBRNS 252 at 258.

Conversion

There is also little doubt that if a receiver sells goods which in fact were subject to a retention of title clause[10] so as to interfere with the property rights of the suppliers of the goods he would be liable in conversion. It is no part of a receiver's function to purport to give title on sale to a purchaser of goods which never were in the ownership of the company. The charge from which his authority is derived also marks out the property which is subject to the charge. The defence of innocence will not help if he is sued for conversion since guilt or innocence is irrelevant in the tort of conversion.[11]

Negligence

The liability of a receiver and manager in negligence[12] is now established in relation to his exercise of the power of sale. A liability in that regard to guarantors of the debt secured by the relevant debenture pursuant to which the receiver and manager was appointed was at first denied by the much criticised decisions of Thesiger J in *Barclays Bank Ltd v Thienel*[13] and of Milmo J in *Latchford v Beirne*[14] but finally acknowledged in *Standard Chartered Bank Ltd v Walker*[15] and confirmed by Mann J in *American Express International Banking Corpn v Hurley*.[16]

Indemnity

Can a receiver-manager guilty of such malpractice claim an indemnity against the debenture holders who appointed him? It is thought that if the negligence can be imputed to him personally there is no reason why he should have any such right to an indemnity. In that situation he stands in no better position than agents,[17] partners[18] or trustees[19] who stand to lose their right of indemnity if the loss they cause can be imputed to their personal negligence.

Where the receiver is entitled to an indemnity from the company it is thought that the receiver will be entitled to count that right as a receivership expense. So on principle he should be able to claim priority in respect of it from the realised assets even against preferential creditors of the company.[20]

---

10 Ie a clause reserving title to the supplier of goods until the price of the goods has been paid in full: see the discussion at p 204.
11 *Hollins v Fowler* (1875) LR 7 HL 757 at 770 and 795–796.
12 See Anu Arora 'Receivers' liability for negligence' (1983) LMCLQ 294.
13 (1978) 122 Sol Jo 472, 247 Estates Gazette 385.
14 [1981] 3 All ER 705.
15 [1982] 3 All ER 938, [1982] 1 WLR 1410.
16 [1985] 3 All ER 564.
17 *Duncan v Hill* (1873) LR 8 Exch 242, 42 LJ Ex 179.
18 *Thomas v Atherton* (1878) 10 Ch D 185, 48 LJ Ch 370, CA.
19 *Buttle v Saunders* [1950] 2 All ER 193.
20 Anu Arora (1983) LMCLQ 294 at 300.

VICARIOUS LIABILITY OF DEBENTURE HOLDER

A debenture holder will be vicariously liable for the acts and defaults of his duly appointed receiver where the latter is acting as agent for the debenture holder. Apart from the rare cases where the receiver is expressly appointed to act as agent of the debenture holder, an agency may also be held to exist where the receiver acts on specific directions or instructions given by the debenture holder.[1]

If the receiver is invalidly appointed the person responsible for that invalid appointment, namely the appointor, will be vicariously liable for the acts and defaults of his purported receiver.[2] The 'receiver' in such a case is an agent for the debenture holder. Walton J suggested in *Bank of Baroda v Panessar*[3] that this was not the case. But his reasoning was on this occasion flawed. He argued from the existence of a statutory indemnity under s 34 of the Insolvency Act 1986 that the relationship could not be one of principal and agent: the statutory provision would have been superfluous had there been an agency because the law in such a case implies an indemnity in any event. It is usually dangerous to imply common law principles from statutory provisions. But this is the more so when the implication runs contrary to authorities which identify the appointor as the de facto principal.[4]

EXCLUSION OR LIMITATION OF LIABILITY

In considering the extent to which the liability of a debenture holder or his receiver may be excluded or limited, it is necessary to see: (i) whether there is a relevant exemption or limitation in the debenture itself which is capable of operating to the benefit of the receiver or guarantor; (ii) whether the exemption, as a matter of construction, covers the breach of duty; and (iii) what is the effect upon the exemption of the Unfair Contract Terms Act 1977.

Privity of contract

As a matter of contract, a mortgagee or debenture holder may effectively exclude or limit his liability to the company for the default of his receiver.[5] But such immunity will not normally enure for the benefit of the receiver. There are,

---

1 *Standard Chartered Bank v Walker* [1982] 1 WLR 1410 at 1416A, CA.

2 *Standard Chartered Bank v Walker* [1982] 3 All ER 938, [1982] 1 WLR 1410; *American Express International Banking Corpn v Hurley* [1985] 3 All ER 564.

3 [1987] Ch 335, [1986] 3 All ER 751.

4 See *Re Goldburg (No 2)* [1912] 1 KB 606 at 610–611; *Re Jaffe Ltd (in liquidation) v Jaffe (No 2)* [1932] NZLR 195.

5 Such a clause will not bind a guarantor under a separate instrument: *MacManus v Royal Bank of Canada* (1983) 47 CBR NS 252 at 257.

however, several ways in which the receiver may achieve immunity or protection all the same:

(a)   where the mortgagee has expressly contracted as agent for the receiver;[6]

(b)   where the mortgagor or guarantor agrees with the mortgagee not to sue the receiver;[7]

(c)   where the mortgagor or guarantor agrees to pay over all the proceeds of a claim against the receiver to the mortgagee;

(d)   where the mortgage empowers the mortgagee to act as agent for the mortgagor or guarantor in agreeing with the receiver on appointment a restricted duty or liability to the mortgagor or guarantor.[8]

Construction and contra proferentem rule

Given the presence in the mortgage of an exemption provision, the next step is to see whether on its true construction it covers the breach of duty in question. Any ambiguity must be construed against the mortgagee or his receiver in accordance with the *contra proferentem* rule.[9] Because of that rule a clause exempting a mortgagee from loss occasioned to the mortgagor by sale is not to be construed as exemption from liability *in negligence*:[10] exclusion from liability in negligence must be expressly conferred.[11] So too exclusion of liability for sales made before the power of sale has arisen does not extend to liability for negligent failure to get the best price.[12] Again in *Standard Chartered Bank v Walker*[13] the debenture provided that the bank should have power to appoint a receiver who could take possession of and sell the company's assets. It contained an express provision that:

> 'Any receiver or receivers so appointed shall be deemed to be the agent or agents of the company and the company shall be solely responsible for his or their acts or defaults and for his or their remuneration.'

The Court of Appeal held that there was a triable issue as to whether the bank had interfered to such an extent as to render it liable for acts or defaults of the receiver. This recognises that the words 'solely responsible' should not be construed to exclude the liability of an interfering debenture holder.

---

6   But such a provision may be ineffective if his identity is unknown at the date of the mortgage: *Expo International Pty Ltd v Chant* [1979] 2 NSWLR 820, 4 ACLR 679; cf *Port Jackson Stevedoring Pty Ltd v Salmond & Spraggon (Australia) Ltd* [1981] 1 WLR 138 (stevedores).
7   *Snelling v John G Snelling Ltd* [1973] QB 87. The mortgagee may enforce the agreement.
8   Treitel *Law of Contract* (10th edn) pp 577–588.
9   Broom's *Legal Maxims* (10th edn) pp 402–410.
10 *American Express International Banking Corpn v Hurley* [1985] 3 All ER 564 at 571D–F.
11 See *Chitty on Contracts* (28th edn) Vol I, 668–670, 14-010–14.012.
12 *Tse Kwok Lam v Wong Chit Sen* [1983] 1 WLR 1349 at 1360.
13 [1982] 3 All ER 938, [1982] 1 WLR 1410.

Unfair Contract Terms Act 1977

The Unfair Contract Terms Act 1977 (UCTA 1977) only extends to a provision in a contract which excludes or restricts the liability of a party to the contract.[14] It could thus apply only if in the first place the mortgagee has contracted as agent for the receiver.[15] Secondly, it will not apply to exemption clauses so far as they seek to exclude liability in negligence in relation to the creation, transfer or termination of interests in land.[16] Such exemption clauses are outside the ambit of the Act. Where the exemption clause does fall within the ambit of the Act, the term must have been a fair and reasonable one to have been included having regard to the circumstances which were in existence, or ought reasonably to have been known to exist or were in the contemplation of the parties when the contract was made.[17]

STATUTORY FORMALITIES ON ACCEPTANCE

The appointment of a person as a receiver or manager of a company's property under powers contained in an instrument is of no effect unless it is accepted by the appointee before the end of the business day next following that on which the instrument of appointment is received by him or on his behalf.[18] Subject to this possibility of invalidation, the appointment is deemed to be made at the time at which the instrument of appointment is received by the appointee or on his behalf.[19]

Administrative receivers are obliged by the Insolvency Rules 1986 to give written confirmation of their acceptance. If two or more persons are appointed jointly as administrative receivers, each of them has to confirm acceptance on his own behalf; but the appointment is effective only when all those jointly appointed have complied with the confirmation requirements.[20] Where a person is appointed as the sole or joint administrative receiver of a company's property under provisions contained in an instrument,[1] the appointee, if he accepts the appointment, must within seven days confirm his acceptance in writing to the appointor unless the appointment was accepted in writing.[2] A duly authorised agent may give the necessary confirmation on the appointee's behalf.[3] In confirming his acceptance, the appointee must state (i) the time and date of his receipt of notice of the appointment, and (ii) the time and date of his acceptance.[4]

---

14 UCTA 1977, s 2(2).
15 See at p 148, above.
16 UCTA 1977, s 1(2) and Sch 1, para 1.
17 UCTA 1977, s 11(1).
18 IA 1986, s 33(1)(a).
19 IA 1986, s 33(1)(b).
20 IR 1986, r 3.1(1).
 1 IR 1986, r 3.1(2).
 2 IR 1986, r 3.1(3).
 3 IR 1986, r 3.1(4).
 4 IR 1986, r 3.1(5).

STATUTORY DUTIES OF AN ADMINISTRATIVE RECEIVER TO ASCERTAIN AND INVESTIGATE THE COMPANY'S AFFAIRS

Two of the aims of the new insolvency legislation in England were: (a) to remedy the lack of involvement of unsecured creditors in receiverships; and (b) to require a receiver to provide the unsecured creditors (as well as others) with information about the likely outcome and progress of his work. These aims are realised by a set of provisions requiring administrative receivers: (i) to notify the company and all the creditors of the company of their appointment;[5] (ii) to require designated persons to submit to the receiver a statement of affairs;[6] (iii) to submit a report to the registrar of companies and to secured and unsecured creditors;[7] and (iv) to furnish information to any duly constituted committee of creditors.[8]

These duties, which are discussed below,[9] do not extend to an administrative receiver appointed to act with an existing administrative receiver or to an administrative receiver appointed in place of an administrative receiver dying or ceasing to act, save to the extent that the predecessor has failed fully to comply with the duty,[10] in which case his successor and any continuing receivers must finish the task. Where the company is being wound up the same duties apply, even though the liquidator and the administrator may be the same person.[11]

Notice to submit statement of affairs

The administrative receiver must require some or all of defined categories of persons to make out or submit the prescribed form of statement.[12] The categories are: (i) those who are or have been officers of the company; (ii) those who have taken part in the company's formation at any time within one year before the date of the appointment of the administrative receiver; (iii) those who are in the company's employment, or have been in its employment within that year, and are in the administrative receiver's opinion capable of giving the information required; and (iv) those who are or have been within that year officers of or in the employment of a company which is, or within that year was, an officer of the company. In this context 'employment' includes employment under a contract for services.[13]

The form of the notice required for the statement of affairs is in Form 3.1B.[14] The persons to whom the notices are in fact sent are referred to in the rules as 'deponents'.[15] The notice must inform each of the deponents of:

5 IA 1986, s 46.
6 IA 1986, s 47.
7 IA 1986, s 48.
8 IA 1986, s 49.
9 See at pp 150–155 below.
10 IA 1986, ss 46(2) and 48(7).
11 IA 1986, s 46(3).
12 IA 1986, s 47(1).
13 IA 1986, s 47(3).
14 See IR 1986, r 3.3(1).
15 See IR 1986, r 3.3(2).

(a)   the names and addresses of all others (if any) to whom the same notice has been sent;

(b)   the time within which the statement must be delivered;

(c)   the effect of any failure to comply with the notice;[16]

(d)   the statutory duty[17] of each of the deponents to co-operate with the administrative receiver by giving him relevant information and attending on him if so required.[18]

The administrative receiver must, on request, furnish each deponent with the forms required for the preparation of the statement of affairs.[19]

Form of statement of affairs and its verification

The statement of affairs must be verified by affidavit by the persons required to submit it and must show (i) particulars of the company's assets, debts and liabilities; (ii) the names and addresses of its creditors; (iii) the securities held by them respectively; (iv) the dates when the securities were respectively given; and (v) such further or other information as may be prescribed.[20] The statement must be in the prescribed form,[1] must contain all the particulars required by that form and must be verified by affidavit by the deponents, using the same form.[2]

The administrative receiver may require any of the persons who may be required to prepare and submit to him a statement of affairs[3] to submit an affidavit of concurrence, stating that he concurs in the statement of affairs.[4] An affidavit of concurrence may be qualified in respect of matters dealt with in the statement of affairs, where the maker of the affidavit is not in agreement with the deponents, or he considers the statement to be erroneous or misleading, or he is without the direct knowledge necessary for concurring with it.[5] The statement of affairs must be delivered to the receiver by the deponent making the affidavit of verification, or by one of them, if more than one, together with a copy of the verified statement.[6] Every affidavit of concurrence must be delivered by the person who makes it, together with a copy.[7] The administrative receiver must retain the verified copy of the statement and the affidavits of concurrence, if any, as part of the records of the receivership.[8]

16 See IA 1986, s 47(6) and Sch 10.
17 IA 1986, s 235.
18 IR 1986, r 3.3(3).
19 IR 1986, r 3.3(4) (amended by SI 1987/1919).
20 IA 1986, s 47(2).
 1 For the prescribed form see IA 1986, SI 1986/1925, rr 3–4, 12.7, Sch 4, Form 3.2.
 2 IR 1986, r 3.4(1).
 3 Ie any of the persons mentioned in IA 1986, s 47(3).
 4 IR 1986, r 3.4(2).
 5 IR 1986, r 3.4(3).
 6 IR 1986, r 3.4(4).
 7 IR 1986, r 3.4(5).
 8 IR 1986, r 3.4(6).

Time for submission of statement of affairs

Subject to any concession by the administrative receiver, pursuant to statute, the time limit for submission of a statement of affairs by the persons required to submit it is until the end of the period of 21 days beginning with the day after that on which the prescribed notice of the requirement is given by the administrative receiver or for such longer period as he may allow.[9] The administrative receiver may, if he thinks fit, at any time release any person, who would otherwise be treated as a deponent, from any obligation to make out and submit a statement of affairs or to provide the statutory details, or he may extend the period of 21 days at the time of giving the statutory notice or subsequently. Where the administrative receiver refuses to grant any such release or extension, the court may, if it thinks fit, intervene and itself grant it.[10]

Limited disclosure

Where the administrative receiver thinks that it would prejudice the conduct of the receivership for the whole or part of the statement of affairs to be disclosed, he may apply to the court for an order of limited disclosure in respect of the statement or a specified part of it.[11] The court may on the application order that the statement or, as the case may be, a specified part of it, be not open to inspection otherwise than with the leave of the court.[12] The court's order may include directions as to the delivery of documents to the registrar of companies and the disclosure of relevant information to other persons.[13]

If a person without reasonable excuse fails to comply with any obligation imposed on him under the above provisions,[14] he is liable on conviction on indictment to a fine, or on summary conviction to a fine not exceeding the statutory maximum and, on conviction after continued contravention, to a daily default fine not exceeding one-tenth of the statutory maximum.[15]

The administrative receiver's power to give a release or to grant an extension of time[16] may be exercised at the receiver's own discretion or at the request of any deponent.[17] A deponent may, if he requests a release or extension of time and it is refused by the receiver, apply to the court for it.[18] The court may, if it thinks that no sufficient cause is shown for the application, dismiss it; but the court must not do so unless the applicant has had an opportunity to attend the court for an ex parte hearing, of which he has been given at least seven days' notice.[19] If the

9 IA 1986, s 47(4).
10 IA 1986, s 47(5).
11 IR 1986, SI 1986/1925, r 3.5(1).
12 IR 1986, r 3.5(2).
13 IR 1986, r 3.5(3).
14 Ie the provisions of IA 1986, s 47.
15 IA 1986, ss 47(6), 430, Sch 10.
16 Ie under the IA 1986, s 47(5): see below.
17 IR 1986, SI 1986/1925, r 3.6(1).
18 IR 1986, r 3.6(2).
19 IR 1986, r 3.6(3).

application is not dismissed, the court must fix a venue[20] for it to be heard and give notice to the deponent accordingly.[1] The deponent must, at least 14 days before the hearing, send to the receiver a notice stating the venue and accompanied by a copy of the application, and of any evidence which he, the deponent, intends to adduce in support of it.[2]

The receiver may appear and be heard on the application; and whether or not he appears, he may file a written report of any matters which he considers ought to be drawn to the court's attention; and if such a report is filed, a copy of it must be sent by the receiver to the deponent, not later than five days before the hearing.[3] Sealed copies of any order made on the application must be sent by the court to the deponent and the receiver.[4]

On any such application the applicant's costs must be paid in any event by him and, unless the court otherwise orders, no allowance towards them may be made out of the assets under the administrative receiver's control.[5]

Expenses of statement of affairs

A deponent[6] making the statement of affairs and affidavit must be allowed, and paid by the administrative receiver out of his receipts, any expenses incurred by the deponent in so doing which the receiver thinks reasonable.[7] Any decision by the receiver under this provision is subject to appeal to the court.[8] Nothing in this provision, however, relieves a deponent from any obligation with respect to the preparation, verification and submission of the statement of affairs, or to the provision of information to the receiver.[9]

Report by administrative receiver

To registrar and secured creditors

The statement of affairs is likely to be a useful and convenient source of information for an administrative receiver performing his statutory duty to prepare a report. According to that statutory duty, an administrative receiver must, within three months (or such longer period as the court may allow), after his appointment send a statutory report to (i) the registrar of companies, and (ii) to any trustee for the *secured* creditors of the company and (iii) (so far as he is aware of their addresses) to all such secured creditors.[10]

20 Ie the date, time and place for the hearing of the application.
 1 IR 1986, r 3.6(3).
 2 IR 1986, r 3.6(4).
 3 IR 1986, r 3.6(5).
 4 IR 1986, r 3.6(6).
 5 IR 1986, r 3.6(7).
 6 For the meaning of 'deponent' see IR 1986, r 3.3(2).
 7 IR 1986, r 3.7(1).
 8 IR 1986, r 3.7(2).
 9 IR 1986, r 3.7(3).
10 IA 1986, s 48(1).

Statute lays down guidelines for the contents of such a report. The matters to be covered comprise:

(a)   the events leading up to the administrative receiver's appointment, so far as he is aware of them;

(b)   the disposal (or proposed disposal) by him of any of the property of the company and the carrying on (or proposed carrying on) by him of any business of the company;

(c)   the amounts of principal and interest payable to the debenture holders by whom, or on whose behalf, he was appointed and the amounts payable to preferential creditors; and

(d)   the amount (if any) likely to be available for the payment of other creditors.[11]

This obligation to submit a report does *not* apply to an administrative receiver succeeding another or assisting an administrative receiver who is already in harness,[12] unless the obligation has been incompletely discharged.

To unsecured creditors

The time limits for the submission of a statutory report apply equally to (i) sending a copy of the report to the unsecured creditors of the company (so far as the receiver is aware of their addresses), and (ii) publication in the prescribed manner of a notice stating an address to which unsecured creditors of the company should write for copies of the report to be sent to them free of charge.[13] In either case, unless the court otherwise directs, the administrative receiver must also lay a copy of the statutory report before a meeting of the company's unsecured creditors summoned for the purpose on not less than 14 days' notice.[14] The court may otherwise direct only if, not less than 14 days before the application is made to the court, the report states the intention of the administrative receiver to apply for such a direction or a copy of the report is sent to the unsecured creditors or a notice to unsecured creditors is published.[15]

Procedure for report to creditors

If the administrative receiver decides not to send a copy of his report to the creditors, but to publish a notice instead, the notice must be published in the newspaper in which the receiver's appointment was published.[16] If he proposes to apply to the court to dispense with the holding of the meeting of unsecured creditors he must, in his report to creditors or (as the case may be) in the

---

11 IA 1986, s 48(1).
12 IA 1986, s 48(7).
13 IA 1986, s 48(2).
14 IA 1986, s 48(2).
15 IA 1986, s 48(3).
16 IR 1986, r 3.8(1).

newspaper notice, state the venue fixed by the court for the hearing of the application.[17] Subject to any order of the court, the copy of the receiver's report to be sent to the registrar of companies must have attached to it a copy of any statement of affairs and copies of any affidavits of concurrence.[18] If the statement of affairs or affidavits of concurrence, if any, have not been submitted to the receiver by the time he sends a copy of his report to the registrar of companies, he must send a copy of the statement and any affidavits of concurrence as soon thereafter as he receives them.[19]

Creditors' meeting and creditors' committee

It has been seen that the administrative receiver, whether within the relevant time limit he sends a copy of his report to unsecured creditors or publishes a notice inviting such creditors to write in for a report, must, unless the court otherwise directs, summon a meeting of the company's unsecured creditors on not less than 14 days' notice.[20] Such a meeting may, if it thinks fit, establish a creditors' committee to exercise the functions conferred on it by or under the legislation.[1] If such a committee is established, the committee may, on giving not less than seven days' notice, require the administrative receiver to attend before it at any reasonable time and furnish it with such information relating to his functions and his performance of them as it may reasonably require.[2] Provision is made in the Insolvency Rules 1986 for the summoning and conduct of creditors' meetings[3] and for the constitution, functions and procedure of the creditors' committee.[4] These matters are covered in a later chapter.

DUTIES IN RESPECT OF ACCOUNTS

An administrative receiver must (i) within two months after the end of 12 months from the date of his appointment, and of every subsequent period of 12 months, and (ii) within two months after he ceases to act as administrative receiver, send to the registrar of companies, to the company and to the person by whom he was appointed and to each member of the creditors' committee, if there is one, the requisite accounts of his receipts and payments as receiver.[5] The court may, on the receiver's application, extend the above period of two months.[6] The relevant court for this purpose, if proceedings have not been commenced in which the

---

17 IR 1986, r 3.8(2).
18 IR 1986, r 3.8(3).
19 IR 1986, r 3.8(4).
20 IA 1986, s 48(2).
 1 IA 1986, s 49(1).
 2 IA 1986, s 49(2).
 3 IR 1986, rr 3.9–3.15.
 4 IR 1986, rr 3.16–3.30A.
 5 IR 1986, r 3.32(1). For the prescribed form of abstract of receipts and payments, see rr 3.32, 12.7, Sch 4, Form 3.6.
 6 IR 1986, r 3.32(2).

application may be made, is the court having the jurisdiction to wind up the company.[7]

The accounts must be in the form of an abstract showing: (i) receipts and payments during the relevant period of 12 months; or (ii) where the receiver has ceased to act, receipts and payments during the period from the end of the last 12-month period to the time when he so ceased; alternatively, if there has been no previous abstract, receipts and payments in the period since his appointment as administrative receiver.[8]

The provisions just summarised are without prejudice to the receiver's duty to render proper accounts otherwise than as stated above.[9]

If the administrative receiver makes default in complying with these provisions, he is liable on summary conviction to a fine not exceeding one-fifth of the statutory maximum and, on conviction after continued contravention, to a daily default fine not exceeding one-fiftieth of the statutory maximum.[10]

DUTY IN RESPECT OF VAT BAD DEBT RELIEF

Issue of certificate of insolvency

It is the duty of an administrative receiver to issue a certificate of insolvency[11] forthwith upon his forming the opinion that the relevant circumstances in which a company is deemed insolvent for the purposes of the provision relating to value added tax bad debt relief are satisfied.[12]

Contents of certificate

There must in the certificate be specified: (i) the name of the company and its registered number; (ii) the name of the administrative receiver and the date of his appointment; and (iii) the date on which the certificate is issued.[13]

The certificate must be intituled CERTIFICATE OF INSOLVENCY FOR THE PURPOSES OF SECTION 22(3)(b) OF THE VALUE ADDED TAX ACT 1983.[14]

Notice of issue

Notice of the issue of the certificate must be given by the administrative receiver within three months of his appointment or within two months of

---

7 IA 1986, s 251, applying CA 1985, s 744.
8 IR 1986, r 3.32(3).
9 IR 1986, r 3.32(4).
10 IR 1986, r 3.32(5), 12.21, Sch 5.
11 In the terms of the Value Added Tax Act 1994, which specifies the circumstances in which a company is deemed insolvent.
12 IR 1986, r 3.36(1).
13 IR 1986, r 3.36(2).
14 IR 1986, r 3.36(3).

issuing the certificate, whichever is the later, to all of the company's un-secured creditors of whose address he is then aware and who have, to his knowledge, made supplies to the company, with a charge to value added tax, at any time before his appointment.[15] Thereafter, he must give the notice to any creditor of whose address and supplies to the company he becomes aware.[16] But he is not under an obligation to provide any creditor with a copy of the certificate.[17]

Retention of certificate with accounting records

The certificate must be retained with the company's accounting records, and the provisions relating to where and for how long records are to be kept[18] apply to this certificate as they apply to those records.[19] Moreover, it is the duty of any administrative receiver on vacating office to bring this retention obligation to the attention of the directors or, as the case may be, any successor of his as admini-strative receiver.[20]

DUTIES ON VACATION OF OFFICE

Vacation of office: formalities

An administrative receiver who vacates office either on completion of the receivership or in consequence of his ceasing to be qualified as an insolvency practitioner must fulfil certain notification formalities. He must forthwith give notice of his vacation of office (i) to the company or, if it is in liquidation, the liquidator, and (ii) to the members of the creditors' committee (if any).[1] Where an administrative receiver vacates office otherwise than by death, he must within 14 days after vacation of office send a notice to that effect to the registrar of companies.[2] Failure to comply with this notification duty without reasonable excuse renders the receiver liable to a fine and, for continued contravention, to a daily default fine.[3] The notice to the registrar may be given by means of an endorsement on the notice required by s 405(2) of the Companies Act 1985, which deals with a notice for the purposes of the register of charges.[4]

---

15 IR 1986, r 3.37(1).
16 IR 1986, r 3.37(2).
17 IR 1986, r 3.37(3).
18 Ie CA 1985, s 222.
19 IR 1986, r 3.38(1).
20 IR 1986, r 3.38(2).
 1 IR 1986, r 3.35(1) as amended by the Insolvency (Amendment) Rules 1987 (I(A)R 1987), SI 1987/1919, r 3(1) and Sch, Pt 1, para 33.
 2 IA 1986, s 45(4).
 3 IA 1986, s 45(5). On penalties, see IA 1986, s 430 and Sch 10.
 4 IR 1986, r 3.35(2).

Formalities of resignation

Before resigning his office, an administrative receiver must give at least seven days' notice of his intention to do so to (i) the person by whom he was appointed, (ii) the company or, if it is then in liquidation, the liquidator, and (iii) in any case, to the members of the creditors' committee (if any).[5] The relevant notice must specify the date on which the receiver intends his resignation to take effect.[6] No notice is, however, necessary if the receiver resigns in consequence of the making of an administrative order.[7]

Death

Death is hardly a consensual event and it automatically terminates the receivership so far as the deceased is concerned. But it is convenient to discuss its consequences here. If an administrative receiver dies, the person by whom he was appointed must forthwith, on his becoming aware of the death, give notice to (i) the registrar of companies, (ii) the company or, if it is in liquidation, the liquidator, and (iii) in any case, to the members of the creditors' committee (if any).[8]

---

5 IR 1986, r 3.33(1) as amended by I(A)R 1987, SI 1987/1919, r 3(1) and Sch, Pt 1, para 31.
6 IR 1986, r 3.33(2).
7 IR 1986, r 3.33(3).
8 IR 1986, r 3.34 as amended by I(A)R 1987, r 3(1) and Sch, Pt 1, para 32. Form 3.7 is the appropriate form.

CHAPTER 11

Trading and commercial contracts

GENERAL

A receiver and manager with powers of management will have to decide at an early stage what to do about trading or commercial contracts made before his appointment. He will also have to decide to what extent he wishes to enter into fresh trading contracts. And he may well be faced with tricky problems of set off as between the company and third parties with whom the company has traded or continued to trade.

EXISTING CONTRACTS

The first truism is that the appointment of a receiver and manager (with the usual plenary powers of management) does not, of itself, bring to an end existing trading or commercial contracts. Sometimes the contract itself will specify that it is to terminate automatically if a receiver and manager is appointed. Sometimes the contract confers an option on the other party to terminate the contract. But what if it does not?

The answer is that the receiver and manager must then consider what the effect of his failure to abide by the contract will be. If it is clear that non-performance will significantly prejudice the goodwill of the company he should not abandon the contract; likewise if non-performance will adversely affect realisation of the assets. Otherwise he is free to disregard or 'adopt' the contract as he wishes. He does not, it seems, owe any duty to the other contracting party to adopt the contract.[1]

A receiver appointed out of court who chooses not to perform an existing contract leaves the other party to the contract with its claim for damages against the company as an unsecured creditor.[2] On the other hand, where an existing contract is one whose breach could be forestalled by the granting of specific

---

1 *Ardmore Studios (Ireland) Ltd v Lynch* [1965] IR 1.
2 *Airline Airspares Ltd v Handley Page Ltd* [1970] Ch 193, [1970] 1 All ER 29n; *Kernohan Estates Ltd v Boyd* [1967] NI 27.

performance or an injunction such relief may also be available to prevent a breach by the receiver.[3]

Moreover, the fact that specific performance would undermine the statutory scheme for distribution of assets and cause hardship to the creditors of a company in receivership which is hopelessly insolvent is not a ground of defence.[4]

In *Re Diesels and Components Pty Ltd*,[5] by the terms of a customs agent's appointment, goods which came into its possession or under its control were to be subject to a special and general lien and pledge for money due for its services. Receivers were appointed under a trading charge given to the bank. The agent became aware of the appointment but obtained possession of goods under its appointment after that time. McPherson J, following *George Barker (Transport) v Eynon*,[6] held that the agent was entitled to assert its pre-receivership contractual right to retain the goods against the receivers. There had been no repudiation of the contract, let alone acceptance of such repudiation, so the contract remained on foot with the lien operating for the benefit of the company.

Any abandonment of a commercial contract will, up to a point, dent the reputation of the company. But it is submitted that only the prospect of a significant loss of goodwill should deter a receiver from determining an existing trading contract. In other words, if the company is intended to trade in the future the receiver must ask himself: will repudiation seriously affect the trading prospects of the company?[7] If he is directing himself to realisation he should ask himself whether this repudiation would adversely affect the realisation.[8] Both these questions were raised by Graham J in *Airline Airspares Ltd v Handley Page Ltd*[9] where an ex parte injunction was discharged on an interlocutory motion. He found on the facts that future trading was most unlikely and that the receiver's decision to hive off the most economically viable part of the business to a newly formed subsidiary was not impeachable.

A receiver, therefore, stands in a stronger position than the company. But since the receiver is normally appointed as agent for the company, by his repudiation the receiver may open up the field for pursuit of the company. The company may not, in this context, be sued for specific performance except in relation to a binding contract to sell land[10] but as the principal standing behind its agent, the receiver, it will be liable for damages:[11] the appointment of a receiver by the

3 *Schering Pty Ltd v Forrest Pharmaceutical Co Pty Ltd* [1982] 1 NSWLR 286; *Freevale Ltd v Metrostore Ltd* [1984] Ch 199, [1984] 1 All ER 495; *Re Diesels & Components Pty Ltd* [1985] 2 Qd R 456, 9 ACLR 825; *Re Atlantic Computers Systems plc* [1992] Ch 505 at 526–527. See WG Guild (1986) 60 ALJ 42; D Milman and S Coneys [1984] Conv 446.

4 *AMEC Properties Ltd v Planning Research and Systems plc* [1992] BCLC 1149, CA.

5 (1985) 9 ACLR 825.

6 [1974] 1 All ER 900, [1974] 1 WLR 462, CA.

7 *Airline Airspares Ltd v Handley Page Ltd* [1970] Ch 193, [1970] 1 All ER 29.

8 [1970] Ch 193, [1970] 1 All ER 29.

9 [1970] Ch 193, [1970] 1 All ER 29.

10 *Macleod v Alexander Sutherland Ltd* 1977 SLT (Notes) 44. See the section, 'Contract for Sale of Land' at p 162, below.

11 *George Barker (Transport) Ltd v Eynon* [1974] 1 WLR 462 at 471.

debenture holder does not necessarily forfeit the rights of the other party to the contract.[12]

NEW CONTRACTS

Despite the fact that the receiver or manager of the property of the company appointed under the powers of any instrument (in other words a *non-administrative* corporate receiver) may be an agent of the company and able to bind it by his contract he will, to the same extent as if he had been appointed by order of the court, be personally liable on any contract entered into by him in the performance of his functions, except in so far as the contract otherwise provides and in respect of that liability he is entitled to indemnity out of the assets. This personal liability and indemnity are spelled out by statute;[13] but nothing in the statutory provision is to be taken as limiting any right to indemnity which he would have apart from it, or as limiting his liability on contracts entered into without authority, or as conferring any right to indemnity in respect of that liability.[14] A similar provision deals with the personal liability and right of indemnity of an *administrative* receiver in the same way.[15]

RATIFICATION OF CONTRACTS

A receiver is entitled to ratify contracts made by others ostensibly as agents for the company. This does not constitute novation of the contract which would in turn involve him in personal liability; and the statutory provision just recited has no application to such a case.[16] The ratification will relate back to the date of the contract.[17]

The statutory assimilation of the position of the privately appointed receiver to that of one appointed by the court broke new ground. Previously, as a general rule,[18] a privately appointed receiver was not personally liable in contract, the liability being that of his principal, in other words of the company or of the debenture holders. That pre-existing liability is not, it is suggested, displaced by the statutory innovation with the result that the third party can pick his defendant.

12 *Aluminium Industrie Vaassen BV v Romalpa Aluminium Ltd* [1976] 2 All ER 552, [1976] 1 WLR 676, CA.
13 IA 1986, s 37(1)(a) and (b).
14 IA 1986, s 37(3). If a solicitor fails to advise the receiver to obtain an indemnity he may be liable in negligence: *RA Price Securities LA v Henderson* [1989] 2 NZLR 257, NZCA.
15 See IA 1986, s 44(1)(b) and (c) and (3). On his vacation of office any indemnity of an administrative receiver is charged on and paid out of any property in or under his control at that time in priority to any security of the debenture holder: IA 1986, s 45(3)(b). A similar rule applies when a non-administrative receiver vacates office: IA 1986, s 37(4)(b).
16 *Lawson v Hosemaster Machine Co Ltd* [1966] 2 All ER 944, [1966] 1 WLR 1300, CA.
17 [1966] 2 All ER 944, [1966] 1 WLR 1300, CA.
18 *Thomas v Todd* [1926] 2 KB 511, 95 LJKB 808.

It remains to be added that the receiver's authority to enter into contracts on behalf of the company is terminated by the commencement of winding up.[19] Thereafter he may be liable for breach of warranty of authority if he negotiates new contracts in the name of the company: his liability is personal. If the relevant document provides that the company alone is to be answerable for his acts, contracts and defaults neither the trustees nor the debenture holders are personally liable in respect of contracts entered into by him, even though they were negotiated after the company went into liquidation.[20]

CONTRACT FOR SALE OF LAND

Where a company has entered into a binding contract to sell land and subsequently a receiver and manager is appointed under a debenture the mere fact of receivership affords no defence to an action for specific performance of the contract at the suit of the purchaser. This was confirmed by the court in *Freevale Ltd v Metrostore Holdings Ltd.*[1] The real question raised in that case as crystallised by the court was:[2] does the appointment out of court of a receiver in respect of a company vendor of land somehow destroy the equitable interest in the land which was vested in the purchaser prior to the appointment of the receiver by virtue of the subsisting valid contract for its sale and purchase, or does the appointment of a receiver alternatively somehow prevent the court perfecting that equitable interest by making an order for specific performance? The decision in *Airline Airspares Ltd v Handley Page Ltd*[3] affords no assistance to the solution of this question because the contract concerned was not one of which the court would, apart from the receivership, grant specific performance.

The decision in the Scottish case of *Macleod v Alexander Sutherland Ltd,*[4] where specific performance of a building contract was not decreed against a receiver, is also distinguishable. The company had become little more than a shell, having ceased its business. The works would only have been carried out if the receiver in exercise of his powers had entered into some other arrangements which would have involved him in personal liability. Not surprisingly the court would not impose a decree of specific performance which would have that effect.

---

19 *Gosling v Gaskell* [1897] AC 575, 66 LJQB 848, HL; *Thomas v Todd* [1926] 2 KB 511, 95 LJKB 808.

20 *Gosling v Gaskell* [1897] AC 575, 66 LJQB 848, HL disapproving the dictum of Lord Esher MR in *Owen & Co v Cronk* [1895] 1 QB 265 at 272, CA, that a receiver was the agent of the trustees. Cf LPA 1925, s 109(2) discussed at p 308.

1 [1984] Ch 199, [1984] 1 All ER 495 (Donald Rattee QC sitting as a deputy High Court judge). Hardship to creditors of hopelessly insolvent company is no defence: *AMEC Properties Ltd v Planning Research and Systems plc* [1992] BCLC 1149, CA.

2 [1984] Ch 199 at 203C–D.

3 [1970] Ch 193.

4 1977 SLT (Notes) 44.

HIRE-PURCHASE AGREEMENTS

Hire-purchase agreements into which the company has entered call for a word or two on their own. A chattel subject to a hire-purchase agreement which becomes annexed to the land is, under the general law, a fixture.[5] Nevertheless the right of the person described as 'owner' in the agreement is given special protection by the courts. If the chattels become fixtures the owner still retains an equitable interest in the land which has priority over any subsequent *equitable* charge[6] such as a debenture. This equitable interest has been held by the Court of Appeal in *Re Morrison, Jones & Taylor Ltd*[7] to give the 'owner' the right, with the leave of the court, to enter and remove the thing hired after the appointment of a receiver. The right will only disappear on payment in full by the debenture holder of the outstanding debt and costs.[8] The hire purchase agreement in question was in fact made before the debentures were issued. But the same prevalence of the supplier's interest (where it is retained) will apply, even where the hire purchase agreement is entered into after the floating charge. The debenture holders only get a charge on the interest that the company has in the relevant chattels.[9] That interest is fettered by the supplier's prior interest.

The position is different where there is a subsequent *legal* mortgage of land where the mortgagee has no notice of the hire purchase agreement affecting the fixtures. Such legal mortgagee will have priority on taking possession.[10]

Assets subject to an existing hire purchase agreement will not be subject to the debenture. It is necessary for the receiver to check that under the relevant agreement the assets are still owned by the supplier. If in fact the title to the assets turns out to have passed under the relevant agreement to the company different considerations will apply; the receiver will then be able to dispose of them. Otherwise the receiver will have to decide whether to adopt the contract or, if (which would be rare) the directors wish to retain custody of them, whether to hand them over to the directors and get confirmation from the owners that this is acceptable.

If there is equity in the goods the receiver may be able to negotiate a settlement figure with the owners of the goods. If there is none because the market value is less than the total future instalments the receiver may decide to surrender the goods to the hire purchase company so long as he is able to do so without affecting adversely his ability to continue trading.

A further possibility is that under the contract the appointment of a receiver terminates the contract and gives the supplier a right to repossess them, or to consolidate all outstanding contracts between the company and the supplier so that the receiver must continue with all or none of them.

---

5 *Hobson v Gorringe* [1897] 1 Ch 182 at 193 and 195, CA.
6 See eg *Re Samuel Allen & Sons Ltd* [1907] 1 Ch 575; *Johnston v International Harvester Co of New Zealand Ltd* [1925] NZLR 529 at 544, CA.
7 [1914] 1 Ch 50, CA.
8 [1914] 1 Ch 50 at 55 per Eve J (at first instance).
9 [1914] 1 Ch 50. This accords with the principle, applied in different circumstances in *Security Trust Co v Royal Bank of Canada* [1976] AC 503, [1976] 1 All ER 381 discussed at p 44 above.
10 *Hobson v Gorringe* [1897] 1 Ch 182; *Reynolds v Ashby* [1904] AC 466, HL; *Ellis v Glover and Hobson Ltd* [1908] 1 KB 388, CA.

CONTRACTS OF INSURANCE

When a receiver and manager of the company's business is appointed, then if the company has entered into contracts of insurance against any liability to third parties, its rights against the insurers in respect of that liability are automatically transferred and vested in the third party. The third party however retains his rights to recover any balance not covered by insurance.[11]

SET-OFF AND LIEN

The rights of set-off and lien can conveniently be dealt with together because, as one commentator[12] has rightly pointed out, they are analogous. The effect of both of them is to avoid circuity of action and both operate to confer rights akin to security, a lien being indeed a form of charge.

In the context of private receiverships rights of set-off and lien assume particular importance[13] because companies in receivership are often making claims against companies and businesses which are themselves hard-pressed. Mutual dealings spawn mutual debts and it is necessary for receiver and third party alike to identify cases where successful claims can be made.

Set off

The circumstances in which rights of set-off can occur are multifarious and probably not capable of exhaustive enumeration.[14] After some initial general-isations the approach to the topic which follows attempts to deal with the commonest examples which have been the subject of express decision or have been touched on in obiter dicta.

First, if a right of set off arose before crystallisation such right can be asserted against the debenture holders and the receiver.[15] This is the case whether or not the claim is a liquidated one so long as it arises out of the same subject matter.[16]

An equitable set off is available in respect of unliquidated claims between the parties[17] but they must be closely related that is to say, in effect, interdependent.[18]

---

11 Third Party (Rights against Insurers) Act 1930, s 1; and see *Murray v Legal and General Assurance Society Ltd* [1970] 2 QB 495, [1969] 3 All ER 794.
12 See JH Farrar 'Some Recent Developments in the Law of Receivers' (1975) JBL 23 at 31.
13 See, generally, James O'Donovan 'Rights of Set-off and Lien in Company Receiverships' (1978) 52 ALJ 562–567.
14 For more extended treatment, see Derham *Set Off* (2nd edn, 1998) McCracken *The Banker's Remedy of Set Off* (2nd edn 1998); and Philip R Wood *English and International Set Off* (1989).
15 *Rother Iron Works Ltd v Canterbury Precision Engineers Ltd* [1974] QB 1, [1973] 1 All ER 394, CA.
16 *Newfoundland Government v Newfoundland Rly Co* (1888) 13 App Cas 199, 57 LJPC 35, PC fold in *Sun Candies Pty Ltd v Polites* [1939] VLR 132.
17 *Hargreaves v Action 2000 Ltd* [1993] BCLC 1111, CA.
18 *Grant v NZMC Ltd* [1989] 1 NZLR 8 at 13. There is doubt about the precise nature of this nexus. Compare Meagher Gummow and Lehane *Equity* (3rd edn) pages 3709–3710 (narrow) with *AWA Ltd v Exicom Australia Pty Ltd* (1990) 19 NSWLR 705 (less restrictive).

Contrariwise a creditor who contracts with the receiver cannot set off against the receiver a debt owed by the company prior to the receivership: there is no mutuality as the parties are not dealing with each other in the same right.[19] Nor is the claimant's position any better if the claim sought to be set off arose after receivership but out of a pre-receivership contract, unless it arose out of the same subject matter.[20]

However, if the competing claims arise out of the same contract or series of contracts since the appointment there is no reason why the doctrine of set-off should not apply.[1] Indeed there seems no good reason in principle that claims arising out of separate and distinct contracts between the receiver and a third party and entered into *after* the receivership should not be set off the one against the other.[2]

Closely connected claims on same contract or on same subject matter

Lord Hobhouse once observed[3] 'there is no universal rule that claims arising out of the same contract may be set off against one another'. On the other hand where the claims arise out of obligations which are closely interrelated they will be set off against each other. Thus in *Newfoundland Government v Newfoundland Rly Co*[4] the opposing claims were (i) a claim by the plaintiff railway company that the Government was bound to pay a certain amount of subsidy and to make grants of land for a completed portion of a railway, though as a whole it was not completed, and (ii) a claim by the Government for damages arising out of the railway company's breach of the contract to construct the railway. The Judicial Committee of the Privy Council, after construing the nature and effect of the contract, held that the Government was entitled to set off a counterclaim for unliquidated damages for the company's breach of contract in not completing the line against the company's claim for the unpaid subsidy. Lord Hobhouse delivering the opinion of the Judicial Committee said:[5]

> 'The two claims under consideration have their origin in the same portion of the same contract, where the obligations which gave rise to them are intertwined in the closest manner. The claim of the Government does not arise from any fresh transaction freely entered into by it after notice of assignment by the company.'

In the result their Lordships had no hesitation in saying that the claims should be set off against each other.

---

19 *NW Robbie & Co Ltd v Witney Warehouse Co Ltd* [1963] 3 All ER 613, [1963] 1 WLR 1324, CA; *Felt and Textiles of New Zealand Ltd v R Hubrich Ltd* [1968] NZLR 716; *Rendell v Doors and Doors Ltd (in liquidation)* [1975] 2 NZLR 191.
20 *Business Computers Ltd v Anglo African Leasing Ltd* [1977] 2 All ER 741, [1972] 1 WLR 578 (claim under a hire purchase agreement consequent upon termination after receivership); and see *TR Hillson Ltd (in receivership) v Beverley Trading Co Ltd* (1987) NZCLC 100,026.
1 *Rendell v Doors and Doors Ltd (in liquidation)* [1975] 2 NZLR 191 at 202; *Leichhardt Emporium Pty Ltd v AGC (Household Finance) Ltd* [1979] 1 NSWLR 701 at 707.
2 *Rendell v Doors and Doors Ltd (in liquidation)* [1975] 2 NZLR 191 at 201.
3 *Newfoundland Government v Newfoundland Rly Co* (1888) 13 App Cas 199 at 212.
4 (1888) 13 App Cas 199.
5 (1888) 13 App Cas 199 at 212.

In *Sun Candies Pty Ltd v Polites*[6] the plaintiff had a liquidated claim for breach of contract and the defendant had an unliquidated counterclaim for breach of contract. The plaintiff's claim was for the balance of purchase money of a business. The defendant's unliquidated claim was for breach of warranty as to the value of the business, which value determined the amount of purchase money. The order made by Mann CJ was judgment for the plaintiff for £350 and for the defendant for £400 on the counterclaim and he directed a set off of the damages and costs between the parties. Before the judgment was entered the plaintiff sought on motion to have the order for set-off omitted from the judgment on the ground that at the time of the contract the plaintiff's assets were subject to a floating charge in favour of a debenture holder and that a week or two after the contract had been entered into a receiver went into possession of the assets. The application failed because, as Mann CJ pointed out, both claims arose on closely related provisions in the *same* contract and the case was therefore within the principles set out in *Newfoundland Government v Newfoundland Rly Co* and already discussed.

In *Rother Iron Works Ltd v Canterbury Precision Engineers Ltd*[7] the plaintiff and the defendant were trading with each other. At a point of time when the plaintiff owed the defendant £124 for goods sold and delivered, the defendant contracted to buy goods to the value of £159 from the plaintiff. Before the goods were delivered or the price became payable, the bank with which the plaintiff had its account appointed a receiver and manager under its debenture and the floating charge over the plaintiff's business crystallised.

The defendant maintained that it was entitled to set off the £124 due to the defendant under the previous contract and so it owed the receiver who was suing in the name of the plaintiff company only £35. The receiver denied that there was any right of set-off. But the claim for a set-off succeeded. Russell LJ delivering the judgment of the court explained the decision thus:[8]

> 'In our judgment the argument of the defendants is to be preferred. It is true that the right of the plaintiff company to sue for the debt due from the defendant company was embraced when it arose, by the debenture charge. But if this was because the chose in action consisting of the rights under the contract became subject to the charge on the appointment of the receiver, then the debenture holder could not be in a better position to assert those rights than had been the assignor plaintiff company. And if the obligation of the defendant company to pay £159 be regarded as a chose in action on its own it never in our view came into existence except subject to a right to set off the £124 as in effect payment in advance. That which became subject to the debenture charge was not £159 but the net claim sustainable by the plaintiff company of £35.'

There is indeed something to be said for the view that a debenture holder who authorises the continuation of the company's business, as distinct from merely the realisation of its assets, should be prepared to accept the normal incidents of

6 [1939] VLR 132.
7 [1974] QB 1, [1973] 1 All ER 394, CA.
8 [1974] QB 1, [1973] 1 All ER 394 at 6.

trading, including the possibility that its debtors may require rights of set off.[9] However that may be, where a lessor is indebted to a lessee who has mortgaged his property (including that debt) to a mortgagee by way of equitable assignment and that mortgagee thereafter causes a receiver to take control of that lessee and causes it to continue in occupation of the demised premises as lessee, a liability for rent subsequently incurred by the lessee may be offset against the debt which the lessor owes.[10]

When a receiver continues to perform a contract which was in existence at the time of his appointment claims under the contract which were in existence before the receivership can be set off against claims arising under the contract after the receivership has begun. This was the course taken by the Privy Council in *Parsons v Sovereign Bank of Canada*,[11] a case involving a receiver appointed by the court rather than by the debenture holder. Their Lordships did not expressly deal with the effect of the crystallisation of the floating charge. But the appointment of the receiver undoubtedly caused the charge to crystallise, even if it had not done so before. And on crystallisation any choses in action held by the company would pass to the debenture holders by way of equitable assignment. Accordingly the set-off solution in the case should be equally applicable where the receivership in question is constituted out of court. The company was a paper manufacturing company which had supplied the appellants with paper under numerous business contracts which were in existence when the court appointed receivers and managers of the company. On 14 June 1907, the receivers and managers had assigned amounts due from the appellants for paper delivered to them to the respondents. Three days later the receivers and managers repudiated the contracts with the appellants. On 27 July 1907, notice of the assignment made on 14 June was for the first time given to the appellants. The respondents as assignees from the receivers sued for the invoice price of the goods purchased by the appellants; the appellants claimed to set off against the purchase price damages for breach of contract. The set-off claim succeeded. The amount sued for was due under the old contracts with the company (which was responsible for the breach) and not under the new contracts with the receivers. A similar result was achieved in a Canadian case.[12] A defendant sought leave to file a defence and counterclaim alleging a set-off to a claim brought by a receiver in the name of the company. The claim was brought under a contract by which the plaintiff agreed to provide management services in connection with four condominium units. The defendant was permitted to claim a set-off with respect to claims which were liquidated at the time the debenture crystallised and to counterclaim in respect of matters which flowed out of and were inseparably connected with the contract which gave rise to the chose in action on which the plaintiff's suit was based. But the defendant was not granted leave to counterclaim in respect of claims arising out of contracts other than the one on which the plaintiff sued.[13]

---

9 *West Street Properties Pty Ltd v Jamison* [1974] 2 NSWLR 435 at 440E per Jeffrey J.
10 [1974] 2 NSWLR 435 at 441D.
11 [1913] AC 160, 82 LJPC 60, PC.
12 *Abacus Cities Ltd v Aboussafy* (1980) 34 CBRNS 195 (Alberta QB).
13 (1980) 34 CBR NS 195 at 199 per HJ Macdonald J.

Lack of mutuality

A creditor who contracts with the receiver cannot set off against the receiver a debt owed by the company prior to the receivership. The parties are not dealing with each other in the same right: there is no mutuality of beneficial interest. That was the position in *Rendell v Doors and Doors Ltd (in liquidation)*[14] where the appellant and the respondent company had, prior to the receivership, traded with each other. At the start of the receivership the receiver took accounts and found a balance to be owing by the company to the appellant. During the receivership the appellant purchased doors from the respondent to the value of $2,046 odd. The respondent sued the appellant for that sum and the appellant claimed to set off the balance found due to the appellant by the respondent at the start of the receivership. As Chilwell J observed, the debt owed by the company to the appellant in no way involved the debenture holder: the appellant was the legal and beneficial owner of that debt or chose in action.[15] On the other hand when the appellant purchased goods from the company during the receivership those goods were impressed with a charge in favour of the debenture holder. Likewise when the goods were sold to the appellant the choses in action consisting of the several debts owing by the appellant for the purchase price on such sale of goods were impressed with the same charge in favour of the debenture holder. The legal title to those choses in action was vested in the company; the beneficial title in the debenture holder until it had been paid off in full. It followed that there was no mutuality of beneficial interest until the debenture holder had been paid in full.[16]

Another illustration of disallowance of a set off because the two debtors were not in the same right is to be found in *Leichhardt Emporium Pty Ltd v AGC (Household Finance) Ltd.*[17] In this case, over a number of years the plaintiffs, a retailer selling from a number of shops, and a financier (AGC) had a business arrangement whereby the latter purchased goods from the former for cash and sold them on hire purchase or leased them to the former's customers. The retailer asked AGC to finance fixtures and fittings in a new store which it was opening and AGC then sold the retailer certain fixtures and fittings on terms. Thereafter the original arrangements continued. Then the retailer gave its bankers an equitable charge over all its assets, receivers were later appointed but the arrangement still continued. At the date of the proceedings the amount owed by the retailer to AGC for fixtures and fittings was exactly the same as the amount owed by AGC in relation to transactions all entered into after the appointment of the receiver in accordance with the original business arrangements. AGC sought to set off its debt against its liability to the plaintiff retailer.

Yeldham J rejected the claim to set off. The effect of the appointment of the receiver was that the AGC's debt owed to the retailer became in equity the property of the bank.[18] Accordingly, the two debts were not in the same right and

---

14 [1975] 2 NZLR 191.
15 [1975] 2 NZLR 191 at 201
16 [1975] 2 NZLR 191 at 202.
17 [1979] 1 NSWLR 701.
18 See *NW Robbie & Co Ltd v Witney Warehouse Co Ltd* [1963] 1 WLR 1324 at 1340; *Ferrier v Bottomer* (1972) 126 CLR 597; *West Street Properties Pty Ltd v Jamison* [1974] 2 NSWLR 435.

the one could not be set off against the other.[19] The two debts were not, he held, so intimately connected with one another that, in equity, set off would be allowed, even though the debt owed by AGC arose only after the equitable assignment.[20] It was argued that 'the intimate connection' test formulated in one of the textbooks[1] was erroneous and not supported by the cases[2] cited in support of the relevant textbook. Yeldham J declined to stigmatise the textbook statement as erroneous[3] although it does appear that the cases do not actually provide support for the statement. He regarded the two debts as being separate and independent, the one not conditional on the other, and 'connected' only in the sense that the parties had previously regularly done business with each other. The case was not one where the plaintiff's debt was incurred by or at the behest of the receiver, or in circumstances which gave the receiver or the debenture holder any benefit of significance.[4] The fact that AGC permitted the fixtures to remain in the premises, rather than repossess them upon default did not constitute a proper ground for set-off.[5]

In *West St Properties Pty Ltd v Jamison*[6] the court, at the invitation of the parties, determined the question of set-off by reference to assumed or admitted facts. The agreed facts were in outline as follows: (a) one of the defendants (Mainline) lent money to the plaintiff under a development agreement; (b) Mainline became the tenant of a portion of the building erected with the help of the loan; (c) the loan became repayable; (d) a receiver was appointed by a bank in whose favour Mainline had executed a mortgage debenture; (e) the receiver as agent of Mainline continued in possession under the lease; (f) rent owing by Mainline to the plaintiff in respect of a period after the appointment of the receiver was owing and unpaid; (g) Mainline declined to pay that rent on the ground that the original loan could be set-off against the unpaid rent. The question of law was whether there was any right of set off on these assumed facts. Jeffrey J held that there was a right of set-off. The plaintiff had argued by reference to *NW Robbie & Co Ltd v Witney Warehouse Co Ltd*[7] and *Lynch v Ardmore Studios (Ireland) Ltd*[8] that a pre-receivership claim could not be set off against a post-receivership indebtedness. The learned judge distinguished these two cases. They did not deal with the situation which existed in the case before him: indeed they were the very converse of it. And, he continued:

19 *NW Robbie & Co Ltd v Witney Warehouse Co Ltd*, above; *Felt and Textiles of New Zealand Ltd v R Hubrich Ltd (in receivership)* [1968] NZLR 716.
20 [1979] 1 NSWLR 701 at 709.
 1 *Kerr on Receivers* (14th edn) p 314; (15th edn) pp 327–328; (16th edn) p 309.
 2 *Collins v Jones* (1830) 10 B & C 777; *McKinnon v Armstrong Bros & Co* (1877) 2 App Cas 531, 36 LT 482, HL.
 3 [1979] 1 NSWLR 701 at 706.
 4 As in *West Street Properties Pty Ltd v Jamison* [1974] 2 NSWLR 435. Where a company in receivership incurred a liability for rent to a lessor which already owed money to that lessee, the rent being incurred for the benefit of the debenture holder; and see *Rendell v Doors and Doors Ltd (in liquidation)* [1975] 2 NZLR 191.
 5 [1979] 1 NSWLR 701 at 707.
 6 [1974] 2 NSWLR 435.
 7 [1963] 3 All ER 613, [1963] 1 WLR 1324, CA.
 8 [1966] IR 133.

'They are cases in which an unsecured creditor of a company has sought to obtain
payment of his debt in priority to the secured creditor by purporting to set it off
against a debt which he owes the company and which in equity belongs to the
secured creditor. An ordinary unsecured creditor of course has no priority over
the rights of the debenture-holder, even though his debt accrued due before the
date of crystallisation or, for that matter, before the date the debenture was given.
The receiver in those cases could not, consistently with his duties as such, pay the
claim which was sought to be set off. The disallowance of such a set-off is upon
a principle similar to that which prevents a cross-action for a legal debt from
being maintained against a plaintiff suing on behalf of an equitable chargee where
the substantial consequence of doing so would be to allow the defendant, as no
more than an unsecured creditor of the plaintiff, to defeat the equitable chargee's
security. But that is a very different case from one in which the receiver on behalf
of a secured creditor causes the company to collect an unsecured debt which in
equity belongs to that secured creditor by setting it off against a liability which
the company incurs. In a case where the debenture-holder elects after crystallisation to cause the company to carry on its business, debts, incurred to existing
debtors of the company in so doing may be met by the pro tanto collection of the
debts owed by them to the company by means of set-off. This is but a method of
recovery alternative to the taking of proceedings at law in the name of the
company, something which, as already observed, the debenture-holder has after
crystallisation, an undoubted right to do. For him to direct that a debt which he
owns should be applied in reduction or extinction of an indebtedness which the
company incurs is merely to exercise his dominion over it. It is one thing to say
that a set-off at law cannot be availed of to defeat or postpone a prior equitable
title to a debt, but quite another to say that it is not available to the equitable
owner who wishes to employ the legal rights over which he has control in order
to collect it.'

Jeffrey J was not satisfied that mutuality in beneficial interest was a universal
requirement in cases of set-off,[9] and he cited examples where courts of equity
had allowed set-off even where mutuality was absent.[10] But on the assumption
that mutuality was necessary he found it 'in the circumstances that the debenture
holder is the equitable owner of the debt owned by West Street and is the party
for whose ultimate benefit and at whose direction the debt owed to West Street is
being incurred'.[11] This concept of mutuality has rightly been described as 'somewhat expansive'.[12]

Crown set-off

All government departments are emanations of one legal entity, that is the
Crown.

The general rule at common law was that the subject could not set off a
debt claimed from the Crown against a debt due to the Crown and stems from

---

9   [1974] 2 NSWLR 435 at 441F.
10 *Ex p Stephens* (1805) 11 Ves 24; *Hamp v Jones* (1840) 9 LJ Ch 258; cf *Bechervaise v Lewis*
    (1872) LR 7 CP 372, 41 LJCP 161.
11 [1974] 2 NSWLR 435 at 441E.
12 Meagher Gummow and Lehane *Equity: Doctrines and Remedies* (3rd edn) para 2869.

the Crown's prerogative.[13] As Rowlatt J pointed out in *A-G v Guy Motors Ltd*:[14]

> 'At the back of the apparently hard rule that there can be no set off in this case[15] against the Crown there lies this fact, that the subject cannot make good a claim against the Crown except in a particular way that is by petition of right and any decision merely shows that he cannot get round that by refusing to pay a debt to the Crown and then asserting his claim by setting it off.'

Since 1947, the right to set off between the Crown and the subject has been governed in England by the Crown Proceedings Act 1947.

In relation to *liquidations* it has been held that the Crown is entitled to set off debits and credits even though they do not arise from contracts. In *Re DH Curtis (Builders) Ltd*[16] a company carrying on business as building contractors went into voluntary liquidation. Among its creditors it numbered the Revenue and the Department of Health and Social Security but at the same time it was owed a balance of excess input tax by the Commissioners of Customs and Excise. The position therefore was that the company was indebted to the Crown through two departments for certain taxes and the Crown through another department was indebted to the company for the repayment of another tax. It was conceded to be irrelevant that three separate government departments were involved. The relevant rules to be applied are those as to set off in bankruptcy which apply to the liquidation of insolvent companies by virtue of s 317 of the Companies Act 1948. It was argued on the strength of a dictum of Vaughan Williams J in *Re Mid-Kent Fruit Factory*[17] that the wording of the relevant bankruptcy section was restricted to mutual debts, mutual credits and mutual dealings which arise out of contract. Brightman J after a searching analysis of the cases in England and elsewhere concluded that the dictum of Vaughan Williams J was wrong. The purpose of the relevant section in the Bankruptcy Act 1914 was to do substantial justice between the debtor and the creditor. It should not therefore be construed as limiting the right of set off to contractual obligations.

The decision in *Re DH Curtis (Builders) Ltd* was approved in *Re Cushla Ltd*,[18] another case involving a company in liquidation.

Both cases it will be noted involved liquidations in which the mandatory provisions of s 31 of the Bankruptcy Act 1914 were imported by statute into the specific context of liquidation.

Again, in *RA Cullen Ltd v Nottingham Health Authority*,[19] the principle of mutuality applied. A health authority had plumbing work done for it and owed money for it to the company which went into liquidation. The company for its part was in debt to the Department of Health and Social Security in respect of arrears of national insurance contributions. This latter debt exceeded the sum due

---

13 *Re Cushla Ltd* [1979] 3 All ER 415, [1979] STC 615.
14 [1928] 2 KB 78 at 80; cf *Re Ind Coope & Co Ltd* [1911] 2 Ch 223 at 235–236.
15 Alleged agreement as to tax refund not set off against undisputed tax assessment.
16 [1978] Ch 162.
17 [1896] 1 Ch 567.
18 [1979] 3 All ER 415, [1979] STC 615.
19 (1986) 2 BCC 99.368, CA.

for the plumbing. Sir Denys Buckley who delivered the leading judgment held that the debts were both mutual: they were between the Crown and the company.

A further refinement is where the Crown is a preferential creditor and a non-preferential creditor but owes money to an insolvent company, as for example in respect of a refund of value added tax. That was the position in *Re Unit 2 Windows Ltd*.[20] The debt owed by the company was to the Department of Health and Social Security and was in part preferential. Walton J held[1] that what is now r 4.90 of the Insolvency Rules had not anticipated such a 'conundrum' and that 'the only logical and sensible solution' was to spread the refund due rateably between the preferential and non-preferential ingredients of the debt.

The position regarding Crown set off in a corporate *receivership* is far from clear. Certainly the Crown, when sued in the name of a government department, may not without leave of the court avail itself of any set-off if the subject matter of the set-off does not relate to the same department.[2] Likewise no set-off may be made or counterclaim pleaded without leave of the court where the Crown is suing for payment in the name of one government department and the set-off or counterclaim is sought by the receiver against another department. But the provisions of s 31 of the Bankruptcy Act 1914 were not applicable to a company in receivership: they apply only to the winding up of solvent companies. Moreover although roughly the same order of preference is accorded to creditors in a receivership as would apply in a winding up the provision which effects that result makes no express mention of the liquidation rules relating to Crown set off.

Lien

A floating security constitutes an incomplete assignment of the assets charged. That incomplete assignment becomes converted into an equitable assignment of those assets and the company's rights. The equitable assignment is subject to pre-existing equities and also to other rights given by the company to outside parties under ordinary trading contracts. On principle crystallisation of a charge on property including property subject to a subsisting lien[3] would leave the receiver unable to assert the debenture holder's interest in priority to the lien.

The principle was extended in *George Barker (Transport) Ltd v Eynon*[4] to a contractual lien. In that case carriers who contracted under the Standard Conditions of the Road Haulage Association were owed over £3,000 by a company for work done over several months. They nevertheless agreed to carry a further load, worth over £7,000, for a charge of £58. After the contract was made but before the carriers had taken delivery of the load at the docks a receiver

20 [1985] 3 All ER 647, [1985] 1 WLR 1383.
 1 Not following *Re EJ Morel Ltd* [1962] Ch 21.
 2 Crown Proceedings Act 1947, s 35(2).
 3 *Re British Tea Table Co (1897) Ltd* (1909) 101 LT 707. Even though the lien claimant may have been aware of the floating charge when he obtained possession: *Brunton v Electrical Engineering Corpn* [1892] 1 Ch 434.
 4 [1974] 1 All ER 900, [1974] 1 WLR 462, CA.

and manager was appointed over the company's undertaking. The Court of Appeal held that the completed equitable assignment on crystallisation was subject to rights already given by the company to outside parties under ordinary trading contracts. These rights included the general contractual lien that became exercisable when the carriers got actual possession of the load. In this connection, Stamp LJ declared: 'contractual rights come into existence at the time of the contract erecting them, notwithstanding that they may not be exercisable on the happening of a future event.'[5]

As one commentator has pointed out a general lien is the right to retain goods until the owner has paid money that is due, which is often for services rendered by the claimant in respect of those and other goods but which may have been in respect of other matters.[6] A lien cannot be claimed, in default of agreement to the contrary, until the services have been rendered.[7] The carrier or other contractor must, therefore, either fully perform his part of the contract before he claims his lien or obtain the agreement of the receiver to a term that he may claim the lien before he would otherwise be entitled to do so. Mocatta J found that such a term was necessarily implied in the particular agreement between the receiver and the carriers when they agreed that the receiver would in any event pay the £58 and would pay the additional £3,000 if the carriers proved they were entitled to claim the lien.[8] The lesson for contractors is plain; first they should do their utmost to secure a special agreement 'advancing' the lien in point of time; otherwise they should complete the carriage to the destination and there withhold delivery for 'a brief and quasi-symbolic period' before they can claim their lien. The receiver's counsel of perfection is both to repudiate and, if he can, physically prevent the contractor from obtaining possession of the goods in pursuance of his contract.[9]

The general lien that was asserted in *Brunton v Electrical Engineering Corpn*[10] in respect of the title deeds of company which had gone into receivership was a solicitor's lien in respect of fees incurred after the receivership. The lien in question did not fall within the prohibitive restriction against the creation of subsequent charges because it was created not by the company but by operation of law.

The primary point at issue in *Majeau Carrying Co Pty Ltd v Coastal Rutile Ltd*[11] was whether the appellant company was entitled to a lien over goods which it still held to secure the payment of cartage and storage charges due in respect of goods which it no longer held. The evidence failed to establish any local trade custom and the majority rejected the existence of any common law

---

5 [1974] 1 WLR 462 at 473B. See also *De Lorean Motor Cars Ltd v Northern Irish Carriers Ltd* [1982] NI 163.

6 Michael Tugendhat 'Receiver/Contractor Relationships – Businessmen should be wary of inducements' [1974] LMCLQ 39 at 40–41.

7 See *Wiltshire Iron Co Ltd v Great Western Rly Co* (1871) LR 6 QB 776; Mocatta J (at first instance) said that he 'would have felt constrained to follow it, albeit with regret' [1973] 3 All ER 374 at 379A.

8 [1973] 3 All ER 374 at 379.

9 [1974] 1 WLR 462 at 473 per Stamp LJ.

10 [1892] 1 Ch 434.

11 (1973) 129 CLR 48, HC of A.

lien independent of custom.[12] The respondent company's receiver and manager therefore succeeded in a claim to recover the goods in question. The receiver and manager failed however in the cross-appeal for repayment of two amounts which he had paid to the appellant. The first amount was an overpayment in connection with a pre-receivership debt and the second was a duplicated payment of a post-receivership debt. The appellant had appropriated the over-payment towards pre-receivership debts other than those intended to be paid by the receiver, and such set off (it was held) could not be disturbed. As for the duplicated payment, the court held that in the absence of any express or implied agreement it could be applied in paying a pre-receivership liability. The moral of the tale is clear. If a receiver and manager goes on dealing with the company's creditors he should specifically earmark the payments he makes as payments of the debts intended to be cleared. Failure on his part to do this may enable a creditor to set off overpayments or accidental payments against debts which the creditor would otherwise have to pursue in the winding-up.

Assume however that possession is obtained by the claimant *after* the charge has crystallised. In such a case the lien will only prevail over the debenture if the company had express, implied or ostensible authority from the debenture holder to allow a lien to arise.[13] A claimant who on taking possession is already aware that the charge has crystallised cannot, in the absence of some express provision such as has been mentioned, assert his lien against the fixed chargee's interest.[14] But if after crystallisation the chargee expressly or impliedly authorises work giving rise to a lien he may be giving that lien priority.

Where the debenture deed does in fact contain a prohibition on the creation of liens a person who has actual or constructive knowledge of the contents of the debenture will be precluded from asserting the priority of his lien unless he can show that the debenture holder assented to the company's action giving rise to the lien.[15]

HIVING DOWN

Description and purpose

An increasingly common practice in company receiverships[16] is to carry out a 'hiving down' operation. The purpose of such an arrangement is to segregate the saleable assets of the company into a clean package, free of obligations whether to staff or creditors, which will be more readily saleable and which if

12 Gibbs J considered that even if there had been a lien at common law it had been abolished and not revived: (1973) 129 CLR 48 at 51.
13 Ie whether there is a clause *prohibiting* the creation of a lien: see *Williams v Allsup* (1861) 10 CBNS 417; *Tappenden v Artus* [1964] 2 QB 185, [1963] 3 All ER 213, CA; *Fisher v Automobile Finance Co of Australia Ltd* (1928) 41 CLR 167, [1928] VLR 496; *Lombard Australia Ltd v Wells Park Motors Pty Ltd* [1960] VR 693.
14 *Brown v Associated British Motors Ltd* [1932] NZLR 655.
15 *Albemarle Supply Co Ltd v Hind & Co* [1928] 1 KB 307, CA.
16 Occasionally also in liquidations.

the transaction is correctly effected may bring to the purchaser certain fiscal advantages.[17] By this means the economically viable part of the business is separated from the unviable part, assets pass without liabilities, and continuity of employment is secured. Occasionally such an agreement is dubbed a 'hiving off' agreement[18] but the expression 'hiving down', though less elegant, accurately describes the process of segregating the saleable assets downwards into a subsidiary. The subsidiary is usually acquired off the peg by the company acting by its receiver, but may be an existing subsidiary.[19] Once the process of hiving down is complete the receiver will at an appropriate time sell the shareholding in the subsidiary, now owning the 'hived down' business, to a purchaser. The consideration to be given by the subsidiary to the receiver for the segregated assets may be shares, or may be such sum as a named firm of accountants 'acting as experts and not as arbitrators shall in due course upon request of either of the parties [to the agreement] certify to be a fair and proper consideration'.[20]

The purchase price to be paid by the subsidiary is usually expressed to be payable on demand. But the demand will not be made until a purchaser has been found for the business. When such a purchaser has been found the receiver will sell the company's shareholding in the subsidiary to the purchaser and the purchaser will pump sufficient cash into the subsidiary to enable it to pay its parent company the consideration specified in the hiving down agreement. The classic end of the operation is the adoption by the company owning the hived down business of a new name, resembling the old name, so as to capitalise on any residual reputation. The appearance is then of 'a phoenix risen from the ashes of the old company'.

Varying methods

There are of course various ways in which a hiving down may be structured. Some versions of the operation leave the employees in the service of their original master; they are then made available at a charge to the hived down company. In other versions the employees are taken over by the hived down company. For reasons which will appear[1] the former variety is the more usual.

Historically, hiving down was a procedure devised to enable a receiver to continue to trade even though an unsecured creditor is intent upon forcing a liquidation. It first came into vogue in the 1950s and gained additional attraction when tax legislation provided that the trading losses of an insolvent company could be transferred to a subsidiary:[2] at the time this represented a particular attraction to purchasers of the subsidiary. But the tax advantages have been progressively eroded.

---

17 *Pambakian v Brentford Nylons Ltd* [1978] ICR 665 at 669H–670, EAT per Phillips J.
18 [1978] ICR 665 at 668G.
19 As in *Re Foster Clark Ltd's Indenture Trusts* [1966] 1 All ER 43, [1966] 1 WLR 125.
20 *Pambakian v Brentford Nylons Ltd* [1978] ICR 665 at 669B.
1 See at p 190 below.
2 Finance Act 1954, s 17.

The method of carrying out the hiving down will need to meet the circumstances of the particular case and reference should be made to the practice manuals for practical advice in this regard.[3]

Potential disadvantages

The practice of hiving down is not without its disadvantages. First, of course, the formalities must be carefully carried out. Secondly, there are now certain unattractive fiscal consequences. On the subsidiary leaving the group there will be corporation tax on capital gains arising on a re-opening of the previous transaction. The purchaser will be likely to seek an indemnity against this liability, while the receiver will be equally likely to resist such a request. The result is often a reduction in the purchase price, an unattractive attribute of this method of sale. Relief for prior tax losses may also be at risk:[4] this too is a further disadvantage.

3 See particularly the excellent discussion in Chilvers and Shewell *Receivership Manual* (2nd edn, 1983) pp 36–38, 64–65.
4 For a discussion of some of the tax problems, see at pp 636–640 below.

CHAPTER 12

Rights of employees under contracts of employment

INTRODUCTION

The rights of employees in the event of a company going into receivership are clearly a matter of the greatest importance both to the employees and to the receiver and manager concerned.[1] Employees will want to know where they stand so that they can do whatever they can to cushion the blow. In particular they will need to know from what date the termination of employment takes place. These matters are of interest and concern to the receiver also both in his dealings with employees and in his financial and management decisions. The position is in certain areas covered by statute, and so far as the United Kingdom is concerned by regulations[2] seeking to implement an EEC Directive. The main areas for analysis are (i) if and when any relevant contract of employment is terminated, (ii) the relevant remedies available to dismissed employees, (iii) the preferential claims of employees, (iv) redundancy fund payments, and (v) residual rights enjoyed by employees.

TERMINATION OF EMPLOYMENT

The general rule is that an out of court appointment[3] of a receiver and manager as agent of the company does not of itself automatically terminate contracts of

---

1 The topic has attracted considerable attention over the last two decades: see David Pollard *Corporate Insolvency Employment and Pension Rights* (2000) and for earlier comment GTE Parsons and WF Ratford *Employees' Rights in Receiverships and Liquidations* (2nd edn, 1984); P Davies and M Freedland 'The Effect of Receiverships upon Employees of Companies' (1980) 9 ILJ 95–113; Diana Kloss and David Milman 'The Rights of Employees on Corporate Insolvency' [1982] Conv 99–117; John McMullen *Business Transfers and Employee Rights* (1987); Grunfeld *Law of Redundancy* (1990).
2 Transfer of Undertakings (Protection of Employment) Regulations 1981, SI 1981/1794.
3 The appointment of a receiver by the court terminates contracts of employment: *Reid v Explosives Co Ltd* (1887) 19 QBD 264, CA; but see for a modern questioning of this principle, *International Harvester Export Co v International Harvester (Australia) Ltd* (1983) 7 ACLR 391.

employment. This was first recognised by Plowman J in *Re Foster Clark Ltd's Indenture Trusts*,[4] who said:

> 'At first sight there appears to be no very good reason why the appointment out of court of a receiver who is agent of the company should determine contracts of employment.'

Indeed there are two very good reasons for the general rule. First, despite the appointment, the company retains the legal title to its assets; secondly, there is the business reality that the employees continue to work at the same premises as part of the same business.[5] There are, however, several recognised exceptions (or qualifications) to the general principle which were emphasised by Lawson J in *Griffiths v Secretary of State for Social Services*.[6]

Thus if the receiver sells off or hives down the business to a purchaser as happened in *Re Foster Clark Ltd's Indenture Trusts*,[7] that act will, at common law, automatically terminate the employees' contracts of employment, though this will not necessarily occur if only *part* of the business is disposed of.[8] The effect of hiving down on employees was the subject matter of judicial[9] as well as academic criticism and has been affected by the Transfer of Undertakings (Protection of Employment) Regulations 1981 discussed below.

The dictum was, however, applied by Pennycuick J in *Re Mack Trucks (Britain) Ltd*[10] where the point directly arose, and later cases have confirmed the existence of a general rule[11] which applies also to the actual or ostensible authority of a solicitor to act for the company.[12]

However, the general rule yields (as such rules usually do) to exceptions. So far three exceptions have been identified.[13] The first qualification of the general proposition is where the appointment is accompanied by a sale or 'hiving down' of the business: the sale or hiving down operates to terminate contracts of employment because there is no longer any business for which the employees can work.[14] That in effect was what happened in *Re Foster Clark Ltd*[15] where the sale was to a subsidiary. But the same would apply where the sale is to a new company incorporated for the very purpose of taking over the business. Secondly, the appointment may have the effect of terminating the contract of

---

4 [1966] 1 WLR 125 at 132. There were textbook statements of such a rule in Hooper *Receivers for Debenture Holders* (1933) p 20; *Palmer's Company Law* (20th edn) p 419 and *Kerr on Receivers* (13th edn) p 315.

5 *Deaway Trading Ltd v Calverley* [1973] 3 All ER 776, [1973] ICR 546 per Sir John Donaldson P.

6 [1974] QB 468, [1973] 3 All ER 1184.

7 [1966] 1 All ER 43, [1966] 1 WLR 125.

8 *Pambakian v Brentford Nylons Ltd* [1978] ICR 665, EAT.

9 [1978] ICR 665 at 673 per Phillips J who called for parliamentary review; cf the cautious reservation of position by Slynn J in *Migwain Ltd v Transport and General Workers Union* [1979] ICR 597 at 600.

10 [1967] 1 All ER 977, [1967] 1 WLR 780.

11 *Deaway Trading Ltd v Calverley* [1973] 3 All ER 776, [1973] ICR 546, NIRC; *Griffiths v Secretary of State for Social Services* [1974] QB 468, [1973] 3 All ER 1184.

12 *Re Peek Winch & Tod Ltd* (1979) 129 NLJ 494, CA.

13 *Griffiths v Secretary of State for Social Services* [1974] QB 468 at 485–486.

14 [1974] QB 468.

15 [1966] 1 All ER 43, [1966] 1 WLR 125.

employment if the receiver and manager enters into a new agreement with a particular employee that may be inconsistent with the continuation of his old service contract. That is an exceptional case indicated but not ruled upon in *Re Mack Trucks (Britain) Ltd*,[16] by Pennycuick J whose obiter dictum was echoed by Lawson J in *Griffiths v Secretary of State for Social Services*:[17] the contract of employment is superseded and ex hypothesi terminated.

A third situation is where the continuation of the employees' services is inconsistent with the role and functions of the receiver and manager. This possibility was recognised by Pennycuick J in *Re Mack Trucks (Britain) Ltd*[18] and followed by Lawson J in the *Griffiths* case, where however the managing director was, on the facts, not in conflict with the role and functions of the receiver who had been appointed.[19] The position where the receiver retains workers without comment is not clear;[20] but where he varies the contractual terms materially he makes himself personally liable.[1]

If the receiver and manager is acting as agent for the debenture holders the appointment will, it is conceived, probably terminate the company's contracts of employment. There is no clear judicial authority for this proposition, which has nevertheless some textbook support.[2] The case of *Hopley Dodd v Highfield Motors (Derby) Ltd*[3] is sometimes cited as authority for the proposition.[4] The issue in that case was whether the employee was entitled to statutory compensation in the form of a redundancy payment. She qualified if the appointment of a receiver and manager automatically determined her employment but did not qualify if her employment continued after the appointment and was ended by mutual agreement. The industrial tribunal decided that her employment had indeed automatically terminated on the appointment by the debenture holders of a receiver and manager. It is not clear whether the receiver and manager was agent for the company. If there was an agency clause the decision is heterodox.

DISMISSAL REMEDIES

The first remedy that any dismissed employee should consider is his or her remedy for wrongful dismissal. If the dismissal amounts to a repudiation of the

16 [1967] 1 WLR 780 at 787.
17 [1974] QB 468 at 486.
18 [1967] 1 WLR 780 at 786.
19 See the analysis of JH Farrar 'Recent Developments in the Law of Receivers' (1975) JBL at 29–30. Normally there might be a conflict. But if the managing director is, factually, under tight control by the board a receivership will not necessarily dismiss him.
20 *Re Mack Trucks (Britain) Ltd* [1967] 1 All ER 977, [1967] 1 WLR 780.
 1 [1967] 1 All ER 977, [1967] 1 WLR 780; and see *O'Rourke v Cork* (1977) an industrial tribunal decision summarised in Parsons and Ratford *Employees' Rights in Receiverships and Liquidations* (1984) (no material variation).
 2 See Hooper *Receivers for Debenture Holders* (1933) 21; *Kerr on Receivers and Administrators* (17th edn) p 415.
 3 (1969) 4 ITR 289.
 4 See James O'Donovan 'Corporate Redundancy' (1976) 4 ABLR 257 at 262–263; Grunfeld *Law of Redundancy* (3rd edn, 1989) pp 84–85 assumes that the receiver and manager was agent for the debenture holders.

contract there is a civil remedy in damages.[5] The fact that the dismissal was involuntary, as in the case of the automatic displacement of the de facto controller of the company by a receiver and manager with plenary powers, is no answer.[6] But of course the employee must mitigate his loss,[7] by accepting any offer of engagement on comparable terms or by looking elsewhere. In many cases the civil remedy may prove a cold comfort particularly if the company goes into liquidation and his claim is reduced to that of an unsecured creditor.

The remedy for wrongful dismissal is also of value when the receiver on his own personal responsibility retains the employee and then wrongfully dismisses the employee. The latter can then sue the receiver personally.

The question whether an employee can bring an action for unfair dismissal, because for example he has been unfairly selected for redundancy[8] or been dismissed as a result of a transfer of business[9] or because the company has failed to observe the statutory consultation periods[10] is an open one. In a case involving a claim for unfair dismissal when a company went into voluntary liquidation the claim (based on a lack of proper notice) failed.[11] The tribunal doubted 'very much if there can be an unfair dismissal in the case of a properly conducted entry into liquidation'.[12] Certainly if an employee's contract of employment is automatically terminated by the appointment of a receiver, in other words by operation of law, there can be no claim for unfair dismissal.

The receiver may decide on his appointment to try and make a go of the company's business, for that purpose retaining the existing staff and workforce. If he is later driven to dispense with their services they can claim redundancy payments in respect of this later dismissal; and, for the purposes of assessing the quantum of that award their periods of employment both before and after the start of the receivership will be taken into account.[13]

With this latter example may be contrasted the position of staff and workforce who are re-engaged in the employment of the receiver (and not of the company). If they are subsequently dismissed they run the risk of losing their redundancy payments unless they have worked for the receiver for more than two years.[14] And their previous service will not count in the assessment of any award.

Provided that a company employee has been employed by the company for at least two years[15] he is entitled to bring a claim for a redundancy payment because

5 *General Billposting Co Ltd v Atkinson* [1909] AC 118, 78 LJ Ch 77, HL.
6 *Reigate v Union Manufacturing Co (Ramsbottom) Ltd* [1918] 1 KB 592, 87 LJKB 724, CA.
7 *Re Gramophone Records Ltd* [1930] WN 42 at 43.
8 See Employment Rights Act 1966 (ERA 1996), s 105.
9 Transfer of Undertakings (Protection of Employment) Regulations 1981, reg 8.
10 Trade Union and Labour Relations (Consolidation) Act 1992, s 188; and see Collective Redundancy and Transfer of Undertakings (Protection of Employment) (Amendment) Regulations 1999, SI 1999 No 1925.
11 *Fox Bros (Clothes) Ltd v Bryant* [1979] ICR 64, EAT.
12 Neither is to be taken to have adopted a contract of employment by reason of anything done or omitted to be done within 14 days after his appointment: IA 1986, s 37(2) (non-administrative receiver); IA 1986, s 44(2) (administrative receiver).
13 IA 1986, s 37(1)(a) (non-administrative receiver); IA 1986, s 44(a)(b) (administrative receiver).
14 They are bound by the decision of the House of Lords in *Powdrill v Watson* [1995] 2 AC 394.
15 [1979] ICR 64 at 67 per Kilner Brown J (EAT).

the mere fact that employment is no longer available or the company going into receivership constitutes constructive dismissal.[16] A fortiori he can bring such a claim if he has been expressly dismissed. A redundancy award, it should be noted, does not qualify as a preferential debt on a distribution of the company's assets. But payment of the award is guaranteed by the state if the employing company fails to pay it.[17]

If a receiver, acting for the company or personally makes an employee redundant that employee will be eligible for a redundancy payment. And if the company goes into receivership then the employees concerned will be entitled to redundancy payments unless the receiver offers them further employment on equally advantageous terms.[18] What constitute equally advantageous terms in this connection depend on the circumstances of each case[19] and the normal principles of construction of contracts.[20]

PERSONAL LIABILITY OF RECEIVER AFTER APPOINTMENT

Introduction

The position of receivers and managers in regard to contracts of employment with a company's employees has had a varied and dramatic history. Awareness of this history is vital to a proper understanding of the current state of the law in this country. Case law rules have been overlaid by statutory reforms which were found to be flawed and there has been further statutory intervention.

There is now a distinction between the respective liabilities of an administrative receiver and those of a non-administrative receiver and manager. Each continues to be personally liable on any contract of employment adopted[1] by him in the carrying out of his receivership functions.[2]

But as a result of amendments urgently introduced in 1994 statute now provides that an administrative receiver (but not a non-administrative receiver) is personally liable only to the extent of any qualifying liability.[3]

The decision in Nicoll v Cutts

The *fons et origo* or fountainhead of all the legislative concern was the decision of the Court of Appeal in 1985 in the case of *Nicoll v Cutts*.[4] It was there held that a receiver appointed out of court had no personal liability for the remuneration of employees retained after his appointment. The employee in that case was at the

16 *Re Mack Trucks (Britain) Ltd* [1967] 1 All ER 977, [1967] 1 WLR 780; *Deaway Trading Ltd v Calverley* [1973] 3 All ER 776, [1973] ICR 546.
17 ERA 1996, s 155.
18 ERA 1996, s 155.
19 ERA 1996, s 139.
20 ERA 1996, s 166.
 1 ERA 1996, ss 141 and 146.
 2 See *Taylor v Kent County Council* [1969] 2 QB 560, [1969] 2 All ER 1080.
 3 *Atkins v Davis* (1970) 5 ITR 203; *Secretary of State for Employment v Rooney* [1977] ICR 440.
 4 [1985] BCLC 322, 1 BCC 99,427, CA.

time of the relevant appointment in hospital as a result of an accident. The receiver visited him in hospital on several occasions but did not dismiss him until two months after his appointment. The question before the court was whether the employee could claim the shortfall between the money paid to him from a redundancy fund and his salary until dismissal. The Court of Appeal held that the appointment of a receiver out of court[5] did not operate as a dismissal: the receiver being the agent of the company, there was no change in the personality of the employer. An appointment in such circumstances, it was held, had no effect on ordinary service contracts and so there was no new contract on which the employee could sue the receiver.

Amendment of insolvency legislation

In order to reverse or mitigate the perceived mischief of *Nicoll v Cutts* two amendments were proposed to the insolvency legislation which found favour. In their present form both the relevant provisions, which deal respectively with non-administrative and administrative receivers, specify that the receiver in each case 'is personally liable on any contract entered into by him in the carrying out of his functions (except in so far as the contract otherwise provides) and on any contract of employment adopted by him in the carrying out of those functions'.[6] It was further provided that such a receiver was not to be taken to have adopted a contract of employment by reason of anything done or omitted to be done within 14 days after his appointment.[7]

Administrative receiver

Meaning of 'adopt'

The precise effect of the meaning of the words 'any contract of employment adopted by' the receiver occasioned considerable discussion.[8] Finally, *quietus* of a kind was achieved, as with dust or powder on swarming bees,[9] by the decision of the Court of Appeal in *Re Paramount Airways Ltd (No 3)*.[10] This unwelcome decision involved an administrator and not a receiver but the concept of adoption of contracts of employment occurs in both scenarios. The Court of Appeal held that adoption could occur simply through the retention of staff without changing the terms of their employment. Prior to that, there had grown up a practice on the part of receivers of issuing a letter disclaiming both personal liability and any adoption of the contracts of employment. The practice of issuing a letter which

---

5 It is otherwise in the case of a court appointment: *Reid v Explosives Co Ltd* (1887) 19 QBD 264.
6 IA 1986, ss 44(1)(b) (administrative receiver) and 37(1)(a) (non-administrative receiver).
7 IA 1986, ss 44(3) (administrative receiver) and 37(3) (non-administrative receiver).
8 For the main protagonists in the debate see the second edition of this book at p 149, n 5.
9 See Virgil Georgics IV 86–87: *Hi motus animorum atque haec certamina tanta Pulveris exigui iactu compressa quiescent.*
10 [1994] BCC 172, CA; affirmed by the House of Lords in *Powdrill v Watson* [1995] 2 AC 394.

was thought to do the trick of negativing adoption was based on the unreported and aberrant decision of Harman J in *Re Specialised Mouldings Ltd.*[11] When announcing his decision upholding a disclaimer letter the judge said his written reasons would follow (the case was a test case). But he never gave his reasons in writing or otherwise, and eventually is understood to have declined to do so because the time limited for appeal had expired and he had been told that no appeal was contemplated. Nevertheless, news of this (as it appeared) successful ploy quickly spread and what became known Specialised Mouldings letters became commonplace.

The transparent sham of retaining staff on the same terms but with the issue of a *Specialised Mouldings* letter[12] unilaterally disclaiming adoption or personal liability would, in the words of Professor Goode 'drive a coach and horse' through the relevant section of the Insolvency Act 1986 and deprive it of any significant meaning.[13] And that view was shared by the Court of Appeal in *Re Paramount Airways (No 3)*. In the trenchant words of Dillon LJ 'the mere assertion by the administrator or receiver[14] that he is not adopting the contracts is mere wind with no legal effect because adoption is a matter not merely of words but of fact'.[15] Accordingly, where a receiver, in a '*Specialised Mouldings*' type letter, in fact treats a contract of employment as remaining in force, despite protestations to the contrary, reality overrides mumbo jumbo. To continue the metaphor, a unilateral incantation cannot cast an effective spell over an obvious reality.

Effect of the Paramount Airways decision

The effect of the decision of the Court of Appeal in *Re Paramount Airways (No 3)* was that administrative receivers who retained staff beyond the initial 14-day period for reflection exposed themselves to personal liability for all accrued and current rights arising under the relevant contracts of employment. That exposure caused consternation among those insolvency practitioners who did administrative receivership work and remedial legislation in the shape of an Insolvency Act 1994 was swiftly introduced.[16]

---

11 (13 February 1987, unreported) but noted in 3 IL&P 123 and discussed in Stewart *Administrative Receivers and Administrators* (1987) pp 96–99, para 512.

12 Goode *Principles of Corporate Insolvency Law* p 102.

13 No distinction can be drawn between the meaning of the word 'adopts' in IA 1986, s 44 (administrative receiver) and in IA 1986, s 19 (administrator): see *Re Leyland DAF Ltd and Re Ferranti International plc* [1994] BCC 658 per Lightman J following the obiter dicta in *Re Paramount Airways (No 3)* [1994] BCC 172, CA and not the view of Evans Lombe J at first instance.

14 *Re Paramount Airways (No 3)* [1994] BCC 172, CA at 180B.

15 The whole saga is dealt with in Mudd (1994) 10 IL&P 38 and in (1995) 11 IL&P 78; and see also Paul Davies 'Employee Claims in Insolvency: Corporate Rescues and Preferential Claims' (1994) 23 ILJ 141–150.

16 This includes 'any sums which, if they had been paid, would have been treated for the purposes of the enactments relating to social security as earnings in respect of that period': IA 1986, s 44(2D).

The 1994 reforms

The gist of the legislation was that where, on or after 15 March 1994, a contract of employment is adopted by an administrative receiver he will only become personally answerable for 'qualifying liabilities'.

Qualifying liabilities

A liability under a contract of employment is a qualifying liability if it is a liability to pay a sum of money by way of wages or salary or contributions to an occupational pension scheme, is incurred while the administrative receiver is in office and is in respect of services rendered wholly or partly after the adoption of the contract.[17] Where the services are rendered partly before and partly after the adoption of the contract of employment, the personal liability of the administrative receiver will only extend to so much of the sum as is payable in respect of services rendered after the adoption.[18] Wages or salary payable in respect of a period of holiday[19] or absence from work through sickness or other good cause are deemed to be wages or (as the case may be) salary in respect of services rendered during that period.[20] So too a sum payable in lieu of holiday money is deemed to be wages or (as the case may be) salary in respect of services rendered in the period by reference to which his holiday entitlement arose.[1]

On the other hand, if he adopts the employment contracts he is not entitled to the relief extended to the administrative receiver by virtue of which the administrative receiver is answerable only for 'qualifying liabilities'.

Time for decision on adoption

A further important aspect of the statutory provision is that it expressly provides that 'the administrative receiver is not to be taken to have adopted a contract of employment by reason of anything done or omitted to be done within 14 days after his appointment'.[2] These words give the receiver a breathing space or period of grace in which to cogitate and make a final decision on adoption or non-adoption. Plainly any interim decision to continue the contracts over the preliminary period will not bind the receiver if at the end of the period he determines not to adopt the contracts of employment.[3]

But what if the interests of the receivership require the receiver to commit himself to adopt the contracts without delay, because, for example, that is the only way of holding on to key employees? In those circumstances, it has been suggested, it is not sensible to read the section as denying full recognition and

---

17 IA 1986, s 44(2C)(a).
18 IA 1986, s 44(2C)(b).
19 (1985) 9 ACLR 825 at 827.
20 There was no question of any appeal and in the event the final judgment was never delivered.
 1 (13 February 1987, unreported). See Stewart *Administrative Receivers and Administrators* (1987) pp 97–99.
 2 See IA 1986, s 44(3).
 3 IA 1986, s 44(3).

effect to a *final* decision to adopt the contract within the two-week period.[4] As against this it is to be noted that the wording of the statute appears to be absolute in terms: 'the administrative receiver is not to be taken to have adopted a contract of employment by reason of *anything* done or omitted to be done within 14 days after his appointment.'[5] The safer course would appear to be for the position to be confirmed at the expiry of the 14-day period.

Non-administrative receiver

A non-administrative receiver (in other words, a receiver or manager appointed under powers contained in an instrument) is, to the same extent as if he had been appointed by order of the court, personally liable on any contract of employment adopted by him in the performance of his functions[6] and he is also entitled in respect of that liability to indemnity out of the assets.[7] It is to be noted that this provision purports to equate the position of such a receiver to a court-appointed receiver[8] so far as personal liability is concerned. The manner in which this is done is by providing that personal liability accrues by reference to his 'adoption' of the previous contract of employment and he is given in any event the same 14-day breathing space to decide on adoption or non-adoption as an administrative receiver is given. The same considerations therefore apply as in the case of an administrative receiver.[9] What constitutes adoption is in both cases the same and the extent of the indemnity is the same.

PREFERENTIAL PAYMENTS

Reference must here be made to the preferential status enjoyed by employees in relation to unpaid remuneration and holiday remuneration due to them at the moment when a company goes into receivership. The question of preferential payments generally is dealt with elsewhere.[10] For present purposes it is, at this point, convenient simply to list the particular types of remuneration upon which preferential status is conferred by the Insolvency Act 1986. The particular preferential status results in the particular payments taking priority to debenture holders secured by a floating charge, both where the company is in receivership[11] or in liquidation.[12]

---

4 See Lightman and Moss *Law of Receivers of Companies* (2nd edn, 1992).
5 IA 1986, s 44(3) (emphasis added).
6 IA 1986, s 37(1)(a).
7 IA 1986, s 37(1)(b).
8 IA 1986, s 37(1). For the position of a court-appointed receiver (who is a principal and not an agent) see *Strapp v Bull Sons & Co* [1895] 2 Ch 1, CA; *Re Glasdir Copper Mines Ltd* [1906] 1 Ch 365, CA; *Moss Steamship Co v Whinney* [1912] AC 254, especially at 259 and 271, HL.
9 See at pp 183–184, above.
10 See at p 262.
11 IA 1986, s 40 and Sch 6, paras 9–15.
12 IA 1986, s 386.

The payments recognised by the Insolvency Act 1986 as deserving of preference are:

(a)   Unpaid salaries for the four months preceding the receivership up to a maximum of £800. Overtime rates[13] and salaries based on commission[14] are included under this head.

(b)   Accrued holiday remuneration.

To this list the Employment Protection (Consolidation) Act 1978 followed by the Employment Rights Act 1996 (ERA 1996) added the following:

(c)   Guarantee payments.

(d)   Medical suspension payments.

(e)   Time off payments.

(f)   Protective awards.[15]

These matters are all considered in more detail elsewhere in this work.[16]

The true test of an employee is that he is employed under a contract of service and his employer retains the right to control the work.[17] For that reason a sub-contractor engaged under a contract for services is not within the preferential class.[18] Hence a building contractor 'on the lump' has no preferential claim.[19]

REDUNDANCY FUND PAYMENTS FROM NATIONAL INSURANCE FUND

When a receiver and manager is duly appointed of the undertaking of a company, the company as employer is treated as 'insolvent' for the purposes of section 184 of the Employment Rights Act 1996.[20] This means that the employee may be able to mount a claim for a payment by the Secretary of State from the National Insurance fund in respect of certain specific preferential debts up to certain limits. A pre-condition of acceptance by the Secretary of State of the relevant claim is that the receiver has made the necessary statement that there is an apparent debt outstanding to the employee on the appropriate date.[1]

13 *Northland Fisheries Ltd v WA Scott & Sons Ltd* [1975] CCL 3113, 56 DLR (3d) 319.
14 *Re Earle's Shipbuilding and Engineering Co Ltd* [1901] WN 78.
15 Employment Protection (Consolidation) Act 1978, s 121; ERA 1996, Sch 1 para 29.
16 See at p 261, below.
17 See the Australian cases of *Zuijs v Wirth Bros Pty Ltd* (1955) 93 CLR 561, [1956] ALR 123; *Graham v Bentley* (1959) 76 WNNSW 603; *Australian Mutual Provident Society v Allan* (1978) 52 ALJR 407, 18 ALR 385, PC.
18 *Re Keith White Development Pty Ltd* [1967] QWN 1.
19 *Re CW & AL Hughes Ltd* [1966] 2 All ER 702, [1966] 1 WLR 1369.
20 ERA 1996, s 183(3).
 1 ERA 1996, s 187(2).

The section applies to the following debts: (a) any arrears of pay in respect of one or more (but not more than eight weeks)[2]; (b) any amount which the employer is liable to pay the employee for the period of notice required by section 86(1) or (2)[3] of the Act or for any failure of the employer to give the period of notice required by section 86(1); (c) any holiday pay in respect of a period or periods of holiday not exceeding six weeks in all, to which the employee became entitled during the 12 months immediately preceding the appropriate date; (d) any basic award of compensation for unfair dismissal;[4] (e) any reasonable sum by way of reimbursement of the whole or part of any fee or premium paid by an apprentice or articled clerk.[5]

Arrears of pay in this particular context are treated as including guarantee payments, medical suspension payments, time off payments and protective awards.[6]

The total amount payable to an employee in respect of any particular[7] debt falling within section 184 where the amount of the debt is referable to a period of time may not exceed the relevant amount[8] as varied by the Secretary of State from time to time.[9]

There is a complaints procedure available to any disgruntled employee whose claim is either rejected or partly rejected by the Secretary of State. The complaint should be presented to an industrial tribunal within three months of communication of the relevant decision or if that is not reasonably practicable within such further period as is reasonable.[10]

Where the Secretary of State makes any payment to any employee in respect of any redundancy fund payment he is subrogated to the right of the employee to the extent of any overlap with the right of the employee to be treated preferentially on a distribution of the company's assets by the receiver.[11]

RESIDUAL RIGHTS

Two residual rights may finally be mentioned. The first is an absolute right: the freedom to compete. The second right depends upon the particular pension arrangements in existence.

2 This is not incompatible with Community law: *Secretary of State for Employment v Mann* [1996] IRLR 4, EAT.
3 Subject to any available set off: *Westwood v Secretary of State for Employment* [1984] IRLR 209, HL (employment benefit deducted).
4 Under ERA 1996, s 119.
5 ERA 1996, s 184(1).
6 ERA 1996, s 184(2). Presumably each of the different types of debt here specified is to be treated separately as arrears and each as subject to a separate maximum of eight weeks of payment in the aggregate: cf Employment Protection Bill 1975, cl 58(2)(f).
7 For a justification of this interpretation, see Drake and Bercusson *Employment Acts 1974–1980* (1981) in their commentary on what is now s 186(2).
8 ERA 1996, s 186(1). Presently £220: see SI 1999 No 586.
9 ERA 1996, s 186(1).
10 ERA 1996, s 124(1).
11 ERA 1996, s 125(1).

Freedom to compete

An employee who has been dismissed because of the appointment of a receiver has at any rate one comfort: he is entirely free to compete with his former corporate employer if it continues to trade. This will be so even if his contract of employment contained a restrictive covenant against competition. Such a covenant could only be enforced by injunction which is an equitable remedy. And as was pointed out by Cozens Hardy MR in *Measures Bros Ltd v Measures*,[12] it would be inequitable to allow equitable relief to a party which has not, whether by reason of misfortune or otherwise, performed and cannot perform its part of the bargain.

Occupational pension schemes

Where a corporate employer has established an occupational pension scheme for its employees the money contained in the fund is held on trust for the employees. That means that the fund does *not* form part of the general assets available for distribution by the receiver.[13]

Statutory provision has been made for the Secretary of State to make good an insolvent employer's contributions to an 'occupational pension scheme'. An 'occupational pension scheme' is 'any scheme or arrangement which provides or is capable of providing, in relation to employees in any description of employment benefits (in the form of pensions or otherwise) payable to or in respect of any such employees on the termination of their employment or on their death or retirement'.[14] The gist of the statutory provision as regards receivers is that if when the receiver is appointed there are employees' or employer's contributions owing to an occupational pension scheme, the Secretary of State will, within specific limits, pay those contributions from the redundancy fund on written application from persons competent to act for the scheme.[15]

TRANSFER OF UNDERTAKINGS (PROTECTION OF EMPLOYMENT) REGULATIONS 1981

The Acquired Rights Directive

The Transfer of Undertakings (Protection of Employment) Regulations 1981[16] came into full force on 1 May 1982.[17] They implemented an EEC

---

12 [1910] 2 Ch 248 at 254, CA.

13 *Re Kayford Ltd* [1975] 1 All ER 604, [1975] 1 WLR 279.

14 ERA 1996, s 46(3) cross-referring to Pension Schemes Act 1993, s 1.

15 Pension Schemes Act 1993, s 124.

16 SI 1981/1794. For a study of the Regulations, see Elias and Bowers *Transfer of Undertakings: The Legal Pitfalls* (5th edn 1994); and see also Paul Davies and Mark Freedland *Transfer of Employment* (1982); Elias (1982) 3 Co Law 147–156. For their interaction with insolvent companies, see David Pollard 'Insolvent Companies and TUPE' (1996) 25 Industrial Law Journal 191–210 and *Corporate Insolvency Employment and Pension Rights* (2000) 107–129.

17 TUPER 1981, reg 1(2).

Directive[18] finally adopted by the EEC Council just over five years beforehand.[19] The history of the making of the Directive and of the stately process of domestic consultation and final enactment in the United Kingdom[20] has been well told elsewhere.[1]

Effect, purpose and status of the regulations

Though having the appearance of subordinate legislation the regulations are on a par with statute law. They amend existing employment legislation. And their importance to receivers, particularly in regard to 'hive down' operations, cannot be underestimated.

The purpose of the regulations is to safeguard employees' rights in the event of transfer of undertaking, businesses and parts of businesses. This is achieved by providing, with one important exception, that on a relevant transfer of a business all the rights and obligations of employment contracts are automatically transferred.

Two preliminary points are worth making though they are more related to the status of the regulations themselves than to the importance of the regulations to receivers. First, the regulations are not capable of amendment in the same way as an Act of Parliament. Secondly, made as they are pursuant to a Directive, the regulations may, in the case of ambiguity, be construed by reference to the Directive.[2] It is necessary also to note that there is an argument[3] that some of the regulations may be ultra vires the present Act, namely the European Communities Act 1972.[4] Moreover, even if the regulations are all intra vires in so far as any of them fall foul of the standards prescribed by the Directive, an attack could be launched by the European Commission taking the British government before the European Court. Another possibility is that the general principle of the Directive could be enforced in the English courts if the case is sufficiently clear.[5]

Both receiverships and administrations whose purposes include survival of the company[6] are thought to be within the Acquired Rights Directive.

In the context of receivership law it must at all material times be borne in mind that the regulations are concerned with a 'transfer of an undertaking'. In other words the regulations *only* operate if there is a relevant transfer of an undertaking as defined. Hiving down does not constitute such a transfer because reg 4 provides that a transfer from a parent company to a subsidiary is deemed not to

---

18 EEC Directive 77/187.
19 On 14 February 1977. For comparison of the draft and final versions of the Directive, see (1976) 5 Industrial Law Journal 197 and (1977) 6 Industrial Law Journal 106 (Hepple).
20 The Regulations, other than regs 11(10) and 13(3) and (4), extend to Northern Ireland: reg 1(3).
1 See Davies and Freedland *Transfer of Employment* (1982).
2 Elias (1982) 3 Co Law 147–149.
3 (1982) 3 Co Law 147–149.
4 European Communities Act 1972, s 2(2).
5 Elias (1982) 3 Co Law 147–149.
6 *Mythen v Employment Appeals Tribunal* [1990] 1 IR 98.

have been effected until immediately before[7] the undertaking is sold to a third party or until the subsidiary ceases to be wholly owned by the parent company, whichever event is the earlier.[8] The practice of leaving the employees on the payroll of the insolvent parent company is thus safeguarded even though the undertaking or part of it is hived down. And the receiver is not even under the duty to consult the employees under reg 11. Accordingly, if a purchaser requires the parent company to dismiss its employees *before* the purchase by the purchaser of the hived down business those employees will not be subject to the automatic transfer principle. The employees will then be left with their claims for redundancy and perhaps for unfair dismissal against the (probably) insolvent parent company. On the other hand if the subsidiary is sold the employees will then have their employment rights against the subsidiary in its new ownership rather than against the former insolvent employers. If the hiving down operation is not successful and the subsidiary company ceases to trade, goes into receivership or has to be wound up by a liquidator the regulations will not apply. The employees' rights will be against the parent company which has continued to employ them: there will not have been any deemed transfer.[9]

The transfer of an undertaking is no justification in itself for dismissal: indeed a dismissal made because of the transfer is treated as an unfair dismissal.[10] But the dismissal can be justified if there is an 'economic, technical or organisational reason entailing changes in the workforce[11] of either the transferor or the transferee either before or after the relevant transfer'.[12] So there must be evidence adduced in support of the alleged reason for dismissal. And furthermore the reason must be shown to be one 'entailing' the change in the workforce. As yet there is no guidance as to whether the word means 'necessitating' or something less connoting 'desirable'; and the other question is whether the courts will accept the employer's bona fide belief that the change is necessary (or desirable) or apply some objective criterion.[13]

Two other matters should be particularly noted. First, those parts of the contract of employment dealing with pensions are not automatically transferred, and this would appear not to give the employee any right to claim constructive dismissal.[14] Secondly, duties are contained in the Regulations to inform[15] and

---

7　Cf *D'Urso v Ercole Marelli Electromeccanica Generale SA* [1992] IRLR 136, ECJ.

8　TUPER 1981, reg 4.

9　See the booklet of the Department of the Environment 'Employment rights on the transfer of an undertaking' at p 4; *Kerry Foods Ltd v Greber* [2000] IRLR 10.

10　TUPER 1981, reg 8(1). But see reg 8(5) added by SI 1995/2587.

11　There is no such change merely because the employee will not accept new terms and conditions: *Delabole Slate v Berriman* [1985] IRLR 305, CA. Cf cases where nature of individual's job changes: *Porter v Queen Medical Centre* [1993] IRLR 486; *Trafford v Sharpe & Fisher (Building Suppliers) Ltd* [1994] IRLR 325; and see *Michael Peters Ltd v Farnfield* [1995] IRLR 190, EAT and *Pollard* at 126–127.

12　TUPER 1981, reg 8(2). As to what falls within reg 8(2) see *Anderson v Dalkeith Engineering Ltd* [1984] IRLR 429; *Kerry Foods Ltd v Greber* [2000] IRLR 10.

13　See Elias (1982) 3 Co Law 153.

14　TUPER 1981, reg 7 (as amended by Trade Union Reform and Employment Rights Act 1993, s 33) and see *Pollard* 128–129.

15　TUPER 1981, reg 10. For the matters on which information is required see reg 10(2).

consult[16] with any recognised trade unions before the transfer takes place.[17] These duties hardly constitute a burden since compliance with the Regulations is not required if it would be unreasonable.[18]

The present Regulations have been much criticised by academic lawyers.[19] particularly those specialising in the field of employment law. The hiving down regulation is said with some force not to be reconcilable with the terms of the Directive. It is relevant to point out that the regulation was introduced after considerable lobbying and pressure from insolvency lawyers and they tend to defend the practice of hiving down and by implication the exemption.[20]

16 TUPER 1981, reg 11. See *Kerry Foods Ltd v Greber* [2000] IRLR 10.
17 Elias (1982) 3 Co Law 150–151.
18 EPCA 1975, ss 99(8) and 100(6); TUPER 1981, reg 10(7).
19 See *Davies and Freedland*; and Elias (1982) 3 Co Law 147 at 155.
20 See Peter Totty and Michael Crystal *Corporate Insolvency* (1982) pp 119–120.

CHAPTER 13

Creditors

EXECUTION CREDITORS

Introduction

Execution is the enforcement of the sentence of the law,[1] or as Lord Denning once put it: 'Execution means quite simply the process of enforcing or giving effect to the judgment of the court'.[2] There are various forms of execution but in relation to receivership one is concerned only with the forms which are exerted on the debtor's property. The various methods which receivers are likely to come across number five:

(a) seizure and sale of goods through a bailiff or sheriff's officers under the writ of fieri facias (usually abbreviated to fi fa);

(b) the attachment of debts due by third parties to the debtor by garnishment proceedings;

(c) obtaining a charging order under the Charging Orders Act 1979;

(d) obtaining an order for the appointment of a receiver by way of equitable execution;

(e) arrest under maritime procedure.

Before turning to the problems which face receivers dealing with judgment creditors pursuing any of these methods of execution it is convenient to restate certain important basic principles which conduce to clear analysis.[3]

First, an execution creditor is in no better position than the judgment debtor so far as the rights of third parties are concerned, save that he is not bound by estoppels binding the judgment debtor. He takes subject to all prior legal or

---

1 3 *Blackstone's Commentaries* 412.
2 *Re Overseas Aviation Engineering (GB) Ltd* [1963] Ch 24 at 39.
3 For recent discussions, see Diane M Hare and David Milman 'Debenture holders and judgment creditors – problems of priority' (1982) LMCLQ 57–80; RJ Calnan 'Priorities between Execution Creditors and Floating Chargees' (1982) 10 NZULR 111–133.

equitable interests, whether by way of charge or lien or whatever.[4] It 'is well settled', as Lord Halsbury LC observed in *Re Standard Manufacturing Co*[5] 'that an execution creditor takes subject to all equities'.

Secondly, rights acquired by creditors in the course of execution are not proprietary interests: execution is a means of enforcing a personal right existing in a debt.[6]

Thirdly, there comes a point of time when the debtor cannot by assignment create further proprietary interests except subject to the rights acquired under the process of execution. This point of time varies as will be seen, with the particular method of execution.

Writ of fieri facias: seizure and sale

The writ of fieri facias[7] is a direction by the Crown to the sheriff 'to make available' a sum of money sufficient to pay the judgment debt and interest and the costs of execution.[8] The procedure, unless terminated by payment on the spot, involves (i) the 'binding' of the chattels; (ii) seizure of the chattels by the sheriff; (iii) sale of the chattels followed by a payment of the proceeds of sale to the judgment creditor.

The chattels are 'bound' by the writ from the moment when the writ is delivered to the sheriff for execution.[9] The debtor still has a general property in the chattels[10] and it would appear that the judgment creditor does not obtain any proprietary interest in them.[11] The sheriff on the other hand does acquire a legal proprietary interest in the chattels when they are bound, for he can, within his bailiwick, seize the goods not only from the debtor but also from anyone claiming an interest in them under a subsequent disposition of the debtor[12] except assignees in bankruptcy or liquidators[13] and persons who obtain legal title to the goods in good faith and for valuable consideration before seizure.[14]

One heterodox decision of the Divisional Court held that the debenture holder's rights prevailed over an execution creditor whose sheriff had seized the goods under a writ of fieri facias, even though the debenture holder had not taken any step to bring about the crystallisation of the floating charge.[15] But it

4 *Richards v Johnston* (1859) 4 H & N 660; *Richards v Jenkins* (1887) 18 QBD 451, CA.

5 [1891] 1 Ch 627 at 641, CA.

6 *Re Standard Manufacturing Co* [1891] 1 Ch 627; *Re Opera Ltd* [1891] 3 Ch 260, CA; *Jennings v Mather* [1902] 1 KB 1, CA.

7 RSC Ord 45, r 1. See also *Civil Procedure* Vol 1, Spring 2000, p 800 et seq.

8 Save where the judgment is for less than £600 and contains no order as to costs: RSC Ord 47, r 4.

9 County Courts Act 1984, s 99.

10 *Anon* (1608) 1 Brownle 41; *Payne v Drewe* (1804) 4 East 523, 1 Smith KB 170.

11 *Payne v Drewe* (1804) 4 East 523, 1 Smith KB 170, cf Hare and Milman (1982) LMCLQ 57 at 60–61 citing *Slater v Pinder* (1871) LR 6 Exch 228; affd (1872) LR 7 Exch 95.

12 *Giles v Grover* (1832) 9 Bing 128, 1 Cl & Fin 72, HL; *Lucas v Nockells* (1833) 10 Bing 157, 7 Bli NS 140, HL.

13 *Re Davies, ex p Williams* (1872) 7 Ch App 314.

14 Supreme Court Act 1981, s 138(2).

15 *Davey & Co v Williamson & Sons Ltd* [1898] 2 QB 194.

has been disapproved of by the Court of Appeal in *Evans v Rival Granite Quarries Ltd*.[16]

There is no case which clearly decides whether a judgment creditor is entitled to the proceeds of sale if the sheriff sells the goods *prior* to crystallisation. In *Re Opera Ltd*[17] where the sheriff had not sold prior to the winding up and it was held that the debenture holder had priority over the judgment creditor Lindley LJ left open the position as to priority had the sheriff sold *before* crystallisation.[18] Romer J in *Robson v Smith*[19] seems to have deduced that the crucial point in *Re Opera Ltd*[20] was that there was a winding up before sale:

> 'and, therefore, before the execution was completed – in other words before the assets seized by the execution creditors had been completely dealt with so as to give any rights therein to the creditors'.

So he thought that sale completed the execution and displaced any uncrystallised claim of the debenture holder. Nor is *Taunton v Sheriff of Warwickshire*[1] any more conclusive. There again sale of the goods and payment of the proceeds to the execution creditor had not taken place and indeed there had been no sale but merely on the facts a deposit of money with the sheriff to abide the event. The case is no authority for the proposition that a judgment creditor can retain the proceeds of sale only if the sheriff has paid them over to him prior to crystallisation.

The authorities are now clear that if a judgment creditor instructs the sheriff to seize goods which are subject to a floating charge and if the charge is crystallised after seizure but before sale, the charge holder will take in priority to the executing creditor.[2] This principle applies even though there may be informalities in the issue of the debentures[3] or even if the debentures have not been actually issued.[4]

A further conundrum occurs if following seizure the company, in order to prevent the sale of the goods by the sheriff, pays the whole or part of the debt to the sheriff. If the floating charge holder later causes his charge to crystallise while the goods are still in the hands of the sheriff he is clearly entitled to the goods in priority to the judgment creditor, but two cases hold that he cannot reclaim payment of the money paid by the company to the sheriff.[5]

The preference accorded to the claims of debenture holders against execution creditors has been subjected to substantial criticism. Some commentators[6]

---

16 [1910] 2 KB 979, CA.

17 [1891] 3 Ch 260, CA.

18 [1891] 3 Ch 260 at 263.

19 [1895] 2 Ch 118.

20 [1891] 3 Ch 260, CA, and also cf *Re Standard Manufacturing Co* [1891] 1 Ch 627, CA.

 1 [1895] 2 Ch 319, CA; and see *Robinson v Burnell's Vienna Bakery Co Ltd* [1904] 2 KB 624 at 626–627; and *Heaton & Dugard Ltd v Cutting Bros Ltd* [1925] 1 KB 655, DC.

 2 *Re Standard Manufacturing Co* [1891] 1 Ch 627, CA; *Re Opera Ltd* [1891] 3 Ch 260, 60 LJ Ch 839, CA; *Re London Pressed Hinge Co Ltd* [1905] 1 Ch 576.

 3 *Duck v Tower Galvanizing Co* [1901] 2 KB 314.

 4 *Simultaneous Colour Printing Syndicate v Foweraker* [1901] 1 KB 771.

 5 *Robinson v Burnell's Vienna Bakery Co Ltd* [1904] 2 KB 624; *Heaton & Dugard Ltd v Cutting Bros Ltd* [1925] 1 KB 655, DC.

 6 Hare and Milman (1981) LMCLQ 57 at 77; RJ Calnan 'Priorities between Execution Creditors and Floating Chargees' (1982) 10 NUZLR 111 at 131.

consider that as a matter of principle a floating chargee should only get priority if the charge crystallises before the execution creditor gets a proprietary interest in the company's property.[7] Assuming that automatic crystallisation is good in law a floating chargee could in any event obtain additional protection by providing in the charge itself for automatic crystallisation on commencement of execution.

Garnishors

The process of execution of a judgment debt by way of garnishee proceedings for the attachment of debts requires no extended discussion here.[8] In essence it enables a creditor to obtain an order against a third party who owes money to the judgment debtor to pay the creditor out of the proceeds.[9] A garnishee order does not create any charge: it earmarks the debt to answer a particular claim and prevents the person to whom the debt is originally due from assigning it, except subject to the garnishee order.[10] The procedure involves first an order nisi then an order absolute.

The order nisi attaches the debt and when served on the garnishee binds the debt in the garnishee's hands,[11] subject to any dispute as to the existence of the debt or any right of set off. It does not operate as an assignment of the debt in equity nor yet a transfer of the debt.[12] The debt, the subject of the order, remains the property of the judgment debtor, and the right of the garnishor under the garnishee order nisi is subject to such rights and equities as already exist over it as the property of the debtor.

The receiver's title prevails even if the garnishee order is made absolute before he is appointed[13] unless the money has been actually paid under the order.[14] Thus in *Cairney v Back*[15] where the sequence of events was order nisi, notice thereof, order absolute and then appointment of a receiver Walton J held, following *Norton v Yates*,[16] that there was no difference between the two cases. In each case the important point is that although the floating charge had not crystallised into a specific charge *before* the date of the relevant order, the earmarked debt was subject to the floating charge in question, which was an *equitable* charge. So the rights of the garnishor were not truly infringed; the garnishor took subject to any

---

7 Cf *Wheatley v Silkstone and Haigh Moor Coal Co* (1885) 29 Ch D 715.

8 See RSC Ord 49; *Choice Investments Ltd v Jeromnimon* [1980] 2 WLR 80 at 83.

9 *Re McMeckan, ex p Oliver* (1896) 22 VLR 271.

10 *Goetze v Aders* (1874) 2 R 150, 12 SLR 121; *Galbraith v Grimshaw* [1910] 1 KB 339, CA; affd [1910] AC 508, HL.

11 See RSC Ord 49, r 3(2); *Derham v Wymond* (1887) 8 ALT 170; *Re McMeckan, ex p Oliver* (1896) 22 VLR 271; *MG Charley Pty Ltd v FH Wells Pty Ltd* (1963) 80 WNNSW 754 at 757; cf *Kare v North Kent Packers Ltd* (1954) 12 WWRNS 358, [1955] 2 DLR 407; revsd (1955) 14 WWRNS 251, [1955] 2 DLR 412.

12 *Norton v Yates* [1906] 1 KB 112, following *Re Combined Weighing and Advertising Machine Co* (1889) 43 Ch D 99, CA.

13 *Cairney v Back* [1906] 2 KB 746 (where the money was paid into court).

14 *Robson v Smith* [1895] 2 Ch 118.

15 [1906] 2 KB 746.

16 [1906] 1 KB 112.

rights or equities which affected the garnished debt, and the floating charge was one such right.

More difficult to justify, perhaps, is the decision of the Divisional Court in *Geisse v Taylor*.[17] A judgment creditor obtained and served upon a limited company a garnishee order absolute attaching debts due from the company to the judgment debtor. The garnishees subsequently borrowed bona fide a sum of money from a person on the security of a debenture covering all their assets and property. Execution against the garnishees was then levied by the garnishor; and the sheriff having seized the goods of the garnishees the debenture holder appointed a receiver and claimed the goods under his debenture. There was an interpleader issue to try the right to the goods seized as between the garnishor and the debenture holder.

It was held by Lord Alverstone CJ, Jelf J and a rather doubtful Kennedy J that the garnishee order did not give the garnishor any legal or equitable right to the goods in priority to the debenture holder who was therefore entitled to succeed in the issue. Whatever other justification may be found for this decision it is not possible to classify it, as Buckley LJ did in *Evans v Rival Granite Quarries Ltd*,[18] as a case where 'either the security had already crystallised or there was an application to crystallise it'. At the relevant date namely the date of the order absolute the floating security had not even been issued let alone crystallised. In the light of the subsequent decision of the House of Lords in *Galbraith v Grimshaw*,[19] that after service of a garnishee order the judgment debtor could only assign the garnished debt subject to the garnishee order, *Geisse v Taylor* must be considered of doubtful authority.

Even a garnishee order absolute does not transfer property in the garnished debt to the garnishor. It stands in this respect on the same footing as a garnishee order nisi: the debt remains the property of the judgment debtor, and the rights of the garnishor are subject to any rights and equities which affected the garnished debt in the hands of the judgment debtor.[20]

One might expect that the fact that a garnishee order earmarks a particular debt[1] would cause it to prevail over a subsequent appointment of a receiver. But the present state of the authorities does not bear out any such expectation.

Where judgment was obtained against a company and the judgment creditor served a garnishee order nisi on a person owing the company a debt which at the time was subject to a floating charge in a debenture it was held by Warrington J in *Norton v Yates*[2] that the title of the debenture holder prevailed over that of the creditor even though the debenture holder's receiver was appointed after the service of the order.

---

17 [1905] 2 KB 658; and see (1906) 22 LQR 11.
18 [1910] 2 KB 979 at 1001, CA (classifying *all* the cases cited by the debenture holder as being cases of that kind).
19 [1910] AC 508, HL (where *Geisse v Taylor* was cited but not commented upon); in the Court of Appeal Kennedy LJ echoed his doubts: see [1910] 1 KB 339 at 345.
20 *Cairney v Back* [1906] 2 KB 746 at 751 explaining *Norton v Yates* [1906] 1 KB 112.
 1 See *Goetz v Aders* (1874) 2 R 150; *Galbraith v Grimshaw* [1910] 1 KB 339, CA; affd [1910] AC 508, HL.
 2 [1906] 1 KB 112.

The competition between garnishee creditors and receivers and managers takes many forms. In *Coopers and Lybrand Ltd v National Caterers Ltd*[3] funds were paid into court by the garnishee following a garnishee order. On the same day, but after the payment in, a receiver and manager of the judgment debtor's assets was appointed by the holder of a debenture containing a floating charge on the assets of the judgment debtor. Subsequently the funds were paid out of court by error. When the error was righted by payment back into court the receiver brought an application for payment out of the funds. The judgment creditor who had obtained the garnishee order contested that application. Locke J held that the receiver had priority over the judgment creditor. Service of a garnishee order does not of itself have the effect of transferring ownership of the debt to the garnishor.[4]

On the other hand in *Mackay and Hughes (1973) Ltd v Martin Potatoes Ltd,*[5] where *Cairney v Back*[6] was not among the list of cases considered by the court, the sequence of events was that the receiver was appointed before the garnishee order was served on the company's debtor. Neither the garnishor nor the debtor company had notice of the appointment of the receiver by the bank. Pursuant to the garnishee order the debtor paid into court the amount it owed to the company (now in receivership). The bank and its receiver brought an application for an order that they were entitled to the money paid into court. Their application failed both before the Master and before O'Brien J sitting in the Ontario Supreme Court. It was held that priority for a receiver appointed under a debenture does not come into existence until the receiver has actually been appointed and notice of his appointment has been given to competing creditors. Crystallisation, to become effective as against the garnishee, required something other than the appointment of the receiver, and notice was an essential requirement. There having been no notice by the receiver until after garnishee proceedings were taken, the judgment creditor had priority.

It is interesting to note how the twin issues of crystallisation and notice were dealt with in this particular contest between floating chargee and garnishor. On the subject of crystallisation O'Brien J quoted two passages from the judgment of the appellate court in *Ontario Development Corpn v Trustee of the Estate of IC Suatac Construction Ltd.*[7] First, on crystallisation Howland JA said:

> 'The first question to be determined is whether the floating charge given by the debenture creates a charge on the property of Suatac at the time when it was given or only from the time when it is crystallised. The answer is that the floating charge creates a *present* security from the time it is given but does not create a specific security until it is crystallised.'

Then a little later on he says:[8]

---

3   (1982) 47 CBRNS 57, BCSC.
4   *General Brake & Clutch Service Ltd v WA Scott & Sons Ltd* (1975) 59 DLR (3d) 741, Man CA.
5   (1981) 15 BLR 312, Ont SC.
6   [1906] 2 KB 746.
7   (1976) 12 OR (2d) 465 at 469–470, Ont CA referring to *Evans v Rival Granite Quarries Ltd* [1910] 2 KB 979 at 999, CA.
8   (1976) 12 OR (2d) 465 at 472.

'It is only when the floating charge crystallises and a receiver and manager is appointed that an execution creditor loses his equity to have his execution paid by the company in the course of carrying on its business. The execution then becomes subject to the higher equity of the debenture holder. If the execution has not been paid at that time nor has there been a sale by the sheriff, it will thereafter be subject to the interest of the debenture holder.'

That led naturally to the next question as to what is the relationship between notice and crystallisation.

As to the relationship between crystallisation and notice O'Brien J in *MacKay and Hughes (1973) Ltd v Martin Potatoes Ltd*[9] looked back, in sympathy, to observations of Osler J in *Bank of Montreal v Woodtown Developments Ltd*.[10] The first of these pointed out that:[11]

'A long line of cases of which perhaps *Re Roundwood Colliery Co*,[12] may be taken as the starting point, has made it clear that a priority for a receiver appointed under the powers contained in a debenture does not come into being until the receiver whether court appointed or creditor appointed, has actually been appointed and it is, if not explicitly stated, inferentially a part of that reasoning that to establish his priority over another creditor seeking to establish a claim, notice of his appointment must be given.'

From these generalities he continued in relation to the particular facts:[13]

'It is clear from the above that in my view as against the landlord, the present defendant, the plaintiff Bank as represented by the receiver had no priority until the landlord had been notified which as I have found was not until November 10th. While the landlord did not properly distrain, it did enter upon the premises and take possession of the stock under claim of right.'

Charging order

The position of a judgment creditor who chooses to enforce his judgment by means of a charging order is clearer, not least because the procedure has recently been revised by the Charging Orders Act 1979. The history of charging orders has been traced elsewhere[14] and needs no further exposition here.

Like the garnishee procedure the procedure by way of charging order involves two stages: an order nisi and an order absolute. But there is this difference. Unlike the garnishee procedure the charging order procedure creates an immediate charge at the order nisi stage.

9 (1981) 15 BLR 312, Ont SC.
10 (1979) 25 OR (2d) 36.
11 (1979) 25 OR (2d) 36, at 40.
12 [1897] 1 Ch 373, CA.
13 (1979) 25 OR (2d) 36 at 41.
14 Law Commission Working Paper No 46, paras 3–8; *Re Overseas Aviation Engineering (GB) Ltd* [1963] Ch 24, [1962] 3 All ER 12, CA.

The Charging Orders Act 1979 (COA 1979) provides a new code[15] of charging orders based on the recommendations of the Law Commission.[16]

Property or assets charged

The appropriate court (as defined in the Act)[17] may by order impose an absolute or conditional charge which the Act specifically calls a charging order on certain specified classes or kinds of property or assets. These comprise any interest held by the debtor beneficially not only in land[18] but also in government stock, stock of any other body (except a building society) incorporated within England and Wales, stock of any body incorporated outside England and Wales or of any state or territory outside the United Kingdom, being stock registered in a register kept at any place within England and Wales, units of any unit trust in respect of which a register of the unit holders is kept at any place within England and Wales, and funds in court.[19] Moreover, the court may also make such an order in respect of any interest held by the debtor under any trust.[20] In any case where a charge is imposed by a charging order in respect of stock within the categories just listed or of units in a unit trust or of funds in court, the court making the order may provide for the charge to extend to any interest or dividend payable in respect of the asset.[1] Power is conferred on the Lord Chancellor to amend by statutory instrument the categories set out in s 2(2) of the Act by adding to, or removing from, the kinds of assets for the time being referred to there, any asset of a kind which in his opinion ought to be added or removed.[2] The result is that former difficulties raised in relation to the charging of interests under trusts for sale[3] have been overcome.[4]

Stock standing in the name of a trustee for the judgment debtor and others may be the subject of a charging order.[5] So too a debtor's contingent interest in one of the specified assets can be charged by the court.[6]

If a judgment or order is made against a trustee as such, then any interest held by him as such trustee in any such assets as are mentioned in s 2(2) of the 1979 Act, including interests under another trust can be so charged.[7] Likewise such trust assets which are held by the judgment debtor as trustee for his sole benefit

---

15 The code consists of the Act itself, together with the rules contained in RSC Ord 50.
16 Report of the Law Commission on Charging Orders, 1976 Cmnd 6412 to which reference may be made to aid interpretation of the code. See *Civil Procedure* Vol 1, 2000, SC 50.0.1 et seq.
17 COA 1979, s 1(2) analysed below.
18 COA 1979, s 2(1)(a)(i), (2)(a); see *National Westminster Bank Ltd v Stockman* [1981] 1 All ER 800, [1981] 1 WLR 67 (beneficial interest in proceeds of trust for sale of land).
19 COA 1979, s 2(1)(a)(i), (2)(b) and (c).
20 COA 1979, s 2(1)(a)(ii).
 1 COA 1979, s 2(3).
 2 COA 1979, s 3(7) and (8).
 3 *Irani Finance Ltd v Singh* [1971] Ch 59, [1970] 3 All ER 199, CA and *National Westminster Bank Ltd v Allen* [1971] 2 QB 718, [1971] 3 All ER 201n.
 4 *National Westminster Bank Ltd v Stockman* [1981] 1 All ER 800, [1981] 1 WLR 67.
 5 *South Western Loan and Discount Co v Robertson* (1881) 8 QBD 17, 51 LJQB 79.
 6 *Cragg v Taylor* (1867) LR 2 Exch 131, 36 LJ Ex 63.
 7 COA 1979, s 2(1)(b)(i).

may be so charged.[8] And where there are two or more debtors both or all of whom are liable to the creditor for the same debt and they together hold the whole beneficial interest under a trust of such assets unencumbered and for their own benefit, a charging order can also be made.[9]

Appropriate court

The appropriate court in the case of a fund lodged in court is the court in which the fund is lodged.[10] If the order to be enforced is a maintenance order[11] of the High Court[12] the appropriate court is either the High Court itself or a county court.[13] Where the judgment or order to be enforced is a judgment or order of the High Court for a sum exceeding the county court limit the appropriate court is the High Court.[14] All other cases should go to the county court[15] with one optional exception: if there is more than one judgment to be enforced and the High Court is the appropriate court for any one of those applications, all can be made there.[16]

Defeasibility of order nisi

The House of Lords reviewed the enforcement of judgments against insolvent companies in *Roberts Petroleum Ltd v Bernard Kenny Ltd*.[17] The court had made a charging order nisi over land owned by a company in favour of a judgment creditor; the court simultaneously appointed a receiver to enforce the charging order. The company thereafter convened a meeting of its shareholders on short notice and resolved on a voluntary liquidation. The question was whether in the decision to make the order nisi into an absolute order the court should exercise its discretion by refusing to make the order absolute because a statutory scheme for dealing with the company's assets was irrevocably imposed by resolution to wind up (and of course by a winding up order). The vagaries of judicial response, until the voices of infallibility spoke unanimously, are striking. Bristow J thought that the court could not, in the proper exercise of its discretion, make the order absolute. The Court of Appeal[18] reached the same conclusion as the district registrar, that is that the court could indeed properly make the order absolute and exercised its discretion to make the order absolute. According to the Court of Appeal the insolvency of a company followed by liquidation was not of itself enough to justify the court in refusing to make absolute the charging order nisi: there had to be some other factor present such as a scheme of arrangement set up

---

8 COA 1979, s 2(1)(b)(ii).
9 COA 1979, s 2(1)(b)(iii).
10 COA 1979, s 1(2)(a).
11 As defined in the Attachment of Earnings Act 1971, s 2(a).
12 RSC Ord 50.
13 COA 1979, s 1(2)(b).
14 COA 1979, s 1(2)(d).
15 COA 1979, s 1(2)(c).
16 COA 1979, s 1(4).
17 [1983] 2 AC 192, [1983] 1 All ER 564, HL.
18 [1982] 1 All ER 685, [1982] 1 WLR 301, CA.

by the main body of creditors which had a reasonable prospect of success before there was 'sufficient cause' not to make the order absolute.

The reasoning underlying the decision of the Court of Appeal, though not the result of that decision, was the subject of some criticism. In particular two commentators[19] placed emphasis on the secured creditor status of a chargee under a charging order nisi[20] and argued that such status should not be undermined by the use of an unfettered judicial discretion.[1] In liquidation, they argued, specific statutory provisions justified interference with vested rights of creditors: no such provisions cover receivership and pre-liquidation situations.[2]

In the House of Lords Lord Brightman agreed with the propositions that the order nisi imposed an immediate charge and that at the date of the commencement of the liquidation the assets were already outside the statutory scheme. But he held that the charge was defeasible[3] and equated charging orders nisi with garnishee orders nisi.[4] The imposition of the statutory scheme was therefore a sufficient cause. By refusing to make the order absolute the court was able to ensure parity of treatment of unsecured creditors. The advantage of the conclusion reached and the principle established was that 'it may help to avert an unseemly scramble of creditors'.[5] It also 'establishes a clear working rule, and avoids the uncertainties of an inquiry whether a scheme of arrangement has been set on foot and has a reasonable prospect of succeeding.'[6] The fact that this view is not universally shared must be noted[7] but unless and until legislation overrules the effect of the House of Lords decision those who are 'chargees nisi' must face the hazards of their defeasible interests. The Cork Committee made no mention of this point and no legislative provision to deal with this point emerged with the Insolvency Act 1986.

Equitable execution

There is conflicting authority on the question whether a judgment creditor obtains a specific charge over corporate property if he succeeds in getting a receiver by way of equitable execution appointed in respect of it. In *Levasseur v Mason & Barry Ltd*[8] it was held by the Court of Appeal that what was in effect a specific charge[9] (subject in the circumstances to an outstanding lien) affected the goods or the proceeds of them at the moment the receiver by way of equitable execution was appointed. Stirling J in *Croshaw v Lyndhurst Ship Co*[10] to whom *Levasseur's*

19 See Diane M Hare and David Milman (1983) 4 Co Lawyer 84–86.
20 Administration of Justice Act 1956 (AJA 1956), s 5(3) re-enacted in COA 1979, s 3(4).
 1 Citing *Burston Finance Ltd v Godfrey* [1976] 1 WLR 719 at 736 per Shaw LJ.
 2 Hare and Milman (1983) 4 Co Lawyer at 85.
 3 See [1983] 1 All ER 564 at 573. There is no reference to the AJA 1956, s 5(3).
 4 See [1983] 1 All ER 564 at 573H–574B.
 5 [1983] 1 All ER 564 at 576.
 6 The test laid down in *Burston Finance Ltd v Godfrey* [1976] 2 All ER 976, [1976] 1 WLR 719.
 7 Hare and Milman (1982) LMCLQ 57; Milman and Hare 'Corporate Insolvency: the Cork Committee Proposals' (1983) 127 Sol Jo 280; cf All ER Rev 1983 at 61–62 (DD Prentice).
 8 [1891] 2 QB 73, CA.
 9 Though the word 'charge' was referred to in argument (which claimed there was no lien or charge) the judgments refer only to right or entitlement.
10 [1897] 2 Ch 154.

case was cited held that an order appointing a receiver by way of equitable execution of money receivable in respect of the debtor's interest in a ship and her freight did not confer on the judgment creditor any charge on the debtor's property so as to make him a secured creditor and was not equivalent to seizure of property in execution. On the subsequent winding up the judgment creditor was therefore not a secured creditor, the judge having refused in the exercise of his discretion to allow the receivership order to be further proceeded with.[11]

Whichever way this conflict of authority is resolved the charge would have to become specific before any floating charge crystallised to override the debenture holder's interest.

Arrest under maritime procedure

An arrest in Admiralty is equivalent to a sequestration. As Sir George Jessel MR pointed out in *Re Australian Direct Steam Navigation Co*:[12]

> 'The term sequestration has no particular technical meaning; it simply means the detention of property by a Court of Justice for the purpose of answering a demand which is made. That is exactly what the arrest of a ship is.'

More recently it has been observed that arrest and sale in Admiralty are 'equivalent to sequestration and execution respectively and are incidents in proceedings in rem'.[13] From the moment the writ is issued entitling the plaintiff to arrest the res in issue, the writ gives the plaintiff secured creditor status over the asset[14] so that satisfaction of any judgment subsequently obtained against a defendant company is guaranteed even in the event of liquidation.[15]

With this procedure may be contrasted the form of pre-trial attachment known as the Mareva injunction.[16] A Mareva injunction does not entitle the applicant to gain secured creditor status as against the company's debenture holders.[17] It simply freezes the assets of the company within the jurisdiction.[18]

---

11 On this view a further order would be needed to impose a specific charge.
12 (1875) LR 20 Eq 325 at 326–327.
13 *The Constellation* [1965] 2 Lloyd's Rep 538 at 543, per Hewson J.
14 *Re Aro Co Ltd* [1980] Ch 196, [1980] 1 All ER 1067, CA.
15 *Re The Zafiro* [1959] 1 Lloyd's Rep 359.
16 *Mareva Compania Naviera SA of Panama v International Bulkcarriers SA* [1975] 2 Lloyd's Rep 509, CA.
17 *Cretanor Maritime Co Ltd v Irish Marine Management Ltd* [1978] 3 All ER 164, [1978] 1 WLR 966, CA.
18 The Mareva injunction, now known as a freezing order, has already attracted a considerable literature: D Powles 'The Mareva injunction expanded' [1981] JBL 415; D Powles 'Mareva round-up' [1982] JBL 489; R Horsfall, 'The Mareva Injunction' [1982] Conv 365–379; M Hetherington 'Inherent Powers and the Mareva injunction' (1983) 10 Sydney LR 77; A Tyree 'Mareva injunctions: the third party problem' (1983) 10 ABLR 375; J Ferris 'Mareva injunctions and innocent third parties' (1981) 1 Lit 311. There are textbooks: M Hetherington *Mareva Injunction* (1983); D Powles *The Mareva Injunction and Associated Orders* (1985); R N Ough and W Flenley *The Mareva Injunction and Anton Piller Order: Practice and Procedure* (2nd edn, 1993); David Copper *Mareva Injunctions* (1988); Mark S W Hoyle *The Mareva Injunction and Related Orders* (3rd edn, 1997).

RESERVATION OF TITLE CREDITOR

Where a receiver and manager is operating under a valid unassailable charge ordinary trade creditors often have a gloomy prospect. The debenture holder, in most cases a bank, is ahead of them in the queue for payment of outstanding debts. In the trenchant words of Templeman LJ in the Court of Appeal: 'Unsecured creditors rank after preferential creditors, mortgagees and the holders of floating charges and they receive a raw deal'.[19] Perhaps, therefore, it is not surprising that at any rate in some cases sympathy has been shown towards 'an invention designed to provide some protection for one class of unsecured creditors, namely unpaid sellers of goods'.[20] The invention in question, which has given considerable trouble to receivers and managers, is the reservation or retention of title clause,[1] often referred to as a Romalpa clause after the name of the defendant in the leading case of *Aluminium Industrie Vaassen BV v Romalpa Aluminium Ltd*[2] (the *Romalpa* case).

The reasoning behind the use of a reservation of title clause is that if the seller of goods can rely on his equitable title to identifiable assets instead of a mere equitable charge over them he is in a commanding position over fellow creditors. In equity he, and not the company, owns the assets. The company cannot charge those assets and its creditors cannot look to them for satisfaction of their debts. Such a trust arrangement has been aptly described as 'a snare for secured and unsecured creditors'[3] for no reasonable investigation would ever reveal the existence of this overriding equitable ownership. Creditors will therefore give or extend credit in ignorance of the true position of the company, to their own detriment.

The Romalpa case

The facts of the *Romalpa* case[4] were simple, and, because of the importance of the case, bear repetition. A Dutch company (AIV) sold aluminium foil to Romalpa. Romalpa got into financial difficulties. When a receiver was appointed it owed AIV over £122,000. The receiver certified that £35,152 was held in an account in his name with Romalpa's bankers, representing the proceeds of the sale of aluminium foil supplied by AIV, which Romalpa had sold to third parties. AIV, who had a reservation of title clause in their conditions of sale, claimed to be entitled to trace the aluminium foil into the proceeds of sale. That claim was

---

19 *Borden (UK) Ltd v Scottish Timber Products Ltd* [1981] Ch 25 at 42F (citing *Business Computers Ltd v Anglo African Leasing Ltd* [1977] 2 All ER 741, [1977] 1 WLR 578).
20 [1981] Ch 25. Templeman LJ added 'although there is no logical reason why this class of creditor should be favoured as against other creditors such as the suppliers of consumables and services'.
1 See generally Gerald McCormack *Reservation of Title* (2nd ed 1995); and see also John Parris *Effective Retention of Title Clauses* (1986). There is a cornucopia of analysis to be found in legal articles: see p 206, n 8. See J Mance QC [1992] LMCLQ 35–39 citing more.
2 [1976] 2 All ER 552, [1976] 1 WLR 676.
3 See W Goodhart and G Jones (1980) 43 MLR 489 at 491.
4 [1976] 1 WLR 676 at 683–686.

upheld by Mocatta J at first instance[5] and by the Court of Appeal.[6] The relevant condition which fell to be construed was couched in outlandish language. This was because it was translated (or rather transliterated) from the Dutch, which was the original language of the contract.

The condition substantially contained two limbs. The first limb, which embodied the provision for reservation of title in respect of the original material delivered was in the following form:

> 'The ownership of the material to be delivered by AIV will only be transferred to the purchaser when he has met all that is owing to AIV, no matter on what grounds. Until the date of payment, purchaser, if AIV so desires, is required to store this material in such a way that it is clearly the property of AIV.'

The second limb spelled out the consequences of using the aluminium foil in connection with other materials:

> 'AIV and purchaser agree that, if purchaser should make (a) new object(s) from the material, mixes this material with (an) other object(s) or if this material in any way whatsoever becomes a constituent of (an) other object(s) AIV will be given the ownership of this (these) new object(s) as surety of the full payment of what purchaser owes AIV. To this end AIV and purchaser now agree that the ownership of the article(s) in question, whether finished or not are to be transferred to AIV and that this transfer of ownership will be considered to have taken place through and at the moment of the single operation or event by which the material is converted into (a) new object(s) or is mixed with or becomes a constituent of (an) other object(s). Until the moment of full payment of what purchaser owes AIV, purchaser shall keep the object(s) in question for AIV in his capacity of fiduciary owner and, if required, shall store this (these) object(s) in such a way that it (they) can be recognised as such. Nevertheless, purchaser will be entitled to sell those objects to a third party within the framework of the normal carrying on of his business and to deliver them on condition that – if AIV so requires – purchaser as long as he has not fully discharged his debt to AIV shall hand over to AIV the claims he has against his buyer emanating from his transaction.'

The defendants conceded that the effect of the condition was to make them *bailees* of the material supplied by AIV until all the debts were paid, but contended that once they had resold the material to bona fide purchasers the relationship between them and AIV was purely that of debtor and creditor. In the absence of any express or constructive trust AIV were not entitled to avail themselves of the equitable remedy of tracing. Roskill LJ considered it obvious that the business purpose of the whole of the condition, read in its context in the general conditions was to secure AIV so far as possible against the risk of non-payment after they had parted with possession of the goods delivered, whether or not those goods retained their identity after delivery. To give effect to what he considered the obvious purpose of the retention of title clause one must imply into the first part of the clause not only the power to sell, but also the obligation to account in accordance with the normal fiduciary relationship of principal and agent, bailor and bailee.

---

5 [1976] 1 WLR 676 at 678.
6 [1976] 1 WLR 676 at 683.

Romalpa decision initially underrated

The importance of the decision of the Court of Appeal in the *Romalpa* case was not at once appreciated. The appellate judges who decided the case totally underestimated the likely effect of their decision in the commercial world. They refused leave to appeal to the House of Lords, no doubt in part because of the unanimity of judicial opinion. But Roskill LJ on refusing leave also described the contract as 'a rather simple contract, not altogether happily expressed in the English language, but which could not govern any other case.'[7] For some time the case was not even reported and when it was reported it was not thought worthy of coverage in the official Law Reports. However once the *Romalpa* case emerged from these shadows, the full light of commercial and legal criticism was directed upon it.[8]

Reservation of beneficial and equitable ownership

The *Romalpa* case concerned aluminium foil. The goods were not mixed with others nor subjected to any manufacturing process: they remained intact as originally sold. In *Re Bond Worth Ltd*[9] what was in issue was synthetic fibre supplied for the manufacture of carpets. The fibre was processed into yarn, and then the yarn was woven into carpets. The claim by the supplier to be the owner of the manufactured carpets by reference to a retention of title clause failed. The contract did not provide that the property should remain with the supplier until the specified sums were paid. In effect, the entire property[10] in the fibre passed to the company and there was no question of any bailment. All that was contemplated was that the equitable and beneficial ownership of the fibre should remain with the supplier and that should the fibre be mixed with other goods in the manufacturing process the supplier should be deemed to have an equitable and beneficial interest in the new product.

Despite the reference to 'equitable and beneficial ownership', Slade J in a long and subtle judgment held that the clause did not create a bare trust in favour of the supplier. The whole purpose of the clause was to afford security for payment of the purchase price under each relevant order, and the necessary existence of an

---

7 See *Borden (UK) Ltd v Scottish Timber Products Ltd* [1981] Ch 25 at 45.
8 There is now a very substantial literature indeed. Articles since 1980 include Iwan Davies 'Reservation of Title Clauses: A Legal Quagmire?' [1984] 1 LMCLQ 49–80; IR Davies 'Romalpa clauses: further developments' [1984] 2 LMCLQ 280–289; Andrew Hicks 'Reservation of title; a pious hope' (1985) 27 Malaya LR 63–112 (which cites three pages of earlier legal articles at 110–112); Garry A Muir 'Recent Developments in "Reservation of Property" Clauses' (1985) 13 ABLR 3–29; D Chalmers 'Romalpa Retention of Title Clauses' (1986) 60 ALJ 545–553; JR Bradgate 'Reservation of Title Ten Years On' [1987] Conv 434–447; Sally E Wheeler 'The Insolvency Act 1986 and Retention of Title' [1987] JBL 180–186; Julie Spencer 'The Commercial Realities of Reservation of Title Clauses' [1989] JBL 220–232; Gerard McCormack 'Reservation of Title – the controversy continues' [1989] LMCLQ 198–215; Professor Dr Everest 'Romalpa Clauses: The Fundamental Flaw' (1994) 68 Australian LJ 404–413. For earlier literature, see the first edition of this book, at pp 125–126.
9 [1980] Ch 228, [1979] 3 All ER 919; and see Michael Burke 'Reservation of Title – The Lessons of Bond Worth' (1979) NLJ 651. Cf *Re W J Hickey Ltd* [1988] IR 126 (identifiable proceeds held in trust).
10 [1980] Ch 228 at 256B.

equity of redemption was quite inconsistent with the existence of a trustee relationship.[11] The charge was necessarily equitable, so that the only remaining question as to its nature was whether it was specific or floating. Slade J held that it was the latter: it was quite incompatible with the existence of a specific charge in equity over specific assets that the alleged trustee should be free to use them as he pleases for his own benefit in the course of his own business.[12]

The learned judge in the *Bond Worth* case further held that the charge was created by the company in receivership and was void for want of registration under what is now s 395 of the Companies Act 1985 against the debenture holder as creditor.[13] The conclusion that it was the company which 'created' the charge followed from the finding that the entire property passed to the company. The classification of the charge as 'floating' was entirely consistent with the analysis that the interest was only to become effective in certain circumstances: the possibility of crystallisation is a mark of the floating charge.[14] What the *Bond Worth* case teaches the prudent supplier is to use a retention of title clause which makes it quite clear that the *legal* title remains with the supplier until payment. It also demonstrates the risk that an attempt to create a security interest not only in the goods supplied in their original form but also in the property in a new manufactured or processed form will be classified as a charge created by the company.[15] Moreover, registration of a clause that is likely to be construed as a floating charge is plainly desirable.

Validity and ambit of the clause

Two fairly frequent assaults on the validity of a Romalpa clause can be mentioned at this point. First, it may be claimed that the clause represents a charge created by the purchaser company within s 396(1) of the Companies Act 1985, so that if it has not been registered it is void against an administrator or liquidator of the company or any person who for value acquires an interest or right over property subsequent to the charge for non-registration under s 399(1) of the Companies Act 1985 as amended. Secondly, depending on the wording of the clause in question, it may be claimed that the relevant clause does not confer such extended rights as are sought to be established by the seller in reliance on its provisions. Retention of title clauses are found in a wide variety of forms. Each clause must be construed according to its terms. In consequence the case law on the subject has become subtle and refined and in the memorable words of Staughton J is 'presently a maze if not a minefield'.[16]

It is particularly importance to remember the caveat of Robert Goff LJ in *Clough Mill Ltd v Martin*[17] that in reading the 'spate' of cases dealing with

---

11 [1980] Ch 228 at 248E–F.
12 [1980] Ch 228 at 266C. For criticism of the decision and the reasoning of Slade J see Parris *Effective Retention of Title Clauses* (1986) pp 69–70.
13 See CA 1985, s 396(1)(f), replacing CA 1948, s 95(2)(e).
14 *Illingworth v Houldsworth* [1904] AC 355, 73 LJ Ch 739, HL.
15 See Cork Committee Report (Cmnd 8558) 364, para 1614.
16 *Hendy Lennox (Industrial Engines) Ltd v Grahame Puttick Ltd* [1984] 1 WLR 485 at 493.
17 *Clough Mill Ltd v Martin* [1985] 1 WLR 111 at 114F–G per Robert Goff LJ.

Romalpa clauses one should bear in mind the differing facts, issues, contractual provisions and concessions of counsel in each case.

As a general proposition, the simpler the clause the more likely it is to succeed. 'All liabilities' clauses have now received the authoritative blessing of the House of Lords.[18] On the other hand, attempts to attach, by contract, new or mixed goods or the proceeds of the sale and or hire generally fail on the basis that the clauses amount to unregistered charges.[19]

Creation of a charge

In *Re Bond Worth Ltd*,[20] Slade J held that the relevant retention clause created a charge. He reached this conclusion by what can be described as a purposive approach, saying that where the purpose of the clause was merely to provide the seller with security for payment of the funds, it must be a charge:[1]

> 'In my judgment, any contract which, by way of security for the payment of a debt, confers an interest in property defeasible or destructible upon payment of such debt, or appropriates such property for the discharge of the debt must necessarily be regarded as creating a mortgage or charge as the case may be.'

However this purposive approach was firmly rejected by the Court of Appeal in *Clough Mill Ltd v Martin*.[2] Oliver LJ questioned the correctness of the assumption that the *whole* purpose of the clause is to give the seller security for the payment of the purchase price and commented:[3]

> 'No doubt that is a part, and an important part, of the purpose of the clause, but put in more general terms its purpose is to protect the [seller] from the insolvency of the buyer in circumstances where the price remains unpaid.'

But Oliver LJ pointed out that even if the whole purpose of the clause was to achieve security, it by no means followed as a necessary or logical consequence that a charge was created. The dictum of Slade J, recited above, which the receiver relied upon was inapplicable. The operative word in that dictum was 'confers' and the whole of Slade J's judgment in *Re Bond Worth* was based upon the fact, as he found, that the legal title to his goods had passed to the buyer.[4] If, in fact, the seller has retained the legal title to the goods, then by definition the buyer cannot have charged them in his favour.[5]

Attempts to create a sale and repurchase contract to circumvent the categorisation of the transaction as a charge are also prone to failure.[6]

---

18 *Armour v Thyssen Edelstahlwerke AG* [1991] 2 AC 339; J Mance QC [1992] LMCLQ 35–39.
19 *Tatung (UK) Ltd v Galex Telesure Ltd* (1985) 5 BCC 325; *Specialist Plant Services Ltd v Braithwaite Ltd* (1987) 3 BCC 119; and see the cases discussed below at 211–216.
20 [1980] Ch 228, [1979] 3 All ER 919.
 1 [1980] Ch 228 at 248.
 2 [1985] 1 WLR 111.
 3 [1985] 1 WLR 111 at 122E–F.
 4 [1985] 1 WLR 111 at 123A–B. The finding that the legal title had passed is highly debatable.
 5 [1985] 1 WLR 111 at 123A; and see at 119C–D per Robert Goff LJ and at 125B–C per Sir John Donaldson MR.
 6 *Curtain Dream plc v Churchill Merchandising Ltd* [1990] BCC 341.

The numerous cases which have been decided in the field of Romalpa clauses can best be discussed under four main headings. They can conveniently be divided into cases of: (i) unmixed and unaltered goods; (ii) mixed and altered goods; (iii) claims to the proceeds of sub-sales; and (iv) claims to recover the sub-sold goods.

Unmixed and unaltered goods

Goods intact

The first situation is where there is a reservation of legal title or ownership and the claim is to identifiable goods which are unmixed and unaltered.

In *Clough Mill Ltd v Martin*,[7] the Court of Appeal was faced with four identically drafted contracts. Each contract provided that the *risk* in the goods (which consisted of yarn) was to pass to the buyer (a manufacturer of fabrics) on delivery. But each contract stipulated by cl 12 that 'the *ownership*' of the yarn was to remain with the supplier who reserved the right to dispose of the yarn until he had been paid in full in accordance with the terms of the contract or until such time as the company sold the yarn to its customers by way of bona fide sale. The clause also contained a right to repossess and resell if payment became overdue and provided that the incorporation of the yarn in (or its use as material for) other goods would result in the property in the whole of the goods being and remaining with the supplier. The bank put in a receiver. A claim to repossess quantities of unsold and unused yarn was made to, and rejected by, the receiver who countered with the assertion that the retention of title clause constituted an unregistered charge void for want of registration under what is now s 395 of the Companies Act 1985. Counsel for the plaintiff supplier who sued in conversion put his case as one which was fairly and squarely on all fours with the *Romalpa* case. Judge O'Donoghue distinguished the case from the *Romalpa* case on two grounds because in that case (as distinct from the case before him) there was no evidence that the first was required for any manufacturing process so that there was nothing to suggest that the buyer was more than a mere bailee as was conceded by the buyer; and secondly because in the case before Judge O'Donoghue (unlike the *Romalpa* case) there was no duty to store the yarn separately and no duty to account for the proceeds of sale of manufactured goods when ultimately sold.

The circumstances were much closer to those in *Re Bond Worth* except that in the *Bond Worth* case equitable and beneficial ownership was reserved while here simply the ownership in the yarn was reserved. The judge declared that in construing a retention of title clause, such as cl 12 of the parties' contract, the court had to establish its true effect by looking at the *purpose* for which the clause had been inserted in the contract. Since the sole purpose of the clause in question was to provide security for the payment of the purchase price, and since the rights conferred on the plaintiff by the clause were for that limited purpose only, the judge held that the contract took effect as a contract for the sale of goods

---

7 [1985] 1 WLR 111, CA. See also *SA Ter Molst International NV v Showcase Furniture (NS) Ltd* (1985) 3 DCR 42, Judge J P Duncan at Otahuhu (claim for unused furniture upholstery fabric: trust of goods and proceeds expressed).

whereby the property in the goods passed to the company on delivery and a charge over the yarn was created by the company in favour of the plaintiff by way of security for the payment of the purchase price.

In upholding the claim and reversing the decision of the judge below, the Court of Appeal made some helpful generalisations about the efficacy of retention of title provisions. Some of these have already been noted. Thus earlier decisions must be treated as not necessarily decisive[8] and the underlying purpose of the contract (eg to create a security) is not determinative of the issue.[9] Five points stand out clearly from the appellate judgments. First, the concept of retention of title is doctrinally acceptable and capable of being formulated contractually.[10] Secondly, concepts such as 'bailment' or 'fiduciary obligation' must not be allowed to override clearly expressed contractual intentions.[11] Thirdly, an orthodox retention of title provision, reserving title over identifiable unmixed goods does not create a registrable charge: the registration principle is applicable only where: (i) the purchasing company creates a charge; and (ii) that charge confers a security over its own property.[12] In the fourth place, the mere fact that the contract envisages ample liberties in the buyer in relation to the goods sold,[13] exercisable before or at the notional time for transmission of property, is not of itself fatal to a reservation of title or to a characterisation of seller and buyer as bailor and bailee.[14] The retention will be effective until the originally retained property must necessarily have disappeared. Lastly, a different provision in the same contract constituting a charge (because despite language to the contrary it cannot take effect feasibly except as a charge) will not necessarily infect another provision with the same characterisation.

Goods affixed or incorporated but substantially intact

The problem facing Staughton J in *Hendy Lennox (Industrial Engines) Ltd v Grahame Puttick Ltd*[15] was logistical as well as knotty. The case was tried in the Winchester Crown Court where, despite efforts by counsel, not all the books which it might have been desirable to cite could be procured. The case is of more than passing interest because the diesel engines subjected to the reservation of title clause were to be incorporated by the buyers into generating sets and sold to sub-buyers with the engines unaltered in substance. The buyers went into receivership and 11 days later the suppliers successfully applied for an interim injunction restraining the buyers from selling or parting with possession of the engines. There were three generating sets on the premises when they were visited by the suppliers' representative. Two were in a deliverable state and their serial

8 See [1985] 1 WLR 111 at 114F–G.
9 See [1985] 1 WLR 111 at 125C–H per Sir John Donaldson MR.
10 [1985] 1 WLR 111 at 121F–122A per Oliver LJ.
11 [1985] 1 WLR 111, at 116G–H per Robert Goff LJ.
12 [1985] 1 WLR 111 at 125A–C per Sir John Donaldson MR: 'The agreement between the plaintiff and the buyer involved the plaintiff *retaining* property in the goods. It did not involve the buyer conferring a charge on any property, but still less on its own property.'
13 [1985] 1 WLR 111, 116F–H.
14 [1985] 1 WLR 111.
15 [1984] 1 WLR 485; cf *Gebrueder Buehler AG v Kwong* [1988] 2 MLJ 69, Sing CA (equipment on affixation subject to mortgage).

numbers had been communicated to the sub-buyers. The third set for which the sub-buyers later paid £1,236.82 was not in a deliverable state. The injunction was discharged a fortnight later on the buyers' undertaking to pay into a joint deposit account of the parties' solicitors the proceeds of sale of the sets.

The learned judge held that the sellers had retained proprietary rights in the goods and that these rights had not been affected because the engines had been wholly or partly incorporated, by bolts and other connections, in the generator sets. There was no right to retake the goods once the property had passed to sub-buyers and on the facts property in two of the generator sets had passed on the relevant date. The engine in the third generator set stood differently: there had been a valid proprietary claim to retake the engine and on its delivery to sub-buyers the claim had been transformed into a claim against the proceeds. It could not be implied from the terms of the agreement between the parties that the buyers occupied a fiduciary position in relation to the proceeds of sale of the two engines:[16] so far as the third was concerned on payment of a sum into the solicitors' joint account a chose in action was created which belonged to the suppliers.

Mixed or altered goods

Many goods sold subject to a retention of title provision are subjected to the purchaser's manufacturing process. It is necessary to consider: (i) cases where the retention clause is silent as to the ownership of mixed goods; and (ii) contractual provisions purporting to affect the ownership of the finished product.

Contract silent

The case of *Borden (UK) Ltd v Scottish Timber Products Ltd*[17] concerned the supply of resin used in the manufacture of chipboard. The supplier claimed at least a proportional interest in the chipboard manufactured with the use of the relevant resin. At first instance it was held that the supplier was entitled to trace the resin supplied into the chipboard manufactured from such resin, or into the proceeds of sale of such chipboard and that the tracing remedy was not a charge created by the company to which the precursor of ss 395 and 396 of the Companies Act 1985 had any application.

On appeal the judgment below[18] was reversed. The Court of Appeal was unable to discern any fiduciary relationship such as that of principal and agent or bailor and bailee. It was admitted that the defendants were to use the resin in the process of manufacture; and that recovery of the resin was impossible and could not be demanded. The fiduciary element said to be present in the *Romalpa* case[19] was therefore absent. From the argument of counsel for the supplier it is clear that it was accepted that the legal concept of property in the resin ceased to have

16 The grounds of distinction from the *Romalpa* case are set out at [1984] 1 WLR 485 at 498–499.
17 [1981] Ch 25, [1979] 3 All ER 961.
18 See [1979] 2 Lloyd's Rep 168 (Judge Rubin sitting as a judge of the Chancery Division).
19 For criticism of the alleged fiduciary element in *Romalpa*, see Alexander Hill Smith 'Updating the Romalpa clause' (1980) NLJ 529.

anything to apply to when the resin as resin ceased to exist.[20] Classification of this acceptance as a 'fatal' concession is the language of hyperbole: the admission was one which simply coincided with the strong and independently formed view of the Court of Appeal. In the words of Templeman LJ referring to the effect of the manufacturing process: 'The plaintiff's title to the resin became meaningless'.[1] The manufacturer had amalgamated the resin and the other ingredients into a new product by an irreversible process and the resin, as resin, could not be recovered for any purpose; for all practical purposes it had ceased to exist and the ownership in that resin must also have ceased to exist.[2] With this loss of identity the resin could no longer be traced into the chipboard or the proceeds of its sale. Equally the interest in or charge on the chipboard in favour of the plaintiffs was expressed to arise under the contract and none could be implied. It is important to note that there was no language in the contract effective to create any interest in or charge over the chipboard or the proceeds of sale. Had there been such language sufficient to raise such a charge it is clear that Buckley and Templeman LJJ would have held that such charge, being unregistered, would be void as against the liquidator and creditors of the defendant under what is now s 395. But both would have viewed the charge as one which, if executed by an individual, would require registration as a bill of sale and not as a floating charge. That view is open to question because a bill of sale for this purpose excludes transfer of goods in the ordinary course of business in any trade or calling and prima facie goods transferred under a Romalpa clause would fall within that designation. The further suggestion by Buckley LJ that the charge could not be a 'floating' charge because it was intended to affect specific goods[3] is likewise open to question. The essence of a floating charge is indeterminacy not of the property involved, but of the time when the charge may crystallise.

The effect of the *Borden* case on the status of the *Romalpa* decision is itself something of a riddle. One now outmoded view is that the *Romalpa* case turned on its own very special facts and the concessions made in the case. In this connection Roskill LJ, in refusing leave to appeal to the House of Lords, observed that it would not govern any other case. Other commentators seek to pick their way through the minefield laid by *Bond Worth* and *Borden* and indeed later cases and suggest that by the use of appropriately detailed provisions a supplier can obtain rights over mixed products. Any such clause would need to ensure that there is a fiduciary relationship by establishing the necessary preconditions for a bailment. Secondly, it would be necessary to avoid any stipulation or hint that the property in the final products shall pass to the supplier on mixing and to ensure that the purchaser performs some new act after the new goods have come into existence, for example by the physical segregation of the new goods and make that the occasion of the passing of the property. The alternative to these subtleties is always to register under s 395 of the Companies Act 1985.

20 [1981] Ch 25 at 31 and 41.
 1 [1981] Ch 25 at 44E.
 2 [1981] Ch 25 at 46A–B per Buckley LJ.
 3 [1981] Ch 25 at 46H–47B.

As can be imagined further problems occur when several suppliers supply goods subject to Romalpa clauses. If the sellers' retention of title interests constitute floating charges they will rank in priority according to the order in which they were created. Whether this is the date when the clause was first agreed to by the relevant parties or the date when the particular delivery was made is an unanswered question. The potential priority of a Romalpa-type charge ranking in priority over a previously made general floating charge can be avoided by an express prohibition against the subsequent creation of Romalpa-type floating charges.

Contractual provisions about ownership of finished product

A specific provision, not infrequently incorporated in Romalpa clauses, is one whereby ownership of the products manufactured with the goods agreed to be sold is to vest in the seller. The efficacy of such a provision is the subject of considerable doubt. Robert Goff LJ in *Clough Mill Ltd v Martin*[4] found it difficult to see why, if the parties agree that the property shall vest in A, that agreement should not be given effect to, and this view was shared by Oliver LJ.[5] However, all three appellate judges were of the opinion that the specific provision in that case whereby 'if any of the material is incorporated in or used as material for other goods before . . . payment the property in the whole of such goods shall be and remain with the seller until such payment has been made' would constitute a charge on the new product in favour of the seller,[6] even though such a conclusion does do violence to the language of the particular provision. They were all affected by the fact that a repossession or a resale pursuant to such a provision would, assuming that the contract of supply was then determined, appear to leave the buyer uncompensated for any contribution of his own in the way of work or added material to the product. The provision could not be constituted as creating a trust. Those who insert Romalpa clauses in their contracts of sale must be aware that other suppliers might do the same; and the prospect of two lots of material, supplied by different sellers, each subject to a Romalpa clause which vests in the seller the legal title in a product manufactured from both lots of material, is not at all sensible.

A less extreme case of alteration is found in *Re Peachdart Ltd.*[7] In that case the microscopic small print, transposed for the benefit of the court into eight pages of foolscap, failed in the event to secure protection for the supplier of leather to a company manufacturing handbags. The handbag company was in receivership, and the receiver applied to the court for determination whether the supplier had, on the appointment of the receiver, an interest or charge on: (i) unused leather on the company's premises unsold at the date of appointment of the receiver; (ii) handbags manufactured by that date and incorporating leather supplied by the supplier; and (iii) uncollected invoices payable to the company in respect of

4 [1985] 1 WLR 111 at 119.
5 [1985] 1 WLR 111 at 124.
6 [1985] 1 WLR 111 at 120, 124, 125.
7 [1984] Ch 131, [1983] 3 All ER 204. Applied in *Ian Chisholm Textiles Ltd v Griffiths* [1994] BCC 96.

handbags manufactured by the company from the supplier's leather. In fact, by the time of the hearing what was in issue was the proper destination of the proceeds of sale of the unused leather, of the proceeds of sale of the completed and uncompleted handbags sold since the receiver's appointment and of the proceeds of sale of the handbags sold before his appointment but for which payment had not been received.

The conditions of sale contained retention of title clauses which provided that until payment was received in full the seller retained the ownership of the leather including a right of resale if payment was overdue and had the right to trace any proceeds of sale by the buyer, including any goods made with the leather, by the creation of a fiduciary relationship between buyer and seller.

Vinelott J rejected a valiant argument that the case was on all fours with the *Romalpa* case. This argument proceeded on the footing that the purchaser was a bailee of the leather and that while there was no obligation to store separately, that was not necessary because any given skin could be identified by a person skilled in the leather trade, as sold under a particular contract. Vinelott J did not decide whether the company was strictly a bailee of the unused leather. But, even assuming there was a bailment when the leather was first delivered, he found that the true construction of the conditions of sale meant that the intention of the parties must have been that at least after a piece of leather had been appropriated to be manufactured into a handbag and work had started on it (when the leather would cease to have any significant value as raw material) the leather would cease to be the exclusive property of the supplier and become the exclusive property of the handbag manufacturers. The supplier, he held, would thereafter have a charge on handbags in course of manufacture and on the distinctive products emerging as the end products. The charge would in due course shift to the proceeds of sale. There being only a charge and it being unregistered, it was void against the receiver, and as regards the book debts against the bank, and as regards completed or partly completed handbags against the preferential creditors.

The effect of the cases thus appears to be that virtually any provision purporting to grant rights to trace into the manufactured product or its proceeds of sale will amount to a charge created by the company and will accordingly, if unregistered, be void as against a receiver of the company's assets.[8]

Proceeds of sub-sales

A retention of title provision (without more) does not impose on the original buyer any obligation to account for sale proceeds.[9] Nor is such a term to be implied as necessary to achieve business efficacy.[10] The only safe way of making

8 *Borden (UK) Ltd v Scottish Timber Products Ltd* [1981] Ch 25, [1979] 3 All ER 961, CA; *Re Bond Worth Ltd* [1980] Ch 228; *Re Peachdart Ltd* [1984] Ch 131, [1983] 3 All ER 204; *Specialist Plant Services Ltd v Braithwaite Ltd* [1987] BCLC 1, CA.

9 *Hendy Lennox (Industrial Engines) Ltd v Grahame Puttick Ltd* [1984] 2 All ER 152, [1984] 1 WLR 485; *Re Andrabell Ltd* [1984] 3 All ER 407.

10 But see for a case where such an obligation was implied, *Len Vidgen Ski & Leisure Ltd v Timara Marine Supplies (1982) Ltd* (1985) 2 NZ Co Law Cas 99, 438, discussed in Peter Watts 'Reservation of Title Clauses in England and New Zealand' 6 Oxford Journal of Legal Studies (1986) 456–464.

the original buyer accountable for the sale proceeds is to see that the retention clause constitutes the original buyer trustee or fiduciary in respect of the proceeds of any sub-sale, with a duty to keep such proceeds in a separate account unmixed with the buyer's own money and identified, therefore, as held for the benefit of the supplier.

The language of bailment or agency on its own is not conclusive since not all bailees or agents are fiduciaries for their bailors or principals. Clearly, therefore, the use of the word 'trustee' or 'fiduciary' is most desirable. An express inhibition on the free use of the proceeds of sale is equally desirable, and it should be borne in mind that where a period of credit is allowed it is normally to be inferred that the buyer will be free to use the proceeds of sale as he wishes.[11]

As has been mentioned already, the mere fact that seller and buyer stand in relation to each other as bailor and bailee does not of itself give rise to a fiduciary duty to account on the part of the buyer-bailee.[12] In *Hendy Lennox (Industrial Engines) Ltd v Grahame Puttick Ltd*[13] and in *Re Andrabell Ltd*[14] the court was unable to identify the necessary fiduciary relationship for the purpose of giving rise to any duty to account on the part of the original buyer. However, it is possible to extract from those two cases and from the *Romalpa* decision itself pointers to the existence of the necessary fiduciary relationship.[15]

So where the goods supplied by a vendor to a company are simply resold by the company without alteration, the contract may by appropriate wording provide that the company is also to be regarded as standing in a fiduciary position to the vendor in relation to any goods sold so that the vendor may then be entitled to trace his goods into the proceeds of sale.[16]

A further refinement would also seem to be necessary. In order to avoid the risk of the provision being held to constitute a charge on the proceeds it is preferable for the supplier to specify that the buyer shall only hold as trustee or fiduciary such *part* of the proceeds of sale as represent or are equivalent to the original price charged by the supplier for the relevant goods.[17]

11 See *Aluminium Industrie Vaassen BV v Romalpa Aluminium Ltd* [1976] 2 All ER 552, [1976] 1 WLR 676; cf *Re Bond Worth Ltd* [1980] Ch 228 at 261 and 263–264 (liberty to mix funds inconsistent with trustee/beneficiary relationship). See further *Hendy Lennox (Industrial Engines) Ltd v Grahame Puttick Ltd*, [1984] 2 All ER 152, [1984] 1 WLR 485 at 497–499 and *Re Andrabell Ltd* [1984] 3 All ER 407 at 414–415.

12 *Hendy Lennox (Industrial Engines) Ltd v Grahame Puttick Ltd* [1984] 1 WLR 485 at 498; *Re Andrabell Ltd* [1984] 3 All ER 407 at 413–414.

13 [1984] 2 All ER 152, [1984] 1 WLR 485.

14 [1984] 3 All ER 407.

15 *Aluminium Industrie Vaassen BV v Romalpa Aluminium Ltd* [1976] 2 All ER 552, [1976] 1 WLR 676.

16 *Aluminium Industrie Vaassen BV v Romalpa Aluminium Ltd* [1976] 2 All ER 552, [1976] 1 WLR 676; CA; cf *Re Andrabell* [1984] 3 All ER 407 (contractual terms made it impossible to imply fiduciary relationship); *Pfeiffer (E) Weinkellerei Weineinkauf GmbH & Co v Arbuthnot Factors Ltd* [1988] 1 WLR 150 (clause providing that claims against sub-purchasers should pass to the vendor until the vendor paid in full held to be charge on book debts void for want of registration). And see *Tatung (UK) Ltd v Galex Telesure Ltd* (1988) 5 BCC 325; *Re Weldtech Ltd* [1991] BCC 16; *Compaq Computer Ltd v Abercorn Group Ltd* [1991] BCC 484; *Modelboard Ltd v Outerbox Ltd (in liquidation)* [1993] BCLC 623. See the discussion of these cases in *McCormack*.

17 *Borden (UK) Ltd v Scottish Timber Products Ltd* [1981] Ch 25 at 45; *Re Bond Worth Ltd* [1980] Ch 228 at 248 and 259.

Where the relevant provision attempts to subject the proceeds of sale of goods manufactured from those originally supplied, the materials and labour supplied by persons other than the original supplier will be likely to lead a court to conjure a charge out of the provision.[18] Such a charge if unregistered will be void for want of registration under s 395(1) of the Companies Act 1985.[19]

Claims against sub-purchasers

Normally the title of sub-purchasers from a buyer will not be affected by the fact that the latter is not owner of the goods.[20] They will get good title to the sub-sold goods under s 25(1) of the Sale of Goods Act 1979[1] or under s 2 of the Factors Act 1889 or because the buyer has the express or implied authority of the seller to sell the goods in the ordinary course of business and to give a good title to the sub-purchasers.[2] Knowledge on the part of the sub-purchaser that the goods are subject to a Romalpa clause will prevent that result,[3] and so will bad faith.[4] Both the statutory provisions deny the claim of a person who purchases in bad faith or with notice of the right of the original seller.

Some Romalpa clauses attempt to extend the rights of the supplier in this situation by providing that if the buyer resells any of the goods subject to the Romalpa clause any claim against the sub-purchaser is to vest immediately in the seller. Such a provision would nevertheless be likely to rank as an assignment by way of charge registrable as a charge on book debts. Even if such a provision were dressed up as a declaration of trust it might still be looked on as a charge on book debts[5] or a floating charge on the specific property.[6]

Other defences to the claim

Receivers faced with Romalpa-type claims have a number of defences which they should as a matter of prudence consider.

Non-incorporation

First, they should consider whether the particular clause relied upon was in fact incorporated into the contract between the supplier and the company.

Such incorporation may be achieved expressly[7] or by implication[8] in such a way that it can be said that the purchaser be treated as having accepted the term

---

18 Cf *Len Vidgen Ski & Leisure Ltd v Timara Marine Supplies (1982) Ltd* (1985) 2 NZ Co Law Cas 99, 438. And see *Tatung (UK) Ltd v Galex Telesure Ltd* (1989) 5 BCC 325.

19 *Borden (UK) Ltd v Scottish Timber Products Ltd* [1981] Ch 25 at 44–45, CA.

20 *Hendy Lennox (Industrial Engines) Ltd v Grahame Puttick Ltd* [1984] 1 WLR 485 at 495.

1 *Re Peachdart Ltd* [1984] Ch 131 at 141; *Archivent Sales and Developments Ltd v Strathclyde Regional Council* (1984) 27 BLR 98; *Four Point Garage Ltd v Carter* [1985] 3 All ER 12.

2 *Re Bond Worth Ltd* [1980] Ch 228 at 246; *Four Point Garage Ltd v Carter* [1985] 3 All ER 12.

3 *Re Interview Ltd* [1975] IR 382 (knowledge that goods were subject to a Romalpa clause).

4 *Feuer Leather Corpn v Frank Johnstone & Sons* [1981] Com LR 251.

5 CA 1985, ss 395(1) and 396(1)(e). See *Re Interview Ltd* [1975] IR 382.

6 *Re Bond Worth Ltd* [1980] Ch 228, [1979] 3 All ER 919.

7 For example in a contractual document: *L'Estrange v Graucob* [1934] 2 KB 394.

8 By a consistent course of dealing, but not otherwise.

in question.[9] The purchaser must have sufficient notice of the term[10] and there may be incorporation from a course of dealing.[11] Some cases turn on a 'battle of standard forms' used on either side: the courts usually allow victory to the form last past the post.[12]

The argument that the supplier has failed to incorporate the relevant retention of title clause into the contract has frequently been raised, but has usually failed.[13] In *Wavin Nederland BV v Excomb Ltd*,[14] however, Leggatt J held that the receiver succeeded on this ground because it was impossible to extract from the confusion of documents any shared contractual intention that the clause should be incorporated into the contract.

Non-identification

Secondly, the receiver will claim that the onus of proof rests on the supplier to show that the goods on the company's premises are the supplier's goods. In this connection, identification may prove very difficult.

Proof of payment

Next, the receiver may require the supplier to prove that the goods in question have not been paid for, again a difficult task if there had been a current account clause and the account has at any time been in credit. But in such a case the supplier may rely on the presumption of regularity and allege that goods received earlier were paid for earlier.[15]

Procedurally, a receiver may be in difficulty in refusing a supplier access to premises on which goods are stored which are subject to a valid Romalpa clause, even where no express right of entry has been reserved under the contract. He might expose himself to personal liability if the Romalpa claim succeeds.[16] Despite suggestions[17] that a supplier might get a mandatory ex parte injunction to enter and recover goods with an order for costs against the receiver personally, that could only happen in a very plain case. Right of entry to inspect can be agreed. From the receiver's point of view it may be preferable to issue a summons

---

9 See McCormack *Reservation of Title* (2nd edn, 1995) 68–72.

10 *John Snow and Co Ltd v D G Woodcroft & Co Ltd* [1985] BCLC 54; *Interfoto Picture Library Ltd v Stiletto Visual Programmes Ltd* [1988] 1 All ER 348. And see the Irish cases summarised in Robert Pearce (1985) 20 Ir Jur (NS) 264 at 267–270.

11 *J Spurling v Bradshaw* [1956] 1 WLR 461; *McCutcheon v David MacBrayne Ltd* [1964] 1 WLR 125; *British Crane Hire Ltd v Ipswich Plant Hire Ltd* [1975] QB 303.

12 *British Road Services Ltd v Arthur Crutchley & Co Ltd* [1968] 1 All ER 811; *Butler Machine Tool Ltd v Ex-Cell-O Corpn (England) Ltd* [1979] 1 WLR 401; *Sauter Automation Ltd v Goodman (Mechanical Services Ltd* [1986] 2 FTLR 239, 34 BLR 81. See the discussion of these cases in *McCracken* pp 68–72.

13 *Aluminium Industrie Vaassen BV v Romalpa Aluminium Ltd* [1976] 2 All ER 552, [1976] 1 WLR 676, CA; *Re Bond Worth Ltd* [1980] Ch 228, [1979] 3 All ER 919; *Sugar Distributors Ltd v Monaghan Cash and Carry Ltd* [1982] ILRM 399; *John Snow & Co Ltd v Woodcroft & Co Ltd* [1985] BCLC 54.

14 (1983) 133 NLJ 937.

15 Parris *Effective Retention of Title Clauses* (1986) pp 137–145, paras 9.05–9.07.

16 *Six Arlington Street Investments Ltd v M J Spencer* (1979) unreported.

17 Parris *Effective Retention of Title Clauses* (1986) p 146, para 9.09.

for directions as to what he should do in the face of a Romalpa claim. The vesting of disputed goods in a hive-down company risks a claim for conversion under the Tort (Interference with Goods) Act 1977. But if he is ignorant of the retention clause, while he may be liable, he will be entitled to an indemnity.[18]

If goods are incorporated into land the seller under a Romalpa clause cannot recover them. A receiver will therefore be astute to see whether there has been the necessary degree of annexation to enable him to repel any claim based on a Romalpa clause and in particular to see whether the seller has reserved any right of entry under the relevant contract.[19]

The company in the Irish case of *Re Interview Ltd*[20] had imported electrical equipment from a German supplier on terms that the supplier should retain title until the equipment had been paid for and the company agreed to assign to the supplier all claims for payment due from sub-purchasers. Kenny J held that the latter assignment, being by way of charge, was void for non-registration as against the company's bank which had registered a floating charge. The bank's appointment of a receiver did not, however, affect the supplier's property in the unsold goods; and in the case of the goods sold to sub-purchasers by the receiver after his appointment the supplier's claim for the prices due to the company in respect of such goods ranked in priority to the claim of the receiver.

'TRUST' CREDITOR

Another device used by trade creditors in trying to achieve some measure of protection against the consequences of corporate insolvency is the trust device. It is exemplified by the case of *Re Kayford Ltd*.[1] There on the advice of accountants a company which had got into financial difficulties declared an express trust on mail order subscriptions and a separate trust account was opened. The conjunction of an express declaration and segregation of the subscriptions was a powerful feature of the case. Sir Robert Megarry V-C was able, without much trouble, to hold that there was indeed a trust with sufficiently certain subject matter. Money subject to that trust did not form part of the company's assets available in its liquidation, and the 'trust' creditors could recover their money.

The device failed, however, in *Re London Wine Co (Shippers) Ltd*,[2] a rather neglected case decided by Oliver J. The case concerned stocks of wine kept in various warehouses by the subject company. A receiver was appointed by the bank. Prior to his appointment the company had acquired substantial stocks of wine which had been deposited in various warehouses and sold to a variety of customers. It was the intention of the company that, on the purchase of the wines by customers those wines should become the property of the customers but be stored by the company at the expense of their customers. To that end when a

18 *Scott v Nesbitt* (1808) 14 Ves 438; *Re Ryland's Glass Co* (1904) 49 Sol Jo 67.
19 For a full and interesting discussion, see Alexander Hill-Smith 'The Romalpa Clause in Relation to Land' (1983) 133 NLJ 207–210.
20 [1975] IR 382.
 1 [1975] 1 All ER 604, [1975] 1 WLR 279.
 2 The decision is noted in (1976) 126 NLJ 977; but see now [1986] PCC 121.

customer paid for the wine invoiced to him the company sent the customer a 'certificate of title'. At the same time the company, in its books, would allocate a particular consignment reference number at a particular warehouse to a customer's purchase. But the warehouse was not told of the sale except where the customer mortgaged his wine. There was never any segregation or appropriation of the wine within the warehouse until actual delivery of the wine to a purchaser. The question was whether, when the floating charge of the bank crystallised, the wine sold belonged to the respective purchasers or remained the property of the company so as to be caught by the bank's fixed charge.

It was submitted on behalf of the purchasers that if the legal title to the wine had not passed to them then either the wine became subject to a valid and effective trust in their favour or that they had a right to specific performance of their contracts, the bank taking subject to that equitable right on the crystallisation of the charge. Oliver J seems to have accepted that there was indeed an intention to create a trust[3] but concluded that the trust failed for uncertainty of subject matter. At the various dates when the beneficial interests were to take effect it was not clear what the composition of the consignments of wine was in respect of which the purchasers' beneficial interests were to take effect. As for the right to specific performance the contracts were not ones in respect of which equity would grant that remedy: the goods in question were not sufficiently identified. Nor even if there had been such a right would the beneficial interest necessarily pass.

In *Re Chelsea Cloisters Ltd*[4] this question arose in relation to a tenants' deposit account. Various flats in a block were let on short-term furnished tenancies. A term of the tenancies was that the tenant should pay a deposit against breakages and dilapidations, returnable if there were none. When the landlord company ran into financial difficulties its accountant recommended that a segregated tenants' deposit account be set up so that deposits would not be spent as part of the company's general cash flow. The Court of Appeal referred to the dictum of Channel J in *Henry v Hammond*:[5]

> 'It is clear that if the terms upon which a person receives the money are that he is bound to keep it separate, either in a bank or elsewhere and to have that money so kept as a separate fund of the person entitled to it, then he is a trustee of that money and must hand it over to that person who is his cestui que trust.'

The range of cases in which a trust device has been held to override the claims of a receiver or liquidator includes examples of great variety.

Loans for particular purpose

Whereas a normal loan, even if made for a particular purpose, will not normally[6] be treated as being money put into trust, it will be otherwise if the

---

3 Reference was made to *Re Kayford Ltd* [1975] 1 All ER 604, [1975] 1 WLR 279.
4 (1980) 41 P & CR 98, 131 NLJ 482, CA following *Re Kayford Ltd* [1975] 1 WLR 279 at 282.
5 [1913] 2 KB 515 at 521.
6 But see *National Bolivian Navigation Co v Wilson* (1880) 5 App Cas 176, HL where money was advanced to trustees for bond holders for the construction of a railroad and was successfully reclaimed by the bondholders on the withdrawal of a crucial government concession.

money is to be segregated from the general assets of the borrower and repaid if the purpose is not carried out. Thus, in *Barclays Bank Ltd v Quistclose Investments Ltd*,[7] money was advanced to a company for the sole purpose of paying a dividend already declared by the company and credited with the full knowledge of the bank to a special account in the company's name. It was held by the House of Lords that there was a primary trust to pay the dividend and since this could not be achieved there was a resulting trust to the lenders. Again, in *Carreras Rothmans Ltd v Freeman Mathews Treasure Ltd*,[8] money advanced for the purpose of paying designated invoices and for that reason placed in a special client account was similarly classified as trust money for particular creditors of the company. When the purpose was incapable of being achieved there was a resulting trust to the lender.

Trusts for investors

Where subscription money is received in a separate account on the footing that it is to be returned if the scheme under which it is paid fails, a trust may be held to exist in that event.[9] Investors may also be held to be protected by a trust where the company itself has established a special redemption fund to repay those investors.[10]

Trusts for employees

The courts have also held in particular cases that sums received under insurance policies for the benefit of employees of a company are held on trust for those employees, so as to escape the claims of the company's receiver.[11] No doubt sick funds and other funds collected for the benefit of employees would be likely to be similarly treated.

Factoring agreements

Where a debt factor having taken an assignment of debts due to the company authorises the company to collect the debts, holding them on trust for the factor, such an arrangement creates a valid trust in favour of the factor which will prevail against any other claims if the company goes into receivership or liquidation.[12]

---

7 [1970] AC 567, [1968] 3 All ER 651, HL.
8 [1985] Ch 207, [1985] 1 All ER 155.
9 *Re Nanwa Gold Mines Ltd* [1955] 3 All ER 219, [1955] 1 WLR 1080.
10 *Elkins v Capital Guarantee Society* (1900) 16 TLR 423, CA.
11 *Re Independent Air Travel Ltd* [1961] 1 Lloyd's Rep 604; and see *Smith v Birrell Ltd* 1968 SLT 174.
12 *International Factors Ltd v Rodriguez* [1979] QB 351, [1979] 1 All ER 17, CA and see *Tay Valley Joinery Ltd v C F Financial Services Ltd* (1987) 3 BCC 71.

Retention money under building contract

Where under a building contract the main contractor holds retention money for sub-contractors this may also create a trust effective against a receiver or liquidator. This was established in *Re Tout and Finch Ltd*[13] and the principle has been upheld in a subsequent line of cases.[14] But the retention fund must have been set up and not merely promised.[15]

Money held on constructive trust

The successful trust device is not always constituted by express agreement. A constructive trust may prevail against a receiver or liquidator. For example, in *Chase Manhattan Bank NA v Israel-British Bank (London) Ltd*[16] the company had knowingly received money paid under a mistake of fact. The circumstances were such as to raise a constructive trust over the relevant money. In *Neste Oy v Lloyds Bank plc*[17] six payments had been made into a special account of an agent handling a ship owner's business in the United Kingdom. The first five payments were not held on trust but at the time of the sixth payment the directors of the agent company knew that the agent company would be going into receivership. Bingham J held that there was a constructive trust since it would be un-conscionable for them not to return the payment.

Statutory trusts

The Secretary of State is to make regulations providing for the establishment of clients' trust accounts to protect investors' funds.[18]

It is an interesting side-light that in Canada various provinces provide by statute that certain claims shall have priority as deemed trusts, among which are wages, vacation pay, retail sales tax and employees' pension deductions.[19]

Certainty of trust

The efficacy of the device, so far as any express trust is alleged, depends on the creditor being able to show that a sufficiently certain and effective trust exists.

---

13 [1954] 1 All ER 127, [1954] 1 WLR 178.
14 *Rayack Construction Ltd v Lampeter Meat Co Ltd* (1979) 12 BLR 30; *Re Saunders Ltd* (1981) 17 BLR 125. Cf *Re Jartray Developments Ltd* (1982) 22 BLR 134.
15 *Mac-Jordan Construction v Brookmount Erosion Ltd* [1992] BCLC 350.
16 [1981] Ch 105, [1979] 3 All ER 1025.
17 [1983] 2 Lloyd's Rep 658 following the principle declared by Cardozo J in *Beatty v Guggenheim Exploration Co* 225 NY 380 (1919) at 386.
18 Financial Services Act 1986, s 55.
19 See Frank Bennett 'Administration of a Corporate Receivership' (1979) 27 CBR (NS) 113 at 133–135, 138, 140.

This must in turn depend upon the drafting of contemporaneous documentation to reflect a clear unequivocal trust.

An express trust must conform in the matter of the three certainties, that is, certainly of intention, certainty of subject matter and certainty of objects. In relation to certainty of intention the court will look to the substance of the agreement[20] and in analysing whether there is certainty of subject matter the court will be concerned to see whether the trust assets are identifiable[1] and in existence at the time the alleged trust came into existence[2] and whether it is unequivocally manifested.[3]

PUBLIC UTILITIES

Non-administrative receiver

The position of a non-administrative receiver in regard to the continued supply of gas and electricity to the company of which he is receiver and manager is that both gas and electricity boards may insist on the payment of outstanding arrears before continuing supplies. A receiver is not a new customer with a statutory right to supply if he is acting as agent of the company, either as regards gas or electricity.[4] But a subsidiary is a new customer, and one of the bonuses of hiving down is that in principle, whatever the reluctance of the boards may be, the subsidiary is entitled to the supply of gas or electricity.[5] Previous favourable terms of supply available to the company will not apply, and the new customer may face demands for a large deposit in advance, or the receiver may be asked to provide a personal guarantee.

In the event of litigation about the right of a board or company supplying facilities such as gas or electricity it is virtually certain that the crucial factor will be held (as it has been in Canada) to be whether the receiver has opened a new account. That was what had happened in *Canada Trust Co v Consumers' Gas Co*[6] where, after the plaintiff had appointed a receiver who had opened a new account with the gas company and paid the current bills, the gas company cut off the gas supply because of the debtor company's arrears. The plaintiff sought an interlocutory injunction to restrain the withholding of gas supply. In the Supreme Court of Ontario Keith J distinguished two earlier English cases namely *Re Smith*[7] and *Paterson v Gas Light and Coke Co*[8] because in those cases no new

20 *Re Kayford Ltd* [1975] 1 All ER 604, [1975] 1 WLR 279; *Swiss Bank Corpn v Lloyds Bank Ltd* [1982] AC 584.
1 *Re London Wine Co (Shippers) Ltd* [1986] PCC 121.
2 *Export Credits Guarantee Department v Turner* 1981 SLT 286.
3 *Re Multi Guarantee Co Ltd* [1987] BCLC 257; *Lord v Australian Elizabethan Theatre Trust* (1991) 5 ACSR 587.
4 See *Paterson v Gas Light and Coke Co* [1896] 2 Ch 476, CA.
5 See the discussion at p 174.
6 (1977) 26 CBRNS 193, 83 DLR (3d) 449.
7 [1893] 1 QB 323, 67 LT 596.
8 [1896] 2 Ch 476, CA.

account had been opened in the name of the receiver. But in the case before him it was otherwise, and applying the old test[9] of a strong prima facie case, Keith J granted the injunction sought.

The decision in *Canada Trust Co v Consumers' Gas Co* was in its turn distinguished in *Peat Marwick Ltd v Consumers' Gas Co*[10] where no new account had been opened in the name of the receiver. Osler J rejected a motion for a mandatory injunction because he considered that at the trial of the action the receiver would probably be held liable. After referring to *Ostrander v Niagara Helicopters Ltd*[11] where Stark J had pointed out that a receiver, not court appointed, is called the agent of the company but is in fact the agent for the mortgagee or other creditor in possession Osler J continued:[12]

> 'In practice, however, the debenture in such cases, as here, provides expressly that the receiver shall be deemed to be the agent of the company. Obviously, this is done for the purpose of making it apparent to third parties that the receiver has authority to deal with and manage the affairs of the company. That being so, it is not surprising that the defendant in the present case should look to the receiver for payment of its account and refuse to enter upon a new contract unless it is paid. That is the result in two English cases dealing with similar situations under very similar legislation namely *Re Smith* [1893] 1 QB 323 and *Paterson v Gas Light and Coke Co* [1896] 2 Ch 476'.

Administrative receiver

An administrative receiver stands differently in these matters because his position is expressly dealt with under s 233 of the Insolvency Act 1986.[13]

LOCAL AUTHORITIES

A company which goes into receivership is very often in arrears with its rates and the local authority will be concerned to recover such arrears. Rating liability is based on occupation and the crucial question in relation to a privately appointed receiver is whether he or the company is in occupation of the relevant premises.

Although a ratepayer cannot be sued in civil proceedings for non-payment of rates, and unpaid rates (with one exception[14]) do not create a charge on land in respect of which the rates have been assessed, the local authority has a powerful weapon at its disposal. It can collect its money by means of a distraint order obtained from a magistrates' court.[15]

9 Ie that applied in England before *American Cyanamid Co v Ethicon Ltd* [1975] AC 396, [1975] 1 All ER 504, HL.
10 (1977) 26 CBRNS 195, 83 DLR (3d) 450.
11 (1973) 19 CBRNS 5, 40 DLR (3d) 161.
12 (1977) 26 CBRNS 195 at 197.
13 See the discussion at p 108.
14 Penal rating surcharges: see Local Government Act 1974, s 19.
15 General Rate Act 1967, s 96.

Previous uncertainties in the law

Whether the appointment of a receiver constitutes a change of occupier for rating purposes is a question on which the authorities were, for a long time, not clear. In *Richards v Kidderminster Overseers*,[16] a deed of floating charge gave power to the trustee to appoint a receiver and manager who was expressed to be the agent of the mortgagor. North J held that on a receiver duly appointed under the power entering into possession of the premises and starting to carry on the business of the company there was a change of occupancy within the meaning of the relevant statutory provisions as to rating with which he was concerned.[17]

In *Re Marriage Neave & Co*,[18] the question in issue was whether entry upon the company's premises by a receiver and manager for the purpose of carrying on the business represented a change of occupation within the wording of a particular statutory provision concerning rates[19] which had been the subject of argument in *Richards v Overseers of Kidderminster*. The receivers had been appointed by the court under an order which did not direct delivery-up of possession to him; but they had in fact gone on to the property to manage and carry on the business. Lindley LJ drew a distinction between an order under which possession was to be given up and the factual position which he was considering. To him it did not appear from the evidence that the receiver and managers had taken possession of the land in any sense at all. He analysed the position in the following way:[20]

> 'What they have done is this: they have gone to the property for the purpose of receiving and managing the income and business of the company, but they have not done anything to change the ostensible possession of the property in any way whatever; and on the facts it appears to me that the possession and occupation have not been changed at all.'

The finding was clearly based on the construction of the order itself. 'The mere fact that a receiver is appointed by an order which does not in fact order the company to give up possession does not dispossess the company.'[1] And Rigby LJ[2] distinguished *Richards v Kidderminster Overseers* because that case concerned a *privately* appointed receiver.

The distinction between *Richards v Kidderminster Overseers*[3] and *Re Marriage Neave & Co Ltd*[4] was explained by Ungoed Thomas J in *Taggs Island Casino Hotel Ltd v Richmond Upon Thames Borough Council*.[5] That case concerned a motion for an interlocutory injunction by the plaintiff ratepayer company and the receiver and manager of its undertaking to prevent the sale by the rating authority of goods of the company to satisfy a rating liability. It was

---

16 [1896] 2 Ch 212, 65 LJ Ch 502.
17 Poor Rate Assessment and Collection Act 1869, s 16; Public Health Act 1875, s 211(3).
18 [1896] 2 Ch 663, CA.
19 Poor Rate Assessment and Collection Act 1869, s 16.
20 [1896] 2 Ch 663 at 672.
 1 [1896] 2 Ch 663.
 2 [1896] 2 Ch 663 at 678.
 3 [1896] 2 Ch 212.
 4 [1896] 2 Ch 663, CA.
 5 [1967] RA 70.

there held, albeit for interlocutory purposes, that although the document under which the receiver is appointed is a very material factor in determining whether or not the receiver had gone into occupation of the premises, the true test is not whether that document required delivery up of possession to him (as distinguished from empowering him to enter into possession) but whether he did take possession in accordance with directions for delivery up of possession contained in the document or did not take up possession at all.

Ungoed Thomas J referring to the two earlier cases had this to say on the point:[6]

> 'There has been a good deal of argument about these cases and their effect. It seems to me, however, on these cases, that the distinguishing feature between the *Richards*[7] case and the *Re Marriage, Neave & Co*[8] case was not that one case required the receiver to go into possession and the other did not, but that in the one case there was, as is so commonly provided in orders of the court, a direction that the receiver should go into possession and that possession be delivered up to the receiver and that this was effected in accordance with the order; and that in the *Marriage Neave* case possession of the land was not taken at all. It seems to me, prima facie at any rate, to be a question of fact whether, when the receiver has authority to go into possession, he does in fact go into possession, and whether the kind of possession which he takes amounts occupation of the premises'.

A receiver was, in one case, held to be an occupier within the meaning of the Factories Act 1937.[9] But in the course of his judgment Lord Caldecote LCJ in the case in question referred to the usual deemed agency clause and observed that it had 'the effect of protecting the debenture holder from liability as mortgagee in possession or as principal'.[10] Ungoed Thomas J concluded that if a receiver was in possession amounting to occupation that occupation was not an occupation on behalf of the company just by reason of the deemed agency clause.

Decision in Ratford and Hayward v Northavon RDC

The law has now been considerably clarified by the decision of the Court of Appeal in *Ratford v Northavon District Council*.[11] This established that where a receiver has been appointed under a debenture with a deemed agency clause and is empowered but not obliged to take possession, the burden of proof shifts from the receiver to the rating authority which must show that the receiver has dispossessed the company or at the least is enjoying possession otherwise than as agent of the company. The facts touching the receiver's presence at the company's premises were in that case consistent with the receiver being in occupation as agent of the company. Slade LJ commented that although it would

---

6 [1967] RA 70 at 77.
7 [1896] 2 Ch 212, 65 LJ Ch 502.
8 [1896] 2 Ch 663, 65 LJ Ch 839.
9 *Meigh v Wickenden* [1942] 2 KB 160, [1942] 2 All ER 68.
10 [1942] 2 KB 160 at 165.
11 [1987] QB 357, [1986] 3 All ER 193, CA.

be possible for a receiver to take independent possession of the premises in practice such cases (he suspected) would be rare.

LANDLORDS

Nowadays leases granted to companies will often, as a precaution, contain a provision that the lease may be forfeited on the appointment of a receiver, so that in that event the landlord may terminate the lease.

Subject to the consequences of such a provision (if present) the general rule is that the appointment of a receiver of a tenant company will not affect the lease or the landlord's rights in any way.

Distress

The landlord can still distrain for rent[12] subject to any prior distress levied by a local authority even though the charge has crystallised.[13] If the local authority distrains first its distress is not subject to the rights which a landlord possesses under s 1 of the Landlord and Tenant Act 1709. Accordingly where the local authority levies its distress first that distress takes priority over a subsequent distress levied by a landlord.

The court may relieve a receiver who innocently sells goods without the knowledge of a distraint.[14]

In contrast to the position where the receiver is court appointed[15] a landlord needs no permission to proceed with the distress. But he must abide by the rules of distress: he must distrain only on a reasonable quantity of goods and his distraint must not be excessive.

Forfeiture

An attempt by the landlord to forfeit a lease for non-payment of rent as against a receiver can be met by a claim to an *absolute* right to avoid forfeiture by payment of the rent arrears in full, even if a court order forfeiting the lease has been made.[16] Where a lease is forfeited on other grounds there may still be a claim to relief against forfeiture.[17] If the lease is expressed to be forfeitable on the appointment of a receiver, the appointment of a receiver will constitute the breach of a

---

12 *Re Roundwood Colliery Co* [1897] 1 Ch 373 at 393 (distress levied but not completed before appointment); *Purcell v Queensland Public Curator* (1922) 31 CLR 220, [1922] St R Qd 25 (where the receiver had been appointed and gone into possession prior to distress).
13 *Purcell v Queensland Public Curator,* above.
14 See *Abingdon RDC v O'Gorman* [1968] 2 QB 811, [1968] 3 All ER 79, CA.
15 As to which see in this respect: *Re New City Constitutional Club Co* (1887) 34 Ch D 646 at 660, CA.
16 Common Law Procedure Amendment Act 1856.
17 See LPA 1925, s 146.

'condition' and not simply the breach of a covenant. Nevertheless a receiver will have a number of strings to his bow. First, he may prompt the company to apply for relief under s 146 of the Law of Property Act 1925, the application being combined with one to assign the lease to a suitable purchaser if there is no chance of the company regaining its solvency. Secondly, the receiver may persuade the holder of any fixed charge including the holder of any crystallised floating charge to apply for relief as a sub-tenant under s 146. Finally, the receiver could apply for relief from forfeiture on equitable grounds.[18] He can do this in the company's name[19] and this power survives the company's liquidation.[20]

Continued occupation

A receiver enjoys no statutory or other right of disclaimer. However, the receiver may not wish to use the leasehold property or pay rent for it or cause the company of which he is receiver to pay rent for it. In such a case there is no compulsion on the receiver. If he does decide to make use of the leasehold premises then plainly he must pay the rent which he will treat as a legitimate outgoing either under the terms of any relevant statutory provision[1] or under the express terms of the debenture. Where he decides to continue in occupation he will in practice pay any arrears in order to avoid distress.

---

18 LPA 1925, s 146.
19 *Goughs Garages Ltd v Pugsley* [1930] 1 KB 615.
20 *Official Custodian for Charities v Parway Estates Developments Ltd* [1985] Ch 151.
 1 See the LPA 1925, s 109(8).

CHAPTER 14

Meetings and committees of creditors in an administrative receivership

INTRODUCTION

The insolvency legislation, now contained in the Insolvency Act 1986 and the Insolvency Rules, introduced a novel concept into receiverships. This is the creditors' meeting. The function of such a meeting, which can be adjourned, is twofold: to consider the receiver's report and, if it thinks fit, to elect a creditors' committee. The duties of an administrative receiver in relation to the compilation and transmission of his report have been considered in an earlier chapter.[1] This chapter is concerned with the detailed rules relating to creditors' meetings and to committees of creditors.

MEETINGS OF CREDITORS

Procedure for summoning meeting

In fixing the venue[2] for a meeting of creditors[3] the administrative receiver must have regard to the convenience of the persons who are invited to attend.[4] The meeting must be summoned for commencement between 10.00 and 16.00 hours on a business day,[5] unless the court otherwise directs.[6] At least 14 days' notice of the venue must be given to all creditors of the company who are identified in the statement of affairs, or are known to the receiver and had claims against the company at the date of his appointment.[7] With the notice summoning the meeting, forms of proxy must be sent out.[8] The notice must include a statement to the effect that creditors whose claims are wholly secured are not entitled to

---

1 See Chapter 10.
2 Ie the date, time and place of the meeting: IR 1986, rr 13.1, 13.6.
3 Summoned pursuant to IA 1986, s 48(2).
4 IR 1986, r 3.9(1).
5 Ie not a Saturday or a Sunday, Christmas Day, Good Friday or a day which is a bank holiday in any part of Great Britain: IR 1986, rr 13.1, 13.13(1) and IA 1986, s 251.
6 IR 1986, r 3.9(2).
7 IR 1986, r 3.9(3).
8 IR 1986, r 3.9(4). For the prescribed form of proxy, see rr 3.9, 12.7, Sch 4, Form 8.3.

attend or be represented at the meeting.[9] Notice of the meeting must also be published in the newspaper in which the receiver's appointment was advertised;[10] and the notice to creditors and the newspaper advertisement must contain a statement of voting rights.[11]

Chairman and quorum

The chairman at the creditors' meeting must be the receiver or a person nominated by him in writing to act in his place.[12] A person so nominated must be either one who is qualified to act as an insolvency practitioner[13] in relation to the company or an employee of the receiver or his firm who is experienced in insolvency matters.[14]

Any meeting of creditors in insolvency proceedings is competent to act if a quorum is present, that is to say in the case of a creditors' meeting, at least *one* creditor entitled to vote.[15] For this purpose the reference to the creditor necessary to constitute a quorum is to any persons present or represented by proxy by any person, including the chairman, and including persons duly represented under the Companies Act 1985.[16]

Where at any meeting of creditors the above provisions as to a quorum being present are satisfied by the attendance of the chairman alone or one other person in addition to the chairman, and the chairman is aware, by virtue of proofs and proxies received or otherwise, that one or more additional persons would, if attending, be entitled to vote, the meeting must not commence until at least the expiry of 15 minutes after the time appointed for its commencement.[17]

The creditors' meeting must not be adjourned, even if no quorum is present, unless the chairman decides that it is desirable; and in that case he must adjourn it to such a date, time and place as he thinks fit.[18] If there is no quorum and the meeting is not adjourned, it is deemed to have been duly summoned and held.[19]

Voting rights

At the creditors' meeting a person is entitled to vote only if: (i) he has given to the receiver, not later than 12 noon on the business day[20] before the day fixed for

9 IR 1986, r 3.9(5).
10 IR 1986, r 3.9(6).
11 IR 1986, r 3.9(7).
12 IR 1986, r 3.10(1).
13 As to insolvency practitioners and their qualifications see pp 53–54.
14 IR 1986, r 3.10(2).
15 IR 1986, r 12.4A(1), (2)(a) (added by SI 1987/1919).
16 IR 1986, r 12.4A(3) (added by SI 1987/1919).
17 IR 1986, r 12.4A(4) (added by SI 1987/1919).
18 IR 1986, r 3.14(1). Rule 3.9(1) and (2) applies, with necessary modifications, to any adjourned meeting: r 3.14(2).
19 IR 1986, r 3.14(3).
20 For the meaning of 'business day' see IR 1986, r 13.13(1) and IA 1986, s 251. See p 229, n 5.

the meeting, details in writing of the debt that he claims to be due to him from the company, and the claim has been duly admitted; and (ii) there has been lodged with the administrative receiver any proxy which the creditor intends to be used on his behalf.[1] The chairman of the meeting may allow a creditor to vote notwithstanding that he failed to comply with (i) above, if satisfied that the failure was due to circumstances beyond the creditor's control.[2] The receiver, or if other, the chairman of the meeting may call for any document or other evidence to be produced to him where he thinks it necessary for the purpose of substantiating the whole or any part of the claim.[3]

Votes are calculated according to the amount of a creditor's debt as at the date of the appointment of the receiver, after deducting any amounts paid in respect of that debt after that date.[4] A creditor may not vote in respect of a debt for an unliquidated amount, or any debt whose value is not ascertained, except where the chairman agrees to put upon the debt an estimated minimum value for the purpose of entitlement to vote and admits the claim for that purpose.[5] A secured creditor is entitled to vote only in respect of the balance, if any, of his debt after deducting the value of his security as estimated by him.[6]

A creditor may not vote in respect of a debt on, or secured by, a current bill of exchange or promissory note, unless he is willing: (i) to treat the liability to him on the bill or note of every person who is liable on it antecedently to the company, and against whom a bankruptcy order has not been made, or, in the case of a company, which has not gone into liquidation, as a security in his hands; and (ii) to estimate the value of the security and, for the purpose of his entitlement to vote, to deduct it from his claim.[7]

Admission and rejection of claims

At the creditors' meeting the chairman has power to admit or reject a creditor's claim for the purpose of his entitlement to vote, and the power is exercisable with respect to the whole or any part of the claim.[8] The chairman's decision under this provision, or in respect of any matter arising in relation to voting rights, is subject to appeal to the court by any creditor.[9] If the chairman is in doubt whether a claim should be admitted or rejected, he should mark it as objected to and allow the creditor to vote, subject to his vote being subsequently declared invalid if the objection to the claim is sustained.[10] If, on an appeal, the chairman's decision is reversed or varied, or a creditor's vote is declared invalid, the court may order that another meeting be summoned, or

---

1 IR 1986, r 3.11(1).
2 IR 1986, r 3.11(2).
3 IR 1986, r 3.11(3).
4 IR 1986, r 3.11(4).
5 IR 1986, r 3.11(5).
6 IR 1986, r 3.11(6).
7 IR 1986, r 3.11(7).
8 IR 1986, r 3.12(1).
9 IR 1986, r 3.12(2).
10 IR 1986, r 3.12(3).

make such other order as it thinks just.[11] Neither the receiver nor any person nominated by him to be chairman is personally liable for costs incurred by any person in respect of any such appeal to the court, unless the court makes an order to that effect.[12]

Resolutions and minutes

At the creditors' meeting, a resolution is passed when a majority, in value, of those present and voting in person or by proxy have voted in favour of it.[13] The chairman of the meeting must cause a record to be made of the proceedings, and kept as part of the records of the receivership.[14] The record must include a list of the creditors who attended, whether personally or by proxy, and, if a creditors' committee has been established, the names and addresses of those elected to be members of the committee.[15]

CREDITORS' COMMITTEE

Establishing a creditors' committee

Where a meeting of creditors is summoned,[16] the meeting may, if it thinks fit, establish a committee ('the creditors' committee') to exercise the functions conferred on it by or under the Insolvency Act 1986.[17] If such a committee is established, it may, on giving not less than seven days' notice, require the administrative receiver to attend before it at any reasonable time and furnish it with such information relating to the carrying out by him of his functions as it may reasonably require.[18]

Constitution of committee

Where it is resolved by the creditors' meeting to establish a creditors' committee, the committee must consist of at least three and not more than five creditors of the company elected at the meeting.[19] Any creditor of the company is eligible to be a member of the committee, so long as his claim has not been rejected for the purpose of his entitlement to vote.[20] A body corporate may be a member of the

11 IR 1986, r 3.12(4).
12 IR 1986, r 3.12(5).
13 IR 1986, r 3.15(1).
14 IR 1986, r 3.15(2).
15 IR 1986, r 3.15(3).
16 Ie under IA 1986, s 48.
17 IA 1986, s 49(1).
18 IA 1986, s 49(2).
19 IR 1986, r 3.16(1).
20 IR 1986, r 3.16(2).

committee, but it cannot act as such otherwise than by a properly appointed[1] representative.[2] 'Body corporate' does not include a corporation sole but includes a company incorporated elsewhere than in Great Britain; it does not include a Scottish firm.[3]

Formalities of establishment

The creditors' committee does not come into being, and accordingly cannot act, until the administrative receiver has issued a certificate of its due constitution.[4]

No person may act as a member of the committee unless and until he has agreed to do so and, unless the relevant proxy or authorisation contains a statement to the contrary, such agreement may be given by his proxy-holder or representative[5] present at the meeting establishing the committee.[6] The receiver's certificate of the committee's due constitution must not issue unless and until at least three of the persons who are to be members of the committee have agreed to act.[7] As and when the others, if any, agree to act, the receiver must issue an amended certificate.[8] The certificate, and any amended certificate, must be sent by the receiver to the registrar of companies.[9] If, after the first establishment of the committee, there is any change in its membership, the receiver must report the change to the registrar of companies.[10]

Functions and meetings of the committee

The creditors' committee must assist the administrative receiver in discharging his functions and act in relation to him in such manner as may be agreed from time to time.[11] Meetings of the committee must be held when and where determined by the receiver.[12] The receiver must, however, call a first meeting of the committee not later than three months after its establishment; and thereafter he must call a meeting: (i) if requested by a member of the committee or his representative, the meeting then to be held within 21 days of the request being received by the receiver; and (ii) for a specified date, if the committee has previously resolved that a meeting be held on that date.[13] The receiver must give

1 Ie appointed under IR 1986, r 3.21.
2 IR 1986, r 3.16(3).
3 IA 1986, s 251 applying CA 1985, s 740.
4 IR 1986, r 3.17(1). For the prescribed form of certificate see rr 3.17, 12.7, Sch 4, Form 3.4.
5 Ie under the Companies Act 1985, s 375.
6 IR 1986, r 3.17(2) (substituted by SI 1987/1919).
7 IR 1986, r 3.17(2A) (added by SI 1987/1919).
8 IR 1986, r 3.17(3). For the prescribed form of amended certificate see rr 3.17, 12.7, Sch 4, Form 3.4.
9 IR 1986, r 3.17(4).
10 IR 1986, r 3.17(5). For the prescribed form of report see rr 3.17, 12.7, Sch 4, Form 3.5.
11 IR 1986, r 3.18(1).
12 IR 1986, r 3.18(2).
13 IR 1986, r 3.18(3).

seven days' written notice of the venue[14] of any meeting to every member, or his representative designated for that purpose, unless in any case the requirement of notice has been waived by or on behalf of any member; and waiver may be signified either at or before the meeting.[15]

The acts of the creditors' committee established for any administrative receivership are valid notwithstanding any defect in the appointment, election or qualifications of any member of the committee or any committee member's representative or in the formalities of its establishment.[16]

The chairman and quorum at meetings

Subject to the exception in the case of a meeting convened for the purpose of obtaining information from the receiver,[17] the chairman at any meeting of the creditors' committee must be the administrative receiver, or a person nominated by him in writing to act.[18] A person so nominated must be either one who is qualified to act as an insolvency practitioner in relation to the company,[19] or an employee of the receiver or his firm who is experienced in insolvency matters.[20]

A meeting of the committee is duly constituted if due notice has been given to all the members, and at least two members are present or represented.[1]

Committee members' representatives

A member of the creditors' committee may, in relation to the business of the committee, be represented by another person duly authorised by him for that purpose.[2] A person acting as a committee member's representative must hold a letter of authority entitling him so to act, either generally or specially, and signed by or on behalf of the committee member.[3] For this purpose any proxy or any authorisation under the Companies Act 1985[4] in relation to any meeting of creditors of the company is, unless it contains a statement to the contrary, to be treated as a letter of authority to act generally, signed by or on behalf of the committee member.[5]

The chairman at any meeting of the committee may call on a person claiming to act as a committee member's representative to produce his letter of authority,

---

14 Ie the date, time and place thereof.
15 IR 1986, r 3.18(4).
16 IR 1986, r 3.30A (added by SI 1987/1919).
17 Ie pursuant to the IR 1986, r 3.28(3): see the references to r 3.28(1)–(3) in Appendix 1, below.
18 IR 1986, r 3.19(1).
19 As to insolvency practitioners and their qualifications see pp 53–54.
20 IR 1986, r 3.19(2).
 1 IR 1986, r 3.20.
 2 IR 1986, r 3.21(1).
 3 IR 1986, r 3.21(2) (amended by SI 1987/1919).
 4 Ie under CA 1985, s 375.
 5 IR 1986, r 3.21(2).

and may exclude him if it appears that his authority is deficient.[6] No member may be represented by a body corporate, or by a person who is an undischarged bankrupt, or is subject to a composition or arrangement with his creditors.[7] No person may act, on the same committee, at one and the same time, as representative of more than one committee member, or act both as a member of the committee and as representative of another member.[8] Where a member's representative signs any document on the member's behalf, the fact that he so signs must be stated below his signature.[9]

Resignation, termination of membership and removal

A member of the creditors' committee may resign by notice in writing delivered to the administrative receiver.[10]

Membership of the creditors' committee is automatically terminated if the member: (i) becomes bankrupt, or compounds or arranges with his creditors; or (ii) at three consecutive meetings of the committee is neither present nor represented, unless at the third of those meetings it is resolved that these provisions shall not apply to his case; or (iii) ceases to be, or is found never to have been, a creditor.[11] However, if the cause of the termination is the member's bankruptcy, his trustee in bankruptcy replaces him as a member of the committee.[12]

A member of the committee may be removed by resolution at a meeting of creditors, at least 14 days' notice having been given of the intention to move that resolution.[13]

Vacancies

If there is a vacancy in the membership of the creditors' committee, such vacancy need not be filled if the administrative receiver and a majority of the remaining members of the committee so agree, provided that the total number of members does not fall below the required minimum.[14] Alternatively, the receiver may appoint any creditor, being qualified[15] to be a member of the committee, to fill the vacancy if a majority of the other members of the committee agree to the appointment and the creditor concerned consents to act.[16]

---

6 IR 1986, r 3.21(3).
7 IR 1986, r 3.21(4).
8 IR 1986, r 3.21(5).
9 IR 1986, r 3.21(6).
10 IR 1986, r 3.22.
11 IR 1986, r 3.23(1).
12 IR 1986, r 3.23(2).
13 IR 1986, r 3.24.
14 IR 1986, r 3.25(1), (2). The required minimum is that required by r 3.16.
15 Ie qualified under the IR 1986 (amended by SI 1986/1919).
16 IR 1986, r 3.25(3).

Procedure at meetings and resolutions by post

At any meeting of the creditors' committee, each member of it, whether present himself or by his representative,[17] has one vote; and a resolution is passed when a majority of the members present or represented have voted in favour of it.[18] Every resolution passed must be recorded in writing, either separately or as part of the minutes of the meeting.[19] A record of each resolution must be signed by the chairman and kept as part of the records of the receivership.[20]

The administrative receiver may, however, seek to obtain the agreement of members of the creditors' committee to a resolution by sending to every member, or his representative designated for the purpose, a copy of the proposed resolution.[1] Where the receiver makes use of such procedure, he must send out to members of the committee or their representatives, as the case may be, a copy of the proposed resolution on which a decision is sought, which must be set out in such a way that agreement with or dissent from each separate resolution may be indicated by the recipient on the copy so sent.[2] Any member of the committee may, within seven business days[3] from the date of the receiver sending out a resolution, require him to summon a meeting of the committee to consider the matters raised by the resolution.[4] In the absence of such a request, the resolution is deemed to have been passed by the committee if and when the receiver is notified in writing by a majority of the members that they concur with it.[5] A copy of every resolution so passed and a note that the committee's concurrence was obtained must be kept with the records of the receivership.[6]

Information from administrative receiver

Where the creditors' committee resolves to require the administrative receiver to attend before it for the purpose of furnishing the committee with such information relating to the carrying out by him of his functions as the committee may reasonably require,[7] the notice to him must be in writing signed by the majority of the members of the committee for the time being; and a member's representative[8] may sign for him.[9] The meeting at which the receiver's attendance is required must be fixed by the committee for a business day,[10] and must be held at

---

17 As to committee members' representatives see above.
18 IR 1986, r 3.26(1).
19 IR 1986, r 3.26(2).
20 IR 1986, r 3.26(3).
 1 IR 1986, r 3.27(1).
 2 IR 1986, r 3.27(2) (amended by SI 1987/1925).
 3 For the meaning of 'business day' see p 229, n 5.
 4 IR 1986, r 3.27(3).
 5 IR 1986, r 3.27(4).
 6 IR 1986, r 3.27(5).
 7 Ie pursuant to the Insolvency Act 1986, s 49(2).
 8 As to committee members' representatives see above.
 9 IR 1986, r 3.28(1).
10 For the meaning of 'business day', see p 229, n 5.

such time and place as he determines.[11] Where the receiver so attends, the members of the committee may elect any one of their number to be chairman of the meeting in place of the receiver or any nominee of his.[12]

Expenses of members

The administrative receiver must, out of the assets of the company, defray any reasonable travelling expenses directly incurred by members of the creditors' committee or their representatives in relation to their attendance at the committee's meetings, or otherwise on the committee's business, as an expense of the receivership;[13] but this provision does not apply to any meeting of the committee held within three months of a previous meeting, unless the meeting in question is summoned at the instance of the administrative receiver.[14]

Members' dealings with the company

Membership of the creditors' committee does not prevent a person from dealing with the company while the receiver is acting, provided that any transactions in the course of such dealings are entered into in good faith and for value.[15] The court may, on the application of any person interested, set aside a transaction which appears to it to be contrary to the above requirements and may give such consequential directions as it thinks fit for compensating the company for any loss which it may have incurred in consequence of the transaction.[16]

11 IR 1986, r 3.28(2).
12 IR 1986, r 3.28(3).
13 IR 1986, r 3.29(1).
14 IR 1986, r 3.29(2).
15 IR 1986, r 3.30(1).
16 IR 1986, r 3.30(2).

CHAPTER 15

Effect of winding up

INTRODUCTION

Where mortgage debentures have been issued charging the whole of the company's assets including future debts and calls, difficult questions may arise as to the effect of liquidation on the rights of the debenture holders, and the respective functions of the liquidator and the receiver.[1] The approach adopted by this chapter is to consider (i) the effect, if any, of a winding up on the right to appoint or on an existing appointment, (ii) the effect of a supervening winding up on the powers of the receiver having regard in particular to his usual position as 'agent' for the company, and (iii) the effect of liquidation on the various duties of a receiver and manager.

EFFECT ON APPOINTMENT

Ordinarily the instrument creating the debenture confers on the holders or their trustees a right to appoint a receiver and manager. A supervening liquidation will not affect their right of appointment.[2] Indeed the standard form of debenture specifies the presentation of a petition or a resolution for a voluntary liquidation as events which give rise to an immediate liability to repay all outstanding principal and interest and to a right to appoint a receiver and manager.

Formerly it was the case that once a liquidator has been appointed in a compulsory winding up the receiver had to get the leave of the court to take possession of the assets, because he would otherwise have been guilty of contempt should he interfere with the possession of an officer of the court.[3] However, in the Australian case of *Re Landmark Corpn Ltd*[4] it was held that leave was

---

1 For an Australian analysis, see James O'Donovan *Company Receivers and Managers* (2nd edn, 1992) ch 13, paras 13.10–13.20. For a Malaysian view, see Samsar Kamis Bin Hj Ab Latif 'Receivership and Liquidation: Interrelationship' [1995] 1 MLJ liii–lxxxvii.
2 *Re Henry Pound, Son & Hutchins* (1889) 42 Ch D 402; *Strong v Carlyle Press* [1893] 1 Ch 268.
3 *Re Henry Pound, Son & Hutchins* (1889) 42 Ch D 402.
4 (1968) 88 WN (Pt 1) (NSW) 195, [1968] 1 NSWR 705. In the ordinary case there is 'no purpose whatever in perpetuating what is, after all, no more than an outmoded practice which involves a pointless expenditure on costs': see (1968) 88 WN (Pt 1) (NSW) 195 at 197 per Street J.

only necessary if there was a dispute as to the right of the receiver to possession of the assets under the de facto control of a liquidator who refuses to give them up. In other respects the right to appoint a receiver is virtually absolute: the debenture holders as secured creditors stand outside the liquidation.[5] Their independent realisation of their security necessarily results in withdrawing the winding up to some extent from the court's control.[6]

Just as the event of liquidation does not prevent the appointment of a receiver, the appointment of a receiver does not prevent a liquidation.

A winding-up order may not now be refused simply on the ground that the assets of the company have been mortgaged to an amount equal to or in excess of their value, or that the company has no assets. The court therefore may make a winding-up order even though there is a receiver in possession and it is plain that the creditors can derive no benefit from the order. In *Re Chic Ltd*[7] the judgment creditors who were petitioning for the winding up of a company were in that position; the company was in receivership and the assets were very small and more than covered by the debentures. The petitioners could not show that there would be any surplus assets or that they would get any advantage from the winding up. But the company could not pay its debts or exercise any control over its business which was being carried on for the benefit of the debenture holders. The receiver was running up large liabilities. In these circumstances it was held that the company should be wound up. A similar order was made in *Re Clandown Colliery Co*[8] where again, the debentures swamped the assets and a receiver and manager was already in harness. The petition was opposed by the great majority in number and amount of the unsecured creditors but no reasons for their opposition were proffered in affidavit or otherwise. The court made a compulsory winding-up order.

The fact that a receiver has been appointed at the instance of a debenture holder does not preclude the debenture holder from petitioning. The remedy given to him to enforce his security upon the undertaking as a going concern does not deprive him of his remedy as a creditor who has obtained a judgment for his debt, but cannot obtain payment.

The commencement of a winding up and in particular the appointment of a liquidator may deter a potential receiver and manager from accepting a proffered appointment if he has reason to suspect that the charge under which his appointment would be made is in any way vulnerable. The charge may be a preference or infringe the statutory provision restricting the creation of floating charges within a certain period prior to a winding up. It may not have been registered or properly executed or there may be some other flaw. Some of these matters have been referred to in an earlier chapter and it is not intended to rehearse them again. But the point which needs to be emphasised is that the classic way for the liquidator to promote the interests of preferred and other creditors is to impugn, if he can, the receiver's title.

5 *Strong v Carlyle Press* [1893] 1 Ch 268; *Ansted v Land Co of Australasia (No 2)* (1894) 4 BC (NSW) 60.
6 *Re Henry Pound, Son & Hutchins* (1889) 42 Ch D 402 at 420 per Cotton LJ; and see *Re High Crest Motors Pty Ltd* (1978) 3 ACLR 564.
7 [1905] 2 Ch 345, 74 LJ Ch 597.
8 [1915] 1 Ch 369, 84 LJ Ch 420.

Prior to the enactment of the Insolvency Act 1986, the charge under which the receiver was appointed could be attacked either on the basis that it was a fraudulent preference or, if it was a floating charge, on the basis that it was statutorily invalid. The law has undergone considerable reform in this area in England. Preferences can still be set aside though on a different basis, and the Insolvency Act 1986 has enlarged the ambit of the provision dealing with the statutory invalidation of floating charges. But there are now additional statutory weapons with which to attack a company charge. The charge in question may be a transaction at an undervalue or an extortionate credit bargain.

The old law relating to fraudulent preferences and to the statutory invalidation of floating charges still survives in some Commonwealth jurisdictions whose companies legislation is derived from the English Companies Acts of 1929 and 1948. Some of the case law remains of assistance in construing expressions which occur in the 1986 legislation and these will be maintained where relevant.

REOPENING TRANSACTIONS ANTECEDENT TO INSOLVENCY[9]

Introduction

Premonitions of an impending insolvency occasionally impel a creditor of a beleaguered company to try and steal a march on fellow creditors. Such premonitions may also tempt those connected with the company to secure their own position to the detriment of the general body of creditors. For both these reasons company legislation in many jurisdictions makes provision for a liquidator to be able to reopen certain antecedent transactions (that is to say transactions entered into at a time preceding the liquidation).

The precise rationale for such provisions is seldom articulated in the cases or by the legislature. Each provision has lived its own independent life and been individually developed and modified without any appeal to any overriding and coherent doctrine. The latest version of the statutory provisions directed to this end in England is contained in the Insolvency Act 1986.

Preferences under the Insolvency Act 1986

Introduction

The old law as to 'fraudulent preferences' as contained in s 615 of the Companies Act 1985 (and s 320 of the 1948 Act) had long been thought to be unsatisfactory. The concept of a fraudulent preference had at its root a dominant intention to prefer one creditor of the company over others.[10] The burden of showing the relevant dominant intention was often difficult for a liquidator to discharge. The

---

9 See Andrew Keay 'The Avoidance of Pre-Liquidation Transactions An Anglo Australian Comparison' [1998] JBL 515–549 (a discussion which covers IA 1986, ss 238–244 and Australian equivalents but not the avoidance of floating charges under the IA 1986, s 245).

10 *Re M Kushler Ltd* [1943] Ch 248, [1943] 2 All ER 22, CA.

aim of the Insolvency Act 1986 was therefore to catch more unfair dispositions. The draftsman has, however, eschewed the term 'voidable preference' recommended by the Cork Committee[11] and has not seen fit to adopt the expression 'undue preference' common in Australia. The Insolvency Act 1986 refers, so far as England and Wales[12] are concerned, simply to 'preferences'. The invalidation or curing of preferences arises in the context of an administration order having been made in relation to a company, or of a winding up.

Avoidance

Where a company has at a relevant time (as defined by the Act) given a preference to any person, the liquidator or administrator[13] may apply to the court for an order under s 239 of the Insolvency Act 1986 and the court must, on such application, make such order as it thinks fit for restoring the position to what it would have been if the company had not given that preference[14]. The terms 'relevant time' and 'preference' are both defined in the Insolvency Act 1986.[15]

Definition of 'preference'

Preference is not limited to the case of a transfer of property. A company gives a preference to a person if (a) that person is one of the company's creditors or a surety or guarantor for any of the company's debts or other liabilities, and (b) the company does anything or suffers anything to be done which (in either case) has the effect of putting that person into a position which, in the event of the company going into insolvent liquidation, will be better than the position he would have been in if that thing had not been done.[16] But the court will only act in relation to a preference given to a person if the company which gave it was influenced in deciding to give it by a desire to produce in relation to that person the effect mentioned in (b).[17] Payments made for the commercial benefit of the company even where there has been creditor pressure may escape classification as preferences.[18]

---

11 (1982) Cmnd 8558, para 1244.
12 But the term 'unfair preference' is applied in Scotland: IA 1986, s 243.
13 Each is an office holder as defined for the purposes of IA 1986, ss 238–245: IA 1986, s 238(1).
14 The court may also decline to make an order: cf *Re Lewis's of Leicester Ltd* [1995] BCC 514 (desire was not to give concessionaires in a department store a preference but rather to prevent store from looking more like a morgue than a market in its final weeks of trading).
15 See below. But no order shall be made in relation to a market contract as defined by CA 1985, s 155, unless the court is satisfied that the person in favour of whom the contract was made knew that a preference was being given: CA 1985, ss 159 and 164(5), (6).
16 IA 1986, s 239(4) and see *Re Thirty-Eight Building Ltd* [1999] 1 BCLC 416 (five trustees of retirement benefit scheme were creditors not beneficiaries themselves). Examples of a preference are: paying the whole or part of a debt, providing security or further security for an existing debt, and returning goods which have been delivered but not paid for: (1982) Cmnd 8558, para 1208. A payment to a third party at the direction of the preferred creditor can be a preference: *Re Exchange Travel (Holdings) Ltd* [1996] BCC 933 at 948 per Rattee J.
17 IA 1986, s 239(5). The desire may be inferred: *Re M C Bacon Ltd* (1990) BCC 78.
18 *Re Ledingham-Smith* [1993] BCLC 635 (to retain services of an accountant); *Re New Generation Engineers* [1993] BCLC 435 (payment to most pressing creditors to save business); *Re Lewis's of Leicester Ltd* [1995] BCC 514 (to protect image and profits over Christmas).

Relevant time

The time at which a company gives a preference is a relevant time for the purposes of this statutory provision if the preference is given: (a) in the case of a preference which is given to a person who is connected with the company at a time in the period of two years ending with the onset of insolvency; or (b) in the case of a preference which is not such a transaction and is not so given, at a time in the period of six months ending with the onset of insolvency; or (c) in either case, at a time between the presentation of a petition for the making of an administration order in relation to the company and the making of such an order on that petition.[19]

Where a company gives a preference at a time mentioned in (a) or (b) above, that time shall not be a relevant time for the purposes of s 239 unless the company (i) is unable to pay its debts within the meaning of s 123 of the Insolvency Act 1986 at that time; or (ii) becomes unable to pay its debts within the meaning of that section in consequence of the preference.[20] Indemnity to pay its debts may also be inferred from the fact that the company has invoices which it has not paid.[1]

Onset of insolvency

For the purposes of (a) above the onset of insolvency is: (i) in a case where this statutory provision applies by reason of the making of an administration order or of a company's going into liquidation immediately upon the discharge of an administration order, the date of the presentation of the petition on which the administration order was made; and (ii) in a case where this section applies by reason of a company's going into liquidation at another time, the date of the commencement of the winding up.[2]

Desire to produce preferential effect

The court must not make an order under this avoidance provision in respect of a preference given to any person unless the company which gave the preference was influenced in deciding to give it by a desire to produce in relation to that person the effect mentioned above. So a *dominant* intention to prefer is no longer necessary.[3]

Nor is it sufficient to establish an intention: there must be a desire to produce the effect mentioned in the section.[4] So a decision by a company to give a bank a charge to secure the company's existing borrowings was not actuated by a

19 IA 1986, s 240(1).
20 IA 1986, s 240(2); *Re D G K Contractors Ltd* [1990] BCC 903.
 1 *Willis v Corfe Joinery Ltd (in liquidation)* [1998] 2 BCLC 75.
 2 IA 1986, s 240(3).
 3 IA 1986, s 239(5). This test is to be contrasted with the previous 'dominant intention to prefer' test. *Re M C Bacon* [1990] BCC 78 at 87 (desire is subjective).
 4 *Re M C Bacon* [1990] BCC 78 at 87. So a decision to put a creditor and a guarantor of that creditor in a better position in the liquidation will, in each case, ground an order: *Re Agriplant Services Ltd* [1997] BCC 842.

positive desire to improve the creditor's position in the event of its own insolvent liquidation but by proper commercial considerations. The only alternative if the bank withdraws its support was liquidation.[5]

A company which has given a preference to a person connected with the company[6] at the time the preference was given is presumed, unless the contrary is shown,[7] to have been influenced in deciding to give it by such desire as aforesaid.[8] This important change, introduced on the recommendation of the Cork Committee, reverses the burden of proof as regards the factor of desire (ie intention) when the person who is preferred is a person connected with the company.

The fact that something has been done in pursuance of the order of a court shall not, without more, prevent the doing or suffering of that thing from constituting the giving of a preference.

Orders

The court has a general discretion about the type of order it may make, but some indication of the possible terms of orders is contained in s 241(1) of the Insolvency Act 1986. Without prejudice to the generality of the new statutory provision, an order under that section with respect to a preference given by a company may:

(a) require any property transferred in connection with the giving of the preference to be vested in the company;

(b) require any property to be so vested if it represents in any person's hands the application either of the proceeds of sale of property so transferred or of money so transferred;

(c) release or discharge (in whole or in part) any security given by the company;

(d) require any person to pay, in respect of benefits received by him from the company, such sums to the office holder[9] as the court may direct;

(e) provide for any surety or guarantor whose obligations to any person were released or discharged (in whole or in part) by the giving of the preference, to be under such new or revived obligations to that person as the court thinks appropriate;

---

5 *Re M C Bacon* [1990] BCC 78 at 87.
6 For persons connected with the company, see IA 1986, s 249(1); and see the definition of 'associate': IA 1986, s 435 on which see *Re Thirty-Eight Building Ltd* [1999] 1 BCLC 416.
7 As in *Re Beacon Leisure Ltd* [1991] BCC 213 *Re Fairway Magazines Ltd* [1992] BCC 924 and *Re Generation Engineers Ltd* [1993] BCLC 435. For cases where the presumption applied, see *Re DGK Contractors Ltd* [1990] BCC 903; *Weisgard v Pilkington* [1995] BCC 1,108; *Re Exchange Travel (Holdings) Ltd (in liquidation)* [1996] BCC 933 and *Wills v Corfe Joinery Ltd (in liquidation)* [1997] BCC 511.
8 IA 1986, s 239(6). For a case where the presumption was not rebutted, see *Katz v McNally* [1999] BCC 291, CA.
9 For the definition of 'office holder', see IA 1986, s 238(1) (liquidator or administrator).

(f) provide for security for the discharge of any obligation imposed by or arising under the order, for such an obligation to be charged on any property for such security or charge to have the same priority as a security or charge released or discharged (in whole or in part) by the giving of the preference; and

(g) provide for the extent to which any person whose property is vested by the order in the company, or on whom obligations are imposed by the order, is to be able to provide in the winding up of the company for debts or other liabilities which arose from, or were released or discharged (in whole or in part) under or by the giving of, the preference.[10]

The form of order that can be made is qualified, in that while an order under s 239 may affect the property of, or impose any obligation on, any person whether or not he is the person to whom the preference was given, such an order:

(a) shall not prejudice any interest in property which was acquired from a person other than the company and was acquired in good faith and for value and without notice of the relevant circumstances, or prejudice any interest deriving from such an interest; and

(b) shall not require a person who received a benefit from the transaction or preference in good faith and for value and without notice of the relevant circumstances, to pay a sum to the office holder, except where the payment is to be in respect of a preference given to that person at a time when he was a creditor of the company.[11]

Where a person has acquired an interest in property from a person other than the company in question, or has received a benefit from the transaction or preference, and at the time of that acquisition or receipt either he had notice of the relevant surrounding circumstances and of the relevant proceedings, or he was connected with, or was an associate of, either the company in question or the person with whom that company entered into the transaction or to whom that company gave the preference, then, unless the contrary is shown, it is statutorily presumed that the interest was acquired or the benefit was received otherwise than in good faith.[12]

The relevant surrounding circumstances, in relation to the presumption of good faith applicable to the provision governing the restriction on orders, are:

(a) the fact that the company in question entered into the transaction at an undervalue, or

(b) the circumstances which amounted to the giving of the preference by the company in question,

10 IA 1986, s 241(1).
11 IA 1986, s 241(2).
12 IA 1986, s 241(2A).

and whether for those purposes a person had notice of the relevant proceedings is determined by further provisions.[13]

It is also to be noted that the provisions of ss 239–241 apply without prejudice to the availability of any other remedy, even in relation to a preference which the company had no power to give.[14] Although the common law doctrine of ultra vires has been abolished for almost all purposes[15] it still has some relevance in regard to charitable companies.[16]

Transactions at undervalue

Not only preferences but also transactions at an undervalue may be set aside by the court on the application of certain office holders.

A company enters into a transaction with a person at an undervalue if:

(a)   the company makes a gift to that person or otherwise enters into a transaction with that person on terms that provide for the company to receive no consideration; or

(b)   the company enters into a transaction with that person for a consideration the value of which, in money or money's worth, is significantly less than the value, in money or money's worth, of the consideration provided by the company.[17]

It is important to identify or ascertain what was the transaction alleged to have been entered into by the company at an undervalue. Such identification of the relevant transaction must be done by reference to the person with whom it was entered into and can only take account of the elements of the transaction between the company and that person. Thus a contract between the company and one person cannot form part of a transaction entered into between the company and another person, unless the transaction has been artificially designed: otherwise two separable but linked transactions involving the company and two different parties cannot be aggregated to save a transaction which on its own is at an undervalue.[18]

The creation of security over a company's assets is not a transaction at an undervalue.[19] Where neither gift nor absence of consideration is relied on, a comparison has to be made between the value obtained by the company for the transaction and the value of the consideration provided by the company. Both values must be measurable in money or money's worth and both must be

---

13   IA 1986, s 241(3) as substituted by I (No 2) A 1994, s 1(1) and (6). The further provisions are in
     IA 1986, s 241(3A)–(3C), which spell out the constituent facts leading to the assumption that a
     person has notice of the relevant proceedings.
14   IA 1986, s 241(4).
15   See CA 1985, s 35(1), as revised by CA 1989, s 108.
16   See Charities Act 1993, s 65.
17   IA 1986, s 238(4).
18   *Phillips v Brewin Dolphin Bell Lawrie Ltd* [1999] 1 BCLC 714, CA (where separate transaction
     was at an undervalue).
19   *Re MC Bacon Ltd* [1990] BCC 78.

considered from the company's point of view.[20] By charging its assets the company appropriates them to meet the liabilities due to the secured creditor and adversely affects the rights of other creditors in the event of insolvency. But it does not deplete its assets or diminish their value. It retains the right to redeem and the right to sell or mortgage the charged assets. All it loses is the ability to apply the proceeds otherwise than in satisfaction of the secured debt, which is not something capable of valuation in monetary terms and is not customarily disposed of for value.[1]

On a parity of reasoning the same would very possibly apply to a guarantee given by a company of the indebtedness of another.[2]

On the other hand, the creation of a trust is not necessarily a diminution of the assets of the company. Thus where the substance of the arrangement by way of trust was the payment of future sums due to concession holders in a department store in respect of trading which was to take place in the future, the transaction was held not to be one at an undervalue.[3]

Such transactions may be avoided, or otherwise subjected to a court order under s 241 of the Insolvency Act 1986, at the instance of a liquidator or administrator,[4] if they were carried out within the relevant time, namely within two years ending with the onset of insolvency.[5] The onset of insolvency in this context means the date of a resolution for voluntary winding-up or the date of the presentation of a petition on which winding-up order is eventually made or the date of any administration order.[6] The court must not, however, make an order in respect of a transaction at an undervalue if it is satisfied (i) that the company which entered into the transaction did so in good faith[7] and for the purpose of carrying on its business, and (ii) that at the time it did so there were reasonable grounds for believing that the transaction would benefit the company.[8] The discussion relating to orders concerning preferences should be referred to in connection with orders concerning transactions of an undervalue.[9]

---

20 [1990] BCC 78 at 92D–E, per Millett J analysing the IA 1986, s 238(4)(b).
1 [1990] BCC 78 at 92E–F.
2 Cf the useful discussion in Louis G Doyle *Administrative Receivership Law and Practice* (1995) citing, inter alia, *Commerce Bank of Kansas City v Achtenberg* [1994] CCH Bank Dec 75, 631.
3 *Re Lewis's of Leicester Ltd* [1995] 1 BCLC 428 at 438–439. Cf. *Re Thirty-Eight Building Ltd* [1999] BCC 260 (declaration of trust held a voidable preference).
4 IA 1986, s 238(1) makes it clear that those are the only office holders who can challenge a transaction at an undervalue.
5 IA 1986, s 240(1).
6 IA 1986, s 240(3).
7 Gifts of a company's property for no proper trading purpose are acts of misfeasance and cannot be in good faith. Likewise, keeping a company afloat by financing its overdraft by circulating cheques is not a transaction carried out in good faith: *Re Barton Manufacturing Co Ltd* [1999] 1 BCLC 740.
8 IA 1986, s 238(5). No order is to be made in relation to a market contract as defined by CA 1989 unless the court is satisfied that a person in favour of whom the contract was made knew at the time he entered into it that it was at an undervalue.
9 See pp 242–245 above.

Avoidance of certain floating charges under the Insolvency Act 1986

The new insolvency legislation has made substantial changes in the avoidance provisions formerly contained in s 617 of the Companies Act 1985 (previously s 322 of the Companies Act 1948). Avoidance of the charge will sabotage the receiver's title.

Extent of invalidity

A floating charge on the company's undertaking or property created at a relevant time (defined below) is invalid, except to the extent of the aggregate of: (i) the value of so much of the consideration for the creation of the charge as consists of money paid, or goods or services supplied,[10] to the company[11] at the same time as, or after, the creation of the charge;[12] (ii) the value of so much of that consideration as consists of the discharge or reduction, at the same time as, or after, the creation of the charge, of any debt of the company; and (iii) the amount of such interest (if any) as is payable on the amount falling within (i) or (ii) above in pursuance of any agreement under which the money was so paid, the goods or services were so supplied or the debt was discharged or reduced.[13]

Floating charge

The nature of a floating charge has already been discussed.[14] The requirement that the impugned charge should be a *floating* charge normally causes no trouble. In most cases it is clear that a charge is indeed a floating charge because the charge follows some common form. But just as Monsieur Jourdain talked prose without realising it[15] parties can create a floating charge also without realising that their arrangement amounts to such a charge.[16]

The operation of the section avoiding floating charges created during the objectionable period is not restricted to general floating charges over the whole undertaking of a company.[17] A particular floating charge over a particular category of the company's assets is void unless registered and there is no reason to suppose that such a particular floating charge is not equally void under another provision in the same Act. Certainly the language of s 245 of the Insolvency Act 1986 is suitably wide in its terms. And a particular floating charge is a floating charge nevertheless.

10 See p 251 below.
11 See *Re Columbian Fireproofing Co Ltd* [1910] 2 Ch 120, CA; *Re F and E Stanton Ltd* [1929] 1 Ch 180. Where a company has an overdrawn account with a bank, cheques paid on that account constitute cash paid to the company: see *Re Yeovil Glove Co Ltd* [1965] Ch 148, [1964] 2 All ER 849, CA. The decision is criticised in the Cork Report, paras 1560–1562.
12 [1929] 1 Ch 139 at 142 per Maugham J; at 145 per Eve J.
13 IA 1986, s 245(2).
14 [1965] Ch 186n.
15 See Molière *Le Bourgeois Gentilhomme* Act 2, Scene 6: 'Par ma foi, il y a plus de quarante ans que je dis de la prose sans que j'en susse rien.'
16 *Re Bond Worth Ltd* [1980] Ch 228, [1979] 3 All ER 919.
17 *Re Bond Worth Ltd* [1980] Ch 228 at 269–271.

Since the section is explicitly directed at floating charges it is axiomatic that a charge which has always been fixed is outside the section.[18] So where a debenture creates a specific fixed charge over the company's real property and fixtures and a floating charge over its remaining assets only the floating charge can be set aside under the section.[19] It is therefore in the interests of a debenture holder to ensure, so far as he can, that the charge which he gets by way of security gives a fixed charge over as much property as possible. There has been an increasing tendency for banks to seek to create fixed charges over assets which were assumed to be capable of being charged only by way of floating charge. The courts have accepted, for instance, that vehicles of a company and its book debts can, by appropriate language, be subjected to fixed charges.[20]

It is not necessary that the charge under attack should be a floating charge when the attack is made. A floating charge crystallises by operation of law on the commencement of a winding up[1] and at that stage ex hypothesi is not floating any longer. But of course the section is designed to give a liquidator the right to call in question the validity of the charge; so that clearly the time for testing the nature of the charge cannot be that time when the challenge is made. In fact the relevant time is the date of the creation of the charge. The statutory language of the 1986 Act now makes this clear beyond peradventure: 'floating charge' is redefined so as to include any charge which was originally created as a floating charge but has since become a fixed charge.[2] If the charge was created as a floating charge the fact that it crystallises prior to the commencement of a winding up, for example on the appointment of a receiver, does not take the charge outside the section. In *Re Post Supermarket Ltd*[3] the charge in question automatically crystallised as soon as it was executed and counsel for the debenture holder ingeniously argued that the charge was not a floating charge within the section but a fixed charge since its creation. Casey J held that the language of the charge made it clear that it was created as a floating charge and that there was a nominal split second of time during which the charge floated before the automatic crystallisation provisions came into effect.[4]

On the other hand the charge must still be in existence. If the receiver has actually gone in, paid off the debenture holders and extinguished the charge there is no room for avoiding the charge.[5] All that remains is the possibility of attacking the payments on the grounds of a fraudulent or voidable preference.[6]

18 *Re Dittmer Gold Mines Ltd* [1954] St R Qd 255.
19 [1983] BCLC 311.
20 *Tudor Heights Ltd v United Dominions Corpn Finance Ltd* [1977] 1 NZLR 532 (specific charge on 'fixed plant and machinery').
 1 *Siebe Gorman & Co Ltd v Barclays Bank Ltd* [1979] 2 Lloyd's Rep 142 at 159, citing *Evans Coleman & Evans Ltd v RA Nelson Construction Ltd* (1958) 16 DLR (2d) 123. There are other *Robin Hood Flour Mills Ltd v Fuller Bakeries Ltd* (1963) 42 WWR 321, 40 DLR (2d) 207. For an unsuccessful attempt see *Kelly v James McMahon Ltd* [1980] IR 347 discussed in (1982) 3 Co Law 136–137 (David Milman).
 2 IA 1986, s 245(2)(b).
 3 *Hodson v Tea Co* (1880) 14 Ch D 859, 49 LJ Ch 234; *Wallace v Universal Automatic Machines Co* [1894] 2 Ch 547, 63 LJ Ch 598; *Re Crompton & Co Ltd* [1914] 1 Ch 954, 83 LJ Ch 666.
 4 [1978] 1 NZLR 330.
 5 [1978] 1 NZLR 330 at 340.
 6 *Re Parkes Garage (Swadlincote) Ltd* [1929] 1 Ch 139.

PAYMENT TO THE COMPANY

Under the statutory predecessor of s 245, the payment had to be to the company. However where a bank paid cash at the request of the company to persons who were creditors of the company, the bank, of course, not being liable itself to those creditors, there was undoubtedly a payment in cash by the bank to the company for the purposes of the section.[7] Equally, where directors of a company who were not guarantors of the overdraft of the company agree to advance money for the purpose of guaranteeing that overdraft, that would be a payment in cash by the directors *to the company* although they in fact paid the money direct to the bank and did not first go through the form of paying it into the company's banking account and then drawing a cheque on that in favour of the bank.[8]

The question whether cash had been paid to the company was also raised in an interesting case before Nourse J. In *Re GT Whyte & Co Ltd,*[9] Company A extended credit to a company which subsequently went into liquidation ('GTW'). The money was in fact provided by Company B, a subsidiary of A. Subsequently a floating charge over GTW's assets was created which had the effect of making it indebted to A rather than A's subsidiary namely B. The charge having in the event been created within 12 months of the winding up it was invalid except as to the amount of any 'cash paid' to GTW. The question arose as to whether the transaction had been for the benefit of GTW or whether it had simply substituted a secured debt for an unsecured debt, to the detriment of other creditors. Nourse J held that for this purpose there was in substance no difference between A and its subsidiary B. The floating charge did not make *new* money available for the use of GTW, and it still owed money to A, as it had in reality, at the outset. The charge thus had the effect of securing the debt owed to A and was neither 'cash paid' to, nor for the benefit of, GTW.

Again, payments to creditors of two companies whose business was conducted by a unit trust constituted for the purpose were not payments to that trust.[10]

Under the new section payments made by the chargee direct to the company's creditors in discharge or reduction of the companies debts is consideration paid to the company.[11]

PAYMENT BY THE DEBENTURE HOLDER

Another interesting question in relation to the payment of cash or money to the company is whether the payment must be made by the person who receives the

7   *Re Thomas Mortimer Ltd* (1925) [1965] Ch 186n at 189 per Romer J.
8   [1965] Ch 186n.
9   [1983] BCLC 311.
10 *M Hoffman Nominees Pty Ltd v Cosmos Fish Processors (International) Pty Ltd* [1983] VR 349.
11 Payments made by the lender direct to the company's bank are not made to the company: *Re Fairway Magazines Ltd* [1992] BCC 924.

charge, in other words by the debenture holder. There is in fact a decision giving an affirmative answer to that question.[12] The debenture holder in the case in question got a charge, but it got it in consideration of a debt owing by the company to a third person. The lender might, it was assumed, have paid money to the company in consideration of a charge but the lender never got a charge. It was held that under the section the money had to be paid in consideration of the charge the validity of which was in issue. It cannot, the court held, avail the holder of the charge to show that he has taken the charge following a payment of cash made in consideration of a charge other than the one he holds.

At the same time as the execution of the charge

Whether the payment of money or the supply of goods or services is made at the same time as the execution of the charge is a question of fact and degree. This was established by *Re Shoe Lace Ltd*[13] (also cited as *Power v Sharp Investments Ltd*) where a debenture was executed several months after a loan had been provided by a company to its insolvent subsidiary. The board of the subsidiary had resolved to issue the debenture but in terms which were too imprecise to constitute an immediate agreement to grant a security and thereby to create an equitable interest at the time. It was held by Hoffmann J and by the Court of Appeal that the loan had not been provided at the same time as the granting of the security by way of floating charge. Subject to a very limited *de minimis* rule changes made at any time *before* the creation of the floating charge will not in future be registered as protected.[14] This time constraint illustrates the difference between the old wording and the new wording.

Value of goods or services

The value of any goods or services supplied by way of consideration for a floating charge is to be treated as the amount in money which at the time they were supplied could reasonably have been expected to be obtained for supplying the goods or services in the ordinary course of business and on the same terms (apart from consideration) as those on which such goods or services were supplied to the company.[15]

Consequences of invalidity

Only the floating charge is invalidated, the covenant to pay is still valid.[16] If the

---

12 *Transrhodes (NR) Ltd v Lusaka Mechanical Plant Ltd* [1956] R & N 36 (Rhodesian Federal Supreme Court).
13 [1993] BCC 609, CA; [1992] BCC 636.
14 The view of this imprecise restriction taken by Mummery J in *Re Fairway Magazines Ltd* [1992] BCC 924 must be looked on as overruled by the decision of the Court of Appeal in *Re Shoe Lace Ltd*. The interval envisaged as sufficiently minimal is a coffee break.
15 IA 1986, s 245(6).
16 *Re Parkes Garage (Swadlincote) Ltd* [1929] 1 Ch 139; *Mace Builders (Glasgow) Ltd v Lunn* [1987] Ch 191, [1986] 3 WLR 921, CA.

sum secured is repaid before the onset of insolvency,[17] the liquidator or administrator cannot recover the sum so paid unless the repayment is set aside as a preference, and transactions effected under the authority of the charge which have been completed before the commencement of the winding up of the company are unaffected.[18]

If, for example, a receiver appointed by the debenture holder realises the mortgaged property by sale before the onset of insolvency, he is not required to pay the proceeds to the liquidator.[19]

Relevant time

The time at which a floating charge is created by a company is a relevant time for the purposes of the avoidance provision if the charge is created:

(a)   in the case of a charge which is created in favour of a person who is *connected* with the company, at a time in the period of two years ending with the onset of insolvency;

(b)   in the case of a charge which is created in favour of any other person (in other words a *non-connected person*), at a time in the period of 12 months ending with that date; or

(c)   in either case, at a time between the presentation of a petition for the making of an administration order in relation to the company and the making of such an order on that petition.[20]

Where a company creates a floating charge at a time mentioned in (b) above, and the person in favour of whom the charge is created is *not* connected with the company, that time shall not be a relevant time for the purposes of this section unless the company (i) is unable to pay its debts within the meaning of s 123 of the Insolvency Act 1986 at that time; or (ii) becomes unable to pay its debts within the meaning of that section in consequence of the transaction under which the charge is created.[1]

Extortionate credit transaction

Statement of rule

A receiver may also be vulnerable to attack on the footing that the security under which he was appointed was part of an extortionate credit transaction.

---

17   Ie, (a) in a case where an administration order has been made, the date of the presentation of the petition on which the order was made; and (b) in a case where the company goes into liquidation, the date of the commencement of the winding up: IA 1986, s 245(5).

18   *Re Parkes Garage (Swadlincote) Ltd* [1929] 1 Ch 139.

19   *Mace Builders (Glasgow) Ltd v Lunn* [1987] Ch 191, [1986] 3 WLR 921.

20   IA 1986, s 245(3).

 1   IA 1986, s 245(4).

Where a company is, or has been, a party to a transaction for, or involving, the provision of credit to the company, the court may, on the application of the liquidator or administrator[2] make an order with respect to the transaction, if the transaction is or was extortionate and was entered into in the period of three years ending with the day on which the administration order was made or (as the case may be) the company went into liquidation.[3]

Definition of 'extortionate'

A transaction is extortionate (in this context) if, having regard to the risk accepted by the person providing the credit:

(a)   the terms of it are or were such as to require grossly exorbitant payments to be made (whether unconditionally or in certain contingencies) in respect of the provision of the credit; or

(b)   it otherwise grossly contravened ordinary principles of fair dealing.

In such circumstances it has to be presumed, unless the contrary is proved, that a transaction with respect to which an application is made under s 244 of the Insolvency Act 1986 is or, as the case may be, was extortionate.[4] The burden of proving that a transaction was not extortionate is thus put squarely, in every case, onto the person who gave the credit.

Extent of court order

If the court finds the credit transaction to be extortionate, any order made by the court may contain any one or more of the following provisions:

(a)   a provision setting aside the whole or part of any obligation created by the transaction;

(b)   a provision otherwise varying the terms of the transaction or varying the terms on which any security for the purposes of the transaction is held;

(c)   a provision requiring any person who is or was a party to the transaction to pay to the liquidator or administrator any sums paid to that person, by virtue of the transaction, by the company;

---

2   Each is an office holder. For the definition of 'office holder', see IA 1986, s 238(1).
3   IA 1986, s 244(1), (2). See also Lionel Bently and Geraint G Howells 'Judicial Treatment of Extortionate Credit Bargains' [1989] Conv 164–174 discussing the parallel provisions in Consumer Credit Act 1974, s 137; and see *Ketley v Scott* [1981] ICR 241; *Wills v Woods* (1984) 128 Sol Jo 222; *Woodstead Finance Ltd v Petrou* [1996] BTLC 267 (42.5% pa, secured); *Davies v Directloans Ltd* [1986] 1 WLR 823 (25.785% pa, secured); *Castle Phillips Finance Co v Williams* [1986] CCLR 13 (48% pa, unsecured).
4   IA 1986, s 244(3). See *Davies v Directloans Ltd* [1986] 2 All ER 783, [1986] 1 WLR 823.

(d)   a provision requiring any person to surrender to the liquidator or receiver
any property held by him as security for the purposes of the transaction;
and/or

(e)   a provision directing accounts to be taken between any persons.[5]

EFFECT ON AGENCY AND POWERS

Agency

Usually the mortgage debenture provides that a receiver and manager, appointed
thereunder shall be the agent of the company.[6] In the case of an administrative
receiver he is statutorily deemed to be the company's agent unless and until the
company goes into liquidation.[7] A compulsory winding up order automatically
terminates that agency.[8] Likewise, the commencement of a voluntary winding
up, by the passing of a resolution to wind up, brings to an end the agency of a
receiver and manager.[9] So far as the receiver is concerned, although he retains his
right to custody and control over the company's assets, the company, whose
agent he is, no longer has full and free capacity to continue its business in terms
of the objects in its memorandum. The company cannot authorise the receiver to
do any act which it is unable to do itself, so that it cannot empower the receiver,
after the date of the liquidation, to carry on its business so as to create debts
provable against the unmortgaged assets of the company; but the receiver can
still continue to exercise his powers in the name of the company although the
company is no longer liable for any debts which he may incur in doing so.[10] In
other words, the termination of the agency does not leave a vacuum. His
'contemplated position as agent of the mortgagor must be regarded as not of the
essence of his position and status as receiver'.[11] The agency ends but not the
receivership. The receiver is still in control. But his position is peculiar and made
more difficult. He cannot bind the company with fresh obligations. Acting, as he
does, as a principal he will be personally liable in respect of fresh contracts,
albeit with a right to indemnity out of the assets of the company. And if despite
the termination of his agency he purports to act in the name of the company he
may be held liable for breach of warranty of authority.

---

5   IA 1986, s 244(4). The powers conferred by s 244 are expressed to be exercisable in relation to
any transaction concurrently with any powers exercisable in relation to that transaction as a
transaction at an undervalue: IA 1986, s 244(5).
6   See David Milman 'Receivers as Agents' (1981) 44 MLR 658–659.
7   IA 1986, s 44(1)(a).
8   *Gosling v Gaskell* [1897] AC 575, HL.
9   *Thomas v Todd* [1926] 2 KB 511.
10 *Visbord v Federal Taxation Comr* (1943) 68 CLR 354 at 352 per Williams J. The company is
'incapacitated by the winding-up order from carrying on business', and the receiver could not
create debts which would be provable in the liquidation against the unmortgaged assets of the
company: see *Gaskell v Gosling* [1896] 1 QB 669 at 699–700, CA per Rigby LJ (dissenting but
upheld in [1897] AC 575, HL).
11 *Re Northern Garage Ltd* [1946] Ch 188 at 192 per Vaisey J.

In some cases a receiver and manager may be content to continue trading because he has extracted a comprehensive (and satisfactory) indemnity from the debenture holders before accepting the appointment.[12] Indeed a prudent receiver and manager will always strive to extract such an indemnity. In rare cases the debenture holders may be liable because the receiver and manager was their agent, either under the express terms of the debenture or by subsequent agreement. In the absence of express agreement it will be difficult to show that the debenture holders have given the appointee authority to act on their behalf. Because of the dangers of personal liability many receivers and managers will, on a liquidation, either cease to trade or hive down the trading business to a subsidiary company immediately.

The purpose of the insolvency legislation, enacted in 1986, is to amend the law in relation to the agency and indemnity against personal liability of receivers. As has been noticed earlier the power of agency is normally included in the modern floating charge but for the avoidance of doubt statute now provides for a receiver to be deemed to be the agent of the debtor company, unless the floating charge expressly provides to the contrary.[13]

It was proposed in the Cork Report that when a company was in receivership and a winding-up petition was presented or a resolution passed that the company should go into voluntary liquidation, a copy of the petition or resolution should be served on the receiver.[14] It was also proposed that the new legislation should enable[15] a receiver who considers that in the circumstances continued trading would be beneficial, to recommend to the debenture holder that an application for the appointment of an administrator[16] should be made. Neither of these proposals was adopted by the Insolvency Act 1986.

Powers

While a compulsory winding-up order or the commencement of a voluntary winding up brings about a cesser of the agency of the receiver and manager, some of his powers survive the death of his agency. He may continue to carry on the company's business, though not so as to impose fresh liabilities on the company.[17] He is of course entitled to take possession of the assets comprised in the debenture;[18] and so that power remains. And he may continue to get in and realise all the company's assets both real and personal comprised in the debenture.[19]

---

12 The authorities do not expressly cover this point. See however O'Donovan (1973) 54 ALJ 264 at 266–267; and see *Re New Vogue Ltd (in liquidation)* [1932] NZLR 1633 at 1641 per Myers CJ; *Re KVE Homes Pty Ltd and the Companies Act* [1979] 1 NSWLR 181 (where management was left in the hands of the receiver and a provisional liquidator was appointed).

13 (1984) Cmnd 9175, para 143.

14 (1984) Cmnd 9175 para 144. See also (1982) Cmnd 8558, paras 467–468.

15 (1984) Cmnd 9175, para 144.

16 As to the administrator procedure, see p 509.

17 *Gosling v Gaskell* [1897] AC 575, 66 LJQB 848, HL.

18 *Re Henry Pound Son & Hutchins* (1889) 42 Ch D 402, 58 LJ Ch 792, CA.

19 *Re Henry Pound Son & Hutchins* (1889) 42 Ch D 402 at 418.

Power to continue proceedings

Again, he retains the power to continue proceedings in the name of the company to get in assets of the company comprised in the debenture. Thus in *Gough's Garages Ltd v Pugsley*[20] the power to continue proceedings started by the receiver in the name of the company to obtain a new lease of business premises was held to survive a winding-up order. It was necessary to bring proceedings in the company's name because the legal title was vested in the company. The same applies where the proceedings were originally started by the company.[1] And it is tolerably clear that just as a receiver can continue proceedings started by him prior to the liquidation he is not precluded from starting an action after liquidation in relation to a chose in action falling fairly within the scope of his appointment.[2]

Power to call uncalled capital

On the other hand there are some powers such as the power to call uncalled capital,[3] or to create debts which would become provable in the liquidation against the uncharged assets of the company which do *not* survive the termination of the agency.[4]

Dispositive and conveyancing powers

Again the termination of the authority of the receiver to act as agent of the company does not affect his power to hold or dispose of property comprised in the debenture.[5] At one time there was debate as to whether the receiver's conveyancing power survives a termination of the agency. One (now recanted) view, unsupported by any citation of authority, was that the determination of his agency entails that he can no longer convey property in the name of the company, even if the debenture so provides.[6] A typical debenture employed by banks and other institutional lenders provides that any appointed receiver exercising a power of sale shall also have a power of attorney to execute any conveyance or

---

20 [1930] 1 KB 615, 99 LJKB 225, CA; followed, perhaps somewhat hesitantly, in *Newman Bros Ltd v Allum* [1934] NZLR 694.
1 *Bacal Contracting Ltd v Modern Engineering (Bristol) Ltd* [1980] 2 All ER 655.
2 *Gough's Garages Ltd v Pugsley* [1930] 1 KB 615 at 621 per Greer LJ and at 625–626 per Romer LJ.
3 *Re Henry Pound Son & Hutchins* (1889) 42 Ch D 402, 58 LJ Ch 792. The proper person to get in uncalled capital in a liquidation is the liquidator: *Fowler v Broad's Patent Night Light Co* [1893] 1 Ch 724, 62 LJ Ch 373. A receiver can apply in the liquidation for an order directing him to get in uncalled capital: *Re Westminster Syndicates Ltd* (1908) 99 LT 924.
4 *Re Henry Pound Son & Hutchins* (1889) 42 Ch D 402; *Thomas v Todd* [1926] 2 KB 511, 95 LJKB 808.
5 *Sowman v David Samuel Trust Ltd (in liquidation)* [1978] 1 WLR 22; *Barrows v Chief Land Registrar* (1977) Times, 20 October. There are Australian cases to the same effect: *Re Landmark Corpn Ltd (in liquidation) and the Companies Act* [1968] 1 NSWR 705; *Re High Crest Motors Pty Ltd* (1978) 3 ACLR 564.
6 See *Kerr on Receivers* (15th edn) p 351; cf (16th edn) pp 332–333.

other instrument in the name of the company.[7] When the Chief Land Registrar, on the basis of advice received, refused to register conveyances by receivers after the commencement of liquidation unless the liquidator was joined as a party, the grounds for his decision were subjected to considerable criticism. One commentator,[8] stressing the absence of any authority for the proposition that the power of attorney to convey in the company's name determined on a compulsory order or voluntary resolution, pointed to the survival, in such circumstances of the power to sue in the company's name.[9] Both powers survived, he suggested, because they were needed to realise assets comprised in the debenture.

Two decisions in 1977 resolved the controversy. First in *Sowman v David Samuel Trust Ltd (in liquidation)*[10] it was held that a receiver could execute a contract to sell a freehold property comprised in the debenture notwithstanding the making of a winding up order. The winding-up order did not affect the power of the receiver to hold and dispose of the company's property, including the power to use the company's name for that purpose. Accordingly his execution of the contract of sale was a valid exercise of that power. The conveyance itself in *Sowman's* case had been executed *by the debenture holder* under a power of attorney contained in the debenture and it was held that this had not been revoked by the winding up.[11] In *Barrows v Chief Land Registrar*[12] the receiver not only executed the contract of sale but also executed the conveyance in the name of the company. It was held that the winding-up order terminated his agency but did not terminate his power to execute or sign documents as receiver in the name of the company. No doubt similar principles would apply where the event triggering the termination was a resolution to wind up. It should be added that a conveyance by the receiver in the name of the company is not a 'disposition of the property of the company' within s 127 of the Insolvency Act 1986 and may validly be made without the leave of the court despite the presentation of a petition for compulsory winding up.[13] Formerly it was thought that after presentation of a petition leave of the court was required to a conveyance by the receiver.[14] But s 127 applies only to dispositions of property which belongs beneficially to the company[15] and after the appointment of a receiver and manager the charged property belongs in equity to the debenture holders.[16]

---

7 See 2 *Forms and Precedents* (4th edn) 853 for an example.
8 PJ Millett QC 'The Conveyancing Powers of Receivers after Liquidation' (1977) 41 Conv NS 83.
9 *Gough's Garages Ltd v Pugsley* [1930] 1 KB 615, 99 LJKB 225, CA.
10 [1978] 1 All ER 616, [1978] 1 WLR 22.
11 An authority coupled with an interest is irrevocable: *Smart v Sandars* (1848) 5 CB 895 at 917; and see also the Powers of Attorney Act 1971, s 4.
12 (1977) Times, 20 October.
13 See PJ Millett QC (1977) 41 Conv NS 83 at 93–95 anticipating the decision in *Sowman v David Samuel Trust Ltd (in liquidation)* [1978] 1 All ER 616, [1978] 1 WLR 22.
14 See *Re Clifton Place Garage Ltd* [1970] Ch 477, [1970] 1 All ER 353, CA.
15 *Sowman v David Samuel Trust Ltd (in liquidation)* [1978] 1 All ER 616, [1978] 1 WLR 22; and see *Re Norman King & Co Pty Ltd* [1960] SRNSW 98, 76 WNNSW 690.
16 *George Barker (Transport) Ltd v Eynon* [1974] 1 WLR 462 at 467; *Biggerstaff v Rowatt's Wharf Ltd* [1896] 2 Ch 93 at 106, CA.

Power to take possession

Mention has already been made of the power of the receiver to take possession of the assets subject to his charge.[17] This power continues to subsist despite the appointment of a liquidator.[18] And nowadays, as has been seen,[19] it is unlikely that a receiver would be driven to get the leave of the court to recover assets in the possession of the liquidator but forming part of the charge. There is no shackle on the receiver's power to dispose of property subject to his charge as a result of the commencement of winding up by the court because the statutory provision[20] requiring leave to dispose of the relevant property after the presentation of a winding-up petition applies only to property which belongs beneficially to the company.[1] On the appointment of a receiver the charged assets belong in equity to the debenture holders and not to the company.[2]

Another power which remains undisturbed by the event of liquidation is the right of the receiver and manager to retain all documents needed to evidence the title of the debenture holders.[3] If these documents have found their way into the hands of a liquidator they can be recovered. That is clearly established in the case of *court* appointments[4] and would appear to apply equally to 'private' appointments.[5]

EFFECT ON DUTIES

As regards the receiver's duties the most important consequence of winding up is in connection with s 40 of the Insolvency Act 1986.[6] This section provides that where in the case of a company registered in England a receiver is appointed[7] on behalf of the holders of any debentures[8] of the company secured by a floating charge, then if the company is not at the time in the course of being wound up the

---

17 See at p 255, above.

18 *Sowman v David Samuel Trust Ltd (in liquidation)* [1978] 1 All ER 616, [1978] 1 WLR 22.

19 See at p 255, above.

20 IA 1986, s 127.

 1 *Sowman v David Samuel Trust Ltd (in liquidation)* [1978] 1 WLR 22 at 30, and see *Re Norman King & Co Pty Ltd* [1960] SRNSW 98, 76 WNNSW 690.

 2 *Biggerstaff v Rowatt's Wharf Ltd* [1896] 2 Ch 93 at 106; *George Barker (Transport) Ltd v Eynon* [1974] 1 WLR 462 at 467.

 3 *Re Landmark Corpn Ltd* (1968) 88 WN (Pt 1) (NSW) 195 at 196–197.

 4 *Engel v South Metropolitan Brewing and Bottling Co* [1892] 1 Ch 442, 61 LJ Ch 369; *Re Ind Coope & Co Ltd* (1909) 26 TLR 11, CA.

 5 See (on the equivalent Australian provisions) *Home v Walsh* [1978] VR 688; sub nom *Re High Crest Motors Pty Ltd* (1978) 3 ACLR 564; *Expo International Pty Ltd v Chant* (1979) 3 ACLR 888.

 6 Cf Hong Kong Companies Ordinance, s 79; Malaysian Companies Act, s 191; Singapore Companies Act, s 226.

 7 The term 'receiver' covers a receiver and manager: see *Re Custom Card (NSW) Pty Ltd, Hunter v Bank of New South Wales* (1979) 38 FLR 354, [1979] 1 NSWLR 241; revsd on other grounds in *Bank of New South Wales v Federal Taxation Comr* (1979) 54 ALJR 129, 79 ATC 4687. The section applies to court and private receivers: *Re Barnby's Ltd* [1899] WN 103.

 8 This includes an equitable mortgage: *Re Tarjan Construction Co Pty Ltd* (1964) 80 WNNSW 1342, [1964] NSWR 1054.

debts which, in every winding up must be paid in priority to all other debts[9] must be paid out of the assets coming to the hands of the receiver in priority to any claim for principal or interest in respect of the debentures.[10]

The phrase 'in the course of being wound up' which occurs in the Australian legislation has been the subject of judicial comment both in England and in Australia in this connection. In *Stein v Saywell*[11] McTiernan and Menzies JJ thought that in the case of a compulsory liquidation a company would not be in the course of being wound up at any time before the actual making of the order. Barwick CJ in the same case took the opposite view. But in *Re Christonette (International) Ltd*,[12] Vinelott J accepted the proposition that until, in the case of a compulsory winding up, an order is made the company is not in the course of being wound up. In a voluntary winding up the liquidator is appointed by the company in general meeting[13] and although it is not legally obligatory this is invariably done at the same meeting as that at which the resolution for voluntary winding up is passed.[14] Strictly then, a company may only be in the course of being wound up if a liquidator, compulsory or voluntary, has been appointed. But with a voluntary winding up because of the almost invariable practice just mentioned the company will be in the course of being wound up as soon as the resolution to wind up is passed.[15] Certainly Vinelott J in *Re Christonette (International) Ltd*[16] held that s 94 'deals with the situation where at the time of the appointment of a receiver or when a debenture holder takes possession of assets of a company no liquidator has been appointed'.[17]

Lastly, in connection with duties of a receiver and manager the liquidator can compel the receiver and manager to perform his statutory duties to render and verify proper accounts of his receipts and payments and to pay over to the liquidator the 'amount properly payable to him'.[18]

The court has power[19] to order in a suitable case the receiver of a company appointed under a debenture to pay the costs of an action carried on by him after the company had been compulsorily wound up and which had been incurred after the winding-up order.[20] A factor which may lead the court to the conclusion that it is just and equitable to make such an order (provided the receiver has recourse against his debenture holders) is that if the proceedings had been brought by the liquidator and not the receiver the successful party's costs would have been accorded priority. It cannot be just to hold that in an action by the

---

9 IA 1986, s 386.
10 IA 1986, s 40(1), replacing CA 1985, s 196 (which replaced CA 1948, s 94).
11 (1969) 121 CLR 529 at 533.
12 [1982] 3 All ER 225, [1982] 1 WLR 1245.
13 At that time under CA 1948, s 133(3); see now IA 1986, s 86.
14 See *James v Evening Standard Newspaper Co Ltd* (1895) 21 VLR 399, 17 ALT 158.
15 See James O'Donovan 'The Interaction of Winding Up and Receivership' (1979) 53 ALJ 264 at 268, which was drawn to the attention of Vinelott J in *Re Christonette (International) Ltd* [1982] 3 All ER 225, [1982] 1 WLR 1245.
16 [1982] 3 All ER 225, [1982] 1 WLR 1245.
17 [1982] 1 WLR 1245 at 1254.
18 IA 1986, s 41.
19 See Supreme Court Act 1981, s 51(1), (2).
20 *Bacal Contracting Ltd v Modern Engineering (Bristol) Ltd* [1980] 2 All ER 655.

liquidator on behalf of the general body of creditors the costs of a successful defendant are secured, whereas in an action by the receiver on behalf of certain favoured creditors the successful defendant is left to rank as an unsecured creditor.[1]

It is naturally otherwise where the receiver is appointed before the liquidator and the latter wrongly impugns the receiver's title. Such costs are preferential costs of the receiver.[2]

---

1 [1980] 2 All ER 655 at 661G.
2 *Re Christonette (International) Ltd* [1982] 3 All ER 225, [1981] 1 WLR 1245.

CHAPTER 16

Distribution

INTRODUCTION

After realisation of the assets of the company comes distribution. Here the order of application is important: each liability has its place. Payments must be in accordance with the relevant pecking order.[1] Distribution from the proceeds of fixed charge realisations are dealt with in the discussion of mortgages in a later chapter. The present analysis is concerned with distribution out of sums realised from assets subject to a floating charge.

Order of payment

When the assets subject to the floating charge (including a crystallised floating charge) have been realised there is a well recognised basic order for the payment of debts and distribution out of the proceeds of all sales.[2] This order is as follows:

(1) the costs of selling the property, collecting the debts and enforcing the claims of the company against third persons so as to realise the security created by the debentures or the relevant trust deed, but not the cost of preserving such assets with a view to realisation;[3]

(2) all other proper expenses of the receiver and manager including, of course, his remuneration;

(3) the costs and expenses of the trustees of the debenture trust deed and also their remuneration if the trust deed directs that it shall be paid before the debenture debt;[4]

(4) where the debentures are secured by a floating charge, the debts of the company which would be preferential payments in a winding up;

(5) the debenture debt with interest on it up to the date of payment;

---

1 See below.
2 See *Re Glyncorrwg Colliery Co* [1926] Ch 951.
3 *Lathom v Greenwich Ferry Co* (1895) 72 LT 790.
4 *Re Piccadilly Hotel Ltd* [1911] 2 Ch 534.

(6)   payment over of the balance to any subsequent debenture holder or in the absence of any subsequent chargee to the liquidator (if the company has gone into liquidation) or to the company.

PREFERENTIAL DEBTS

General

Section 40 of the Insolvency Act 1986 provides as follows:

'40(1) The following applies, in the case of a company, where a receiver is appointed on behalf of the holders of any debentures of the company secured by a charge which, as created, was a floating charge.

(2) If the company is not at the time in course of being wound up, its preferential debts (within the meaning given to that expression by section 386 in Part XII) shall be paid out of assets coming to the hands of the receiver in priority to any claims for principal or interest in respect of the debentures.

(3) Payments made under this section shall be recouped as far as may be out of the assets of the company available for payment of general creditors.'

The effect of these subsections is to impose on every receiver appointed to enforce a floating charge a positive obligation to pay preferential debts. A preferential debt must be satisfied by the receiver in priority to the claims of a holder of a floating charge and in priority to any other creditor who does not have a fixed charge. Then the receiver recoups so far as he can an equivalent sum from the general assets of the company. In this way the ordinary unsecured creditors of the company are the ones who, in effect, subsidise the preferential claimants.

The preferential claimants enjoy priority over the debenture holders only in relation to assets falling within the floating charge and not in relation to assets falling within a fixed charge.[5] This among other things is made clear by the language of s 40(1) of the Insolvency Act 1986, which provides that the section is to apply when the charge under which the receiver is appointed was, *as created*, a floating charge.

As between themselves the preferential debts rank equally under the Insolvency Act 1986.

While the legislation may create new preferential claims, as it has done since the enactment of the Insolvency Act 1986, the courts will not do so off their own bat.[6]

Protection of preferential creditors

The actual decision in *Re Brightlife Ltd*[7] favoured the debenture holder against the preferential creditor. However, in England reform of the insolvency law has

---

5   *IRC v Goldblatt* [1972] Ch 498, [1972] 2 All ER 202.
6   *Re Rafidain Bank* [1992] BCC 376.
7   [1987] Ch 200, [1986] 3 All ER 673. See also *Re Permanent Houses (Holdings) Ltd* [1988] BCLC 563 (demand was event of default on which floating charge crystallised *before* receiver was appointed so that the debenture holder secured priority over preferential creditors).

put an end to the ability of a lender under a floating charge to steal a march on preferential creditors by the device of including an automatic (or semi-automatic) crystallisation clause in the charge. Statute has achieved this result by providing that both in the Insolvency Act 1986 and in the Companies Act 1985 a floating charge means a charge which *as created* was a floating charge.[8] Accordingly, preferential debts now have priority over a floating charge whether those debts arise before or after crystallisation and they may be paid out of assets which are subject to the crystallised floating charge. A receiver appointed under a floating charge (as thereby defined) is statute-bound to pay preferential creditors out of the assets coming into his hands, in priority to the claims of the debenture holder.[9] But assets coming into his hands other than from under the floating charge, for example assets derived from a fixed charge under which he was also appointed receiver, are not available for preferential creditors.[10] So in the case of a surplus arising from a fixed charge realisation the surplus must go to the company or, if the company is in liquidation, to the liquidator.[11] Fixed plant[12] and machinery[13] over which a specific charge has been given will therefore not be available to satisfy preferential claims.

The priority of these preferential payments applies, in the case of a charge that is partly specific and partly floating, only to the assets secured by the floating charge.[14] The preferential payments do not enjoy priority over all other payments such as the costs of realisation and the receiver's remuneration, but they do rank immediately before the principal and interest secured by the debentures.[15]

While preferential claims have no inherent priority over a fixed charge, such priority can arise if the fixed chargee surrenders priority in respect of the charged assets to a floating chargee without formulating an effective subrogation agreement. So a simple postponement agreement can lead to a fixed chargee unwittingly surrendering priority to preferential claimants.[16]

A receiver and manager who ignores this scheme of priorities does so at his peril. He will be liable in damages to the preferential creditors if he exhausts the assets in carrying on the company's business on behalf of the debenture holder by paying ordinary debts without first paying the preferential debts.[17] A similar prospect of litigation will await a receiver who collects the assets and then hands them over to the company with the knowledge that it will transfer them to the

---

8 IA 1986, ss 40(1), 251; CA 1985, s 196 as amended by IA 1986, s 439(1) and Sch 13.
9 IA 1986, s 40(2).
10 *Re Lewis Merthyr Consolidated Collieries Ltd* [1929] 1 Ch 498; *Re GL Saunders Ltd* [1986] 1 WLR 215. See the discussion at p 296, below.
11 *Re Lewis Merthyr Consolidated Collieries Ltd* [1929] 1 Ch 498; *Re GL Saunders Ltd* [1986] 1 WLR 215. See the discussion at p 296, below.
12 As to what is included in this term see *Tudor Heights Ltd (in liquidation) v United Dominions Corpn Finance Ltd* [1977] 1 NZLR 532.
13 As to what is fixed machinery, see *Re Hi Fi Equipment (Cabinets) Ltd* [1988] BCLC 65 (heavy freestanding machinery held not to be fixed machinery).
14 *Re Lewis Merthyr Consolidated Collieries Ltd* [1929] 1 Ch 498, CA; cf *Re Griffin Hotel Co Ltd* [1941] Ch 129, [1940] 4 All ER 324.
15 *Re Glyncorrwg Colliery Co Ltd* [1926] Ch 951.
16 *Re Portbase (Clothing) Ltd* [1993] Ch 388.
17 *Woods v Winskill* [1913] 2 Ch 303; *Westminster Corpn v Haste* [1950] Ch 442, [1950] 2 All ER 65; *Re Tarjan Construction Co Pty Ltd* [1964] NSWR 1054.

debenture holder in satisfaction of his claim without any provision being made for payment of the preferential debts.[18] An action in tort by a preferential creditor for damages for failing to pay the debt out of available assets is not barred by lapse of time if the receiver had sufficient money to satisfy the demand at any time within six years[19] before the bringing of the action.[20]

Any payments made in respect of such preferential debts out of the assets charged by the floating charge must be recouped, so far as they may be out of the assets of the company available for the payment of general creditors.[1]

The statutory duty to account to preferential creditors out of floating charge assets is not a duty which is limited to those debentures under which the receiver is actually appointed: it extends to any debentures of the company served by a charge which as created, was a floating charge.[2]

Relevant date

There are six categories of preferential debt which are listed in Schedule 6 to the Insolvency Act 1986. All but the fourth category include a reference to 'the relevant date'. This expression means in the case of receivership (as opposed to liquidation or an administration order) the date of the receiver's appointment.[3]

Debts due to the Inland Revenue

This category does not, in relation to any receivership starting on or after 29 December 1986, consist of *any* debts due to the Inland Revenue. Only two specific types of debt due to the Inland Revenue are now classified as preferential.

First, are sums due from the debtor company in respect of Pay As You Earn (PAYE) deductions made under s 203 of the Taxes Act 1988 from employees' wages paid in the 12-month period before the 'relevant date'. From such sums must be deducted the amount of the repayments of income tax which the debtor was liable to make in the six-month period. The resultant balance is the preferential debt.[4]

The second type of debt to the Inland Revenue accorded preferential status comprises sums due at the relevant date from the debtor company in respect of such deductions as are required to be made by the debtor company for the six-month period under ss 559 and 560 of the Taxes Act 1988 (sections which impose deductions from payments to sub-contractors in the construction industry.[5]

---

18 *IRC v Goldblatt* [1972] Ch 498, [1972] 2 All ER 202.
19 Limitation Act 1980, s 2.
20 *Westminster Corpn v Haste* [1950] Ch 442.
 1 IA 1986, s 386 and Sch 6; and see *Re Mannesmann Tube Co Ltd* [1901] 2 Ch 93, 70 LJCh 565.
 2 *Re H & K Medway Ltd* [1997] 1 BCLC 545 not following *Griffiths v Yorkshire Bank plc* [1994] 1 WLR 1427.
 3 IA 1986, s 387.
 4 IA 1986, Sch 6, Category 1, para 1.
 5 IA 1986, Sch 6, Category 1, para 2.

Debts due to Customs and Excise

Value added tax

Any value added tax (VAT) which is referable to the six-month period prior to the appointment of the receiver ranks as a preferential debt. If the whole of the prescribed accounting period, to which any value added tax is attributable, falls within the six-month period the whole amount of that tax is referable to that period. Otherwise it is the proportion of the tax equal to such proportion (if any) of the accounting reference period in question as falls within the six-month period.[6] 'Prescribed' in this context means prescribed by regulations under the Value Added Tax Act 1994.

Insurance premium tax

Any insurance premium tax which is referable to the six-month period prior to the appointment of the receiver likewise ranks as a preferential debt. If the whole of the accounting period[7] to which any insurance premium tax is attributable falls within the six-month period, the whole of that tax is referable to that period. Otherwise it is the proportion of the tax which is equal to such proportion (if any) of the 'accounting period' in question as falls within the six-month period.[8]

Landfill tax

So too, any landfill tax which is referable to the six-month period prior to the appointment of the receiver ranks as a preferential debt. Similar apportionment rules apply as obtain in the case of insurance premium tax the relevant 'accounting period' being construed in accordance with Part IV of the Finance Act 1996.[9]

Car tax

The next sub-category of debt to the Customs and Excise categorised as preferential is the amount of any car tax which is due at the relevant date (the commencement of the receivership) from the debtor and which became due within a period of 12 months next before that date.[10]

Betting and gaming duties

Preferential status is also conferred upon any amount due from the debtor at the commencement of the receivership (the relevant date) and which became due

---

6 IA 1986, Sch 6, Category 2, para 3. Where a group of companies has opted for group treatment the whole amount of the tax owed by the group may be treated as a preferential debt: *Re Nadler Enterprises Ltd* [1980] 3 All ER 350, [1981] 1 WLR 23.
7 References to accounting periods are to be construed in accordance with Part III of the Finance Act 1994.
8 IA 1986, Sch 6, Category 2, para 3A, inserted by FA 1994, Sch 7, para 2.
9 IA 1986, Sch 6, Category 2, para 3B, inserted by FA 1996, s 60 and Sch 6, Part III, para 12(1).
10 IA 1986, Sch 6, Category 2, para 4.

within the period of twelve months next before that date in relation to designated betting and gaming duties.[11] The relevant imposts are: (a) general betting duty or bingo duty, (b) general betting duty and pool betting duty recoverable from an agent collecting stakes[12] and (c) gaming licence duty.[13]

Excise duty on beer

The amount of any excise duty on beer which is due at the date of the receiver's appointment and which became due within the six-month period prior to that date is also a preferential debt.[14]

Lottery duty

Any amount which is due by way of lottery duty from the company at the date of the receiver's appointment and which became due in the period of 12 months preceding that date is a preferential debt.[15]

Air passenger duty

Last under this category of preferential debts is any amount which is due by way of air passenger duty from the company at the date of the receiver's appointment and which became due in the preceding six-month period.[16]

Social security contributions

The third category of preferential debts comprises: (1) all sums which at the date of the receiver's appointment are due from the debtor on account of Class 1 or Class 2 National Insurance contributions[17] under the Social Security Contributions and Benefits Act 1992 or the Social Security Contributions and Benefits (Northern Ireland) Act 1992 and which became due from the debtor in the 12 months next before the date of the appointment of the receiver;[18] (2) all sums which at the date of the receiver's appointment have been assessed and are due from the debtor on account of Class 4 contributions under either of those Acts, being sums which (a) are due to the Commissioners of Inland Revenue (rather than to the Secretary of State or a Northern Ireland department) and (b)

---

11 IA 1986, Category 3, para 5.
12 Betting and Gaming Duties Act 1981, s 12(1).
13 Betting and Gaming Duties Act 1981, s 14 and Sch 2.
14 IA 1986, Sch 6, Category 2, para 5A, inserted by FA 1991, Sch 2, para 22.
15 IA 1986, Sch 6, Category 2, para 5B, inserted by FA 1993, s 36(2); see SI 1993/2842 for start date (1 December 1993).
16 IA 1986, Sch 6, Category 2, para 5C, inserted by FA 1994, Sch 7, para (31(1) from 31 October 1994.
17 Both classes of contribution are defined: see Social Security Contributions and Benefits Act 1992, ss 1(2), 6, 11, 15 and Social Security Contributions and Benefits (Northern Ireland) Act 1992, ss 1(2), 6, 11, 15.
18 IA 1986, Sch 6, Category 3, para 6.

are assessed on the debtor up to 5 April next before the receiver's appointment but not exceeding, in the whole, any one year's assessment.[19]

Contributions to occupational pension schemes and state scheme provisions

Any sum which is owed by the company and is a sum to which Schedule 4 to the Pension Schemes Act 1993 applies (contributions and occupational pension schemes and state pension schemes) is a preferential debt.[20]

Remuneration of employees

The fifth category of preferential debt relates to accrued remuneration or accrued holiday remuneration of employees and money advanced and applied for such remuneration. The category comprises:[1]

(1) accrued remuneration payable to employees in respect of the whole or any part of the period of four months next before 'the relevant date' (subject to an upper limit to be prescribed by the Secretary of State);[2]

(2) any accrued holiday remuneration in respect of any period of employment before the relevant date regardless of the date of termination of employment (subject also to the upper limit to be prescribed by the Secretary of State);[3]

(3) so much of any sum advanced and applied for the payment of debts which would otherwise have been preferential under (1) or (2).[4]

A creditor claiming such priority has to show that four conditions are satisfied, namely (1) that he is an employee, in other words that he has the relevant status (2) to whom remuneration is due (3) in respect of services rendered by him to the company (4) before 'the relevant date'.

Relevant status

In England a claimant for priority in respect of wages or salary formerly had to show that he was either a clerk or servant or a workman or labourer. These job descriptions were generalised by some Commonwealth statutes into the perhaps more embracing description 'employee', and that term is now used in the relevant provisions of the Insolvency Act 1986.

---

19 IA 1986, Sch 6, para 7.
20 IA 1986, Sch 6, Category 4, para 8.
 1 IA 1986, Sch 6, Category 5, para 9.
 2 IA 1986, Sch 6, para 10.
 3 IA 1986, Sch 6, para 11.
 4 IA 1986, s 387.

The two claimants in *Re Ashley & Smith Ltd* were outside contributors to a newspaper called the *Sportsman* and had been selected as representative of two categories of contributors to the newspaper in question who were claiming preferential status. Sargant J asked himself the question whether the main indications of service were present or not and concluded that neither of the claimants was a servant of the company.

Sargant J noted in particular four circumstances of relevance in the case before him:[5]

> 'In the first place, they were working entirely away from the company, and not in the office of the company at all. Secondly, they were not exclusively employed in the service of the company, but they might have taken up any amount of other work for other persons, and I think it is highly probable that they did so. Thirdly, they were not bound to render services generally but only a particular class of service. Fourthly, and most important of all, they might perform the service in question practically as they pleased; they were not working under the control of the company or subject to the command of the master under whom they worked.'

The learned judge added that he was not saying that any one of those four circumstances 'except possibly the last would be entirely conclusive'.[6] The element of control has been identified as a criterion for distinguishing servants from independent contractors in the law of torts[7] and Plowman J referred to the degree of control test in tort in order to exclude in *Re CW & AL Hughes Ltd*[8] the claims of labour only sub-contractors to rank as 'servants' within section 319. But it is questionable whether in modern conditions the control test is a universal or necessarily meaningful solvent. Certainly, as various Canadian authorities show, the element of control and supervision exercised may be a strong indication that the relationship in question is one of employment.

Three of the four circumstances mentioned by Sargant J were present also in *Re Benalpha Products Ltd*[9] where the claimant was a consulting engineer. He was employed by a company under a contract made by letter: his remuneration was expressed to be £60 per month plus all travelling and incidental expenses; he was to devote such time and attention as might be necessary for establishing a continuous production process at a particular factory; his contract was to be terminable on six months' notice; and in the event of a cesser of business his claim for arrears was not to exceed the extent of the assets of the syndicate. Pursuant to the contract the engineer, once the factory opened, attended daily at the premises from 10 am to 4 pm. From time to time he had to refer to the general manager but he did not work under his direct orders. There was no other expert of the same calibre employed by the company. He himself was the sole judge of the time and attention which it was necessary to devote to the company and there was nothing to stop him from carrying on other employment. It was held that this

---

5 [1918] 2 Ch 378 at 383.
6 [1918] 2 Ch 378 at 383.
7 See *Salmond and Heuston on Torts* (21st edn) 435–438; Fleming *Law of Torts* (9th edn) 414–420.
8 [1966] 2 All ER 702, [1966] 1 WLR 1369.
9 (1946) 115 LJ Ch 193.

was not a contract of service. His employment was that of an expert and he was not therefore a servant of the company so as to rank as a preferential creditor.

But just as in the law of torts the test of control sometimes proves inadequate[10] so it is likely to prove inadequate in the context of section 319. The test of whether the person is employed as part of the business and his work is done as an integral part of the business has been suggested[11] and criticised.[12]

Cooke J in *Market Investigations Ltd v Minister of Social Security*[13] attempted a classification of the main considerations upon which the issue whether a given situation produces a contract of service or a contract for services depends, saying:

> 'The observations of Lord Wright, of Denning LJ and of the judges of the Supreme Court suggest that the fundamental test to be applied is this: "Is the person who has engaged himself to perform these services performing them as a person in business on his own account?" If the answer to that question is "yes" then the contract is a contract for services. If the answer is "no" then the contract is a contract of service. No exhaustive list has been compiled and perhaps no exhaustive list can be compiled of the considerations which are relevant in determining that question, nor can strict rules be laid down as to the relative weight which the various considerations should carry in particular cases. The most that can be said is that control will no doubt always have to be considered, although it can no longer be regarded as the sole determining factor; and that factors which may be of importance are such matters as whether the man performing the services provides his own equipment, whether he hires his own helpers, what degree of financial risk he takes, what degree of responsibility for investment and management he has, and whether and how far he has an opportunity of profiting from sound management in the performance of his task.'

This approach treats the question 'contract of service or no?' as inevitably a mixed question of law and fact.[14]

The number and elaboration of the judgments on this point have evoked the academic heart-cry[15] that it seems that there is still no real alternative to the view of Somervell LJ that 'one perhaps cannot get beyond this. "Was this contract a contract of service within the meaning which an ordinary person would give to those words?"'[16] The test: 'What would the view of an ordinary person be who learned of the facts?'[17] certainly reserves the widest possible discretion to the judge coming to determine the matter, for the view of the ordinary person might

---

10 See *Clerk and Lindsell on Torts* (17th edn) 166–170 paras 5.05–5.10.
11 *Stevenson Jordan and Harrison Ltd v MacDonald* [1952] 1 TLR 101 at 111, CA per Denning LJ. In *Bank voor Handel en Scheepvaart NV v Slatford* [1953] 1 QB 248 at 295, Denning LJ said 'It depends on whether the person is part and parcel of the organisation'.
12 *Ready Mixed Concrete (South East) Ltd v Minister of Pensions and National Insurance* [1968] 2 QB 497 at 524 per MacKenna J.
13 [1969] 2 QB 173 at 184; and see *Construction Industry Training Board v Labour Force Ltd* [1970] 3 All ER 220 at 224 per Cooke J.
14 See *Global Plant Ltd v Secretary of State for Health and Social Security* [1972] 1 QB 139 at 152–155 where Lord Widgery LCJ reviewed the authorities.
15 *Clerk and Lindsell on Torts* (17th edn) 169–170 para 5.09.
16 *Cassidy v Ministry of Health* [1951] 2 KB 343 at 352–353, CA quoting Buckley LJ in *Simmons v Heath Laundry Co* [1910] 1 KB 543 at 553, CA.
17 *Inglefield v Macey* (1967) 2 KIR 146 at 152 per Ashworth J.

well be one of perplexity in a finely balanced case. The criteria spelled out by Cooke J provide a more detailed guide and with their reference to financial risk and opportunity of profit afford plausible yardsticks for determining whether preferential treatment should be given to persons claiming to have the relevant status as against ordinary trade creditors, who also take financial risks.

With all these considerations in mind one can turn appropriately to concrete examples in the decided cases.

A spare time agent appointed to obtain purchasers of the company's wireless sets, to install them and to attend to and repair those sets, who is paid by commission, where there is no right of action on either side to enforce continuance of the relationship, is not an employee of the company but simply an independent contractor.[18] A fashion editor of a newspaper at a fixed salary with a seat in the office and duties of a general nature was held to be an employee; but in the same case contributors to the same newspaper who were employed part time at a fixed salary were held not to be employed.[19]

An opera singer engaged to sing during a season at a certain sum for each performance has been held to be a 'servant' so as to entitle him to priority of payment of his remuneration;[20] so too a chemist employed at a weekly wage for regular hours for part of the week even though he had other employment for the rest of the time.[1]

Wages or salary

The two terms 'wages' and 'salary' no doubt reflect the old fashioned dichotomy between the non-manual clerk or servant and the manual workman or labourer.[2] However that may be, if priority is successfully to be claimed the amount claimed must be wages or salary.

Commissions and allowances were, under the old law, capable of amounting to wages or salary. Thus the commission of a commercial traveller who is in fact a servant of the company counts as a salary.[3] So too the commission paid to workmen according to the tonnage of ships turned out was held to be wages even though the amount payable was not fixed but varied in proportion to the work actually done.[4]

An allowance payable to an employee in respect of living expenses has been held to constitute wages or salary so as to rank for priority accordingly.[5] On the

---

18 *Re General Radio Co Ltd* [1929] WN 172.
19 *Re Beeton & Co Ltd* [1913] 2 Ch 279; *Re Ashley & Smith Ltd* [1918] 2 Ch 378.
20 *Re Winter German Opera Ltd* (1907) 23 TLR 662; cf *Ryan v Wills* (1918) 44 DLR 634 (actress paid a weekly salary); and see *Narich Pty Ltd v Pay-roll Tax Comr* [1984] ICR 286, PC (Weight Watchers lecturer).
 1 *Re GH Morison & Co Ltd* (1912) 106 LT 731.
 2 The dichotomy was identified in *Re London Casino Ltd* (1942) 167 LT 66.
 3 *Re Klein* (1906) 22 TLR 664; *Re Hartwick Fur Co* (1914) 17 DLR 853. In Canada a salaried commercial traveller qualified for the priority: *Re Morlock & Cline Ltd* (1911) 23 OLR 165. But a selling agent not subject to any contract did not: *Re Parkin Elevator Co* (1916) 37 OLR 277, 31 DLR 123.
 4 *Re Earle's Shipbuilding and Engineering Co* [1901] WN 78.
 5 *Re R McGaffin Ltd* [1938] NZLR 764.

other hand damages due in lieu of proper notice do not have the requisite characteristics.[6] But payments in respect of proper notice are wages or salary within the meaning of the preferential provision.[7]

The reference to wages or salary in Sch 6 to the Insolvency Act 1986 is a reference to the *gross* amount of such wages or salary before statutory deductions for Pay As You Earn (PAYE) or National Insurance contributions; and the limit on the sum to which priority is to be given is necessarily a limit on the sum in respect of *gross* wages or salary before deductions.

The practical consequence of so interpreting the words 'wages' and 'salary' is that the procedure which needs to be adopted in dealing with the employee's proof is as follows:

(1)   The employee proves for the whole of the gross amount of wages or salary due to him.

(2)   The employee will rank as a preferential creditor for that part of the claim which represents arrears of gross wages or salary which accrued due in respect of services rendered to the company during the period of four months next before the relevant date up to the statutory maximum.[8] The employee will rank as an ordinary non-preferential creditor for any balance.

(3)   In paying dividends, whether preferential or not, the receiver must deduct PAYE and National Insurance contributions from the sums paid to the employee, and account for the sums deducted.

(4)   Additionally there may be preferential claims by the Revenue in respect of PAYE deductions made by the company and not paid over before the relevant date.

'Remuneration'

A sum is payable by the debtor to a person by way of remuneration in respect of a period if (a) it is paid as wages or salary (whether payable for time or for piecework or earned wholly or partly by way of commission), in respect of services rendered to the debtor in that period,[9] or (b) it is a guarantee payment,[10] remuneration on suspension on medical grounds or on maternity grounds,[11] a time-off payment in respect of looking for work (or for making arrangements for training) after notice of dismissal for redundancy, or in respect of ante-natal care, for time off for carrying out trade union duties,[12] or

---

6   *Re VIP Insurances Ltd* [1978] 2 NSWLR 297, 3 ACLR 751.
7   *Re Leeds Twentieth Century Decorators* [1962] CLY 365.
8   Originally £200, now £800.
9   IA 1986, Sch 6, para 13(1)(a).
10   See Employment Rights Act 1996, Part III.
11   See ERA 1996, Pt VII.
12   See ERA 1996, ss 53 (looking for work), and 56 (ante-natal care) and Trade Union and Labour Relations (Consolidation) Act 1992 (carrying out trade union duties).

remuneration under a protective award,[13] payable in each case by the debtor in respect of that period.[14]

Holiday remuneration is deemed to have accrued to an employee where employment has been terminated in consequence of his company employer going into receivership under s 40 of the Insolvency Act 1986 if by virtue of his contract of employment or of any enactment[15] that remuneration would have accrued in respect of that period had his employment continued until he became entitled to be allowed the holiday.[16] Lastly, any remuneration payable by the debtor to a person in respect of a period of holiday or of absence from work through sickness or other good cause is deemed to be wages or salary in respect of services rendered to the debtor in that period.[17]

Services rendered to the company

The wages or salary in question must be in respect of services rendered to the company. In *Re General Radio Co Ltd*[18] the company in question carried on the business of making and selling wireless apparatus. It organised a number of persons to find purchasers and to install and repair sets sold to them. On the facts Clauson J held these persons to be independent contractors but he considered that even had they been employees the sums claimed as preferential could not rank as preferential debts because their services were rendered not to the company but to customers by arrangement with the company.

Time

The services must have been rendered to the company during the four months prior to the appointment of the receiver for the payment to rank as a preferential debt payable out of assets coming in to the hands of the receiver. This of course assumes that no liquidator has previously been appointed. Where after the appointment of a receiver a liquidator is appointed either by resolution in a voluntary winding up or by a compulsory winding-up order the preferential claim against the liquidator will only be in respect of wages and salary accruing for services rendered after the receivership and up to the appointment of the liquidator.[19]

---

13 See Trade Union and Labour Relations (Consolidation) Act 1992, s 189.

14 IA 1986, Sch 6, para 13(1)(b) and (2) (as amended by Employment Rights Act 1998, Sch 1, para 29).

15 Or any order or direction under any enactment: IA 1986, Sch 6, para 14(3).

16 IA 1986, Sch 6, para 14.

17 IA 1986, Sch 6, para 15(a). Remuneration in respect of a period of holiday includes any sum which, if it had been paid, would have been treated for the purposes of emoluments relating to social security as earnings in respect of that period: IA 1986, Sch 6, para 15(b).

18 [1929] WN 172.

19 *Re Christonette (International) Ltd* [1982] 3 All ER 225, [1982] 1 WLR 1245. Cf *Re Portbase Clothing Ltd* [1993] Ch 388 at 396.

Levies on coal and steel

A further category of preferential debt has been added by the Insolvency (ECSC Levy Debts) Regulations 1987,[20] namely any sums due at the relevant date from the debtor in respect of (a) the levies on the production of coal and steel referred to in Articles 49 and 50 of the ECSC Treaty, or (b) any surcharge for delay provided for in Article 50(3) of that Treaty and Article 6 of Division 3/52 of the High Authority of the Coal and Steel Community.

---

20 SI 1987/2093 made by the Secretary of State for Trade pursuant to power in European Communities Act 1972, s 2(2).

CHAPTER 17

Remuneration and indemnity

INTRODUCTION

In addition to satisfying himself as to the validity of his appointment a receiver should obviously be concerned to see that there is provision for his remuneration and that the provision is adequate. At the same time he needs to reassure himself that he will be properly indemnified against any liability which he may incur in and about his receivership. The discussion which follows deals both with remuneration and indemnity.[1]

REMUNERATION

As regards remuneration the receiver needs to know who is his paymaster, the basis upon which his remuneration is calculated, how far that basis may be varied and when he may deduct his remuneration. In addition he should have it in mind that in certain circumstances he can be deprived of his remuneration.

Appointment a pre-condition

In order to claim remuneration under an express provision for remuneration of a receiver in a debenture deed the claimant must actually have been appointed receiver. This elementary point arose in *Re Gabriel Controls Pty Ltd*[2] where a debenture holder purported to appoint one Campbell from the well-known international firm of Touche Ross & Co to be receiver and manager of the company. In the event Campbell declined to proceed under the appointment without a court order. No court order appointing him or any other member of his firm was ever sought or obtained. Subsequently another person was appointed receiver and manager. The remuneration provision was to be spelled out of two clauses of the

---

1 For a discussion of the Australian position, see O'Donovan *Company Receivers and Managers* (2nd edn, 1992, with updates) ch 12, expanding upon James O'Donovan 'Company receivers and managers: remuneration and indemnity' (1979) 5 The Queensland Lawyer 37.
2 (1982) 6 ACLR 684 (Sup Ct of South Australia).

deed. First, in applying assets collected there was provision for preferential 'payment of commission to such receiver at a rate to be fixed by the lender not exceeding five per centum of the gross amount of the moneys collected or got in by him or at such higher rate as may be fixed on an application to the Supreme Court'. And in the only other relevant clause the lender was stated to be under no liability to the receiver for his remuneration and costs charges or expenses or otherwise, save as provided in the deed.

The firm of Touche Ross in due course claimed payment for 'professional services' in respect of 'the proposed receivership' of the company. Legoe J rejected the claim. The evidence did not establish that the firm had ever been appointed as receiver. In any event crystallisation of the floating charge was not complete unless and until the person appointed, eligible though he might be, had accepted the appointment. The execution of the documents purporting to appoint Campbell was no more than a unilateral action requiring the confirmation of the appointee before the appointment could be said to be complete. The work done was in any case outside the provision of the deed because it was admitted to be in respect of a *proposed* receivership. And in any case it could not be said to be in accordance with the method of calculation laid down by the deed. Each of the recited reasons was fatal to the application.

Who pays?

The receiver's remuneration is usually payable by the company.[3] Some debentures have an express provision that the company shall be liable for the receiver's remuneration. More frequently the debenture will provide that any receiver and manager appointed thereunder shall be the agent of the company and that the company shall be responsible for such receiver's acts and defaults and for his remuneration.[4] Such a provision constitutes the company the appointee's principal, and therefore his paymaster. In the absence of such an express provision it is a question of construction whether the receiver is the agent of the company or of the debenture holder who appointed him. If the receiver is the agent of the debenture holders then they are responsible for his remuneration.

It has long been the practice to incorporate in the document constituting the security provisions analogous to those in the statutory provision under which the receiver is deemed to be the agent of the mortgagor. The question of construction will then be how far the instrument under consideration by adopting, extending or excluding the relevant statutory provisions has in fact constituted the receiver the agent of the company.

The actual decision in *Deyes v Wood*[5] was that the debenture holders who appointed the receiver were liable for his remuneration on the footing that he was their agent. The debentures incorporated provisions of the Conveyancing Act

---

3 As in *United Malayan Banking Corpn Bhd v Roland Choong Shin Cheong* (1991) 1 MSCLC 90,697 (provision absolving debenture holder from liability for remuneration).

4 *Re Gabriel Controls Pte Ltd* (1982) 6 ACLR 684; *Gomba Holdings UK Ltd v Minories Finance Ltd* [1988] 1 WLR 1231, CA.

5 [1911] 1 KB 806, CA.

1881 relating to receivers but also conferred powers that went beyond those conferred by the Act. The debenture omitted to express the well-known provision that the receiver should be the agent of the company mortgagor. Incorporation of the statutory provisions which included inter alia a provision that a receiver appointed under the statutory powers should be deemed to be the agent of the mortgagor does not necessarily incorporate the latter provision because the provision applies 'unless the mortgage deed otherwise provides'. The extended powers to carry on the business and to realise the capital assets of the business were held to represent a sufficient contrary provision so that the receiver and manager was the agent of, and could look for remuneration from, the debenture holders.

Out of what fund?

The question who pays the receiver should be distinguished from the question: against or from what fund is the remuneration to be charged or paid, as the case may be?[6] In *Deyes v Wood*[7] for example the issue was not whether the receiver was entitled to deduct and retain his remuneration out of the fund realised, but rather whether the receiver was limited to looking to the fund or could look also to the debenture holders, he being their agent.[8]

The question which arose in *Moodemere Pty Ltd v Waters*[9] was not so much whether the receivers were entitled to look to the debenture holder for that remuneration and reimbursement of costs, charges and expenses of realisation but rather whether they were, as a matter of law, entitled to deduct and retain out of the fund realised costs, charges, expenses and remuneration earned relating to the realisation in priority to and even against the debenture holder, the liquidator and the creditors generally. The emphasis in the decided cases is that the costs of realising assets and creating a fund from which to satisfy a secured debt are payable out of the fund so credited before the debt itself is satisfied.[10]

In the *Moodemere* case, Murphy J, after discussing some of the earlier cases, said:[11]

> 'I think it follows that where a company charges its assets and a default occurs so that the creditor becomes entitled in equity to the assets charged, a person, validly appointed to realise the assets so as to provide a fund to satisfy the debt, is entitled

---

6 See *Moodemere Pty Ltd v Waters* [1988] VR 215 at 219 per Murphy J commenting on the discussion in the first edition of this book at 177.

7 [1911] 1 KB 806 above.

8 See [1911] KB 806 at 814 per Scrutton J. The debenture deed did not contain a clause stating that the receiver should be the agent of the company.

9 [1988] VR 215.

10 *Re Oriental Hotels Co* (1871) LR 12 Eq 126 (where the liquidator in his capacity as receiver got his expenses of realisation: (1871) LR 12 Eq 126 at 132 and 135); *Re Regent's Canal Ironworks Co* (1875) 3 Ch D 411 at 427 (liquidator); *Batten v Wedgwood Coal and Iron Co* (1884) 28 Ch D 317: *Re Universal Distributing Co Ltd* (1933) 48 CLR 171 (liquidator); *Moodemere Pty Ltd v Waters* [1988] VR 215 (receiver).

11 [1988] VR 215 at 221.

to look to the fund itself to reimburse his proper costs, charges and expenses of realisation and his just remuneration attendant on the realisation, before even the creditor is paid his secured debt out of the fund.'

This principle applies whether the receiver is appointed by the court or not, and even if he also be the liquidator of the company.[12] So that even if the fund is insufficient to pay both the just costs of realisation of the receiver, and the debt owed to the debenture holder, the receiver remains entitled to deduct and retain his moneys first.

Basis and rate

The basis and rate of the remuneration payable to a receiver and manager are usually spelled out expressly in the mortgage debenture or document of appointment.

Most jurisdictions have enacted a statutory provision dealing with the remuneration of a receiver appointed by a mortgagee out of court in the following terms:[13]

'The Receiver shall be entitled to retain out of any money received by him, for his remuneration, and in satisfaction of all costs, charges and expenses incurred by him as Receiver, a commission at such rate not exceeding five per centum on the gross amount of all money received, as is specified in his appointment, and if no rate is so specified then at the rate of five per centum on that gross amount, or at such other rate as the Court thinks fit to allow, on application made by him for that purpose.'

This provision in its statutory context applies to a receiver appointed under a mortgage who is the receiver of *income* only. Where, as frequently happens, a debenture incorporates this statutory provision or reproduces it, then, in the absence of any other provision in the debenture touching on the remuneration of the receiver, the receiver will presumably be entitled to five per cent not only on the income received but also on the gross proceeds of sales or sale of the property. There is no authority in point. But commentators assume that where the debenture itself gives the receiver power to sell he is entitled to remuneration calculated by reference to the sale proceeds.[14] A commission at a percentage rate 'on the gross amount of all money received' must be payable only on the money received by him *qua* receiver. Taking an extreme case, it cannot have been the intention of the legislature that commission should be payable on money mistakenly, improperly or fortuitously received by the receiver.[15] Remuneration

---

12 A liquidator was appointed receiver in *Perry v Oriental Hotels Co* (1870) 5 Ch App 420 to replace a court receiver appointed when the company was already in liquidation.

13 LPA 1925, s 109(6).

14 *Kerr on Receivers and Administrators* (17th edn) 346–347; Hooper *Receivers for Debenture Holders* (1933) 42; James O'Donovan 'Company receivers and managers: remuneration and indemnity' (1979) 5 The Queensland Lawyer 37 at 38.

15 *Banstead Road Garage Ltd v AG Buchan and Cleveland Petroleum Co Ltd* (17 June 1971, unreported), per Ungoed Thomas J.

for work done as a receiver must, logically, be tied to money received by him as receiver.[16] Accordingly, where the debenture itself gives the receiver power to sell he receives the sale proceeds in his capacity as receiver. On the other hand if the power of sale is delegated to the receiver, who is otherwise acting as agent for the company, it is strongly arguable (and the better view) that the receiver then accepts the sale proceeds as agent of the debenture holder and not as receiver. In such a case commission could only be claimed on the basis of his acting as an agent of the mortgagee, and would be at the rate fixed by the appointment or by the power of attorney delegating the power of sale.

If no rate is specified in his appointment and the receiver is appointed pursuant to the statutory power contained in the Law of Property Act 1925 the rate of remuneration will be at a rate (not exceeding 5 per cent) on such amount or at such other rate as the court sees fit to allow on an application by the receiver made for that purpose. Only when the receiver wants to get a rate of remuneration in excess of 5 per cent will an application to the court be necessary.[17]

In the statutory provision already referred to the 5 per cent rate is expressed to cover not merely the receiver's remuneration but also all costs, charges and expenses incurred by him in his receivership. In some cases the statutory maximum scarcely gives any remuneration to a receiver and barely covers his overheads. Accordingly some debentures separate remuneration from 'costs charges and expenses incurred'[18] and provide for a higher rate of remuneration. Despite the emphatic wording in the section, which specifies 5 per cent as a maximum, some practitioners assume that there is liberty to vary the rate by virtue of the provision that 'any ... section regulating the exercise of [the power to appoint a receiver] may be varied or extended by the mortgage deed'.[19] Others doubt the possibility of exceeding what is a statutory maximum, at any rate where the appointment is made under the statutory power. This nice point can be neatly side-stepped by conferring on the debenture holder an *express* power to appoint a receiver and manager and by also including in the debenture a provision for remuneration in accordance with a professional scale.

A straight percentage basis has its drawbacks. Where the company has an enormous turnover or very substantial realisable assets a percentage basis may overline the receiver's pocket.

At the other end of the spectrum, where the company has an abnormally low turnover and has already sold off many of its realisable assets a percentage basis of remuneration may be unfair to the receiver: even a percentage of the amount which he realises may yield a niggardly return. For these reasons some debentures leave the debenture holder with a discretion as to the remuneration to be specified in the appointment, with a proviso linked to the permissible statutory (or deemed statutory) maximum. So, for example, it may be provided[1] (in such a proviso) that 'such remuneration shall not be at a higher rate than that from time

---

16 *Semble* he cannot charge commission on collections made after he should have finished his job: *Expo International Pty Ltd v Chant (No 2)* (1980) 5 ACLR 193.
17 *Marshall v Cottingham* [1982] Ch 82, [1981] 3 All ER 8.
18 See 6 Encyclopaedia of Forms and Precedents (4th edn) 1184 Form 18:27, Clause 7(2).
19 LPA 1925, s 101(3).
1 6 Forms and Precedents (4th edn) 1184 Form 18.27 (Clause 7(2)).

to time in force under the scale of professional charges for the management collection of rents and lettings of property laid down by the Chartered Auctioneers'
and Estate Agents' Institute (and sub-s (6) of s 109 of the Law of Property Act
1925 shall be varied accordingly)'.[2]

There are pitfalls for debenture holder and receiver alike in this field. A
debenture holder should beware of agreeing a professional scale fee in excess of
any basis sanctioned by the debenture; for if he does, he will be personally liable
to the receiver for any excess over the permissible limit. A receiver and manager
may be left high and dry if the debenture specifies that the remuneration payable
shall be such as the debenture holders determine and then the debenture holders
fail to reach a decision.[3] In practice, of course, the remuneration is usually agreed
between the receiver and the debenture holder or holders before the appointment
is taken up.[4] Failure to agree the remuneration at that stage may preclude a claim
for a quantum meruit if the proper analysis is that there is a binding contract. This
is because an express contract is inconsistent with any such claim.[5] However, if
the agreement between the debenture holder and the receiver is for a
remuneration to be mutually arranged between the parties there is no contract
and a claim for quantum meruit may be maintained.[6]

But what if the debenture is totally silent on the matter of remuneration? In
such a case there is obviously room for implication. Because the appointee is
almost always an accountant or other professional person the court will usually
be prepared to imply a right to remuneration.[7] The next step is to identify the
criteria for fixing the remuneration. In fact all the circumstances of the case are
material: the nature of the business, the length and complexity (or otherwise) of
the receivership, and the going rate for comparable receiverships should be
considered. The court in fixing a reasonable remuneration will have regard to all
these factors and any other relevant circumstances.

Theoretically the ultimate fall back of a receiver who has been 'worthy of his
hire' and who derives no comfort from the debenture, is the restitutionary claim
of quantum meruit.[8] But the very nature of receivership renders it almost
inconceivable that a receiver should be driven to those lengths. The court, in the
absence of any express term as to remuneration, would, it is suggested, be almost
certainly constrained to imply some term as to remuneration.

Naturally where the debenture contains an explicit provision dealing with the
receiver's remuneration there is little, if any, room for implying a right to a

---

2 Ibid.
3 Hooper *Receivers for Debenture Holders* (1933) 43.
4 *Re Richmond Gate Property Co Ltd* [1965] 1 WLR 335 at 338 (express contract between
   directors and managing director).
5 *Re Richmond Gate Property Co Ltd* [1965] 1 WLR 335 at 338.
6 *Way v Latilla* [1937] 3 All ER 759, HL; and see Goff and Jones *Law of Restitution* (5th edn)
   592–596.
7 *Gibbon v Budd* (1863) 2 H & C 92; *Prior v Bagster* (1887) 57 LT 760 (5% of assets recovered);
   Turner v Reeve (1901) 17 TLR 592.
8 See Goff and Jones *Law of Restitution* (5th edn) 240–252; PB Birks 'Restitution for Services'
   (1974) 27 CLP 13; Gareth Jones 'Restitutionary Claims for Services Rendered' (1977) 93 LQR
   273; *Prior v Bagster* (1887) 57 LT 760.

higher remuneration than that stipulated:[9] *expressum facit cessare tacitum*.[10] That is not to say that extra remuneration can never be claimed. For instance, extra duties may justify extra remuneration; so that if the debenture holder asks the receiver and manager to perform additional services, outside the scope of the duties laid down by the instrument of appointment, the debenture holder will be liable to pay him additional remuneration. The receiver and manager stands in the position of a paid agent and the basis upon which a paid agent can ask for more is helpfully discussed by Kekewich J in *Williamson v Hine*[11] a case involving the managing owner of a ship:

'A paid agent . . . is bound to discharge all those duties multifarious or otherwise, and onerous or otherwise, which the terms of that agency cover. He must make his own bargain with his principal, and it is his duty to do all that bargain entails and to be content with his remuneration. If he is called upon to do anything outside the terms of his agency, he is entitled to make a special bargain, or he can decline to do it unless he is remunerated on a special footing; or he may do the work, and, provided everything is fair and above-board, he probably would be allowed some fair remuneration according to some recognised measurement of the value. But if he does anything within the terms of his agency, however uncompensated it may seem to him personally, he can neither charge for it in his account nor can he secretly take any commission for it.'

Variation

There is a limited right, conferred upon a *liquidator*, to apply to the court to fix the amount to be paid by way of remuneration to any person who, under the powers contained in any instrument, has been appointed a receiver or manager of the property of a company.[12] Once such an order has been made either the liquidator or the receiver and manager whose remuneration is in question may apply to the court to vary or amend the order.[13] This statutory right, it will be observed, is only enjoyed where the receiver or manager has been appointed under the powers contained in some instrument. It is not available where the receiver was appointed under some statutory power. However debentures almost invariably contain express powers to appoint a receiver and manager so that the statutory right to apply to the court to fix his remuneration can be exercised by the liquidator, or (if an order has previously been made and requires amendment) by the receiver and manager himself.

Where no previous order has been made under the relevant statutory provision the power of the court (1) extends to fixing the remuneration for any period before the making of the order or the application therefor,[14] (2) is exercisable even though

9 *Kofi Sunkersette Obu v A Strauss & Co Ltd* [1951] AC 243.
10 The maxim is discussed in Broom's *Legal Maxims* (10th edn) 443–454.
11 [1891] 1 Ch 390 at 395.
12 IA 1988, s 36. For an unsuccessful application, see *Re Potters Oils Ltd (No 2)* [1986] 1 All ER 890, [1986] 1 WLR 201.
13 IA 1986, s 36(3).
14 IA 1986, s 36(2)(a).

the receiver or manager has died or ceased to act before the making of the order or the application therefor,[15] (3) can be exercised so as to require the receiver or manager or his personal representative to account for any remuneration in excess of the amount fixed by the court for any period before the making of the order.[16]

Where a previous order has been made under the relevant statutory provision the court may vary or amend that order, at the instance either of the liquidator or of the receiver and manager.[17]

The amount which the court will sanction as proper very much depends upon the particular circumstances of the case: there is no fixed scale, and each case is dealt with on its merits.

In a compulsory winding up the liquidator will make the relevant application to the court by a summons in the winding up.[18] Where the winding up is a voluntary winding up the proper course is for the liquidator to issue an originating summons. The relevant process should in each case be served on the receiver or manager.

The question remains: does a receiver or manager appointed out of court have a right to apply to the court for an increase in the remuneration stipulated by the debenture or by the document appointing him? One writer has suggested that a privately appointed receiver or manager 'can apply to the court for authority to retain additional remuneration if the circumstances warrant such a course being adopted'.[19] No authority is cited for the proposition and there is no trace of it in the other monographs.[20]

In *Re Odessa Promotions Pty Ltd (in liquidation)*[1] there was an express provision in the debenture deed specifying that the remuneration of the receiver was to be fixed at a rate not exceeding 5 per cent of the gross sum of all moneys received. Shortly after accepting their appointment the receivers wrote to the debenture holder stating that their charges would be at scale rates and the debenture holder agreed to this. The company went into liquidation and the liquidator pointed to the letter of the deed: 5 per cent. The Supreme Court of Victoria held that it had no statutory power to ride roughshod over the express bargain contained in the debenture deed.

Disallowance

It is a principle of the law of agency that an agent is not entitled to remuneration for transactions in relation to which he is in breach of his duties as agent where the breach goes to the root of the contract or otherwise justifies the principal's

15 IA 1986, s 36(2)(b).
16 IA 1986, s 36(2). But the court will not exact any excess for any period prior to the application unless special circumstances justify such a course: IA 1986, s 36(2) proviso.
17 IA 1986, s 36(3); HK Companies Ordinance 1933–76, s 300; Singapore CA, s 219(3); MCA, s 184(3).
18 See 10(1) *Court Forms* (1999 Issue) and Forms 213 and 214 for originating application and statement in support.
19 Hooper *Receivers for Debenture Holders* (1933) 43.
20 *Kerr on Receivers and Administrators* (17th edn) 434–435; Riviere *Law Relating to Receivers and Managers* (1912) 197.
 1 (1979) ACLC 49–253.

repudiation of the liability to pay.[2] In accordance with this principle a receiver and manager may by his acts or omissions forfeit his right to commission or remuneration.

What, then, is a breach of duty such as will justify a refusal of remuneration to a receiver and manager? Few of the cases touching on this point concern receivers and managers. Guidance is, however, to be found in cases involving ordinary agents. From these one appreciates that a relevant breach may be described in various ways. A wrongful delegation of receivership duties may be described as a wrongful breach of the duty not to delegate, serious enough to justify forfeiture of a right to remuneration;[3] or the right may be denied on the simple ground that the commission has not been earned. In other cases the relevant breach goes to the root of the contract or is a repudiatory breach.[4]

The acceptance of a bribe in connection with his receivership flies in the face of the duties of good faith owed by a receiver, and is a breach which goes to the root of his contract, so as to disentitle him in any event to remuneration.[5] Likewise a receiver who sells property subject to the debenture and obtains a secret profit from the purchaser will not only have to account for that profit, but is not entitled to any commission.[6] In some exceptional cases the court has ruled that the taking of a secret profit was not a bar to a claim for commission[7] either on the basis that the agent acted in good faith[8] or on the ground that the alleged profit was not connected with the relevant obligation of the agent.[9] A receiver and manager who is misguided enough to exercise a power of sale in favour of himself or a partner of his or a company in which he is substantially interested would also forfeit his right to commission on the sale, whether or not any loss had been suffered by reason of his conduct.[10] In all these cases it could equally be said that the relevant conduct was outside the scope of the receiver's authority.[11]

The disentitling breach may consist of (and be described as) gross neglect or gross misconduct[12] or dishonesty. An example of dishonesty is where a receiver

---

2 *Bowstead and Reynolds on Agency* (16th edn) 317–322; Powell *Law of Agency* (2nd edn) 327; Fridman *Law of Agency* (7th edn) 200–201.

3 *Beable v Dickerson* (1885) 1 TLR 654. As to what receivership functions may be delegated, see at pp 120–124.

4 *Thornton Hall & Partners v Wembley Electrical Appliances Ltd* [1947] 2 All ER 630 at 634, CA; cf *Keppel v Wheeler* [1927] 1 KB 577 at 592, CA.

5 *Harrington v Victoria Graving Dock Co* (1878) 3 QBD 549; see also ER Hardy Ivamy 'The bribery of agents' (1949) 16 The Solicitor 245.

6 *Andrews v Ramsay & Co* [1903] 2 KB 635, 72 LJKB 865; *Manitoba and North-Westerland Corpn v Davidson* (1903) 34 SCR 255; *Levin v Levy* 1917 TPD 702.

7 *Hippisley v Knee Bros* [1905] 1 KB 1. The decision was 'slightly regretted' at the time and the circumstances were 'very exceptional': see (1905) 21 LQR 102; and see *John D Rosart Real Estate Co Ltd v Horvath* (1961) 29 DLR (2d) 205 at 208.

8 *Hippisley v Knee Bros* supra; and see *Complin v Beggs* (1913) 24 Man LR 596, 13 DLR 27.

9 *Calgary Realty Co v Reid* (1911) 19 WLR 649, 1 WWR 218; *Westergaard v Weyl* (1912) 21 WLR 403, 7 DLR 847; *Mack v McLeod* [1925] 2 DLR 1201.

10 *Lunghi v Sinclair* [1966] WAR 172; noted in [1967] ASCL 331–332 (partner); *Salomons v Pender* (1865) 3 H & C 639, 6 New Rep 43 (company).

11 *Salomons v Pender* supra; *Andrews v Ramsay & Co* supra.

12 *White v Lady Lincoln* (1803) 8 Ves 363 (gross neglect in keeping accounts); *White v Chapman* (1815) 1 Stark 113 (gross misconduct by factor); *United Agency and Trust Co v Amm Bros* 1917 TPD 439.

and manager in the exercise of a power of sale colludes with a prospective purchaser.[13] In *Greenwood v Harvey*[14] no receiver was involved but a selling agent colluded with two competing purchasers with the object of holding down the price. His duty of economic loyalty to his principal was of course to obtain the best available price. 'The rule of undivided loyalty is relentless and supreme':[15] its violation disentitled the agent to any commission. Lack of skill or due diligence, or simply negligence, may have the same result: loss of the right to remuneration.[16] Nor is commission chargeable in relation to transactions which are abortive due to some default on the receiver's part.[17] Thus if a receiver and manager were to start legal proceedings and through mismanagement they achieved nothing any commission attributable to the time wasted would be irrecoverable.[18]

Commission will, moreover, only be payable where the transaction in question was expressly or impliedly authorised,[19] or is later ratified by the receiver and manager's principal.[20] In the context of ratification it will be remembered that after the commencement of the winding up the receiver and manager ceases to be the agent of the company[1] and so ratification after that point of time will not be possible.

Where the course of the receivership includes a number of severable transactions the rule depriving the receiver and manager of commission or remuneration will only apply to those in respect of which he is in breach of duty.[2] Thus a receiver and manager who negligently mishandles a sale of one item of the company's property so that the sale is at a gross undervalue may forfeit the agreed percentage of commission on that sale, while remaining entitled to the relevant percentage on all other receipts. Alternatively if the basis of his remuneration is by reference to time spent, the time appropriated to the mis-handled sale will be disregarded.

Attack on amount of remuneration

The liquidator in *Re Potters Oils (No 2)*[3] alleged that the appointment of a receiver in that case was unnecessary and that the receiver's claim for remuneration and disbursements was in any event excessive.

---

13 *Andrews v Ramsay & Co* [1903] 2 KB 635.
14 [1965] NSWR 1489, discussed by R Baxt (1967) Aus Lawyer 55.
15 *Meinherd v Salmon* 249 NY 456 at 464 (1928) per Cardozo J.
16 *Denew v Daverell* (1813) 3 Camp 451 (sale became nugatory); *Moneypenny v Hartland* (1824) 1 C & P 352; *Dalton v Irvin* (1830) 4 C & P 289.
17 *Denew v Daverell* supra.
18 *Huntley v Bulwer* (1839) 6 Bing NC 111, 8 Scott 325.
19 *Marsh v Jelf* (1862) 3 F & F 234 (sale by private treaty instead of auction).
20 Ibid (no ratification). If the debenture holder ratifies or adopts a mishandled sale the receiver and manager may get his commission: *Keppel v Wheeler* [1927] 1 KB 577, CA; *Harrods Ltd v Lemon* [1931] 2 KB 157, CA.
 1 *Gosling v Gaskell* [1897] AC 575, 66 LJQB 848, HL.
 2 *Nitedals Taendstik fabrik v Bruster* [1906] 2 Ch 671; cf *Headway Construction Co Ltd v Downham* (1974) 233 Estates Gazette 675.
 3 [1986] 1 WLR 201 at 207.

Hoffmann J rejected the argument to the effect that the appointment was unnecessary because a liquidator was in the saddle. The debenture gave an unfettered contractual right to appoint a receiver at any time after the loan had become repayable. That right was to enable the debenture holder to protect his own interests.

As to the claim that the remuneration was excessive, he pointed out that s 36 of the Insolvency Act 1986 confers two separate discretions. The first is a discretion as to whether to interfere at all. The second, once the decision has been made to fix the remuneration, is a discretion as to the amount. Both appear to be entirely unfettered. In exercising those discretions the judge bore in mind three considerations. First, the exercise of the power involves interference with the contractual rights in the interest of unsecured creditors. Accordingly interference should be confined rather than take the form of a routine taxation by the court of receivers' remuneration. Secondly, the court is ill-equipped to conduct a detailed investigation of a receiver's charges on an itemised basis. Thirdly, the debenture contemplated remuneration as a percentage of the sum realised by the receiver. That, of course, was not of itself a reason for not interfering. But in the case before him, there was nothing to show that either a percentage calculation or the 5 per cent maximum was unreasonable. Guidance might, he thought, be obtained from the fact that the fees of liquidators and trustees in bankruptcy are ordinarily calculated as a percentage of the moneys which pass through their hands.

Further guidance, it is suggested, can be gleaned from the decisions concerning the remuneration of court-appointed receivers[4] and in particular the review of the relevant considerations in *Mirror Group Newspapers plc v Maxwell (No 2)*.[5]

Turning to the claim for disbursements, the judge noted that the section was confined to the receiver's remuneration. It conferred no jurisdiction to interfere with his right to indemnity for disbursements. That right remained subject to the ordinary law of agency.[6]

INDEMNITY

Importance of indemnity

The importance to a receiver and manager of a proper right of indemnity can hardly be over-stated. Good remuneration loses much of its gilt when matched by an inadequate right of indemnity. The court will, in certain circumstances, imply a right to an indemnity. But, for reasons which will appear, a receiver and manager is better advised to extract express indemnities. In that way he can cover, as far as possible, all reasonable contingencies, whereas if he relies on an implied right of indemnity he may, in the event, find it to be a cold comfort.

---

4 See at 477–482 below.
5 [1998] 1 BCLC 638.
6 [1986] 1 WLR 201.

A receiver and manager may have a right of indemnity against the company whose assets are charged or against the debenture holders or debenture holder who appointed him.

Extent

It will be remembered that in most debentures it is provided that any receiver and manager appointed by the debenture holder shall be the agent of the company. In the case of an administrative receiver of a company, such administrative receiver is deemed to be the agent of the company unless and until the company goes into liquidation.[7]

As between principal and agent there is usually an implied obligation on the part of the principal to indemnify the agent for expenses and liabilities properly incurred by the agent in the performance of his duties. Where, therefore, the debenture specifies that any receiver and manager shall be the agent of the company the court will, in the absence of any express indemnity or any provision including a right of indemnity, usually imply an indemnity to that effect. Presumably the same principle applies to the deemed statutory agency.

The implication only arises if such expenses and liabilities are in fact occasioned by his employment and does not arise at all if the contract between the parties expressly excludes any right of reimbursement or indemnity. While in some contracts of agency express exclusion of a right to reimbursement and indemnity may be found no sane receiver and manager would accept such an inhibition. The right is not affected by the fact that the payment for which the agent seeks to be indemnified is not one for which the principal could be made liable.[8] On the other hand the right to indemnity does not apply to a liability such as income tax incurred in respect of a profit made by the agent acting as principal.[9]

The indemnity or reimbursement is a full indemnity or reimbursement. Thus where a receiver and manager is sued and the facts support a right to be indemnified for his costs in that litigation, the scale of his reimbursement is that of costs on a common fund basis and not simply party and party, for he would then be out of pocket.[10] For the same reason if a receiver and manager has succeeded in the litigation but has only recovered party and party costs he is entitled to be reimbursed the difference between those costs and costs on the common fund basis.[11]

The right of indemnity and reimbursement naturally applies to liabilities arising out of the premature revocation of the authority of the receiver and manager.[12] Thus in *Hill v Venning*[13] a receiver and manager whose appointment

---

7 IA 1986, s 44.
8 *Brittain v Lloyd* (1845) 14 M & W 762, 15 LJ Ex 43; *Adams v Morgan & Co Ltd* [1924] 1 KB 751, CA.
9 *Re Hollebone's Agreement* [1959] 2 All ER 152, [1959] 1 WLR 536, CA.
10 *Williams v Lister & Co* (1913) 109 LT 699, CA.
11 *Re Famatina Development Corpn Ltd* [1914] 2 Ch 271, CA.
12 *Warlow v Harrison* (1859) 1 E & E 309 at 317 per Martin B. Revocation by the appointor is no longer possible in the case of an administrative receivership.
13 (1979) 4 ACLR 555.

had been revoked claimed in addition to his remuneration a lien on the assets subject to the debenture for amounts for which he had become personally liable in the performance of his duties as receiver. Connolly J granted him an interlocutory injunction until trial over the assets in respect of which he claimed a lien. The right of indemnity covers not merely those losses which the receiver actually sustained but also in accordance with equitable principles the full amount of the liabilities incurred by him, even though they may never in fact be enforced.[14]

Liability in this context is not confined to legal liability.[15] But a possibility of a future claim is not enough.[16] The extent to which a receiver may obtain an indemnity for possible damages which might be claimed against him in the future arising out of his management of the undertaking was at issue in *Dyson v Peat*.[17] The receiver and manager of a colliery was within three weeks of his appointment appointed liquidator under a voluntary winding up. He later sold the colliery and was accountable to the debenture holders for the proceeds of sale. He claimed the right to retain this money as an indemnity fund against any future claims which might be made against him for damage to the surface arising out of his working of the coal. It was held by Eve J that he had no such lien at law and no equitable lien either on principle or authority. The money did not come from his discharge of duties as agent of the debenture holder. The plaintiffs did not deny that he would have been entitled to be indemnified by them against any claims which might have been made against him for damage to the surface arising out of his working of the coal. But any lien even on those moneys which came to him as agent would be inconsistent with the activities which he was carrying out on his principal's behalf. A receiver has no right of indemnity against remote contingencies. Nor unless he has applied to the court for directions in relation to prospective litigation will he have an indemnity for his costs incurred in defending a case, certainly if he loses and has made no such application he will be at risk that the court will not allow his costs. Of course if he wins, his costs will be treated as an incident of his proper administration in respect of which he will be entitled to his indemnity.[18] The right of indemnity extends to cases where the relevant liabilities were incurred under an honest error of judgment.[19] It is of course immaterial whether or not an agent (and by extension a receiver and manager) professes to be acting as agent for his principal if he is in fact so acting: his right to indemnity or reimbursement depends on deeds not words.[20]

Lastly, it should be noted that the indemnity and lien can be claimed by a subsequent debenture holder's receiver in priority to the first debenture if the receiver has been left by the first debenture holder to manage and recover the assets of the company.[1]

---

14 *Lacey v Hill, Crowley's Claim* (1874) LR 18 Eq 182.
15 *Rhodes v Fielder, Jones and Harrison* (1919) 89 LJKB 15 (barrister's fees).
16 *Dyson v Peat* [1917] 1 Ch 99, 115 LT 700.
17 [1917] 1 Ch 99.
18 *Expo International Pty Ltd v Chant (No 2)* (1980) 5 ACLR 193.
19 *Broom v Hall* (1859) 7 CBNS 503, 34 LTOS 66; *Pettman v Keble* (1850) 9 CB 701.
20 *Re Fox, Walker & Co, ex p Bishop* (1880) 15 Ch D 400, CA; *Re Rogers, ex p Rogers* (1880) 15 Ch D 207, 43 LT 163, CA.
 1 *National Australia Bank Ltd v Composite Buyers Ltd* (1991) 6 ACSR 94.

Out of what assets?

The next question is: out of what assets may the indemnity be claimed? The appointment of a receiver and manager crystallises the floating charge and perfects the equitable assignment of the assets subject to the charge. In other words after the appointment the charged assets belong in equity to the debenture holder or holders. On principle one would expect any implied indemnity only to be capable of being enforced against unencumbered assets of the company, unless there had been some agreement to the contrary. But that, of course, could turn out to be a very hollow indemnity indeed. The classic debenture charges all the property of the company. And even when it does not the amount of unencumbered assets may well be insufficient to meet the indemnity in question. In practice the question rarely arises. This is because the matter is usually dealt with by express agreement. The standard form of mortgage debenture gives the receiver and manager a claim against the assets subject to the charge. And it is conceived that where a receiver incurs a personal liability in the course of his duties and while acting in good faith, he will in any event have a right to indemnity out of the charged assets.[2] The indemnity will survive repayment of the debenture and the execution of a release of the security.[3]

Disallowance

A receiver and manager is not entitled to reimbursement or indemnity where the relevant expenses or liabilities were incurred in the sort of circumstances which would operate to deprive him of any right to remuneration. So he will have no right to any indemnity or reimbursement where he incurred the relevant expense or liability as a result of his own default[4] or breach of duty[5] or through transactions which are outside the scope of his authority and have not been ratified by his principal.[6] Likewise there is in general no right of indemnity against the consequences of transactions which fall foul of the criminal law.[7] The rule prohibiting indemnity or reimbursement where the conduct of the receiver and manager is illegal only applies where his act is obviously or manifestly unlawful or where he knows that it is unlawful,[8] or

---

2 Cf *Jennings v Mather* [1902] 1 KB 1 at 6; and see *Savage v Union Bank of Australia Ltd* (1906) 3 CLR 1170 at 1186.
3 See *Hill v Venning* (1979) 4 ACLR 555 (dismissed receiver); *Re Rylands Glass and Engineering Co Ltd* (1904) 118 LT Jo 87 and *Re Arctic Electric Supplies* (1932) 48 TLR 350 (both cases where private receiver replaced by court receiver).
4 *Thacker v Hardy* (1878) 4 QBD 685 at 687; *Lewis v Samuel* (1846) 8 QB 685; *Duncan v Hill* (1873) LR 8 Exch 242.
5 *Ellis v Pond* [1898] 1 QB 426, CA (premature sale); *Solloway v McLaughlin* [1938] AC 247, [1937] 4 All ER 328, PC (fraud of agent).
6 *Beaumont v Boultbee* (1805) 11 Ves 358; *Bowlby v Bell* (1846) 3 CB 284.
7 *Burrows v Rhodes* [1899] 1 QB 816 at 829; *Haseldine v Hosken* [1933] 1 KB 822, CA.
8 *Burrows v Rhodes* [1899] 1 QB 816 at 829; *Haseldine v Hosken* [1933] 1 KB 822, CA.

where the act or transaction is unlawful by virtue of legislation imposing strict liability.[9] Nor as Kennedy J pointed out in *Burrows v Rhodes*[10] 'can there be any valid claim to indemnity where the doer of the act which constitutes the offence has done it with knowledge of all the circumstances necessary to constitute the act an offence, but in ignorance that the act done under those circumstances constituted an offence. A man is presumed to know the law'. Accordingly a receiver who makes a contract which is prohibited by statute[11] or who makes a payment which it is criminally illegal for him to make, as for example a bribe,[12] is not only precluded from recovering any remuneration but is also not entitled to any indemnity against his expenses in such a transaction. Where, however, the indemnity is sought in respect of expenses which are distinct from the illegal transaction it is a different matter: the right to an indemnity is not affected.[13]

It seems to be implicit in the reasoning of those cases which deny an indemnity to an agent who knowingly conducts himself in an illegal way that if the agent does not know of some circumstance which renders his act illegal he is still entitled to his indemnity. That has certainly been held to be the case where the agent is able to prove that he was positively misled by his principal as to some crucial factor in the transaction.[14] On a parity of reasoning the same should apply where without fault on his part he was unaware of the particular circumstance which made the transaction a criminal offence, unless (it has been suggested)[15] it is known that the act is morally a wrong act. In *Allen v Allen*[16] an agent was held entitled to an indemnity in respect of money expended by him in ignorance that the purpose of the expenditure was in fact illegal. His ignorance was one of fact not law. A receiver and manager in like circumstances would doubtless also be entitled to an indemnity.

Where the conduct of a receiver and manager amounts to a tort but not a crime, he is at common law, like any other agent, entitled to be indemnified against expenses and liabilities if the transaction in question was not manifestly tortious or tortious to his knowledge.[17] And where he incurs liability to a third party in respect of a tort committed with the authority of the debenture holder as principal he is entitled to such contribution from the latter as the court considers to be just and equitable having regard to the extent of their respective responsibility for the damage.[18] Such contribution may take the form of a complete indemnity.[19]

---

9 See *Bowstead and Reynolds on Agency* (16th edn) 7-062, 7-066, 7-069.
10 [1899] 1 QB 816 at 829.
11 *Ex p Mather* (1797) 3 Ves 373; *Warwick v Slade* (1811) 3 Camp 127.
12 *Josephs v Pebrer* (1825) 3 B & C 639, 1 C & P 507.
13 *Lindo v Smith* (1858) 5 CBNS 587.
14 *Burrows v Rhodes* [1899] 1 QB 816 at 829–830.
15 [1899] 1 QB 816 at 830.
16 (1954) 55 SRNSW 75, 72 WN 1.
17 *Adamson v Jarvis* (1827) 4 Bing 66, 12 Moore CP 241; *Betts v Gibbins* (1834) 2 Ad & El 57; *W Cory & Son Ltd v Lambton and Hetton Collieries Ltd* (1916) 86 LJKB 401, 115 LT 738, CA.
18 Law Reform (Married Women and Tortfeasors) Act 1935, s 6(1)(c), (2).
19 Law Reform (Married Women and Tortfeasors) Act 1935, s 6(2).

Enforcement of the right to reimbursement and indemnity

A receiver and manager may like any other agent enforce his rights of reimbursement and indemnity by action or by the exercise of his lien,[20] or the receiver may seek the discretions of the Court[1] and if appropriate a declaration as to his right to an indemnity.[2] In those rare cases where a receiver is sued by his principal he may assert his right to reimbursement or indemnity by way of set off or counterclaim.[3]

20 *Hill v Venning* (1979) 4 ACLR 555 (Qld Sup Ct) (interlocutory injunction granted to receiver and manager to secure his lien).
 1 Under IA 1986, s 35.
 2 *Re Therm-a-Stor Ltd* [1996] 2 BCLC 400. The section is wide enough to embrace any dispute concerning the receiver's remuneration.
 3 *Curtis v Barclay* (1826) 5 B & C 141, 7 Dow & Ry KB 539.

CHAPTER 18

Termination

A receiver and manager appointed out of court has a defined object: to secure the repayment of the sum due to the creditor who appointed him. Once that goal is reached he will want to be discharged entirely from his responsibilities. This chapter considers the circumstances of termination of receivership, and rehearses the residual duties, liabilities and rights of a receiver on termination.[1]

CIRCUMSTANCES

A receivership may be determined by the parties themselves, by death, by the court or automatically.

By the parties

The most obvious and frequent circumstance where a receivership ends is where the receiver's job is done and his appointor, expressly or tacitly, discharges him. Such termination is either entirely or in effect consensual, and occurs after the receivership has run its course. But termination may also take place prematurely in the event of the death, resignation or dismissal of the receiver.

Dismissal

An initial point to note is that although the receiver under the conventional debenture is expressed to be the agent of the company, that special and limited[2] agency does not invest the company with any powers to dismiss the receiver. The right was conventionally reserved to the debenture holder, usually linked with a notice in writing which took effect on communication. A non-administrative receiver appears to have no remedy if he is dismissed unless he was appointed

---

1 See *Company Receivers and Managers* (2nd edn 1992, with updates) ch 15, expanding and updating O'Donovan 'Termination of Receivership' (1979) Chartered Accountant in Australia (September) 47 (available in Library of Institute of Chartered Accountants).
2 *R v Board of Trade, ex p St Martin Preserving Co Ltd* [1965] 1 QB 603, [1964] 2 All ER 561.

for a fixed period in which case he might claim damages for wrongful dismissal. An administrative receiver, however, can now only be removed by the court.[3]

Resignation

An administrative receiver now has a statutory right in England to resign from his receivership.[4] In default, however, of a contractual provision in the debenture enabling him to resign, a non-administrative receiver can only lawfully resign with the consent of the debenture holder who appointed him. Without such consent his resignation would constitute a breach of contract for which he might be held liable in damages. He would not, however, be compelled to complete his receivership because the courts set their face against specific enforcement directly or indirectly of a contract to perform personal services.[5]

On the resignation or removal of a receiver the full management powers and authorities of the directors are revised[6] or if the company is in liquidation pass to the liquidator.

By the court

The court may in the exercise of its inherent jurisdiction remove a non-administrative receiver in a proper case. An application to the court to achieve that end would be brought by the person or persons who appointed him.

A power for a debenture holder of a company to appoint a receiver conferred by a debenture which states that all the debentures are to rank 'pari passu' is a fiduciary power and must be exercised for the benefit of all the debenture holders. If such a power is exercised by a debenture holder not in the interests of all the debenture holders, but with a view to the benefit of the shareholders of the company the court has jurisdiction to appoint and will appoint its own receiver.[7] The court may also interfere where the receiver and manager has not on a true analysis of the position been appointed by a majority in value of the debenture holders if that is a condition of the appointment.[8] Another clear example is where a disqualified person is purportedly appointed: the court will hold the purported appointment a nullity and any acts done by the disqualified receiver will likewise lack the proper legal effect that would otherwise have been attributed to them.[9]

---

3 IA 1986, s 45(1).
4 IA 1986, s 45(1).
5 See *Chinnock v Sainsbury* (1860) 3 LT 258; *Morris v Delobbel-Flipo* [1892] 2 Ch 352. The rule is not absolute but very special circumstances are needed to escape it: see *Hill v C A Parsons & Co Ltd* [1972] Ch 305, [1971] 3 All ER 1345, CA; Pettit *Equity and the Law of Trusts* (8th edn) 619–622.
6 *Re Geneva Finance Ltd: Quigley v Cook* (1991) 7 ACSR 415.
7 *Re Maskelyne British Typewriter Ltd* [1898] 1 Ch 133, 67 LJ Ch 125, CA.
8 *Re Slogger Automatic Feeder Co Ltd* [1915] 1 Ch 478, 84 LJ Ch 587.
9 *Portman Building Society v Gallwey* [1955] 1 All ER 227, [1955] 1 WLR 96 (body corporate appointed receiver).

No doubt sufficiently serious misconduct or a flagrant breach of duty casting doubt on the safety of the security in the receiver's hands would also cause the court to intervene.[10]

An administrative receiver may at any time be removed from office by order of the court.[11]

Automatically

The title of a receiver and manager is no better than the title of the debenture holder who appointed him. Where therefore a prior incumbrancer comes forward and appoints his own receiver and manager the appointee of the later incumbrancer will perforce be replaced. This replacement is automatic[12] and requires no order of the court unless of course there is a dispute as to priorities. An administrative receiver must vacate his office if he ceases to be qualified to act as an insolvency practitioner.[13] He must also vacate office if an administration order is made.[14]

EFFECT OF TERMINATION

Prior to the Insolvency Act 1986 most debentures contained an express provision enabling the debenture holder to replace the receiver whom he had appointed by another receiver. The main use of a provision of this kind was to deal with the situation that arose if the receiver died or resigned. But it also served a purpose in the case of misconduct or a basic difference of opinion between the debenture holder and the receiver.

In the case of an administrative receiver the appointing creditor can no longer rely on such a clause to effect the removal of the administrative receiver. There is only one way for a debenture holder to secure the removal of an administrative receiver, that is by applying to the court.

Moreover in the absence of any such provision it must clearly be open to a debenture holder to appoint a fresh receiver in place of the one who dies, retires by agreement, or is removed by the court. If within a reasonable time a substitute receiver is found and appointed there will be no break in the continuity of the receivership.[15] Were it otherwise serious consequences might ensue. The company might try to deal with the assets subject to the charge or the employees' contracts of employment might be affected. As it is any attempt to interfere with the assets in the continuing receivership can be protected by injunction.[16]

---

10 *Re Neon Signs (Australasia) Ltd* [1965] VR 125.
11 IA 1986, s 45(1).
12 This is deducible from *Re Metropolitan Amalgamated Estates* [1912] 2 Ch 497 at 502 (where, however, an order was necessary because the subsequent incumbrancer was court-appointed).
13 IA 1986, s 45(2).
14 IA 1986, s 11(1)(b). See the discussion at 524.
15 *Re R W Hill Ltd and Simmons' Contract* [1920] WN 386.
16 *Bayly v Went* (1884) 51 LT 764.

If there is a smooth hand-over of the receivership no problem should arise in relation to the liability to pay preferential creditors. It is true that the receiver cannot avoid his liability by handing over the assets to the company or to the debenture holders, and will be liable in damages to unpaid preferential creditors, if he fails to settle their debts.[17] On the other hand the statutory provision dealing with the receiver's liability for preferential debts simply requires the preferential debtors to be paid out of the assets coming to the hands of the receiver. There is a suggestion in *IRC v Goldblatt*[18] that the receiver's liability in this regard is a personal one. But it is thought that the term 'receiver' could justifiably be held to cover a substitute receiver in the circumstances of a smooth and rapid transference of responsibilities. Where on the other hand the element of continuity is absent the old receiver would have to pay the preferential creditors before releasing funds in his hands.

TERMINAL DUTIES AND PROCEDURES

Once the receiver and manager has sufficient funds to pay off the debenture holder's debt and his own remuneration and the costs, charges and outgoings incurred in the proper exercise of his powers a receiver and manager should call a halt to his management of the company.[19] His job is done and if he goes beyond this point he may be liable to account as a trespasser,[20] as well as running the risk of getting no reward[1] or even indemnity[2] for his labours or expenditure.

If there are not enough funds left to cover all these payments the receiver and manager is usually entitled under the common forms of mortgage debenture to retain an amount to meet his own remuneration and proper expenses.[3] The balance goes to the debenture holder.[4]

Where at any time an administrative receiver vacates office, his remuneration and any expenses properly incurred by him and any indemnity to which he is entitled out of the assets of the company will be charged on and paid out of any property of the company which is in his custody or under his control at the time in priority to any security held by the person by or on whose behalf he was appointed.[5]

---

17 *Woods v Winskill* [1913] 2 Ch 303; *Westminster Corpn v Haste* [1950] Ch 442 at 447; *IRC v Goldblatt* [1972] Ch 498, [1972] 2 All ER 202.
18 [1972] Ch 498, [1972] 2 All ER 202.
19 *Expo International Pty Ltd v Chant* [1979] 2 NSWLR 820, 4 ACLR 679.
20 *Re Goldburg (No 2), ex p Page* [1912] 1 KB 606.
 1 *Marsh v Jelf* (1862) 3 F & F 234; *Gillow & Co v Lord Aberdare* (1892) 9 TLR 12, CA.
 2 *Duncan v Hill* (1873) LR 8 Exch 242, 42 LJ Ex 179; *Thacker v Hardy* (1878) 4 QBD 685 at 687. *New Zealand Farmers' Co-operative Distributing Co Ltd v National Mortgage and Agency Co of New Zealand Ltd* [1961] NZLR 969.
 3 *Bank of New South Wales v Federal Taxation Comr* (1979) 54 ALJR 129, 79 ATC 4687; *Hill v Venning* (1979) 4 ACLR 555.
 4 *Expo International Pty Ltd v Chant* [1979] 2 NSWLR 820, 4 ACLR 679.
 5 IA 1986, s 45(3). There is a similar provision covering the case of an administrative receiver who ceases to hold office on the making of an administration order, see IA 1986, s 11(4).

The discharge of the receiver does not allow him to escape from the possibility of penalties. Thus if a receiver fails to pay the final balance due from him he may, notwithstanding his discharge, be made to account for it and be compelled to repay the amount he was allowed as remuneration with interest.[6] But time will tell against an applicant for the reopening of accounts. Once accounts have been passed, it was held, they will not be reopened for the purpose of charging a receiver with interest or disallowing or clawing back his remuneration, unless the application is made promptly.[7] Presumably a similar result would ensue now that the passing of accounts has been replaced by examination.

SURPLUS AFTER SALE UNDER FIXED AND FLOATING CHARGE

Until the decision of Nourse J in *Re GL Saunders Ltd*[8] it was a vexed question[9] what should happen where a receiver appointed under a fixed and floating charge debenture realised from the sale simply of property subject to the fixed charge more than enough to settle the debt due to the debenture holder.

What then happens to the surplus? Is the balance remaining in the receiver's hands after satisfying the debenture holder in full to be paid to the company or to the preferential creditors? The question has provoked different opinions among practitioners and it may be convenient to set out the arguments in favour of (1) payment to the company and (2) payment to the preferential creditors, before turning to the decision in *Re GL Saunders Ltd* itself.

PAYMENT TO THE COMPANY

One should start with the position under the law of mortgages. The sale proceeds of mortgaged property received by a mortgagee are by statute applicable first in the payment of all costs, charges and expenses properly incurred by him as an incident to the sale; secondly in discharge of the mortgage money, interest, and costs and other money, if any, due under the mortgage; and the residue is payable to 'the person entitled to the mortgaged property or authorised to give receipts for the sale thereof'.[10] The words in inverted commas embrace a second or subsequent mortgagee, or if none, the mortgagor. Accordingly unless there is anything to the contrary in s 40(2) of the Insolvency Act 1986 the surplus proceeds of sale arising after the satisfaction of the debt due to the debenture holder are payable to a second or subsequent incumbrancer or, if none, to the

---

6 *Harrison v Boydell* (1833) 6 Sim 211.
7 *Ward v Swift* (1848) 8 Hare 139, 12 LTOS 190.
8 [1986] 1 WLR 215.
9 See R Hatton and T Cooke 'Fixed Charge Surplus—The Argument is Over' (1985) Ins L & P 137–139; and see Gordon Stewart *Administrative Receivers and Administrators* (1987) 117–118, paras 603–604.
10 LPA 1925, s 105.

company and not to preferential creditors in the receivership constituted pursuant to the combined fixed and floating charge.

Section 40(2) of the Insolvency Act 1986 (formerly s 94 of the Companies Act 1948) provides that, where a receiver is appointed on behalf of the holders of any debentures of a company secured by a floating charge, the preferential debts must be paid out of any assets coming to the hands of the receiver in priority to any claim for principal or interest in respect of the debentures. In *Re Lewis Merthyr Consolidated Collieries Ltd*[11] both Tomlin J and the Court of Appeal held that on the true construction of the statutory predecessor of s 40(2) the priority given to the preferential debts applies only to those assets coming to the hands of the receiver which are derived from the subject of the floating charge, and does not extend to assets coming to his hands which are subject to the fixed charge.

PAYMENT TO PREFERENTIAL CREDITORS

The contrary argument proceeds on the footing that it is wrong to regard s 40(2) as merely containing a negative prohibition not to pay the debenture holder and thus having no significance if there is no 'claim for principal or interest in respect of the debentures' in priority to which the preferential creditors are to be paid. There is, it is asserted, clear judicial support for the view that the provision is positive:

> 'It is a provision which requires [the receiver] to pay the preferential creditors out of any assets coming to his hand . . . as receiver.'[12]

The contrary argument also supposes that the surplus of the proceeds of sale of property subject to the fixed charge is, after satisfaction of the debt due to the debenture holder, itself caught by the floating charge and is thus within s 40(2).

This line of argument requires the receiver in his role as receiver under the floating charge to be classified as 'the next subsequent incumbrancer'. That status is deduced from the fact that the floating charge receiver will be known to have or be capable of having the next succeeding proprietary interest by reason of his statutory indemnity 'out of the assets'.[13] The fixed charge receiver need not concern himself with the state of account between the company and the floating charge receiver; still less is it for him to pay to him only that to which he is entitled under his statutory indemnity. So long as he has knowledge of the subsequent incumbrancer he is bound to transfer the *whole* balance to him, or at the very least, if he pays anyone else he does so at his peril. Then when the floating charge receiver has received the whole surplus under the fixed charge s 40(2) comes into play.

11 [1929] 1 Ch 498, CA.
12 *Westminster Corpn v Haste* [1950] Ch 442 at 447 approved in *IRC v Goldblatt* [1972] Ch 498 at 505.
13 IA 1986, s 37(1)(b).

PREFERRED VIEW

The argument that the surplus upon sale of assets subject to a fixed charge is itself caught by the floating charge granted simultaneously to secure the same debt is, upon proper analysis, unattractive and one to be rejected. It overlooks the fact that there is only one, single debt owed to the debenture holder and secured by both the fixed and the floating charge. Accordingly the discharge of the one by payment of the secured debt necessarily discharges the other.

The proper view is that the *whole* of the proceeds of sale of property subject to the fixed charge (and not merely a sufficient part thereof to discharge the debt to the debenture holder), constitute assets subject to the fixed charge, fall outside s 40(2) and are payable to the debenture holder in discharge of the debt due to him and subject thereto to the next incumbrancer or, if none, the company.

Two considerations in particular drive one to this conclusion. First, even if the language of any particular debenture is wide enough to bring within the scope of a floating charge, *while it still subsists*, a fund of money, despite the fact that historically it represents the proceeds of sale of property formerly subject to the fixed charge, yet it cannot possibly extend to a fund which cannot come into being until the debt for which the floating security itself is a security has been repaid in full. Such an extension would have the effect of including within the scope of the floating charge its own equity of redemption. Any analogy with the case where there are two or more successive mortgages on the same property does not really help. In such a case the equity of redemption of the first mortgage is subsequently made the subject of a second mortgage to secure a different debt owed by the mortgagor, whether to the same or (more usually) a different mortgagee. But in the case of a fixed and floating charge there are two mortgages, on different properties, to serve a single debt. In such a case, neither can include the equity of redemption of the other; for that in the context involves including in each mortgage its own equity of redemption.

Secondly, s 40(2) (and its predecessor) imposes a positive duty upon the receiver.[14] However this positive duty is only a duty to pay the claims of the preferential creditors 'out of the assets which would otherwise go to the debenture holders in discharge of their principal and interest'.[15] That is why the receiver's costs and expenses and his remuneration have priority to the claims of preferential creditors. But the same reasoning demonstrates that the claims of the preferential creditors to be paid *by the receiver* (as distinct from the company) depend on the continued subsistence of the debt due to the debenture holder. It follows that s 40(2) can have no possible application once the claims of the debenture holder have been paid in full, and the contest over the fixed charge surplus is between the preferential creditors and the company.

---

14 *Westminster Corpn v Haste* [1950] Ch 442 at 447; *IRC v Goldblatt* [1972] Ch 498, [1972] 2 All ER 202.
15 *Re Glyncorrwg Colliery Co* [1926] Ch 951.

A helpful analogy which confirms the approach just adopted is the case where there are two properties subject to a fixed charge. Suppose the receiver goes into possession of one and sells it, realising enough to discharge the debt due to the debenture holder. Suppose, too, that he never goes into possession of the other property. What is the position in relation to that other property? It was formerly subject to a fixed charge in favour of the debenture holder, but that has been discharged. It has never been subject to a floating charge. What is there in those circumstances to defeat the company's claim to retain possession? The answer must be nothing. Section 40(2) can have no possible application: (1) because the property has never been subject to a floating charge; (2) because the receiver has not taken possession of the property in question (and his only duty is to pay preferential debts 'out of assets coming to his hands'); (3) because the property would not 'otherwise go to the debenture holder'; (and his only duty is to pay preferential debts out of such property). Yet if s 40(2) does not apply to this property, being property subject to a fixed charge which is not needed to satisfy the claims of the debenture holder, it is very hard to see how it can apply to the surplus proceeds of sale of the first mentioned property. The two are in *pari materia*.

DECISION IN RE GL SAUNDERS LTD

In *Re GL Saunders Ltd*[16] Nourse J held that a fixed charge surplus in a receivership should be handed to a company or its liquidator and was not available to meet the claims of preferential creditors in accordance with what is now section 40(2) of the Insolvency Act 1986.[17] He reached his conclusion by reference to the provisions of section 105 of the Law of Property Act 1925 and also following a dictum of Lawrence LJ in *Re Lewis Merthyr Consolidated Collieries Ltd*,[18] who in discussing the statutory precursor of s 40(2) of the Insolvency Act 1986 said:[19]

> 'In my judgment the fact that the debenture in the present case is one which combined with the floating charge a fixed charge does not bring the section into operation as against the assets comprised in a fixed charge. Such assets are outside the scope and purview of the section.'

Nor would the preferential creditors derive assistance from the argument that assets subject to the floating charge would precede the equity of redemption in the assets subject to the fixed charge. Once there was a surplus and both charges were extinguished the equity of redemption in the fixed assets would be enlarged into the assets themselves and would cease to exist as such.[20] Nourse J moreover expressly endorsed the preferred view set out above.[1]

16 [1986] 1 WLR 215.
17 Then CA 1948, s 94.
18 [1929] 1 Ch 498.
19 [1929] 1 Ch 498 at 512. See also dictum of Tomlin J at [1929] 1 Ch 498 at 507.
20 [1986] 1 WLR 215 at 220.
 1 Citing the first edition of this book.

TERMINATION OF RECEIVER'S POWERS

Once the receiver has paid all preferential debts and the debenture holder and any other creditors who rank ahead of the debenture and once he has been able to receive in his receiver's account sufficient funds to cover his remaining liabilities, remuneration and expenses, his work (like old Kaspar's[2]) is done: he is *functus officio*. There is no residual duty on him, after that point has been reached, to distribute the property of the company among unsecured claimants ranking behind the debenture holder.[3] And any further activities may expose him to a claim in trespass[4] and any attempt to proceed with sales of further property may be restrained by injunction.[5]

2 Robert Southey 'The Battle of Blenheim' (1800) line 2.
3 *Bank of New South Wales v Federal Taxation Comr* (1979) 145 CLR 438; *Re Arnold Trading Co Ltd* [1983] NZLR 445 at 451, CA.
4 *Bank of New South Wales v Federal Taxation Comr* (1979) 145 CLR 438 at 454.
5 *Rothenberg v Monjack* [1993] BCLC 374.

CHAPTER 19

Mortgages and statutory charges

MORTGAGES

Introduction

Before 1860 a mortgagee had no power to appoint a receiver out of court unless he had expressly stipulated for such a power in the mortgage. As a consequence if in the absence of such an express power he did appoint a receiver it was equivalent to going into possession and the receiver was his agent.[1] Going into possession has substantial drawbacks because it imposes personal liability on the mortgagee and because very onerous duties to account for receipts and management are imposed by the court on a mortgagee in possession. Well drawn mortgages side-stepped these difficulties by including a power for the mortgagee to appoint a receiver and also a statement that any receiver appointed pursuant to the power was to be considered the agent of the mortgagor. Rigby LJ analysed the position in *Gaskell v Gosling*.[2] Although his judgment in the Court of Appeal was a dissenting one it was unanimously upheld by a strong House of Lords[3] and it has been described in relatively recent times as a masterly statement.[4] After referring to the problems confronting a mortgagee in possession he continued:

> 'The Courts also favoured any means which would enable the mortgagee to obtain the advantages of possession without its drawbacks. Mortgagees began to insist upon the appointment by the mortgagor of a receiver to receive the income, keep down the interest on encumbrances, and hold the surplus, if any, for the mortgagor, and to stipulate often that the receiver should have extensive powers of management. Presently mortgagees stipulated that they themselves should in place of the mortgagor appoint the receiver to act as the mortgagor's agent. This made no difference in the receiver's position and imposed no liability on the mortgagee appointing. Though it was the mortgagee who in fact appointed the receiver, yet in making the appointment the mortgagee acted, and it was the object of the parties that he should act as agent for the mortgagor.'

---

1 *Quarrell v Beckford* (1816) 1 Madd 269.
2 [1896] 1 QB 669, 65 LJQB 435, CA.
3 [1897] AC 575, 66 LJQB 848, HL.
4 *Lawson v Hosemaster Machine Co Ltd* [1966] 1 WLR 1300 at 1315, CA.

The deed which Rigby LJ was considering expressly provided that the receiver appointed should be the agent of the mortgagor and it is now well established that so long as those words are included in the mortgage a receiver will be the agent of the mortgagor so that the mortgagee will not incur liability by his actions. Equally by virtue of making such an appointment the mortgagee does not become a mortgagee in possession.

What conveyancers expressed statute came to imply. In 1860 the Trustees, Mortgagees etc Powers Act 1860, more frequently referred to as Lord Cranworth's Act,[5] made the power to appoint receivers statutory for mortgages created by deed. The power was limited to the case of rents and profits from land, but the receiver was deemed to be the agent of the mortgagor. The scope of the power was widened by section 19 of the Conveyancing Act 1881 which was in turn replaced by section 101 of the Law of Property Act 1925.

The current position in England and Wales[6] is that all mortgages by deed executed after 1881 are governed by the provisions now to be found in sections 101 and 109 of the Law of Property Act 1925. These provisions, it should be stressed, constitute a statutory recognition of a well established conveyancing practice and for that reason contain powers to vary or extend the statutory scheme.

It should be observed that where a mortgagee appoints a receiver out of court the appointment does not of itself preclude the mortgagee from subsequently issuing a writ indorsed with a statement of claim and obtaining summary judgment[7] provided that no money has come to the hands of the receiver.[8] But if the receiver has received money, and there is a question as to what on the true state of the account as between mortgagor and mortgagee is due to the mortgagee leave to defend must be granted.[9] Moreover if the receiver has been appointed by the court in a foreclosure action the subsequent issue of a specially indorsed writ and a claim for summary judgment is unnecessary and improper because the mortgagee in a foreclosure action obtains a personal order for payment of the principal with interest down to the date of the certificate and so has a complete remedy in the foreclosure action.[10]

Who may appoint

The power to appoint a receiver is conferred on mortgagees whose mortgages are created by *deed* and this applies to most legal mortgagees and registered chargees.[11] A mortgagee by deed who is already in possession may nevertheless

---

5 23 & 24 Vict, c 45, s 11.

6 Section 19 of the Conveyancing Act 1881 continues to apply in both parts of Ireland.

7 Under RSC Ord 14. The proceedings must be started in the Chancery Division: see RSC Ord 88, r 2.

8 *Lynde v Waithman* [1895] 2 QB 180 at 188, CA.

9 *Lynde v Waithman* [1895] 2 QB 180, CA; and see *Rice v Kinghorn* (1895) 17 PR 1.

10 *Earl Poulett v Viscount Hill* [1893] 1 Ch 277, CA; *Williams v Hunt* [1905] 1 KB 512, CA.

11 The term mortgagee includes a chargee by way of legal mortgage and a person from time to time deriving title under the original mortgagee or by LPA 1925, s 205(1)(xvi) entitled to redeem the mortgage.

appoint a receiver who will take over possession.[12] A second or subsequent mortgagee by deed can also appoint a receiver subject always to the rights of prior incumbrancers,[13] who may substitute their own receiver for one appointed by the subsequent mortgagee. Although an equitable mortgagee has no right, except under a court order, to enter into possession of the mortgaged property he can always appoint a receiver of the income thereof, provided always that the equitable mortgage was effected by deed.[14] However if the mortgage or charge was not created by deed the equitable mortgagee or chargee can only secure the appointment of a receiver by applying to the court.

When power arises

The statutory power to appoint a receiver out of court arises when the mortgage money is due[15] and even then is only exercisable if certain other specified conditions are satisfied.[16] The power which arises on the mortgage money becoming due is a power to appoint a receiver of the income of the mortgaged property or any part thereof, or if the mortgaged property consists of an interest in income, or of a rent charge or an annual or other periodical sum, a receiver of that property or any part thereof.[17] The statutory provisions concerning the time when the power arises may be varied or extended by the mortgage deed, and as so varied and extended will as far as may be operate as if the variations or extensions were contained in the statute itself.[18] If there is any inconsistency between the statutory provisions and the express provisions of the mortgage deed, the latter prevail.[19]

Conditions for exercise of statutory powers

Even though the power to appoint a receiver may have arisen it does not normally become exercisable until one of the three events specified by statute for the exercise of the power of sale occurs.[20] In other words apart from express provision in the deed itself[1] the appointment cannot be made unless and until (1) notice has been served on the mortgagor or one of several mortgagors requiring payment of the mortgage money and there has been a default in payment of the money or part thereof for three months after service,[2] or (2) some interest under

12 *Refuge Assurance Co Ltd v Pearlberg* [1938] Ch 687, [1938] 3 All ER 231.
13 *Vacuum Oil Co v Ellis* [1914] 1 KB 693 at 703, CA.
14 LPA 1925, s 205(1)(xvi).
15 LPA 1925, s 101(1)(iii).
16 See infra.
17 LPA 1925, s 101(1)(iii).
18 LPA 1925, s 101(3).
19 LPA 1925, s 101(4).
20 LPA 1925, s 109(1) cross-referring to s 103.
 1 See LPA 1925, s 101(4).
 2 LPA 1925, s 103(1)(i). Notice cannot be served until after the principal money has become due. The notice can in the alternative demand payment in three months' time if the mortgagee is unpaid, he may then exercise his remedy: *Barker v Illingworth* [1908] 2 Ch 20.

the mortgage is in arrear and unpaid for two months after becoming due,[3] or (3) there has been a breach of a provision contained in the mortgage deed or in the statute (other than the covenant for the payment of the mortgage money or interest) on the part of the mortgagor or some other person concurring in the mortgage.[4]

Because these conditions are not always commercially acceptable mortgagees will often stipulate for an earlier appointment. In the case of a mortgage of short leasehold property or of other property held or existing for a limited period or where the loan is short term the receiver is often expressed to be capable of being appointed on the execution of the mortgage.[5]

Mode of appointment

A receiver appointed under the statutory power is appointed by writing under the hand of the mortgagee.[6] For this purpose an invalid or possibly invalid, deed can serve as the relevant 'writing'.[7] The procedure governing appointment applies equally to the removal of a receiver and the appointment of a new receiver in his place.[8] There is no statutorily prescribed form of appointment in this country[9] although some jurisdictions[10] require an appointment made by the mortgagee in writing to be in a prescribed form.

Where the statutory power is untrammelled by express variations in the mortgage deed a formal demand is not a pre-condition to the exercise of the power: default is enough.[11] But if the deed provides for formal demand before exercise of the power that formality must be observed. Failure to make the formal demand could, in such a case, vitiate the statutory effect of the appointment, leaving the receiver as agent of the mortgagee rather than of the mortgagor.[12] That in turn makes the mortgagee liable for the receiver's acts and omissions.

Most frequently the mortgage deed specifies an abridged timetable for the exercise of the power after default. For example in the case of debentures and other company charges it is usually provided that the power shall be exercisable as soon as the principal is due or if any interest shall be more than a specified number of days in arrear or within a specified number of days after payment of principal or capital has been demanded and not paid.

---

3 LPA 1925, s 103(1)(ii).
4 LPA 1925, s 103(1)(iii).
5 See *United Realization Co Ltd v IRC* [1899] 1 QB 361, 68 LJQB 218; *Portman Building Society v Gallwey* [1955] 1 All ER 227, [1955] 1 WLR 96.
6 LPA 1925, s 109(1).
7 *Windsor Refrigerator Co Ltd v Branch Nominees Ltd* [1961] Ch 375, [1961] 1 All ER 277, CA.
8 LPA 1925, s 109(5); and see the discussion at p 77, infra.
9 For forms of appointment see 28 *Forms and Precedents* (5th edn) 344–348.
10 Notably New South Wales and Queensland: see James O'Donovan 'The Statutory Power to Appoint a Company Receiver in Australia' (1978) 13 UWA Law Rev 434 at 439.
11 See LPA 1925, s 109.
12 *Barclays Bank Ltd v Kiley* [1961] 2 All ER 849, [1961] 1 WLR 1050. And consider the cases about formal demand discussed at p 78, supra.

As has already been said any such variations operate as though contained in the statute and where inconsistent with the statutory provisions take precedence over them.[13]

Where the statutory or express power for a mortgagee to appoint a receiver is made exercisable by reason of the mortgagor committing an act of bankruptcy or being adjudged bankrupt or entering into liquidation by arrangement or in the case of a company being wound up, the power is not exercisable on that account alone without leave of the court. If any other event has caused the power to be exercisable leave is not required even though after the triggering event bankruptcy or winding up has occurred.

Validity of appointment

A person paying money to a statutorily appointed receiver is not concerned to inquire whether any case has occurred to authorise the receiver to act.[14]

While this measure of protection is afforded to a person paying money to a receiver whose title is vulnerable an invalid appointment has more serious repercussions for the mortgagee. A receiver appointed under the statute is deemed to be an agent for the mortgagor; and the mortgagor is solely responsible for the receiver's acts and defaults unless the mortgage deed otherwise provides.[15] But if the appointment is not under the statutory powers the deemed agency for the mortgagor is not brought into play. The receiver in such a case remains the agent of the *mortgagee*, who in turn will be liable for his acts and defaults.

An attack on the validity of the appointment might be in the interests of the mortgagor or some other mortgagee. Such an attack may be mounted (1) if the mortgage deed is not validly executed or is not a deed for the purposes of the statutory power, or (2) if the power was not in fact exercisable at the time of the appointment, or (3) if the formal requirements of an appointment have not been complied with. In some jurisdictions the appointment can be attacked because the receiver is disqualified by statutory provision.

Termination of the appointment

The mortgagor cannot dismiss the receiver:[16] that power is reserved to the mortgagee. The receiver will be displaced by the appointment of a receiver by a prior mortgagee but not by the liquidation of a company mortgagor which will only terminate his agency for the mortgagor.[17]

---

13 LPA 1925, ss 110 and 205(1)(i).
14 LPA 1925, s 109(4).
15 LPA 1925, s 109(2).
16 *Gomba Holdings Ltd v Minories Finance Ltd* [1988] 1 WLR 1231, CA.
17 *Gosling v Gaskell* [1897] AC 575; *Sowman v David Samuel Trust Ltd (in liquidation)* [1978] 1 WLR 22, CA; *American Express International Banking Corpn v Hurley* [1986] BCLC 52.

Duties of mortgagee in relation to the receivership

A mortgagee owes a general duty to subsequent incumbrances and to the mortgagor to use his powers for the sole purpose of securing repayments of the moneys owing under his mortgage and a duty to act in good faith.[18]

A mortgagee is not bound to exercise his powers even if advised to do so, although the mortgaged property is depreciating and however advantageous it may be to the mortgagor.[19] He can decide if and when to exercise his powers on the basis of his own interests. There is, in short, no obligation on him to enforce his security: he may instead rely on the personal covenant for payment. If he decides to enforce his security by appointing a receiver he can choose when to make the appointment, having regard to his own interests, even though the timing of the appointment may be disadvantageous to the mortgagor or unsecured creditors.[20]

A mortgagee is not responsible for the acts of a receiver unless the latter is acting as his agent (rather than as deemed agent of the mortgagor). However an express provision may constitute the receiver agent for the mortgagee. And if the mortgagee directs or interferes with the receiver's activities, the receiver may be treated as the agent of the mortgagee, and the latter may be liable for his acts.[1]

The equitable duties which a mortgagee and by extension his receiver owe in respect of exercising any power of sale or in running the business subjected to receivership have been discussed earlier.[2] A receiver who decides to carry on the mortgaged business must do so with reasonable competence.[3]

Powers of a statutory appointee

A receiver appointed under the statute has a statutory power to demand and recover all the income of which he is appointed receiver.[4] This he may do in the name of the mortgagor or the mortgagee to the full extent of the interest which the mortgagor could dispose of. He is also empowered to give effectual receipts for the income which he demands and recovers under the statute.[5]

The income of which the receiver is appointed receiver may consist of income from trust property, income arising under the statutory trusts from an undivided

---

18 *Downsview Nominees Ltd v First City Corpn Ltd* [1993] AC 295. Proof of bad faith on the part of the mortgagee may nevertheless render him liable in circumstances where he could otherwise not have been: ibid.

19 *Palk v Mortgage Services Funding plc* [1993] Ch 330, CA; *Lloyds Bank v Bryant* [1996] NPC 31, CA. See also *China and South Sea Bank Ltd v Tan* [1990] 1 AC 536.

20 *Shamji v Johnson Matthey Bankers Ltd* [1986] BCLC 278; affd [1991] BCLC 36, CA; *Re Potters Oils Ltd (No 2)* [1986] 1 WLR 201.

1 *Downsview Nominees Ltd v First City Corpn Ltd* [1993] AC 295; *Gomba Holdings Ltd v Minories Finance Ltd* [1988] 1 WLR 1231, CA.

2 See at 130–139 above. For a recent case see *Skipton Building Society v Stott* [2000] 2 All ER 779 (surety successfully impeached receiver's sale).

3 *Medforth v Blake* [1999] 2 BCLC 221, CA.

4 LPA 1925, s 109(3).

5 LPA 1925.

share to which the mortgagor is entitled, income from mortgaged shares or other personalty and of course the rents and profits of land that has been mortgaged.

As regards rent, the receiver should at the earliest opportunity after his appointment give the tenants notice to pay their rents to him, arrears as well as future rents. Until the receiver does give such notice the tenants can obtain a valid discharge from the mortgagor even though they know of the appointment.[6] Only rents attributable to the mortgaged property are so recoverable by the receiver. So where the mortgagor has leased land together with furniture or other chattels and the mortgage only extended to the land the rent must be apportioned between the land and the chattels.[7] If the court has appointed a receiver on the application of a subsequent incumbrancer, a receiver appointed under the statute by a prior incumbrancer cannot claim the future rents until the leave of the court has been obtained, unless the order expressly reserves his right to do so.[8] Obviously such an express reservation is desirable.

The property must be seen to be within the scope of the charge in question. A debenture holder's charge may cover uncalled capital but debentures often exclude uncalled capital from the scope of the receiver's appointment because the liquidator is usually better poised to get in unpaid calls.[9]

It remains to point out that the charge in question must be valid. Elsewhere in this work there is discussion of the validity of company charges: such charges are invalid if not properly executed or if the charge is not properly registered[10] or constituted a fraudulent preference[11] or was floating charge infringing s 245 of the Insolvency Act 1986.[12] In relation to other charges they must not infringe public policy[13] or, in the case of charities, the restrictions on dealings contained in the Charities Act 1993.[14]

Once the mortgagee has appointed a receiver the mortgagor cannot distrain, even though he alleges negligence on the part of the receiver.[15] Indeed a distress by the mortgagor in such circumstances is illegal.[16] A person paying money to the receiver is afforded some statutory protection: he is not concerned to inquire whether any case has happened to authorise the receiver to act.[17]

The receiver's power to distrain, it should be noted, comes to an end when the mortgagee's interest is determined. In *Serjeant v Nash, Field & Co*[18] the lessee of premises created a yearly tenancy under which the plaintiff became a tenant and

6 *Vacuum Oil Co Ltd v Ellis* [1914] 1 KB 693, 83 LJKB 479, CA.
7 *Salmon v Matthews* (1841) 8 M & W 827, 11 LJ Ex 59; *Charles Hoare & Co v Hove Bungalows Ltd* (1912) 56 Sol Jo 686, CA.
8 See *Re Metropolitan Amalgamated Estates Ltd* [1912] 2 Ch 497, 81 LJ Ch 745.
9 *Australian Industry Development Corpn v Co-operative Farmers and Graziers Direct Meat Supply Ltd* [1978] VR 633, [1978] 3 ACLR 543.
10 CA 1985, s 395.
11 See the discussion at p 241.
12 See the discussion at p 248.
13 *Horwood v Millar's Timber and Trading Co Ltd* [1917] 1 KB 305; *A Schroeder Music Publishing Co Ltd v Macaulay* [1974] 3 All ER 616, [1974] 1 WLR 1308, HL.
14 Charities Act 1993, s 36.
15 *Bayly v Went* (1884) 51 LT 764.
16 *Woolston v Ross* [1900] 1 Ch 788.
17 LPA 1925, s 109(4).
18 [1903] 2 KB 304, CA.

occupier on the same day the lessee mortgaged the premises by sub-demise. The lease contained a covenant against assigning, sub-letting or parting with possession without the written consent of the lessor. That prior written consent had not been obtained in the case of the mortgage. The mortgagor was adjudicated bankrupt. The mortgagee appointed a receiver to whom one quarter's rent was paid. Before the next quarterly payment the lessor issued a writ for possession, and served it on the occupier. The receiver distrained for rent but it was held an illegal distress because the mortgagee's interest had been brought to an end by the issue and service of the writ.

Under the statutory power a receiver may be appointed of the income of the mortgaged property or any part thereof.[19]

Where book debts are included in the mortgage and the receiver is given power to collect debts or get in other money in the nature of capital included in the mortgage a receiver appointed under the statutory power should forthwith give notice to the debtors or other persons liable to the mortgagor, or holding the property in trust for him, requiring the debt or other money to be paid to the receiver. In the absence of such a notice the debts remaining within the order and disposition of the mortgagor are available for distribution in the mortgagor's bankruptcy or liquidation.[20]

A receiver appointed under the statutory power has the power to exercise any powers which may have been delegated to him by the mortgagee pursuant to the statute.[1] The following powers in England and Wales have been expressly marked out by the statute as delegable to the receiver: (1) the leasing powers available to a mortgagor or a mortgagee in possession,[2] (2) power to accept a surrender for the purpose of enabling new leases to be granted[3] and (3) power to insure up to two-thirds of the sum required to rebuild unless there is a provision in the mortgage deed expressly negativing the need to insure or unless an insurance is kept up by the mortgagor in accordance with the mortgage deed or under an agreement with the mortgagee up to the full amount specified.[4] The power to lease and accept surrenders of leases is restricted by the words 'as if such mortgagee were in possession of the land'.[5] It should be noted that unless the mortgage deed otherwise provides an equitable mortgagee is not entitled to possession, and so cannot grant a lease or accept surrenders of leases. It follows that he cannot delegate such powers.

Where the receiver is appointed under the statutory power he is deemed to be the mortgagor's agent, and the mortgagor is solely responsible for the receiver's acts or defaults unless the mortgage deed otherwise provides.[6] However his agency may be modified by the terms of the mortgage deed.[7] And the statutory

---

19 LPA 1925, s 101(1)(iii).
20 See *Rutter v Everett* [1895] 2 Ch 872; *Re Pawson's Settlement* [1917] 1 Ch 541.
1 LPA 1925, s 109(3).
2 LPA 1925, s 99(2)–(10) and (19).
3 LPA 1925, s 100.
4 LPA 1925, s 109(7).
5 LPA 1925, ss 99(19) and 100(13).
6 LPA 1925, s 109(2).
7 *Richards v Kidderminster Overseers* [1896] 2 Ch 212 at 220.

agency will cease if the receiver appointed under the statute is transmogrified into a court receiver: he is then the agent of no one, but is an officer of the court.[8]

The death of the mortgagor does not effect any revocation of the power to appoint a receiver.[9] In such a case the receiver may be allowed to sue in the name of the mortgagor's personal representatives on giving indemnity.[10]

In the absence of express extensions of the statutory powers the position of a receiver appointed under the statute is very circumscribed. He is not as a rule entitled to carry on the mortgagor's business[11] so that he may not make a payment on account of an unsecured debt.[12] Again although he can collect income he cannot, unless expressly authorised, collect assets such as book debts.[13] As regards tenants his powers are also hamstrung: he cannot recover possession, bring an action for ejectment, terminate a tenancy or increase the rent; and his powers to collect rent produced by foreign property are ineffective. As has also been seen unless expressly authorised by the mortgagee he may not insure the mortgaged property or even carry out necessary repairs. The mortgagee, of course, has an overriding interest in seeing that income is applied to the reduction of the mortgagor's debt and this explains why the receiver's position is so circumscribed.[14] Consistently with this logic a receiver who without authority expends money on insurance, repairs or litigation against tenants is accountable for that expenditure to the mortgagee.

Whatever the underlying rationale of the circumscribed position of the statutorily appointed receiver commercial convenience often dictates that he should be armed with ampler powers. The statute itself expressly recognises that the statutory provisions take effect *subject* to the terms of the mortgage deed. So a deed enlarging the receiver's powers from their statutory slimness is not for that reason invalidated.[15] But extensions of the statutory powers can result in the receiver no longer being deemed to be an agent of the mortgagor.[16] That result can always be avoided by an express provision in the mortgage deed itself making it clear that the receiver remains the agent of the mortgagor and that the mortgagor will be solely responsible for the acts and defaults of the receiver.

Prior mortgagees

If a prior mortgagee having in his hands a surplus over and above the amount owing to him derived from the mortgaged property indicates that he intends to apply that surplus in wrongfully paying off one puisne mortgagee in preference

---

8   *Hand v Blow* [1901] 2 Ch 721 at 732, CA.
9   *Re Hale* [1899] 2 Ch 107 at 117, CA.
10 *Fairholme and Palliser v Kennedy* (1890) 24 LR Ir 498.
11 *Richards v Kidderminster Overseers* [1896] 2 Ch 212; *Harold Meggitt Ltd v Discount Finance Ltd* (1939) 38 WNNSW 23.
12 *Re Hale* [1899] 2 Ch 107 at 119, CA.
13 *Rutter v Everett* [1895] 2 Ch 872 at 882.
14 *Visbord v Federal Taxation Comr* (1943) 68 CLR 354 at 385.
15 *Richards v Kidderminster Overseers* [1896] 2 Ch 212 at 219.
16 *Richards v Kidderminster Overseers* [1896] 2 Ch 212 at 219.

to the mortgagee next in entitlement, a receiver will be appointed on the application of the injured puisne mortgagee.[17]

A mortgagee of land who is also tenant of that land cannot set up his possession *qua* tenant in opposition to an application by a subsequent mortgagee for the appointment of a receiver. The quality of possession which can prevent the appointment is such a possession as clothes the prior mortgagee with the right to receive the rents and profits in his capacity as mortgagee. Mere possession as tenant is not good enough.[18]

While as a general rule a receiver will not be appointed against a prior legal mortgagee in possession the general rule will yield to special circumstances. Thus in a clear case of gross mismanagement by the prior mortgagee in possession the latter may be deprived of his possession by the appointment of a receiver at the instance of a subsequent mortgagee.[19]

Equitable mortgagees

An equitable mortgagee has no legal right to take possession or to demand payment to himself of the rents of the property subject to the mortgage. But, subject to the rights of any prior mortgagee, he can take possession and enter into receipt of the rents in either one of two ways: (a) in an action to enforce his security he can obtain an order appointing a receiver or (b) under the statutory provision he can himself appoint a receiver. In the one case he obtains judicially, and in the other contractually and by virtue of the statute, a right to take rents by the hand of a receiver. If he serves notice on the tenant requiring the tenant to pay rent to him, the tenant may refuse payment, for he will get no discharge.[20] The equitable mortgagee could not sue the tenant for the rent.[1] He has no legal right in the land demised. If the tenant has paid the rent to him an equitable mortgagee cannot be compelled to refund it to the tenant.[2] A receiver appointed by an equitable mortgagee is entitled to rents as against a person obtaining a garnishee order but he does not obtain priority simply by virtue of his appointment if he has not given notice to the tenants.[3]

Debentures and other equitable mortgages often expressly empower a receiver to sell the mortgaged property and convey the legal estate in the name of the mortgagor or mortgagee. The statutory power of sale is in fact exercisable 'by any person for the time being entitled to receive and give a discharge for the mortgage money'.[4] A statutorily appointed receiver answers that description and,

---

17 *Gouthwaite v Rippon* (1838) 8 LJ Ch 139, 3 Jur 7.
18 *Archdeacon v Bowes* (1796) 3 Anst 752.
19 *Rowe v Wood* (1822) 2 Jac & W 553.
20 *Vacuum Oil Co Ltd v Ellis* [1914] 1 KB 693 at 703 per Buckley LJ.
 1 [1914] 1 KB 693 and at 708 per Kennedy LJ.
 2 [1914] 1 KB 693 citing *Finck v Tranter* [1905] 1 KB 427.
 3 [1914] 1 KB 693, CA. The mortgagee in the case was a second mortgagee who prior to 1926 could only be an equitable mortgagee. Most second mortgagees are *legal* mortgagees nowadays and so can give an effective notice to tenants.
 4 LPA 1925, s 106(1).

despite what is asserted in some works,[5] would appear to have a power of sale independently of any delegation. However that may be, many mortgages do expressly empower the receiver to sell and convey the legal estate in the name of the mortgagor or mortgagee.

Remuneration

Mention is made elsewhere of the statutory provisions relating to remuneration in the property legislation.[6] It is sufficient at this point to note that if no rate of remuneration is specified in the mortgage a statutorily appointed receiver may apply to the court for his remuneration to be fixed[7] and should certainly also do so if he wishes to recover a rate exceeding the statutory ceiling of 5 per cent.[8]

The court can fix the remuneration of a receiver of the property of a company in liquidation or on an application by the liquidator[9] or on the fixing of an account between the mortgagor and the mortgagee.[10]

APPLICATION OF RECEIPTS

Subject to the statutory provisions as to the application of insurance money[11] the receiver who has been appointed pursuant to the statutory power of appointment must apply all money received by him according to a prescribed statutory order,[12] unless that mode of application is varied by the consent of the parties concerned.[13]

He must first apply the money received by him 'in discharge of all rents, taxes, rates and outgoings whatever affecting the mortgaged property'. This provision does not impose on the receiver a statutory duty to pay rates so as to enable the local authority to sue for damages for breach of statutory duty if the rates are not paid.[14] Tax, it should be added, includes VAT on rent paid to the receiver in respect of mortgaged property.[15] The provision has indeed been described as no more than a power and obligation to be read into the mortgage deed. It is part of the powers incident to the estate or interest of the mortgagee, and for the sake of clarity is there stated rather than being fully written out in the mortgage deed as between the parties to the mortgage. It follows then that there is no semblance of a statutory duty to the corporation, no breach of that statutory duty and no

5 See eg *Kerr on Receivers and Administrators* (17th edn) 350.
6 Ie LPA 1925, s 109(6) discussed at p 278 above.
7 LPA 1925, s 109(6).
8 *Marshall v Cottingham* [1982] Ch 82, [1981] 3 All ER 8.
9 IA 1986, s 36.
10 See *Gomba Holdings Ltd v Minories Finance Ltd (No 2)* [1993] Ch 171, CA.
11 LPA 1925, s 108.
12 LPA 1925, s 109(8).
13 *Yourell v Hibernian Bank Ltd* [1918] AC 372, HL.
14 *Liverpool Corpn v Hope* [1938] 1 KB 751, [1938] 1 All ER 492, CA.
15 *Sargent v Customs and Excise Comrs* [1994] 1 WLR 235; affd in part [1995] 1 WLR 821, CA.

damages flowing from it.[16] The purpose of the provision is to preserve the property in the interest of the mortgagee and the mortgagor by ensuring that normal outgoings are duly discharged.[17]

Putting it another way the section means that if the receiver applies money received by him in the discharge of taxes affecting the mortgaged property he cannot be charged by the debenture holder or by the person entitled to the property subject to the charge with having made an improper payment. In *Re John Willment (Ashford) Ltd*[18] Brightman J conceded that in many circumstances it may be correct in theory to say that a receiver has a discretion under s 109(8).[19] He was faced with a claim that a receiver and manager appointed under a debenture had a discretion whether he does or does not pay to the Customs and Excise Commissioners value added tax for the period of the receivership. He concluded that there was only one way in which that discretion could properly be exercised in relation to value added tax, so perhaps it was not correct to describe it as a discretion at all. 'The reason for this conclusion is that if the receiver does not pay the tax he will cause the company to commit a criminal offence.'[20]

A mortgagor can, it should be noted, sue the receiver to recover any damages caused by the receiver's failure to pay the rates and taxes.[1]

Next he must keep down annual sums or other payments, and interest on all principal sums, having priority to the mortgage in right of which he is receiver.[2]

Thirdly, he must apply receipts in payment of his commission, and of the premiums on fire, life or other insurances, if any, properly payable under the mortgage deed or under the Law of Property Act 1925 and the cost of executing proper repairs directed in writing by the mortgagee.[3] After deducting his commission, the rate, content and variation of which are discussed elsewhere,[4] and the premiums on various policies as designated, he then has to pay the costs of executing necessary or proper repairs directed by the mortgagee.[5]

Next in line comes payment of the interest accruing due in respect of any principal moneys due under the mortgage.[6] The receiver is bound to pay any arrears of interest outstanding at the date of his appointment as well as interest subsequently accruing due.[7] But only interest which is due and recoverable falls

---

16 *Liverpool Corpn v Hope* [1938] 1 KB 751 at 755 per Slesser LJ.
17 *Sargent v Customs and Excise Comrs* [1994] 1 WLR 235; affd in part [1995] 1 WLR 821, CA.
18 [1979] 2 All ER 615, [1980] 1 WLR 73.
19 [1980] 1 WLR 73 at 77.
20 [1980] 1 WLR 73 at 78.
 1 *Visbord v Federal Comr of Taxation* (1943) 68 CLR 354 at 385.
 2 LPA 1925, s 109(8)(ii). Statute barred interest cannot be paid by the receiver: *Hibernian Bank v Yourell (No 2)* [1919] 1 IR 310.
 3 LPA 1925, s 109(8)(iii).
 4 See at p 238; and see *Marshall v Cottingham* [1982] Ch 82. An application to vary remuneration upwards can be made in foreclosure or redemption proceedings (if on foot) but otherwise by originating summons to which mortgagor and mortgagee would be respondents: LPA 1925, s 203(2)(a).
 5 For a case where there was no such direction, see *White v Metcalf* [1903] 2 Ch 567.
 6 LPA 1925, s 109(8)(iv).
 7 *National Bank v Kenney* [1898] IR 197. If he overpays the mortgagor, unless time barred, can reclaim against the mortgagee: *Re Jones Estate* [1914] IR 188.

within the statutory precept: he is in breach of his statutory duties if he pays statute barred interest.[8]

Last in this listing is payment in or towards the discharge of the principal money if so directed in writing by the mortgagee.[9]

The statutory order as well as being variable by consent[10] can be extended by the mortgage deed so as, for example, to empower the receiver and manager of a business to pay unsecured debts.[11]

The discharge of interest and capital is for the benefit of the mortgagee as well as for that of the mortgagor, and he may maintain an action against the receiver for failure to perform those statutory duties.[12]

APPLICATION OF SURPLUS

Any surplus or residue left of the money received by the receiver must be paid to the person who, but for the possession of the receiver, would have been entitled to receive the income of which he is appointed receiver or who is otherwise entitled to the mortgaged property.[13] Usually the person entitled is the mortgagor[14] or his assigns or his personal representatives or their assigns if he or they retain the right to possession.

If a later incumbrancer has appointed a receiver the surplus must be paid to that receiver. Likewise if the subsequent mortgagee has taken possession he is entitled to be paid the surplus. In the case of a mortgagee in possession who has appointed a receiver and is still in possession at the end of the receivership when the residue is determined that mortgagee in possession will be the appropriate person to receive the residue.

For the purpose of paying over the balance to the person entitled to it he will of course have to keep proper accounts and have to produce them to the person entitled to receive the balance.[15] A first mortgagee is not entitled to retain the surplus proceeds and asserts on behalf of a third mortgagee or the mortgagor a right to be paid the whole surplus after payment to the second mortgagee of the principal moneys owing on the second mortgage and six years' arrears of interest only.[16]

When the receiver is in doubt as to whom the balance should go or if the mortgagor is untraceable and there is no pending action he might raise the question for determination under Ord 85 r 2 of the Rules of the Supreme Court or alternatively pay the balance into court under the Trustee Act 1925.[17]

---

8 *Hibernian Bank v Yourell (No 2)* [1919] 1 IR 310.
9 LPA 1925, s 109(8)(v).
10 *Yourell v Hibernian Bank Ltd* [1918] AC 372.
11 *Re Hale* [1899] 2 Ch 107 at 118, CA.
12 *Leicester Permanent Building Society v Butt* [1943] Ch 308, [1943] 2 All ER 523 (mortgagee entitled to an account).
13 LPA 1925, s 109(8).
14 *Kenny v Employers' Liability Association* [1901] 1 IR 301.
15 *Smiths Ltd v Middleton* [1979] 3 All ER 842A–B.
16 *Re Thomson's Mortgage Trusts* [1920] 1 Ch 508.
17 TA 1925, s 63.

Mortgagees are trustees of the surplus proceeds of sale[18] and payment into court under the predecessor of s 63 of the Trustee Act 1925 has been allowed.[19]

STATUTORY CHARGES

Local authorities

Local authorities have in relation to certain expenditure which they are able to recover from the owners of premises a statutory charge on the premises. One of the remedies under such a charge is that of appointing a receiver because the powers and remedies enjoyed by a mortgagee by deed under the Law of Property Act 1925 are conferred on the local authority. The charge operates in relation to expenses recoverable[20] by a local authority for works done by the local authority under s 107 of the Building Act 1984.[1] As from the date of the completion of the works the expenses and accrued interest are, until recovered, a charge on the premises and on all estates and interests in them.[2] For the purpose of enforcing the charge the local authority has all the same powers and remedies under the Law of Property Act 1925 and otherwise as if they were mortgagees by deed having powers of sale and leasing, of accepting surrenders of leases and of appointing a receiver.[3] The charge must be registered as a local land charge.[4]

There is a like provision in respect of sums recoverable in respect of work done by a local housing authority under s 193 of the Housing Act 1985. The section in question provides that where a repair notice has not been complied with a local housing authority may recover expenses reasonably incurred by the authority in carrying out works required to be carried out under the notices.[5] The expenses recoverable by the authority together with the interest due are, until recovered, a charge on the premises to which the notice related,[6] and the charge takes effect when the demand for the expenses and interest becomes operative.[7] For the purpose of enforcing the charge the authority has the same powers and remedies under the Law of Property Act 1925 and otherwise as if the authority were mortgagee by deed having powers of sale and leasing, accepting surrenders of leases and of appointing a receiver.[8]

18 *Re Walhampton's Estate* (1884) 26 Ch D 391.
19 *Banner v Berridge* (1881) 18 Ch D 254.
20 Expenses will not rank as recoverable unless they have been formally demonstrated in writing, signed by the appropriate officer of the council and properly served: see Building Act 1984, ss 92–94.
 1 Building Act 1984, s 107(1).
 2 Building Act 1984, s 107(1).
 3 Building Act 1984, s 107(2).
 4 Local Land Charges Act 1975, s 1(1)(a).
 5 Housing Act 1985, s 193(3) and Sch 10, para 1.
 6 Housing Act 1985, Sch 10, para 7(1).
 7 Housing Act 1985, Sch 10, para 7(2).
 8 Housing Act 1985, Sch 10, para 7(3).

Rent charge

If a rent charge or other annual sum (not being a rent incident to a reversion) is charged on another rent charge and the annual sum or any part of it is at any time unpaid for 21 days the person entitled to receive the annual sum has a statutory power to appoint a receiver of the annual sum charged or any part of it.[9] The power is without prejudice to any prior interest or charge[10] and its nature is spelled out by reference to a mortgagee's statutory rights. The statutory provisions relating to the appointment, powers, remuneration and duties of a receiver apply in like manner as if the person making the appointment were a mortgagee entitled to exercise his statutory power of sale, the annual sum charged were the mortgaged property and the person entitled to it were the mortgagor.[11] This power operates in lieu of the remedies conferred on the holder of a rent charge under s 121 of the Law of Property Act 1925.

9 LPA 1925, s 122(2).
10 LPA 1925.
11 LPA 1925.

Part 2

Court receivers and managers

CHAPTER 20

Jurisdiction

PARTICULAR COURTS

The origins of the court's equitable jurisdiction to appoint a receiver or a receiver and manager have already been mentioned.[1] The equitable jurisdiction is now enshrined in statute. By virtue of the Supreme Court Act 1981 the High Court presently enjoys a statutory jurisdiction to appoint a receiver by an interlocutory or final order in all cases in which it appears to the court to be just and convenient to do so.[2] Previously statute had restricted the jurisdiction to interlocutory orders and used the phrase 'just *or* convenient' rather than 'just and convenient'.[3] The words 'just or convenient' were interpreted as meaning 'where it is practicable and the interests of justice require it'.[4]

Any order made under the statutory jurisdiction may be made either unconditionally or on such terms and conditions as the court thinks just.[5] The appointment may be made either before or after judgment, and of course by the judgment itself or at the hearing of the action.[6]

In the result the jurisdiction to appoint a receiver, formerly exercised only by the old Court of Chancery, now extends to all divisions of the High Court.[7] The jurisdiction to appoint a receiver is also exercisable by the Court of Appeal and an original motion before the Court of Appeal for the appointment of a receiver may be made by the special leave of the court.[8]

---

1 See at p 3, above. See also *Mercantile Group (Europe) AG v Aiyela* [1994] 1 All ER 110.
2 Supreme Court Act 1981, s 37(1).
3 See the Supreme Court of Judicature (Consolidation) Act 1925, s 45(1).
4 *Edwards & Co v Picard* [1909] 2 KB 903 at 907, CA per Fletcher Moulton LJ (dissenting though not on this point).
5 Supreme Court Act 1981, s 37(2). See *Parker v Camden London Borough Council* [1986] Ch 162 at 172–173, 177 and 179.
6 *Beddow v Beddow* (1878) 9 Ch D 89 at 93; *Anglo-Italian Bank v Davies* (1878) 9 Ch D 275 at 286, CA; *Re Prytherch* (1889) 42 Ch D 590 at 600.
7 See Supreme Court Act 1981, s 19(2)(b).
8 Supreme Court Act 1981, ss 15(3), 16(1), 49; and see *Civil Procedure*, Vol 1, Spring 2000, 9A–45. For older cases in the Court of Appeal in Chancery, see *Brenan v Preston* (1852) 2 De GM & G 813; *Chaplin v Young* (1862) 6 LT 97; and see also *Hyde v Warden* (1876) 1 Ex D 309, CA (receiver and manager appointed no previous application having been made to the Divisional Court or a judge).

The jurisdiction is also exercisable in the county courts as regards causes of action within the limits of county court jurisdiction.[9] A county court may for example appoint a receiver of the rents and profits of an equity of redemption by way of equitable execution, even though it could not have issued the now abolished writ of elegit which under the previous practice of the High Court was a necessary preliminary to such an appointment.[10]

It goes without saying that anything the Court of Appeal can do, the ultimate court of appeal, the House of Lords, can do. In *Houlditch v Marquess of Donegal*[11] the House of Lords held itself to have a power to appoint a receiver on the failure of a lower court to appoint, the court in question at the time being the Court of Chancery in Ireland.

EXERCISE OF JURISDICTION IN HIGH COURT

Chancery Division

Not unnaturally in the light of the history of the remedy, of all the three divisions of the High Court now enjoying receivership jurisdiction, the Chancery Division is the most frequently approached forum by applicants for the appointment of a receiver.[12]

Following the transfer of contentious probate proceedings to the Chancery Division[13] it is now that division which exercises the statutory jurisdiction[14] to appoint an administrator pending suit[15] where probate proceedings are pending. Previously, except in special circumstances[16] the Chancery Court would not entertain an application for the appointment of a receiver if probate proceedings were pending. Once an administrator pending suit had been appointed in probate proceedings the Chancery Court would not appoint a receiver at all.[17]

Other subtleties obtained which were dictated by the wish of the respective courts not to tread on jurisdictional toes. Where no proceedings were pending a receiver might still be appointed in a creditor's administration action in the Chancery Division[18] if the appointment had been claimed by the writ[19] even if the

---

9 County Courts Act 1984, s 38; RSC, Ord 32, p 1(1) (as substituted).

10 *R v Selfe* [1908] 2 KB 121.

11 (1834) 2 Cl & Fin 470, 8 Bli NS 301, HL.

12 A master of the Chancery Division may appoint a receiver: see *Practice Direction* [1975] 1 All ER 255, [1975] 1 WLR 129, para 3(f).

13 See Supreme Court Act 1981, s 61(1), Sch 1, para 1(h).

14 The jurisdiction under the Supreme Court Act 1981, s 117.

15 *Horrell v Witts and Plumley* (1866) LR 1 P & D 103; *Re Messiter-Terry's Goods* (1908) 24 TLR 465; *Re Shorter's Goods* [1911] P 184.

16 *Re Wright* (1888) 32 Sol Jo 721 (urgent case in vacation); *Re Evans's Goods* (1890) 15 PD 215 (undue delay in Probate Division and notice of trial withdrawn). In earlier times the Court of Chancery often appointed receivers in such cases.

17 *Veret v Duprez* (1868) LR 6 Eq 329.

18 *Re Baker* (1882) 26 Sol Jo 682; *Re Cleaver's Estate* [1905] P 319.

19 *Re Wenge* [1911] WN 129, 55 Sol Jo 553.

probate action was started after the motion for a receiver had been launched.[20] The Probate Division would appoint an administrator pending suit after the appointment of a receiver in Chancery[1] but, out of diplomacy, would not appoint any one but the Chancery receiver except for special reasons.[2] When such an appointment was made the Chancery Division would discharge its own receiver (thereby avoiding any conflict of jurisdiction) but would keep some residual control over him in his capacity as administrator, making appropriate orders within its discretion, for example for the payment of particular debts.[3]

Now that the Chancery Division has power to make an appointment of an administrator pending suit as well as to appoint a receiver much of this refined learning is likely to become obsolete. Theoretically, of course, the same principles apply where there is any question as to whether a receiver or an administrator pending suit should be appointed.[4] But the problems and refinements really arose out of the two jurisdictions being in separate courts. In practice it must be unlikely that the court will consider that it is appropriate to appoint or continue in office a receiver when there is jurisdiction to appoint an administrator pending suit.

The power to appoint receivers is not restricted to the period between the start of proceedings and final judgment.[5] The court may therefore appoint a receiver at the trial of the action[6] or, indeed, after a final judgment so long as that judgment is still unsatisfied,[7] because the process of the court can still be prayed in aid to enforce the judgment. But once an order absolute has been made in foreclosure proceedings no receiver can be appointed in those proceedings since the order absolute has concluded the proceedings so far as the court is concerned.[8] It is otherwise where there has been an order for administration or for foreclosure nisi and a proper case is made out: there is nothing to preclude the court in that event from appointing a receiver.[9]

Family Division

In the Family Division receivers are sometimes appointed by way of equitable execution in divorce cases.[10] In *S v S*[11] a receiving order was made as the most

---

20 *Re Oakes* [1917] 1 Ch 230. The parties wanting to obtain representation should be before the court: *Re Henderson* (1886) 2 TLR 322.

1 *Tichborne v Tichborne, ex p Norris* (1869) LR 1 P & D 730; *Re Evans's Goods* (1890) 15 PD 215; *Re Cleaver's Estate* [1905] P 319.

2 *Tichborne v Tichborne* above; *Re Evans* above.

3 *Tichborne v Tichborne* above.

4 The procedure on both applications is similar: cf RSC Ord 30 and Ord 76, r 14 applying rr 2, 4, 6.

5 *Smith v Cowell* (1880) 6 QBD 75, CA; *Edwards & Co v Picard* [1909] 2 KB 903 at 907, CA.

6 *Re Prytherch* (1889) 42 Ch D 590.

7 *Anglo-Italian Bank v Davies* (1878) 9 Ch D 275 at 286, CA; *Salt v Cooper* (1880) 16 Ch D 544, CA.

8 *Wills v Luff* (1888) 38 Ch D 197; cf *Ingham v Sutherland* (1890) 63 LT 614.

9 *Bowman v Bell* (1844) 14 Sim 392; *Thomas v Davies* (1847) 11 Beav 29; *Re Bywater's Estate* (1855) 1 Jur NS 227; *Brooker v Brooker* (1857) 3 Sm & G 475, 26 LJ Ch 411; *Weston v Levy* [1887] WN 76, 31 Sol Jo 364.

10 See *Gordon v Gordon* (1912) Times, 26 November.

11 (1973) Times, 23 June.

appropriate remedy against a husband who had persistently defaulted in maintenance payments although there was no reported precedent in the Family Division or its predecessor the Probate Divorce and Admiralty Division for making such an order.

Queen's Bench Division

The most frequent example of appointing a receiver to be found in the Queen's Bench Division is the appointment of a receiver by way of equitable execution.[12] Receivers are now rarely encountered outside that particular field. However the Admiralty jurisdiction now exercised in the Queen's Bench Division must not be overlooked. In one case a receiver has been appointed under the Admiralty jurisdiction in an action of co-ownership at the instance of one of two co-owners.[13] Another illustration occurred in an action by an equitable mortgagee of ship and freight.[14]

District registries

A word or two is in place concerning applications for receivership in the district registries of the High Court. Formerly, applications in an action pending in the district registry which may be disposed of in London by a master in the Chancery Division or the Queen's Bench Division or by a registrar in an Admiralty action could be made to a district registrar.[15] Thus an application for a receiver by way of equitable execution could be made to a district registrar.[16] Other cases where a Chancery master would exercise jurisdiction to appoint a receiver in chambers are where the application is (1) to appoint a receiver in place of a deceased or retired receiver, (2) on the hearing of a mortgagee's originating summons in chambers for sale or foreclosure or (3) by consent. These applications could also be dealt with by a district registrar.

The position is now regulated under the Civil Procedure Rules 1998 which provide that except where an enactment rule or practice direction provides otherwise any act which the Court may perform may be performed in relation to proceedings in the High Court by any judge Master or district judge and in relation to proceedings in a county court by any judge or district judge.[17] A district judge or Master may impose an injunctive order in connection with, or as ancillary to, an order appointing a receiver by way of equitable execution.[18]

---

12 For discussion of equitable execution, see p 345.
13 *The Ampthill* (1880) 5 PD 224.
14 *Burn v Herlofson and Siemensen, The Faust* (1887) 56 LT 722, CA; and see *The Edderside* (1887) 31 Sol Jo 744.
15 See the previous (ie 2nd edn) of this book at 274.
16 This was always so: see *Walker v Robinson* (1876) 34 LT 229; *Re Smith* (1877) 6 Ch D 692, 36 LT 178; *Re Capper* (1878) 26 WR 434.
17 CPR 1998, r 2.4.
18 *Civil Procedure*, Vol 1, Spring 2000, 2 BPD-001–002.

JUSTICE OF THE PEACE

Finally, one must note that in the case of companies carrying on an undertaking of a public nature mortgagees and holders of debenture stock may in certain circumstances apply to two justices for the appointment of a receiver without starting any action.[19]

These statutory provisions do not oust the ordinary jurisdiction of the High Court to appoint a receiver in a proper case.[20]

19 Companies Clauses Consolidation Act 1845, ss 53 and 54; Commissioners Clauses Act 1847, ss 86 and 87; Companies Clauses Act 1863, ss 25 and 26.
20 *Fripp v Chard Rly Co, Fripp v Bridgewater and Taunton Canal Co* (1853) 11 Hare 241 at 259. Supreme Court Act 1981, s 37. As a rule the court will not appoint a *manager* of an undertaking of a public nature: *Marshall v South Staffordshire Tramways Co* [1895] 2 Ch 36, CA.

CHAPTER 21

Grounds for appointment

PERSONS UNDER DISABILITY

Minors

Prior to 1926 a minor (then conventionally referred to as an infant) was capable of holding both legal estates and equitable interests in land. Since 1926 a legal estate in land can no longer be vested in a minor[1] although he can hold an equitable interest. A minor now attains his majority at the age of 18.[2]

The old practice of applying on petition (without any action being on foot) for the appointment of a receiver to protect a minor's property, which was at one time frequent,[3] is now obsolete. Such applications are now made in an action to which the trustees are parties.

Where a minor is beneficially entitled to any property the court may with a view to the application of the capital or income of that property for his maintenance, education or benefit appoint a person to convey the property or vest the right to transfer stock or shares or things in action or to receive dividends or recover a thing in action on such terms as the court thinks fit.[4] This power enables the court to appoint a person to convey land belonging to a minor tenant in tail so as to give a mortgagee an effective charge on the fee simple.[5] In cases covered by the power in section 53 of the Trustee Act 1925 an application under that section and not for a receiver is the appropriate course.

Mental infirmity

The court has always exercised jurisdiction to appoint a receiver of the property

---

1 LPA 1925, s 1(6).
2 Family Law Reform Act 1969, s 1.
3 *Dillon v Lady Mount-Cashell* (1727) 4 Bro Parl Cas 306, HL; *Re Cormicks (minors)* (1840) 2 I Eq R 264; *Whitelaw v Sandys* (1848) 12 I Eq R 393; *Re Leeming* (1851) 20 LJ Ch 550.
4 TA 1925, s 53. On the position prior to 1926: see 4 Wolstenholme and Cherry *Conveyancing Statutes* (13th edn) 81–82.
5 *Re Gower's Settlement* [1934] Ch 365, 103 LJ Ch 164 (entailed interest in remainder); *Re Coke* [1935] C No 1730 cited in 4 Wolstenholme and Cherry op cit at 82; and see *Re Meux, Gilmour v Gilmour* [1958] Ch 154, [1957] 2 All ER 630 (disentailment and resettlement held 'an application of capital').

of a mentally infirm person. The jurisdiction, however, is now, except in the case of trustees, exercised in the Court of Protection under the provisions of the Mental Health Act 1983. It is beyond the scope of this work to cover the code of practice in the Court of Protection whose rules are very much sui generis.

PRESERVATION OF PROPERTY

The most frequent ground for the appointment of a receiver by the court is the protection or preservation of property for the benefit of persons who have an interest in it.[6] Receivers have, in the past, often been appointed on this ground pending the trial of an action[7] or an interpleader issue[8] or pending proceedings in another court[9] or a reference to arbitration[10] or pending the constitution of the legal representative of a deceased person.[11] A receiver may also be appointed at the instance of tenants of property where the landlord neither collects the rents due nor performs his repairing covenants and the property is deteriorating.[12]

PARTNERSHIP

General

Another application, indeed perhaps the most common application, of the principle that the court has power to appoint a receiver or receiver and manager whenever it is just and convenient to do so, arises in the case of partnership disputes. The court will exercise its jurisdiction in appropriate cases on the application of any partner, whether plaintiff or defendant,[13] or indeed of any other person interested in the partnership assets.[14] For example, the personal repre-

---

6 See *Wingfield v Wingfield* [1919] 1 Ch 462, CA where an action in which an order for the appointment of a receiver had been obtained having been discontinued, a charging order for the costs of obtaining the appointment was refused.

7 *Free v Hinde* (1827) 2 Sim 7; *Richards v Goold* (1827) 1 Mol 22; *Tullett v Armstrong* (1836) 1 Keen 428; *Dawson v Yates* (1838) 1 Beav 301; *Kelly v Butler* (1839) 1 I Eq R 435; *Bartley v Bartley* (1845) 9 Jur 224; *Bainbrigge v Bainbrigge* (1850) 20 LJ Ch 139; *Fripp v Chard Rly Co* (1853) 11 Hare 241; *White v Smale* (1856) 22 Beav 72; *Taylor v Eckersley* (1876) 2 Ch D 302, CA; *Re Bechstein's Business Trusts* (1914) 58 Sol Jo 864 (alien enemy firm). As to an action being not maintainable by an agent, cf *Re Gaudig and Blum* (1915) 31 TLR 153.

8 *Howell v Dawson* (1884) 13 QBD 67, DC.

9 *Brenan v Preston* (1852) 2 De GM & G 813 at 839–840; *Wright v Vernon* (1855) 3 Drew 112; *Transatlantic Co v Pietroni* (1860) John 604, 2 LT 726 (foreign court).

10 See the Arbitration Act 1996, s 44(2)(e); *Plews v Baker* (1873) LR 16 Eq 564 at 573; *Halsey v Windham* [1882] WN 108; *Compagnie du Senegal v Woods & Co* (1883) 53 LJ Ch 166, 49 LT 527; *Pini v Roncoroni* [1892] 1 Ch 633.

11 *King v King* (1801) 6 Ves 172; *Wood v Hitchings* (1840) 2 Beav 289; *Owen and Gutch v Homan* (1853) 4 HL Cas 997 at 1032; *Nothard v Proctor* (1875) 1 Ch D 4, CA; *Re Shephard* (1889) 43 Ch D 131 at 132, CA; *Re Messiter-Terry's Goods* (1908) 24 TLR 465.

12 *Hart v Emelkirk Ltd* [1983] 3 All ER 15, [1983] 1 WLR 1289.

13 *Katsch v Schenck* (1849) 18 LJ Ch 386.

14 *Davis v Amer* (1854) 3 Drew 64.

sentatives of a deceased partner may apply to the court for a receiver, particularly if the surviving partner has failed to get in the partnership assets.[15]

The court also has power to appoint a manager,[16] a function usually (but not necessarily) combined with that of receiver. The function of a manager is to carry on the partnership business under the direction of the court. A receiver does not have this power unless he is also appointed manager.[17]

As a general rule the court is antipathetic to the idea of interfering in partnership matters during the continuance of the partnership business.[18] There are sound reasons for its chariness in this regard. The intervention of a receiver and manager is likely to have a traumatic effect: business is inevitably affected by a change in management, and many businesses can do without the draining extra expense of a court-appointed manager. Normally therefore the court will only appoint a receiver and manager after an order for dissolution has been made[19] or where dissolution has in fact been effected by the service of a writ[20] or if the partnership has expired by effluxion of time and one of the partners is dragging his feet over the winding up and realisation of the business.[1]

Dissolution

In former times dissolution alone was not considered an automatic passport to the appointment of a receiver and manager, it being thought that some breach of duty was required.[2] However this view is hardly in tune with later cases which seem to show that once a partnership is dissolved the appointment of a receiver and manager follows almost as a matter of course.[3] In the Australian case of *Tate v Barry*[4] Long Innes J said that it was 'settled that in a suit instituted in equity for the winding up of a partnership already dissolved or for the dissolution of an admitted partnership in which it is clear that dissolution will be granted at the hearing, the plaintiff is entitled, as a general rule, and practically as a matter of course, to the appointment of an interim receiver'. Dissolution by the death of *one* partner is not a ground for the appointment of a receiver and manager on the application of the representatives of the deceased without some breach of the partnership agreement or some neglect of duty on the part of the surviving partner or partners.[5] On the other hand a receiver and manager is appointed more or less automatically when a dissolution occurs by virtue of the death of *both*

---

15 *Estwick v Conningsby* (1682) 1 Vern 118.

16 *Lees v Jones* (1857) 3 Jur NS 954; *Sargant v Read* (1876) 1 Ch D 600.

17 *Re Manchester and Milford Rly Co, ex p Cambrian Rly Co* (1880) 14 Ch D 645 at 653; CA; *Taylor v Neate* (1888) 39 Ch D 538 at 543.

18 *Hall v Hall* (1850) 3 Mac & G 79; *Le Roy v Herrenschmidt* (1876) 2 VLR (Eq) 189.

19 *Gregory v Welch* (1871) 2 VR (Eq) 129.

20 Service of a writ dissolves a partnership at will.

 1 *Pini v Roncoroni* [1892] 1 Ch 633.

 2 *Harding v Glover* (1810) 18 Ves 281 (continuing breach after dissolution).

 3 *Baxter v West* (1858) 28 LJ Ch 169, 32 LTOS 155; *Pini v Roncoroni* [1892] 1 Ch 633; *Embree v McCurdy* (1907) 14 OLR 325, Ont CA.

 4 (1928) 28 SRNSW 380 at 383 citing *Baxter v West* supra.

 5 *Philips v Atkinson* (1787) 2 Bro CC 272; *Collins v Young* (1853) 1 Macq 385, HL.

partners[6] for there is not the same mutual confidence between partners' personal representatives as between partners themselves.

Retirement stands on a different footing. There is no right to the appointment of a receiver where one partner has retired leaving the remaining partners to carry on the partnership business.[7]

While, therefore, dissolution raises at the very least a strong prima facie case for the appointment of a receiver and manager it is not necessary that the proceedings in which the appointment of a receiver and manager is claimed should expressly ask for a dissolution in the prayer for relief.[8] Conversely, dissolution in fact is not a sine qua non of a court appointment. Danger to the partnership assets is a ground for the appointment of a receiver before dissolution.[9]

A receiver may be appointed in an action for dissolution even though the partnership agreement provides for reference of disputes to arbitration.[10] But it may now be more convenient to apply in the arbitration for the appointment of a receiver.[11]

Existence of partnership in dispute

Often, of course, the issue comes before the court at the interlocutory stage with a motion for the appointment of a receiver and manager. If there is a conflict of evidence on the very existence of a partnership the court may nevertheless appoint a receiver and manager. In *Tucker v Prior*[12] it was held by Charles J that a receiver would not be appointed where the existence of the partnership was in question. But if the assets are in danger there may still be a case for the appointment of a receiver and manager.[13] And in *Floydd v Cheney*[14] Megarry J doubted whether the principle stated in *Tucker v Prior* was correct, and said that there was no general rule of practice that when the existence of a partnership was in question a receiver would not be appointed of the assets until the question had been determined.[15] In proper cases the court will make such an appointment.[16] The presence of jeopardy or misconduct will have an important bearing on the attitude of the court. That also applies where dissolution of the partnership is disputed. In the absence of prospective damage to the plaintiff the court will not, on motion, appoint a receiver and manager where there is a substantial issue as to whether the partnership has been dissolved[17] or has come to an end because it

6 *Philips v Atkinson* (1787) 2 Bro CC 272.
7 *Sobell v Boston* [1975] 2 All ER 282, [1975] 1 WLR 1587.
8 *Sheppard v Oxenford* (1855) 1 K & J 491, 25 LTOS 63.
9 *Evans v Coventry* (1854) 5 De GM & G 911, 24 LTOS 186; revsg 3 Drew 75 (secretary had made away with some of the funds).
10 *Halsey v Windham* [1882] WN 108; *Compagnie du Senegal v Smith & Co* [1883] WN 180; *Pini v Roncoroni* [1892] 1 Ch 633; *Machin v Bennett* [1900] WN 146.
11 Arbitration Act 1996, s 44(2)(e).
12 (1887) 31 Sol Jo 784.
13 *Longbottom v Woodhead* (1887) 31 Sol Jo 796.
14 [1970] Ch 602, [1970] 1 All ER 446.
15 See *Tate v Barry* (1928) 28 SRNSW 380.
16 [1970] Ch 602 at 610; and see *Tate v Barry* (1928) 28 SRNSW 380.
17 *Fairburn v Pearson* (1850) 2 Mac & G 144; *Bowker v Henry* (1862) 6 LT 43.

was for a fixed term but will rather direct the issue to be tried first.[18] It should, however, be noted that a defendant in an action for dissolution of a partnership who claims to own the whole business cannot move in the action for the appointment of a receiver.[19]

Misconduct

Misconduct by one partner is not of itself a ground for the appointment of a receiver and manager.[20] It is a qualitative matter. There is misconduct and misconduct, and only if the misconduct in question puts the partnership assets in jeopardy, or raises a substantial doubt as to the security of the partnership business, will the court make an appointment.

There must be something more than a partnership squabble. And mere non-cooperation by one partner, which throws the burden of responsibility on to his fellow partner, is not enough to justify an appointment.[1] The same applies to cases of complete deadlock.[2] However, a refusal to co-operate may in the circumstances be serious enough to justify the appointment of a receiver. Thus in *Barrett v Snowball*[3] four out of five partners who owned coal mines and brickfields in Tasmania successfully applied for an injunction to restrain the fifth partner who managed the partnership business in Melbourne from interfering in the business, and for a receiver over the partnership property in Melbourne; and Tasmanian property was not subjected to the receivership. The defendant in that case was completely refusing to co-operate in any way with his fellow partners. Certainly any breach or action calculated to destroy the mutual trust and confidence which should obtain between partners will induce the court to intervene. Thus if a partner uses partnership assets for carrying on trade on his own account,[4] or tries to divert goodwill of the partnership to himself,[5] or refrains from getting in debts due to the partnership to oblige debtors who were customers of another business carried on by that same partner,[6] an appointment will be made. The most extreme case is where a partner steals partnership assets[7] or makes away with some of them.[8] But a case will also arise where the partnership itself was induced by fraud.[9]

---

18 *Baxter v West* (1858) 28 LJ Ch 169, 32 LTOS 155.
19 *Hardy v Hardy* (1917) 62 Sol Jo 142.
20 *Baxter v West* (1858) 28 LJ Ch 169, 32 LTOS 155.
1 *Roberts v Eberhardt* (1853) Kay 148, 23 LJ Ch 201; *Rowe v Wood* (1822) 2 Jac & W 553; cf *Jefferys v Smith* (1820) 1 Jac & W 298.
2 *Re Yenidje Tobacco Co Ltd* [1916] 2 Ch 426, CA.
3 (1870) 1 AJR 8.
4 *Smith v Jeyes* (1841) 4 Beav 503; and see *Chapman v Beach* (1820) 1 Jac & W 594n.
5 *Harding v Glover* (1810) 18 Ves 281.
6 *Young v Buckett* (1882) 51 LJ Ch 504, 46 LT 266 (surviving partner sued by representative of deceased partner).
7 *Estwick v Conningsby* (1682) 1 Vern 118.
8 *Oliver v Hamilton* (1794) 2 Anst 453. *Evans v Coventry* (1854) 5 De GM & G 911, 24 LTOS 186; *Sheppard v Oxenford* (1855) 1 K & J 491, 25 LTOS 90 (property already abroad: partner absconded abroad).
9 *Re Hooper, ex p Broome* (1811) 1 Rose 69.

Exclusion

Even though there may be no misconduct jeopardising the partnership assets the court will as a rule appoint a receiver and manager if one partner wrongfully excludes his fellow partner from the management of the partnership business.[10] This is, as a Canadian court observed, perhaps the most prominent point on which the court acts in appointing a receiver and manager of a partnership concern.[11] There are certainly numerous cases in various jurisdictions illustrating the principle,[12] and not infrequently the exclusion giving rise to the appointment is linked with a claim that the defendant is solely entitled to the entire partnership property. Sometimes it is alleged that the plaintiff is not a partner[13] or that he has no interest in the partnership assets.[14] Where the court is unable to reach a finding on that issue adverse to the plaintiff it will appoint a receiver and manager.

The court will not appoint a receiver and manager where the exclusion of a partner, is according to the terms of the partnership agreement.[15] But where dissolution has taken place and one of the partners excludes the other on the basis of an oral agreement which the other denies an interim receiver may be appointed until the issue can be tried.[16]

Illegality

Sometimes a defendant is in a position to rely on illegality as a defence to an action. If the illegality is established then, presumably, the court cannot interfere. But if the position is unclear at the interlocutory stage the court may appoint a receiver and manager to protect the property *pendente lite* and the character of the defence will frequently enable the court to overcome any scruples which it might otherwise have about intervening. A case in point is *Hale v Hale*[17] where the partners had for many years carried on business as brewers. The plaintiff started proceedings for dissolution of the partnership and the defendant denied the plaintiff's right to any remedy or relief whatever on the ground that the partnership was illegal. The defendant relied among other things on the maximum '*in pari delicto potior est conditio defendentis*'. Lord Langdale MR treated exclusion on the ground of illegality as reason enough for the appoint-

---

10 *Floydd v Cheney* [1970] Ch 602, [1970] 1 All ER 446.
11 *Prentiss v Brennan* (1850) 1 Gr 371, CA.
12 *Wilson v Greenwood* (1818) 1 Swan 471 at 481; *Goodman v Whitcomb* (1820) 1 Jac & W 589 at 592; *Rowe v Wood* (1822) 2 Jac & W 533; [1814–1923] All ER Rep 360; *Const v Harris* (1824) Turn & R 496 at 525; *Hale v Hale* (1841) 4 Beav 369; *Naish v Ody* (1897) 41 Sol Jo 726. Australia: *Mitchell v Simons* (1862) 1 SCRNSW Eq 70; *Boyle v Willis* (1880) 1 ALT 189; Canada; *Steele v Grossmith* (1872) 19 Gr 141; New Zealand: *Redwood v Redwood* (1908) 28 NZLR 260.
13 *Peacock v Peacock* (1809) 16 Ves 49; *Blakeney v Dufaur* (1851) 15 Beav 40.
14 *Wilson v Greenwood* (1818) 1 Swan 471, 1 Wils Ch 223; *Clegg v Fishwick* (1849) 1 Mac & G 294 (lease granted to surviving partners but pursuant to covenant in previous lease in which deceased interested).
15 *Blakeney v Dufaur* (1851) 15 Beav 40.
16 *Steele v Grossmith* (1872) 19 Gr 141.
17 (1841) 4 Beav 369.

ment of a receiver and manager. Again, in *Sheppard v Oxenford*[18] a receiver was appointed although the legality of the partnership was denied. Illegality in this context includes the case of a partnership business whose object is contrary to public policy, as for example a business whose object would involve the breach of the law of a friendly state. Despite the decision of Fletcher Moulton LJ in one case[19] a partnership between bookmakers had been held not to be per se illegal[20] although a receiver would not be appointed to get in gaming debts which of their nature are irrecoverable.

CREDITOR AGAINST DEBTOR

The most commonly encountered case of a receiver being appointed in aid of a general creditor is that of equitable execution[1] where a receiver is appointed to enable a judgment creditor to obtain the benefit of his judgment at law. Leaving that case aside, in a limited number of cases the court will appoint a receiver for the protection of unsecured creditors.

A plaintiff who is seeking to establish a claim as a general creditor against a defendant is not usually entitled to have, before trial, a receiver appointed over a specific fund or property of the defendant, unless the evidence is very clearly in his favour and the risk of injury to the defendant is very small. Of course where the creditor has the right to have his debt paid out of a particular fund even though he has no charge or security of any kind over the fund a receiver may exceptionally be appointed.[2] Particular jeopardy to the plaintiff's general interest must be shown. Thus if property is in no one's possession,[3] as where a grant of probate or administration is still pending, a receiver may be appointed to preserve the property until the parties' respective rights are substantially determined.[4] And the same will apply where although an executor is in the saddle he is dissipating the estate.[4]

It has been held that an order for maintenance in divorce proceedings constitutes the wife a judgment creditor, so that she may be entitled to have a receiver appointed over her husband's interest under a settlement.[5] Whatever may have been the position in the past[6] having regard to the exclusive jurisdiction of the Family Division to enforce its own orders such an application should be made in that division.[7]

---

18 (1855) 1 K & J 491, 25 LTOS 63.
19 *Hyams v Stuart King* [1908] 2 KB 696 at 718, CA.
20 *Thwaites v Coulthwaite* [1896] 1 Ch 496; *Keen v Price* [1914] 2 Ch 98; *Jeffrey v Bamford* [1921] 2 KB 351; and see now Betting, Gaming and Lotteries Act 1963.
1 See the discussion at p 375.
2 *Cummins v Perkins* [1899] 1 Ch 16, CA (debt payable by a married woman out of her separate estate).
3 *Higginson v German Athenaeum Ltd* (1916) 32 TLR 277 (club in suspended animation).
4 *Owen and Gutch v Homan* (1853) 4 HL Cas 997, 1 Eq Rep 370, HL.
5 *Oliver v Lowther* (1880) 42 LT 47, 28 WR 381 (application in Chancery Division).
6 *Oliver v Lowther* (1880) 42 LT 47, 28 WR 381.
7 See *Ivimey v Ivimey* [1908] 2 KB 260, 77 LJKB 714, CA; cf *Re Hedderwick* [1933] Ch 669; and Matrimonial Causes Rules 1977, SI 1977/344, r 86; and see Supreme Court Practice 1988, para 42/1/9.

INDEPENDENT RAILWAY COMPANIES

The section which follows discusses the remedy of receivership in respect of these railway companies not swept up into the bucket of the nationalised railway system introduced by the Transport Act 1947. The functions and powers of these relics of Victorian enthusiasm are regulated by special Acts and subject to one exception,[8] public general legislation passed since 1947 does not apply to these undertakings.

Until 1867 the court had no power to appoint a receiver and manager of a railway company.[9] The natural result of this inability to grant that remedy was that a judgment creditor of a railway company could deliver a writ of fieri facias against the company, seize all its rolling stock and other goods and thus effectively strangle the whole undertaking.[10] This dire situation was remedied by the passing of the Railway Companies Act 1867 which protected the rolling stock and plant of a railway company from execution by a judgment creditor and so enabled such a company to carry on its business as a going concern for the benefit of both the public and its creditors.[11] Obviously creditors then had a better chance of being paid than if the whole undertaking was broken up and sold.[12]

The term 'railway company' is statutorily defined. For the purposes of the Act, a railway company is a company constituted by Act of Parliament, or by certificate under an Act, for the purpose of constructing, maintaining or working a railway, either alone or in conjunction with any other purpose,[13] whether or not the railway is the principal purpose.[14] Whether by reason of this definition the Act applies to the British Railways Board is not entirely clear. The Transport Act 1962 which established the British Railways Board[15] repealed all the remaining provisions of the Railway Companies Act 1867[16] except ss 1 to 5 whose application to the British Railways Board was not specifically excluded. As against this it can be said that the surviving provisions of the 1867 Act are inappropriate to, and do not mesh very satisfactorily with, the present constitution of the Board.

A person (and that term includes a corporation)[17] who has obtained a judgment[18] against a railway company, as statutorily defined, but who is deprived of his right of having the company's property taken in execution has a statutory right to obtain the appointment of a receiver and, if necessary, a manager of the undertaking.[19] The appointment of a manager is necessary if the railway business

---

8 Transport Act 1962, s 43(1)(b), (2)–(7).
9 *Gardner v London Chatham and Dover Rly Co* (1867) 2 Ch App 201.
10 See *Re Eastern and Midland Rly Co* (1890) 45 Ch D 367 at 378.
11 Railway Companies Act 1867, s 4.
12 See *Re Eastern and Midlands Rly Co* (1890) 45 Ch D 367, 63 LT 604, CA; *Re Wrexham Mold and Connah's Quay Rly Co* [1900] 2 Ch 436 at 439.
13 Railway Companies Act 1867, s 3.
14 *Great Northern Rly Co v Tahourdin* (1883) 13 QBD 320, CA. See also *Re East and West India Dock Co* (1888) 38 Ch D 576, CA.
15 Transport Act 1962, s 1.
16 See Transport Act 1962, s 95(1), Sch 12, Pt I (repealed).
17 Railway Companies Act 1867, s 3.
18 'Judgment' includes decree, order or rule: Railway Companies Act 1867, s 3.
19 Railway Companies Act 1867, s 4.

is being carried on.[20] A railway company which has never acquired any land or constructed any works is not an 'undertaking' for this purpose.[1]

It is doubtful whether the court has jurisdiction to appoint a receiver of the undertaking of a railway company before the line has been opened for traffic, but, in any case, it ought not to do so.[2] But it can appoint a receiver of part of the line where that part only is open for traffic.[3] It is not a pre-condition to the jurisdiction of the court that the company should itself be working its traffic, as the line may be leased, or there may be arrangements for working with another company, or the company may only take tolls for carriages passing over its line.[4] Nor is it necessary that the company should possess rolling stock which, but for the Act, might be taken in execution.[5]

In this connection a receiver and manager may be appointed of the under-taking of a company originally formed for other purposes, but afterwards authorised by statute to make a short piece of line over its land in connection with the line of a railway company and to work it for through traffic.[5] But if appointed the receiver and manager must be appointed in respect of the whole undertaking of the company and not merely the piece of line.[6]

The procedure for applying for a receiver under the statutory jurisdiction conferred by the Railway Companies Act 1867 was by way of petition in the Chancery Division of the High Court.[7] The only evidence required in support of the petition was an affidavit showing that the petitioner was a judgment creditor, that his judgment was unsatisfied, and that the company was a going concern.[8] Under the Woolf procedural reforms, the proper procedure is a claim form followed by an application notice with a supporting witness statement.

When appointing a receiver and manager in this context the court exercises its discretion for the benefit of all creditors and is not fettered in this regard by the existence of any contract between the company and any other party.[9] As long as the company is a going concern, debenture holders have no voice in deciding who is to be manager or what is to be his salary.[10]

And clearly a receiver should not be appointed where there is no money for him to receive.[11]

Where the railway company's officers are acting fairly, they may be appointed managers.[12] In those circumstances they have the same management powers

---

20 *Re Manchester and Milford Rly Co* (1880) 14 Ch D 645, 49 LJ Ch 365, CA.
1 *Re Birmingham and Lichfield Junction Rly Co* (1881) 18 Ch D 155, 50 LJ Ch 594.
2 *Re Knott End Railway Act 1898* [1901] 2 Ch 8, 70 LJ Ch 463, CA.
3 *Re Southern Rly Co* (1880) 5 LR Ir 165.
4 *Re Manchester and Milford Rly Co* (1880) 14 Ch D 645 at 652.
5 *Re Manchester and Milford Rly Co* (1880) 14 Ch D 645 at 652.
6 *Re East and West India Dock Co* (1888) 38 Ch D 576, 57 LJ Ch 1053, CA.
7 *Re East and West India Dock Co* (1888) 38 Ch D 576, 57 LJ Ch 1053, CA.
8 Railway Companies Act 1867, s 4.
9 *Re Manchester and Milford Rly Co* (1880) 14 Ch D 645, CA.
10 *Re Hull, Barnsley and West Riding Junction Rly and Dock Co* (1887) 57 LT 82.
11 *Re Hull, Barnsley and West Riding Junction Rly and Dock Co* (1887) 57 LT 82.
12 *Re Knott End Railway Act 1898* [1901] 2 Ch 8, 70 LJ Ch 463, CA.

which they previously enjoyed but must exercise them as officers of the court and under the court's directions not as the company's officers.[13]

All money received by a receiver or by a receiver and manager of a railway company as defined by the statute must be applied in the order laid down in the statute.[14] It has been held that money received, for this purpose, includes the proceeds of sale of rolling stock sold to another company under the provisions of a statutory agreement authorised after the receiver's appointment.[15] The priority is spelled out in s 4 of the 1867 Act.

First, the receiver must make due provision for the working expenses of the railway and other proper outgoings in respect of the undertaking. This priority comes before all else: a judgment creditor gains no priority over those expenses and outgoings by obtaining a receivership order.[16] And indeed for this same reason where an order for a receiver has been made on the petition of one judgment creditor a petition by a second judgment creditor should be refused.[17]

Plainly it is important to identify what are properly expenses and outgoings qualifying for such preferential treatment.

Working expenses may compendiously be defined as such expenses as are fairly necessary to enable the railway to work efficiently, such as wages, necessary repairs and, in the case of steam engines, coal.[18] Judged by this test payments for rolling stock bought under a hire purchase agreement are working expenses.[19] But a debt for rails supplied before the appointment of a receiver is not a working expense;[20] nor is the cost of promoting a bill in Parliament for power to substitute electricity for steam in working the railway;[1] nor is a judgment debt for damages obtained against the company for negligence.[2]

'Proper outgoings' includes payments which must be made if the railway is to be kept working, as for example in respect of rates and taxes.[3] Costs incurred in the course of litigation may run the risk of being beyond the pale. So in one case where a contractor was owed money by a company and the court gave leave for him to proceed with an action against the company and for the company to defend the action and the result of the action was that there was a substantial reduction in the sum payable, it was, nevertheless, held that the company's costs were not 'proper outgoings'.[4]

---

13 *Re Manchester and Milford Rly Co* (1880) 14 Ch D 645, 49 LJ Ch 365, CA.
14 *Re Eastern and Midlands Rly Co (No 2)* (1891) 66 LT 153; *Whadcoat v Shropshire Rlys Co* (1893) 9 TLR 589.
15 *Re Liskeard and Caradon Rly Co* [1903] 2 Ch 681.
16 *Re Wrexham Mold and Connah's Quay Rly Co* [1900] 2 Ch 436, CA (judgment for damages for negligence with costs); and see the earlier cases of *Re Mersey Rly Co* (1888) 37 Ch D 610, CA; *Devas v East and West India Dock Co* (1889) 58 LJ Ch 522, 61 LT 217.
17 *Re Mersey Rly Co* (1888) 37 Ch D 610, CA.
18 *Re Wrexham Mold and Connah's Quay Rly Co* [1900] 2 Ch 436.
19 *Re Cornwall Minerals Rly Co* (1882) 48 LT 41, CA; *Re Eastern and Midlands Rly Co* (2) (1891) 66 LT 153.
20 *Re Navan and Kingscourt Rly Co* (1885) 17 LR Ir 398, Ir CA.
 1 *Re Mersey Rly Co* (1895) 64 LJ Ch 623, 72 LT 535; affd [1895] 2 Ch 287, CA.
 2 *Re Wrexham Mold and Connah's Quay Rly Co* [1900] 2 Ch 436.
 3 *Re Wrexham Mold and Connah's Quay Rly Co* [1900] 2 Ch 436.
 4 *Re Wrexham Mold and Connah's Quay Rly Co* [1900] 1 Ch 261, CA.

EXECUTORS AND TRUSTEES

The equitable remedy of receivership is available against both executors and trustees where the circumstances make it appropriate. The criteria for the appointment of a receiver to displace these fiduciaries are almost identical. Primarily it is jeopardy or the risk of jeopardy that justifies an application to the court. Assessing the degree of jeopardy or risk involves a qualitative judgment. A proper case must be made out: the court will not dispossess an executor or a trustee of the trust estate in favour of a receiver on slight grounds. The testator or other creator of the trust is presumed to have known what he was about; and normally the court respects the expressed wishes as to who should administer the trust estate.

What then constitutes a proper case? The cases warrant the assertion that it should be a strong case,[5] and it must be borne in mind that receivership is a drastic and not inexpensive remedy, with the possibilities of further expensive applications to the court for directions.

Misconduct is obviously a prime ground for the appointment of a receiver where the misconduct is sufficiently grave. A strong case is necessary.[6] Where *one* of several executors or trustees is guilty of misconduct the court will not, as a general rule, appoint a receiver on the interlocutory application of the beneficiaries without the consent of all the other trustees,[7] though it seems that the court might dispense with the consent of a trustee living abroad, or one who had practically ceased to act.

On the other hand wherever all the executors or trustees are, or a sole executor or trustee is, guilty of such conduct as to endanger the property, the court will appoint a receiver.[8] Thus in *Clarke v Heathfield (No 2)*[9] trustees of a trade union who were thwarting court orders and putting union funds to the jeopardy of substantial depletion were removed and replaced by an interlocutory receiver.

If part of a trust fund has been lost, that is prima facie evidence of a breach of duty by the trustee, sufficient to justify the interference of the court by the appointment of a receiver for the purpose of preserving the remainder of the fund on the interlocutory application of a beneficiary.[10] The fact that a sole executor or trustee is under some personal disability[11] or is of such a character as is likely to lead to the jeopardy of the trust fund is sufficient ground for the appointment of a receiver, as for example if he is of violent conduct and drunken habits.[12] If the maladministration is sufficiently serious the absence of any corrupt motive is by

---

5 *Middleton v Dodswell* (1806) 13 Ves 266 (executor); *Smith v Smith* (1836) 2 Y & C Ex 353; *Bainbridge v Blair* (1835) 4 LJ Ch 207.

6 *Middleton v Dodswell* (1806) 13 Ves 266; *Browell v Reed* (1842) 1 Hare 434.

7 *Tidd v Lister* (1820) 5 Madd 429.

8 *Anon* (1806) 12 Ves 4; *Richards v Perkins* (1838) 8 LJ Ex Eq 57, 3 Y & C Ex 299; *Brooker v Brooker* (1857) 3 Sm & G 475; *Rawson v Rawson* (1864) 11 LT 595; *Harris v Harris* (1887) 56 LJ Ch 754, 35 WR 710.

9 [1985] ICR 606. An earlier ex parte appointment (ie an appointment not on notice) was upheld by the Court of Appeal: *Clarke v Heathfield* [1985] ICR 203, CA.

10 *Evans v Coventry* (1854) 5 De GM & G 911, 3 Eq Rep 545.

11 *Brooker v Brooker* (1857) 3 Sm & G 475 at 477.

12 *Everett v Prythergch* (1841) 12 Sim 363.

the by. Thus in *Whitehead v Bennett*[13] a sole trustee who had been guilty of improvident expenditure and wilful waste in converting farming lands into a race course was guilty of conduct justifying his replacement by a receiver.

The fact that executors or trustees are, or that a sole executor or trustee is, in poor circumstances, is not in itself a ground for the appointment of a receiver,[14] particularly if the testator or settlor appointed them without regard to their circumstances.[15] However, if the poverty in fact leads to the jeopardy of the assets, as for example if the sheriff seizes part of the property to satisfy a debt of the executor, the court will interfere by the appointment of a receiver.[16] The fact that a sole executor has since the testator's death had execution issued against him, and a return of nulla bona made may be a ground for the appointment of a receiver.[17]

It is not necessarily a sufficient ground for appointing a receiver that an insolvent debtor has been named as a trustee by the creator of a trust.[18] Normally, however, the insolvency of an executor or administrator is a ground for the appointment of a receiver at the instance of either beneficiaries or creditors,[19] and this is so even if the insolvency occurs before the testator's death unless it is clearly shown that the testator was well aware of the insolvency at the date of the will or deliberately refrained from altering his choice after knowledge of the true facts. The court will not infer from the mere fact of the will not having been changed after the testator became aware of his nominated executor's bankruptcy that the testator intended to entrust his estate to an insolvent executor.[20] The court may refuse to appoint a receiver on the ground of bankruptcy of an executor or trustee if the application is interlocutory and several of the persons interested in the property refuse to join in the application.[1]

It is not the practice of the court to appoint a receiver on the ground that one of several executors or trustees is out of the jurisdiction[2] though, again, such an appointment may be made with the consent of the other trustees.[3]

However the court will generally be prepared to appoint a receiver if a sole executor or trustee remains out of the jurisdiction.[4] In one old case the court made an appointment where the husband of an executrix was out of the jurisdiction, and the beneficiaries would on this account have been unable to get redress if the assets had been misappropriated by the executrix.[5]

---

13 (1845) 6 LTOS 185, 10 Jur 3; and see *Re Moxley's Goods* [1916] 2 IR 145.

14 *Hathornthwaite v Russel* (1740) 2 Atk 126, Barn Ch 334; *Knight v Duplessis* (1749) 1 Ves Sen 324; *Anon* (1806) 12 Ves 4; *Howard v Papera* (1815) 1 Madd 142; *Manners v Furze* (1847) 11 Beav 30 at 31.

15 *Hathornthwaite v Russel* (1740) 2 Atk 126, Barn Ch 334; *Howard v Papera* (1815) 1 Madd 142.

16 *Rawson v Rawson* (1864) 11 LT 595.

17 *Gawthorpe v Gawthorpe* [1878] WN 91.

18 *Stainton v Carron Co* (1854) 18 Beav 146 at 161 per Romilly MR.

19 *Re Winsmore, ex p Ellis* (1742) 1 Atk 101; *Shore v Shore* (1859) 4 Drew 501, 28 LJ Ch 940; *Re Johnson* (1866) 1 Ch App 325, 14 LT 242; *Gawthorpe v Gawthorpe* [1878] WN 91; *Re Hopkins* (1881) 19 Ch D 61, 30 WR 601, CA.

20 *Langley v Hawk* (1820) 5 Madd 46.

 1 *Smith v Smith* (1836) 2 Y & C Ex 353.

 2 *Browell v Reed* (1842) 1 Hare 434 at 435.

 3 *Tidd v Lister* (1820) 5 Madd 429.

 4 *Noad v Backhouse* (1843) 2 Y & C Ch Cas 529; *Dickins v Harris* [1866] WN 93.

 5 *Taylor v Allen* (1741) 2 Atk 213.

Another case in which the court will be prepared to step in and appoint a receiver in trust or estate matters is in the event of a dispute between trustees or executors leading to a deadlock, or to some trustees acting to the exclusion of others:[6] in such cases the trustees may be made to pay the costs of the appointment.[7]

An executor could, it is conceived, before probate obtain in the Chancery Division leave to initiate a claim against his co-executor claiming the appointment of a receiver where such co-executor has intermeddled with the estate and made preparations for sale of the assets without the consent of such executor[8] or where the assets are in the possession of the co-executor and he refuses to account for them.[9]

The court may appoint a receiver on the interlocutory application of all the beneficiaries where any of a set of trustees refuses to act.[10] But this will only be done with the consent of the remaining trustees or trustee, as the disclaimer of one does not affect the estate of the others, and it is not the practice of the court to appoint a receiver solely because one of several trustees has disclaimed or is inactive.[11] That practice yielded in *Tait v Jenkins*[12] where one of two trustees of real estate declined to act and the court appointed a receiver on behalf of the infant beneficiaries but with liberty to either of the trustees to offer himself. In *Tidd v Lister*[13] where one trustee was abroad and a second had played a minimal role in the trust the court, with the consent of a third trustee on whom the brunt of the trust administration had almost exclusively fallen, appointed a receiver on the application of the beneficiaries.

If a sole executor or trustee refuses to act[14] or fails to get the trust fund into his possession[15] the court may likewise interfere on behalf of a legatee before probate or administration in the absence of the persons with the right to take out probate or letters of administration and where there is no danger to the assets.[16]

A receiver and manager may be appointed by the court of the business of a deceased person pending the grant of probate[17] or letters of administration.[18] The purpose of an application for such an appointment is to protect assets of the estate which of their very nature require the attentions of a manager.[19] If a sole

---

6 *Wilson v Wilson* (1838) 2 Keen 249; *Bagot v Bagot* (1841) 10 LJ Ch 116; *Swale v Swale* (1856) 22 Beav 584.
7 *Wilson v Wilson* above.
8 *Re Moore's Goods* (1888) 13 PD 36, 57 LJP 37.
9 *Pemberton v McGill* (1855) 3 WR 557.
10 *Brodie v Barry* (1811) 3 Mer 695.
11 *Browell v Reed* (1842) 1 Hare 434, 11 LJ Ch 272.
12 (1842) 1 Y & C Ch Cas 492.
13 (1820) 5 Madd 429.
14 *Palmer v Wright* (1846) 10 Beav 234 at 237.
15 *Kirwan v Kirwan* (1836) Donnelly 71.
16 *Re Henderson* (1886) 2 TLR 322.
17 *Re Wenge* [1911] WN 129, 55 Sol Jo 553; *Re Oakes* [1917] 1 Ch 230; *Re Sutcliffe* [1942] Ch 453, [1942] 2 All ER 296; and see *Re Wright* (1888) 32 Sol Jo 721.
18 *Steer v Steer* (1864) 2 Drew & Sm 311, 11 LT 502; *Overington v Ward* (1865) 34 Beav 175; *Blackett v Blackett* (1871) 24 LT 276; *Re Baker* (1882) 26 Sol Jo 682.
19 That is certainly the case as regards a receiver without powers of management: *Re Parker* (1879) 12 Ch D 293, 48 LJ Ch 691; *Re Clark* [1910] WN 234.

executor dies, a receiver and manager may likewise be appointed pending a fresh grant of probate. A manager may also be appointed to manage the business of a testator pending sale in an administration action.[20] Moreover the court will fill the management gap by appointing a manager not only where there is no manager in office, but also where the person in fact entrusted with management is not, or considers himself not to be, up to the job. Thus in *Hart v Denham*[1] two out of three trustees under a will, a surgeon (the plaintiff in the action) and a warehouseman, admitted that they were not competent to manage the business of the testator, which was that of pin and needle maker. The third trustee was the testator's widow who had managed the business on her own for a while, to the dissatisfaction of the plaintiff. It was held by Sir John Romilly MR that in default of agreement as to the appointment of a manager it should be referred to chambers to appoint a proper person as receiver and manager with liberty to the widow, against whom there was no evidence of incompetence, to propose herself for the office.

The appointment of a receiver in an administration action deprives the executor of his right to take possession of the assets.[2]

TENANT FOR LIFE

Under the old law obtaining before the property legislation of 1925 a receiver could be appointed against a tenant for life of renewable leaseholds who threatened to allow the lease to expire without providing for renewal.[3] Equally a tenant for life who by refusing to produce title deeds prevented the raising of portions having priority to his life estate might have a receiver appointed against him.[4]

The tenant for life has since 1926 been under a statutory obligation to give effect to all equitable interests by mortgage or other disposition. Accordingly if he refuses or neglects or is unable to do so a vesting order transferring or creating the requisite legal estate can be obtained.[5] No doubt where the interests of the persons entitled to beneficial interests are put in peril by the failure or refusal of the tenant for life to perform his obligations a receiver may still be appointed pending the making of a vesting or other appropriate order. So a receiver will be appointed against a tenant for life who fails to apply income in keeping down incumbrances[6] or to keep leaseholds in repair according to the relevant covenants in the leases.[7]

---

20 *Re Hodges* [1899] 1 IR 480; *Ramsay v Simpson* [1899] 1 IR 194, Ir CA.

 1 [1871] WN 2.

 2 *Kirk v Houston* (1843) 5 I Eq R 498; *Minford v Carse and Hunter* [1912] 2 IR 245 at 273, Ir CA.

 3 *Bennett v Colley* (1833) 2 My & K 225, Coop temp Brough 248 (where the theoretical right to a receiver grounded a later claim to compensation).

 4 *Brigstocke v Mansel* (1818) 3 Madd 47.

 5 Settled Land Act 1925, s 16.

 6 *Giffard v Hort* (1804) 1 Sch & Lef 386 at 407; cf *Garnett's Executors v Pratt* (1833) Hayes & Jo 303 (arrears of interest during previous life tenancy).

 7 *Re Fowler* (1881) 16 Ch D 723, 44 LT 99.

Subject to certain exceptions, however, no settlement created on or after 1 January 1997 is a strict settlement and no such settlement is deemed to be made thereafter.[8]

CHARITIES

The law of receivership has impinged upon charity administration in several cases. A neglected nineteenth-century example occurred in *A-G v St Cross Hospital*.[9] An information was filed by the Attorney-General in 1849 to correct alleged abuses and praying a scheme. At the hearing in 1853 it was argued that the Earl of Guildford who had been appointed master of the foundation was not accountable for any of the rents received by him. The court was not prepared to make him account for the period prior to the filing of the information but ordered an account of rents received after the filing of the information and appointed a receiver.[10] After the appointment of a receiver a cleric who had been much concerned in the reformation of the abuses at St Cross insisted that the chapel within the hospital was part of the church of St Faith of which he was churchwarden. He was restrained by injunction from interfering with the possession of the receiver and interfering with the chaplain's performance of divine services without prejudice to his right to litigate his complaint in any court he might be advised.

A more recent example of the aptness of appointing a court receiver and manager occurred in *A-G v Schonfeld*[11] which involved a tangle of trust deeds executed by the late Dr Solomon Schonfeld. He had been the moving force in the Jewish Secondary Schools Movement which ran five schools. Litigation was started by originating summons by three persons who were or claimed to be trustees of the charity. They sought determination of two main problems: who were the trustees and by what trusts it was governed. The charity was additionally in serious financial difficulties and there were also disquieting reports of the way in which the schools for which it was responsible were being run. The Attorney-General, who was necessarily a party to the proceedings, took out a separate summons for the appointment of a receiver and manager. The purpose of the application was temporarily to put the affairs of the charity into the hands of a person responsible to the court, and thus to safeguard the assets and to protect the educational welfare of the school children.

Walton J recognising that the circumstances were extremely unusual made an order granting the application until the hearing of the main action or a further order. He also authorised the appointment of advisers, including in particular an educational adviser.

In the case of the girls' school the power of appointing a new head teacher was in the trustees and Megarry V-C held that the receiver had power to advertise a

---

8 See Trusts of Land and Appointment of Trustees Act 1996, s 2.
9 (1854) 18 Beav 601.
10 (1853) 17 Beav 435.
11 [1979] Ch Com Rep 19, paras 46–51. The case subsequently came before Whitford J who directed that the appointment of a receiver and manager should continue until a scheme was directed.

vacancy in the post of head teacher and on taking proper advice to appoint a suitable person to that post.[12] The boys' school presented a greater difficulty because it was run by foundation governors appointed by the trustees of the charity and representative governors appointed and removable by the local education authority. Megarry V-C rejected the argument that the receiver enjoyed a similar power. But the receiver's powers to manage the affairs of the charity obviously included making proper provision for what was to be done by others and thus ensuring that there were effective foundation governors able to join the representative governors in appointing a new headmaster. Accordingly the learned Vice-Chancellor was prepared to declare that the receiver had the power to remove the foundation governors and replace them and could properly exercise that power after taking advice.[13]

In *A-G v Wright*[14] a receiver and manager of a charity school was again appointed by the court and the grant of an injunction in favour of the Attorney-General was made conditional on the giving of a cross-undertaking by the receiver limited to such amount, if any, as the receiver should be entitled and able to recover by way of indemnity from the funds of the charity.

Though outside the purview of the present discussion, mention can be made here of the power statutorily conferred upon the Charity Commissioners to appoint a receiver and manager in respect of the property and affairs of a charity.[15] It is provided that where at any time after they have instituted an inquiry under s 8 of the Charities Act 1993 with respect to any charity (other than an exempt charity) the Charity Commissioners are satisfied that there is or has been any misconduct or mismanagement in the administration of the charity or alternatively that it is necessary or desirable to act for the purpose of protecting the property of the charity or securing a proper application for the purposes of the charity of that property or of property coming to the charity, they may of their own motion, inter alia, appoint a receiver and manager in respect of the property and affairs of the charity.[16] The power is a judicial power giving the Commissioners a concurrent jurisdiction with the High Court in the circumstances posited by the statutory provision.[17]

LANDLORD AND TENANT

Recent developments

In certain circumstances a tenant may be able to obtain from the court an order appointing a receiver to collect the rents and manage the demised premises

---

12 *Re Jewish Secondary Schools Movement Trusts* (24 October 1979, unreported) referred to in *A-G v Schonfeld* [1980] 1 WLR 1182 at 1186C–D.
13 *A-G v Schonfeld* [1980] 1 WLR 1182; see finally [1982] Ch Com Rep 44–45, paras 1–3.
14 [1987] 3 All ER 579, [1988] 1 WLR 164.
15 See Charitites Act 1993, s 18(1(vii), 19(2) and (3). See also the Charities (Receiver and Manager) Regulations 1992, SI 1992/2355.
16 Charities Act 1993, s 18(1)(vii).
17 For further discussion of the ambit of this power and jurisdiction, see Picarda *Law and Practice Relating to Charities* (3rd edn, 1999) 592–593, 595–596; and for a recent case see *Weth v A-G* [1999] 1 WLR 686, CA.

pending trial.[18] This is done on the usual basis that the High Court may by order (whether interlocutory or final) appoint a receiver in all cases in which it appears to the court to be just and convenient to do so.[19] There are several cases in which such an application has been successfully made. But it is important to note that there is now also a special statutory code which, in certain cases, displaces the court's jurisdiction under the Supreme Court Act 1981, substituting for that jurisdiction a jurisdiction to appoint a manager under the Landlord and Tenant Act 1987.

All the cases which have arisen so far have been cases involving blocks of flats where the landlord has been in breach of covenant and in consequence the building has fallen into disrepair.[20] The statutory code is expressly directed to cases where the premises consist of the whole or part of a building if the building or part contains two or more flats.

A receiver may be appointed where the property is in effect abandoned by the lessor[1] or where he is only carrying out some of his duties.[2] In the case of disrepair, the usual reason for applying for a receivership, the nature of the works, the need for them, the probability of their being done and the objection to doing them, will all be factors to be taken into consideration.[3] Indeed, if the income or any other property or money to be put under the control of the receiver is plainly inadequate to meet the cost of repair the receivership is likely to prove ineffective and may even frustrate the carrying out of repairs that the landlord is willing to do.[4] For that reason a receiver ought not to take office unless he is satisfied that the assets of which he is appointed receiver will be adequate to meet his remuneration or that his remuneration will be covered by an enforceable indemnity by a party to the litigation.[5]

The statutory code to which reference has already been made is contained in Part II of the Landlord and Tenant Act 1987. The relevant provisions are set out in ss 21 to 24 of the 1987 Act. Their general effect is to confer in certain circumstances upon the tenant of a flat the right to apply to the court for the appointment of a manager to act in relation to the premises in which the flat is contained.

A manager may be appointed by the court where the premises consist of the whole or part of a building if the building or part contains two or more flats.[6] But the statutory case does not apply to any such premises at a time when:

---

18 Such order can be registered in the register of writs and orders, or if the land is registered land protected by a caution: *Clayhope Properties Ltd v Evans* [1986] 2 All ER 795, [1986] 1 WLR 1223, CA.

19 Supreme Court Act 1981, s 37(1).

20 See also *Parker v Camden London Borough Council* [1986] Ch 162, [1985] 2 All ER 141, CA and *Newman v Camden London Borough Council* [1986] Ch 162, [1985] 2 All ER 141, CA.

 1 *Hart v Emelkirk Ltd* [1983] 3 All ER 15, [1983] 1 WLR 1289 (landlords not collecting rents and not complying with their insurance covenants).

 2 *Daiches v Bluelake Investments Ltd* (1985) 51 P & CR 51 (landlord not carrying out major repairs but fulfilling some duties).

 3 *Daiches v Bluelake Investments Ltd* (1985) 51 P & CR 51; and see *Blawdziewicz v Diadon Establishment* [1988] 35 EG 83 (construction of penthouse apartments by landlord overlapped with repairs required by tenant).

 4 *Evans v Clayhope Properties Ltd* [1987] 1 WLR 225 at 230G–231B per Vinelott J.

 5 *Evans v Clayhope Properties Ltd* [1988] 1 All ER 444, [1988] 1 WLR 358, CA, affirming [1987] 2 All ER 40, [1987] 1 WLR 225.

 6 LTA 1987, s 21(2). For the definition of 'flat', see LTA 1987, s 60(1).

(a)   the interest of the landlord in the premises is held by an exempt landlord[7] or a resident landlord;[8] or

(b)   the premises are included within the functional land of any charity.[9]

Moreover the term 'tenant' does not include references to a tenant under a tenancy to which Part II of the Landlord and Tenant Act 1954 applies.[10] On the other hand, where the statutory code applies, it ousts any other jurisdiction the court has to appoint a receiver and manager.[11]

VENDOR AND PURCHASER

In an action by a vendor for specific performance of a contract for sale where the purchase money is unpaid and the purchaser has gone into possession, a receiver may be appointed on the application of the vendor pending a reference as to title where the property requires expenditure and attention.[12]

A receiver ought also to be appointed on the vendor's application where there is evidence that the purchaser in possession is insolvent and has tried to dispose of the property,[13] or is using the property in a way inconsistent with its ordinary usage or contrary to the usual course of husbandry,[14] or is putting the property in jeopardy.[15]

The fact that the property is partly in the possession of the vendor and partly in that of the purchaser, will not prevent the court making an appointment.[16]

If a vendor succeeds at the trial, but the purchaser, who is in possession of the property, appeals, the vendor will be entitled to a receiver pending the appeal, if the property is such as requires to be kept as a going concern, for example a farm or business.[17]

As an unpaid vendor is in the position of an equitable incumbrancer he is, apart from any action for specific performance, entitled to the appointment of a receiver if the purchaser is in possession, and there is danger to the property.[18]

Where a purchaser has been discharged by the court from his bargain because of the inability of the vendor to make a title, the purchaser may secure the

---

7   Exempt landlords are defined in LTA 1987, ss 60 and 58(1). They include various councils, development organisations the Housing Corporation and charitable housing trusts and certain defined housing associations.

8   A resident landlord is one with his principal or only residence in the block which must not be purpose built: LTA 1987, ss 60 and 58(2).

9   LTA 1987, s 21(3). The functional land of a charity is that land which it occupies for its very charitable activity: see Charities Act 1960, 529 (repealed).

10 LTA 1987, s 21(7).

11 LTA 1987, s 21(6).

12 *Boehm v Wood* (1820) 2 Jac & W 236.

13 *Hall v Jenkinson* (1813) 2 Ves & B 125.

14 *Osborne v Harvey* (1841) 1 Y & C Ch Cas 116.

15 *Taylor v Eckersley* (1876) 2 Ch D 302, CA.

16 *Hall v Jenkinson* supra.

17 *Hyde v Warden* (1876) 1 Ex D 309, CA.

18 *Boyle v Bettws Llantwit Colliery Co* (1876) 2 Ch D 726, 45 LJ Ch 748.

appointment of a receiver of the rents of the property in order to satisfy his costs and expenses out of those rents should there be no money in court out of which they can be paid.[19]

A railway company, which has contracted to buy land, will in an action for specific performance by the vendor be treated like any other purchaser in regard to the appointment of a receiver,[20] except that in such a case a receiver will not be appointed on an interlocutory application, even if the company admits liability.[1]

If a vendor brings an action against a purchaser to have the transaction between them set aside on the ground of fraud or misrepresentation, and the purchaser is in possession, the court will not, as a general rule, appoint a receiver of the property on an application of the vendor until the transaction has actually been set aside by the court, unless it is clearly shown that the property is likely to perish from the neglect or misconduct of the defendant.[2] Nevertheless in such a case a receiver may be appointed before the transaction is set aside if it is necessary for the preservation of the property, for example if there is a danger of leasehold property being forfeited owing to non-payment of rent.[3]

DISPUTED TITLE

Formerly in cases of disputed title to land, equity would not as a rule, interfere with the party in possession by appointing a receiver unless his title was obviously defective[4] or was affected by some equity,[5] or the rents were in danger of being lost[6] or the property was in danger of destruction.[7] Now, however, the court will entertain an interlocutory application for a receiver by a person asserting a purely legal title and a receiver may be appointed if the court takes the view

19 *Hill v Kirwan* (1824) 1 Hog 175.
20 *Cosens v Bognor Rly Co* (1866) 1 Ch App 594; *Bishop of Winchester v Mid-Hants Rly Co* (1867) LR 5 Eq 17; *Munns v Isle of Wight Rly Co* (1870) 5 Ch App 414.
 1 *Pell v Northampton and Banbury Junction Rly Co* (1866) 2 Ch App 100; *Latimer v Aylesbury and Buckingham Rly Co* (1878) 9 Ch D 385, 39 LT 460, CA.
 2 *George v Evans* (1840) 4 Y & C Ex 211.
 3 *Cook v Andrews* [1897] 1 Ch 266.
 4 *Metcalfe v Pulvertoft* (1812) 1 Ves & B 180; *Earl of Fingal v Blake* (1828) 1 Mol 113; subsequent proceedings (1828) 2 Mol 50.
 5 *Stitwell v Williams* (1821) 6 Madd 49, Jac 280; *Podmore v Gunning* (1832) 5 Sim 485; *Clegg v Fishwick* (1849) 1 Mac & G 294, 19 LJ Ch 49. See also *Bainbrigge v Baddeley* (1851) 13 Beav 355 at 361 per Lord Langdale MR; *Berry v Keen* (1882) 51 LJ Ch 912, CA.
 6 *Mordaunt v Hooper* (1756) Amb 311; and see also *Knight v Duplessis* (1749) 1 Ves Sen 324; *Clark v Dew* (1829) 1 Russ & M 103; *Lloyd v Lord Trimleston* (1829) 2 Mol 81; *Lancashire v Lancashire* (1845) 9 Beav 120, 15 LJ Ch 54.
 7 See generally, *Ridgway v Roberts* (1844) 4 Hare 106 (disputed title to ship); *Dobbin v Adams* (1845) 8 I Eq R 157; *Fetherstone v Mitchell* (1846) 9 I Eq R 480; *Bainbrigge v Baddeley* (1851) 3 Mac & G 413, 13 Beav 355; *Earl Talbot v Hope Scott* (1858) 4 K & J 96; *Campbell v Campbell* (1864) 4 Macq 711, HL; *Carrow v Ferrior, Dunn v Ferrior* (1868) 3 Ch App 719, 37 LJ Ch 569; *Hitchen v Birks* (1870) LR 10 Eq 471, 23 LT 335; *Parkin v Seddons* (1873) LR 16 Eq 34.

that the plaintiff will probably succeed at the hearing and that, in all the circumstances of the case, the appointment is just and convenient.[8]

In an action for recovery of land, the jurisdiction is exercised with great caution, and if the defendant is in occupation the court will only appoint a receiver in special circumstances: otherwise the substantive issue might in effect be determined by evidence of a kind only admissible on interlocutory application. Thus in one case the fact that the defendant who was in occupation could show only a shadowy title and was without means was held by the Court of Appeal an insufficient reason for exercising the court's discretion to appoint a receiver.[9] Moreover a defendant in such an action may be deprived of the privilege of relying on his occupation without disclosing his title.[10]

The court will consider the length of the defendant's possession[11] and the position of the tenants, who might be called upon to pay their rents over again if the party in possession were not solvent.[12] Similarly, a landlord suing to recover possession of demised premises for breach of covenant may secure the appointment of a receiver of the rents and profits pending trial if he shows a probability of success at the hearing and that the appointment is necessary to preserve the property, for example where there are licences which are endangered.[13]

The title in dispute may be as to goods. In one case an owner sued for the return of goods from a banker who claimed a lien and a receiver was appointed who was empowered to allow the owner to use the goods.[14]

COMPANIES

The appointment by the court of a receiver and manager of the assets and undertaking of a company was in the past often made on an application of a debenture holder.[15] Nowadays, however, the provisions of debentures confer such ample powers upon the debenture holder that a curial appointment will normally not be needed: the receiver appointed out of court can equally well protect the debenture holder's interest. Only if there is some inadequacy in the debenture provisions or there is need for a remedy backed-up by committal powers is it in practice necessary to apply to the court for a receiver. An example of this is where the security is in jeopardy and although the power to appoint a receiver

---

8 *Crane v Jullion* (1876) 2 Ch D 220; *Real and Personal Advance Co v McCarthy and Smith* (1879) 40 LT 878; *Berry v Keen* (1882) 51 LJ Ch 912, CA; *John v John* [1898] 2 Ch 573, CA (distinguishing *Foxwell v Van Grutten* [1897] 1 Ch 64, CA.)
9 *Marshall v Charteris* [1920] 1 Ch 520, CA.
10 *John v John* [1898] 2 Ch 573 at 580, CA.
11 *John v John* [1898] 2 Ch 573, CA; and see also *Jones v Jones* (1817) 3 Mer 161.
12 *John v John* [1898] 2 Ch 573, CA; and see also *Hitchen v Birks* (1870) LR 10 Eq 471, 23 LT 355.
13 *Gwatkin v Bird* (1882) 52 LJQB 263, DC; *Charrington & Co Ltd v Camp* [1902] 1 Ch 386; *Leney & Sons Ltd v Callingham and Thompson* [1908] 1 KB 79, CA.
14 *Hatton v Car Maintenance Co Ltd* [1915] 1 Ch 621; and see *Doulton Potteries Ltd v Bronotte* [1971] 1 NSWLR 591 at 599.
15 *Moss Steamship Co Ltd v Whinney* [1912] AC 254, HL; *Parsons v Sovereign Bank of Canada* [1913] AC 160, PC.

has been reserved it has not yet become exercisable.[16] Such jeopardy might be constituted by a threat by the company that it will distribute all its assets among its shareholders[17] or by the fact that it has ceased to be a going concern.[18] But it is not enough that the security is insufficient.[19]

But the court has been prepared to appoint a receiver and manager of a company's assets and undertaking in a minority shareholders' action where the complaint was that the majority were conducting the business of the company in a prejudicial manner. This happened in the Australian case of *Duffy v Super Centre Development Corpn Ltd*[20] where a receiver was given very wide powers to manage the business. In that capacity the receiver was fulfilling the function of preserving the company's business so that eventually it could be taken over again by the board of directors.

An appointment may also be made by the court on the application of shareholders or indeed of the company itself where for instance there is no governing body, or there are such disputes between the directors that the management is paralysed.[1]

EQUITABLE EXECUTION

In certain cases the court can appoint a receiver as a method of enforcing a judgment or order. Such a receiver is frequently referred to as a receiver by way of equitable execution.[2]

The process of so-called[3] equitable execution was devised by the old Court of Chancery prior to the Judicature Acts. The principle underlying the process is that equity will not suffer a wrong to be without a remedy. From early times equity would step in to give equitable relief to judgment creditors who were unable to reap the fruits of their judgment by taking out execution at law. Originally, perhaps, the relief was confined to setting aside conveyances made by debtors for the purpose of putting their property out of a creditor's reach.[4] But it was soon extended to all cases where the debtor had an equitable interest which (if it had been legal) could have been touched at law.[5]

---

16 *McMahon v North Kent Ironworks Co* [1891] 2 Ch 148.
17 *Re Tilt Cover Copper Co Ltd* [1913] 2 Ch 588.
18 *Hubbuck v Helms* (1887) 56 LJ Ch 536, 56 LT 232.
19 *Re New York Taxicab Co Ltd* [1913] 1 Ch 1.
20 [1967] 1 NSWR 382.
 1 *Trade Auxiliary Co v Vickers* (1873) LR 16 Eq 298; *Stanfield v Gibbon* [1925] WN 11. For a recent example see, *Re a Company (No 00596 of 1986)* (1986) 2 BCC 99, 063 (petition for relief based on unfair prejudice).
 2 The best modern survey of the English law is, paradoxically, a Canadian work, CRB Dunlop *Creditor Debtor Law in Canada* (1981) 277–306; see also M Cababe *Attachment of Debts and Equitable Execution* (1888, 2nd edn); *Attachments Receivers and Charging Orders* (1900, 3rd edn).
 3 The expression has been called a misnomer: see *Re Shephard* (1889) 43 Ch D 131 at 138, CA.
 4 *Smithier v Lewis* (1686) 1 Vern 398; *Higgins v York Buildings Co* (1740) 2 Atk 107; *Stileman v Ashdown* (1742) 2 Atk 477.
 5 *Balch v Wastall* (1718) 1 P Wms 445; *Shirley v Watts* (1744) 3 Atk 200.

In the leading case of *Re Shephard*[6] Cotton LJ defines a receivership of this kind as 'a taking out of the way a hindrance which prevents execution at common law'. By 'hindrance' in this context the learned Lord Justice meant hindrance arising from the nature of the property. The point was made more clearly in the same case by Fry LJ when he said,[7] in relation to the old law prior to the Judicature Acts:

'A receiver was appointed by the Court of Chancery in aid of a judgment at law when the plaintiff shewed that he had sued out the proper writ of execution, and was met by certain difficulties arising from the nature of the property which prevented his obtaining possession at law, and in these circumstances only did the Court of Chancery interfere in aid of a legal judgment for a legal debt.'

An even more explicit statement is to be found in *Holmes v Millage*,[8] another decision of the Court of Appeal, where Lindley LJ declared the judgment of the two members sitting. The defendant who had no assets in this country was a foreign correspondent for a London morning newspaper living in Paris and was paid a weekly salary through bankers in Paris. Garnishee proceedings failed because no weekly payments were in arrear. Next the plaintiff applied at Chambers for the appointment of a receiver of the defendant's salary by way of equitable execution. The judge dismissed the application; the Divisional Court reversed that decision and appointed a receiver; the Court of Appeal in turn reversed the decision of the Divisional Court. Lindley LJ said:[9]

'The only cases of this kind in which courts of equity ever interfered were cases in which the judgment debtor had an equitable interest in property which could have been reached at law, if he had had the legal interest in it, instead of an equitable interest only. . . . It is an old mistake to suppose that because there is no effectual remedy at law, there must be one in equity.'

The old Court of Chancery had no jurisdiction to prevent a man from earning his living or from receiving his earnings, unless he had himself assigned or charged them. The position under the Judicature Act was the same: that Act did not give power to appoint a receiver where the Courts of Equity could not appoint one before.[9] It follows that the court has no jurisdiction to appoint a receiver simply because, under the circumstances of the case it would be a more convenient mode of obtaining satisfaction of a judgment than the usual modes of execution. But there are references in the cases[10] to the possible availability of receivership where there are special circumstances. Those circumstances must, however, be such circumstances as would have enabled the Court of Chancery before the Judicature Acts to have interfered by way of injunction or receiver at the suit of the judgment creditor.[11]

6 (1889) 43 Ch D 131 at 135–136, CA.
7 (1889) 43 Ch D 131 at 138.
8 [1893] 1 QB 551.
9 [1893] 1 QB 551 at 555; and see *Salt v Cooper* (1880) 16 Ch D 544, CA.
10 Eg *Harris v Beauchamp Bros* [1894] 1 QB 801, CA.
11 See *Manchester and Liverpool District Banking Co v Parkinson* (1888) 22 QBD 173, CA; *Harris v Beauchamp Bros* [1894] 1 QB 801, CA.

The principles of 'equitable execution' have been affected by statute. The Judicature Acts put an end to the Chancery monopoly of the remedy and simplified the procedure.[12] The Administration of Justice Act 1956 extended the power of the Court to appoint a receiver by way of equitable execution so as to operate in relation to all legal estates and interests in land. And the provisions of the 1956 Act extending the ambit of equitable execution have themselves been further supplemented by the Charging Orders Act 1979.

The Judicature Act 1873 conferred jurisdiction on all divisions of the High Court to grant injunctive relief or to appoint a receiver in all cases in which it appeared just and convenient to do so,[13] and a similar jurisdiction was conferred on the county court.[14] At first blush the wording of the relevant provision, s 25(8), which says that an injunction may be granted or a receiver may be appointed 'by an interlocutory order of the court in all cases in which it shall appear to the court to be just or convenient that such an order should be made' appears to be so wide as to give the court power to do what neither a Court of Law nor a Court of Equity could have done before the Act.[15] In *North London Rly Co v Great Northern Rly Co*[16] it was decided that the phrase 'just or convenient' did *not* justify the granting of an injunction in a case in which no injunction could be granted by any court before the Judicature Acts came into operation. In *Holmes v Millage*[17] Lindley LJ said that the same reasoning obviously applied to the appointment of receivers as well as to the grant of injunctions and continued:[18]

> 'Although injunctions are granted and receivers are appointed more readily than they were before the passing of the Judicature Acts, and some inconvenient rules formerly observed have been very properly relaxed, yet the principles upon which the jurisdiction of the Court of Chancery rested have not been changed.'

Many other cases decided before the Administration of Justice Act 1956 came into force underline the principle that as a general rule a receiver by way of equitable execution would only be appointed in such circumstances as would have enabled the Court of Chancery before the Judicature Acts to have interfered by way of injunction or receiver at the suit of a judgment creditor.[19]

An important feature of the pre-1873 process was eliminated. The courts no longer required the creditor to go through the motions of levying an execution at law if it could be shown that to do so would simply be a waste of time.[20]

---

12 *Morgan v Hart* [1914] 2 KB 183 at 191, CA.
13 Judicature Act 1873, s 25(8).
14 Judicature Act 1873, s 83.
15 See *Manchester and Liverpool District Banking Co v Parkinson* (1888) 22 QBD 173 at 175, CA per Lord Esher MR citing *Smith v Cowell* (1880) 6 QBD 75, CA and see the dissenting judgment of Fletcher Moulton LJ in *Edwards & Co v Picard* [1909] 2 KB 903 at 908, CA.
16 (1883) 11 QBD 30, CA.
17 [1893] 1 QB 551.
18 [1893] 1 QB 551 at 557.
19 *Aslatt v Southampton Corpn* (1880) 16 Ch D 143 at 148; *Manchester and Liverpool District Banking Co v Parkinson* (1888) 22 QBD 173, CA; *Harris v Beauchamp Bros* [1894] 1 QB 801, CA; *Cadogan v Lyric Theatre Ltd* [1894] 3 Ch 338, CA; *Edwards & Co v Picard* [1909] 2 KB 903, CA (Fletcher Moulton LJ dissenting); *Morgan v Hart* [1914] 2 KB 183, CA.
20 *Anglo-Italian Bank v Davies* (1878) 9 Ch D 275 at 285; *Re Whiteley* (1887) 56 LT 846.

The most recent review of equitable execution was made by Millett J in *Maclaine Watson & Co Ltd v International Tin Council.*[1] In that case it was held that a receiver by way of equitable execution would not be appointed to enforce an award and judgment against the International Tin Council ('ITC'). This was because the rights of indemnity or contribution assumed to be exercisable against the states comprising its membership were not justiciable in the English courts, being founded on the interpretation of the construction of a treaty between sovereign states: it followed that, so far as they were assets of ITC, they were not susceptible to equitable execution.

It was submitted that the court had no jurisdiction to appoint such a receiver except where the interest of the judgment debtor in the alleged asset is an equitable interest only which, if it had been a legal interest, could have been reached by execution at law. This was inconsistent with *Bourne v Colodense Ltd*[2] where the debtor's asset was a *legal* chose in action, namely a claim to be indemnified on demand, and a receiver was appointed. Execution at law was not available, since a claim to be indemnified is not an attachable debt and cannot be made the subject of a garnishee order.[3] The difficulty was overcome by the appointment of a receiver. So the asset does not have to be an equitable interest.

MORTGAGES

Before the Judicature Act 1873 the court would not, as a general rule, appoint a receiver in favour of a legal mortgagee.[4] The rationale of this general disinclination of the court to intervene was that it was always open to a legal mortgagee to take possession under his legal title.[5] The court would, however, exceptionally grant receivership relief if the security was in jeopardy.[6] Likewise if there was anything which prevented the mortgagee from availing himself of his legal remedy the court would appoint a receiver for him.[7] For the same reason namely that no legal remedy was open to him, the court would appoint a receiver for an equitable mortgagee[8] or for the owner of an equitable rent charge.[9] So too where the remedy of distress or other legal remedy given to the owner of an annuity or rent charge could not effectively be used, the court would appoint a receiver.[10] Where on the other hand the owner of an annuity or rent charge charged on

1 [1988] Ch 1, [1987] 3 All ER 787; affd [1989] Ch 253, [1989] 3 All ER 523, HL.
2 [1985] ICR 291; see also *Goldschmidt v Oberrheinische Metallwerke* [1906] 1 KB 373 at 375.
3 *Johnson v Diamond* (1855) 11 Exch 73.
4 *Berney v Sewell* (1820) 1 Jac & W 647; *Ackland v Gravener* (1862) 31 Beav 482 at 484; *Sollory v Leaver* (1869) LR 9 Eq 22; *Re Pope* (1886) 17 QBD 743 at 749, CA; *Re Prytherch* (1889) 42 Ch D 590 at 600.
5 See the cases cited in the previous footnote.
6 *Stevens v Lord* (1838) 2 Jur 92.
7 *Ackland v Gravener* (1862) 31 Beav 482.
8 *Metcalfe v Archbishop of York* (1836) 1 My & Cr 547 at 558; *Re Pope* (1886) 17 QBD 743 at 749, CA.
9 *Pritchard v Fleetwood* (1815) 1 Mer 54.
10 *Cupit v Jackson* (1824) M'Cle 495, 13 Price 721; *Shee v Harris* (1844) 1 Jo & Lat 91; *White v Smale* (1856) 22 Beav 72.

property had either by statute or under an express power an effective remedy by way of distress the court would not appoint a receiver.[11] And the mere fact that the tenants of mortgaged property were numerous and the rents difficult to collect would not induce the court to appoint a receiver on behalf of a legal mortgagee.[12]

With the enactment of the Judicature Act 1873,[13] and in the case of Ireland of the Judicature (Ireland) Act 1877,[14] legal mortgagees were placed on the same footing as equitable mortgagees. Accordingly the court can appoint a receiver on the application of a legal as well as of an equitable mortgagee[15] and can take that course where the mortgage includes both legal estates and equitable interests.[16]

Since the Judicature Act 1873 (replaced successively by the Supreme Court of Judicature (Consolidation) Act 1925 and the Supreme Court Act 1981) the court has been empowered to grant a receiver by interlocutory orders whenever it should appear just or convenient to do so.[17] The effect of this enlargement of jurisdiction was considered in the context of mortgages by the Court of Appeal in *Re Pope*[18] where it was held that a receiver could now be appointed by the court at the instance of a legal mortgagee in the same way as at the instance of an equitable mortgagee. The court is prepared to take this course because although a legal mortgagee has power to take possession yet there are obvious conveniences in appointing a receiver, not the least of which is the avoidance of the invidious consequences of being a mortgagee in possession. Accordingly the mortgagee may apply for the appointment of a receiver wherever the mortgagor breaks any of his obligations whether it be his covenant to pay principal[19] or interest[20] (even though the mortgagee may have covenanted not to call in his loan until some future date)[1] or some other covenant.[2] The court will grant relief if a relevant default is established at the hearing even if there was no evidence of default when the proceedings were started.[3]

In practice occasions for the exercise of the court's jurisdiction to appoint a receiver at the instance of a mortgagee are relatively rare. Most company charges confer an express power to appoint a receiver and manager with powers of

11 *Sollory v Leaver* (1869) LR 9 Eq 22; *Kelsey v Kelsey* (1874) LR 17 Eq 495, 30 LT 82.
12 *Sturch v Young* (1842) 5 Beav 557.
13 Judicature Act 1873, s 25(8) now re-enacted in Supreme Court Act 1981, s 37.
14 Judicature (Ireland) Act 1877, s 28(8).
15 *Truman & Co v Redgrave* (1881) 18 Ch D 547; *Tillett v Nixon* (1883) 25 Ch D 238; *Re Pope* (1886) 17 QBD 743 at 749, CA; *Re Whiteley* (1887) 56 LT 846 at 847; *Duke of Grafton v Taylor* (1891) 7 TLR 588. For Irish cases, see *Church Temporalities Comrs of Ireland v Harrington* (1883) 11 LR Ir 127; *Kenealy v O'Keeffe* (1900) 34 ILTR 75; *McCausland v O'Callaghan* (1903) 3 NIJR 144; *Langdale Chemical Manure Co v Ginty* (1907) 41 ILTR 40; *Butler v Butler* [1925] 1 IR 185; *National Bank Ltd v Barry* (1966) 100 ILT 185.
16 *Pease v Fletcher* (1875) 1 Ch D 273.
17 Judicature Act 1873, s 25(8).
18 (1886) 17 QBD 743 at 749 per Cotton LJ; and see *Tillett v Nixon* (1883) 25 Ch D 238.
19 *Curling v Marquis of Townshend* (1816) 19 Ves 628 at 633; *Hopkins v Worcester and Birmingham Canal Proprietors* (1868) LR 6 Eq 437.
20 *Bissill v Bradford Tramways Co Ltd* [1891] WN 51; *Strong v Carlyle Press* [1893] 1 Ch 268, CA.
 1 *Burrowes v Molloy* (1845) 2 Jo & Lat 521, 8 I Eq R 482.
 2 *Free v Hinde* (1827) 2 Sim 7 (covenant to disentail); and see *Leney & Sons Ltd v Callingham* [1908] 1 KB 79, CA.
 3 *Re New Publishing Co Ltd* (1897) 41 Sol Jo 839; *Re Carshalton Park Estate Ltd* [1908] 2 Ch 62.

management which are certainly as wide as if not wider than those which a court would grant; and the power is, in general, exercisable not merely in cases where there is some default in the payment or principal or interest but also on the happening of a comprehensive series of events which might endanger the security. In the case of legal and equitable mortgages the majority are effected by deed and so incorporate the statutory power and often an express wider power too. But the curial remedy still retains a useful place in some situations. Chief of these is where the security is in jeopardy but the express or statutorily implied power of appointment is not yet exercisable. Another situation for a court appointment is where, despite the availability of an express or implied power, the receiver appointed pursuant to the power would not have sufficiently wide powers: a case in point is where the mortgage includes a business, and the only power is the statutory power, which carries no powers of management.

In extreme cases of mismanagement a receiver may even be appointed against a mortgagee in possession on the application of the mortgagor. There is no authority precisely in point but the suggestion is canvassed in an Australian case. In *Hayward v Martin*,[4] a decision in the Victoria Supreme Court, Molesworth J said that where a mortgagee in possession is charged with mismanaging the estate the court, although having, it would seem, the power in extreme cases, will not appoint a receiver so long as there is a margin of debt to protect the mortgagor. Usually there is a sufficient remedy in the taking of accounts where the mortgagee may be charged with wilful default. But if the mortgagor could establish a real risk that his right to an account would in the circumstances be fruitless presumably a receiver could be appointed.

The fact that mortgages are created under the provisions of a statute which expressly provides for the appointment of a receiver otherwise than with the help of the court does not prevent a court appointment.[5] Similarly the fact that the mortgagee has either an express or a statutory power himself to appoint a receiver does not inhibit the court from making an appointment on the mortgagee's application even if he has already appointed a receiver under such power.[6] Indeed where foreclosure proceedings are pending the court considers it more desirable that a receiver should be appointed by the court than by the mortgagee.[7] The court will not, as a rule, assist a mortgagee in possession to get rid of his liabilities by appointing a receiver.[8] But this disinclination is not a matter of law, simply one of discretion, and the court may come to the conclusion that the appointment of a receiver is just and convenient.[9] The court will be especially inclined to appoint a receiver at the instance of a mortgagee who has

---

4 (1883) 9 VLR (E) 143.

5 *Fripp v Chard Rly Co* (1853) 11 Hare 241, 2 LJ Ch 1084.

6 *Bord v Tollemache* (1862) 1 New Rep 177, 7 LT 526; *Re Prytherch* (1889) 42 Ch D 590; *McMahon v North Kent Ironworks Co* [1891] 2 Ch 148; *County of Gloucester Bank v Rudry Merthyr Steam and House Coal Colliery Co* [1895] 1 Ch 629, CA.

7 *Tillett v Nixon* (1883) 25 Ch D 238.

8 *Re Prytherch* (1889) 42 Ch D 590; *County of Gloucester Bank v Rudry Merthyr Steam and House Coal Colliery Co* [1895] 1 Ch 629, CA.

9 *County of Gloucester Bank v Rudry Merthyr Steam and House Coal Colliery Co* [1895] 1 Ch 629, CA.

gone into possession if the action is one for foreclosure and the costs of the receiver will consequently fall upon the mortgagee.[10]

The question of appointment is however in the discretion of the court and a mortgagee is not entitled to such an appointment as of right.[11] The principles on which the court exercises its jurisdiction are well defined. Save in very special cases the court will not make an appointment unless an action is pending.[12] For this purpose proceedings on an originating summons constitute an action.[13] Once an action is pending it is desirable that any appointment should be made by the court and not by the mortgagee pursuant any power which he may have.[14]

Default on the part of the mortgagor is not the only handle to an application for a receiver. If the security is in jeopardy the court will appoint a receiver on the application of a mortgagee[15] even though the principal money may not have become due and no interest is in arrear and there is no breach of contract.[16] The cases which illustrate this point are mostly cases where the charge in question is a company charge and the application is by a debenture holder.[17] That was the position in *McMahon v North Kent Ironworks Co*[18] where on the unopposed application of a debenture holder alleging jeopardy Kekewich J appointed a receiver and said:[19] 'As a matter of principle a mortgagee has a right to the protection of his security if it is in jeopardy'. Conversely, in the absence of jeopardy and of default the consent of the mortgagor is not sufficient to induce the court to appoint a receiver.[20]

The position prior to the Judicature Act 1873 was, as has already been mentioned, that an equitable mortgagee[1] or chargee[2] was, as a rule, entitled to a receiver provided that the court was satisfied of the equitable right in the applicant.[3] The position in Ireland prior to the Judicature (Ireland) Act 1877 was the same.[4] The applicant had therefore to make out a prima facie case of an equitable mortgage or charge, prove that money was due thereon, and bring an

---

10 *Tillett v Nixon* (1883) 25 Ch D 238; *Mason v Westoby* (1886) 32 Ch D 206; *Re Prytherch* (1889) 42 Ch D 590 at 601.

11 *Re Prytherch* (1889) 42 Ch D 590.

12 For example the mental disorder of the mortgagee.

13 *Ex p Mountfort* (1809) 15 Ves 445; *Taylor v Emerson* (1843) 6 I Eq R 224; and see *Gasson and Hallagan Ltd v Jell* [1940] Ch 248.

14 *Re Fawsitt* (1885) 30 Ch D 231, CA.

15 *Duke of Grafton v Taylor* (1891) 7 TLR 588.

16 *Wildy v Mid-Hants Rly Co* (1868) 18 LT 73, 16 WR 409; *Re London Pressed Hinge Co Ltd* [1905] 1 Ch 576.

17 See further at p 394 below.

18 [1891] 2 Ch 148.

19 [1891] 2 Ch 148 at 150.

20 *Re London Pressed Hinge Co Ltd* [1905] 1 Ch 576 at 583.

1 *Shakel v Duke of Marlborough* (1819) 4 Madd 463 (agreement for mortgage); *Berney v Sewell* (1820) 1 Jac & W 647; *Sollory v Leaver* (1869) LR 9 Eq 22; *Coulthurst v Smith* (1873) 29 LT 714.

2 *Curling v Marquis of Townshend* (1816) 19 Ves 628; *Tanfield v Irvine* (1826) 2 Russ 149; *Metcalfe v Archbishop of York* (1836) 1 My & Cr 547 at 558.

3 *Davis v Duke of Marlborough* (1819) 2 Swan 108 at 138; *Greville v Fleming* (1845) 2 Jo & Lat 335.

4 *Marchioness of Downshire v Tyrrell* (1831) Hayes 354; *Weldon v O'Reilly* (1841) Fl & K 320; *Barker v Rowe* (1842) Long & T 655.

action inter alia to enforce the security.[5] A mortgagee by deposit of title deeds was entitled, like any other equitable mortgagee, to the appointment of a receiver[6] and the mere possession of the deeds by the applicant was (and is) sufficient to enable the court to appoint on an interlocutory application.[7]

Where there are two or more mortgagees subsequent mortgagees may obtain the appointment of a receiver but such appointment will be made without prejudice to the right of the prior mortgagees to take possession.[8] The words usually inserted in an order which also reserves the rights of prior mortgagees are 'without prejudice to the rights of prior incumbrancers who may think fit to take possession by virtue of their respective securities'.[9] If the order contains no such reservation, prior mortgagees cannot interfere with a court-appointed receiver without first applying to the court, for the receiver is an officer of the court.[10]

If a prior mortgagee is in possession the court will not in general on the application of a subsequent mortgagee or other creditor appoint a receiver so long as anything remains due to the prior mortgagee, unless the latter refuses to accept what he alleges to be due.[11] To avoid the appointment being made he must be able to swear that something, however small the amount, is due to him and then the court will not interfere with his possession;[12] but that rule will not be able to prevail in a case where the conduct of the mortgagee himself has made it impossible for any person to ascertain whether anything is due to him or not.[13] A prior mortgagee must, it seems, swear that some *definite* sum is due: a statement on oath that he believes that when accounts are taken it will be found that a large sum remains due to him will not be enough to stave off the appointment of a receiver.[14] Time may be given to a mortgagee whose accounts are in a mess to make an affidavit of the debt.[15] Once a definite sum is sworn to, the court will not try the matter on affidavit.[16]

Where no prior mortgagee is in possession the court may on the application of a subsequent mortgagee appoint a receiver without prejudice to the rights of that prior mortgagee.[17] The receivership order may in such a case recite that it is 'without prejudice to the rights of any prior incumbrancers'.[18] An up-to-date

5 *Union Bank of Canada v Engen* [1917] 2 WWR 395 (Can).
6 *Aberdeen v Chitty* (1839) 3 Y & C Ex 379, 8 LJ Ex Eq 30.
7 *Bodger v Bodger (No 2)* (1862) 11 WR 160.
8 *Bryan v Cormick* (1788) 1 Cox Eq Cas 422; *Dalmer v Dashwood* (1793) 2 Cox Eq Cas 378; *Berney v Sewell* (1820) 1 Jac & W 647; *Smith v Egan* (1837) Sau & Sc 238.
9 Seton *Judgments and Orders* (7th edn) 765 and 798.
10 *Aston v Heron* (1834) 2 My & K 390, 3 LJ Ch 194; *Re Metropolitan Amalgamated Estates Ltd* [1912] 2 Ch 497.
11 *Berney v Sewell* (1820) 1 Jac & W 647.
12 *Chambers v Goldwin* (1804) 5 Ves 834, cited (1804) 13 Ves 377 at 378; *Quarrell v Beckford* (1807) 13 Ves 377 at 378; *Rowe v Wood* (1822) 2 Jac & W 553 at 557.
13 *Codrington v Parker* (1810) 16 Ves 469; *Hiles v Moore* (1852) 15 Beav 175.
14 *Hiles v Moore* (1852) 15 Beav 175.
15 *Codrington v Parker* (1810) 16 Ves 469.
16 *Rowe v Wood* (1822) 2 Jac & W 553.
17 *Bryan v Cormick* (1788) 1 Cox Eq Cas 422; *Dalmer v Dashwood* (1793) 2 Cox Eq Cas 378; *Davis v Duke of Marlborough* (1819) 2 Swan 108 at 137, 165; *Berney v Sewell* (1820) 1 Jac & W 647; *Tanfield v Irvine* (1826) 2 Russ 149 at 151; *Smith v Egan* (1837) Sau & Sc 238.
18 See *Underhay v Read* (1887) 20 QBD 209, CA.

formulation of the qualification is 'without prejudice to the rights of any prior incumbrancers to receive the rents and profits receivable in respect of the interests of the defendants in the said mortgaged property or in the proceeds of sale thereof'.[19]

Among the rights of a prior mortgagee is his right to take possession, and where his rights have been expressly saved by a receivership order he can in fact take possession without the leave of the court,[20] although formerly it was considered that leave was required and application for leave was usually made.[1] Indeed some still think that it is at least desirable for the sake of good order that in every case an application should be made to the court to assert the prior right.[2] The application would generally be granted as a matter of course on evidence that the prior incumbrancer was unpaid and that there has been a default. Naturally leave will be required when there has been no express saving of the prior mortgagee's right in the order.[3]

If a receiver has been appointed in the absence of a prior mortgagee he will be discharged and the prior mortgagee, though he be only an equitable mortgagee, will be let into possession.[4] Where other incumbrances are known to exist the appointment may be accompanied by an inquiry as to the priority of the several incumbrances.[5] The court will not allow a prior mortgagee to object to the appointment of a receiver at the instance of a subsequent mortgagee unless the prior mortgagee is prepared to exercise his legal right of entry and take possession of the property.[6]

A receiver will be appointed against the owner of the legal estate who refuses to satisfy equitable interests[7] or if there is a strong prima facie case for setting the sale to him aside.[8] Otherwise he will only be appointed if the rents and profits are in danger.[9]

19 See 28 *Court Forms* (2nd edn) (1997 Issue) 169, Form 65.
20 *Underhay v Read* (1887) 20 QBD 209 at 219, CA; *Engel v South Metropolitan Brewing and Bottling Co* [1891] WN 31.
 1 *Preston v Tunbridge Wells Opera House Ltd* [1903] 2 Ch 323, 72 LJ Ch 774; *Re Metropolitan Amalgamated Estates Ltd* [1912] 2 Ch 497 at 502.
 2 RH Moldaver 'Abuse of Power by Receivers and the Appointment of Receivers as a Remedy' Law Society of Upper Canada Special Lectures (1979) Abuse of Power p 237; and see *Gowar v Bennett* (1847) 9 LTOS 310.
 3 *Berney v Sewell* (1820) 1 Jac & W 647.
 4 *Langton v Langton* (1885) 7 De GM & G 30.
 5 *Davis v Duke of Marlborough* (1819) 2 Swan 108 at 138; *Metcalfe v Archbishop of York* (1833) 6 Sim 224; affd 1 My & Cr 547; *Hiles v Moore* (1852) 15 Beav 175 at 179.
 6 *Silver v Bishop of Norwich* (1816) 3 Swan 112n.
 7 *Pritchard v Fleetwood* (1815) 1 Mer 54.
 8 *Hugonin v Baseley* (1806) 13 Ves 105; *Stilwell v Wilkins* (1821) Jac 280; *George v Evans* (1840) 4 Y & C Ex 211.
 9 *Lancashire v Lancashire* (1845) 9 Beav 120 at 129.

CHAPTER 22

Selection and eligibility of receiver

GENERAL

In the selection of a person to act as receiver the court acts in the exercise of its judicial discretion, taking account of the circumstances of the case and the comparative fitness of the parties proposed, and will choose such person as it considers will best serve the rights and interests of all parties to the dispute.[1] The questions to be considered by the court have been summarised conveniently in an American case in the following way:[2]

> 'It [the court] places the property in the hands of a receiver whose duty it is to preserve it, prevent deterioration, and so manage it that the rights of its real owner will be prejudiced as little as possible. The person selected for this duty must possess integrity of character, business experience, a knowledge of affairs, a capacity for the examination into and comprehension of accounts, must not be partisan, and must have no pecuniary interest in any one of the classes of creditors whose claims come before the court.'

The person most fit to fill the office should be appointed without regard to who may propose or recommend him.[3]

One should also approach the matter of appointment with negative factors as well as positive factors in mind. A person will not be appointed if from any cause his duties as receiver would conflict with his own interest.[4] This is a well known principle in relation to fiduciaries: they should not put themselves in a position where their duties and interest conflict.[5] Equally the court should try to avoid putting a person in that dilemma. So the person whose duty it would be to check the receiver's accounts will not be appointed.[6]

---

1 *Thomas v Dawkin* (1792) 1 Ves 452, 3 Bro CC 508; *Morison v Morison* (1838) 4 My & Cr 215; *Perry v Oriental Hotels Co* (1870) 5 Ch App 420, 23 LT 525.
2 See *Farmers' Loan and Trust Co v Cape Fear and Yadkin Valley Railroad Co* 62 Fed 675 at 677 (1884).
3 *Lespinasse v Bell* (1821) 2 Jac & W 436.
4 *Fripp v Chard Rly Co* (1853) 11 Hare 241. But see *Cookes v Cookes* (1865) 2 De GJ & Sm 526.
5 See Finn *Fiduciary Obligations* (1977) 199–251.
6 *Garland v Garland* (1793) 2 Ves 137; *Anon* (1797) 3 Ves 515; *Re Lloyd* (1879) 12 Ch D 447, 41 LT 171, CA.

The court will obviously prefer a nominee who is fully competent to act on his own initiative. So it will not appoint a person who from ignorance of the kind of property over which it is proposed to appoint him receiver would have to act under the advice of another person.[7] In this connection in the ordinary case of a receivership of the rents and profits of land it is not a fatal objection that the nominee has no experience of estate management provided he is otherwise qualified.[8] But the court would surely now blanch at appointing an illiterate a receiver.[9] The court will also set some considerable store by the availability of the person in question and while any real doubt as to availability is not an absolute disqualification the court will obviously take it into account.[10] Thus it is an objection that the person proposed will be unable to give personal attention to the duties of the office because his daily affairs give him no time to do so.[11] Depending on the circumstances, the distance which a receiver or manager lives from the estate or business may be of importance: it will no doubt depend on the nature of the property whether constant attention is necessary or not and it may be the case that other factors outweigh the disadvantages.[12]

PARTIES TO THE ACTION

Any party to the action may be appointed receiver, but it is an established rule that one of the parties to the action shall not be appointed receiver without the consent of the other party, unless a special case is made out.[13]

If in a partnership action one of the parties has been in effect the managing partner, and the nature of the business is a personal one, and such that an indifferent person cannot be found to carry it on effectually, such party will be appointed receiver though his appointment is opposed by the other partner.[14]

If one party is entitled to a heavily preponderant interest in the property, and the property is in jeopardy, that party may be appointed receiver.[15] And another special case is where there is immediate danger to property: the plaintiff may be appointed interim receiver for a set period, or until a receiver is appointed under the order for the appointment of a receiver.[16]

---

7 *Lupton v Stephenson* (1848) 11 I Eq R 484.

8 *Wilkins v Williams* (1798) 3 Ves 588; *Bagot v Bagot* (1841) 10 LJ Ch 116 at 120.

9 Cf *Chaytor v Maclean* (1848) 11 LTOS 2.

10 *Wynne v Lord Newborough* (1808) 15 Ves 283.

11 *Re Errington, ex p Fermor* (1821) Jac 404. But with modern communications distance may be a less relevant factor: *Re Carshalton Park Estate Ltd* [1908] 2 Ch 62 at 68.

12 *Wynne v Lord Newborough* (1808) 15 Ves 283.

13 *Sargant v Read* (1876) 1 Ch D 600; *Re Lloyd* (1879) 12 Ch D 447, 41 LT 171, CA; *Budgett v Improved Patent Forced Draught Furnace Syndicate Ltd* [1901] WN 23.

14 *Sargant v Read* above.

15 *Hoffman v Duncan* (1853) 18 Jur 69; *Boyle v Bettws Llantwit Colliery Co* (1876) 2 Ch D 726.

16 *Chaplin v Young* (1862) 6 LT 97; *Taylor v Eckersley* (1876) 2 Ch D 302, CA.

PARTICULAR PERSONS

A solicitor may certainly act as a receiver, but the solicitor to the plaintiff in the action will not be appointed,[17] nor will a solicitor in the action acting for all parties.[18]

A trustee may be appointed receiver, but the court will as a rule avoid making such an appointment,[19] whether the trustee be a sole trustee or one acting jointly with others.[20] However, an exception may be made if no other person can be found by whom the estate is likely to be equally well managed, or the trustee is willing to act without remuneration,[1] or if the terms of the trust are such that he is, as trustee, entitled to be paid out of the trust estate.[2]

A partner is frequently appointed receiver and manager of the partnership assets and business in a partnership action, provided he is solvent and there is no reason to distrust him.[3] So too a retired partner having an interest in the assets may also be appointed.[4]

A mortgagee may be appointed,[5] and likewise a person having a lien on the property, as, for example, an unpaid vendor.[6]

A liquidator of a company may be appointed receiver and manager of the assets and business of the company,[7] as also may be a director[8] and a managing director.[9] But it would seem that a managing director will not be appointed where the debenture holders want to intervene and protect the property for themselves.[10] A debenture holder may be in those circumstances appointed.[11]

A practising barrister may be appointed so long as no trading is envisaged[12] and so may a member of the House of Commons,[13] and it is doubtful whether the court in these days would in choosing a receiver regard these facts as drawbacks in a case where estates distant from London had to be managed. For example in *Wiggin v Anderson*[14] Walton J appointed the plaintiff in a partnership action to be receiver despite the fact that he was a member of Parliament, the duties actually requiring to be performed by the receiver not being such as to be incompatible with his parliamentary duties. With a business requiring constant supervision

---

17 *Re Lloyd* (1879) 12 Ch D 447, 41 LT 171, CA.
18 *Garland v Garland* (1793) 2 Ves 137.
19 *Sutton v Jones* (1809) 15 Ves 584; *Re Bignell* [1892] 1 Ch 59, CA.
20 *Anon v Jolland* (1802) 8 Ves 72.
 1 *Sykes v Hastings* (1805) 11 Ves 363.
 2 *Re Bignell* above.
 3 *Collins v Barker* [1893] 1 Ch 578, 62 LJ Ch 316; *Davy v Scarth* [1906] 1 Ch 55.
 4 *Hoffman v Duncan* (1853) 18 Jur 69.
 5 *Re Prytherch* (1889) 42 Ch D 590.
 6 *Boyle v Bettws Llantwit Colliery Co* (1876) 2 Ch D 726.
 7 *Re Henry Pound* (1889) 42 Ch D 402.
 8 *Budgett v Improved Patent Forced Draught Furnace Syndicate Ltd* [1901] WN 23.
 9 *Makins v Percy Ibotson & Sons* [1891] 1 Ch 133.
10 *Re Carshalton Park Estate Ltd* [1908] 2 Ch 62 at 68.
11 *Budgett v Improved Patent Forced Draught Furnace Syndicate Ltd* supra.
12 *Garland v Garland* (1793) 2 Ves 137; *Wynne v Lord Newborough* (1808) 15 Ves 283.
13 *Wynne v Lord Newborough* supra.
14 (19 March 1982, unreported). I am obliged to Mr Thomas Baxendale of the Chancery Bar for details of this case.

different considerations will apply, for both occupations are demanding and in the case of a barrister (and one may add a student of the Inns of Court) being engaged in trading is forbidden.

The directors or secretary of a railway company can and generally will be appointed managers of the undertaking of the company when a manager is appointed under section 4 of the Railway Companies Act 1867.[15]

In one old case it was held that a peer would not be appointed as he could not be committed if found guilty of misconduct.[16] But both a peer and a member of Parliament can be committed for contempt if the proceedings are of a punitive nature.[17] The next friend of an infant plaintiff will not be appointed,[18] nor will the receiver-general of a county.[19]

CREDITORS OR THEIR NOMINEES

A judgment creditor or mortgagee will not himself be appointed receiver unless he agrees to act without a salary, for payment of a salary to the creditor might have a tendency to usury.[20]

As a general rule a judgment creditor or an incumbrancer is entitled to have his own nominee appointed on satisfying the court by affidavit of the nominee's fitness for the office.[1] However, if the value of the equity of redemption is as great as that of the mortgage debt, and the master chooses to appoint the nominee of the mortgagor his discretion will not be overridden just because the mortgagee's nominee is better qualified.[2]

WHO NOMINATES?

The receiver may be appointed at the hearing by the judge in court or in chambers[3] or an order may be made referring it to the master to appoint a fit and proper person.

The right to propose the person to be appointed belongs, in the first instance, to the parties interested in the action.[4] But a stranger has no right to propose the person to be appointed.[5]

---

15 *Re Manchester and Milford Rly Co* (1880) 14 Ch D 645, CA.
16 *A-G v Gee* (1813) 2 Ves & B 208.
17 *Re Gent* (1888) 40 Ch D 190; *Earl of Aylesford v Earl Poulett* [1892] 2 Ch 60, 61 LJ Ch 406.
18 *Stone v Wishart* (1817) 2 Madd 64.
19 *A-G v Day* (1817) 2 Madd 246.
20 *Sayers v Whitfield* (1829) 1 Knapp 133 at 142 per Lord Wynford; *Cummins v Perkins* [1899] 1 Ch 16 at 18, CA. See also *Cox v Champneys* (1822) Jac 576; *Davis v Barrett* (1844) 13 LJ Ch 304; *M'Garry v White* (1885) 16 LR Ir 322; *Beamish v Stephenson* (1886) 18 LR Ir 319; *Gilroy v Conn* (1912) 1 DLR 580, 21 OWR 526; on appeal 2 DLR 131.
1 *Bowersbank v Colasseau* (1796) 3 Ves 164; *Wilkins v Williams* (1798) 3 Ves 588; *Anderson v Kemshead* (1852) 16 Beav 329 at 344–345.
2 *Thomas v Dawkin* (1792) 1 Ves 452, 3 Bro CC 508.
3 *Re Llewellyn, Lane v Lane* (1883) 25 Ch D 66.
4 *A-G v Day* (1817) 2 Madd 246; *Bord v Tollemache* (1862) 1 New Rep 177, 7 LT 526.
5 *A-G v Day* above.

Even if the parties interested fail to nominate a proper person, the master should not himself propose anyone, at any rate until a further reasonable time has been given to the parties interested to make a proposal.[6]

The court will not disturb the master's choice unless there is some substantial objection as to the propriety of the choice, or there is some other substantial objection in point of principle to induce the court to overturn the appointment made by the master.[7]

Similarly, the Court of Appeal will not interfere with an appointment made by a judge except on the grounds upon which it would be proper for a judge to disturb a master's choice: in other words the Court of Appeal is guided by similar considerations when asked to review an appointment by a judge.[8]

6 *A-G v Day.*

7 *A-G v Day; Thomas v Dawkin* (1792) 1 Ves 452, 3 Bro CC 508; *Bowersbank v Colasseau* (1796) 3 Ves 164; *Tharpe v Tharpe* (1806) 12 Ves 317; *Wynne v Lord Newborough* (1808) 15 Ves 283.

8 *Lupton v Stephenson* (1848) 11 I Eq R 484; *Cookes v Cookes* (1865) 2 De GJ & Sm 526; *Nothard v Proctor* (1875) 1 Ch D 4 at 8, CA.

CHAPTER 23

Managers

IN WHAT CASES APPOINTED

As has already been remarked the jurisdiction of the court to appoint a manager is far more modern than the jurisdiction to appoint a receiver only.[1]

The court will not appoint a manager for the purpose of making a profit.[2] Except where the appointment is to preserve the status quo until trial the court will only appoint a manager with a view to a sale as a going concern.[3] Thus the court will not, on behalf of an incumbrancer, appoint a manager of the undertaking of a company which because of its public nature cannot be sold.[4] For the same reason, until the passing of the Railway Companies Act 1867, the court would not appoint a manager of the undertaking of a railway company.[5]

The prospective sale need not be immediate or absolutely certain to take place. Accordingly the court may appoint a manager of the business carried on by a company on the application of debenture holders whose charge has not yet crystallised by the debt having become due, where their security is in jeopardy.[6]

In the case of partnerships, as has already been seen, where a dissolution has taken place, or is imminent, the court will appoint a manager of the partnership business in order to preserve it with a view to a sale as a going concern.[7] Indeed a manager may be appointed even where a dissolution is not claimed, if it is

---

1 *Re Newdigate Colliery Ltd* [1912] 1 Ch 468 at 472, CA.

2 *Re Leas Hotel Co* [1902] 1 Ch 332.

3 *Waters v Taylor* (1808) 15 Ves 10; *Gardner v London, Chatham and Dover Rly Co* (1867) 2 Ch App 201 at 212; *Whitley v Challis* [1892] 1 Ch 64 at 69, CA; *Re Victoria Steamboats Ltd* [1897] 1 Ch 158; *Re Leas Hotel Co* supra; *Boehm v Goodall* [1911] 1 Ch 155 at 158; *Re Newdigate Colliery Co Ltd* [1912] 1 Ch 468 at 472, CA.

4 See the cases on tramways and waterworks: *Marshall v South Staffordshire Tramways Co* [1895] 2 Ch 36, CA disapproving *Hope v Croydon and Norwood Tramways Co* (1887) 34 Ch D 730 and *Bartlett v West Metropolitan Tramways Co* [1893] 3 Ch 437; affd [1894] 2 Ch 286; *Pegge v Neath District Tramways Co* [1895] 2 Ch 508; *Blaker v Herts and Essex Waterworks Co* (1889) 41 Ch D 399.

5 *Gardner v London, Chatham and Dover Rly Co* (1867) 2 Ch App 201.

6 *Re Victoria Steamboats Ltd* [1897] 1 Ch 158.

7 *Jefferys v Smith* (1820) 1 Jac & W 298; *Roberts v Eberhardt* (1853) Kay 148, 2 Eq Rep 780; *Sargant v Read* (1876) 1 Ch D 600; *Taylor v Neate* (1888) 39 Ch D 538.

necessary to preserve the partnership business, and the proceedings have an ultimate dissolution as their object.[8]

If trustees of a business, who hold it upon trust for sale with power of postponement, are not in fact qualified to manage such business, and cannot reach agreement on the appointment of a manager, the court may appoint a manager on the application of one of them.[9] Another example of the court's exercise of its power to appoint a manager is that a manager may be appointed of the business of an intestate pending the grant of letters of administration and the sale of the business.[10]

It appears that, though there may be no sale in view, the court will appoint a manager of a business if such appointment is the only means of preserving the same as a going concern pending the settlement of some disputed point by the court. Thus, the court will appoint a manager of a business pending a dispute between a vendor and purchaser of that business.[11]

It remains to be added that the appointment of a manager is, as a rule, made for a limited period only.[12]

OF WHAT PROPERTY APPOINTED

The court will not appoint a manager except of a trade or business. Subject to that it may appoint a manager of any kind of business, as, for example, the business connected with a theatre,[13] an hotel,[14] a colliery,[15] a farm,[16] a newspaper,[17] the business of engineers,[18] distillers and wine merchants,[19] or paper manufacturers.[20]

A manager may be appointed of a business out of the jurisdiction.[1]

CHOICE OF MANAGER

The same person may be appointed receiver and manager, or one person may be appointed receiver and another manager; or the same person may be appointed

---

8 *Sheppard v Oxenford* (1855) 1 K & J 491, 25 LTOS 63. For further examples of appointments of managers in cases of partnership, see p 326 et seq.
9 *Hart v Denham* [1871] WN 2.
10 *Steer v Steer* (1864) 2 Drew & Sm 311, 11 LT 502.
11 *Gibbs v David* (1875) LR 20 Eq 373; *Hyde v Warden* (1876) 1 Ex D 309, CA.
12 *Day v Sykes, Walker & Co Ltd* [1886] WN 209; *Re Victoria Steamboats Ltd* [1897] 1 Ch 158.
13 *Ex p O'Reily* (1790) 1 Ves 112; *Waters v Taylor* (1808) 15 Ves 10.
14 *Truman & Co v Redgrave* (1881) 18 Ch D 547; *Whitley v Challis* [1892] 1 Ch 64, CA.
15 *Campbell v Lloyd's Barnett's and Bosanquet's Bank Ltd* [1891] 1 Ch 136n; *Gloucester County Bank v Rudry Merthyr Steam and House Coal Colliery Co* [1895] 1 Ch 629, CA.
16 *Hyde v Warden* (1876) LR 1 Ex D 309, CA.
17 *Chaplin v Young* (1862) 6 LT 97.
18 *Taylor v Neate* (1888) 39 Ch D 538.
19 *Collins v Barker* [1893] 1 Ch 578.
20 *Makins v Percy Ibotson & Sons* [1891] 1 Ch 133.
1 *Re Huinac Copper Mines Ltd* [1910] WN 218.

receiver and manager, and another person may be appointed to act jointly with him in both capacities, or in one of such capacities.[2]

DUTIES OF MANAGER

It is the duty of a manager to carry on the business over which he is appointed in the ordinary way according to the general course of business adopted in the particular trade. He must not enter into speculative transactions, but he may enter into such new contracts as may be reasonable, with a view to preserving the business as a going concern.[3]

TITLE OF APPLICANT

The question will sometimes arise whether the person applying for a manager has an interest in the business in question, or only in the subject matter of the business, or the premises on which the business is carried on, as the court cannot appoint a manager of the business where the person applying is interested only in such subject matter or premises.[4]

A floating charge given by a company on all its property, both present and future, or on the undertaking and property of the company, will amount to a charge on the company's business so as to entitle the chargees to the appointment of a receiver and manager.[5]

The words 'all the property and effects whatsoever' of an hotel company,[6] 'the assets' of a partnership,[7] and 'the effects and securities' of a partnership,[8] have all been held to include the goodwill of the business.

A mortgage of a colliery[9] and a steamship[10] have also been held to include the business connected with the mortgaged property in each case by implication, so as to entitle the mortgagee to seek the appointment of a receiver and manager.

But a mortgage of a hotel and buildings does not ordinarily include the business carried on there.[11]

---

2 *Collins v Barker* [1893] 1 Ch 578.

3 *Taylor v Neate* (1888) 39 Ch D 538.

4 *Whitley v Challis* [1892] 1 Ch 64; *Gloucester County Bank v Rudry etc Colliery Co* [1895] 1 Ch 629; *Lenney & Sons v Callingham* [1908] 1 KB 79, CA.

5 *Peek v Trinsmaran Iron Co* (1876) 2 Ch D 115; *Makins v Percy Ibotson & Sons* [1891] 1 Ch 133; *Edwards v Standard Rolling Stock Syndicate* [1893] 1 Ch 574.

6 *Re Leas Hotel Co* [1902] 1 Ch 332.

7 *Jennings v Jennings* [1898] 1 Ch 378.

8 *Re David and Matthews* [1899] 1 Ch 378.

9 *Jefferys v Smith* (1820) 1 Jac & W 298; *Campbell v Lloyd's Bank* [1891] 1 Ch 136n; *Gloucester County Bank v Rudry etc Colliery Co* [1895] 1 Ch 629.

10 *Fairfield Shipbuilding & Co Ltd v London & Steamship Co Ltd* [1895] WN 64.

11 *Whitley v Challis* [1892] 1 Ch 64; *Leney & Sons Ltd v Callingham* [1908] 1 KB 79; *Palmer v Barclays Bank Ltd* (1971) 23 P & CR 30, 220 Estates Gazette 1871.

GENERAL EFFECT

The appointment of a manager by the court does not dissolve or annihilate any existing firm or company. It simply takes the conduct of the *business* out of the hands of those who previously carried it on and vests entire control in the manager.[12] The company's affairs do not cease to be its affairs and become solely those of the receiver and manager[13] and the appointment does not necessarily strip the company of the power to pursue an action.[14] In no case is a manager appointed by the court to be regarded as the agent or employee of the individual, firm or company whom he displaces.[15] It is for this reason, incidentally, that service on a receiver and manager appointed in a partnership action is not good service on the partners: the court's receiver and manager is not an agent for that or any other purpose. That is in sharp contradistinction to the position of a manager appointed out of court who as has been seen may be regarded as the agent of the debtor.[16]

Although a receiver and manager appointed by the court acts as an officer of the court, he does not necessarily, by carrying on the business, dispossess the previous owner or occupier of the business premises, unless, perhaps where he has taken possession by direction of the court. He is to be regarded rather as a custodian or caretaker on behalf of the owners. Thus, he is unable to resist a distraint for rates some portion of which is due in respect of a period before his appointment;[17] nor may he insist on a continuance of a supply of gas or electricity to the premises without paying arrears due to the supplier.[18] The appointment of a receiver and manager of a business will not generally operate to determine trade contracts.[19]

EFFECT ON EMPLOYEES

Because it effects a change in the personality of the employer, the appointment of a manager in a debenture holder's action operates, as a general rule, as a

---

12 *Moss Steamship Co Ltd v Whinney* [1912] AC 254, HL; *Minford v Carse and Hunter* [1912] 2 IR 245 at 273, Ir CA; *Parsons v Sovereign Bank of Canada* [1913] AC 160, PC.

13 *R v Board of Trade, ex p St Martins Preserving Co Ltd* [1965] 1 QB 603, [1964] 2 All ER 561, DC.

14 *Newhart Developments Ltd v Co-operative Commercial Bank Ltd* [1978] QB 814, [1978] 2 All ER 896, CA.

15 *De Grelle & Co v Bull and Ward* (1894) 10 TLR 198; *Burt, Boulton and Hayward v Bull* [1895] 1 QB 276 at 279, CA; *Re Newdigate Colliery Ltd* [1912] 1 Ch 468 at 470, CA; *Re Flowers & Co* [1897] 1 QB 14, CA (a bankruptcy case).

16 *Channel Airways Ltd v Manchester Corpn* [1974] 1 Lloyd's Rep 456.

17 *Re Marriage, Neave & Co* [1896] 2 Ch 663, CA (distinguishing *Richards v Kidderminster Overseers, Richards v Kidderminster Corpn* [1896] 2 Ch 212, where the receiver and manager had been appointed out of court under the provisions of a debenture trust deed); *Gyton v Palmour* [1945] KB 426, [1944] 2 All ER 540, DC. See also *De Montmorency v Pratt* (1849) 12 I Eq R 411.

18 *Paterson v Gas Light and Coke Co* [1896] 2 Ch 476, CA (distinguished in *Granger v South Wales Electrical Power Distribution Co* [1931] 1 Ch 551); *Husey v London Electric Supply Corpn* [1902] 1 Ch 411, CA.

19 *Parsons v Sovereign Bank of Canada* [1913] AC 160, PC. See also *Re British Tea Table Co (1897) Ltd* (1909) 101 LT 707 (payment of solicitor out of money in his hands).

dismissal of the employees of the company,[20] although possibly not in all cases,[1] and may give rise, in the case of any employees whose services are not retained by the manager, to a claim against the company for damages for wrongful dismissal or breach of contract.[2] It does not, however, affect the position of directors or disentitle them to their ordinary remuneration[3] nor does it necessarily determine the right of debenture trustees to remuneration.[4]

20 *Reid v Explosives Co* (1887) 19 QBD 264, CA; *Midland Counties District Bank Ltd v Attwood* [1905] 1 Ch 357 at 362; *Robinson Printing Co Ltd v Chic Ltd* [1905] 2 Ch 123 at 134; *Measures Bros Ltd v Measures* [1910] 2 Ch 248 at 256, CA. The same principle appears to apply where the appointment is made over a partnership business.
 1 *Parsons v Sovereign Bank of Canada* [1913] AC 160 at 171, PC (labourers on an agricultural estate). Cf *Reid v Explosives Co* (1887) 19 QBD 264 at 269, CA.
 2 *Reid v Explosives Co* (1887) 19 QBD 264, CA; *Measures Bros Ltd v Measures* [1910] 1 Ch 336 at 344; *Parsons v Sovereign Bank of Canada* [1913] AC 160, PC. Although where a new contract of employment with the receiver is made only nominal damages may be recovered: *Brace v Calder* [1895] 2 QB 253 at 261, CA. Dismissal by a receiver does not release an employee from covenants against trade competition which have been imposed for the protection of goodwill: *Welstead v Hadley* (1904) 21 TLR 165, CA.
 3 *Re South Western of Venezuela (Barquisimeto) Rly Co* [1902] 1 Ch 701, 71 LJ Ch 407.
 4 The terms of the trust deed must be considered in each case: *Re Anglo-Canadian Lands (1912) Ltd* [1918] 2 Ch 287, distinguishing *Re Locke and Smith Ltd* [1914] 1 Ch 687, CA.

CHAPTER 24

Over what property?

INTRODUCTION

The question discussed in this chapter is whether or not particular types of property are amenable to a receivership order. To analyse that question it is necessary to analyse the nature of the applicant's title.

A distinction must be drawn between (1) those cases where the applicant applies for a receiver because property in dispute is in jeopardy and it is desired to preserve that property pending resolution of the dispute, (2) claims by incumbrancers to enforce their security and (3) those cases where a receiver by way of equitable execution is claimed. Many of the cases about assignability, which is a pre-condition of enforcing a charge and of equitable execution, are relevant under each of those two heads but the two heads must still be distinguished.

PROPERTY IN DISPUTE

When the court is asked to appoint a receiver or receiver and manager of property in dispute it will of course only appoint its officer over those assets which actually are in dispute.[1] That requires analysis of the ambit of the dispute. The point is conveniently illustrated by *Clydesdale v McManus*,[2] where the dispute concerned land on which a hotel was built, the hotel building itself and some of the hotel furniture; it did not, however, concern the hotel business and accordingly the court refused to appoint a receiver over that business.

PRESERVATION OF SECURITY

Where the aim of the proceedings is to preserve property which is in jeopardy until the hearing of the substantive action it will usually be found that the plaintiff is in fact an incumbrancer whose security is at risk. In that sort of case it

---

1 *Hatton v Car Maintenance Co Ltd* [1915] 1 Ch 621.
2 (1934) 36 WALR 89.

must be shown that the property in question is assignable and that a prima facie valid assignment or charge has been made; otherwise the applicant will have no title to mount his action.

PROPERTY ASSIGNABLE BY NATURE

Naturally land and tangible assets cause little difficulty, except where the owner is subject to restrictions on dealing.

So far as land is concerned it matters not whether the land is held in possession or reversion. But it appears that if the interest is reversionary the receiver should be appointed to receive the rents and profits receivable in respect of the reversionary interest not of the land.[3] A receiver may be appointed of a rent charge or of a fee farm rent.[4]

A receiver may be appointed of furniture,[5] chattels comprised in a bill of sale,[6] the surplus proceeds of sale of mortgaged chattels,[7] rent paid in respect of furniture,[8] and heirlooms.[9] So also a motor car,[10] and cabs used with the business of a cab owner[11] may be subjected to a receivership order.

A receiver may also be appointed pending an action for trespass;[12] or on the application of a legal mortgagee;[13] or in respect of the rents and profits of land vested in joint tenants, even though no case of exclusion be made out;[14] or of the estate of a deceased person despite the fact that no legal representative has been constituted and no probate proceedings are pending;[15] or on the application of a judgment creditor even though he has not followed up his legal remedies,[16] so long as the circumstances make it just and convenient;[17] or to enforce the payment of money into court.[18]

---

3 See *Re Harrison and Bottomley* [1899] 1 Ch 465 at 467, CA.

4 *Manly v Hawkins* (1838) 1 Dr & Wal 363; *Stevelly v Murphy* (1840) 2 I Eq R 448.

5 *Manchester and Liverpool District Banking Co v Parkinson* (1888) 22 QBD 173, CA; *Whitaker v Cohen* (1893) 69 LT 451.

6 *Taylor v Eckersley* (1876) 2 Ch D 302, CA.

7 *Gouthwaite v Rippon* (1838) 8 LJ Ch 139.

8 *Hamilton v Brogden* [1891] WN 14; *Charles Hoare & Co v Hove Bungalows Ltd* (1912) 56 Sol Jo 686, CA.

9 *Earl of Shaftesbury v Duke of Marlborough* (1820) 1 *Seton's Judgments and Orders* (7th edn) 734.

10 *Hatton v Car Maintenance Co Ltd* [1915] 1 Ch 621.

11 *Howell v Dawson* (1884) 13 QBD 67.

12 *Percy v Thomas* (1884) 28 Sol Jo 533, DC; *Cummins v Perkins* [1899] 1 Ch 16 at 20, CA.

13 As to such appointment, see p 348.

14 *Porter v Lopes* (1877) 7 Ch D 358; *Hills v Webber* (1901) 17 TLR 513, CA; and see *The Ampthill* (1880) 5 PD 224 (co-owners of ship). In the case of land the legal interest of joint tenants is that of trustees for sale: see LPA 1925, s 36.

15 *Re Parker, Dearing v Brooks* (1885) 54 LJ Ch 694; *Re Dawson, Clarke v Dawson* (1906) 75 LJ Ch 201, 94 LT 130.

16 *Bryant v Bull, Bull v Bryant* (1878) 10 Ch D 153; *Re Watkins, ex p Evans* (1879) 13 Ch D 252, 49 LJ Bcy 7, CA; *Re Pope* (1886) 17 QBD 743, CA; *Re Whiteley* (1887) 56 LT 846.

17 *Manchester and Liverpool District Banking Co v Parkinson* (1888) 22 QBD 173, CA. As to the meaning of 'just and convenient', see *Edwards & Co v Picard* [1909] 2 KB 903 at 907, CA.

18 *Stanger Leathes v Stanger Leathes* [1882] WN 71; *Re Coney, Coney v Bennett* (1885) 29 Ch D 993; *Re Whiteley* (1887) 56 LT 846.

Again, in actions for the specific performance or rescission of contracts for the sale of land, and particularly of mining property, a receiver, and if need be a manager, is often appointed to safeguard the property until the substantive rights of the parties are decided.[19] Equally an unpaid vendor may apply for the appointment of a receiver with a view to enforcing his unpaid vendor's lien.[20] But an unpaid vendor will not be able to secure the appointment of an interim receiver against a railway company: 'an interlocutory application to restrain a railway company from running their trains is monstrous'.[1] Usually an unpaid vendor of a business is entitled to an indemnity in respect of any expense incurred in carrying on the business until completion.[2] This right would, no doubt, ground his right to apply for the appointment of a receiver.[3] In a partnership dispute, the fact that the surviving partner is trying to divert the goodwill of the business to himself is in itself ground enough for the appointment of a receiver and manager on the application of the representative of a deceased partner.[4] But, as a rule, a receiver will not be appointed on the application of a retiring partner if it was contemplated that other partners would continue the partnership business after dissolution.[5] So too any plaintiff who has a right to be paid out of a particular fund is entitled to an injunction of a receiver to prevent that fund being dissipated so as to defeat his rights.[6]

A receiver may be appointed of a ship.[7] Thus the court will where an action for co-ownership is brought by one owner claiming a moiety against the other co-owner appoint a receiver where circumstances exist which in the opinion of the court render such a course just and convenient.[8] Want of good faith on the part of persons in possession is an obvious ground for the appointment of a receiver in this context.[9] But where the legal title to a ship is in issue and the plaintiff has no equitable title the court will not interfere by appointing a receiver.[10]

It follows, since the greater includes the less, that a person's interest in a ship[11] or the equity of redemption of the shares of a ship[12] may be the subject matter of a receivership. Receivers have also been appointed of the gear[13] of a ship, and of

---

19 *Boehm v Wood* (1820) 2 Jac & W 236; *Stilwell v Wilkins* (1821) Jac 280; *Portman v Mill* (1839) 8 LJ Ch 161, 3 Jur 356; *Gibbs v David* (1875) LR 20 Eq 373 (rescission); *Hyde v Warden* (1876) 1 Ex D 309, CA; *Cook v Andrews* [1897] 1 Ch 266 (rescission).
20 *Munns v Isle of Wight Rly Co* (1870) 5 Ch App 414; *Earl of St Germans v Crystal Palace Rly Co* (1871) LR 11 Eq 568, 24 LT 288; *Williams v Aylesbury and Buckingham Rly Co* (1873) 28 LT 547; *Boyle v Bettws Llantwit Colliery Co* (1876) 2 Ch D 726; *Poole v Downes* (1897) 76 LT 110.
1 *Latimer v Aylesbury and Buckingham Rly Co* (1878) 9 Ch D 385 at 387, 39 LT 460, CA.
2 *Golden Bread Co Ltd v Hemmings* [1922] 1 Ch 162.
3 See *Hyde v Warden* (1876) 1 Ex D 309, CA.
4 *Young v Buckett* (1882) 51 LJ Ch 504, 46 LT 266.
5 *Sobell v Boston* [1975] 2 All ER 282, [1975] 1 WLR 1587.
6 *Cummins v Perkins* [1899] 1 Ch 16 at 19, CA.
7 *Liverpool Marine Credit Co v Wilson* (1872) 7 Ch App 507 at 511; *Keith v Burrows* (1876) 1 CPD 722 at 736; on appeal 2 App Cas 636, HL; *The Edderside* (1887) 31 Sol Jo 744.
8 *The Ampthill* (1880) 5 PD 224.
9 *Brenan v Preston* (1852) 2 De GM & G 813.
10 *Ridgway v Roberts* (1844) 4 Hare 106.
11 *Croshaw v Lyndhurst Ship Co* [1897] 2 Ch 154.
12 *Wilson Bros v Donald* (1899) 7 BCR 33.
13 *Compagnie de Senegal v Woods & Co* [1883] WN 180 (ship and her gear).

the machinery of a ship temporarily at an engineer's for repairs.[14] So too the freight[15] or cargo[16] of a ship may be subjected to a receivership order.

The interest over which a court receiver (other than by way of equitable execution) is claimed must, however, be a genuine right of property. Thus a receiver will not be appointed of a purely voluntary allowance, as for example income of property held on discretionary trusts for the benefit of a judgment debtor.[17] Nor will a receiver be appointed of rates not yet assessed, for until an assessment has been made there is nothing to collect.[18]

ASSIGNMENTS CONTRARY TO PUBLIC POLICY

Public policy forbids certain assignments of pay. It is contrary to public policy for a public officer to assign the salary payable to him for the purpose of maintaining the dignity of his office or to assure the due discharge of the duties of that office.[19] But it is important to note that this doctrine does not apply to assignments of or charges on salary which has accrued due.[20] It only applies in the context of assignments of salary to future instalments of pay. That principle is certainly established so far as the future salary and pay of military and naval officers,[1] and extends naturally to policemen.[2] But it almost certainly goes further.

Normally both the present and future earnings of an individual or of a business are capable of assignment. But this is only a general rule and the assignment may not be valid for all purposes.[3] Thus an assignment by a member of a profession of his future earnings is void against a trustee in bankruptcy as regards receipts after commencement of the bankruptcy.[4] Moreover, as will be seen later, a receiver cannot be appointed by way of equitable execution of *future* earnings.[5] On the other hand a receiver by way of equitable execution may be appointed in

---

14 *Brenan v Preston* (1852) 2 De GM & G 813.

15 *Roberts v Roberts* (1854) 1 *Seton's Judgments and Orders* (7th edn) 772; *The Bloomer* (1864) 11 LT 46; *Burn v Herlofson and Siemensen, The Faust* (1887) 56 LT 722, CA.

16 *Peruvian Guano Co Ltd v Dreyfus Bros & Co* [1892] AC 166, HL (guano).

17 *R v Lincolnshire County Court Judge* (1887) 20 QBD 167, DC.

18 *Drewry v Barnes* (1826) 3 Russ 94, 5 LJOS Ch 47 (rates for parking and lighting expenses).

19 See DW Logan 'A Civil Servant and his Pay' (1945) 61 LQR 240–267.

20 *Flarty v Odlum* (1790) 3 Term Rep 681 at 683 per Buller J; *Barwick v Reade* (1791) 1 Hy Bl 627 (for *future* services); *Picton v Cullen* [1900] 2 IR 612 at 614, CA per Ashbourne LC; *Price v Lovett* (1851) 20 LJ Ch 270.

 1 *Flarty v Odlum* supra; *Barwick v Reade* supra. Naval officers: *Apthorpe v Apthorpe* (1887) 12 PD 192, 57 LT 518, CA.

 2 *Hobbs v Howell* (1914) 29 WLR 650, 7 WWR 256 (sergeant in Royal North West Mounted Police).

 3 *Holmes v Millage* [1893] 1 QB 551 at 559, CA; *Horwood v Millar's Timber and Trading Co Ltd* [1917] 1 KB 305, CA. An assignment by an individual must not strip him of his only means of support; *King v Michael Faraday & Partners Ltd* [1939] 2 KB 753, [1939] 2 All ER 478.

 4 *Re de Marney* [1943] Ch 126, [1943] 1 All ER 275.

 5 *Holmes v Millage* [1893] 1 QB 551, CA (journalist's earnings); *Cadogan v Lyric Theatre Ltd* [1894] 3 Ch 338, CA (theatre takings): *Re Johnson* [1898] 2 IR 551; see at p 345 above.

respect of *outstanding* salary or earnings,[6] because normally wages, salary and earnings already due are assignable.[7]

It is conventionally (if not dogmatically) asserted in various textbooks that the salary of a civil servant or a public officer paid out of national funds is also un-assignable.[8] No case in fact goes so far as to hold that salary already accrued or in arrear and due to such a person is unassignable. And indeed the English case law is curiously inconclusive. The case of *Cooper v Reilly*[9] for example did not decide that the salary of an assistant parliamentary counsel to the Treasury cannot be assigned. From both reports of the case it is apparent that Sir John Leach MR thought the question whether or not such a salary was assignable 'one of doubt and difficulty', and he adopted the course, not uncommon at the time,[10] of directing a case to be stated for the opinion of the Court of Common Pleas. There were, it seems, no further proceedings pursuant to that direction. Although the purpose of directing a case to be stated was to settle disputes about facts, the Court of Chancery not infrequently framed the issue so as 'to leave the question of law, as well as of fact, to the consideration of a Court of Law'.[11]

In *Palmer v Bate*,[12] which is conventionally quoted as authority for the proposition that the salary of a clerk of the peace cannot be assigned, there is equal ambiguity.[13] An issue, involving both law and fact,[14] was directed for the opinion of the Court of Common Pleas which returned the issue with a certificate that the assignment was bad without indicating whether that conclusion was one on the evidence or one of law.

In *Picton v Cullen*[15] the Irish Court of Appeal conceded for the purpose of argument that the doctrine of public policy preventing the assignment or charging of the salary of a public officer applied to *future* instalments of the salary of a teacher paid from national funds. As to salary already accrued Ashbourne LC said:[16]

> 'I put aside questions of future instalments and assignments and confine myself to the narrow limits of this case, where a national schoolmaster, who is owed £10 3s 6d by the Commissioners of National Education for work already done, and pay already due, has an order made against him appointing the judgment creditor receiver by way of [equitable] execution over that sum. In my opinion there is no principle of law or public policy to safeguard that from execution.'

---

6 *Picton v Cullen* [1900] 2 IR 612.
7 *Russell & Co Ltd v Austin Fryers* (1909) 25 TLR 414, DC (money due under contract for services); *Crouch v Martin and Harris* (1707) 2 Vern 595 (seaman's wages). The situation in the last case is now covered by Merchant Shipping Act 1970, s 11(1)(b).
8 Treitel *Law of Contract* (10th edn) 644–645.
9 (1829) 2 Sim 560; affd 1 Russ & M 560.
10 The practice was ended by the Chancery Procedure Amendment Act 1852.
11 *Hambrooke v Simmons* (1827) 4 Russ 25 at 27.
12 (1821) 2 Brod & Bing 673, 6 Moore CP 28. For earlier proceedings: see *Palmer v Vaughan* (1818) 3 Swan 173.
13 The case may have really turned on a statute of 1552 involving the sale of judicial offices, ie 5 & 6 Edw 6, c 16.
14 The Court of Chancery was not averse to framing an issue to leave both law and fact at large: see *Hambrooke v Simmons* (1827) 4 Russ 25 at 27.
15 [1900] 2 IR 612.
16 [1900] 2 IR 612 at 614.

The status of the assignability of the *future* salary of a civil servant was squarely in issue in the Irish case of *M'Creery v Bennett*.[17] In that case a petty sessions clerk covenanted to assign his official salary to the plaintiff to secure an annuity. The plaintiff brought an action for the appointment of a receiver by way of equitable execution over the future salary of the clerk, and Barton J held that the assignment of the salary was unenforceable.[18]

The doctrine that the *future* pay of a public servant is unassignable on grounds of public policy was pressed to extraordinary limits in the Scottish case of *Mulvenna v Admiralty*.[19] There the wages of a telephone attendant at a royal dockyard were held unassignable, with the consequence that a court order for the maintenance of his wife and family could not be enforced. Lord Blackburn said[20] that the terms of service of a public servant:

> 'are subject to certain qualifications dictated by public policy, no matter to what service the servant may belong, whether it be naval, military, or civil, and no matter what position he holds in the service, whether exalted or humble.'

He went on to say that it was enough that the servant was a public servant, and that public policy, no matter on what ground it was based, demanded the qualification. In Canada it has been held more realistically that the rule of law that salaries of public officers cannot be assigned as being contrary to public policy does not extend to a junior clerk in the civil service.[1]

Again the case of *Arbuthnot v Norton*[2] is not conclusive. It concerned the assignment by a puisne judge of the Supreme Court of Madras of the sum (equal to six months' salary) which would be payable to his legal personal representative if he died after more than six months in office. The Privy Council obviously thought that the assignment of a salary would have been contrary to public policy but held that the sum in question was not 'salary'. Equally the decision of the Court of Exchequer in *Wells v Foster*[3] did not concern the salary of a clerk in the Audit Office but the allowance by way of compensation for his removal from office, and in particular the assignability of future instalments of that allowance. In this case too the judges clearly considered that the doctrine of public policy applied to the salary of a civil servant as well as to his retiring allowance.

There is, therefore, no English case which deals directly with the validity of an assignment of the *future* salary of a civil servant. Even in *Lucas v Lucas*[4] what was in issue was the accrued salary of an Indian civil servant so that any appeal to the doctrine of public policy was misdirected, and the actual decision in the case was not as to the assignability of the salary but as to whether the salary was owing or accruing to the civil servant for the purposes of garnishee proceedings.

Nevertheless it is tolerably plain that underlying many of the English decisions is the notion or belief that the future salary of a civil servant could not

17 [1904] 2 IR 69.
18 [1904] 2 IR 69 at 73.
19 1926 SC 842.
20 1926 SC 842 at 859.
 1 *Traders Bank v McKay* (1909) Alta LR 31.
 2 (1846) 5 Moo PCC 219, 10 Jur 145.
 3 (1841) 8 M & W 149.
 4 [1943] P 68, [1943] 2 All ER 110.

be assigned or attached. As already noted, in Canada the application of a judgment creditor for the appointment of a receiver to receive the cheques for salary not yet due of the judgment debtor, a Dominion civil servant, was dismissed.[5]

Why, it may be asked, is it contrary to public policy for future instalments of salary payable to a public officer to be assignable? Various reasons have been put forward in the books. Thus it has been said that a public officer ought not to be deprived of the means to maintain the dignity of his office. It is fit that the public servant should retain the means of a decent subsistence without being exposed to the temptations of poverty.[6] A public officer must not be allowed to fall into such a situation as to make it difficult for him in consequence of any pecuniary embarrassment to maintain the dignity of his office.[7] Whether a salary is assignable on the ground of public policy depends on the nature of the duty and the interest of the public to secure the payment of the salary to the person by whom the duty is to be performed. The public is interested not only in the performance from time to time of the duties but also in the fit state of preparation of the party having to perform them.[8] If therefore they were permitted to deprive themselves of their salaries they might be rendered unable promptly to enter upon their duties when called upon and the public service would be thereby greatly injured.

The principle or 'doctrine' has nevertheless been severely criticised.[9] The doctrine, it has been suggested, was evolved to meet a certain set of conditions in the public service which have long since vanished. There have certainly been judicial rumblings against the continuing usefulness and desirability of the doctrine. Thus Gibson J in *Hamilton v Coningham*[10] was unwilling to 'assent to the principle that any public servant, if his salary is sufficient, can be permitted to treat his office under the Crown as clothing him with the ancient privileges of Alsatia against his creditors'. And in a judgment rejecting the claim of an Irish Member of Parliament that the doctrine should be extended so as to prevent his Member's salary from being treated as part of his assets for the benefit of his creditors Lord Parker said:[11]

> 'I am not sure that public policy has not on this occasion justified its reputation as an unruly horse, for while, on the one hand, the public is undoubtedly interested in every man paying his lawful debts, it is, on the other hand, by no means clear that either the dignity or efficiency of a member of Parliament would be enhanced by his being placed in a better position to defeat creditors than the rest of His Majesty's subjects.'

Equally it may be argued that there can be no good reason for putting a civil servant in any better position than a Member of Parliament.

---

5 *Forin v Wagner* (1908) 9 WLR 593. Other Canadian cases hold that the salary of a government officer (*Cane v MacDonald* (1903) 10 BCR 444) and of a public officer (*Powell v R* (1905) 25 CLT 140, 9 Exch CR 364) are not assignable.
6 *Wells v Foster* (1841) 8 M & W 149 at 151 per Lord Ainger CB.
7 *Grenfell v Dean and Canons of Windsor* (1840) 2 Beav 544 at 550 per Lord Langdale citing the opinion of Lord Eldon in *Davis v Duke of Marlborough* (1818) 1 Swan 74 at 79.
8 (1840) 2 Beav 544 at 549.
9 See (1945) 61 LQR 240.
10 [1903] 2 IR 564 at 568.
11 *Hollinshead v Hazleton* [1916] 1 AC 428 at 461; and see per Lord Atkinson at 439.

Public policy also precludes certain pensions from being assigned. Where a pension is granted to one who though not for the time engaged in any active duties, is still liable to be called to active service and is therefore to be considered in the service of the Crown, the pension is to be considered as to some extent granted in order to maintain the grantee until he is called on to serve again.[12] Thus compensation paid to a civil servant on reduction in office is not assignable since he is liable to be called upon to serve again.[13] For the very same reason the half-pay of an army officer was not assignable either in law or in equity.[14] Sometimes, as in the case of some pensions granted to former members of the Indian civil service, there is no question of a recall to duty and such a pension is assignable.[15] A pension having for its object a perpetual memorial of natural gratitude for public services is not alienable,[16] nor is the pension of a Lord Chancellor.[17]

In the absence of any statutory bar a man may assign a pension given to him entirely for past services whether the pension was granted to him for life or during pleasure. A receiver by way of equitable execution may thus be appointed of the pension of a former county court judge[18] of an Indian naval officer's pension,[19] of a civil service pension[20] and of the pension of a retired colonial judge.[1] Likewise such a receiver may be appointed of the pension of an officer of the Royal Irish Constabulary[2] or of a railway employee who is not liable to be called on to resume his duties[3] or of an annual sum granted as compensation for abolition of the post of receiver of first fruits and Crown rents.[4]

ASSIGNMENT PROHIBITED BY STATUTE

Many pensions are specifically denied assignability and naturally such pensions cannot be subjected to equitable execution.

The assignment of naval, military and air force pensions is of course expressly forbidden by statute.[5] Other non-assignable pensions and allowances, whose non-assignability stems from statutory prohibition, include: benefits under civil

---

12 *Wells v Foster* (1841) 8 M & W 149 at 152.
13 *Wells v Foster* supra (clerk in the Audit Office).
14 *Flarty v Odlum* (1790) 3 Term Rep 681; *Lidderdale v Duke of Montrose* (1791) 4 Term Rep 248; *McCarthy v Goold* (1810) 1 Ball & B 387. At one stage it was thought to be assignable in equity: *Stuart v Tucker* (1777) 2 Wm Bl 1137. Later cases denied this: *Stone v Lidderdale* (1795) 2 Anst 533; *McCarthy v Goold* supra.
15 *Knill v Dumergue* [1911] 2 Ch 199, CA.
16 *Davis v Duke of Marlborough* (1818) 1 Swan 74.
17 (1818) 1 Swan 74 at 79.
18 *Willcock v Terrell* (1878) 3 Ex D 323, 39 LT 84, CA.
19 *Dent v Dent* (1867) LR 1 P & D 366.
20 *Sansom v Sansom* (1879) 4 PD 69; *Molony v Cruise* (1892) 30 LR Ir 99.
 1 *Re Huggins, ex p Huggins* (1882) 21 Ch D 85, CA.
 2 *Murphy v Green* (1890) 26 LR Ir 610; *Manning v Mullins* [1898] 2 IR 34. But not of the pension of a prison officer: *Blair v Coghlan* (1898) 33 ILTR 20.
 3 *Crouch v Victorian Rly Comrs* [1907] VLR 80 (retirement allowance).
 4 *Johnson v Mason* (1850) 2 Ir Jur 170.
 5 Naval and Marine Pay and Pensions Act 1865, s 4; Army Act 1955, s 203; Air Force Act 1955, s 203.

service superannuation schemes;[6] parliamentary pensions;[7] pensions of retired clergy;[8] police pensions;[9] firemen's pensions;[10] superannuation benefits payable out of funds maintained by local authorities[11] and superannuation benefits payable to school teachers.[12]

Child benefit is not assignable,[13] nor is industrial injury benefit;[14] benefit under the National Insurance legislation;[15] benefit under the Supplementary Benefits Act 1976.[16]

EQUITABLE EXECUTION

Introduction

As has already been said, the property over which a receiver by way of equitable execution may be appointed is more restricted.

A distinction must be made between land and interests in land where the position is governed by statute and other forms of property where other rules apply.

The court must, in the first place and in any event, be satisfied that the property in question is capable of assignment.[17] In the case of land and interests in land there can be no doubt on the matter. But certain other rights are not assignable and in respect of these equitable execution is not available.[18] Secondly, the court must be satisfied, in the case of property other than land, that the property in question cannot be reached through legal execution.[19]

The power of the High Court and of the county courts to appoint a receiver by way of equitable execution has now been regulated by statute so as to operate indisputably in respect of all legal estates and equitable interests in land.[20] Prior

---

6 Superannuation Act 1972, s 5.
7 Parliamentary and other Pensions Act 1972, s 20. For pensions payable to former United Kingdom representatives in the European Parliament, see European Assembly (Pay and Pension) Act 1979, s 4; European Assembly (United Kingdom Representatives) Pension Order 1980, SI 1980/1450, art 22. And see Pensions Act 1995, s 91 (right to pension under occupational pension scheme).
8 Clergy Pensions Measure 1961, s 35(2); and see *Gathercole v Smith* (1881) 17 Ch D 1, 50 LJ Ch 671, CA; *Gathercole v Smith* (1881) 7 QBD 626, CA.
9 Police Pensions Act 1976, s 203.
10 Fire Services Act 1947, s 26(1), (2); Fire Services Act 1951, s 1; Firemen's Pension Scheme Order 1973, SI 1973/966, App 2, art 70 as amended by SI 1975/1717.
11 Superannuation Act 1972, s 29(2), Sch 7, para 5.
12 Superannuation Act 1972, Sch 7, para 6; Teachers' Superannuation Regulations 1976, SI 1976/1987, reg 95(1).
13 Social Security Administration Act 1992, s 187(1)(c).
14 Social Security Administration Act 1992, s 187(1)(a).
15 Social Security Administration Act 1992, s 87.
16 Supplementary Benefit Act 1976, s 16.
17 See at pp 368 and 378–380.
18 See at pp 370–375 and 380–381.
19 *Re Shephard* (1889) 43 Ch D 131, CA; *Holmes v Millage* [1893] 1 QB 551; *Harris v Beauchamp Bros* [1894] 1 QB 801, CA. *Morgan v Hart* [1914] 2 KB 183, CA.
20 Administration of Justice Act 1956, s 36(1) replaced as regards county courts by similar provisions in the County Courts Act 1984, s 107(1) and see Charging Orders Act 1979, s 2(2).

to the intervention of statute the position was unclear. While some authorities doubted whether an appointment could be made over a debtor's legal interest in land[1] it appears to have been assumed in *Re Pope*[2] that equitable execution was available against both legal and equitable interests in land. In jurisdictions where the matter has not been resolved by statute it is suggested that equitable execution over legal property will be available if it can be shown that because of special circumstances, such as the inadequacy of the security, other methods of execution would be inadequate or extremely inconvenient.[3]

The power may be exercised in relation to an estate or interest in land, whether or not a charge has been imposed on that land,[4] for the purpose of enforcing the judgment, decree, order or award in question; and the power is in addition to and not in derogation of any power of the court to appoint a receiver in proceedings for enforcing such a charge.[5]

The normal remedy, since the abolition of the writ of elegit, of a judgment creditor against land on an interest in land of the debtor is either by application for a charging order or land[6] or an interest in the proceeds of sale of land[7] or for a receiver by way of equitable execution as appears most convenient or both. So as to protect the judgment creditor both types of order should be registered under the Land Charges Act 1972,[8] or, if the land is registered land, under the Land Registration Act 1925.[9] Where an order has been made and duly registered under the Land Charges Act 1972 the provisions which avoid the order (if unregistered) as against a purchaser do not apply to an order made appointing a receiver for enforcing the charge or by way of equitable execution.[10]

Historical perspective

The approach of the judges to the kind of assets which could be reached by equitable execution has vacillated. It may be broadly stated that until the last decade or so of the nineteenth century the approach of the judges was expansive and liberal in regard to the kind of property available to a receiver appointed by way of equitable execution, but that with a series of Court of Appeal decisions post-dating the Judicature Acts a form of *rigor aequitatis* set in not merely in England but also in other jurisdictions.

Despite the apparent liberality of approach practised in the nineteenth century a change of policy is discernible in the reluctance of twentieth-century judges to

1 *Re Bueb* [1927] WN 299 per Clauson J; cf *Smith v Tsakyris* [1929] WN 39, CA.
2 (1886) 17 QBD 743, CA.
3 *Hills v Webber* (1901) 17 TLR 513, CA; *Borough of Parramatta v Powell* (1905) 22 WN NSW 218.
4 Under Supreme Court Act 1981, s 152(4), Sch 7. An interest in land at one time did not include an interest in the proceeds of sale: *Irani Finance Ltd v Singh* [1971] Ch 59, [1970] 3 All ER 199, CA.
5 Supreme Court Act 1981, s 37(4), (5); County Courts Act 1984, s 107(2).
6 Charging Orders Act 1979, s 2(2).
7 Charging Orders Act 1979, s 2(1)(a).
8 LCA 1972, s 6.
9 LRA 1925, s 59(1).
10 LCA 1972, s 6(4).

spread the net of receivership by way of equitable execution even as far as their predecessors had done. This is not the place in which to narrate the history of this change of heart or to speculate about the rationale.[11] It may be sufficient to say that after the decision in the Court of Appeal in *Re Shephard*[12] the English courts exhibited a tendency to discover alternative available procedures militating against the supplementary justice of equity.[13] Two categories of assets were held to fall outside the pale of equitable execution: (1) assets already susceptible to execution or garnishment and (2) assets which could not be seized at common law or in equity prior to the Judicature Acts. In the latter category fell the future profits of a business,[14] the future earnings of a judgment debtor[15] and the patentee's rights under an undeveloped patent.[16]

A similar process of rigidification is observable in other jurisdictions of which the best chronicled is the Canadian experience. The wide wording of the Judicature Act (mirrored by Canadian statute law) was seen as potentially dangerous to the interests of the community unless given a less 'exaggerated' interpretation.

The general paring down of nineteenth-century notions started with the forthright decision of Meredith J in *Re Asselin and Cleghorn*[17] where a judgment creditor tried unsuccessfully to obtain equitable execution over a wide range of the debtor's assets. Four paragraphs of the judgment of Meredith J are particularly worth quoting:[18]

> 'It is strange that the introduction of the words "a receiver" may be "appointed . . . in all cases in which it shall appear to the Court to be just or convenient that such order should be made," should have given such exaggerated notions to some creditors of new means of enforcement of their claims as seems to have prevailed among them: means by which they might acquire not only the property of the debtor usually seized under execution, but also every sort of property, right, or interest, no matter how remote or contingent, that he might have, as well as all that he might acquire until the debt was fully paid, including all sorts of rights of action.
>
> There was no good excuse for such notions; they were but the offspring of rapacity. The law is reasonable in regard to enforcement of payment of debts; it does not permit of enslaving or casting into prison of honest debtors; it gives reasonable exemptions from seizure for the benefit of the debtor and his family, and safeguards his eligible property against needless sacrifice. On the other hand, it provides ample punishment for dishonest debtors.

---

11 See CRB Dunlop *Creditor-Debtor Law in Canada* (1981) 278–303 especially at 288–291 and 298–303.

12 (1889) 43 Ch D 131 at 138, CA.

13 See *Harris v Beauchamp Bros* [1894] 1 QB 801, CA (assets could be reached by fi fa or garnishment); *Morgan v Hart* [1914] 2 KB 183, CA (examination in aid of execution would have enabled seizure of furniture); cf *Goldschmidt v Oberrheinische Metallwerke* [1906] 1 KB 373, CA discussed in *Dunlop* 289–290.

14 *Manchester and Liverpool District Banking Co v Parkinson* (1888) 22 QBD 173, CA; *Cadogan v Lyric Theatre Ltd* [1894] 3 Ch 338, CA.

15 *Holmes v Millage* [1893] 1 QB 551, CA.

16 *Edwards & Co v Picard* [1909] 2 KB 903, CA; *British Mutoscope and Biograph Co Ltd v Homer* [1901] 1 Ch 671.

17 (1903) 6 OLR 170.

18 (1903) 6 OLR 170 at 171–172.

It is not in the public interest, nor indeed really in a creditor's interest, that the debtor should be denuded of all that he possesses; all interests require that an honest debtor should not be deprived of the means of earning a livelihood and of all means of acquiring money to pay his debts. Too great rapacity in creditors may defeat rather than further their object.

It would be a reversal of the whole trend of modern legislation if the enactment before mentioned had any such wide-spread effect. The words quoted give no sort of real encouragement to the notion. The purpose of them was, so far as they apply to such a case as this, merely to expressly confer upon all the courts the jurisdiction which, under the designation of equitable execution, had, before the fusion of law and equity, been exercised by the Court of Chancery alone.'

This decision heralded a tougher approach to judgment creditors invoking equitable execution. The Canadian courts trod a similar path to that chosen by the English courts. They rejected receivership where fi fa or garnishment was available[19] or where even some other remedy was available.[20] And they refused to grant equitable execution, save in some exceptional cases, where the assets in question had not historically ever been subject to legal (or statutory) execution.

Assets available for equitable execution

Equitable execution can be used to reach money ordered to be paid to a trustee in bankruptcy,[1] goods subject to a possessory lien,[2] property held in joint tenancy,[3] a tenancy in common in the proceeds of sale[4] and rental income from leased furniture.[5] Equally subject to this form of relief are leasehold property subject to a mortgage[6] and an equity of redemption under a bill of sale.[7]

Other interests susceptible to equitable execution have been held to include the arrears of income owing to a wife under a marriage settlement with (the now antique) restraint on anticipation,[8] an amount awarded to a debtor by an arbitrator[9] and even the debtor's legal interest in property subject to an equitable mortgage.[10] Overseas jurisdictions multiply or mirror the examples. In Australia

---

19 *Nova Scotia Mining Co v Greener* (1898) 31 NSR 189; *O'Donnell v Faulkner* (1901) 1 OLR 21; *Davidge v Kirby* (1903) 10 BCR 231; *Hodgman v Tudhope* (1922) 22 OWN 33; *Royal Trust Co v Kritzwiser* [1924] 3 DLR 596, [1924] 2 WWR 760, Sask CA; *Stoehr and McPherson v Morgan* [1929] 4 DLR 301, Sask CA.

20 *Stuart Bros Co v Saskatoon Bottling Co* (1962) 41 WWR 446, Sask QB.

1 *Re Goudie, ex p Official Receiver* [1896] 2 QB 481.

2 *Levasseur v Mason & Barry Ltd* [1891] 2 QB 73, CA.

3 *Hills v Webber* (1901) 17 TLR 513, CA.

4 *Stevens v Hutchinson* [1953] Ch 299, [1953] 1 All ER 699 (where receiver was then denied an order for sale).

5 *Hoare & Co v Hove Bungalows Ltd* (1912) 56 Sol Jo 686, CA.

6 *Smith v Cowell* (1880) 6 QBD 75, CA.

7 See *Re Dickinson, ex p Charrington & Co* (1888) 22 QBD 187 at 192, CA per Fry LJ.

8 *Hyde v Hyde* (1888) 13 PD 166, CA; cf *Hood Barrs v Cathcart* [1894] 2 QB 559, CA; *Bolitho & Co Ltd v Gidley* [1905] AC 98, HL.

9 *Duncan v Scaife* (1888) 4 TLR 716.

10 *Re Pope* (1886) 17 QBD 743, CA; cf *Hills v Webber* (1901) 17 TLR 513, CA.

receivers have been appointed of an interest under a will,[11] an equitable interest in land,[12] and a fund in an equity court payable to the judgment debtor.[13] Canadian courts have likewise embraced as within the remedy a variegated collection of interests: annuities,[14] residuary interests in estates,[15] life insurance policies,[16] debts not yet due and owing and therefore not available for garnishment,[17] and personalty not vulnerable to legal execution.[18]

A receiver by way of equitable execution may be appointed of a legacy or share of residue under a will[19] or, as has been mentioned, of an interest under a settlement of personalty[20] even if reversionary.[1] A share as next of kin under an intestacy can also be taken,[2] and the personal representatives restrained by injunction from parting with the money until the receiver can be properly appointed.[3] Where the judgment debtor has no right to receive anything under the terms of the relevant trusts a receiver will not, however, be appointed.[4]

The courts had little difficulty in granting a receivership order by way of equitable execution over an interest in a term of years that turned out to be an equitable interest,[5] or in respect of moneys in court payable to the judgment debtor such as a deposit paid on presentation of a notice of appeal,[6] moneys taken on an earlier sequestration[7] and moneys payable to the judgment debtor from an estate being administered by the court.[8] Other assets held to be within the catchment of a receiver by way of equitable execution include choses in action.[9] Creditors could therefore look to equity to grant a receiver by way of equitable

11 *Sandford v King* (1900) 26 VLR 387, 22 ALT 68.
12 *Mosman v Sachs* (1885) 2 QLJ 57.
13 *Church v Arnold* (1902) 2 SRNSW Eq 127, 19 WN 199.
14 *Moot v Gibson* (1891) 21 OR 248.
15 *McLean v Bruce* (1891) 14 PR 190, CA; *Allen v Furness* (1892) 20 OAR 34; *Smith v Egan* (1896) 17 PR 330; cf *Gilbert v Jarvis* (1869) 16 Gr 265, Ont CA.
16 *Weekes v Frawley* (1893) 23 OR 235, Ont CA; *Canadian Mutual Loan and Investment Co v Nisbet* (1900) 31 OR 562, CA.
17 *Stuart v Grough* (1888) 15 OAR 299; *Exley v Dey* (1893) 15 PR 353; *Smith v Egan* (1896) 17 PR 330, *Imperial Bank v Motton* (1897) 29 NSR 368, NSCA.
18 *Peto v Welland Rly Co* (1862) 9 Gr 455 (tolls and earnings of a railway company); *Weekes v Frawley* (1893) 23 OR 235, Ont CA; *Fisher v Cook* (1899) 32 NSR 266, NSCA.
19 *Macnicoll v Parnell* (1887) 35 WR 773; *Re McNulty* (1893) 31 LR Ir 391; *Re Marquis of Anglesey* [1903] 2 Ch 727.
20 *Oliver v Lowther* (1880) 42 LT 47; *Webb v Stenton* (1883) 11 QBD 518, CA; *Ideal Bedding Co Ltd v Holland* [1907] 2 Ch 157.
1 *Fuggle v Bland* (1883) 11 QBD 711 (will); *Tyrrell v Painton* [1895] 1 QB 202, CA (will).
2 *Mullen v Ahern* (1891) 28 LR Ir 105.
3 *Archer v Archer* [1886] WN 66.
4 *Whitaker v Cohen* (1893) 69 LT 451, DC; *Brown v Dimbleby* [1904] 1 KB 28, CA; *Birmingham Excelsior Money Society v Lane* [1904] 1 KB 35, CA.
5 *Gore v Bowser* (1855) 3 Sm & G 1; affd 3 Eq Rep 561, CA.
6 *Conn v Gerland* (1873) 9 Ch App 101.
7 *Etherington v Big Blow Gold Mines Ltd* [1897] WN 21; *Romilly v Romilly* [1964] P 22, [1963] 3 All ER 607.
8 *Claydon v Finch* (1873) LR 15 Eq 266; *Re Slade* (1881) 18 Ch D 653; *Westhead v Riley* (1883) 25 Ch D 413 (where a further application was made to the former Lancaster Palatine Court which held the fund was necessary).
9 *Wilson v Metcalfe* (1839) 1 Beav 263.

execution to receive pensions,[10] bank accounts,[11] moneys held by a stakeholder,[12] dividends on stock held by trustees,[13] the income for life from a post-nuptial settlement[14] or a reversionary interest of a debtor under a will.[15]

Assets not available

It is convenient to catalogue here some examples of the court's refusal to grant receivership by way of equitable execution.

There is copious authority for the proposition that the court will not by way of equitable execution appoint a receiver of future wages or salary. The principle was established in the decision of the English Court of Appeal in *Holmes v Millage*[16] which concerned the future earnings of a journalist. It was applied in the Irish case of *Re Johnson*[17] to earnings under a road contract and followed in a plethora of Canadian cases.[18] There appears to be a dual rationale. First, equitable execution over future earnings was not warranted either by the Judicature Act or the Rules or by any principle by which the courts of law or equity were guided before the Act. A second rationale is stated in several of the cases to be the public interest:[19] 'An order depriving a man of his whole means of living is patently contrary to public policy.'[20] The future takings of a theatre have been similarly treated as beyond the judgment creditor's reach. Although in Canada some early cases permitted equitable execution against future business earnings[1] cases in this century disclose a divergence of view, some granting[2] and some refusing[3] a receivership order.

A receiver will not be appointed by way of equitable execution of untaxed costs,[4] of unliquidated damages in a pending action,[5] or of rents profits and moneys receivable in respect of an interest in patents.[6] Nor will equitable

10 *McCarthy v Goold* (1810) 1 Ball & B 387; *Willcock v Terrell* (1878) 3 Ex D 323, 39 LT 84, CA; *Sansom v Sansom* (1879) 4 PD 69; *Knill v Dumergue* [1911] 2 Ch 199, CA.
11 *Manton v Manton* (1870) 40 LJ Ch 93; *Miller v Huddlestone* (1882) 22 Ch D 233.
12 *Ward v Booth* (1872) LR 14 Eq 195.
13 *Bryant v Bull* (1878) 10 Ch D 153; and see *Lehane v Porteous* [1917] 2 WWR 560.
14 *Oliver v Lowther* (1880) 42 LT 47.
15 *Fuggle v Bland* (1883) 11 QBD 711.
16 [1893] 1 QB 551, 62 LJQB 380, CA.
17 [1898] 2 IR 551.
18 See the cases cited in *Re Noriega* (1979) 23 OR (2d) 520; *Commerce Capital Mortgage Corpn v Leung* (1979) 32 CBRNS 182 (Ont SC) and Dunlop *Creditor-Debtor Law in Canada* (1981) 301.
19 For example *Bedell v Gefaell* [1938] OWN 437, CA; *Re Noriega* (1979) 23 OR (2d) 520.
20 *Sculthorpe v Manion* (1922) 21 OWN 348 per Logie J.
 1 *Simpson v Ottawa Rly Co* (1868) 2 Chy Chrs 226; *Peto v Welland Rly Co* (1862) 9 Gr 455.
 2 *Desaulnier v Johnston* (1910) 15 WLR 205; *Boucher v Viala* [1947] 2 WWR 227; *Shafer v Jones* [1950] 2 WWR 625.
 3 *Bedell v Gefaell* [1938] OWN 437, CA; *Collins v Hall* [1938] OWN 477.
 4 *Willis v Cooper* (1900) 44 Sol Jo 698. But if the costs are to be paid out of a specified fund which is in jeopardy a receiver may be appointed on that ground over the fund: *Cummins v Perkins* [1899] 1 Ch 16, CA.
 5 *Central Bank of Canada v Ellis* (1896) 27 OR 583.
 6 *Edwards & Co v Picard* [1909] 2 KB 903, CA (Fletcher Moulton LJ dissenting).

execution lie against a sum the payment of which to the debtor is wholly contingent and dependent on the will of another person[7] or against a judgment debtor's property generally.[8]

A receiver cannot be appointed by way of equitable execution of inalienable property such as a weekly sum payable to a wife under the order of a magistrates' court[9] or periodical payments ordered in matrimonial proceedings.[10]

The position regarding future earnings is that while they are generally assignable[11] they are not liable to be subjected to a receivership by way of equitable execution.[12] A fortiori where future earnings are not assignable on the grounds of public policy a receiver by way of equitable execution may not be appointed over them.[13]

A receiver by way of equitable execution will not be appointed in respect of the book debts of a business which have been got in and expended[14] or where a judgment creditor has begun an action to administer the debtor's estate.[15]

In the context of equitable execution a receiver will not be appointed over another receiver. In such a case the proper order would appear to be for the powers of the receiver already appointed to be extended.[16]

7 *R v Lincolnshire County Court Judge* (1887) 20 QBD 167.
8 *Hamilton v Brogden* [1891] WN 36.
9 *Paquine v Snary* [1909] 1 KB 688, CA (separation order).
10 *J Walls Ltd v Legge* [1923] 2 KB 240, CA; and see *Watkins v Watkins* [1896] P 222, CA (permanent alimony on judicial separation).
11 *Holmes v Millage* [1893] 1 QB 551 at 559, CA; *Horwood v Millar's Timber and Trading Co Ltd* [1917] 1 KB 305, CA.
12 *Hamilton v Brogden* [1891] WN 36; *Holmes v Millage* [1893] 1 QB 551 at 554 (journalist's earnings); *Cadogan v Lyric Theatre Ltd* [1894] 3 Ch 338, CA (box office takings); *Re Johnson* [1898] 2 IR 551; and see *M'Creery v Bennett* [1904] 2 IR 69 (where public policy prevented an order).
13 As to cases of non-assignability on the grounds of public policy, see p 371.
14 *Harper v McIntyre* (1907) 51 Sol Jo 701.
15 *Re Cave* [1892] WN 142, CA; but see *Waddell v Waddell* [1892] P 226; *Re Shephard* (1889) 43 Ch D 131, CA.
16 *Valle v O'Reilly* (1824) 1 Hog 199.

CHAPTER 25

Mode of appointment

INTRODUCTION

Applications for the appointment of a receiver fall into four broad categories: (1) applications to protect disputed property that is in jeopardy; (2) applications in mortgage proceedings; (3) applications by way of equitable execution; and (4) applications in debenture holders' actions.

Before examining the appropriate procedure in each case some general points can conveniently be made. The sequence of procedural steps is important, as is the nature of the documentation which needs to be before the court. These general points are effectively the governing considerations where the receiver is appointed to protect property in jeopardy but have relevance mutatis mutandis in the other categories of application.

General rule: there must be a pending action

The general rule is that the court has no jurisdiction to appoint a receiver to preserve properties unless an action is pending.[1] An action in this context included under the old procedure, an originating summons,[2] an originating motion, a petition and, of course, a writ.[3] Most proceedings now, of course, are started by the issue of a claim form.[4] But caveat proceedings in a probate case do not constitute a pending action. There are exceptional cases where a pending action is not a prerequisite of an application to the court for a receiver. A receiver may be appointed pending a reference to arbitration and certainly after a reference has been made for the arbitrator can now appoint a receiver.[5] Another

---

1 *Salter v Salter* [1896] P 291, 65 LJP 117, CA; and see *Gasson and Hallagan Ltd v Jell* [1940] Ch 248. There is a like principle in Canada: *Ex p Peillon* (1858) 3 NSR 405, CA.
2 *Gee v Bell* (1887) 35 Ch D 160; *Re Francke* (1888) 57 LJ Ch 437, 58 LT 305; *Browne v Bowden* (1904) 4 SRNSW 740 per Simpson CJ in Eq; *Salter v Salter* [1896] P 291, 65 LJP 117, CA; *Law v Garrett* (1878) 8 Ch D 26, 38 LT 3; *Halsey v Windham* [1882] WN 108.
3 Supreme Court Act 1981, s 151 defining 'action'; and RSC Ord 5, r 1.
4 *Civil Procedure*, Vol 1, Spring 2000, Part 7, 7.0.2.
5 Arbitration Act 1996, s 44(2)(e).

exception is where a judgment creditor of a railway company applies for a receiver in connection with the execution of his judgment.[6] As we shall see, receivers appointed by way of equitable execution are in this respect a law unto themselves: ex hypothesi there is no pending action, for the action is over and done with except for executing (or enforcing) the judgment. Again in cases of mental infirmity the court has consistently exercised a jurisdiction to appoint a receiver even though no action is pending.[7]

As a rule the relevant claim form should be served on the defendant *before* a receiver can be appointed.[8] A receiver may be appointed before the defendant has given a acknowledgement of service[9] and if the case be really urgent even before service of the claim.[10] However, a receiver is not usually appointed if the persons principally interested in the property are not before the court.[11] For this and other reasons the court will as a rule only appoint a receiver after the defendant has been given due notice of the application to the court for the appointment of a receiver.

It is not necessary to the appointment of a receiver that there should be an express claim for a receiver in the writ or originating summons or indeed in the statement of claim. But if such appointment is the substantial object of the proceedings then it ought to be expressly claimed in the relevant originating process.[12] Indeed the wisest course where it is appreciated that receivership relief may become appropriate is to keep that option always open by claiming it in the first place. But the absence of such a claim is not fatal: the court can appoint a receiver notwithstanding the absence of a claim for a receiver in that originating process[13] or may give leave for that process to be amended.[14] So too a receiver may be appointed in the Court of Appeal even though that relief was not sought in the court below.[13]

Quite frequently a notice of an application for the appointment of a receiver is served at the same time as the claim form initiating proceedings. But a notice of motion can be served at any time after service of the originating process, whether before or after the time limited for the defendant to acknowledge service and whether or not the defendant has in fact acknowledged service. In general there must be three clear days elapsing between the service of the notice and the return date specified in the application, in other words the hearing date.[15] 'Clear days' means working days excluding Saturdays and

---

6 Railway Companies Act 1867, s 4; and see p 332.
7 *Ex p Whitfield* (1742) 2 Atk 315.
8 *Stratton v Davidson* (1830) 1 Russ & M 484; *Brown v Blount* (1830) 2 Russ & M 83.
9 *Tanfield v Irvine* (1826) 2 Russ 149; *Meaden v Sealey* (1849) 6 Hare 620; *Taylor v Eckersley* (1876) 2 Ch D 302, CA.
10 *Re H's Estate* (1875) 1 Ch D 276.
11 *Shaw v Shore* (1835) 5 LJ Ch 79; and see also the cases about alien enemies: *Ellis & Everard Ltd v Hochberg* (1914) 58 Sol Jo 809; *J Wild & Co Ltd v F Krupps AG* (1914) 58 Sol Jo 867.
12 *Colebourne v Colebourne* (1876) 1 Ch D 690.
13 *Malcolm v Montgomery* (1824) 2 Mol 500; *Osborne v Harvey* (1841) 1 Y & C Ch Cas 116; *Bowman v Bell* (1844) 14 Sim 392; *Wright v Vernon* (1855) 3 Drew 112; *Brooker v Brooker* (1857) 3 Sm & G 475 at 477; *Salt v Cooper* (1880) 16 Ch D 544, CA.
14 *Re Lloyd* (1879) 12 Ch D 447, 41 LT 171, CA.
15 *Civil Procedure*, Vol 1, Spring 2000, Section A, Civil Procedure Rules, Part 23, 23.7.

Sundays.[16] If an application notice is served but the period of notice is shorter than the period required by the Rules or a practice direction the court may direct that, in the circumstances of the case, sufficient notice has been given, and hear the application.[17] The application notice should be served personally on the party concerned unless a solicitor is authorised to accept such service or has notified the applicant that he is authorised to accept service.[18] In such cases personal service is disallowed.[19]

After service of a claim form notice should, if possible, be given to the defendant of any intended application for a receiver.[20] Indeed even on an application without notice most judges of the Chancery Division will ask whether any intimation at all of the hearing has been given to 'the other side'. And even if a defendant has not acknowledged service of the main proceedings an attempt should still be made to serve that defendant with notice of any motion or summons for a receiver.

In *Re Day and Night Advertising Co*[1] it was held that even if the defendant admits particular allegations in the plaintiff's statement of claim in the defence the plaintiff must still verify those allegations by appropriate affidavit evidence. It has been held that no such act of supererogation is required where the plaintiff's title is admitted;[2] and one takes leave to doubt whether a court would nowadays take such a pedantic view in the case of any other fact admitted in the pleadings but not verified by affidavit evidence.

Examples of the sort of facts usually deposed to on a receivership application include allegations that a company is insolvent,[3] that there has been a failure to pay principal or interest that is due,[4] that the secured property is for some reason in jeopardy[5] or that there is some other special reason calling for the appointment of a receiver.[6]

Save in the most extraordinary circumstances a receiver ought not to be appointed ex parte.[7] Nevertheless there are numerous examples in the books of cases where the court has been able to find that the circumstances of the case take it out of the general rule and make the appointment a matter of 'extreme urgency'.[8] The appointment of a receiver ex parte has been held to be justified in the following cases:

---

16 *Civil Procedure*, Vol 1, Spring 2000, Section A, Civil Procedure Rules, Part 2, 2.8; *Brammall v Mutual Industrial Corpn* [1915] WN 78.
17 *Civil Procedure*, Vol 1, Spring 2000, Section A, Civil Procedure Rules, Part 23, 23.7(4).
18 *Civil Procedure*, Vol 1, Spring 2000, Section A, Civil Procedure Rules, Part 6, 6.4(1) and (2).
19 *Civil Procedure*, Vol 1, Spring 2000, para 6.4.1.
20 As will shortly appear, ex parte receiverships (appointments without notice to the other side) are rarely ordered.
1 (1900) 48 WR 362.
2 See *Norway v Rowe* (1812) 19 Ves 144.
3 *Re Day and Night Advertising Co* (1900) 48 WR 362.
4 *Trusts and Guarantee Co v Drumheller Power Co* [1924] 2 DLR 208, [1924] 1 WWR 1029.
5 *Re Day and Night Advertising Co* supra.
6 *Middleton v Dodswell* (1806) 13 Ves 266.
7 *Lucas v Harris* (1886) 18 QBD 127 at 134, CA; *Re Patrick* (1888) 32 Sol Jo 798; *Re Potts* [1893] 1 QB 648, CA; *Re Connolly Bros Ltd* [1911] 1 Ch 731, CA.
8 *Piperno v Harmston* (1886) 3 TLR 219 at 220 per Lindley LJ; *Chapman v Rose-Snider Fur Co* (1922) 69 DLR 639, 51 QLR 603.

(1)   where the property is put in jeopardy whether as a result of the misconduct,[9] mental disorder,[10] bankruptcy[11] or absence[12] of the person having the control of the same or from the non-existence of any person to control the same[13] or from some other reason;[14]

(2)   where notice to the defendant would enable him to frustrate the plaintiff's rights;[15]

(3)   where the defendant has absconded to avoid service of proceedings;[16]

(4)   where the defendant has disappeared;[17]

(5)   where the defendant is abroad;[18]

(6)   where a receiver already appointed has died.[19]

Where the urgency prompting an application without notice arises from the danger that the defendant will make off with the property, the more usual course is to apply without notice for an injunction until the hearing of the application for a receiver rather than to apply without notice for a receiver. And the court may itself decide to grant such substitute relief on an application for receivership made without notice.[20]

When a proposed defendant to contemplated proceedings is out of the jurisdiction so that the claim form cannot be issued without leave[1] and a case of emergency can be made out presumably a receiver could be appointed on an application without notice and leave given for the issue of the writ by the same order. Such a course has been taken in relation to injunctive relief[2] and should equally be taken as regards receivership.

An application for the appointment of a receiver may be made by any party to the relevant proceedings. Mention has already been made of the ability of a plaintiff in an urgent case to obtain the appointment of a receiver even before service of the writ or summons. A defendant, however, can only apply after he has acknowledged service of the proceedings.[3] In *Daw v Herring*[4] Henn Collins J

---

9   *Rawson v Rawson* (1864) 11 LT 595; *Taylor v Eckersley* (1876) 2 Ch D 302, 45 LJ Ch 527, CA.

10   *Re Pountain* (1888) 37 Ch D 609, CA.

11   *Re H's Estate* (1875) 1 Ch D 276.

12   *Dickins v Harris* [1866] WN 93, 14 LT 98.

13   *Blackett v Blackett* (1871) 24 LT 276 (receiver and manager of intestate's business).

14   *Re Potts* [1893] 1 QB 648 at 662; *Minter v Kent, Sussex and General Land Society* (1895) 72 LT 186, CA.

15   *Angliss v Angliss* (1893) 69 LT 462, 1 R 532; *Evans v Lloyd* [1889] WN 171; *Re Lough Neagh Ship Co* [1896] 1 IR 29 at 33.

16   *Maquire v Allen* (1809) 1 Ball & B 75; *Dowling v Hudson* (1851) 14 Beav 423.

17   *London and South Western Bank Ltd v Facey* (1871) 24 LT 126, 19 WR 676.

18   *Dickens v Harris* [1866] WN 93, 14 LT 98; *Tanfield v Irvine* (1826) 2 Russ 149.

19   *Molloy v Hamilton* (1874) IR 8 Eq 499; *Re Stone* (1875) IR 9 Eq 404.

20   *Lloyds Bank Ltd v Medway Upper Navigation Co* [1905] 2 KB 359, CA.

1   *Civil Procedure*, Vol 1, Spring 2000, Section A, Civil Procedure Rules, r 6.20.

2   *Young v Brassey* (1875) 1 Ch D 277.

3   *Daw v Herring* (1891) 35 Sol Jo 752.

4   (1891) 35 Sol Jo 752.

stated that in addition a defendant could only secure the appointment of a receiver on notice given to the plaintiff. But that suggestion is too sweeping. In cases of special urgency a defendant should stand in no worse position than a plaintiff and should be able to apply without notice (ex parte). At any rate in *Hicks v Lockwood*[5] (which was not, incidentally, cited in *Daw v Herring*) a defendant was granted ex parte receivership relief. The defendant's receivership relief must however be related to the relief sought by the plaintiff, or to relief sought in his counterclaim or by a fresh action.[6]

An appointment cannot be made after an order for foreclosure absolute has been made, even though the conveyance of the property may not yet have been executed.[7] In such a case the action is at an end. In a proper case however, for example where special circumstances are shown, the court may reopen the forfeiture.[8]

Form of application

An application for the appointment of a receiver in existing proceedings must be made in accordance with Pt 23 of the Civil Procedure Rules 1998 and the practice supplementing that part.[9] An application for an injunction ancillary or incidental to an order appointing a receiver may be joined to the application for such an order.[10] The application will usually be made to the Master or district judge. But the Master or district judge will not make an injunction unless in connection with or ancillary to an order appointing a receiver by way of equitable execution.[11] The relevant practice direction will apply to an application for the immediate grant of such an injunction.[12]

The procedure for appointment of a receiver by way of equitable execution is the same as that for the appointment of receivers generally. Application is therefore made in accordance with Pt 23 of the Civil Procedure Rules 1998 and forms can be adapted to the needs of the case.

The general rule is that an application must be made to the court where the claim is started[13] or likely to be started,[14] and that the applicant must file an application notice[15] that is to say a document in which the applicant states his intention to seek a court order.[16] If an application is made after proceedings to enforce judgment are begun, it must be made to any court which is dealing with

---

5 [1883] WN 48.
6 *Carter v Fey* [1894] 2 Ch 541, CA.
7 *Wills v Luff* (1888) 38 Ch D 197.
8 *Wills v Luff* (1888) 38 Ch D 197.
9 *Civil Procedure*, Vol 1, Spring 2000, Section A, sc30.1.
10 *Civil Procedure*, Vol 1, Spring 2000, Section A, sc30.1(2).
11 CPR/PD Pt 2, para. 2.3(c).
12 *Civil Procedure*, Vol 1, Spring 2000, Section A, sc30.1(3).
13 CPR, Pt 23, 23.2(1). If the case has been transferred since it was started it should be made to the court named in the transfer order or where the trial is to take place: 23.2(2) and (3).
14 CPR, Pt 23, r 23.2(4).
15 CPR, r 23.3(1).
16 CPR, Pt 23, r 23.1.

the enforcement of the judgment unless any rule or practice direction provides otherwise.[17]

Service of application notice and evidence in support

Upon receiving from the court a time and date for the hearing, the applicant must then serve a copy of the application notice on each respondent[18] as soon as practicable after it has been filed and issued[19] and in any event at least three days before the court is to deal with the application except where some other time limit is specified.[20] There must in addition be served together with the application notice a copy of (a) any written evidence (ie witness statement) in support (if it has not already been served) and (b) any draft order attached to the notice.[1] A party may also rely on matters set out in his statement of case or in his application notice as evidence if such matters or the document or documents in which they are contained are verified by a statement of truth.[2]

Applications without notice

An application under Pt 23 may be made without serving a copy of the application notice if this is permitted by a rule, a practice direction, or a court order. One example of a rule dispensing with the need for an application notice is contained in the rule that the court may grant an interim remedy on an application made without notice if it appears to the court that there are good reasons for not giving notice.[3] Other circumstances in which an application may be made without service of an application notice are set out in the practice direction about applications under Pt 23. They are (a) where the court permits (b) where the parties consent (c) where there is 'exceptional urgency' and (d) where the overriding objective is best furthered by doing so.[4] The general rule that the applicant must file the application notice applies to applications made without notice.[5]

Time when the application should be made

Every application for the appointment of a receiver or receiver and manager should be made as soon as it is apparent that it is necessary or desirable to make it. Wherever possible, applications should be made so that they can be

17 CPR, r 23.2(5).
18 CPR, r 23.4(1).
19 CPR, r 23.7(1)(a) and Practice Direction (Applications) para 4.1 (see *Civil Procedure*, Vol 1, Spring 2000, para 23PD-004).
20 CPR, r 23.7(1)(b).
 1 CPR, r 23.7(3) and (5).
 2 CPR, r 32.6.
 3 CPR, r 25.3.
 4 Practice Direction (Applications) para 3; *Civil Procedure*, Vol 1, Spring 2000, para 23PD-003.
 5 CPR, r 23.3.1.

considered at any other hearing for which a date has already been fixed or for which a date is about to be fixed (particularly where case management conferences, allocation hearings, listing hearings or pre-trial reviews have been fixed.[6]

Hearing of the application

The normal course with an application for a court order under Pt 23 is that it is dealt with at a hearing. However, the court may deal with the application without a hearing in the circumstances in certain defined circumstances. These are where (a) the parties agree as to the terms of the order sought (b) the parties agree that the court should dispose of the matter without a hearing or (c) the court does not consider that a hearing would be appropriate.[7]

In any case where the court holds a hearing for the purposes of dealing with an application in the course of proceedings, the parties must be prepared for the likelihood or possibility that the court may wish to review the conduct of the case as a whole and to give any necessary case management directions. In concrete terms this means that at such a hearing the parties should be ready to assist the court in doing so and to answer any questions the court may ask for this purpose.[8]

Except in the case of the simplest of applications, the applicant should bring to any hearing the draft of the order sought.[9] The judge should of course keep a note of the proceedings on the application.[10]

Most applications for the appointment of a receiver or receiver and manager will be heard in accordance with the general rule for Pt 23 applications, in other words the hearing will be a hearing in public.[11] However a hearing may be in private (a) if publicity would defeat the purpose of the application or (b) the application involves confidential information and publicity would damage that confidentiality or (c) the application was made without notice and it would be unjust to any respondent for there to be a public hearing.[12] The court may also order that an application or part of an application should be dealt with by a 'telephone hearing'.[13]

As already noted the procedure for the appointment of a receiver by way of equitable execution is the same as that for the appointment of receivers generally. Accordingly application is made in accordance with Pt 23 of the Civil Procedure Rules 1998.

---

6 Practice Direction (Applications), paras 2.7 and 2.8.
7 CPR, r 23.8.
8 Practice Direction (Applications), para 2.9 as to which see *Civil Procedure*, Vol 1, Spring 2000, para 23PD-002.
9 Practice Direction (Applications), para 6.1 (see *Civil Procedure*, Vol 1, Spring 2000, para 23PD-006.
10 Practice Direction (Applications), para 8; *Civil Procedure*, Vol 1, Spring 2000, para 23PD-008.
11 CPR, r 39(2)(1).
12 CPR, r 39(2); and see Practice Direction (Miscellaneous Provisions Relating to Hearings), para 1.5 and *Civil Procedure*, Vol 1, Spring 2000, para 39PD-001.
13 For the practice regarding telephone hearings see Practice Direction (Applications), para 6(1) and see *Civil Procedure*, Vol 1, Spring 2000, para 23PD-006.

An order for the appointment of a receiver by way of equitable execution can be made 'without notice' or *ex parte* as the lawyers prior to the Woolf reforms put it. In cases where there is a danger of the property being dissipated prior to the hearing an injunction ancillary to or incidental to the equitable execution may be granted to restrain the dealing. Both of these remedies can be granted by a Master.[14]

Where an applicant seeks an interim injunction he applies without notice. But the application must be supported by evidence in the form of a witness statement containing a statement of truth or an affidavit. The supporting evidence should contain the following:[15]

(1) date and particulars of the judgment, stating that it remains wholly unsatisfied, or to what extent it remains unsatisfied;

(2) particulars and result of any execution which has been issued, stating the nature of the sheriff's return (if any);

(3) that the defendant has no property which can be taken by the ordinary process of execution. If he has, give reasons showing that legal execution would be futile;

(4) particulars of the property as to which it is proposed to appoint a receiver;

(5) the name and address of the receiver proposed to be appointed and stating that in the deponent's judgment he is a fit and proper person to be appointed receiver;

(6) that the defendant is in pecuniary difficulties (that the immediate commitment of a receiver without the delay of giving security is of great importance (and that the deponent firmly believes that the defendant may assign or dispose of his estate or interest in the said (description of property) unless restrained from doing so by the order and injunction of the court.

Supporting evidence

An affidavit sworn on a witness statement compiled before the action is even started is valueless even though filed after the issue of the claim.[16] Nevertheless the court will sometimes make an order on such a statement or affidavit on terms that the applicant undertakes to have it resworn and refiled.[17] Moreover, exceptionally, when the defendant to a contemplated action is out of the jurisdiction and a claim cannot therefore be issued without leave of the court,[18] a witness statement or affidavit in support of the appli-

---

14 *Civil Procedure*, Vol 1, Spring 2000, Section A, Sch 1 sc 51.2.

15 *Civil Procedure*, Vol 1, Spring 2000, Section A, sc 51.3.7 which has notes on other procedural points of interest.

16 *Silber v Lewin* (1889) 33 Sol Jo 757.

17 *Green v Prior* [1886] WN 50; *Re Abbott's Trade Mark No 8656* (1904) 48 Sol Jo 351.

18 *Civil Procedure*, Vol 1, Spring 2000, Section A, Civil Procedure Rules, r 6.20.

cation may be read entitled in the matter of the Supreme Court Act 1981 and of the contemplated action.[19]

It should be borne in mind that where affidavits are used in proceedings in the Chancery Division they must express dates and sums of money in figures not words[20] and ought to eschew the inelegant expression 'and/or'.[1]

The evidence deposed to in support of an application for a receiver should show (1) the nature of the applicant's interest in the property and (2) the grounds on which it is alleged that it is just and convenient that a receiver should be appointed.[2] Obviously as regards the first of these matters there is no need for evidence to be adduced where there is already an admission, for example on the pleadings,[3] of the applicant's title sufficient to give the applicant a locus standi. The law is generally disinclined to require a litigant to knock on an open door; and proof of admitted title is an act of supererogation of that kind. In some old cases it is laid down that evidence should be confined to allegations made in the pleadings (if any) so that evidence going beyond those allegations might be disregarded.[4] But this unduly restrictive approach probably no longer applies: if evidence is relevant it should be adduced and answered and the court will take it into account.

Usually an application will specifically propose a particular person as receiver. In such a case evidence of fitness is required. In other words a witness statement or an affidavit deposing to the fitness of the person proposed to act as a receiver.[5] Such evidence ought not to be given by the solicitor to the applicant or by the solicitor acting for the proposed receiver in the application; but it may be adduced by a solicitor or some other professional person who knows the proposed receiver personally. There should also be before the court evidence that the nominated person is actually willing to act. This can be in the form of a written consent duly verified by a witness statement of an attesting witness.

Naturally evidence as to fitness should be scrupulously accurate and indeed if it is misleading that may be a ground for the discharge of the receiver.[6] The deponent should give an accurate description both of his own status and of the status of the proposed receiver. 'Director of public companies' or 'merchant' is not a proper description of a deponent giving an affidavit of fitness.[7] And it is fundamentally misleading to dub someone an accountant when he has merely worked on the account books of some of his employers.[8]

---

19 See *Young v Brassey* (1875) 1 Ch D 277, 45 LJ Ch 142 (injunction).
20 *Civil Procedure*, Vol 1, Spring 2000, Section A, CPR, Pt 32, 6.1(6). As to when affidavits rather than witness statements should be used see CPR, r 32.15.
1 [1940] WN 188.
2 For an adaptable precedent, see 33 *Court Forms* (2nd edn) (1997 Issue) 103, Form 3.
3 *Norway v Rowe* (1812) 19 Ves 144.
4 See *Dawson v Yates* (1838) 1 Beav 301, 2 Jur 960; *Cremen v Hawkes* (1845) 2 Jo & Lat 674, 8 I Eq R 503; *Wright v Vernon* (1855) 3 Drew 112; *Purves v Lang* (1856) 2 Legge 955 at 957.
5 For a form of precedent see 33 *Court Forms* (1997 Issue) 198, Form 6; *Re Hoyland Silkstone Colliery Co Ltd* (1883) 53 LJ Ch 352, 49 LT 567. For Australian cases see *Fleming v Tooth* (1861) 1 QSCR 32; *Watt v McCunnie* (1899) 5 ALR (CN) 13.
6 *Re Church Press Ltd* (1917) 116 LT 247.
7 *Re Church Press Ltd* (1917) 116 LT 247.
8 *Re Church Press Ltd* (1917) 116 LT 247.

MORTGAGE PROCEEDINGS

A mortgagee may apply[9] for the appointment of a receiver where the mortgagor breaks any of his obligations[10] or the security is in jeopardy[11] or derelict.[12]

A receiver will not however be appointed unless an action is pending,[13] it being understood that for this purpose proceedings on originating summons constitute an action.[14] In addition the court will not assist a mortgagee in possession to rid himself of the burdensome liabilities of that possession by appointing a receiver.[15]

The appointment may be made immediately after service of the originating summons[16] or at the hearing of the summons[17] or at any time before foreclosure absolute.[18] The fact that an action is pending does not prevent the mortgagee from making an out of court appointment under the mortgage[19] but it is nevertheless considered preferable that the court perform this function in such circumstances.[20]

Unless the mortgage security either expressly or impliedly includes the business carried on upon the mortgaged premises the court may not, in an action for foreclosure or sale appoint a receiver and manager of the business.[1]

EQUITABLE EXECUTION

An application for the appointment of a receiver by way of equitable execution used to be made by summons or motion[2] although the latter procedure was in fact seldom encountered, being more expensive. The application should be made in the action in which the judgment or order for payment was obtained, since it is not generally necessary to start a fresh action to get the benefit of equitable execution.[3] In practice the application is nowadays almost inevitably made by an

---

9 For a precedent which can be adapted, see 28 *Court Forms* (1997 Issue) 67, Form 6 paragraphs 8 and 9, and 1997, *Form 15* (originating summons based on mortgagor's bankruptcy). For a claim form, see 28 *Court Forms* (1997 Issue) 117, Form 31 paragraph (4); and for an order see op cit 169, Form 65 paragraph 1.
10 *Strong v Carlyle Press* [1893] 1 Ch 268, 62 LJ Ch 541, CA.
11 *Stevens v Lord* (1838) 2 Jur 92.
12 *Higginson v German Athenaeum Ltd* (1916) 32 TLR 277.
13 *Ex p Mountfort* (1809) 15 Ves 445; *Taylor v Emerson* (1843) 6 I Eq R 224; *Gasson and Hallagan Ltd v Jell* [1940] Ch 248. See the discussion above at 351–352.
14 *Re Fawsitt* (1885) 30 Ch D 231, CA.
15 *Re Prytherch* (1889) 42 Ch D 590.
16 *Re Francke* (1888) 57 LJ Ch 437.
17 *Re Prytherch* (1889) 42 Ch D 590.
18 *Wills v Luff* (1888) 38 Ch D 197.
19 Either under an express power or under the statutory power if the mortgage is by deed: see LPA 1925, s 101(1)(iii).
20 *Tillett v Nixon* (1883) 25 Ch D 238.
 1 *Whitley v Challis* [1892] 1 Ch 64, CA.
 2 RSC Ord 30, r 1(1), Ord 51, r 3. For a form of order see 33 *Court Forms* (1997 Issue) 210–215, Forms 22 and 27.
 3 See *Re Watkins, ex p Evans* (1879) 13 Ch D 252, CA; *Re Peace and Waller* (1883) 24 Ch D 405, 49 LT 637, CA.

application[4] returnable before a master[5] or in the Family Division before a district judge[6] each of whom may grant an injunction if, and only so far as, it is ancillary or incidental to the order appointing the receiver.[7] If the original proceedings are in a district registry the application will be to the district judge.[8]

Where the application is made by a party other than the plaintiff, it must be served on the plaintiff.[9] If no acknowledgement of service has been made and judgment has been given in default the application cannot be served by being filed in default, but must be served personally on the defendant,[10] or leave for substituted service should be obtained.[11]

In other respects since the procedure in these matters is founded on the equitable jurisdiction of the court, the practice in the Queen's Bench Division and the Family Division follows that in the Chancery Division as closely as possible.[12]

The procedure in the Chancery Division is that the applicant takes the original summons together with a copy summons, the judgment and the affidavit in support[13] to the appropriate master's summons clerk for issuing. The summons is then issued and served and the parties attend before the master on the return day in the usual way. If an ancillary or incidental injunction[14] is required leave to serve short notice of the summons may be obtained ex parte on affidavit[15] from the master who may in very urgent cases and on sufficient evidence that the judgment debtor may dispose of his estate or interest in property unless restrained,[16] grant an interim ex parte injunction pending the hearing of the summons itself.[17]

In the Queen's Bench Division the forms of summons and affidavit in support are similar to those in the Chancery Division, but if an interim injunction is also required and is to be asked for by the summons application is made ex parte on affidavit to a master for leave to issue the summons. The affidavit is taken to the

---

4 See *Re Hartley* (1892) 66 LT 588; and for a form of application see 33 *Court Forms* (1997 Issue) 211–212, Form 24. Formerly it was usual to apply by motion: see *Blackburrow v Ravenhill* (1852) 22 LJ Ch 108, 16 Jur 1085; *Booth v Colton* (1868) 18 LT 384, 16 WR 683; *Fuggle v Bland* (1883) 11 QBD 711; *Re Francke* (1888) 57 LJ Ch 437, 58 LT 305.

5 *Re Hartley* (1892) 66 LT 588 (Chancery master). In an Admiralty matter the application is made to the Admiralty Registrar: see RSC Ord 1, r 4A; Ord 51, r 2.

6 RSC Ord 1, r 2.

7 RSC Ord 1, r 2. A master has power to appoint a receiver both by way of equitable execution and to enforce a charging order. In other cases an appointment is usually ordered by a judge because of the injunctive quality of a court appointment in such other cases: *Barclays Bank Ltd v Moore* [1967] 3 All ER 34, [1967] 1 WLR 1201, CA. In uncontroversial cases a Chancery master may appoint; see Supreme Court Practice 1988 para 30/1/6; and see at fn 5 above.

8 RSC Ord 33, r 23.

9 RSC Ord 33, r 3.

10 *Tilling Ltd v Blythe* [1899] 1 QB 557, CA.

11 As to substituted service see RSC Ord 65, r 4.

12 *Walmsley v Mundy* (1884) 13 QBD 807, CA.

13 For a precedent capable of adaptation, see 33 Court Forms (1997 Issue) 114, Form 12.

14 RSC Ord 51, r 1.

15 RSC Ord 30, r 1(3); see 33 Court Forms (1997 Issue) 114, Form 12.

16 *Lloyds Bank Ltd v Medway Upper Navigation Co* [1905] 2 KB 359, CA.

17 For a form of order, see 33 Court Forms (1997 Issue) 116, Form 14. See also RSC note 51/1–317 and *Practice Direction* [1975] 1 All ER 255, [1975] 1 WLR 129 para 3(t), (u)(ii).

Masters' Secretary's Department, and will be laid before the master, whose decision is available on the following day, although in very urgent cases the matter can be dealt with forthwith.[18]

APPLICATION BY DEBENTURE HOLDER

The debenture holder's action, though still the subject of lip service in the texts dealing with company law, is very rarely encountered in practice in England.[19] This fact is reflected in the absence of any precedents relating to such proceedings in the latest encyclopaedia of court precedents.[20]

A debenture holder's action is commenced by claim form which is entitled 'In the matter of' the particular company.[20] As a rule the plaintiff is a debenture holder suing on behalf of himself and all other debenture holders of the class to which he belongs[1] and the defendants are the company, and any other incumbrancers on the same property, as in the case of proceedings to enforce ordinary mortgages.[2]

The appointment of a receiver and manager by the court may be obtained on an originating summons but it is generally obtained by application in an action. As well as claiming receivership relief the claim form will claim enforcement of the debentures by foreclosure or sale and seek accounts and inquiries, which will include an account of what is due to the debenture holders upon the security of the debentures, and an inquiry as to what is comprised in or charged by the debentures.

Service of the proceedings is effected by leaving the claim form at, or posting it to, the registered office of the defendant company,[3] or if the company for some reason has no such office to its head office or principal place of business. The accompanying application will usually be served together with the claim form.

The person appointed receiver by the court is usually the person nominated by the plaintiff in the action to enforce the security.[4] Where sufficient grounds are shown the usual practice is to make the appointment on evidence of fitness[5] on the hearing of the application asking for the appointment and not on a reference of the matter to chambers. If the evidence of fitness proves to have been misleading the receiver who has been appointed will be removed.[6]

---

18 For orders, see 33 *Court Forms* (1997 Issue) 211–213, Forms 23 and 25.
19 It appears to have more vitality in Canada: See Canadian Bankruptcy Reports New Series, passim.
20 See for an adaptable precedent 10 *Court Forms* (2nd edn) Form 195 (*not* reproduced in 10 *Court Forms* (1995 Issue)).
1 *Marshall v South Staffordshire Tramways Co* [1895] 2 Ch 36, CA.
2 *Re Wilcox & Co (late WH Fox & Co) Ltd* [1903] WN 64.
3 CA 1985, s 725.
4 See *Budgett v Improved Patent Forced Draught Furnace Syndicate Ltd* [1901] WN 23 (plaintiff appointed receiver).
5 See 10 *Court Forms* (2nd edn) 362, Form 209, *not* reproduced in the (1995 Issue).
6 *Re Church Press Ltd* (1917) 116 LT 247.

If no one is nominated by the notice of motion or an affidavit of fitness is not forthcoming an order is made for the appointment of a receiver and the matter of who should be appointed is referred to chambers. In this context anyone putting forward a person as a receiver will bear in mind the statutory disqualifications.[7]

7 These are discussed in Chapter 4 at p 52, above (Commonwealth).

CHAPTER 26

Refusal of remedy

REFUSAL

The remedy of receivership, or management by a court manager, is granted according to equitable principles. So far discussion has centred upon the grounds upon which an appointment may be made. It is now convenient to set out the reasons most frequently fixed upon by the courts for refusing to appoint a receiver or manager. Some of the instances reflect a disinclination on the part of the court to inflict what is a disruptive solution except in a strong case. Other examples demonstrate the applicability of well-known equitable defences. The commonest grounds for refusing to grant a receivership or management order are (1) absence of necessity, (2) absence of benefit, (3) other adequate remedy, (4) improper purpose, (5) absence of assets, (6) laches and acquiescence, (7) hardship, (8) unwillingness of plaintiff to do equity, and (9) lack of clean hands. Each of these merits a brief mention, as does the effect of the absence or the objection of parties. A preliminary point needs to be made concerning the attitude of the court to the case where the appointment of a receiver is sought against a party who is in possession.

PARTY IN POSSESSION

One principle emerges clearly from the decided cases. To dispossess a party who is interested and who has the legal title in favour of a receiver requires a strong case to be made out.[1] Where a prior legal mortgagee is in possession, for example, the court will not appoint a receiver as against that mortgagee unless the whole of that mortgagee's debt has been satisfied.[2] The legal title, however,

---

1 *Andrews v Powys* (1723) 2 Bro Parl Cas 504; *Vann v Barnett* (1787) 2 Bro CC 157; *Hugonin v Baseley* (1806) 13 Ves 105; *Middleton v Dodswell* (1806) 13 Ves 266; *Lloyd v Passingham* (1809) 16 Ves 59; *Rutherford v Douglas* (1822) Sim & St 111n; *Smith v Smith* (1836) 2 Y & C Ex 353; *Bainbrigge v Baddeley* (1851) 3 Mac & G 413 at 420; *Campbell v Campbell* (1864) 4 Macq 711, HL; *Baird v Walker* (1890) 35 Sol Jo 56.
2 *Quarrell v Beckford* (1807) 13 Ves 377; *Codrington v Parker* (1810) 16 Ves 469; *Berney v Sewell* (1820) 1 Jac & W 647; *Faulkner v Daniel* (1840) 3 Hare 204n; *Re Southern Rly Co, ex p Robson* (1885) 17 LR Ir 121 at 140, Ir CA.

does not confer blanket protection for a party in possession, since if the legal title has been acquired subject to an existing equitable interest which he has failed to respect a receiver may still be appointed.[3] Nor will it refuse a claim for a receiver where the legal title was acquired with notice of a pending action.[4]

ABSENCE OF PARTIES

The general rule is that even if all necessary parties are not before the court a receiver may be appointed so long as the appointment does not or cannot prejudice their interests.[5] One important exception is where a trust is a public or charitable trust when the receiver may not be appointed in the absence of the Attorney-General.[6]

An example of the relevance of parties having been absent is where the property over which the receiver is appointed is in mortgage and the mortgagees are not before the court: their rights will not be prejudiced by the order.[7]

OBJECTION

Certainly the court will not decline to make an appointment simply because the majority of those interested in the property oppose the idea,[8] or because a prior incumbrancer objects.[9] That is not to say that the court will necessarily disregard objections: it will in particular be astute to protect any subsisting rights in the property other than those of the applicant.[10] This is often achieved by making the relevant order without prejudice to rights of mortgagees[11] and prior incumbrancers,[12] an inquiry as to priorities being directed if necessary. The rule was expressed in general terms in the following way by Lord Eldon in *Davis v Duke of Marlborough*:[13]

> 'The court will on motion appoint a receiver for an equitable creditor, or a person having an equitable estate, without prejudice to persons who have prior estates; in this sense, without prejudice to persons having prior title that it will not prevent their proceeding to obtain possession if they think proper; and with regard to

---

3 *Pritchard v Fleetwood* (1815) 1 Mer 54 (purchaser of legal estate subject to equitable rent charge refused to pay rent charge).
4 *Landon v Morris* (1832) 5 Sim 247 at 264.
5 *Holmes v Bell* (1840) 2 Beav 298; *Hamp v Robinson* (1865) 3 De GJ & Sm 97 at 109.
6 *Skinners' Co v Irish Society* (1836) 1 My & Cr 162.
7 *Bryant v Bull* (1878) 10 Ch D 153. See also *Re Johnson* (1866) 1 Ch App 325, 14 LT 242 (absence of trustee in bankruptcy of defendant in administration proceedings no bar to appointment of receiver, though effectual prosecution of action may not be possible).
8 *Fripp v Chard Rly Co* (1853) 11 Hare 241 at 259.
9 *Silver v Bishop of Norwich* (1816) 3 Swan 112n at 114n.
10 *Contract Corpn v Tottenham and Hampstead Junction Rly Co* [1868] WN 242.
11 *Wells v Kilpin* (1874) LR 18 Eq 298; *Underhay v Read* (1887) 20 QBD 209 at 210, CA; *Croshaw v Lyndhurst Ship Co* [1897] 2 Ch 154.
12 *Re Ind Coope & Co Ltd* [1911] 2 Ch 223 at 226.
13 (1819) 2 Swan 108 at 137–138.

persons having prior equitable estates, the court takes care in appointing a receiver not to disturb prior equities and for that purpose directs inquiries to determine priorities among equitable incumbrancers; permitting legal creditors to act against the estates at law, and settling the priorities of equitable creditors.'

It follows that the court will not appoint a receiver if by so doing the interests of other are exposed to great risks.[14]

The court will for that reason be reluctant to put in jeopardy the reputation of a professional partnership by appointing a receiver, particularly where the integrity of the partners is not in question.[15]

GROUNDS

Absence of necessity

Receivership under court order operates as an injunction as does a court order appointing a manager. The latter remedy is particularly interfering and because disturbance of a court officer carries the possibility of committal for contempt of court a proper case for relief must be made out. Sometimes an injunction alone will suffice. In other cases no real necessity for intervention by the court is made out. The court must therefore be satisfied of the need for receivership or management relief.

Absence of benefit

Although not numbered among the 12 apostolic maxims of equity[16] the equitable maxim 'equity does nothing in vain' finds a counterpart in the equitable remedy of receivership. A receiver will not be appointed if the appointment would be nugatory, as would be the case if the appointment is likely to prove ineffective[17] or indeed destructive of the very property to which it relates.[18] Even more obvious is the case of property which is valueless.[19] And the paradigm example of this respect for reality is that a receiver will not be appointed of an interest under a will which would be forfeited by the very fact of the appointment.[20]

The fact that there is no person in whose name the receiver could bring proceedings to recover the property is not a sufficient ground for refusing a

---

14 *Re Cave* [1892] WN 142, CA.
15 *Floydd v Cheney* [1970] Ch 602, [1970] 1 All ER 446; *Sobell v Boston* [1975] 2 All ER 282, [1975] 1 WLR 1587.
16 As to the maxims see Roscoe Pound *Cambridge Legal Essays* (1926) 259 et seq.
17 *Mercantile Investment and General Trust Co v River Plate Trust, Loan and Agency Co* [1892] 2 Ch 303, 61 LJ Ch 473; *Edwards & Co v Picard* [1909] 2 KB 903, CA.
18 *Cooper v Reilly* (1830) 1 Russ & M 560; *Hamilton v Brogden* [1891] WN 36.
19 *J Walls Ltd v Legge* [1923] 2 KB 240, CA; *Re Thame Borough Council* [1932] NZLR 1323.
20 See *Campbell v Campbell and Davies* (1895) 72 LT 294 (where the appointment of a receiver did not trigger a forfeiture).

receiver,[1] for at the very least the appointment operates as an injunction[2] against receipt of the property by any party to the action.

Where the court cannot act usefully in the appointment of a receiver it should not act at all.[3] Thus in the Canadian case of *Canada Life Assurance Co v Coughlan* the court refused to make an appointment in a mortgage action where it appeared that no substantial benefit would accrue from such appointment.[4]

Other adequate remedy

Equitable remedies are appropriate where the remedy at law is inadequate.[5] Thus equity will not grant specific performance if damages at law afford the plaintiff full compensation for the wrong he has suffered.[6] In relation to injunctions Lindley LJ said in one case:[7]

> 'The very first principle of injunction law is that prima facie you do not obtain injunctions to restrain actionable wrongs for which damages are the proper remedy.'

An order appointing a receivership operates as an injunction for some purposes and the principles relating to the grant of injunctions are relevant[8] when the appropriateness of receivership relief is being considered. But jeopardy and the enforcement of a security or judgment debt are not situations in which an award of damages is likely to be an adequate alternative. There are, however, frequently cases of alleged jeopardy where the court finds the interlocutory position to be too indeterminate to impose what may be the drastic solution of appointing a receiver and manager. In such cases the court may consider it sufficient to grant an injunction for the price of an undertaking in damages by the plaintiff. But receivership may be appropriate on terms. 'Any ex parte order appointing a receiver, operating in effect as an injunction should contain an undertaking as to damages'.[9]

Equity will allow a receiver in aid of a judgment of law where it can be shown that the legal remedies are insufficient.[10] The converse also applies: if there are available and effective legal remedies there is no need for equitable execution.

---

1 *Wood v Hitchings* (1840) 2 Beav 289; *Acheson v Hodges* (1841) 3 I Eq R 516; *Kirk v Houston* (1843) 5 I Eq R 498.
2 For the operation of the appointment as an injunction, see at p 410.
3 *Smith v Port Dover and Lake Huron Rly Co* (1884) 8 OR 256; affd 12 OAR 288.
4 [1935] 3 WWR 38, 50 BCR 194.
5 *Hutton v Watling* [1948] Ch 26 at 36; affd [1948] Ch 398, [1948] 1 All ER 803, CA (specific performance).
6 *Harnett v Yielding* (1805) 2 Sch & Lef 549 at 552.
7 *London and Blackwell Rly Co v Cross* (1886) 31 Ch D 354 at 369.
8 *Cummins v Perkins* [1899] 1 Ch 16 at 20, CA.
9 *Chapman v Rose-Snider Fur Co* (1922) 69 DLR 639 per Middleton J.
10 *Holmes v Millage* [1893] 1 QB 551, CA; *Borough of Parramatta v Powell* (1905) 22 WNNSW 218.

Improper purpose

Equity will not aid an improper purpose. This rule applies even where the circumstances might otherwise call for the appointment of a receiver. Accordingly a partner will not be allowed by getting himself appointed as receiver of the partnership assets to obtain powers in excess of those authorised by the partnership articles.[11] Equally a director may not obtain a receiver of his own property with a view to his preventing his creditors from taking possession.[12] Nor, before the executor's right of retainer or performance among creditors of the same degree was abolished[13] would a receiver be appointed simply for the purpose of defeating either right.[14]

The court will not normally grant an interlocutory receiver where it can do so only if it prejudices the action itself.[15] However, where the existence of a partnership is a core issue that is only one of the factors which must be weighed and taken into account in appointing a receiver.[16]

Absence of assets

It is a pre-condition both of a quia timet application for a receiver and of an application for a receiver by way of equitable execution that the subject matter sought to be subjected to the order is in existence and within the reach of the order. If the property is of its nature inalienable, or outside the scope of the security sought to be enforced, or of negligible value no order will be made. The office furniture of a local branch of a trade union was held to fall within the last category and the court in *Colter v Osbourne*[17] refused to make an order appointing a receiver accordingly.

It is the function of a receiver or manager appointed by the court to carry out the duties assigned to him by the court and by statute in relation to the assets subjected to the court's order. If there are no available assets there is nothing upon which the order can bite.

What then are 'available' assets? Certainly the interest affected must be a genuine right of property. And so a receiver will not be appointed of a purely voluntary allowance such as the income of property held on discretionary trusts,[18] nor of rates not yet assessed,[19] nor yet of a patent which is not being worked.[20]

---

11 *Niemann v Niemann* (1889) 43 Ch D 198, CA.
12 *Piers v Latouche* (1825) 1 Hog 310.
13 See AEA 1971, ss 10(1), 12(6), 14(2).
14 *Re Wells* (1890) 45 Ch D 569; *Baird v Walker* (1890) 35 Sol Jo 56 (retainer); *Philips v Jones* (1884) 28 Sol Jo 360, CA.
15 *Skinners' Co v Irish Society* (1836) 1 My & Cr 162; *Baxter v West* (1858) 28 LJ Ch 169, 32 LTOS 155; *Tucker v Prior* (1887) 31 Sol Jo 784.
16 *Floydd v Cheney* [1970] Ch 602, [1970] 1 All ER 446.
17 (1909) 19 Man LJ 145.
18 *R v Lincolnshire County Court Judge* (1887) 20 QBD 167, DC.
19 *Drewry v Barnes* (1826) 3 Russ 94.
20 *Edwards & Co v Picard* [1909] 2 KB 903, CA.

Property which a debtor can make his own by exercising a power of appointment is not available for equitable execution if the power has not been exercised.[1]

Quite apart from rights which are expressly made unassignable or which are unassignable because of public policy[2] and which therefore cannot be subjected to receivership by way of equitable execution, a receiver cannot, of course, be appointed at the instance of a security holder over assets which are not included in the security. Thus a mortgage of a hotel does not enable the court to appoint a manager of the business carried on in the hotel, as such business is not included in the security either in express terms or by implication.[3] On the other hand, a mortgage of a colliery includes by implication the business carried on there and so opens the way to the appointment of a receiver and manager of that business.[4] One case where the court was prevailed upon to appoint a receiver outside the scope of the plaintiff's charge occurred in *Hope v Croydon and Norwood Tramways Co*[5] where North J, in a debenture holders' action where a receiver had been appointed, confirmed and extended a previous order appointing a receiver by way of equitable execution so as to cover property not falling within the scope of the debentures.

Property held in trust by a company for customers who had paid for goods not delivered by the company is not part of the general assets of the company available to the liquidator or to a receiver howsoever appointed.[6]

Where a receiver is being appointed not to enforce a security or judgment, but to keep jeopardised property in a satisfactory limbo, only the property actually in dispute may be subjected to receivership. In the Australian case of *Clydesdale v McManus*[7] the property actually in dispute was land on which stood a hotel and certain chattels in the hotel and the court refused to appoint a receiver over the hotel business.

Laches or acquiescence

Laches (or delay) and acquiescence are universally applicable equitable defences. And they avail in connection with the equitable remedy of receivership, so that if the applicant for the appointment of a receiver is guilty of laches or acquiescence relief may be refused.[8] In *Norway v Rowe*[9] for example, one of several co-adventurers in a mining concern, who had never interfered or asserted his title while it was running at a loss, claimed the appointment of a receiver on the ground of mismanagement and exclusion when the business was prospering.

---

1 *Whitaker v Cohen* (1893) 69 LT 451.
2 See at p 371 et seq.
3 *Whitley v Challis* [1892] 1 Ch 64, 61 LJ Ch 307, CA; see further the discussion at p 362.
4 *Campbell v Lloyd's, Barnett's & Bosanquet's Bank Ltd* [1891] 1 Ch 136n; *Gloucester County Bank v Rudry Merthyr Steam and House Coal Colliery Co* [1895] 1 Ch 629, CA.
5 (1887) 34 Ch D 730.
6 *Re Kayford Ltd* [1975] 1 All ER 604, [1975] 1 WLR 279.
7 (1934) 36 WALR 89.
8 *Gray v Chaplin* (1826) 2 Russ 126 at 142 (47 years' acquiescence); *Skinners' Co v Irish Society* (1836) 1 My & Cr 162 (long series of years).
9 (1812) 19 Ves 144.

The application was refused. Delay or acquiescence by the plaintiff may result in the defendant having materially altered his position: in such a case the appointment of a receiver may be refused also.[10] The court must weigh the relevance of the acquiescence or delay. Although it has been said that parties 'who have acquiesced in property being enjoyed against their own alleged rights *cannot* come to the court for a receiver'[11], this goes too far. Where the time has not been unreasonably long, and where the court is convinced that there has been improper conduct on the defendant's part, the court will not be influenced by the delay.[12]

Hardship

The appointment of a receiver or receiver and manager is a costly procedure from the viewpoint of a judgment debtor. That consideration will be taken into account by a court in the exercise of its discretion as to whether to grant equitable execution; and undue cost and inconvenience may sabotage an application for a receiver by way of equitable execution.[13]

The appointment of a receiver and manager of a partnership may cause great hardship to a business if the partnership is not in fact going to be dissolved[14] and a fortiori if the very existence of the partnership is denied. The court sets its face against a one-sided irreparable injury in the case of an application for an interim injunction. And equally the court will not, as a rule, appoint a receiver or manager 'in a case where such appointment would inflict irreparable injury upon a defendant who might succeed at the hearing, or when adequate protection can be otherwise afforded to the plaintiff'.[15]

Plaintiff unwilling to do equity

A court of equity in considering whether to grant equitable relief will act on the maxim that he who seeks equity must do equity.[16] In the context of the equitable remedy of receivership the maxim was considered in *Davis v Duke of Marlborough*[17] where Lord Eldon LC said: 'The principle of this court is not to give relief to those who will not do equity'. In that case it was sought to

---

10 *Thomson v Anderson* (1870) LR 9 Eq 523 at 533.

11 *Keating v Olsen* (1905) 2 WLR 497 (Yuk Terr) per Macaulay J (emphasis added).

12 (1905) 2 WLR 497 (Yuk Terr).

13 *Walls Ltd v Legge* [1923] 2 KB 240, where in addition Scrutton LJ considered the whole subject matter inalienable.

14 *Hall v Hall* (1850) 3 Mac & G 79, 20 LJ Ch 585; *Waters v Taylor* (1808) 15 Ves 10; *Tate v Barry* (1928) 28 SRNSW 380, 45 WN 83.

15 *Tate v Barry* (1928) SRNSW 380 at 387 per Long Innes J; and see *Floydd v Cheyney* [1970] Ch 602 at 609–610 per Megarry J. For a Canadian case to the same effect, see *Reynolds v Urquhart* (1902) 5 Terr LR 413 (injury to a defendant outweighing benefit to the plaintiff and plaintiff's right of action not entirely free from doubt).

16 For a general discussion of this maxim, see Keeton and Sheridan *Equity* (3rd edn) 23–25.

17 (1819) 2 Swan 108 at 157.

discharge a receiver on grounds that the deed giving rise to his appointment was oppressive as a bargain with an expectant heir and Lord Eldon would only entertain the application on terms that there was a tender of the purchase money and interest.[18] One equity which the court may extract is an undertaking from a plaintiff to be answerable for what the appointed receiver shall receive or become liable to pay until he shall have given security as directed by the order.[19] There are many examples of the maxim in operation: it pervades almost everywhere in equity and there will no doubt be other factual situations in which a receiver will only be appointed at the price of some equitable act or account.

Lack of clean hands

The principle that he who comes to equity must come with clean hands is sometimes stated as though it were the equivalent of the principle that he who seeks equity must do equity. Thus in 1786 Lord Mansfield CJ said 'that in an equitable action the plaintiff must "come with clean hands" according to the principle that those who seek equity must do equity.'[20] But this is a confusion. A court of equity will refuse equitable relief to a plaintiff whose conduct in relation to the subject matter of the litigation has been improper. Impropriety goes further than a failure to do equity or is, at least, an extreme example of such a failure. It does not mean a general depravity; it must have an immediate and necessary relation to the equity sued for.[1] It bears resemblance to the maxim *ex turpi causa non oritur actio* which applies both in equity and at law. But where the latter maxim is applicable there is no need to rely on lack of clean hands.

The defence may be available wherever equitable relief is claimed. It was considered in relation to injunctive relief in *Duchess of Argyll v Duke of Argyll*[2] where Ungoed-Thomas J said:

> 'A person coming to equity for relief—and this is equitable relief which the plaintiff seeks—must come with clean hands; but the cleanliness required is to be judged in relation to the relief that is sought.'

The defence of 'clean hands' failed because the plaintiff's past immoral attitude to marriage was irrelevant to the issue of breach of confidence. The appointment of a receiver operates as an injunction[3] but any claim that the plaintiff

---

18 (1819) 2 Swan 108 at 166–167. For a short modern example, see *Automobile and General Finance Co Ltd v Hoskins Investments Ltd* (1934) 34 SRNSW 375, 51 WN 129.
19 See eg 33 *Court Forms* (1997 Issue) 106, Form 5.
20 See *Fitzroy v Gwillim* (1786) 1 Term Rep 153. The two maxims are not infrequently lumped together: see eg 16 *Halsbury's Laws of England* (4th edn) paras 1303–1305. But doing equity is prospective and the principle of clean hands is retrospective.
1 *Dering v Earl of Winchelsea* (1787) 1 Cox Eq Cas 318 at 319 per Eyre CB.
2 [1967] Ch 302, [1965] 1 All ER 611 (injunction granted to restrain disclosure of marital confidences).
3 See at p 410.

seeking such relief has unclean hands would have to be directly related to the subject matter of the action to be successful as a defence. Thus a receiver or manager would presumably not be appointed of an undertaking of an immoral nature[4] or of an illegal company[5] or of the copyright in libellous or pornographic material.[6]

4 *Smith v White* (1866) LR 1 Eq 626; and see *Gill v Lewis* [1956] 2 QB 1, [1956] 1 All ER 844, CA.
5 *Re South Wales Atlantic Steamship Co* (1876) 2 Ch D 763, CA.
6 *Walcot v Walker* (1802) 7 Ves 1.

CHAPTER 27

Effect of appointment

IN GENERAL

The effect or results of the appointment of a receiver by the court are far reaching and impinge upon many different rights and problems. Of course the first approach to the appointment must be, to spell out the effect on the appointee himself; he becomes the receiver and it is necessary to analyse his status. The status of the order itself, namely its manner of operation, is another effect requiring consideration. In those cases where there is a forfeiture clause it is necessary to determine what effect the appointment has upon such a clause. The effect of a receivership order on third parties is the widest topic of all. Here arise questions regarding parties claiming possession, the landlord of premises leased by the chargor, parties having paramount rights, judgment creditors, those enjoying liens, and other assorted claimants.

STATUS OF RECEIVER

The status of a receiver appointed by the court has been defined and analysed on many occasions. He is of course first and foremost an officer of the court. A receiver, in the words of Viscount Haldane LC, 'is an officer of the Court put in to discharge certain duties prescribed by the order appointing him'.[1] 'Unquestionably a receiver is an officer of the Court, because appointed by the Court.'[2] He is 'nothing more than the hand of the Court'[3] and 'is a servant of the court and has only such power and authority as the court may choose to give him.'[4] Statements such as these tell the truth, but not the whole truth. 'Usually the receiver appointed by the Court is an officer of the Court and represents neither the plaintiff nor the defendant.'[5] He is in addition appointed for the benefit of all

---

1 *Parsons v Sovereign Bank of Canada* [1913] AC 160. For earlier Canadian cases, see *Forfar v Sage* (1902) 5 Terr LR 255; *Bottoms v Pacific North West Lumber Co* [1929] 4 DLR 415, BC.
2 *McMeckan v Aitken* (1895) 21 VLR 65 at 69 per Holroyd J.
3 *Wilkinson v Gangadhar Sirkar* (1871) 6 BLR 486, Ind.
4 *Manick Lall Seal v Surrut Coomaree Dassee* (1895) ILR 22 Calc 648, Ind.
5 *Trusts and Guarantee Co v Grand Valley Rly Co* (1915) 24 DLR 171 at 173 per Hodgins JA.

parties to the action.[6] In some cases he has been described as being in a sense in the position of trustee or quasi-trustee to all,[7] but these descriptions are heterodox.

The traditional view is that until the rights and wrongs have been determined he is neither agent nor trustee for either party. In a mortgage case it was said that he 'takes possession of assets in which the mortgagee and mortgagor are both interested with the duty of dealing with them finally in the interest of both parties'.[8] The same is true of other cases where property is in dispute. 'A receiver is not an agent for any other person, and a receiver is not a trustee. The receiver is appointed by the order of the court and is responsible to the court and cannot obey the directions of the parties in the action, and in no sense does he stand in the position of agent to the parties who are interested at the suit of whom or one of whom he has been appointed.'[9]

It is then the corollary of the receiver being appointed for the benefit of all parties that he is, as a rule, in no sense an agent or trustee for the party or any of the parties at whose instance the appointment is made.[10] Thus he will not be discharged merely on the application of the party on whose application he was appointed.[11] On the other hand in certain cases a receiver will, after the disputed right has been determined, be considered the receiver of the person entitled. So as between vendor and purchaser the possession by a receiver appointed at the instance of the vendor is attributed to the purchaser from the date at which the purchase ought to have been completed,[12] and to the vendor from the date when it is established that he cannot make out his title.[13]

A receiver and manager appointed by the court over company property is not an agent of the company. They do not appoint him; he is not bound to obey their directions; and they cannot dismiss him, however much they may disapprove of the mode in which he is carrying on the business. Only the court can dismiss him or give him directions as to the mode of carrying on the business, or interfere with him, if he is not carrying on the business properly. The incidents of his relation to the court are such as would, if they existed as between him and an ordinary person, constitute him an agent for such person; but it is of course impossible to suppose that the relation of agent and principal exists between him and the court. The inference which necessarily arises is that the intention is that he shall act in pursuance of his appointment on his own responsibility and not as an agent, because otherwise nobody would be responsible for his acts. The

---

6 *Davis v Duke of Marlborough* (1819) 2 Swan 108 at 118; *Searle v Smales* (1855) 25 LTOS 106, 3 WR 437; *Bertrand v Davies* (1862) 31 Beav 429 at 436; *Seagram v Tuck* (1881) 18 Ch D 296; *Davy v Scarth* [1906] 1 Ch 55 at 57; *Re Newdigate Colliery Co Ltd* [1912] 1 Ch 468, CA; *Viola v Anglo-American Cold Storage Co* [1912] 2 Ch 305 at 311.

7 *Simpson v Ottawa and Prescott Rly* (1860) 1 Chy Chrs 99 per Spragge V-C (trustee); *Brown v Perry* (1865) 1 Chy Chrs 253 per Spragge V-C (quasi-trustee).

8 *Re Newdigate Colliery Co Ltd* [1912] 1 Ch 468 at 478.

9 *Bacup Corpn v Smith* (1890) 44 Ch D 395 at 398 per Chitty J.

10 *Angel v Smith* (1804) 9 Ves 335; *Bacup Corpn v Smith* (1890) 44 Ch D 395, CA; *Ingham v Sutherland* (1890) 63 LT 614; *Boehm v Goddall* [1911] 1 Ch 155.

11 *Bainbrigge v Blair* (1841) 3 Beav 421 at 423.

12 *Boehm v Wood* (1823) Turn & R 332 at 345 (purchaser compelled to accept title).

13 *McLeod v Phelps* (1838) 2 Jur 962.

company cannot be liable for he is not their agent, and the court clearly cannot be liable.[14]

A receiver does not acquire any title or estate from the order appointing him. Nor does the order vest in him any rights of action.[15] Thus a receiver of a company has no right to bring an action in his own name for a debt due to the company since no cause of action is vested in him.[16] As one judge has put it:[17]

'The receiver is the proper person to collect and get in the outstanding debts. . . . But if litigation is needed to recover the alleged debt it must be prosecuted in the name of the person having title to recover at law. The receiver is no more than an officer of the Court who becomes custodian of the assets when received, and has no right to sue in his own name for a debt.'

The principle is not restricted to actions to recover debts: it applies to the recovery of property generally[18] so that a receiver cannot maintain an action for conversion of property the legal title to which was never vested in him and of which he has never had actual possession.[19]

The receiver acts in relation to the property subjected to a court receivership on the titles of the persons who are parties to the action. So the appointment of a receiver by way of equitable execution over a debtor's interest under a will does not constitute on the part of the debtor an attempted alienation or charge or vesting of the interest in anyone else so as to create a forfeiture of that interest: in such a case neither the receiver nor the creditor takes any property or estate.[20] Again a receiver is not personally liable to the landlord to pay out rent in respect of leaseholds over which he is appointed, as no estate is vested in him.[1]

Equally the order does not effect an automatic change of possession.[2] Clearly an appointment over property out of the jurisdiction cannot of itself change the possession[3] but the same principle applies to property within the jurisdiction.[4]

The appointment by the court of a receiver over the estate of the defendant does not change the correlative rights of landlord and tenant previously subsisting between the defendant and his tenants, although the court acquires, by the appointment, additional powers of enforcing the landlord's rights.[5]

A receiver appointed in respect of land which is tenanted is entitled to the rents payable by the tenant or tenants.[6] Usually the order itself will contain an express provision for the payment of rents to the receiver[7] or a provision for attornment

14 *Burt Boulton and Hayward v Bull* [1895] 1 QB 276 at 279 per Lord Esher MR.
15 *Shallcross v Garesche* (1897) 5 BCR 320, BCCA: *Bolton v Darling Downs Building Society* [1935] SR Qd 237.
16 *Franco-Belgium Investment Co v Dubuc* [1918] 2 WWR 684 at 686, Alta.
17 *McGuin v Fretts* (1887) 13 OR 699 at 702, Ont CA per Boyd C.
18 *Re Scottish Properties Pty Ltd* (1977) 2 ACLR 264 at 271 per Needham J.
19 *Dickey v McCaul* (1887) 14 AR 166; *Stuart v Grough* (1887) 14 OR 255.
20 *Re Beaumont* [1910] WN 181.
 1 *Justice v James* (1899) 15 TLR 181 at 182, CA.
 2 *Pratchett v Drew* [1924] 1 Ch 280, 93 LJ Ch 137.
 3 *Re Huinac Copper Mines Ltd* [1910] WN 218.
 4 *Pratchett v Drew* [1924] 1 Ch 280, 93 LJ Ch 137.
 5 *Church Temporalities Comrs of Ireland v Harrington* (1883) 11 LR Ir 127 at 136.
 6 *McDonnel v White* (1865) 11 HL Cas 570 at 583; *Re Lord Annaly* (1891) 27 LR Ir 523.
 7 *Seton's Judgments and Orders* (7th edn) 725; *Underhay v Read* (1887) 20 QBD 209 at 210, CA.

by the tenant to the receiver[8] or both. However, until the order has been obtained and served on the tenants, payment of the rent to the receiver cannot be enforced.[9] It is convenient to discuss the enforcement of the payment of rent and of the requirement of attornment by the tenants in turn.

OPERATION AS INJUNCTION

The appointment of a receiver, as Lindslay LJ had occasion to remark in several cases,[10] operates as an injunction,[11] restraining the parties to the action from receiving any part of the property affected by the appointment.[12] Thus the appointment of a receiver operates as an injunction against the execution debtor receiving anything from his co-partners and if his co-partners pay over to him anything with knowledge of the appointment of the receiver they may get into trouble.[13] An order obtained by a judgment creditor appointing a receiver by way of equitable execution operates as an injunction to restrain the judgment debtor from himself receiving money over which the receiver is appointed and prevents him from dealing with the money to the prejudice of the execution creditor.[14]

DATE FROM WHICH THE ORDER SPEAKS

The order appointing a receiver, or for that matter a receiver and manager, speaks from the moment it is made:[15] it never relates back to the date of the application nor indeed does it have any retrospective effect.[16] That is not to say that the date of the application is of necessity entirely irrelevant: it may well be material for crystallising priorities as, for example, in a debenture holder's action.[17] But from the date of the court's announcement the receiver is an officer and representative

8 For a form of notice to attorn, see 33 Atkin's Court Forms (2nd edn) (1997 Issue) 167, Form 57.

9 *Mitchel v Duke of Manchester* (1750) 2 Dick 787; *Hobhouse v Hollcombe* (1848) 2 De G & Sm 208; *Hollier v Hedges* (1853) 2 I Ch R 370; *Hobson v Sherwood* (1854) 19 Beav 575; *Mullarkey v Donohoe* (1885) 16 LR Ir 365.

10 *Re Sartoris' Estate* [1892] 1 Ch 11 at 22; *Tyrrell v Painton* [1895] 1 QB 202, CA; *Brown Janson & Co v Hutchinson & Co* [1895] 1 QB 737 at 739; *Re Harrison and Bottomley* [1899] 1 Ch 465 at 471 per Lindley MR.

11 See also *Baxter v West* (1858) 28 LJ Ch 169, 32 LTOS 155.

12 *Re Marquis of Anglesey* [1903] 2 Ch 727; *Ridout v Fowler* [1904] 1 Ch 658 at 663–664; *Ideal Bedding Co Ltd v Holland* [1907] 2 Ch 157; *Re A Debtor* [1909] 1 KB 430, CA.

13 *Brown Janson & Co v Hutchinson & Co* [1895] 1 QB 737, CA.

14 *Re Marquis of Anglesey* [1903] 2 Ch 727.

15 That is, announced in court: *Re Bristow* [1906] 2 IR 215, 40 ILTR 30; *Levasseur v Mason & Barry Ltd* [1891] 2 QB 73, 60 LJQB 659, CA (equitable execution is immediate although payment at a later date is directed).

16 *Re Clarke* [1898] 1 Ch 336 at 339, CA.

17 *Industrial Development Bank v Valley Dairy Ltd* [1953] 1 DLR 788, [1953] OR 70; *Great Lakes Petroleum Co Ltd v Border Cities Oil Co Ltd* [1934] 2 DLR 743, [1934] OR 244, CA.

of the court.[18] How quickly he can grind into action will depend upon whether under the order he is immediately equipped with all the necessary authority. That will usually turn on whether he has been required to give security or not. If he has been required to give security his authority to proceed is only complete when he has given security and that security has been perfected.[19] On the other hand if no security is required under the order the receiver has the necessary status to proceed without further ado even though his appointment is extended by a further order of the court requiring him to provide security.[20]

In *Re Watkins*[1] it was held that the appointment of a receiver of the rents of land at the instance of a judgment creditor, though conditional upon the receiver's giving security, operates as an immediate delivery of the land in execution. When the security is afterwards given the order relates back to the date when it was made. In the course of argument James LJ commented[2] that the only point decided in *Edwards v Edwards*[3] was that it was not a contempt of court for an execution creditor to seize chattels after an order appointing a receiver on his giving security, but before the security had been given or possession taken. Referring to *Edwards v Edwards*, he said, 'The case relates to chattels and not to land'. Certainly 'it is settled, as regards personalty, that when the order is in the form of appointing a receiver upon giving security his appointment is not effectual until the security is given'.[4] But it has to be borne in mind that the only real point in *Re Watkins* was whether an order for the appointment of a receiver was really an equitable execution, an actual 'delivery in execution by virtue of other lawful authority'.[5]

TENANTS

If land over which a receiver is appointed by the court is in the possession of tenants the receiver is entitled to an order for attornment and payment of the relevant rent to him. This is because a receiver of land never takes actual possession: he only receives the rents.[6] Usually an express provision for attornment and payment will be inserted in the order of appointment itself,[7] although, naturally

18 *Aston v Heron* (1834) 2 My & K 390; *Owen v Homan* (1853) 4 HL Cas 997 at 1032, HL; *Smart v Flood & Co* (1883) 49 LT 467; *McMeckan v Aitken* (1895) 21 VLR 65 at 60; *Boehm v Goodall* [1911] 1 Ch 155; *Parsons v Sovereign Bank of Canada* [1913] AC 160 at 167, PC.
19 *Defries v Creed* (1865) 6 New Rep 17, 34 LJ Ch 607; *Edwards v Edwards* (1876) 2 Ch D 291; *Re Sims & Woods Ltd* [1916] WN 223 (where appointment lapsed); *Ridout v Fowler* [1904] 1 Ch 658 at 662; affd [1904] 2 Ch 93, CA; *Freeman v Trimble* (1906) 6 SRNSW 133.
20 *Morrison v Skerne Ironworks Co Ltd* (1889) 60 LT 588.
 1 (1879) 13 Ch D 252, CA; *Re Shephard* (1889) 43 Ch D 131 at 135, CA; *Ridout v Fowler* [1904] 1 Ch 658 at 661.
 2 (1879) 13 Ch D 252 at 255.
 3 (1876) 2 Ch D 291, CA.
 4 *Ridout v Fowler* [1904] 1 Ch 658 at 662.
 5 A statutory formulation in 27 & 28 Vict c112, s 1.
 6 *Re Watkins, ex p Evans* (1879) 13 Ch D 252 at 255, CA per James LJ arguendo.
 7 *Seton's Judgments and Orders* (7th edn) 725; *Underhay v Read* (1887) 20 QBD 209, CA; 33 *Court Forms* (1989 Issue) 200, Form 8.

enough, payment cannot be enforced until the order has been made and served on the tenants.[8]

Formerly an order directing a tenant to pay rent to the receiver could be enforced by attachment.[9] Sequestration is however still available as a method of enforcement.[10]

If the defendant is in possession or personal occupation of premises the receivership order will direct him to give up his possession or occupation to the receiver[11] or attorn tenant to the receiver at an occupation rent.[12] However the court has no jurisdiction to order a person in possession of land to attorn to a receiver where the tenancy is not clear, or where a right of purchase is set up by such person.[13] An appropriate course for the court to take where there is ambiguity or contentiousness of that kind might be to refer the matter to the master to inquire and report what steps should be taken against the party in possession.[14] The occupation rent itself is determined on a reference to chambers or to the master.[15] In the case of the order directing the defendant to give up possession or to attorn tenant,[16] occupation rent is payable from the date of the order;[17] but if the order is silent in this respect occupation rent is only payable from the date when the receiver demands it.[18] The receiver is not entitled, at any rate until the rights of the parties have been determined in the action, to any payment in respect of the defendant's possession prior to the order.[19] And a receiver may not distrain upon goods of a defendant in possession who has been constituted tenant.[20]

If despite service of the order a tenant refuses to pay the rent to the court's designated receiver, the receiver may obtain leave to distrain[1] or to bring an

---

8 *Mitchel v Duke of Manchester* (1750) 2 Dick 787; *Hobhouse v Hollcombe* (1848) 2 De G & Sm 208; *Hollier v Hedges* (1853) 2 I Ch R 370; *Hobson v Sherwood* (1854) 19 Beav 575; *Mullarkey v Donohoe* (1885) 16 LR Ir 365. For a form of notice to attorn, see 33 *Court Forms* (1989 Issue) 232, Form 2.

9 *Mitchel v Duke of Manchester* supra; *Batchelor v Blake* (1824) 1 Hog 98; *Anon* (1824) 2 Mol 499; *Brown v O'Connor* (1828) 2 Hog 77; *Brennan v Kenny* (1852) 2 I Ch R 579; *Williams v Williams* (1863) 11 WR 635.

10 *Church Temporalities Comrs of Ireland v Harrington* (1883) 11 LR Ir 127 at 136.

11 *Griffith v Griffith* (1751) 2 Ves Sen 400; *Hawkes v Holland* [1881] WN 128, CA; *Edgell v Wilson* [1893] WN 145.

12 *Re Maudslay Sons & Field* [1900] 1 Ch 602 at 611 per Cozens Hardy J; *Leney & Sons Ltd v Callingham and Thompson* [1908] 1 KB 79; *Pratchett v Drew* [1924] 1 Ch 280; *Masters v Crouch* (1927) 63 L Jo 557 (plaintiff was a second mortgagee).

13 *Brydon v Innes* (1868) 5 WW & AB (Eq) 189, Vic Sup Ct per Molesworth J.

14 (1868) 5 WW & AB (Eq) 189.

15 *Re Burchnall* [1893] WN 171, 38 Sol Jo 59.

16 *Everett v Belding* (1852) 22 LJ Ch 75, 20 LTOS 136; *Randfield v Randfield* (1859) 7 WR 651; *Real and Personal Advance Co v M'Carthy and Smith* (1879) 40 LT 878; *Re Burchnall* [1893] WN 171, 38 Sol Jo 59.

17 *Yorkshire Banking Co v Mullan* (1887) 35 Ch D 125; *Re Burchnall* [1893] WN 171.

18 *Yorkshire Banking Co v Mullan* (1887) 35 Ch D 125.

19 (1887) 35 Ch D 125; and see also *Lloyd v Mason* (1837) 2 My & Cr 487.

20 *Griffith v Griffith* (1751) 2 Ves Sen 400.

1 *Mills v Fry* (1815) Coop G 107, 19 Ves 277; *Fitzpatrick v Eyre* (1824) 1 Hog 171; *Anon* (1826) 1 Hog 335; *Lucas v Mayne* (1826) 1 Hog 394; *Langley v Aylmer, Spiller v Mellifont* (1841) 3 I Eq R 492.

action for the recovery of the land.[2] In exercising his right to distrain he may exercise his own discretion as to the time of enforcing the rent but he must not act oppressively.[3] Distress cannot of course be proceeded with if in fact at the date when leave to distrain was given the tenancy had already been determined some six months.[4]

The remedy of recovery of the land is available against a defendant who is in possession under a collusive tenancy agreement at an inadequate rent.[5] If the alleged tenant took possession after and with notice of the order he may be brought before the court to justify his refusal to pay rent without going through the procedural hoop of being made a party to the action.[6]

Liability of tenant after notice

As a general rule a tenant who has not been served with an order directing payment of rent to a receiver is justified in continuing to pay rent to his landlord.[7] Nevertheless if in point of fact he has notice of the appointment and so knows that the landlord is no longer entitled to receive the rent he will be compelled to pay the rent over again to the receiver,[8] unless he can plead compulsion of law, or some other maintainable defence. In *Underhay v Read*,[9] for example, the order appointing a receiver of mortgaged premises, which had been let after the mortgage, expressly preserved 'the rights of any prior incumbrancers who may think proper to take possession of the same by virtue of their respective securities'. The receiver was appointed at the instance of a judgment creditor. Rent was outstanding at the date of the appointment and the mortgagee threatened the tenant with proceedings and thereby extracted the rent from him. The decision of the Court of Appeal relied both on the reservation of the rights of prior incumbrancers and on the fact that the tenant paid under compulsion of law and in consequence of his lessor's default as grounds for absolving the tenant from liability to the receiver.

If a tenant or other person in possession pays no attention to an order to attorn to the receiver the proper course is to serve him personally with a copy of the order and any certificate there may be completing the appointment,[10] together with a written notice signed by the receiver requiring him to attorn and pay out.[11]

2 *Lord Mansfield v Hamilton, Hobhouse v Hamilton* (1804) 2 Sch & Lef 28; *Fitzgerald v Fitzgerald* (1843) 5 I Eq R 525; cf *Murtin v Walker* (1837) Sau & Sc 139 (leave refused on special grounds).
3 *Lucas v Mayne* (1826) 1 Hog 394.
4 *Paxton v Dryden* (1873) 6 PR 127, Can.
5 *Comyn v Smith* (1823) 1 Hog 81.
6 *Reid v Middleton* (1823) Turn & R 455.
7 *Codrington v Johnstone* (1838) 1 Beav 520; *Russell v Russell* (1853) 2 I Ch R 574; *McDonnel v White* (1865) 11 HL Cas 570.
8 *Brown v O'Connor* (1828) 2 Hog 77; *Mullarkey v Donohoe* (1885) 16 LR Ir 365.
9 (1887) 20 QBD 209, CA following *Johnson v Jones* (1839) 9 Ad & El 809, 1 Per & Dav 651; and see also *Church Temporalities Comrs of Ireland v Harrington* (1883) 11 LR Ir 127.
10 See 33 *Court Forms* (1997 Issue) 126, Form 26 (certificate by master that receiver has given security).
11 33 *Court Forms* (1997 Issue) 232, Form 62.

In the event of continuing recalcitrance the next step is to serve the tenant or other person in possession with an application to attorn and pay rent within a stipulated period.[12] The application should be backed up by evidence showing service of the order and certificate (if any) and non-compliance with the order. If he fails to appear on the summons the master will make an appropriate four-day order[13] and this should be served on the defaulting tenant or person in possession personally, indorsed with a penal notice. The final move to deal with continuing default is for the plaintiff to move for committal or a writ of sequestration.[14]

Arrears

A receiver of rents is entitled to all arrears of rent unpaid when the order appointing him is made,[15] and the tenant will be ordered to pay those arrears even though the tenant has not attorned to the receiver.[16] It has been held that tenants who pay such arrears to their landlord before they have notice of the order ought not be compelled to pay the rent a second time to the receiver. But it is otherwise with a party to the action who having notice of the order, collects arrears of rent or takes securities for the amount due: such a person may be ordered to hand over the rents to the receiver.[17]

Where arrears of rent have been specifically assigned the receiver's right to reclaim them from the assignees may well depend upon whether the rent issued out of land specifically mortgaged or out of land simply forming part of a floating charge. Arrears attributed to specifically mortgaged land will be recoverable by the receiver from the assignees.[18]

The terms of any order requiring an occupant of land to pay an occupation rent must be carefully considered by the receiver. If, for example, the order directs payment of an occupation rent by a defendant in occupation of any part of the premises,[19] he will be a tenant only from the date of the relevant order. An order in that form does not entitle the receiver, at any rate until the rights of the parties have been sorted out in the action itself, to any payment in respect of his previous possession.[1] On a parity of reasoning a receiver should not distrain upon the goods of a defendant in possession who has not been constituted a tenant.[2]

---

12 33 *Court Forms* (1997 Issue) 131, Form 31.
13 33 *Court Forms* (1997 Issue), 131, Form 32.
14 RSC Ord 45, r 5(1).
15 *Codrington v Johnstone* (1838) 1 Beav 520 at 524; *Abbot v Stratton* (1846) 9 I Eq R 233 at 243; *Moore v Marquis of Donegal* (1847) 11 I Eq R 364 at 368; *Russell v Russell* (1853) 2 I Ch R 574; *Re Lord Annaly* (1891) 27 LR Ir 523.
16 *Hobson v Sherwood* (1854) 19 Beav 575.
17 *Hollier v Hedges* (1853) 2 I Ch R 370; *Russell v Russell* (1853) 2 I Ch R 574.
18 *Re Ind Coope & Co Ltd* [1911] 2 Ch 223.
19 *Everett v Belding* (1852) 22 LJ Ch 75, 20 LTOS 136; *Randfield v Randfield* (1859) 7 WR 651; *Re Burchnall* [1893] WN 171.
 1 *Lloyd v Mason* (1837) 2 My & Cr 487; *Yorkshire Banking Co v Mullan* (1887) 35 Ch D 125.
 2 *Griffith v Griffith* (1751) 2 Ves Sen 400.

THIRD PARTIES IN OR CLAIMING POSSESSION

As against a stranger to the action who is in *actual* possession, the appointment of a receiver is of no effect.[3] Thus in *Salt v Cooper*[4] the legal possession of a receiver of the Court of Bankruptcy was sufficient to fend off the claims of a receiver appointed by an execution creditor.

Again an order appointing a receiver and any delivery in execution or other proceedings pursuant to the order are void against a purchaser of land to which the order relates unless it is registered as a land charge[5] or, if the land is registered land, unless a caution has been registered.[6]

Where the stranger is *not* in possession at the date of the receiver's appointment, although his rights are not affected, he will not be allowed to assert them without leave of the court,[7] unless the order is made without prejudice to his rights.[8]

Accordingly an action for possession may not be brought against the receiver without the leave of the court.[9] Moreover even when such an action has been brought by leave of the court against the receiver and judgment has been recovered, the judgment cannot, without leave be enforced by writ of possession as against the receiver.[10] In the older cases we find instances of actions being restrained by injunction.[11] Where an action could formerly have been restrained by injunction a stay of proceedings may now be obtained.[12]

Likewise when a receiver has been appointed over leaseholders, the landlord may not distrain for rent without the leave of the court.[13] Nor after an appointment may a distraint for rates be levied without leave.[14]

Again moving to another field a receiver appointed in an administration action may not recover rent from the executors.[15]

JUDGMENT CREDITORS

The appointment of a receiver in that rarity a debenture holder's action causes

---

3 *Davis v Duke of Marlborough* (1819) 2 Swan 108 at 116; *Johnes v Claughton* (1822) Jac 573; *Morrogh v Hoare* (1842) 5 I Eq R 195 at 199; *Evelyn v Lewis* (1844) 3 Hare 472.
4 (1880) 16 Ch D 544, CA; see also *Underhay v Read* (1887) 20 QBD 209, CA; *Engel v South Metropolitan Brewing and Bottling Co* [1891] WN 31.
5 LCA 1972, ss 6 and 8.
6 LRA 1925, s 59.
7 See *Searle v Choat* (1884) 25 Ch D 723, CA; *Re Henry Pound, Sons & Hutchins* (1889) 42 Ch D 402 at 420 and 422.
8 *Davis v Duke of Marlborough* (1819) 2 Swan 108 at 115; *Underhay v Read* (1887) 20 QBD 209, CA.
9 *Bryan v Cormick* (1788) Cox Eq Cas 422; *Angel v Smith* (1804) 9 Ves 335; *Brooks v Greathed* (1820) 1 Jac & W 176; *Hawkins v Gathercole* (1852) 1 Drew 12 at 18; *Re Battersby's Estate* (1892) 31 LR Ir 73.
10 *Morris v Baker* (1903) 73 LJ Ch 143.
11 *Lees v Waring* (1825) 1 Hog 216; *Evelyn v Lewis* (1844) 3 Hare 472.
12 See Supreme Court of Judicature (Consolidation) Act 1925, s 41 (repealed).
13 *Russell v East Anglian Rly* (1850) 3 Mac & G 104 at 118; *Re New City Constitutional Club Co* (1887) 34 Ch D 646 at 660, CA.
14 *Re British Fullers' Earth Co Ltd* (1901) 17 TLR 232.
15 *Minford v Carse and Hunter* [1912] 2 IR 245, Ir CA.

the debenture holder's floating charge to crystallise, puts an end to the company's authority to carry on its business and so prevents the company from making fresh charges on its assets, and also from paying its creditors in the ordinary course of business. The floating charge becomes a fixed equitable charge and an execution creditor takes subject to all prior equities.[16]

The relative priorities which obtain between a receiver and a debtor's execution creditors are the same for private and court receivers. A judgment creditor who has levied, but not completed, execution at the time of the appointment is usually stopped in his tracks: the receiver has the edge in priority.[17]

There is, however, in the case of a court-appointed receiver this additional restriction: that as the receiver is an officer of the court, steps taken against him have to observe proper formalities.

Accordingly a judgment creditor ought not, without the leave of the court, to levy execution on property which is in the hands of the receiver,[18] albeit that his judgment was obtained *before* the appointment of the receiver.[19] Nor, in the absence of leave from the court, should a judgment creditor seek to attach money in the hands of the receiver which has been directed to be paid to the judgment debtor[20] or retain possession of any goods he may have seized.[1] Nor is the judgment debtor allowed to sue the receiver for damages for seizure of goods:[2] his proper remedy is to apply for the relief to the court which appointed the receiver.[3]

The receiver's right will prevail if all that has happened in the execution process is that the sheriff, pursuant to a writ of fieri facias, has taken possession of the goods, and the receiver has been appointed.[4] However, if following seizure the company pays the whole or part of the debt to prevent a sale the judgment creditor will usually be entitled to the whole[5] or part[6] of the sum paid, even though at the point of crystallisation the money is still in the sheriff's hands. Whether a judgment creditor is entitled to the proceeds of sale if the sheriff actually sells the goods prior to crystallisation is not entirely clear.[7] In a winding up such a sequence of events would give the judgment creditor priority[8] and the same is probably the case even where there is no winding up.

In *Taunton v Sheriff of Warwickshire*[9] a company created a floating charge over its assets. Just over two and a half years later execution was levied on the chattels of the company. A flurry of events ensued. Two days after the levying of

---

16 *Re Marquis of Anglesey* [1903] 2 Ch 727.
17 *Evans v Rival Granite Quarries Ltd* [1910] 2 KB 979 at 990, 997 and 1000, CA.
18 *Russell v East Anglian Rly Co* (1850) 3 Mac & G 104; *Potts v Warwick and Birmingham Canal Navigation Co* (1853) Kay 142 (execution held subject to prior incumbrancers).
19 *Ames v Birkenhead Docks Trustees* (1855) 20 Beav 332.
20 *De Winton v Brecon Corpn (No 2)* (1860) 28 Beav 200.
 1 *Morrison v Skerne Ironworks Co Ltd* (1889) 60 LT 588.
 2 *Re Potter, ex p Day* (1883) 48 LT 912.
 3 *Re Potter, ex p Day* (1883) 48 LT 912.
 4 *Re Standard Manufacturing Co* [1891] 1 Ch 627, CA; *Re Opera Ltd* [1891] 3 Ch 260, CA.
 5 *Heaton and Dugard Ltd v Cutting Bros Ltd* [1925] 1 KB 655.
 6 *Robinson v Burnell's Vienna Bakery Co* [1904] 2 KB 624.
 7 *Re Opera Ltd* [1891] 3 Ch 260, CA.
 8 IA 1986, s 183(1).
 9 [1895] 2 Ch 319, CA.

execution the debenture holders started an action to enforce their securities by the appointment of a receiver; two days after that, notice of the action was given and the sheriff was informed that the debenture holders claimed the goods he had seized; and two days later the debenture holders in their turn were informed that the sheriff would sell the next day. This information prompted a fresh writ and an ex parte injunction the following day, extending till the next day. A receiver was in fact appointed in the prior action on the day the ex parte injunction was (unless renewed) due to expire. The floating charge constituted by the debentures thereupon crystallised. Meanwhile on the day on which the ex parte injunction was granted the solicitor for the debenture holders had paid to the sheriff the amount of the debt and costs due to the judgment creditor with an accompanying letter stating that the lodgement of money was under protest and without prejudice to the rights of the debenture holders. At first instance Kekewich J held the money so deposited to be proceeds of sale but gave priority to the claim of the debenture holders because the sale proceeds had not been paid to the judgment creditor before crystallisation.[10] The Court of Appeal found that the chattels had never been sold and that the money in the hands of the sheriff did not represent sale proceeds but was money deposited with the sheriff to abide the result of the action for a receiver. The floating charge having crystallised before any sale the debenture holders had priority. Two members of the appellate court left open the question whether the result would have been the same had the floating charge crystallised after a sale by the sheriff but before any proceeds had been paid to the judgment creditor.[11]

Whether if a debenture holder or a receiver on his behalf does not interfere until the execution is completed and the execution creditor has got the money in his own hands his interference would be too late was left open also in *Robinson v Burnell's Vienna Bakery Co*.[12] There too money was paid to a sheriff who had taken goods in execution under a writ of fi fa. The payment had been made by the judgment debtor to avoid a sale and to enable the debtor to carry on business. Afterwards a receiver was appointed in a debenture holders' action while the money was still in the hands of the sheriff and had not been handed over to the judgment creditor. Channell J felt some little difficulty about the case but held that the claim of the execution creditor must prevail over that of the debenture holders. The true effect of the transaction was that the money was paid to the sheriff as part of the debt owing to the execution creditor.

Where a judgment creditor secures a garnishee order against a debtor of a company over whose assets the court appoints a receiver, the claim of the receiver will prevail if the money has not actually been paid to the judgment creditor before crystallisation.[13] The rights of a debenture holder are not displaced by a garnishee order nisi.[14] And the equitable rights of the holder of a floating charge will not be displaced by a garnishee order, even when made absolute, if before actual payment the charge crystallises and the holder applies

---

10 [1895] 1 Ch 734.
11 See [1895] 2 Ch 319 at 322 per Lindley LJ and Lopes LJ.
12 [1904] 2 KB 624.
13 *Norton v Yates* [1906] 1 KB 112; *Cairney v Back* [1906] 2 KB 746.
14 *Sinnott v Bowden* [1912] 2 Ch 414 at 421 per Parker J.

for relief.[15] A receiver may not, however, claim money paid to the garnishor prior to crystallisation of the floating charge.[16]

The receiver's right similarly prevails over that of a solicitor to whom a sum of money has been handed to meet costs not yet incurred.[17]

A receiver appointed by the court over leasehold property is not, in the absence of default, *personally* liable to the landlord for the rent due under the lease.[18] But he is bound to pay the rent due to the landlord out of the rents and profits coming to his hands.[19] In the Irish case of *Balfe v Blake*[20] a receiver had been appointed in an administration action and had for several years duly paid to the head landlord of certain lands the head-rent, subject to which the defendant held those lands. The receiver had received from the sub-tenants sums of money considerably exceeding the amount due for head-rent. The head-rent having fallen into arrear, application was made by the landlord that the receiver be directed to pay these arrears and the court made an order to that effect.

Brady LC put the case in this way:[1]

> 'This Court is bound to act with honesty both to landlord and tenant; and being placed in the position of tenant, to do as a just and honest tenant would do. It holds the rents received from the sub-tenants in usum jus habentium. It is responsible in the first instance to the landlord, it being the primary duty of the tenant, and therefore of a receiver over that tenant's interest, to keep down the head rent. So clear is the receiver's duty in this respect, that if, in consequence of his default, the landlord is compelled to institute proceedings for the recovery of his rent the receiver is held liable for costs if rents have reached his hands. The Court is bound to protect all parties, and were it through its officer to apply the rents received from the sub-tenants to purposes other than those to which they ought to be applied, and leave the head-rent unpaid, the landlord might distrain the lands in the possession of the sub-tenants, who would have already paid the receiver. To such a hardship the Court cannot expose them, nor, on the other hand, is it to deprive the landlord of his due. The receiver is the officer upon whom the performance of the obligations imposed by the possession of the land is devolved. His primary duty is to pay the head-rent, and this he is bound to do without any special order of the Court to that effect.'

PERSONS WITH PARAMOUNT RIGHTS

An order appointing a receiver or receiver and manager usually expressly specifies that the appointment is subject to any existing paramount

15 *Norton v Yates* [1906] 1 KB 112; *Cairney v Back* [1906] 2 KB 746; and see *Evans v Rival Granite Quarries Ltd* [1910] 2 KB 979, CA (where no receiver had been appointed and a garnishee order absolute was refused).
16 *Robson v Smith* [1895] 2 Ch 118.
17 *Re British Tea Table Co (1897) Ltd* (1909) 101 LT 707.
18 *Consolidated Entertainments Ltd v Taylor* [1937] 4 All ER 432.
19 *Jacobs v Van Boolen* (1889) 34 Sol Jo 97. There is a plethora of Irish authority on the point: *Hamilton v Lighton* (1810) 2 Mol 499; *Betagh v Concannon* (1830) 2 Hog 205; *Walsh v Walsh* (1839) 1 I Eq R 209; *Saunderson v Stoney* (1839) 2 I Eq R 153; *Elliott v Elliott* (1849) 1 Ir Jur 165.
20 (1850) 1 I Ch R 365.
1 (1850) 1 I Ch R 365 at 367.

rights.[2] But no such saving clause will be added to an appointment grounded upon the misconduct of the very person who has the paramount right. Thus where a first mortgagee in possession abuses his position the court may accede to an application by the second mortgagee for the appointment of a receiver and order delivery up of possession to the court's appointee.

The appointment of a receiver by the court does not affect or prejudice persons with paramount rights who are actually in possession of those rights in their enjoyment of those rights.[3] In such a case possession is ten tenths of the law and no application to the court on the part of the person actually in possession of the right is necessary. Such an application is necessary if the person with a paramount right is not actually in possession. The application will be for leave to exercise the relevant paramount right or rights, and will not be refused.[4]

There are several cases where a right to distrain has been held to be paramount to the claim of a receiver and the court has accordingly granted leave for the exercise of the right to distrain in question. Thus leave to distrain has been given where the right was conferred by deed,[5] by an order of the court[6] or by statute.[7] A gas board may be given leave to exercise a statutory right of distress for default in paying for gas.[8] The right must of course be paramount to the right of the parties.[9]

The owner of a rent charge on land secured by a right of re-entry was in one case held entitled to leave to enter against a receiver of an undertaking appointed by the court.[10] The grantee of an annuity secured by a term, with a right paramount to that of the parties to the action may get leave to sue for possession.[11] As a rule, however, the court will scrutinise a claim under an alleged adverse possession title before giving leave for the initiation of proceedings.[12]

Procedure for obtaining leave

Any application to the court for leave to enforce rights or raise questions against the court's receiver should be made in the action in which the receiver was appointed and not as a rule by independent proceedings.[13] Before the Judicature Acts the consequences of allowing any such questions to be ventilated in

---

2 *Evelyn v Lewis* (1844) 3 Hare 472. For a form of order, see *Seton's Judgments and Orders* (7th edn) 732.
3 *Evelyn v Lewis* (1844) 3 Hare 472.
4 *Re Metropolitan Amalgamated Estates Ltd* [1912] 2 Ch 497.
5 *Eyton v Denbigh Ruthin and Corwen Rly Co* (1868) LR 6 Eq 14.
6 *Pegge v Neath District Tramways Co* [1895] 2 Ch 508 (order by justices to distrain in respect of unpaid penalties for non-repair).
7 *Re Marriage, Neave & Co* [1896] 2 Ch 663, CA (rates); and see *Reeve v Medway (Upper) Navigation Co* (1905) 21 TLR 400 (non-payment of sum for repair of highway).
8 *Re Adolphe Crosbie Ltd* (1909) 74 JP 25.
9 *Reeve v Medway (Upper) Navigation Co* (1905) 21 TLR 400.
10 *Forster v Manchester and Milford Rly Co* (1880) 49 LJ Ch 454.
11 *Brooks v Greathed* (1820) 1 Jac & W 176.
12 *Angel v Smith* (1804) 9 Ves 335; *Houlditch v Wallace* (1838) 5 Cl & Fin 629 at 667, HL.
13 *Morgan v Smith* (1830) 1 Mol 541; *Smith v Earl of Effingham* (1839) 2 Beav 232 at 235 per Lord Landgale MR; *De Montmorency v Pratt* (1849) 12 I Eq R 411.

different courts might have resulted in a conflict between the jurisdiction of a court of common law and an equity court 'which would have brought each court seeking to maintain its own jurisdiction into a position of extreme difficulty'.[14] But the persistence of the general rule after the Judicature Acts is evidenced by, among other cases, the decision of Neville J in *Re Maidstone Palace of Varieties Ltd*.[15] The applicant in that case was a receiver appointed in the Chancery Division in a debenture holder's action and by virtue of that appointment he had the management of a theatre known as the Maidstone Palace of Varieties. In the course of management he made use of certain plant which was claimed by an electric company as their property, the plant having been supplied under a hire purchase agreement. They claimed that he had no right to use it except on the terms of paying them a rent and they claimed a considerable sum, threatening proceedings in the King's Bench Division. Neville J, citing *Aston v Heron*,[16] made the following observations on the procedural proprieties:[17]

> 'It appears to me that a dispute of that kind is one which . . . the Court will deal with itself, and that it will not allow its officer to be subject to an action in another Court with reference to his conduct in the discharge of the duties of his office, whether right or wrong. The proper remedy for any one aggrieved by his conduct is to apply to this Court in the action in which he was appointed. If any wrong has been done by the officer, the Court will no doubt see that justice is done, but no one has a right to sue such an officer in another Court without the sanction of this Court.'

This principle applies whether the action complained of is done by the receiver within the scope of the order appointing him or not.[18] In certain exceptional cases a fresh action may be appropriate as for example where the security of a prior incumbrancer includes property other than that of a subsequent incumbrancer who has appointed a receiver or where an incumbrancer has a charge over property in addition to that subjected to receivership in a partnership action. Independent proceedings may also be allowed to continue if they do not prejudice the rights of the parties to the action in which the receiver has been appointed.[19]

A person applying for leave to bring an action, despite the appointment of a receiver does not need to show a clear legal right.[20] And it should be noted that even the person at whose instance the receiver was appointed may apply for and be granted leave to bring an action against the receiver;[1] without such leave an action against the receiver by a person at whose instance he was appointed by the

---

14 *Russell v East Anglian Rly Co* (1850) 3 Mac & G 104 at 114–115 per Lord Truro LC.
15 [1909] 2 Ch 283; and see *Searle v Choat* (1884) 25 Ch D 723, CA where the impact of the Judicature Acts is expressly discussed.
16 (1834) 2 My & K 390, 3 LJ Ch 194.
17 [1909] 2 Ch 283 at 286.
18 *Searle v Choat* (1884) 25 Ch D 723, CA; *Ames v Richards* (1905) 40 L Jo 66.
19 *Lewis v Lord Zouche* (1828) 2 Sim 388; *Gowar v Bennett* (1847) 9 LTOS 310. But the position may have been altered by the Judicature Acts; see *Searle v Choat* (1884) 25 Ch D 723, CA.
20 *Lane v Capsey* [1891] 3 Ch 411 (just a tenable claim).
 1 *LP Arthur (Insurance) Ltd v Sisson* [1966] 2 All ER 1003, [1966] 1 WLR 1384.

court 'cannot be endured'.[2] The receiver is not usually a necessary party to any properly sanctioned new action.[3]

An application for leave for a third party to bring proceedings against a court receiver was formerly by summons[4] in the receivership action or by notice of motion[5] in that action.[6] It will now be by application on notice.

Court officer must do equity

The court is rightly sensitive about the conduct of its officers and requires of them strict standards. It requires any receiver appointed by the court to observe a high degree of equitable conduct. There are therefore examples to be found in the cases in which the court has granted relief against its own appointed receiver which would not have been obtained against a private litigant. This point was discussed by Kekewich J when the case of *Re Opera Ltd*[7] was before him at first instance.[8] After remarking that when the court 'comes to deal with an officer of its own, it will do that which it cannot make an ordinary litigant do—that is to say, avoid doing the shabby thing, and do what is really honest',[9] he considered the judgment of Lord Esher MR in *Re Carnac, ex p Simmonds*,[10] which concerned a trustee in bankruptcy. He said:[11]

'I do not understand the Master of the Rolls suggested a question of casuistry, or that a mere sentimental honesty is to prevail, nor that we are to examine delicate questions of ethics, because he uses more than once the phrase "high-minded". Where a man of ordinary honesty, intending to do his duty, is in possession of money of which he would not have been in possession if someone else had not made a mistake—made an erroneous payment or taken a wrong step in honest error—then, as a high-minded man, he sets the matter right, notwithstanding that, if proceedings had been taken in a Court of Law, he would have been held to be rightly in possession.'

If the assets in the hands of an officer of the court, on behalf of creditors or others, have been increased by a transaction occasioned by an honest mistake of law, then, notwithstanding such mistake is not capable of rectification as between ordinary adverse litigants, the court will compel its officer to recognise the rules of honesty as between man and man, and to act accordingly.[12] If the sum is no

---

2 *Re Potter, ex p Day* (1883) 43 LT 912.
3 *Smith v Earl of Effingham* (1839) 2 Beav 232.
4 *Richards v Richards* (1859) John 255; *O'Hagan v North Wingfield Colliery Co* (1882) 26 Sol Jo 671.
5 *Ames v Richards* (1905) 40 L Jo 66 (the motion failed).
6 For a form of summons or notice of motion (which can be adopted), see 33 *Court Forms* (1997 Issue) 131, Form 30.
7 [1891] 2 Ch 154; revsd [1891] 3 Ch 260, CA.
8 His comments on this issue were not disapproved in the Court of Appeal.
9 [1891] 2 Ch 154 at 161.
10 (1885) 16 QBD 308, CA; and see *Re Condon, ex p James* (1874) 9 Ch App 609, 43 LJ Bcy 107.
11 [1891] 2 Ch 154 at 161.
12 [1891] 2 Ch 154 at 162.

longer in his hands he may be ordered to repay the amount in question out of subsequent receipts.[13] Nor is this principle restricted to cases of money paid under a mistake: it applies to any case where the receiver has in his hands money (or presumably other property) which as Buckley LJ in *Re Tyler* put it 'in point of normal justice and honest dealing belongs to some one else'.[14] But the honour of the court cannot be satisfied at the expense of somebody else, who is not in point of law or in point of equity bound to satisfy it out of his own means.[15] For example there is no equity entitling a head lessor to claim payment from the receiver by reason of the latter having been put into use or occupation as an officer of the court, even though he has, by the direction of the court, sold off the mortgagor's goods on the premises and so deprived the head lessor of his landlord's remedy by distress.[16]

Rights of landlord against receiver

The appointment of a receiver over property which is leasehold, and in respect of which rent has to be paid to the landlord or lessor of the land, does not in any way subvert the rights of the landlord or lessor. He continues to retain his rights, albeit that the *enforcement* of those rights will require the leave of the court.[17] Putting it another way the appointment suspends the landlord's rights so that he can, following the appointment, exercise those rights only with the leave of the court.[18] Accordingly a landlord who has obtained judgment for the recovery of land against a debtor whose assets have been made the subject of a receivership order may not proceed to enforce his judgment. It is not enough to have leave to start ejectment proceedings against the debtor. The landlord should also apply to the court which appointed the receiver[19] for leave to issue a writ for possession against the receiver[20] or to take any other procedural step that is appropriate. The court will as a rule be ready to grant leave to the landlord to recover possession unless there are special circumstances to justify a different course.[1] Thus in *Ryan v Ryan*[2] the lease of premises was a partnership asset and a receiver and manager of the partnership assets had been appointed by the court. Roper CJ in Equity held that it was necessary for the landlord to obtain the leave of the court before proceeding to recover possession of the premises.

Provided he follows the right procedure, namely that already discussed, a landlord whose rent is in arrear may be granted either an order on the receiver for

13 *Re Carnac, ex p Simmonds* (1885) 16 QBD 308, 66 LJQB 74, CA.
14 [1907] 1 KB 865 at 873, CA (trustee in bankruptcy).
15 *Re Regent's Canal Ironworks Co, ex p Grissell* (1875) 3 Ch D 411 at 419–420, CA per James LJ.
16 *Hand v Blow* [1901] 2 Ch 721 at 730, CA per Stirling J citing *Re Regent's Canal Ironworks Co, ex p Grissell* (1875) 3 Ch D 411 at 419. The judgment of Stirling J was affirmed by the Court of Appeal without calling on counsel for the receiver: see [1901] 2 Ch at 734.
17 *Re Sutton's Estate* (1863) 32 LJ Ch 437 at 438.
18 *Hand v Blow* [1901] 2 Ch 721 at 735, CA.
19 See *Searle v Choat* (1884) 25 Ch D 723, CA where a first mortgagee sought to restrain the receiver from collecting rents due to the first mortgagee.
20 *Morris v Baker* (1903) 73 LJ Ch 143.
 1 *Brenner v Rose* [1973] 1 WLR 443 at 446.
 2 (1950) 68 WNNSW 33, NSW Sup Ct.

payment out of money received by him[3] or leave to distrain[4] or to proceed under a writ of possession[5] or to re-enter.[6] He may alternatively be granted leave in more general terms, in other words he may be granted leave generally to take such proceedings as he may be advised.[7]

Other cases

The vendor of machinery under a hire purchase agreement who has retained title to the machinery may, notwithstanding that it is on premises occupied by a receiver and manager, get the leave of the court to take it away from the premises. On this principle a machine erected at a colliery by a firm of engine makers with a reservation of title until the whole purchase price should be paid was recoverable despite the appointment of a receiver and manager over the company which was lessee of the colliery, and even though it was a trade fixture.[8] In *Re Morrison, Jones & Taylor Ltd*[9] the effect of the hire purchase agreement was to confer upon the vendors an interest in the land to which the patent automatic sprinkler which they supplied was affixed. It was held that the effect of the agreement was also to authorise them in the events which had happened to enter and remove it: the interests of debenture holders who had a subsequent floating security over the purchaser company being equitable interests, the ordinary principles of priorities applied and the floating charge being subsequent in date was therefore postponed to the interests of the vendors.

Where the title in goods or at any rate the right to take possession of them has passed to a purchaser but the goods have been left on the company's premises the purchaser's right prevails over a debenture holder's receiver.[10]

A person or company wishing to carry out construction works authorised by statute on land over which a receiver has been appointed may be given leave to make proposals in chambers for acquiring such rights or interests as might be necessary.[11] The court may also, in favour of a prior mortgagee, make an order discharging the receiver and letting the prior mortgagee into possession even though he may have been a defendant in the proceedings in which the receiver

---

3 *Neate v Pink* (1846) 15 Sim 450 at 452; on appeal 3 Mac & G 476; *Balfe v Blake* (1850) 1 I Ch R 365; *Great Eastern Rly Co v East London Rly Co* (1881) 44 LT 903, CA; *O'Hagan v North Wingfield Colliery Co* (1882) 26 Sol Jo 671; *Jacobs v Van Boolen, ex p Roberts* (1889) 34 Sol Jo 97, DC.

4 *Russell v East Anglian Rly Co* (1850) 3 Mac & G 104 at 118; *Hand v Blow* [1901] 2 Ch 721 at 737, CA.

5 *Morris v Baker* (1903) 73 LJ Ch 143.

6 *General Share and Trust Co v Wetley Brick and Pottery Co* (1882) 20 Ch D 260, CA; *Hand v Blow* [1901] 2 Ch 721 at 724 and 737, CA.

7 *Walsh v Walsh* (1839) 1 I Eq R 209; *Cramer v Griffith* (1840) 3 I Eq R 230.

8 *Cumberland Union Banking Co v Maryport Hematite Iron and Steel Co* [1892] 1 Ch 415 (where the receiver wished to give up possession of the colliery).

9 [1914] 1 Ch 50, 83 LJ Ch 129, CA.

10 *Hamer v London City and Midland Bank Ltd* (1918) 87 LJKB 973, 118 LT 571 (fixed machinery).

11 *Tink v Rundle* (1847) 10 Beav 318 (railway construction); *Richards v Richards* (1859) John 255 (canal works).

was appointed, so long as there has been no question of his having submitted to be bound by the proceedings.[12] After a company has gone into liquidation a liquidator may, on sufficient grounds, apply for the discharge of a receiver appointed in a debenture holders' action.[13]

By virtue of the order the court does, however, assume control of the property affected and from that time the parties to the action retain possession only as custodians for the court.[14]

Unless a receiver is authorised as a matter of urgency to take possession at once[15] the order will normally appoint the receiver conditionally on giving security and his appointment will not be complete, and he consequently cannot go into possession, until he has given security.[16] Even on giving security he cannot compel delivery of possession unless an order directing delivery of possession has been obtained and served on the parties.[17] Such a direction is usually put in the order[18] whether made at the trial or at some interlocutory stage.[19]

The order appointing a receiver of land will either include a direction for possession specifying a date for the delivery of possession[20] or a direction that the person in possession do attorn at an occupation rent. In the commonest form of order, known as a *Pratchett v Drew* order,[1] provision is made for both possibilities and possession is ordered to be given either forthwith, or on or before a certain date, or within four days of service of the order. If the time limit is not complied with a question of enforcement then arises.

The enforcement of the receiver's right of possession is achieved by various remedies. These were conveniently summarised by Cozens-Hardy J in *Re Maudslay, Sons and Field*:[2]

> 'A receiver is an officer of the Court, and the Court does not allow the possession of its officer to be interfered with without its leave. When the Court appoints a receiver it requires the parties to the action to give up possession to the receiver of all property comprised in the order, and treats them as guilty of contempt if they refuse to do so. The Court will grant a receiver a writ of possession or a writ of assistance to enable him to recover possession and will order tenants to attorn to the receiver.'

12 *Langton v Langton* (1855) 7 De GM & G 30, 24 LJ Ch 625; *Walmsley v Mundy* (1884) 13 QBD 807 at 817, CA; *Re Metropolitan Amalgamated Estates Ltd* [1912] 2 Ch 497.

13 *Re Compagnie Générale de Bellegarde* (1876) 2 Ch D 181; *Tottenham v Swansea Zinc Ore Co Ltd* (1884) 53 LJ Ch 776, 51 LT 61; *Bartlett v Northumberland Avenue Hotel Co Ltd* (1885) 53 LT 611, CA.

14 *Peruvian Guano Co Ltd v Dreyfus Bros Co* [1892] AC 166 at 187, HL.

15 *Morrison v Skerne Ironworks Co Ltd* (1889) 60 LT 588.

16 *Defries v Creed* (1865) 6 New Rep 17, 34 LJ Ch 607; *Edwards v Edwards* (1876) 2 Ch D 291, CA; *Re Rollason* (1887) 56 LT 303; *Re Roundwood Colliery Co* [1897] 1 Ch 373, CA; *Ridout v Fowler* [1904] 1 Ch 658; affd on other grounds [1904] 2 Ch 93, CA.

17 *Dove v Dove* (1784) 4 My & Cr 585, 2 Dick 617; *Ferguson v Tadman* (1819) cited in 2 Sim 401; *Green v Green* (1829) 2 Sim 430; *Crow v Wood* (1850) 13 Beav 271; *Randfield v Randfield* (1859) 7 WR 651; *Re Della Rocella's Estate* (1892) 29 LR Ir 464.

18 *Hawkes v Holland* [1881] WN 128, CA; *Edgell v Wilson* [1893] WN 145.

19 *Ind Coope & Co v Mee* [1895] WN 8 (interlocutory application).

20 *Savage v Bentley* (1904) 90 LT 641.

1 See *Pratchett v Drew* [1924] 1 Ch 280, 93 LJ Ch 137. For an example, see 33 *Court Forms* (1989 Issue) 200, Form 9 (not repeated in 1997 Issue).

2 [1900] 1 Ch 602 at 610.

Each of these possibilities merits some discussion.

A person who refuses to deliver possession to a receiver after being ordered by the court to give such possession may be proceeded against for contempt of court.[3] The same applies where a person interferes with the possession of a receiver after he has gone into possession.[4]

On a refusal or failure to deliver up possession of land in accordance with the order the receiver should report that fact to the solicitor of the party having the conduct of the proceedings who should take the necessary steps to enforce the order. This will entail as a first step serving the defaulting party personally with a copy of the order directing the delivery up of possession.[5] The order must specify the time within which possession is to be delivered up,[6] and the copy of it must be indorsed with a notice that failure to comply within the time specified will result in a process of execution to compel compliance.[7] Enforcement is conditional on a copy of the order having been served before the expiration of the time limited by the order.[8]

If this achieves nothing an application for leave to issue a writ for possession is the next step.[9] In the Queen's Bench Division the application is made ex parte to the Practice Master on affidavit: in the Chancery Division the application is made ex parte by motion to the judge, again supported by affidavit. The affidavit will recite service of the order and non-compliance.

The court will lend its assistance in other ways to enable a receiver to go into rightful possession. In *Re Huinac Copper Mines*[10] a receiver and manager had been appointed by the court in a debenture holder's action of all the company's property in Peru. A firm in Lima held the power of attorney of the defendant company when the receivership order was made and acting under that power took possession of the company's copper mine on behalf of the receiver. Some 20 months later the defendant company revoked the power of attorney and granted a fresh one to an individual who ousted the previous attorney from possession of the mine and started working it. Neville J ordered the company to revoke the latter power of attorney and to execute a power of attorney appointing one or more partners in the firm previously acting as attorneys to do so again and take possession of the mine on behalf of the receiver, the plaintiff indemnifying the company in respect of the acts of such attorney.

Although the writ of assistance has been superseded by the writ of possession in the case of land a writ of assistance may still be issued for the purpose of putting a receiver in possession of specific chattels ordered to be delivered to him. A writ of assistance may thus issue for goods which are locked up,[11] or

---

3 See *Civil Procedure*, Vol 1, Spring 2000, Section A, para sc52.1. See also *Mullarkey v Donohoe* (1885) 16 LR Ir 365; *Re Sacker* (1888) 22 QBD 179 at 185, CA.
4 *Broad v Wickham* (1831) 4 Sim 511.
5 *Green v Green* (1829) 2 Sim 430.
6 RSC Ord 52; *Savage v Bentley* (1904) 90 LT 641.
7 RSC Ord 45, r 7; *Civil Procedure*, Vol 1, Spring 2000, Section A, Civil Procedure Rules, Sch 1, sc45.7.
8 RSC Ord 45, r 7(2) and (3).
9 RSC Ord 45, r 3.
10 [1910] WN 218.
11 *Cazet de la Borde v Othon* (1874) 23 WR 110.

where documents are in peril and a receiver appointed by the court is unable to serve the respondent or obtain possession because the respondent has decamped and his clerks are declining to give up the custody of the documents,[12] or where the respondent is in prison for contempt and the mortgage securities are in his possession or in a locked safe in his office.[13]

12 *Wyman v Knight* (1888) 39 Ch D 165.
13 *Re Taylor* [1913] WN 212.

CHAPTER 28

Rights, powers and duties

COLLECTION OF PROPERTY

The classic form of order appointing a receiver empowers him to 'collect, get in and receive'[1] the property comprised in the plaintiff's security or which is in jeopardy. This form of order conferring an express power to 'collect' is but a reminder of the primary duty of a receiver, which is to collect the property of which he is appointed receiver and to pay all money received into court or as the court may direct.[2]

The express power impliedly authorises acts incidental to, or consequential upon, the carrying out of the object encompassed by the express powers.[3] But it does not impliedly authorise a sale, even where the property forms the security and the receiver is appointed at the instance of the security holder.[4]

Normally a receiver will be empowered to collect only the assets which are in dispute or form part of the charge which the receiver is appointed to enforce. However in one case, a debenture holder's action, the court by declaration extended the receiver's power to collect to include all property of the company capable of being taken in execution.[5]

Certainly, the receiver is under a duty to collect as much of the property as possible.[6] And generally he must in discharging his duty of collection 'take the same care with respect to it as a reasonable attention to his own affairs would dictate to him if it was for himself'.[7]

A little leeway is given in some quarters. Thus a receiver appointed to collect and get in debts may exercise a reasonable discretion in giving time for payment,

---

1 See 33 *Court Forms* (1997 Issue) 106, Form 5.
2 *Aston v Heron* (1834) 2 My & K 390; *Chaytor v Maclean* (1848) 11 LTOS 2; *Re Flowers & Co* [1897] 1 QB 14, CA.
3 See *Pole v Leask* (1860) 28 Beav 562.
4 *Australian Industry Development Corpn v Co-operative Farmers' and Graziers' Direct Meat Supply Ltd* (1978) 3 ACLR 543.
5 *Hope v Croydon and Norwood Tramways Co* (1887) 34 Ch D 730.
6 See *Newman v Mills* (1825) 1 Hog 291 (collection of rents).
7 *Massey v Banner* (1820) 1 Jac & W 241 at 247 per Lord Eldon LC.

especially if by that concession he gains some collateral advantage for the creditor, such as security or additional security.[8]

The order will usually direct persons in possession of any real or personal property comprised in the appointment to deliver it up to the appointee or to attorn tenant to him.[9] The receiver should in writing call on the parties in possession to comply with the direction in the order. If they refuse to comply he should report their refusal to the party having the conduct of the action so that the necessary steps can be taken to enforce the order.[10] The party having the carriage of the order will then serve the recalcitrant tenant personally with a copy of the order of appointment of a receiver, and of the order or certificate completing the appointment, requiring him to pay the arrears of rent to the receiver.[11] If despite all this the tenant still will not budge in the direction of payment, he should be served with a summons to pay within a limited time of the service of the order to be made on the summons.[12]

It is not incumbent on a person ordered to deliver a deed or chattel to a receiver to deliver them to the receiver wherever he may be. Where a place is not named in the order the receiver should in person or by duly accredited agent go to the place where the respondent is detaining the deed or chattel and there demand delivery. Where a deed or chattel is not handed over to a receiver in accordance with a decree ordering delivery by all persons generally the proper course for the receiver to pursue is to move on notice to the alleged defaulting party for an order directing him by name to make delivery within a specified limited time and at a specified place.[13]

The court has no jurisdiction to order a person in possession of land to attorn to a receiver, where the tenancy is not clear, or where a right of purchase is set up by such a person.[14]

Naturally an order appointing a receiver should describe the property subjected to the order with accuracy. Otherwise he may not be able to institute successfully proceedings for contempt of court on the basis of interference with his right to collect particular property, for he may not be able to show clearly that the property in question is plainly within the scope of the order. Inadequacy of description is sometimes encountered where a receiver is appointed generally over a trust fund invested in the names of trustees and he may not be able to collect dividends payable on shares or money payable on redemption of debentures held by the company under the terms of the trust. In that event it may be necessary to obtain a further order expressly referring to the property to compel the company declaring the dividend or redeeming the debenture to make payments to the receiver rather than to the trustees under their legal title.

---

8 *Willatts v Kennedy* (1831) 8 Bing 5, 1 Moo & S 35.
9 *Seton's Judgments and Orders* (7th edn) 725; and see *Re Maudslay Sons & Field* [1900] 1 Ch 602.
10 *Daniell's Chancery Practice* (8th edn) 1481.
11 *Daniell's Chancery Practice* (8th edn) 1481.
12 For a form of summons see 33 *Court Forms* (1997 Issue) 131–132, Forms 31 and 32.
13 *Freeman v Trimble* (1906) 6 SRNSW 133 per Simpson CJ in Eq.
14 *Brydon v Innes* (1868) 5 WW & A'B (Eq) 189 a decision of the Victoria Supreme Court (Molesworth J).

RENT, RATES, TAXES AND DUTIES

A receiver is justified in paying head rent,[15] rates,[16] taxes and other outgoings properly chargeable against him in respect of the property of which he is in occupation.[17] Similarly, to keep the ball rolling (so to speak) a receiver of licensed premises may, and indeed should, pay any duties necessary to preserve the licences.[18]

Where it appears desirable on the ground of convenience that documents of title should be produced to, 'or handed over to, the receiver' the court may order their production or delivery on such terms as may be thought fit, despite the opposition of the person legally entitled to hold them. Thus in *Re Ind Coope & Co Ltd*[19] trustees for the debenture holders objected to handing over the deeds of property specifically mortgaged to them but it was held that upon the receiver's undertaking to redeliver the deeds to the trustees when they had served their purpose and subject to a direction that the receiver should grant to the trustees complete access to the deeds, justice was on the particular facts of the case best served by ordering delivery of the deeds to the receiver.

REPAIRS

A receiver appointed by the court without express powers of management is not in general justified in incurring expenditure of whatever nature without the sanction of the court.[20] Nevertheless he may be allowed in his accounts any expenditure which is shown to have been beneficial to the parties interested.[1] This general rule applies to repairs and improvements to property but is not confined to those items. For example, in Ireland at a time of general scarcity and distress the receiver of a minor's estate was authorised to lay out a sum of money in relieving and employing the poor tenantry.[2] So too a receiver may be authorised to incur expenditure in cutting and selling timber for repairs,[3] or in selling timber which has blown down.[4]

An application for leave to effect repairs to house property is made by summons.[5] The application should be made by the plaintiff or other person having the carriage of the order appointing the receiver and not by the receiver, except on the plaintiff's

15 *Walsh v Walsh* (1839) 1 I Eq R 209: *Balfe v Blake* (1850) 1 I Ch R 365; *Jacobs v Van Boolen, ex p Roberts* (1889) 34 Sol Jo 97, DC.

16 See *Re Mannesmann Tube Co Ltd* [1901] 2 Ch 93.

17 *Madden v Wilson* (1854) 6 Ir Jur 129.

18 *Re Hoy's Estate* (1892) 31 LR Ir 66.

19 (1909) 26 TLR 11, CA.

20 *Fletcher v Dodd* (1789) 1 Ves 85.

 1 *Tempest v Ord* (1816) 2 Mer 55; *Whitley v Lowe* (1858) 25 Beav 421, 31 LTOS 5; affd 2 De G & J 704, 4 Jur NS 815; *Re Gomersall* (1875) LR 20 Eq 291, 44 LJ Bcy 97; *Macartney v Walsh* (1830) Hayes 29n.

 2 *Re Jackson* (1831) 2 Hog 238.

 3 *A-G v Boothby* (1860) 1 *Seton's Judgments and Orders* (7th edn) 766.

 4 *Crofts v Poe* (1839) Jo & Car 193.

 5 For a form of summons, see 33 *Court Forms* (1997 Issue) 127–128, Forms 27 and 29.

default or in other special circumstances. Accordingly, where he wants the property put into a proper state of repair and the likely cost exceeds the prescribed amount for which no leave is required, the receiver should, in the first place, apply to the solicitor acting for the plaintiff or other person having carriage of the receivership order to take out the requisite summons. The affidavit in support of the summons should give full particulars of the nature, urgency and likely cost of the repairs proposed, and state the reasons for their becoming necessary. Should the repairs proposed be extensive in scale it may be necessary to enlist the support of a surveyor to give expert evidence on the point in affidavit form.

An inquiry will be directed, if necessary, into the circumstances of the case to determine whether the expenditure has been reasonable and beneficial to the parties interested.[6] However an order for an inquiry was refused in *Garland v Garland*:[7] the receiver in that case had persisted in spending large sums in repairs after prior sums had been allowed him in passing his accounts with a caution from the master not to lay out any more. Because he had disregarded the master's direction the further payments made by him were disallowed. The decision is an application of the wider principle that a receiver must abide strictly by the terms of the order appointing him and any further directions of the court.[8] A receiver should be similarly astute not to exceed any limits placed by the court on his expenditure on repairs or improvements.[9] For if he overspends then there is a risk of his being left out of pocket.[10]

Proper repairs of real estate fall within the scope of the receiver's duty: he is allowed to do certain repairs without even coming to the court. In fact he may at his own risk execute repairs of a more extensive kind. There is no exact rule as to the amount that he may do on his own responsibility, but of course what he does upon his own responsibility is liable to be questioned, unless he has obtained the previous sanction of the court.[11]

Accordingly, unless the proposed repairs are ordinary[12] and of small cost[13] a receiver should obtain the leave of the court to do the repairs. Leave is not required for small repairs estimated to cost not more than £150 in any one accounting period but if the limit is exceeded the master may allow the excess if the receiver satisfies the master that he acted reasonably.[14] Obviously, therefore, if a receiver undertakes major repairs or (which comes to the same thing) spends any considerable sum on repairs without the previous sanction of the court he

---

6 *Blunt v Clitherow* (1802) 6 Ves 799 (expenditure was for lasting benefit of the estate); *A-G v Vigor* (1805) 11 Ves 563 (inquiry as to reasonableness of repairs); and see *Tempest v Ord* (1816) 2 Mer 55 where there was an inquiry whether *new* buildings were fit and necessary and for the benefit of the persons interested in the collieries over which receiver and manager had been appointed.

7 An undated decision cited in *Blunt v Clitherow* (1802) 6 Ves 799 at 800–801.

8 See *De Winton v Brecon Corpn (No 2)* (1860) 28 Beav 200.

9 For an example of such a limitation see *Seton's Judgments and Orders* (7th edn) 765, Form 10.

10 *Simson v Simson* (1863) 2 W & W (E) 97.

11 *Re Graham* [1895] 1 Ch 66 at 72 per Chitty J. Formerly the court never permitted a receiver to lay out money without a previous order of the court; *Tempest v Ord* (1816) 2 Mer 55 per Lord Eldon LC.

12 *Thornhill v Thornhill* (1845) 14 Sim 600; *Re Graham* [1895] 1 Ch 66 at 72.

13 *Blunt v Clitherow* (1802) 6 Ves 799; *A-G v Vigor* (1805) 11 Ves 563.

14 *Practice Direction* [1970] 1 All ER 671, [1970] 1 WLR 520.

runs the risk of footing the whole bill or some part of it himself.[15] Nor should he volunteer to apply to the court for directions when the repairs are the responsibility of somebody else, for example a tenant.[16]

FIRE INSURANCE

A court-appointed receiver may insure premises against loss or damage by fire either in his own name or in the name of persons beneficially interested, or he may keep on foot an existing policy.[17] When he does so he is allowed these premiums on examination of his accounts.[18] Taking out and maintaining such insurance is consistent with his duty as receiver.[19] What is not clear is how far a receiver is liable for his failure to insure. There is no suggestion of a specific duty to insure but a receiver does, of course, have a duty to exercise reasonable care and skill to preserve the property over which he is appointed. A failure to insure may constitute a breach of this wider duty, depending on the circumstances of the case, and in particular on the nature of the property, the known risks and the availability of funds.

The logic of the receiver keeping up the premiums is that he should be entitled to call for the proceeds of the policy to be applied in reinstatement. The receiver would appear to be a person interested in the property over which he is appointed receiver by the court and so entitled to claim reinstatement under the Fires Prevention (Metropolis) Act 1774.[20]

CREATION, DETERMINATION AND SUPERVISION OF LEASES

Creation

When the court appoints a receiver of the rents and profits of land, it is not the practice to insert in the order an express power of leasing. If it is thought reasonable to grant a lease the approval of the court may be obtained by summons at chambers, though the court may give a general authority to create leases or tenancies within proper limits.[1] The proposition that a receiver could let without the sanction of the court for a period not exceeding three years[2] can no longer be considered good law.[3]

---

15 *Re Graham* [1895] 1 Ch 66 at 72. So much of the amount as is considered excessive will be disallowed in his accounts.
16 *Duke of Dorset v Crosbie* (1837) Sau & Sc 683.
17 *Re Graham* [1895] 1 Ch 66 at 71 per Chitty J.
18 *Re Graham* [1895] 1 Ch 66.
19 *Re Graham* [1895] 1 Ch 66. The duty referred to is his duty to preserve the property.
20 Cf *Sinnott v Bowden* [1912] 2 Ch 414.
 1 *Morris v Elme* (1790) 1 Ves 139; *Wynne v Lord Newborough* (1790) 1 Ves 164; and see *Neale v Bealing* (1744) 3 Swan 304n.
 2 *Shuff v Holdaway* (1863) 2 *Daniell's Chancery Practice* (8th edn) 1487n; and see Riviere *Law Relating to Receivers and Managers* (1912) 127.
 3 *Stamford, Spalding and Boston Banking Co v Keeble* [1913] 2 Ch 96.

The court may also sanction a lease after the term has in fact started.[4] Where the land in question is situate abroad the court may, with a view to preventing or cutting down the delay and expense of applications to the English courts, direct an inquiry as to what should be the term beyond which the receiver ought not to let without leave.[5]

When the receiver is responsible for letting the property subject to the court appointment he is bound to let the estate to the best advantage.[6] For all that it would seem that a receiver is not justified in dispossessing tenants without the leave of the court merely for the purpose of raising rents or of dividing the estate into fewer and larger holdings.[7] Nor does the court allow rents to be reduced or arrears to be forgiven or compounded for, unless the parties interested consent.[8]

So that the legal estate in the term shall pass (that is to say the *true* legal estate, and not some legal estate by estoppel) the lease must be made in the name of the party who would have been able to grant the demise had the receiver not been appointed. In fact where a receiver is in possession the court in practice directs the lease to be made by the legal owner or by the person in whom a statutory or conventional power of leasing is vested.[9]

Where the title is in dispute the receiver may be authorised by the court, as was the receiver in *Dancer v Hastings*,[10] to grant a lease in his own name. Once the tenant has accepted the lease he cannot turn round and say that there was no lease: he is estopped from doing that. Likewise if the receiver grants a lease without the court's sanction, as between the receiver and the tenant there is a lease binding by estoppel.[11] Again where the person in possession attorns tenant to the receiver, that creates a tenancy under the receiver by estoppel and gives the receiver the legal powers of a landlord, even though it does not enure for the benefit of the legal estate.[12]

DETERMINATION OF TENANCIES

The receiver does not require the leave of the court to determine tenancies from year to year by a proper notice to quit. An appointment conferring on the receiver a general authority to let lands to tenants from year to year carries with it an implied authority to determine such tenancies on proper notice.[13] And

---

4 *Re Liabilities (War-time Adjustment) Act 1941, Re Cripps* [1946] Ch 265, CA.
5 —— *v Lindsey* (1808) 15 Ves 91.
6 *Wynne v Lord Newborough* (1790) 1 Ves 164.
7 *Wynne v Lord Newborough* (1790) 1 Ves 164; *Lord Mansfield v Hamilton, Hobhouse v Hamilton* (1804) 2 Sch & Lef 28; *Alven v Bond* (1841) Fl & K 196 at 223.
8 *Evans v Taylor* (1837) Sau & Sc 681; *Davis v Cotter* (1837) Sau & Sc 685.
9 *Shuff v Holdaway* (1863) 2 *Daniell's Chancery Practice* (8th edn) 1487n and see *Gibbins v Howell* (1818) 3 Madd 469.
10 (1826) 4 Bing 2, 12 Moore CP 34.
11 *Dancer v Hastings* (1826) 4 Bing 2, 12 Moore CP 34.
12 *Evans v Mathias* (1857) 7 E & B 590.
13 *Doe d Marsack v Read* (1810) 12 East 57 at 60; followed in *Doe d Earl Manvers v Mizem* (1837) 2 Mood & R 56 at 57 per Patterson J; *Crosbie's Lessee v Barry* (1839) Jo & Car 106.

indeed the receiver is similarly placed even though the tenancies have been created before his appointment and the tenants have not attorned to him.[14] On the other hand in *Doe d Marsack v Read*[15] counsel appearing for the tenant expressed a doubt whether by the practice of the Court of Chancery the receiver had power to determine a subsisting lease without the leave and direction of the court. The judgment did not touch on this point. Yet in *Wynne v Lord Newborough*[16] Lord Thurlow LC appears to have had few doubts about the necessity for leave to be given to a receiver who wishes to determine an existing lease or to evict tenants. Indeed Lord Thurlow LC went further (and, as later cases show, too far) when he said that he did 'not know how to make a distinction between leases for one year and others'.[17] The true contrast is between cases where the court in effect gives authority to terminate leases and cases where the order is silent and the position of the receiver does not give rise to any implication. A mere receiver of rents, as such, has no general authority to give a notice to determine a tenancy.[18]

A notice to quit served by the receiver in his own name is a demand for possession by the landlord or his lawfully authorised agent sufficient to support a claim for double value[19] in case of holding over.[20] Before any surrender of a lease is accepted the sanction of the court should be obtained.[1]

Supervision of leases

A receiver is bound to let the estate over which the court appointed him receiver to the best advantage and to get the best terms he can.[2] But this does not mean that he is justified in dispossessing tenants without leave of the court simply for the purpose of increasing rental income or of dividing the estate into fewer and larger holdings.[3] Nor without the leave of the court and the consent of all parties beneficially interested may he abate the rent or forgive or compound for arrears.[4] Thus a reference as to the propriety of abating the rents of tenants and forgiving their arrears was refused on the motion of the receiver alone, but was afterwards granted upon the concurrence of all parties.[5]

---

14 *Doe d Marsack v Read* supra.
15 (1810) 12 East 57.
16 (1790) 1 Ves 164.
17 *Wynne v Lord Newborough* (1790) 1 Ves 164 at 165.
18 *Doe d Mann v Walters* (1830) 10 B & C 626 at 633 per Parke J.
19 Under Landlord and Tenant Act 1730, s 1.
20 *Wilkinson v Colley* (1771) 5 Burr 2694; *Doe d Marsack v Read* (1810) 12 East 57; and see *Jones v Phipps* (1868) LR 3 QB 567 at 572.
 1 *Davidson v Armstrong* (1837) Sau & Sc 135.
 2 *Wynne v Lord Newborough* (1790) 1 Ves 164 at 165 per Lord Thurlow LC.
 3 *Wynne v Lord Newborough* (1790) 1 Ves 164; *Lord Mansfield v Hamilton, Hobhouse v Hamilton* (1804) 2 Sch & Lef 28; *Alven v Bond* (1841) Fl & K 196 at 223.
 4 *Evans v Taylor* (1837) Sau & Sc 681; *Davis v Cotter* (1837) Sau & Sc 685.
 5 *Evans v Taylor* (1837) Sau & Sc 681.

RULE AGAINST SELF-DEALING

A consequence of the fiduciary position of a court-appointed receiver is that he is bound by the rule concisely, if inelegantly, described as the rule against self-dealing. The derivation of the term 'self-dealing' is American.[6] But its convenience to describe a whole range of situations in which a fiduciary can feather his own personal nest, in one way or another, is considerable enough to overcome any stylistic objection.

The rule has many applications both in relation to purchases and the taking of leases.

First, a receiver may not purchase, either in his own name or through the interposition of a trustee, any part of the property over which he is appointed without the sanction of the court.[7] Furthermore the court will not authorise the receiver to bid at a sale unless very special circumstances are shown or unless all persons interested in the property are sui juris and consent.[8] The rationale is simple: a receiver has many opportunities of discovering and putting to use information accessible only to himself and the court might be at a disadvantage if it were to inquire in every case whether the receiver had in fact taken advantage of his privileged position and the opportunities offered by it.[9]

It seems that a receiver could not plead the Limitation Act 1980 if the purchase were later attacked.[10]

Even where the purchase has been at a fair price, and without any circumstances of fraud, concealment, non-disclosure or undue advantage taken, a receiver is not permitted to retain the benefit of his purchase as against the parties interested other than the vendor who elects to stand by his bargain.[11] Indeed it seems that the vendor himself may have the transaction set aside on the grounds of public policy without praying in aid any of the usual grounds for rescission.[12]

In cases where all the interested parties are sui juris they may of course decide to affirm the sale.[13] But if any of them is under a disability or objects to the sale the court either sets aside the transaction in toto[14] or declares that the receiver holds the property in trust for the persons who would be entitled had the sale never taken place.[15] A declaration will not be made to the prejudice of a vendor who repudiates the sale.[16]

The receiver in such cases is entitled to have a charge on the property with interest for any purchase money he may have actually paid[17] and he is also given

---

6   See *Scott on Trusts* (4th edn) para 170 et seq.

7   *Alven v Bond* (1841) Fl & K 196, 3 I Eq R 365; *Nugent v Nugent* [1908] 1 Ch 546, CA.

8   *Anderson v Anderson* (1846) 9 I Eq R 23.

9   *Alven v Bond* supra; *Eyre v M'Donnell* (1864) 15 I Ch R 534; *Nugent v Nugent* supra.

10 See *Re Cornish, ex p Board of Trade* [1896] 1 QB 99 at 104, CA where the wording of the statutory predecessor of Limitation Act 1980 was slightly different.

11 *Boddington v Langford* (1845) 15 I Ch R 558n; *Nugent v Nugent* supra.

12 *Re Ronaynes Estate* (1863) 13 I Ch R 444 at 450; *Eyre v M'Donnell* (1864) 15 I Ch R 534.

13 *White v Tommy* (1836) cited in Fl & K 224.

14 *Cary v Cary* (1804) 2 Sch & Lef 173.

15 *Nugent v Nugent* [1907] 2 Ch 292 at 295.

16 *Boddington v Langford* (1845) 15 I Ch R 558n.

17 *Nugent v Nugent* supra. The court would probably allow a higher percentage than the 4 per cent granted in *Nugent v Nugent*.

credit for what he has spent on the property since his purchase provided (and to the extent) that his expenditure has benefited the estate.[18]

Nor in general can the receiver evade the consequence of this rule by selling to his wife[19] or his agent[20] or a company under his control.[1] Here as in the case of a sale by a trustee equity looks beneath the surface and applies its doctrine to cases where although in form a fiduciary has not sold to himself in substance he has.[2]

LITIGATION

A receiver appointed in an action is appointed to take charge of and receive the property put under his charge. But he is not at liberty, and is not entitled, to bring an action in his own name.[3] Certainly no property or title vests in the receiver on his appointment either at law or in equity.[4] And equally by virtue of his appointment he is not thereby automatically entitled to have the subject matter of the receivership order transferred into his name.[5]

18 *Cary v Cary* (1804) 2 Sch & Lef 173 (fine on renewal of lease recouped).
19 In the case of a *trust* there is no absolute rule placing a purchase by the wife of a trustee in the same category as a sale by a trustee to himself: *Burrell v Burrell's Trustees* 1915 SC 333; *Re King's Will Trusts* (1959) 173 Estates Gazette 627 where Harman J upheld the conveyance in question; *Re McNally* [1967] NZLR 521. The court can authorise such a sale but requires to be satisfied that it is in the real interests of the beneficiaries under the trust that the sale should take place in this way. The clearest evidence is required why this should be so: *Re McNally* [1967] NZLR 521 at 523 per Tompkins J. The decision in *Burrell v Burrell's Trustees* 1915 SC 333 was at one time subjected to strong criticism: see *Robertson v Robertson* [1924] NZLR 552 at 555 per Salmond J obiter and *Tanti v Carlson* [1948] VLR 401 at 406–407 per Herring CJ. But it has been followed, and the principle is now well established: such a purchase is not void but is highly suspect, and unless the attendant suspicions are dispersed the court will set aside the transaction: *Watkins v Lestrange* (1863) 2 SCRNSW Eq 85 at 86; *Heywood v Pryor* (1905) 23 WNNSW 44; *Robertson v Robertson* [1924] NZLR 552; *Re Douglas* (1928) 29 SRNSW 48 at 50–51; *Re Frampton's Will Trusts* [1943] QWN 29; *Tanti v Carlson* [1948] VLR 401; *Glennon v Taxation Comr* (1972) 127 CLR 503. As Megarry V-C has pointed out 'manifestly there are wives and wives': *Tito v Waddell No 2* [1977] 3 All ER 129 at 241. For the American cases, see *Scott on Trusts* (4th edn) Vol IIA para 170.6 at 330–334, where cases on sales by a female trustee to her husband are also cited; and see note 'Validity of life tenant's exercise of power of sale as affected by the fact that conveyance is, directly or indirectly, to him his spouse or his relative', 89 ALR 2d 649 (1963). In *Dowager Duchess of Sutherland v Duke of Sutherland* [1893] 3 Ch 169 at 196, Romer J was 'by no means prepared to accede to the argument that the leases are bad of necessity . . . on the ground that [the tenant for life] cannot lease under any terms or circumstances to his wife'.
20 *Watkins v Lestrange* (1863) 2 SCRNSW Eq 85 at 86. In the case of a trust a purchase in the *Michoud v Girod* 4 How 503 (1846); *Lewis v Hillman* (1852) 3 HL Cas 607, 19 LTOS 329.
1 *Silkstone and Haigh Moor Coal Co v Edey* [1900] 1 Ch 167, 69 LJ Ch 73; *Re Clark* (1920) 150 LT Jo 94; *Re Magadi Soda Co Ltd* (1925) 94 LJ Ch 217; *Farrar v Farrars Ltd* (1888) 40 Ch D 395; and see especially *Tse Kwong Lam v Wong Chit Sen* [1983] 3 All ER 54, [1983] 1 WLR 1349. In the case of a *trust* a purchase by a company of which the trustee is president, general manager or other principal officer has been set aside in some American cases: see *Scott on Trusts* (4th edn) Vol IIA para 170.10 at 346–348.
2 *Tito v Waddell No 2* [1977] 3 All ER 129 at 241 (where the reference is to a trustee).
3 *Re Sartoris's Estate* [1892] 1 Ch 11; on appeal [1892] 1 Ch 11 at 19.
4 *Bolton v Darling Downs Building Society* [1935] SR Qd 237; *Re Scottish Properties Pty Ltd* (1977) 2 ACLR 264 at 271 per Needham J.
5 *Re Scottish Properties Pty Ltd* (1977) 2 ACLR 264 at 271.

The classic order appointing a receiver usually empowers him to 'get in collect or receive' the property comprised in the plaintiff's security.[6] That express wording necessarily and by implication authorises any incidental or consequential acts. The power does not, however, permit a sale of the secured property:[7] that requires even more express phraseology.

A receiver who is not in a position to bring an action in his own name against a debtor is not entitled to launch a bankruptcy petition as a petitioning creditor, since he is not a 'creditor'.[8] On the other hand if he is in a position to bring an action in his own name as where, for example, he is assignee of a debt or holder of a bill of exchange he is entitled to present a bankruptcy petition against the debtor.[9] And he does not need to obtain the leave of the court before doing so.[10]

Where a receiver considers that proceedings have become necessary, for example to recover a debt or property or to enforce compliance with a court order, he should, in the first instance, apply to the party or parties having the conduct of the action.[11] The party having the conduct of the action in which the receiver has been appointed is the proper person to apply to the court.[12] A receiver should not make an application in his own name unless the parties to the action have neglected or refused to do so[13] or have no locus standi.[14] In *Chater v Maclean*[15] a receiver who had been appointed for the plaintiff in an action paid large sums of money to the solicitors for the plaintiff who were also the solicitors acting for the receiver. Some of the money was misappropriated by one of the parties in the firm who absconded. The plaintiff's motion to compel the other partners to bring the money so misapplied into court was dismissed partly on the ground that the proper plaintiff in the circumstances was the receiver.

The application to the court, made by the proper applicant, is usually by application notice (instead of by summons)[16] but an application without notice (ex parte) may be permissible.[17]

If there is no person in whose name the action can be brought, it may be that there would be jurisdiction to direct the action to be in the name of the receiver.[18] But subject to this possibility the practice seems well established that a receiver should not appear as a party to the litigation.[19] Where a receiver has been

6   See *Australian Industry Development Corpn v Co-operative Farmers and Graziers' Direct Meat Supply Ltd* (1978) 3 ACLR 543.
7   (1978) 3 ACLR 543.
8   *Re Sacker* (1888) 22 QBD 179, 58 LJQB 4, CA following *Re Muirhead* (1876) 2 Ch D 22, CA.
9   *Re Lewis, ex p Harris* (1876) 2 Ch D 423 (holder of bill of exchange); *Re Macoun* [1904] 2 KB 700, CA (assignee of debt).
10 *Armstrong v Armstrong* (1871) LR 12 Eq 614, 25 LT 199.
11 *Ward v Swift* (1848) 6 Hare 309, 12 Jur 173; *Re Sacker* (1888) 22 QBD 179 at 185; *Windschuegl v Irish Polishes Ltd* [1914] 1 IR 33.
12 *Re Sacker* (1888) 22 QBD 179 at 185 per Fry LJ.
13 *Miller v Elkins* (1825) 3 LJOS Ch 128; *Ireland v Eade* (1844) 7 Beav 55; *Parker v Dunn* (1845) 8 Beav 497.
14 *Chater v Maclean* (1855) 3 Eq Rep 375, 1 Jur NS 175.
15 (1855) 3 Eq Rep 375, 1 Jur NS 175.
16 See 33 *Court Forms* (1997 Issue) 127, Form 27.
17 *Dyson v Jack* (1894) 16 ALT 1.
18 *McGuin v Fretts* (1887) 13 OR 699, Ont CA.
19 *Mones & Co v McCallum* (1897) 17 PR 398.

substituted without objection as a plaintiff the court can add a plaintiff with a proper interest[20] and the receiver himself can apply for the proper person to be joined even without the latter's consent and contrary to his wishes.[1]

While a receiver appointed by the court acquires no right of action by virtue of his appointment he may subsequently acquire an independent cause of action. In such a case the fact that he is a receiver does not disqualify him from suing, and suing in his own name. His cause of action may arise from his possession, or through his management if he is a receiver and manager. Thus if he is possessed of chattels as receiver and those chattels are unlawfully detained from him he can maintain an action to recover them as being the person in possession of them, quite independently of the fact that he is a receiver: in such a case he does not sue in his character of receiver.[2] He may for example sue as the holder of a bill of exchange or promissory note[3] or as the occupier of business premises[4] or as the bailee of chattels to whom possession has been delivered[5] by order of the court or as the assignee of a debt under a completed assignment.[6]

A receiver may also sue as landlord, if the letting has been in his name pursuant to a power to lease conferred by an order of the court;[7] and he may sue on a covenant for payment of rent to himself, even though he is not a party to the lease.[8]

A receiver and manager often acquires rights of action in the course of managing the business and may sue for the recovery of goods improperly detained by an alleged lien-holder[9] or for the price of goods sold and delivered by him or delivered under a contract which has been assigned to him, although as assignee of the contract his claim will be subject to any right of set off enjoyed by the other party to the contract.[10]

Where a receiver is claimant in interpleader proceedings and the property in dispute is in his possession he is not required to pay the value of the property into court in the usual way: such a course is considered unnecessary because as an

---

20 *Stuart v Grough* (1887) 14 OR 255.
1 *Ritchie v Canadian Bank of Commerce* (1905) 1 WLR 499 (Yukon Terr).
2 *Re Sacker* (1888) 22 QBD 179 at 185, CA per Fry LJ.
3 *Re Lewis, ex p Harris* (1876) 2 Ch D 423; *Re Sacker* (1888) 22 QBD 179 at 183 per Lord Esher MR (winding up petition); *O'Reilly v Connor* [1904] 2 IR 601, Ir CA; *Kettle v Dunster and Wakefield* (1927) 138 LT 158.
4 *Husey v London Electric Supply Corpn* [1902] 1 Ch 411, Ir CA (action to restrain cutting off electricity supply to hotel).
5 *Hills v Reeves* (1882) 31 WR 209, CA per Jessel MR; and see *Purkiss v Holland* (1887) 31 Sol Jo 702, CA; *Re Rollason* (1887) 34 Ch D 495 (where receiver was claimant in interpleader proceedings concerning pawned goods in sheriff's possession).
6 *Re Macoun* [1904] 2 KB 700, CA.
7 *Dancer v Hastings* (1826) 4 Bing 2, 12 Moore CP 34. For an example of an order, see *Palmer's Company Precedents* (16th edn) Part III 653.
8 See Law of Property Act 1925, s 56(1); *Lloyd v Bryne* (1888) 22 LR Ir 269, Ir CA. He may sue for rent in the name of the mortgagor or mortgagee where he has been appointed under the mortgagee's statutory powers: see Law of Property Act 1925, s 109(3).
9 *Moss Steamship Co Ltd v Whinney* [1912] AC 254, HL.
10 *Forster v Nixon's Navigation Co Ltd* (1906) 23 TLR 138; *Rother Iron Works Ltd v Canterbury Precision Engineers Ltd* [1974] QB 1, [1973] 1 All ER 394, CA; cf *NW Robbie & Co v Witney Warehouse Co Ltd* [1963] 3 All ER 613, [1963] 1 WLR 1324, CA.

officer of the court he is in a position to undertake to hold the property subject to the order of the court.[11]

The general rule is that a receiver should not defend proceedings unless he has first obtained the leave of the court.[12] And he should make his application for leave in good time and not, for example, wait to apply for leave until just before trial.[13] Failure on his part to apply for leave to defend may put his costs at risk. If his defence does not succeed he will not be entitled to an indemnity in respect of his costs of the action. Thus in *Swaby v Dickon*[14] a receiver without the sanction of the court defended certain actions arising out of a distress for rent made by him on a tenant of the estate and his defence failed. The court refused to allow him an indemnity for his costs of the action. On the other hand if a receiver defends an action without having first obtained the leave of the court and his defence is successful and the costs of the defence have not exceeded those which he would have incurred if he had applied for leave he may be allowed his costs.[15] A successful defence is not, however, an automatic passport to an indemnity for costs. The defence of the action must be for the benefit of property subject to the receivership. So when an action alleges personal fraud and misconduct against a receiver, but otherwise has no relation to the estate except insofar as the acts complained of are done by him as an officer of the court, the receiver is not entitled to be indemnified against the costs incurred in successfully defending the action.[16]

The lesson from all this is simple. To be on the safe side a receiver should obtain the leave of the court before defending proceedings.

The procedure to be adopted by a receiver who wishes to defend proceedings is the same as that which he has to follow if he wants proceedings initiated.[17] First he should approach the plaintiff or other person in the receivership proceedings who has carriage of the order and should ask him to apply for liberty for the proceedings to be defended.[18] Any resulting application will be by application notice supported by evidence.[19] If necessary, an inquiry will be directed whether it will be in the interest of all parties that the proceedings should be defended.[20] The possibility of such an inquiry explains why it is vital to make the application as soon as possible: otherwise there will be insufficient time for the inquiry to be completed before trial.[1]

There are occasions where it is necessary to join the receiver as a defendant to proceedings in a cause. An example occurred in *Chater v MacLean*[2] which

---

11 *Purkiss v Holland* (1887) 31 Sol Jo 702, CA.
12 *Anon* (1801) 6 Ves 287; *Swaby v Dickon* (1833) 5 Sim 629; *Bristowe v Needham* (1847) 2 Ph 190, 9 LTOS 69.
13 *Anon* (1801) 6 Ves 287.
14 (1833) 5 Sim 629.
15 *Bristowe v Needham* (1847) 2 Ph 190, 9 LTOS 69; and see *Fitzgerald v Fitzgerald* (1843) 5 I Eq R 525; *Re Neill* (1881) 9 PR 176 (Can).
16 *Re Dunn* [1904] 1 Ch 648.
17 See at p 436, above.
18 See 33 *Court Forms* (1997 Issue) 85.
19 See 33 *Court Forms* (1997 Issue) 128, Form 29.
20 *Anon* (1801) 6 Ves 287.
 1 *Anon* (1801) 6 Ves 287 at 288 per Lord Eldon LC.
 2 (1855) 3 Eq Rep 375, 25 LTOS 77. Moreover the plaintiff in such circumstances cannot get summary relief against the firm of solicitors: *Dixon v Wilkinson* (1859) 4 Drew 614, 33 LTOS 39.

concerned an interlocutory motion in an action. The plaintiff's receiver used the same firm of solicitors as the plaintiff who paid out large sums of money to the solicitors in question with no specific instructions. One of the partners in the firm of solicitors misappropriated some of the money and absconded. It was held that the receiver was a necessary party to the motion that the other partners in the firm should bring the misapplied money into court. This was because the money was deemed to be received by the firm as agents for the receiver and not on behalf of the plaintiff.

A plaintiff should indorse his writ or originating summons with a specific claim for a receiver when that relief is a substantial object of the action.[3] But a receiver may be appointed even in the absence of a claim for such relief.[4] If necessary leave to amend the relevant originating process will be given.[5] A receiver may be appointed in the Court of Appeal even though the appointment was not asked for in the court below.[6]

In the Chancery Division, which is the most usual forum for such applications, and where the appointment of a receiver is frequently required before trial, or the substantive hearing of a claim, the application is made in open court. Where an application is made without notice, again it is usually heard in open court. But in a very urgent case it could no doubt be heard by a judge sitting in chambers.

POWER TO EMPLOY AGENTS

A receiver or manager may at all times employ and pay such agents as may be reasonably necessary to enable him to carry out his duties in connection with his receivership or managership.

A receiver appointed by the court on the application of the plaintiff should not employ the plaintiff's solicitor to act for him in matters in which the interests of the plaintiff and the receiver are conflicting. In such a case it may be right for him to employ the defendant's solicitor.[7]

Where a manager is absent from the property, he is entitled to employ agents to manage in his absence, and will be allowed any reasonable remuneration paid to such agents, though he will not be allowed commission for himself during the same period,[8] and the court may appoint a receiver on the express understanding that the management of distant estates shall be in the hands of an agent.[9]

In the case of a receiver appointed out of court by all parties interested, he will be entitled to employ all agents, whose employment may, from the circumstances

---

3 *Colebourne v Colebourne* (1876) 1 Ch D 690.

4 *Malcolm v Montgomery* (1824) 2 Mol 500; *Osborne v Harvey* (1841) 1 Y & C Ch Cas 116; *Bowman v Bell* (1844) 14 Sim 392; *Wright v Vernon* (1855) 3 Drew 112; *Brooker v Brooker* (1857) 3 Sm & G 475 at 477; *Salt v Cooper* (1880) 16 Ch D 544, CA.

5 *Re Lloyd* (1879) 12 Ch D 447, 41 LT 171, CA.

6 As to an appointment in the Court of Appeal, see p 319.

7 *Bloomer v Currie* (1907) 51 Sol Jo 277.

8 *Chambers v Goldwin* (1801) 5 Ves 834; on appeal 9 Ves 254, 1 Smith KB 252; *Forrest v Elwes* (1816) 2 Mer 68.

9 —— *v Lindsey* (1808) 15 Ves 91.

and the deed appointing him, be judged to have been within the contemplation of the parties.[10]

POWER TO CARRY ON BUSINESS

By virtue of his appointment, a court-appointed receiver and manager or manager has power to buy and sell, to discharge outgoings, to engage and dismiss employees,[11] to provide for the payment of current expenses,[12] and, unless expressly prohibited, to enter into fresh contracts in the usual course of business.[13] He must carry on the business in the usual way, but without entering into any speculative dealings[14] or undertakings in which his personal interest may conflict with his duty.[15] He must strictly observe the terms of his appointment and will be disallowed expenditure incurred and remuneration after the expiration of the term of his appointment.[16] He is frequently authorised to appoint a sub-manager or to employ agents to conduct the business under his supervision.[17]

It is the manager's duty to preserve the goodwill as well as the assets of the business, and he is not allowed, therefore, as a rule, to disregard contracts entered into before his appointment, even though the assets could be realised to much greater advantage if contracts were disregarded.[18] The receiver and manager may, however, repudiate a contract where repudiation would not adversely affect the realisation of assets or seriously affect the future trading prospects of the company. If he causes the company to fulfil existing contracts, he does so subject to any rights which would otherwise have affected the company, such as rights of set-off[19] or contractual lien.[20] For the protection of goodwill a receiver and manager may properly bind his employees, within legal limits, not to compete in business.[1] On the other hand a purchaser of a business from a receiver and

---

10 *Gilbert v Dyneley* (1841) 3 Man & G 12, 3 Scott NR 364.
11 *Taylor v Neate* (1888) 39 Ch D 538; *Howard v Danner* (1901) 17 TLR 548; *Welstead v Hadley* (1904) 21 TLR 165, CA. Cf *A-G v Schonfeld* [1980] 3 All ER 1, [1980] 1 WLR 1182.
12 *Re Manchester and Milford Rly Co, ex p Cambrian Rly Co* (1880) 14 Ch D 645 at 653, CA.
13 The powers of management are sometimes confined to contracts subsisting at the date of appointment (*Strapp v Bull, Sons & Co, Shaw v London School Board* [1895] 2 Ch 1, 64 LJ Ch 658, CA), or to contracts not involving more than a certain expenditure (*Taylor v Neate* (1888) 39 Ch D 538 at 545).
14 *Taylor v Neate* (1888) 39 Ch D 538 at 544; *Re British Power Traction and Lighting Co Ltd* [1907] 1 Ch 528 at 535.
15 *Re Eastern and Midlands Rly Co* (1890) 7 TLR 17.
16 *Re Wood Green and Hornsey Steam Laundry Ltd* [1918] 1 Ch 423.
17 See *Re Herricks* (1853) 3 I Ch R 183 at 185, and the orders in *Porter v Corbett* (1900) and *Trevy v Tilley* (1900) 1 *Seton's Judgments and Orders* (7th edn) 731.
18 *Re Newdigate Colliery Co Ltd* [1912] 1 Ch 468, CA; *Airlines Airspares Ltd v Handley Page Ltd* [1970] Ch 193, [1970] 1 All ER 29n.
19 *Rother Iron Works Ltd v Canterbury Precision Engineers Ltd* [1974] QB 1, [1973] 1 All ER 394, CA. Cf *NW Robbie & Co Ltd v Witney Warehouse Co Ltd* [1963] 3 All ER 613, [1963] 1 WLR 1324, CA, where under the debenture, the debts owed to a company were assigned in equity to the debenture holder as they arose, so that cross-claims not existing when the debts arose could not be set off against them.
20 *George Barker (Transport) Ltd v Eynon* [1974] 1 All ER 900, [1974] 1 WLR 462, CA.
1 *Howard v Danner* (1901) 17 TLR 548.

manager may not insist on a covenant by the receiver and manager not to carry on a competing business.[2]

A receiver and manager is entitled to an order for delivery of all books relating to the conduct of the business;[3] but a receiver and manager appointed in a debenture holder's action may not insist on retaining such books as against a liquidator, where the business and management have come to an end.[4]

POWER TO BORROW

A receiver, or receiver and manager, appointed by the court should obtain the leave of the court before borrowing. Where the order appointing him is silent as to borrowing for general purposes, he will be entitled to an indemnity for sums borrowed to meet expenses incurred in the ordinary course of the business, which would be treated as prima facie having been properly incurred, whether he obtains the leave of the court or not. If, however, the order empowers him to borrow for general purposes up to a certain amount, and he borrows beyond that amount without the leave of the court, he will only be allowed indemnity against such sums as to which he shall satisfy the judge that, having regard to all the circumstances under which the same were borrowed, he was justified in so doing without obtaining the leave of the judge, the effect of the order empowering him to borrow up to a certain amount being to limit his authority.[5] What circumstances would justify him in increasing the expenses without leave cannot be defined in general terms, but must be determined in each particular case. Certainly it will not be enough for him to show that the liability was incurred bona fide, and in the ordinary course of business.[6]

The court may, where money is required for the preservation of the property, give power to a receiver appointed in a debenture holder's action to borrow, and give a charge for the same, ranking in priority to all the debentures.[7] But it will not give such leave unless it is convinced that the proposed expenditure is likely to be beneficial to all parties.[8]

Where a power to borrow a certain sum for the purposes of the undertaking has been given to a manager by the court, the power will not necessarily be discharged pro tanto if part of the sum is raised and subsequently paid off.[9]

Where it is a proper case for borrowing, the receiver may lend the money himself. Where he applies to the court for leave to do so, the court will

---

2 *Re Irish* (1888) 40 Ch D 49, commented on in *Boorne v Wicker* [1927] 1 Ch 667. See also *Re Gent* (1892) 40 WR 267.

3 1 *Seton's Judgments and Orders* (7th edn) 728.

4 *Engel v South Metropolitan Brewing and Bottling Co* [1892] 1 Ch 442.

5 *Re British Power, Traction and Lighting Co Ltd* [1906] 1 Ch 497; *(No 2)* [1907] 1 Ch 528. See 33 *Court Forms* (1997 Issue) 128, Form 29.

6 *Re British Power, Traction and Lighting Co Ltd* [1906] 1 Ch 497, *(No 2)* [1907] 1 Ch 528.

7 *Greenwood v Algesiras (Gibraltar) Rly Co* [1894] 2 Ch 205, CA.

8 *Securities and Properties Corpn Ltd v Brighton Alhambra Ltd* (1893) 62 LJ Ch 566; *Re Thames Ironworks, Shipbuilding and Engineering Co Ltd* (1912) 106 LT 674, 28 TLR 273.

9 *Milward v Avill & Smart Ltd* [1897] WN 162, 4 Mans 403.

generally allow him interest at the rate of 5 per cent, and give him a charge on the assets.[10]

A receiver appointed by the court in a debenture holder's action cannot, without the leave of the court, give an effective charge on the assets as security for moneys owing by the company prior to the appointment of the receiver.[11]

EMERGENCY BORROWING

In an action by a debenture holder on behalf of himself and all other debenture holders, the court will in the case of an emergency empower the receiver to borrow money as a first charge on the undertaking in priority to the debentures for the preservation of the property. The first reported case[12] where this was established was the decision of the Court of Appeal in *Greenwood v Algesiras (Gibraltar) Rly Co*[13] where very serious land slips had put in jeopardy the future of the railway and the company running it, and an order sanctioning the borrowing of money for the purposes of preservation was made. Such an order will not, in fact, be made unless a case of salvage is established. One example of the principle in operation in a different context occurred in *Chaplin v Barnett*,[14] where the receiver of the estate of a mentally disordered person was allowed to raise, by a charge on the property, a sum of money needed to enable him to effect a transfer of mortgages, the holders of which were pressing for payment.

POWER TO SELL

A court-appointed receiver does not acquire any power of sale by virtue of his office.[15] In most cases, however, the court has power to order a sale of the property over which the receivership extends. Admittedly there is an important exception in cases of equitable execution: the court has no jurisdiction to authorise a sale in such cases.[16] But where an appointment has been made in an action by a mortgagee for foreclosure, redemption or sale,[17] or in a debenture holder's action,[18] or in the administration of the estate of a deceased person[19] the court does have power to direct a sale of the property which is subject to the receivership.

The Rules of the Supreme Court give the court a power on the application of any party to make an order for sale by any person and in any manner of any goods, wares or merchandise which may be of a perishable nature or likely to

10 *Re Bushell, ex p Izard* (1883) 23 Ch D 75, CA.
11 *Whinney v Moss Steamship Co Ltd* [1910] 2 KB 813, CA; affd [1912] AC 254, HL.
12 There had been numerous unreported cases.
13 [1894] 2 Ch 205, CA.
14 (1912) 28 TLR 256, CA.
15 *Australian Industry Development Corpn v Co-operative Farmers' and Graziers' Direct Meat Supply Ltd* (1978) 3 ACLR 543 (receiver and manager).
16 *Flegg v Prentis* [1892] 2 Ch 428; *De Peyrecave v Nicholson* (1894) 71 LT 255.
17 Law of Property Act 1925, ss 90 and 91.
18 *Wood v Woodhouse and Rawson United* [1896] WN 4.
19 RSC Ord 85, r 2(3)(d).

injure from keeping or which for any other just and sufficient reason it may be desirable to have sold at once.[20] The court also has power to order a sale or enforce a charge over land under the Supreme Court Act 1981 even though a receiver may have been appointed under such a charge.[1]

Where the plaintiff or other party is a legal mortgagee the order for sale may authorise him to convey the fee simple or leasehold term to any purchaser.[2] But what if the order, impersonally, authorises a sale of the property? If the contract was entered into by the receiver the conveyance of land for giving effect to that contract must be made by the persons able to convey the legal estate free from incumbrances. Yet the first legal mortgagee cannot normally convey the fee simple or leasehold term on his own.[3] The subsequent legal incumbrancers, if any, and the mortgagor must also concur in the conveyance: otherwise a vesting order must be obtained.[4] The consent of persons with only equitable interests such as debenture holders with a floating charge is not necessary if they are parties to the action or bound by the order. It is otherwise if they are not parties or not bound by the order; but such an eventuality is unlikely.

POWER TO SEEK DIRECTIONS

A receiver appointed by the court may at any time request the court to give him directions and such a request must state in writing the matters with regard to which directions are required.[5] This will be by letter addressed to the master. In simple cases he will give directions, but in cases of difficulty or dispute may order an application notice to be issued.[6]

---

20 RSC Ord 29, r 4.
 1 Law of Property Act 1925, s 90.
 2 See Law of Property Act 1925, s 91(7).
 3 A sale pursuant to a court order is not subject to the provisions contained in Law of Property Act 1925, s 104. That section only applies to sale pursuant to the mortgagee's statutory powers of sale.
 4 Law of Property Act 1925, s 91(7).
 5 RSC Ord 30, r 8.
 6 *Civil Procedure*, Vol 1, Spring 2000, Section A, Schedule 1, sc30.8.1.

CHAPTER 29

Liabilities

LOSSES AND IMPROPER PAYMENTS

A receiver appointed by the court is prima facie liable to account to the parties to the action for all money coming to his hands,[1] or which ought to have come to his hands but for his own negligence or default.[2] So if a receiver is guilty of delay in passing his accounts and paying his balances and the delay causes a loss to the estate owing to a fall in the price of stocks he may be held personally liable. Lord Eldon LC in *Anon v Jolland*[3] indicated that if such a case were brought before him the delinquent receiver might be held liable for the loss. In the Canadian case of *Emerson Town v Wright*[4] the receiver of a town municipality was held responsible to the corporation for loss of interest occasioned by his neglect to deposit in the bank money collected by him for the town.

This liability to account binds a receiver whether or not he has completed his security.[5] The principle that the appointment of a receiver is merely conditional until his security is perfected, applies only to cases where the question is as to his title as against third parties. It has no application where the question is as to his own liability, or that of his sureties, in respect of money received or expenses incurred by him. Equally the liability continues to bind him even after his appointment has ended, for while his discharge will prevent him from receiving anything further it will not put an end to his liability to account for what he has (or ought to have) received.[6] Being in a fiduciary position the receiver, cannot, as against the parties, take any limitation point in an action in respect of any fraud to which he was a party or in an action to recover from him funds still retained by him or previously received by him and converted to his use.[7] As an officer of

---

1 *Hamilton v Lighton* (1810) 2 Mol 499; *Wilkins v Lynch* (1823) 2 Mol 499; *Re Skerretts* (1829) 2 Hog 192.
2 *Beytagh v Concannon* (1847) 10 I Eq R 351.
3 (1802) 8 Ves 72.
4 (1907) 5 WLR 365.
5 *Smart v Flood & Co* (1883) 49 LT 467.
6 *M'Can v O'Ferrall* (1841) 8 Cl & Fin 30, HL; *Seagram v Tuck* (1881) 18 Ch D 296, 50 LJ Ch 572; *Re Gent* (1888) 40 Ch D 190, 58 LJ Ch 162. For a form of order in such a case see *Practice Note* [1943] WN 71.
7 Limitation Act 1980, s 21(1); cf *Re Cornish* [1896] 1 QB 99 at 104, CA where Kay LJ was considering different statutory wording and the position of a trustee in bankruptcy.

the court it would also seem that he cannot avail himself of lapse of time as a defence in any action. Where as is usually the case he is paid remuneration he is not, it seems, entitled to claim relief from personal liability under s 61 of the Trustee Act 1925[8] since he is a paid trustee.[9]

The question whether the mere fact of allowing an excessive balance to accumulate is an account would disentitle the receiver to relief was raised in the course of the judgment of Lord Brougham LC in *White v Baugh*[10] but not decided.

The receiver should deposit receivership money in a special receivership account or earmark it in some other appropriate way. If he fails to pay the money into a separate account, but puts it with his own personal account and mixes it with his own money, he will be liable for any loss consequent on the failure of the bank.[11] A similar liability accrues if he accepts for his own use interest on balances standing to the credit of the receivership bank account and the bank fails.[12]

Again a receiver will be liable if money for which he is answerable does not reach its proper destination, unless he can show that he has acted with perfect regularity and without negligence. The standard of care expected of him is the care which an ordinary prudent man of business would take in managing similar affairs of his own[13] and not the actual care with which the receiver does in fact transact his own personal business.[14] Several cases bear on the receiver's duty of care in the use of bank accounts. If for instance he pays money temporarily into a bank to a separate receiver's account and the bank fails he will not as a rule be answerable for the loss of that money.[15] But in *Drever v Maudesley*[16] although the receiver kept a special receivership account he was in default in passing his accounts and paying the balance and he was deriving a personal profit from the account. This was sufficient to take the case out of the general rule and make him liable for the loss on the failure of the bank.

A receiver is liable for anything done by him in disobedience of an order of the court. Such disobedience amounts to wilful default. If money has been lost by his wilful default and placing it in what he knew at the time to be improper hands the court will oblige a receiver to answer the loss out of his own pocket.[17] Apart from cases where the receiver pays away a sum contrary to an order of the court,[18] he

---

8 For a comprehensive discussion of s 61 of Trustee Act 1925, see *Underhill's Law of Trusts and Trustees* (15th edn) 881–887.

9 See the comparable case of a liquidator: *Re Windsor Steam Coal Co 1901 Ltd* [1929] 1 Ch 151 at 164–165, CA per Lawrence LJ.

10 (1835) 3 Cl & Fin 44 at 57–58. A similar avoidance of the question occurred in the court below: (1831) 2 Russ & M 215 at 217–218.

11 *Wren v Kirton* (1805) 11 Ves 377.

12 *Drever v Maudesley* (1844) 13 LJ Ch 433, 3 LTOS 157.

13 *Massey v Banner* (1820) 1 Jac & W 241 at 247 per Lord Eldon LC; *Salway v Salway* (1831) 2 Russ & M 215 at 220; *Re Mitchell* (1884) 54 LJ Ch 342.

14 *Re Mitchell* (1884) 54 LJ Ch 342, 52 LT 178.

15 See *White v Baugh* (1835) 3 Cl & Fin 44 at 66 per Lord Lyndhurst; and *Drever v Maudesley* (1844) 13 LJ Ch 433, 3 LTOS 157 per Lord Lyndhurst In *White v Baugh* supra the receiver was held liable because he had not retained control of the account.

16 (1844) 13 LJ Ch 433, 3 LTOS 157.

17 *Knight v Earl of Plymouth* (1747) 1 Dick 120, 3 Atk 480.

18 *Delfosse v Crawshay* (1834) 4 LJ Ch 32; *Re Browne's Estate* (1886) 19 LR Ir 132; *Ind Coope & Co Ltd v Kidd* (1894) 63 LJQB 726, 71 LT 203 (receiver paid plaintiff's solicitors instead of creditors).

will also be personally liable if, contrary to some order or direction of the court, he fails to invest money as directed,[19] or allows a business to be carried on instead of winding it up,[20] or fails to account at the time fixed for him to account, and loss results.[1]

Since the duty of a receiver is to take possession of the property covered by the order appointing him receiver, his parting with control of that property will constitute a breach of duty. If loss ensues from that breach of duty he may be liable for it, even though the particular breach of duty may not have been the immediate and proximate cause of the loss in question.[2] In *Salway v Salway* a receiver paid into a banking house the sums he received to the joint account of his sureties, under an arrangement with them that all drafts on the money so deposited should be written by a solicitor partner of one of the sureties and signed by the receiver. This arrangement effectively deprived the receiver of absolute control by giving the solicitor a veto. The bank failed and a considerable sum was lost. Then the arrangement was repeated with another bank which also failed. When the case reached the House of Lords under the name of *White v Baugh*[3] it was pressed in argument that 'the loss did not arise from the circumstance'. Lord Lyndhurst considered the point to be altogether immaterial:[4]

> 'The party who is paid for the discharge of his duty comes to be relieved from the liability. The Court says "You cannot be relieved from your liability unless your conduct has been strictly regular, whether the loss has been occasioned by the irregularity of your conduct or not". Cases were cited at the bar, and it might be sufficient to refer to the ordinary case where a receiver mixes the trust money with his own money of the banker's; the banker fails, the receiver is obliged to make good the loss. Why? Because he ought not to have mixed the trust money with his own money, but to have placed it in a separate account.[5] If it had been in a separate account this would not have taken place. In precisely the same way it is, because the party has conducted himself irregularly and improperly, that the Court will not relieve him here. The Court exercises the strictest vigilance over receivers; they are paid, be it remembered, for the performance of their duty; they are bound to perform that duty strictly, and when they come to the Court for a favour, the Court has a right to say, that they cannot have that favour unless their conduct has been strictly regular.'

EXCEEDING AUTHORITY

Personal liability is visited upon a receiver who acts in excess of his authority. For example a receiver will be personally liable for taking possession of assets

19 *Hicks v Hicks* (1744) 3 Atk 274 (government or other securities directed).
20 *Re Plant* [1881] WN 115, 45 LT 326, CA.
 1 *Potts v Leighton* (1808) 15 Ves 273; *Bristowe v Needham* (1863) 8 LT 652, 9 Jur NS 1168.
 2 *Salway v Salway* (1831) 2 Russ & M 215; affd sub nom *White v Baugh* (1835) 9 Bli NS 181, 3 Cl & Fin 44.
 3 (1835) 9 Bli NS 181, 3 Cl & Fin 44.
 4 (1835) 3 Cl & Fin 44 at 66.
 5 *Wren v Kirton* (1805) 11 Ves 377.

which were not in fact included in the receivership order. In *Neate v Pink*[6] receivers and managers took possession of property not included in the assets of the testator which they had been appointed to collect. The plaintiffs in the suit argued that the receivers and managers could not claim against the funds in court to recoup themselves for losses sustained by an estate which they were not entitled to receive. However it was held that since the receivers' action was acquiesced in by the beneficiaries who had had the benefit of it the receivers were entitled to an indemnity.[7]

BREACH OF STATUTORY DUTY

A receiver is also personally liable for breach of a statutory duty: he is liable in tort to the person to whom he owes the duty. Thus if a receiver and manager with notice of preferential debts exhausts assets in paying other creditors he is liable in damages in tort to the preferential creditors who have suffered by his breach of duty.[8] The liability will only be in respect of damages which are the natural consequence of the breach of duty.[9]

A receiver and manager is likewise guilty of a statutory breach of duty if having collected assets he hands them over to the company with the knowledge that it will transfer them to the debenture holder in satisfaction of his claim without any provision being made for payment of the preferential debt.[10] In this connection it should be mentioned that an action in tort by a preferential creditor for damages occasioned by the failure of the receiver to pay his debt out of available assets is not barred by lapse of time if the receiver had sufficient assets to pay the debt at any time within six years[11] before the bringing of the action.[12]

A further example of a breach of statutory duty by a receiver giving rise to tortious liability in damages occurs in the case of mortgages where a receiver fails to apply money in his hands as required by statute[13] in payment of interest accruing due in respect of any principal money due under the mortgage[14] or in or towards discharge of the principal money if so directed by the mortgagee.[15] These duties are for the mortgagee's benefit as well as for the mortgagor's, and he may maintain an action against the receiver for failure to perform them.[16]

Where a receiver appointed in an administrative action distributes the assets without directions from the court, an inquiry may be directed as to whether the payments were properly made.[17]

6　(1851) 3 Mac & G 476.
7　(1851) 3 Mac & G 476 at 484.
8　*Woods v Winskill* [1913] 2 Ch 303; *Westminster Corpn v Haste* [1950] Ch 442, [1950] 2 All ER 65.
9　See *Argylls Ltd v Coxeter* (1913) 29 TLR 355 (liquidator).
10　*IRC v Goldblatt* [1972] Ch 498, [1972] 2 All ER 202.
11　Limitation Act 1980.
12　*Westminster Corpn v Haste* [1950] Ch 442, [1950] 2 All ER 65.
13　LPA 1925, s 109(8).
14　LPA 1925, s 109(8)(iv).
15　LPA 1925, s 109(8)(v).
16　*Leicester Permanent Building Society v Butt* [1943] Ch 308, [1943] 2 All ER 523.
17　*Cross v Ormerod* (1801) cited in 6 Ves 800; *Armitage v Forbes* (1831) Hayes 222 at 229.

The non-payment of rates by a receiver is not a breach of a statutory duty for which the local authority can sue.[18]

A receiver and manager of an estate or business is not to blame for trading losses so long as he carries on the business in a usual and proper manner in accordance with the directions of the court. In *Morison v Morison*[19] two persons were successively appointed as court consignees in this country of the testator's West India estates which consisted of plantations, slaves and hereditaments. Each of the consignees was absolved from any responsibility for losses which occurred. The court in the words of Knight Bruce LJ[20] 'sanctioned a series of payments made by the appointed consignees as servants of the court for the time being, and a servant or agent of the court, not affected with fraud or improper conduct, is not answerable for the wisdom correctness or propriety of the orders which he receives, or for the directions by which his acts are sanctioned'. There was in that case no reason to doubt the good faith of either of the two consignees and their respective claims in the accounts were allowed. What a receiver and manager properly expends in discharge of his duty even though the expenditure be not directly sanctioned by the court ought to be allowed him on passing his accounts, and to be recoverable out of the property entrusted to his care, the necessity of the expenditure being in each case the measure of its propriety.[1] He is not generally entitled to be indemnified by the parties personally.[2]

The criterion, then, is the propriety of the expenditure.[3] The beneficial nature of the expenditure is not enough: it must have been 'proper'. Thus any expenses which are incurred by a receiver in open disregard of the orders of the court are disallowed whether they are beneficial to the property or not.[4]

LIABILITIES TO LANDLORD

The appointment of a receiver over leasehold property does not of itself constitute him an assignee of the lease or make him personally liable for the performance of the covenants[5] any more than for the payment of rent.[6] Nor does a receiver who pays rent in his own name become liable as a tenant by estoppel if the landlord has not been induced by such payment to believe that the lease has been assigned to him.[7]

---

18 *Liverpool Corpn v Hope* [1938] 1 KB 751, [1938] 1 All ER 492, CA.
19 (1855) 7 De GM & G 214. As to consignees, see *Seton's Judgments and Orders* (7th edn) 777.
20 (1855) 7 De GM & G 214 at 223.
1 *Securities and Properties Corpn Ltd v Brighton Alhambra Ltd* (1893) 62 LJ Ch 566 at 567, 68 LT 249 per Kekewich J.
2 See *Boehm v Goodall* [1911] 1 Ch 155, 80 LJ Ch 86.
3 See also *Re Bushell, ex p Izard* (1883) 23 Ch D 75 at 80, CA.
4 *Garland v Garland* (undated) cited in 6 Ves at 800; *Re Langham* (1847) 2 Ph 299 (committee of a mentally disordered person).
5 *Hay v Swedish and Norwegian Rly Co Ltd* (1892) 8 TLR 775.
6 (1892) 8 TLR 775; *Consolidated Entertainments Ltd v Taylor* [1937] 4 All ER 432 (receiver and manager).
7 *Justice v James* (1898) 14 TLR 385; affd 15 TLR 181, CA.

Where the receiver is appointed by the court at the instance of a mortgagee by sub-demise there is no privity of estate between him and the head-lessor; neither the receiver nor the mortgagee is *liable* to the head-lessor for rent or under the convenants.[8] Nor in these circumstances is there any equity giving the lessor any right to a charge on a fund in court representing proceeds of sale of the leaseholder's goods which otherwise might have been distrained.[9] This factual situation arose in *Hand v Blow*,[10] a debenture holder's action against the trustees of a trust deed who were mortgagees from the company by sub-demise of four shops in the Edgware Road, London of which the company were lessees. The Court of Appeal affirming the decision of Stirling J disallowed a claim by the head-lessor against the receiver appointed by the court to payment out of the proceeds of the company's goods sold by the receiver while in occupation of the premises of rent in respect of the occupation and of damages for a breach of the company's covenant in the head lease to repair. One of the arguments advanced[11] was that the possession of the receiver having been by the direction of the court, and he having by order of the court sold and removed the chattels the head landlords had an equity that out of the moneys in his hands which were assets of the company the rent due from the company should be paid. In this connection reliance was placed on *Great Eastern Rly Co v East London Rly Co* where it was held that the receiver of the tolls of the defendant company was bound to pay to the plaintiff company rent for the beneficial use of their land in priority to the claims of the debenture holders. None of the members of the court referred to that case in their judgments. Rigby LJ in the course of argument simply distinguished it as a case of direct liability on the part of the defendant company, and not a case of mortgage by sub-demise.

A receiver of leasehold property should nevertheless pay the rent out of assets coming into his hands without applying to the court.[12] Moreover, if the landlord is entitled to the rent and the receiver by his non-payment drives the landlord to take proceedings to recover it, the receiver may be ordered to pay the costs of such proceedings.[13]

If the landlord's property has been retained and occupied for the more beneficial realisation of the assets generally, the landlord's right to recover his rent will rank as against such assets in priority to the claims of all persons for whose benefit such assets are being realised,[14] although not in priority to the costs of the appointment of the receiver.[15]

---

8 *Hand v Blow* [1901] 2 Ch 721, 70 LJ Ch 687, CA. But a payment may well be needed to avoid forfeiture.

9 [1901] 2 Ch 721.

10 [1901] 2 Ch 721, CA.

11 [1901] 2 Ch 721 at 733.

12 *Balfe v Blake* (1850) 1 I Ch R 365.

13 *Walsh v Walsh* (1839) 1 I Eq R 209; *Callaghan v Callaghan* (1849) 1 Ir Jur 42; *Balfe v Blake* (1850) 1 I Ch R 365; *Re Suffield, ex p Brown* (1888) 36 WR 303 (receiver personally liable).

14 *Great Eastern Rly Co v East London Rly Co* (1881) 44 LT 903; *Lathom v Greenwich Ferry Co* (1895) 72 LT 790.

15 *Read v Corcoran* (1851) 1 I Ch R 235.

Apart from his liability to the landlord for the costs of proceedings instituted by the landlord to recover rent which should have been paid,[16] the receiver who his paid away sub-rents without providing for the head-rent and who has no assets in the receivership enabling him to meet the landlord's claim,[17] will be compelled to pay the arrears of head-rent of his own pocket.[18] Nevertheless if the receiver has acted in good faith and in accordance with the directions of the court he will be entitled to an indemnity.[19]

A receiver only accounts for the rent which fell due before the rent day immediately preceding the time of his accounting.[20] In exceptional cases there may be a charge which has priority over the head-rent in which case the receiver must pay that charge first.[1]

COSTS IN LEGAL PROCEEDINGS

The costs of all proceedings in the High Court are in the discretion of the court.[2] Accordingly, where the circumstances warrant it, a receiver like any other party may find himself penalised personally for costs. That unwelcome liability is visited upon a receiver who causes unnecessary proceedings or litigious expense. Thus a receiver who occasions an unnecessary application or appearance may be mulcted in costs for the trouble he has caused.[3] And a similarly adverse order may be granted against a receiver who by his misconduct or default precipitates proceedings based on that misconduct or default.[4] So a receiver who renders accounts very irregularly in point of time,[5] or who publishes a libel[6] or suffers costs to accrue which he ought to have prevented[7] will be made to pay the costs thereby caused. A modern illustration of the principle that the court will use the sanction of an adverse order in costs against a receiver is to be found in *Bacal Contracting Ltd v Modern Engineering (Bristol) Ltd*.[8] The receiver of a company appointed under a debenture carried on an action, which the company had

16 *Walsh v Walsh* (1839) 1 I Eq R 209; *Callaghan v Callaghan* (1849) 1 Ir Jur 42; *Re Suffield, ex p Brown* (1888) 36 WR 303.
17 In some of the cases it would appear that there were sufficient assets: see *Jacobs v Van Boolen* (1889) 34 Sol Jo 97 and the following Irish cases: *Donovan v Sweeny* (1849) 1 Ir Jur 165; *Elliott v Elliott* (1849) 1 Ir Jur 165; *Sherlock v Roe* (1849) 1 Ir Jur 177.
18 *Balfe v Blake* (1850) 1 I Ch R 365; *Jacobs v Van Boolen* supra.
19 *Balfe v Blake* (1850) 1 I Ch R 365; *Walsh v Walsh* (1839) 1 I Eq R 209.
20 *Betagh v Concannon* (1830) 2 Hog 205.
 1 *Madden v Wilson* (1854) 6 Ir Jur 129 (tithe rent charge).
 2 Supreme Court Act 1981, s 51(1); RSC Ord 62, r 2(4).
 3 *Rowan v Dawson* (1831) 4 Ir L Rec 1st Ser 126; *O'Kelly v Gregg* (1838) Jo & Car 76 (wasted application for an injunction); *Re Doolan* (1843) 2 Con & Law 232; *Payne v Lamb* (1844) 8 I Eq R 517; *De Motmorency v Pratt* (1849) 12 I Eq R 411; *Delacherois v Wrixon* (1850) 2 Ir Jur 66.
 4 *Re Suffield and Watts, ex p Brown* (1888) 36 WR 303 (revsd on another point 20 QBD 693, 58 LT 911, CA).
 5 *Bertie v Lord Abingdon* (1845) 8 Beav 53.
 6 *Re Stubbs* (1866) 15 LT 312.
 7 *Cook v Sharman* (1844) 8 I Eq R 515.
 8 [1980] 2 All ER 655.

started, claiming damages for the loss sustained on the collapse of a partially erected building. A winding up order was made against the company but the receiver continued the action nonetheless. It was held that the statutory provision[9] confirming that costs were in the discretion of the court enabled an order to be made against the receiver personally where it was just and equitable to do so.

CONTRACTUAL LIABILITY

A court-appointed receiver is not an agent: until the rights of the parties are finally established he does not hold or deal with the property primarily for the benefit of any one party or as agent for any party. As Chitty J observed in *Bacup Corpn v Smith*:[10]

> 'A receiver is not an agent for any other person, and a receiver is not a trustee. The receiver is responsible to the Court, and cannot obey the directions of the parties in the action, and in no sense does he stand in the position of agent to the parties who are interested at the suit of whom or one of whom he has been appointed.'

The denial of any kind of agency consequent upon a court appointment is universal.[11] A consequence of that is that he is contracting normally, as a principal, and is therefore personally liable on any contract which he enters into as receiver or manager.[12]

The insistence of the English courts upon personal liability of receivers generally, in contract and in tort, is due to the tendency, often exemplified in the nineteenth century, to refuse a privileged position so far as possible to any official dealing with the public.[13]

Freedom of contract permits a receiver appointed by the court to stipulate in any particular contract that he is not to be held personally liable.[14] The fact that there is no express exclusion of personal liability is not conclusive of the matter if the right inference to draw from the nature of the transaction is that the receiver did not intend to pledge his personal credit and the creditor did not rely upon it.[15] Thus in *Re A Boynton Ltd*[16] where a bank lent money to a receiver and manager

---

9 Namely the provision which is now Supreme Court Act 1981, s 51(1).

10 (1890) 44 Ch D 395 at 398.

11 See *Re Flowers & Co* [1897] 1 QB 14, CA; *Re Glasdir Copper Mines Ltd* [1906] 1 Ch 365 at 375, CA per Vaughan Williams LJ; *Re British Power Traction and Lighting Co Ltd* [1910] 2 Ch 470; *Boehm v Goodall* [1911] 1 Ch 155.

For classification of a receiver and manager in a debenture holder's action as a *trustee*, see *Moss Steamship Co Ltd v Whinney* [1912] AC 254 at 259 per Lord Loreburn. 'Fiduciary' seems a better description: see Meagher Gummow and Lehane *Equity: Doctrines and Remedies* (3rd edn) para 2837.

12 *Moss Steamship Co Ltd v Whinney* [1912] AC 254 at 259.

13 See Ralph E Clark 'English and American Theories of Receivers' Liabilities' (1927) 27 Col LR 679 at 680.

14 *Re Glasdir Copper Mines Ltd* [1906] 1 Ch 365, 75 LJ Ch 109, CA.

15 *Re A Boynton Ltd* [1910] 1 Ch 519 at 524.

16 [1910] 1 Ch 519 at 525.

appointed in a debenture holder's action the recitals in the charge given to the bank and the charge itself indicated that the bank were content to look to their security and to that alone, and that they were dealing with the receiver as a receiver and as an officer of the court. The last mentioned factor, namely that the creditor knows that he is dealing with a receiver and manager as such, is not in itself decisive. Accordingly the mere addition of the words 'receiver and manager' after the signature of the receiver and manager is not enough to rebut the presumption of personal liability.[17]

TORT

A tort committed by a person before he is appointed a receiver by the court is not a tort committed by an officer of the court. A receiver who is sued in respect of a tort committed by him before the receivership began cannot pray in aid his status as an officer of the court in relation to an act which ex hypothesi was done by him when he was not an officer of the court.[18]

A court-appointed receiver is not an agent of anyone. He is, rather, a principal acting on his own responsibility. As a result he is personally liable to third parties for any torts committed by him in the course of his receivership or by persons in his employment in the ordinary course of their duties. However the receiver has a right of indemnity against the assets which are subject to his appointment. Yet there are limits to the right of indemnity too: it does not extend to the costs of defending an action in which (1) personal fraud and misconduct are alleged against the receiver *and* (2) the conduct in question had no relation to the estate except so far as the acts complained of were acts done by him while acting as receiver.[19]

A common tort in receivership is where the receiver is guilty of a wrongful distress or trespass or conversion.[20] Certainly the cloak of office which the court puts upon him does not procure him immunity from liability for trespass or conversion. And he may be liable if he proceeds with a wrongful distress[1] or if he takes possession of property not within the ambit of his appointment.[2]

Particular caution must be exercised by a person who complains of an act done by the receiver with the express authority of the court. The complainant must in such a case first obtain the leave of the court to bring proceedings against the receiver for otherwise the complainant might be seeming to flout the court's authority.[3] And indeed a plaintiff who in such a case proceeds without the leave

---

17 *De Grelle & Co v Bull and Ward* (1894) 10 TLR 198; *Burt, Boulton and Hayward v Bull* [1895] 1 QB 276, CA; *Moss Steamship Co Ltd v Whinney* [1912] AC 254 at 258–259 and 263; and see *Justice v James* (1899) 15 TLR 181 at 182, CA.
18 *Fenton Textile Association Ltd v Lodge* [1928] 1 KB 1, CA.
19 *Re Dunn* [1904] 1 Ch 648.
20 See the discussion of a privately appointed receiver's liability in conversion at p 143.
1 *Serjeant v Nash Field & Co* [1903] 2 KB 304, CA; *Parr v Bell* (1846) 9 I Eq R 55.
2 *Parr v Bell* (1846) 9 I Eq R 55; and see *Re Goldberg (No 2)* [1912] 1 KB 606.
3 *Aston v Heron* (1834) 2 My & K 390, 3 LJ Ch 194; and see *Simpson v Hutchinson* (1859) 7 Gr 308.

of the court runs the risk of punishment for contempt of court. If the act complained of was not specifically authorised by the court but was merely committed in the course of the receiver's performance of his duties the court has a discretion as to whether or not the plaintiff should have leave to proceed with his action for trespass.

As a rule the court will by injunction restrain the plaintiff from continuing his action and may require him to apply in the action in which the receiver was appointed.[4] That is certainly the line taken where the act complained of was done under the express directions of the court. The court will then transfer the question of what compensation should be awarded to the master. When quantified the compensation will be the personal liability of the receiver although the latter may be allowed to claim it in his accounts if he acted at the instigation of the parties.[5]

In cases where it is clear that the receiver has done the acts complained of deliberately and maliciously or mala fide or has, for example, intentionally levied an excessive distress the court may allow a separate action to proceed against the receiver for substantial damages.[6]

4   *Parr v Bell* (1846) 9 I Eq R 55; *Re Maidstone Palace of Varieties Ltd* [1909] 2 Ch 283; *Chalie v Pickering* (1836) 1 Keen 749, 5 LJ Ch 308. For an Australian example see: *A 'Beckett v Robinson* (1856) 1 VLT 160; 2 VLT 251.
5   *A 'Beckett v Robinson* (1856) 1 VLT 160; 2 VLT 251.
6   See *Parr v Bell* (1846) 9 I Eq R 55.

CHAPTER 30

Interference with court receiver

GENERAL PRINCIPLES

A receiver, receiver and manager, or manager appointed by the court is, as has been stressed, an officer of the court. There is a general principle of wide application that interference with persons having duties to perform in a court of justice amounts to contempt of court. The principle was explained by Bowen LJ in *Re Johnson*:[1]

> 'The law has armed the High Court of Justice with the power and imposed on it the duty of preventing brevi manu and by summary proceedings any attempt to interfere with the administration of justice. It is on that ground, and not on any exaggerated notions of the dignity of individuals that insults to judges are not allowed. The principle is that those who have duties to discharge in a court of justice are protected by the law, and shielded on their way to the discharge of such duties, while discharging them, and on their return therefrom, in order that such persons may safely have resort to courts of justice.'

The phrase 'persons having duties to discharge in a court of justice' is widely interpreted and includes a court-appointed receiver or manager.

Interference with the possession of a receiver or manager was discussed by Lord Romilly in *Ames v Birkenhead Docks Trustees*:[2]

> 'There is no question but that this Court will not permit a receiver appointed by its authority, and who is therefore its officer, to be interfered with or dispossessed of the property he is directed to receive, by anyone, although the order appointing him may be perfectly erroneous; this Court requires and insists that application should be made to the Court, for permission to take possession of any property of which the Receiver either has taken or is directed to take possession.'

It follows from this that any interference with the possession of the receiver without the permission of the court is a contempt.[3] Certain other interferences

---

1 (1887) 20 QBD 68 at 74, CA.
2 (1855) 20 Beav 332 at 353; and see *Russell v East Anglian Rly Co* (1850) 3 Mac & G 104 per Lord Truro LC.
3 *Ames v Birkenhead Docks Trustees* (1855) 20 Beav 332 at 352; *Defries v Creed* (1865) 6 New Rep 17; *Tai Kwong Goldsmiths & Jewellers (under receivership) v Yap Kooi Hee* [1995] 1 MLJ 1.

with the receiver's rights may also amount to a contempt. In this connection the identity or status of the 'meddler' is of importance and one must distinguish between the position of a party to the action and that of a stranger to the action.

INTERFERENCE BY A PARTY

Interference with property over which a receiver has been appointed by the court at the instance of a party to the action in which the receiver is appointed and whether or not the appointment has been perfected by the provision of security is a contempt.[4] Accordingly a party who is present throughout the hearing of an application for the appointment of a receiver, hears the order appointing a receiver being made and then tries to forestall it by removing the subject matter before the order is drawn up is guilty of contempt.[5]

INTERFERENCE BY A STRANGER

On the other hand an interference by a stranger to the action will constitute a contempt only if the receiver has gone into possession[6] and has also, if he was appointed conditionally upon giving security, perfected his security,[7] and there is nothing further to be done to perfect the order.[8]

CONTUMACIOUS INTERFERENCE

What then constitutes an interference amounting to a contempt? The clearest examples in the cases involve deliberate knowing interferences with the receiver's possession. The following acts, when done without the leave of the court in respect of property over which the court has appointed a receiver, may amount to a contempt of court and justify the court's intervention for the protection of its officer: bringing an action for possession of the land in receivership;[9] taking forcible possession of estates over the rents and profits of which a receiver has been appointed;[10] entering under a claim of right on the land in the

---

4 *Langford v Langford* (1835) 5 LJ Ch 60; *Re Maudslay, Sons & Field* [1900] 1 Ch 602 at 611.
5 *Skip v Harwood* (1747) 3 Atk 564, 2 Swan 586 per Lord Hardwicke LC.
6 *Russell v East Anglian Rly Co* (1850) 3 Mac & G 104; *Defries v Creed* (1865) 6 New Rep 17 (seizure under fi fa before order); *Re Maudslay, Sons & Field* [1900] 1 Ch 602 (order did not put foreign property into possession of receiver).
7 *Edwards v Edwards* (1876) 2 Ch D 291, CA.
8 *Re Maudslay, Sons & Field* supra (no contempt where something else has to be done to perfect order).
9 *Angel v Smith* (1804) 9 Ves 335; *Re Battersby's Estates* (1892) 31 LR Ir 73.
10 *Broad v Wickham* (1831) 4 Sim 511.

receiver's possession;[11] re-entering on property under a power to that effect;[12] and attempting to collect rents receivable by the court's appointee.[13]

Further examples involving flagrant interferences include: trying to steal a march on the receiver by removing chattels after hearing a receivership order pronounced and injunctive relief granted;[14] taking forcible possession, as holder of a bill of sale, of chattels in the receiver's possession;[15] and offering or threatening personal violence to the receiver.[16]

Execution of a judgment debt may also constitute a contempt of court. Thus the attachment of debts due to a company after a receiver has been appointed in a debenture holder's action has been held a contempt[17] as has the levying of execution upon partnership assets in the possession of a receiver.[18] In *Re Cowan's Estate*,[19] however, attachment of money not yet in the receiver's hands was not subverted by the existence of a receivership. A receiver appointed by the court of an estate under administration was ordered to pay the rents and an annuity to a person entitled for life. It was held that the sums so payable, including sums payable thereafter and not yet in the receiver's hands were subject to attachment to ensure a judgment debt of the beneficiary. But a sheriff carrying out execution may be guilty of contempt,[20] although not if he has seized assets under a writ of fi fa before the receiver was actually appointed by order.[1] Furthermore the sheriff is answerable for his under-sheriff or other subordinate who acts in the execution without reference to the sheriff himself.[2]

The sheriff who does seize property subject to a receivership order will be ordered to return it to the receiver.[3] The form of order usually directs the receiver to deliver a list of the property subject to the receivership and the sheriff will be ordered to withdraw.[4] If the execution creditor is before the court he may be restrained from claiming the property from the sheriff,[5] and if the sheriff

11 *Fripp v Bridgewater and Taunton Canal and Stolford Rly and Harbour Co* (1853) 11 Hare 241; and see *Tink v Rundle* (1847) 10 Beav 318 (taking possession under compulsory powers conferred by statute).

12 *Forster v Manchester and Milford Rly Co* [1880] WN 63.

13 *Anon* (1824) 2 Mol 499; *Langford v Langford* (1835) 5 LJ Ch 60; *Thomas v Thomas* (1842) Fl & K 621; *Crow v Wood* (1850) 13 Beav 271; *Delacherois v Wrixon* (1850) 2 Ir Jur 66 at 89; *Hollier v Hedges* (1853) 2 I Ch R 370; *Mullarkey v Donohoe* (1885) 16 LR Ir 365.

14 *Skip v Harwood* (1747) 3 Atk 564, 2 Swan 586.

15 *Re Mead, ex p Cochrane* (1875) LR 20 Eq 282.

16 *Fitzpatrick v Eyre* (1824) 1 Hog 171; *Harvey v Wallis* (1851) 3 Ir Jur 409.

17 *Re Derwent Rolling Mills Co Ltd* (1904) 21 TLR 81; affd 21 TLR 701, CA. Injunctive relief claimed in consequence of the contempt was, however, refused because of the conduct of the applicant. See also *Jogendra Nath Gossain v Debendra Nath Gossain* (1899) ILR 26 Calc 127 (Ind).

18 *Lane v Sterne* (1862) 3 Giff 629, 9 Jur NS 320.

19 (1880) 14 Ch D 638; cf *De Winton v Brecon Corpn (No 2)* (1860) 28 Beav 200 (where money was in hands of receiver).

20 *Russell v East Anglian Rly Co* (1850) 3 Mac & G 104; *Try v Try* (1851) 13 Beav 422; *Lane v Sterne* (1862) 3 Giff 629, 9 Jur NS 320.

1 *Defries v Creed* (1865) 6 New Rep 17.

2 *Russell v East Anglian Rly Co* (1850) 3 Mac & G 104 at 112.

3 *Try v Try* (1851) 13 Beav 422.

4 *Wilmer v Kidd* (1853) 1 *Seton's Judgments & Orders* 7th edn 729.

5 *Russell v East Anglian Rly Co* (1850) 3 Mac & G 104.

surrenders the property to the receiver he in turn will be protected from any complaint by an execution creditor who was not before the court.[6]

Levying a distress may also constitute a contempt[7] although not if the distress was begun before the appointment of the receiver.[8] Obtaining the appointment of a sequestrator against the living of a beneficed clergyman already subject to a receivership even if the possession of the receiver is not actually disturbed is a contempt.[9] So is preventing a clergyman preaching in a chapel on charity property over which a receiver has been appointed.[10] The granting of a lease by a tenant for life of the property within the ambit of the receivership order may be a contumacious interference.[11]

When a receiver is appointed of the rents of land situate abroad, a defendant who prevents payment to the receiver is in contempt of court, and, if he is not himself within the jurisdiction any property of his which is within the jurisdiction may be sequestrated until he purges his contempt.[12] It is not, however, a contempt for a stranger to the action to try to gain possession of foreign assets in priority to the receiver.[13] This is because the court appointment does not automatically place the receiver in possession of foreign property: he has to take further steps in the relevant foreign jurisdiction to get possession of assets subjected to the receivership, and until he has taken those further steps a stranger, at any rate, can race ahead of the receiver.[13]

In *Re Plant, ex p Hayward*,[14] a firm of merchants having filed a petition for liquidation, a receiver was appointed by the court. The receiver sent out the usual notices to the creditors informing them of his appointment and asking for particulars of claims, and he sent out applications to some of the debtors for the debts due. The debtor's solicitor then told the receiver not to collect or apply for any further debts as it would ruin the business and goodwill. He also told the receiver that it was unnecessary for him to interfere with the management beyond holding possession and doing what the solicitor would from time to time direct, as the business was being carried on under his superintendence. The receiver demurred. The solicitor then told the receiver that he as the solicitor would see to the management and he offered in writing an indemnity to the receiver. The Court of Appeal unanimously held this action to be a contempt. Both Lord Selborne LC and Brett LJ laid emphasis on the fact that the solicitor by offering an indemnity knew perfectly well that he was asking the receiver to do something which was wrong. Brett LJ indeed described the interference as 'of the gravest kind'. Cotton LJ said:

---

6 (1850) 3 Mac & G 104.
7 *Re Sutton's Estate* (1863) 8 LT 343; *Eyton v Denbigh, Ruthin and Corwen Rly Co* (1868) LR 6 Eq 14 and 488.
8 *Engel v South Metropolitan Brewing and Bottling Co* [1891] WN 31.
9 *Hawkins v Gathercole* (1855) 6 De GM & G 1 (where the sequestrator had priority because the receiver ought not to have been appointed). A receiver will not be appointed of a living already subject to sequestration: *Bates v Brothers* (1854) 2 Sm & G 509, 23 LJ Ch 782.
10 *A-G v St Cross Hospital* (1854) 18 Beav 601, 24 LJ Ch 148.
11 *Vine v Raleigh* (1883) 24 Ch D 238 at 243.
12 *Langford v Langford* (1835) 5 LJ Ch 60.
13 *Re Huinac Copper Mines Ltd* [1910] WN 218; *Re Maudslay, Sons & Field* [1900] 1 Ch 602 at 611–612.
14 (1881) 45 LT 326, CA.

'It is not for giving bad advice that the [solicitor] is to be held liable but for his interference. It has been clearly shown that the order of the Court was stopped to some extent from having effect by what was done. The proper method, if the order was not considered to be right, was to apply to have such order altered. The solicitor, however, did not take that view of the case. He in fact said to the receiver "Do not act under that order, but do as I tell you to do, and I will indemnify you from the consequences of your disobedience". That appears to me to have been a contempt of Court.'

Contumacious interference with a receiver may be committed by less direct means. Thus in *Helmore v Smith (No 2)*[15] a receiver was appointed pending an appeal against the dissolution of a partnership, in order to keep the business as a going concern. Helmore was a former employee of the partnership but, having been dismissed, set up his own firm. After the receiver had been appointed, Helmore wrote a letter to the customers of the firm, the effect of which, according to Kay J, was to say:[16] 'The business is at the end, subject to the chance of an appeal from the Vice-Chancellor's judgment; send your orders to me'. The Court of Appeal held that Helmore had committed a gross contempt. As Bowen LJ said:[17]

'I will not discuss the cases as to what interference with a receiver and manager will justify the Court in interfering, or lay down any rule upon the subject. All I say is that this was a wrongful act calculated to destroy property under the management of this Court, and that it was done deliberately. Are the hands of the Court so tied that it cannot protect its officers, and must relegate them to the ordinary legal remedy, and the consequent delay of execution? Where it is necessary for the protection of its officers or of the property itself the Court must show that it has a long arm.'

When a receiver and manager of a partnership business has been appointed, a partner who starts a competing business in such a manner as to be likely to injure the original business, for example by issuing circulars that the original business is no longer being carried on, may be punished by committal for contempt of court[18] or at the very least subjected to an appropriate injunction.[19]

Another example of contumacious interference in the context of a partnership dispute where a receiver has been appointed is to be found in the Australian case of *Horne v Leigh*.[20] One of the parties to a partnership action with notice that a receiver had been appointed of certain property mortgaged a portion of that property and thereby gave the mortgagee power on default being made to enter into possession and effect a lease of the mortgaged property. Street J held the party guilty of a contempt of court in interfering or attempting to interfere with the receiver in the performance of his duties. The learned judge offered the guilty party a chance to repent, giving the plaintiff leave to issue a writ of attachment

15 (1886) 35 Ch D 449, CA.
16 (1886) 35 Ch D 449 at 451.
17 (1886) 35 Ch D 449 at 457.
18 *King v Dopson* (1911) 56 Sol Jo 51.
19 *Dixon v Dixon* [1904] 1 Ch 161.
20 (1906) 7 SRNSW 51, 23 WN 242, NSW Sup Ct.

but directing that its operation should be suspended for 14 days; if by the deadline the defendant had not secured the release of the mortgage or put the receiver in funds to enable the latter to discharge the mortgage the attachment was to proceed.

DEFENCES TO CONTEMPT PROCEEDINGS

The complete answer to a charge that there has been impermissible interference with the receiver's rights and thus with the will of the court is, of course, that there has been no interference. Other pleas have been raised in the cases. And it will be convenient to isolate, first, in particular, those defences which have failed to carry the day, and then to identify what legitimate counter-arguments there are to the charge of contempt of court. So there are ineffective defences or pleas, and effective ones. That is not to say that an ineffective defence has no impact at all. When the court comes to consider how to deal with the contempt the matters relied upon by way of unsuccessful defence may mitigate the gravity of the contempt.

The idea that a person who acts under what appears to be a pardonable mistake is not guilty of contempt has been hinted at in one or two cases.[1] The stress laid in some instances on the fact that particular conduct was a 'deliberate act' might appear to have a similar tendency.[2] But conduct of an innocent or unintentional kind which *in fact* interferes with the receiver's possession will constitute a contempt nonetheless. The court can always deal appropriately with a 'technical' contempt when it comes to consider what action to take on the contempt being drawn to its attention.

The consent or submission of the receiver to what is being done will not prevent the interference being a contempt of court.[3] Nor is it any answer to the charge of contempt that the interference was by a person claiming by a paramount title,[4] unless the receiver's appointment was expressly made without prejudice to the rights of such a person.[5] Again, the fact that the appointment of the receiver has been improperly obtained, or has been made on some erroneous basis, does not justify interference with his possession, and such interference will still constitute a contempt of court.[6] Interference by one receiver with another without leave of the court will be as much a contempt as interference by a private individual.[7]

Where the order appointing the receiver does not clearly state over what property the receiver is appointed, interference with his possession under a claim

---

1 *Ward v Swift* (1848) 6 Hare 309; *Fripp v Bridgewater and Taunton Canal Co* (1855) 3 WR 356.
2 See eg *Dixon v Dixon* [1904] 1 Ch 161 at 163.
3 *De Winton v Brecon Corpn (No 2)* (1860) 28 Beav 200; *Re Plant, ex p Hayward* [1881] WN 115, 45 LT 326, CA.
4 *Evelyn v Lewis* (1844) 3 Hare 472; *Randfield v Randfield* (1860) 1 Drew & Sm 310.
5 *Underhay v Read* (1887) 20 QBD 209, CA. See the discussion at pp 418 and 460–461.
6 *Ames v Birkenhead Docks Trustees* (1855) 20 Beav 332, 24 LJ Ch 540; *Russell v East Anglian Rly Co* (1850) 3 Mac & G 104.
7 *Ward v Swift* (1848) 6 Hare 309 at 312.

of right will not be restrained.[8] In some cases, too, the property in question may in fact be property over which the receiver cannot be appointed. An example is the unpaid capital of a railway undertaking:[9] attachment of that unpaid capital does not amount to interference with the possession of the receiver.[10]

Again if the appointment of a receiver is conditional (as it usually is) upon his giving security, interference with him before he completes his security will not constitute a contempt.[11]

If the interest in respect of which a receiver has been appointed determines, as for example where a life interest or a term of years falls in, it will not be contempt of court for the persons entitled to the property expectant on the determination of that interest to resume possession of the property without the leave of the court after such determination.[12]

Two cases involving tenants who paid rent otherwise than to the receiver provide instances of non-contumacious actions. A tenant who knows that a receiver has been appointed but who has not actually been served with notice of the appointment may continue to pay rent to his landlord without being guilty of contempt.[13] And in *Underhay v Read*[14] a tenant who, after an order had been made appointing a receiver of the rents of certain premises, paid rent to a mortgagee, whose rights were reserved under the receivership order and who was threatening proceedings, was held not guilty of contempt. Fry LJ referred to the form of the order which was expressed to be 'without prejudice to the rights of any prior incumbrancers upon the said premises who may think proper to take possession of the same by virtue of their respective securities'.[15] He then continued:[16]

> 'I think the form of order is designed to sanction the payment to such prior incumbrancers of any sums to which they may be entitled without any further application to the Court; and that, whatever their rights may be, they may enforce them without being guilty of a contempt of court. It is no doubt true that this form of order is of modern invention, but a similar form is by no means modern by which, when it came to the knowledge of the Court of Chancery that the property in respect of which a receiver was to be appointed was subject to a prior mortgage, the Court reserved the rights of the mortgagees. No case can be produced in which a person has ever been committed for enforcing such prior rights. I therefore think that, whatever the rights of the prior incumbrancers were, they were entitled to enforce them, and that the tenant is making a payment to them to which they were entitled would not commit a contempt of the order of the Court.'

8 *Crow v Wood* (1850) 13 Beav 271.
9 *Re Birmingham and Lichfield Junction Rly Co* (1881) 18 Ch D 155, 50 LJ Ch 594.
10 Companies Clauses Consolidation Act 1845, s 36; *Re West Lancashire Rly Co* (1890) 63 LT 56 (receiver sued for calls on unpaid shares held by him in his private capacity as a shareholder: no contempt).
11 *Defries v Creed* (1865) 6 New Rep 17; *Edwards v Edwards* (1876) 2 Ch D 291.
12 *Britton v McDonnell* (1843) 5 I Eq R 275; *Kenny v Clarke* (1843) 5 I Eq R 280 at 282; *Re Stack* (1862) 13 I Ch R 213.
13 *Mullarkey v Donohoe* (1885) 16 LR Ir 365.
14 (1887) 20 QBD 209, CA.
15 The form of the order is set out at (1887) 20 QBD 209 at 210–211.
16 (1887) 20 QBD 209 at 219 per Fry LJ.

According to one old case it will not be viewed as a contempt of court for all the parties interested to evict a receiver who has been guilty of waste without the leave of the court.[17] More recently it has been held that no contempt is committed by a third party who unwittingly buys property which is sold in breach of an agreement between the vendor and the receiver.[18]

Looking at the matter from the viewpoint of the receiver appointed by the court, a receiver appointed on behalf of debenture holders is entitled to take possession of all assets comprised in their security. This right of the courtappointed receiver prevails over the right of a judgment creditor who has taken goods in execution but has not actually sold them.[19] Equally the right of the receiver prevails over that of a judgment creditor who has attached debts by garnishee proceedings but has not actually obtained payment.[20] His right also ranks before that of a solicitor to whom a sum of money has been handed to meet costs not yet incurred.[1]

The arm of the receiver is however not always long enough. Thus he has no right to money paid to the sheriff to release goods[2] nor has he any claim to money paid to the garnishor before crystallisation of the security of the debenture holders.[3]

SANCTIONS

Committal

The most condign punishment for a contempt of court is, of course, committal. But the court avoids committal if it can do so without compromising justice and reserves its extreme power to imprison the intermeddler for cases which cry out for such a punishment. As Sir James Wigram V-C said, 'The authority of the Court is best vindicated by reserving its extreme powers for cases which imperatively call for them'.[4] Prison is not the right place for a 'technical' contemnor.

It follows that where the interference arises out of an excusable mistake[5] or is of a kind which the court would, on a timeous application, have sanctioned,[6] the court will not normally punish the offender. The same applies where the appointment of a receiver was the result of a mistake.[7] Certainly an application for committal ought not to be pursued on the ground of interference with possession

---

17 *Bell v Spereman* (1726) Sel Cas in Ch 169, Cas temp King 59.
18 *Densham v Rays, Re Humphrey* (1920) 55 L Jo 52.
19 *Re Standard Manufacturing Co* [1891] 1 Ch 627, CA; *Taunton v Sheriff of Warwickshire* [1895] 2 Ch 319 at 323, CA.
20 *Norton v Yates* [1906] 1 KB 112; *Cairney v Back* [1906] 2 KB 746; *Sinnott v Bowden* [1912] 2 Ch 414 at 421.
 1 *Re British Tea Table Co (1897) Ltd* (1909) 101 LT 707.
 2 *Robinson v Burnell's Vienna Bakery Co Ltd* [1904] 2 KB 624; *Heaton and Dugard Ltd v Cutting Bros Ltd* [1925] 1 KB 655, DC.
 3 *Robson v Smith* [1895] 2 Ch 118.
 4 *Ward v Swift* (1848) 6 Hare 309 at 314.
 5 (1848) 6 Hare 309.
 6 *Hawkins v Gathercole* (1852) 1 Drew 12.
 7 *Russell v East Anglian Rly Co* (1850) 3 Mac & G 104.

where the question of possession has been disposed of, and the only object is to compel payment of the costs and expenses caused by the interference.[8]

On the other hand where the act in question was one which deliberately flouted or defied the receiver's authority the extreme punishment may be appropriate. In *Broad v Wickham*[9] a person had taken forcible possession of estates over which a receiver had been appointed. Sir Lancelot Shadwell V-C ruled that an order nisi need not be drawn up against the party who, though served with the notice of motion had not condescended to appear, and that an order for commitment should be drawn up. Another example of gross contempt was the wilful and persistent obduracy in *Helmore v Smith (No 2)*[10] of the plaintiff's son in refusing to give an undertaking not to repeat his offence of libelling the business carried on by the receiver and manager, despite being afforded an opportunity to give that undertaking by the court itself.

Where committal is appropriate the motion to commit should be issued promptly.[11] Because of the gravity of the sanction it should not be used for any collateral motive or purpose. Thus an application for committal should not be mounted on the basis of a disturbance of possession where that question has already been dealt with and the only object of the application is to compel payment of the costs and expenses caused by such disturbance.[12]

Injunction

An injunction to restrain further interference with a receiver is often settled upon as the best technique of dealing, at any rate at the preliminary stages, with an interference with the receiver.[13] That remedy is both a warning shot and constitutes a further and perhaps more obvious court order breach of which will be followed by committal for persistence in the offence.[14]

The court may also grant an injunction to restrain a person from proceeding with another action, whether within the jurisdiction or elsewhere, which involves an interference with the possession of a receiver appointed by the court within the jurisdiction.[15]

Penal costs order

The court may in all the circumstances decide that no further punishment is necessary than an order that the contemnor shall be mulcted for the costs

---

8 *Ward v Swift* above.
9 (1831) 4 Sim 511.
10 (1886) 35 Ch D 449 discussed at p 459, above.
11 *Ward v Swift* (1848) 6 Hare 309.
12 *Ward v Swift* supra.
13 *Evelyn v Lewis* (1844) 3 Hare 472; *Tink v Rundle* (1847) 10 Beav 318; *A-G v St Cross Hospital* (1854) 18 Beav 601; *Winkle v Bailey* [1897] 1 Ch 123; *Dixon v Dixon* [1904] 1 Ch 161 (dismissed partner competing with receiver-manager).
14 *Johnes v Claughton* (1822) Jac 573.
15 *Re Derwent Rolling Mills Co Ltd* (1904) 21 TLR 81; affd 21 TLR 701, CA; *Jopson v James* (1908) 77 LJ Ch 824, CA; *Re Connolly Bros Ltd* [1911] 1 Ch 731, CA.

and expenses caused by his interference.[16] That result will usually ensue where the interference has been on the part of a sheriff seizing on an execution.[17] In such cases the court may order that not only the person actually interfering but also the person who instigated the interference, shall pay the costs.[18]

ENFORCEMENT OF RIGHTS AGAINST RECEIVER

General

It is a rule of the court, well established, and which is essential for the due protection of its officers, that no action shall be allowed to be prosecuted against a receiver, or those in possession under him, without the leave (or as it now has to be called permission) of the court.[19]

A person therefore who wishes to enforce rights against property in the hands of a receiver, and to avoid being in contempt of court, *must* apply to the court for permission to enforce such rights or for leave to be examined *pro interesse suo*. The court may on such an application decide the right claimed by the applicant there and then, and if the finding is in his favour give him consequential relief against the property. Where there is a doubtful legal question it may give the permission asked for and absolve the applicant from all contempt of court by reason of any proceedings on his part.[20]

If a person wishes to enforce a right against property belonging to a stranger to the action over which the receiver has been appointed by mistake, he should not apply to the court for permission to enforce such right, but should apply for the discharge of the order appointing the receiver so far as it relates to such property.[1]

Granting of permission

If it is necessary to ask for permission, the court must have credit for never refusing it where it ought to be granted.[2] It is not in accordance with the practice of the court to refuse leave to try a right which is claimed against its receiver

---

16 *Russell v East Anglian Rly Co* (1850) 3 Mac & G 104; *Hawkins v Gathercole* (1852) 1 Drew 12; *Harvey v Wallis* (1851) 3 Ir Jur 409; *Lane v Sterne* (1862) 3 Giff 629.
17 *Russell v East Anglian Rly Co* supra; *Lane v Sterne* supra.
18 *Lane v Sterne* supra.
19 See the Canadian cases of *Coleman v Glanville* (1871) 18 Gr 42 per Strong V-C; *Stephens v Royal Trust Co* (1917) 25 BCR 77, BCCA; *Trusts and Guarantee Co v Oakword Clubs* (1931) 40 OWN 581.
20 *Randfield v Randfield* (1860) 1 Drew & Sm 310, 30 LJ Ch 18; *Walmsley v Mundy* (1884) 13 QBD 807 at 816, CA.
 1 *Fowler v Haynes* (1863) 2 New Rep 156.
 2 *Angel v Smith* (1804) 9 Ves 335 at 339 per Lord Eldon LC.

unless it is perfectly clear that there is no foundation for the claim;[3] and the court will apply this principle in considering the application of any person for leave to take any action which may disturb the possession of its receiver.[4]

The court may while granting leave impose conditions upon the applicant,[5] and disobedience to such conditions, even if such conditions have been improperly or unreasonably imposed, will be a contempt of court, and may be punished accordingly.[6]

The cases show that the court has been prepared to give permission to a person to bring an action for ejectment,[7] or to levy execution on property in the possession of a receiver;[8] or to distrain upon such property;[9] or to re-enter under a power;[10] or will permit him to be examined *pro interesse suo*;[11] or to abate an obstruction on property in the possession of a receiver.[12]

Effect and extent of leave

The permission of the court can of necessity only authorise the applicants to pursue any remedies or do any acts which the applicants may lawfully take or do. It will not release them from the normal legal consequences of their acts, including legal liability.[13]

Where the court gives permission to a lessor to bring an action for recovery of land against the lessee, that permission will not entitle the lessor, after obtaining judgment in such action, to proceed to recover possession against the receiver in possession by means of a writ of possession without further permission of the court.[14]

Modes of enforcing rights

There is no general principle that a person who is not a party to the action, and to whom the receiver owes money, may apply in the action for satisfaction of his

---

3 *Hawkins v Gathercole* (1852) 1 Drew 12, 21 LJ Ch 617; *Randfield v Randfield* (1861) 3 De GF & J 766; *Re Henry Pound, Son & Hutchins* (1889) 42 Ch D 402 at 422 (leave to take possession without prejudice to any question as to the powers of the receiver); *Dichl v Caritt, ex p Clement* (1907) 15 OLR 202.

4 *Russell v East Anglian Rly Co* (1850) 3 Mac & G 104 at 118; *Lane v Capsey* [1891] 3 Ch 411.

5 *Hawkins v Gathercole* (1852) 1 Drew 12 at 19; *Re Battersby's Estates* (1892) 31 LR Ir 73.

6 *Re Battersby's Estates* supra.

7 *Angel v Smith* (1804) 9 Ves 335; *Brooks v Greathed* (1820) 1 Jac & W 176.

8 *Russell v East Anglian Rly Co* supra; *Gooch v Haworth* (1841) 3 Beav 428.

9 *Eyton v Denbigh Ruthin and Corwen Rly Co* (1868) LR 6 Eq 14 and 488; *Re Sutton's Estate* (1863) 1 New Rep 464.

10 *Forster v Manchester and Milford Rly Co* [1880] WN 63; *Hand v Blow* [1901] 2 Ch 721 at 737, CA.

11 *Brooks v Greathed* (1820) 1 Jac & W 176.

12 *Lane v Capsey* [1891] 3 Ch 411.

13 [1891] 3 Ch 411 at 417.

14 *Morris v Baker* (1903) 73 LJ Ch 143.

claim out of the funds in court, representing the profits received by the receiver.[15] The court may, however, allow this right to a person not a party to the action in exceptional cases.[16]

The court may give a charge upon property in the possession of a receiver appointed in an action for dissolution of partnership to a judgment creditor of the firm on his undertaking to deal with the charge according to the order of the court, as the court in appointing a receiver aims at equality among the creditors.[17] Such a charge only operates as among the creditors of the partnership themselves, not against the several partners of the firm.[18]

The court may also make an order for the attachment of sums payable by a receiver under order of the court in favour of a creditor of the person to whom such sums are so payable.[19]

15 *Brocklebank v East London Rly Co* (1879) 12 Ch D 839.
16 *Neate v Pink* (1846) 15 Sim 450.
17 *Kewney v Attrill* (1886) 34 Ch D 345 at 346 per Kay J.
18 *Ridd v Thorne* [1902] 2 Ch 344.
19 *Re Cowan's Estate* (1880) 14 Ch D 638.

CHAPTER 31

Sureties

REQUIREMENTS OF SECURITY

Because a receiver appointed by the court is personally liable for his acts and omissions[1] such a receiver may be required to give security approved by the court duly to account for what he receives as receiver and to deal with his receipts as directed by the court.[2] The fact that the receiver may have already provided a security in some other capacity is of course irrelevant.[3]

It should be emphasised that the court has a discretion under the relevant rule whether or not to require a security to be given. The judgment or order directing the appointment of a receiver *may* include such directions as the court thinks fit as to the giving of security by the person appointed.[4] Where a person is appointed receiver by the court is required to give security he must give security approved by the court duly to account for what he receives as receiver and to deal with his receipts as the court directs.[5] Unless the court otherwise directs the security will be by guarantee.[6] The guarantee must be fixed in the office or registry of the court in which the claim is proceeding and must be kept as a record until duly vacated.[7]

The security is fixed by the Master or district judge on an application notice to proceed supported by an evidence as to the nature and value of the property.[8] Such application notice should also deal with the receiver's remuneration. Where the order authorises the receiver to take possession at once, but does not expressly direct security to be given, the possession of the receiver will be lawful and valid against a judgment creditor who subsequently levies execution despite the fact that security has not been given.[9] But this is not the case if the receiver is not empowered to act at once and his appointment is 'upon first giving security'.[10]

1 *Mead v Lord Orrery* (1745) 3 Atk 235 at 244.
2 RSC Ord 30, r 2(1), (2).
3 *Tottenham v Swansea Zinc Ore Co Ltd* (1884) 53 LJ Ch 776, 51 LT 61; *Bartlett v Northumberland Avenue Hotel Co Ltd* (1885) 53 LT 611, CA.
4 RSC Ord 30, r 2(1).
5 RSC Ord 30, r 2(2).
6 RSC Ord 30, r 2(3).
7 RSC Ord 30, r 2(4).
8 33 *Court Forms* (2nd edn) (1997 Issue) 120–121, Forms 17 (application) and 18 (affidavit).
9 *Morrisson v Skerne Ironworks Co Ltd* (1889) 60 LT 588.
10 *Re Rollason* (1887) 34 Ch D 495; *Re Roundwood Colliery Co* [1897] 1 Ch 373 at 393, CA; *Ridout v Fowler* [1904] 1 Ch 658, 73 LJ Ch 325; affd on other grounds [1904] 2 Ch 93, CA.

The time for furnishing security is fixed by the order with a provision unless the security is completed within the stipulated period,[11] or any extension thereof will forthwith determine. Any necessary extension period is within the discretion of the court: three weeks is usual[12] but a shorter period may be appropriate.[13] A receiver may be re-appointed where security is not completed in time.[14]

Although the new rules give great flexibility in relation to directions as to security no doubt attention will be paid to the pre-existing practice of the Chancery Division. In particular the court may take into account the practice which obtained so far as the reduction or increase of security is concerned.

It is therefore open to the court in order to reduce the amount of security which it sees fit to direct to order that money that would otherwise come into the hands of the receiver shall be paid into court.[15]

Likewise where the property over which the receiver is appointed is extended or appreciates substantially in value the court could require additional security[16] and might be prepared to direct a reduction in the security in the event of a substantial diminution in the value of the relevant property.

On being appointed receiver on behalf of debenture holders, the liquidator of a company can be required to give security in respect of his new capacity.[17]

Where the matter is proceeding in the county court the selfsame rules apply.[18]

Since the procedure for the appointment of a receiver by way of equitable execution is the same as that for the appointment of receivers generally, the giving of security is governed by the same rule, albeit with certain refinements tailored to fit receivers by way of equitable execution.[19]

QUALIFICATION AND DISQUALIFICATION

In the Chancery Division the security is usually given by a guarantee society.[20] The important thing is that the surety should be impartial and disinterested.[1] In

---

11 *Re Sims & Woods Ltd* [1916] WN 223; *Rowley v Desborough* (1916) 60 Sol Jo 429.
12 *Re Sims & Woods Ltd* supra.
13 *Re H's Estate* (1875) 1 Ch D 276 (10 days).
14 For a form, see 109 L Jo 659.
15 *Poole v Wood* (1832) 1 *Seton's Judgments & Orders* (7th edn) 741; *Re Eagle* (1847) 2 Ph 201; *Gardner v London Chatham and Dover Rly Co (No 2)* (1867) 2 Ch App 201 at 219.
16 *Marchioness of Downshire v Tyrrell* (1831) Hayes 354; *Wise v Ashe* (1839) 1 I Eq R 210; *Haigh v Grattan* (1839) 1 Beav 201; *Wrixon v Vize* (1842) 5 I Eq R 276; *Kelly v Rutledge* (1845) 8 I Eq R 228 at 230.
17 See above.
18 See *Civil Procedure*, Vol 1, Spring 2000, Section A, Sch 1, sc 30.A1, which applies Order 30 to the county court as to the High Court.
19 Ie by RSC Ord 30, r 2. For details of the procedure to be followed in fixing an appointment before the Master and in proposing securities and in what amount see *Civil Procedure*, Vol 1, Spring 2000, Section A, Sch 1, sc 51.3.8.
20 *Colemore v North* (1872) 42 LJ Ch 4, 27 LT 405; *Harris v Sleep* [1897] 2 Ch 80, CA; *Re Spiritine Ltd* (1902) 18 TLR 679, CA; and see *Hobhouse v Hamilton* (1850) 15 LTOS 372, Ir. So too in the old Probate Division: *Carpenter v Queen's Proctor* (1882) 7 PD 235.
 1 *Panton v Labertouche* (1843) 1 Ph 265; *Re Karamelli and Barnett Ltd* [1917] 1 Ch 203.

the Irish case of *Ryder v Dickson*[2] a party to the action was exceptionally accepted as surety but a solicitor having the conduct of the cause was rejected. A business partner of the receiver is likewise normally unacceptable.

If there is any doubt as to the solvency of sureties the opposing solicitor can attend at the time for settling the security and examine the sureties as to their solvency.[3] Certainly a surety cannot enter into a valid agreement with a receiver to be indemnified out of the property itself.[4] If the security required is particularly substantial it may be split among a number of sureties.[5]

Where individuals are proposed as sureties they must as a rule be resident within the jurisdiction.[6] In the case of corporations, however, some latitude is allowed. Thus the bond of a Scottish guarantee company may be accepted provided that the requirements of the master in any particular case are complied with.[7] Reference should be made to the Chief Master's Secretariat in the Chancery Division[8] or to the master's secretary in the Queen's Bench Division, to ascertain whether the necessary resolutions have been passed and lodged and, if not, as to the procedure to be adopted.[9] The bond of a foreign company may be accepted, subject again to compliance with the master's requirements, if it has assets within the jurisdiction and the court is satisfied as to its solvency.[10] Certainly there is no general rule precluding such acceptance.[11]

A supervening loss of the relevant qualification may effect a disqualification of the surety. Thus if a surety goes abroad[12] or becomes insolvent or obtains his discharge[13] a substitute must be found and a fresh guarantee entered into. But death does not automatically entail the provision of a substitute surety. It depends on whether the estate of the deceased surety is or is not sufficient to cover the liability under the original surety. If the surety dies leaving property bound by his recognisance his death is no ground for requiring the receiver to procure a new surety.[14] But where it is clear that the deceased has not left any property which could be made available for the purpose of satisfying the recognizance a new surety will be required.[15] Where for any of these reasons a new surety is required application for the receiver to provide a substitute surety is made by summons.[16]

---

2 (1835) cited in *Bennett on Receivers* 107.
3 *Smith on Receivers* (1836) 18.
4 *White v Baugh* (1835) 3 Cl & Fin 44 at 59, 65, HL.
5 *Acheson v Hodges* (1841) 3 I Eq R 516; *Re Macdonaghs* (1876) 10 IR Eq 269.
6 *Cockburn v Raphael* (1825) 2 Sim & St 453.
7 See Civil Procedure, Vol I, Spring 2000, Section A, Sch 1, s 30.2; and see fn 10 below.
8 Room 169, 2nd Floor, East Wing, Royal Courts of Justice.
9 Usually annual evidence of solvency is required if the company concerned is to be retained on the list of acceptable sureties.
10 *Re Venezuela Goldfields* (undated) cited in *Aldrich v British Griffin Chilled Iron and Steel Co Ltd* [1904] 2 KB 850 at 852, CA; *Boyle v Rothschild* (1908) 12 OWR 104 (bond of foreign guarantee company refused where insufficient assets available in Canada).
11 *Aldrich v British Griffin Chilled Iron and Steel Co Ltd* supra.
12 *Lane v Townsend* (1852) 2 I Ch R 120.
13 *Vaughan v Vaughan* (1743) 1 Dick 90; *Blois v Betts* (1760) 1 Dick 336.
14 *Averall v Wade* (1841) Fl & K 341.
15 (1841) FL & K 341.
16 For a summons which also asks for consequential variation or discharge of the bond or undertaking; see *Daniell's Chancery Forms* (7th edn) 788 (death or bankruptcy). For an order, see *Seton's Judgments and Orders* (7th edn) 772.

CONTROL OF ASSETS

A surety has no right to control the receivership assets for it is the duty of the receiver to keep those assets in his own hands and not to pass control of them or even joint control of them to anyone else.[17] Nor, as a rule, is a surety entitled to attend at the examination of the receiver's accounts, still less to have them re-opened once they have been submitted.[18] Nevertheless where the receiver has become bankrupt or has died insolvent[19] or it is reasonably certain that he will not be able to pay the balance due from him[20] the surety may obtain an order giving him permission to attend the examination of accounts at his own expense.[1] And whereas a surety is not entitled to have the accounts re-opened merely on the ground that he was not given notice that the account was to be taken, in a proper case he may obtain a re-opening on the conditions of paying the costs of such re-opening and new account and also interest from the date of the order on the sum which he may eventually be called on to pay.[2]

LIABILITY

On any default by a receiver to pay what is due from him in his capacity as receiver his sureties immediately become liable at law up to the limit fixed by the relevant guarantee or bond.[3] However, equitable relief may be available if a penal sum is fixed by the bond, provided that the sureties pay not only any balance due from the receiver but also all sums for which the receiver would have been properly accountable to the court.[4] A surety asking for such equitable relief will apply to the court by which the receiver has been appointed to have the account taken by such court. On taking the account the court does not necessarily exact the full amount of the sum nominated in the recognisance; but the court, when it looks into the case, and considers the nature of the office of the receiver in the circumstances, applies not a principle of contract but a principle of equity, to the account, and relieves the sureties against demands which the court, on a full consideration of the matter, thinks the sureties ought to have allowed in their favour,[5] since it is always in the discretion of the court whether it will allow recourse to be had to the sureties or not.[6]

---

17 *White v Bough* (1835) 3 Cl & Fin 44 at 59 and 63, HL affg. *Salway v Salway* (1831) 2 Russ & M 215.
18 *Re Birmingham Brewing Malting and Distilling Co Ltd* (1883) 52 LJ Ch 358, 48 LT 632 (surety for liquidator).
19 *Simmons v Rose* (1860) and *Sharp v Wright* (1878) cited in *Daniell's Chancery Practice* 8th ed 1501.
20 *Dawson v Raynes* (1826) 2 Russ 466.
 1 See also *Shuff v Holdaway* (1863) cited in 2 *Daniell's Chancery Practice* (8th edn) 1487n and *National Bank v Kenney* [1898] 1 IR 197.
 2 *Re Birmingham Brewing Malting and Distilling Co Ltd* (1883) 52 LJ Ch 358, 48 LT 632.
 3 *Watters v Watters* (1847) 11 I Eq R 335.
 4 *Dawson v Raynes* (1826) 2 Russ 466; *Re Graham* [1895] 1 Ch 66; *Kenney v Employers Liability Assurance Corpn* [1901] 1 IR 301, Ir CA.
 5 *Re Graham* [1895] 1 Ch 66 at 70 per Chitty J.
 6 *Ludgater v Channell* (1851) Mac & G 175 at 178.

As a general rule the court will not hold a surety liable until the amount for which the receiver is liable has been ascertained and the receiver has been called on for such an amount.[7] But if the receiver, after having made default in relation to his accounts and in paying the balance into court, has absconded or become bankrupt or died, or if for any other reason it is impracticable to pursue him, proceedings may be started against the surety even before the actual balance due from the receiver has been ascertained.[8]

Where a surety is sued on his guarantee he may obtain an order for the stay of such proceedings on paying into court the maximum sum guaranteed[9] or balance found due from the receiver.[10] On making such a payment a surety may have the security vacated so far as he is concerned.[11] The court may on any such application allow the balance due to be paid by instalments.[12] Payment to the plaintiffs solicitor is insufficient in the absence of evidence of the solicitor's authority to receive it.[13]

In accordance with these principles the sureties of a receiver are plainly liable up to the amount secured by their recognisance for such principal sum[14] as the receiver is liable to pay and usually for interest which the receiver is liable to pay.[15] In *Re Graham*,[16] for example, Chitty J held a surety of a receiver of rents and profits of real estate liable for (1) moneys paid under a fire insurance policy taken out by the receiver in respect of some farm buildings; (2) dividends on funds in court (invested in consols) representing proceeds of sale of real estate; and (3) a sum paid to the receiver out of personal estate for the purposes of repairs, all of which had been misappropriated by the receiver. While the sureties are normally accountable for interest on balances improperly retained in the receivers hands the court does have a discretion in the matter and may in particular circumstances exercise that discretion in favour of the surety and decline to charge him interest.[17] Laches on the part of parties to the proceedings may make it inequitable for payment of interest to be enforced. For example in *Dawson v Raynes*[18] the parties to the action had for a considerable period failed to ensure that the receiver's accounts were duly passed. This dallying cost them dear for the court declined to award interest against the sureties.

The terms of the security must obviously be considered for the purpose of spelling out the liability of the surety. A receiver who undertakes to account for what the receiver 'should recover and become liable to pay as such receiver' is liable to account for *all* moneys coming into the hands of the receiver as receiver

7 *Ludgater v Channell* (1851) Mac & G 175, 16 LTOS 337; *Brandon v Brandon* (1859) 3 De G & J 524, 28 LJ Ch 147.
8 *Ludgater v Channell* (1851) Mac & G 175, 16 LTOS 337; *Brandon v Brandon* (1859) 3 De G & J 524, 28 LJ Ch 147.
9 *Watters v Watters* (1847) 11 I Eq R 335.
10 *Maunsell v Egan* (1845) 8 I Eq R 372; affd 3 Jo & Lat 251, 9 I Eq R 283.
11 See *Webb v Cashel* (1847) 11 I Eq R 558.
12 *Walker v Wild* (1816) 1 Madd 528 (by consent).
13 *Mann v Stennett* (1845) 8 Beav 189.
14 *Dawson v Raynes* (1826) 2 Russ 466; *Re Graham* [1895] 1 Ch 66.
15 *Dawson v Raynes* supra; *Re Graham* supra.
16 [1895] 1 Ch 66.
17 *Re Herricks* (1853) 3 I Ch R 183 at 187.
18 (1826) 2 Russ 466.

at any time, whether before or after the date of perfecting his security.[19] On the other hand the terms of the security may specifically cut down the surety's liability. Thus the recognisance may be expressed to be void if the receiver duly performs his duties including his duty to account.[20]

The surety will not be liable in respect of property received by the receiver in any capacity other than his capacity as receiver, unless the circumstances of the receipt are such as to estop the receiver from denying that he received such property in his capacity as receiver. So where a receiver of a mentally disordered person made away with the rents received by him after the death of that person his surety will not be held liable for the sums so made away with, for the receiver was not under any duty to collect those rents.[1] Nor is a surety bound to make good to trade creditors who have supplied goods to a receiver for the benefit of the estate of which he is receiver any loss occasioned to them by reason of the receiver having misappropriated funds. The surety's liability in such a case is limited to reimbursing the estate for any loss for which the receiver is responsible; or, putting it another way, his suretyship bond is given to serve the estate and not the receiver's creditors.[2]

Sureties are also liable for the costs of any proceedings necessarily or properly incurred in consequence of the receiver's default. Thus in *Maunsell v Egan*[3] it was held that a surety was answerable for (1) the costs of an attachment against the receiver for not accounting, (2) the costs of appointing a new receiver and discharging the old one,[4] and (3) the costs of the order to the tenants to pay their rents to such a new receiver. A surety is also liable for any other costs of proceedings taken to enforce the security for which the receiver would have been liable.[5] Thus he may be liable to pay the costs of proceedings which the receiver ought to have paid even if the order in those proceedings omits to order the receiver to pay them.[6] But sureties are not, it seems, liable for any money for which the receiver although accountable cannot be made to account in the action.[7] And of course they are only liable up to the amount named in their security.[8]

When a receiver who has been appointed manager for a limited time continues to act as manager beyond that time without the authority of the court his sureties are nevertheless liable for the profits of such management which come to the hands of the receiver as receiver.[9] Likewise sureties are liable for money coming to the hands of a receiver before his appointment is perfected by the completion

---

19 *Smart v Flood & Co* (1883) 49 LT 467.
20 *Maunsell v Egan* (1846) 3 Jo & Lat 251, 9 I Eq R 283.
 1 *Re Walker* [1907] 2 Ch 120, CA.
 2 *Re British Power Traction and Lighting Co Ltd* [1910] 2 Ch 470.
 3 (1845) 8 I Eq R 372; affd 3 Jo & Lat 251, 9 I Eq R 283.
 4 See also *Dawson v Raynes* (1826) 2 Russ 466; *Re Lockey* (1845) 1 Ph 509, 14 LJ Ch 164; *Re Graham* [1895] 1 Ch 66.
 5 *Re Nugent's Estate* [1897] 1 IR 464; and see *Keily v Murphy* (1837) Sau & Sc 479.
 6 *Re Nugent's Estate* supra.
 7 *Re Walker* [1907] 2 Ch 120, CA; *Board of Trade v Employers Liability Assurance Corpn Ltd* [1910] 2 KB 649, CA.
 8 *Shakel v Duke of Marlborough* (1819) 4 Madd 463; *Watters v Watters* (1847) 11 I Eq R 335.
 9 *Re Herricks* (1853) 3 I Ch R 183 at 186.

of his security.[10] The principle that the appointment of a receiver is merely conditional until his security is perfected applies only to cases where the question is as to his title against third parties. It has no application where the question is as to his own liability or that of his sureties in respect of moneys received and expended by him as receiver.[11]

The security given by the guarantee of a surety is not a continuing security. It usually comes to an end on the death of the receiver except as to some outstanding default or some default by personal representatives in that administration of the receiver's estate.[12] When, after the receiver's death judgment has been recovered against a surety, and the judgment has been satisfied he is freed from any further liability, except perhaps for costs.[13]

RIGHT TO INDEMNITY OR CONTRIBUTION

Against principal

It has already been noted in another context that a surety must not attempt to protect himself by any means which will enable him to control the dealings of the receiver with the property.[14] Thus by having the receiver's receipts paid into the bank to the joint account of himself and the receiver as a sort of indemnity is objectionable and if the money is lost, even by the default of a third party, the surety will be liable to make good the loss.[15]

As a matter of general suretyship law until the surety has paid the creditor the surety's right of indemnification against the principal debtor does not constitute a debt owed to the surety by the principal debtor.[16] There must be an accrued liability on the surety which could be enforced by the court before the surety can come to court and claim an indemnity.[17]

Against other parties

A surety who has been called upon to make any payment is entitled to be indemnified by his principal in that capacity in respect of the whole amount of the payments which he makes.[18] And he can also look to his co-sureties in

---

10 *Smart v Flood & Co* (1883) 49 LT 467.
11 (1883) 49 LT 467.
12 See *Clements v Beresford* (1846) 7 LTOS 450, 10 Jur 771 where the rate of interest on a default by the executors of the receiver was not the penal rate.
13 *Re Herricks* (1853) 3 I Ch R 183 at 194; but see *Keily v Murphy* (1837) Sau & Sc 479; *Watters v Watters* (1847) 11 I Eq R 335.
14 See at p 470, above.
15 *Salway v Salway* (1831) 2 Russ & M 215; affd sub nom *White v Baugh* 9 Bli NS 181, 3 Cl & Fin 44.
16 (1826) 2 Russ 466.
17 *Re Ledgard* [1922] WN 105 at 106 per Eve J.
18 See the form of guarantee *Chancery Masters' Practice Forms*, PF 30 CA.

proportion to the amount for which each surety has made himself liable.[19] His right in this regard is an equitable one in the absence of express provision or of any contract between the parties.[20] The right of indemnity against principal and co-sureties is not limited to the actual sums disbursed, but extends to interest at 4 per cent and to the costs of enforcing the claim.[1]

By way of recourse against any beneficial interest of the receiver himself in the property to which the order relates, a surety is entitled to an order declaring that beneficial interest liable to make good the amount he has been compelled to pay.[2] And he is entitled to a lien for his disbursements on any balance payable to the receiver out of court, and may obtain an injunction restraining the receiver from taking out such balance without discharging the surety's claim.[3]

DISCHARGE

As a general rule a surety cannot get his recognisance vacated during the continuance of the receivership at his own request.[4] Equally he will not, without cause, be discharged from his suretyship which he has voluntarily assumed.[5] However in one case a surety was discharged on showing that he had become a surety not realising that to do so was in breach of his own partnership articles.[6] In another case proof of underhand practice in which the person secured was implicated was held to justify an application by a surety for discharge.[7] And an exception will also be made to the general rule where it is clearly for the benefit of all parties that the surety should be discharged.[8] So too an application may be justified on some ground anticipated and prescribed by the terms of the guarantee itself. Moreover a surety may be discharged with the consent of all parties including any co-surety and the receiver.[9] Where there is such consent the order will, as a matter of prudence, be made without prejudice to the liability of the receiver and any other surety for any past or future defaults of the receiver.[10] The order should also declare that the consenting parties will not rely on the vacating of the recognisance by one of them in any proceedings against them on the

---

19 *Re MacDonaghs* (1876) 10 IR Iq 269.
20 *Dering v Earl of Winchelsea* (1787) 1 Cox Eq Cas 318, 2 Bos & P 270; and see *Brandon v Brandon* (1859) 3 De G & J 524 (where the certain property of a receiver, which had been expressly excluded from an assignment to his sureties by way of indemnity, was nevertheless held liable to them on general equitable principles).
1 *Brandon v Brandon* (1859) 3 De G & J 524; *Re Swan's Estate* (1869) IR 4 Eq 209, CA; *Salkeld v Abbott* (1832) Hayes & Jo 110.
2 *Brandon v Brandon* (1859) 3 De G & J 524.
3 *Glossop v Harrison and Hawkes* (1814) Coop G 61; and see *Wright v Morley, Morley v St Alban* (1805) 11 Ves 12.
4 *Griffith v Griffith* (1751) 2 Ves Sen 400.
5 Ibid. But the receiver on applying to vacate his recognisance should give notice to all parties: *Brown v Perry* (1865) 1 Chy Chrs 253 (Can).
6 *Swain v Smith* (1827) 1 *Seton's Judgments & Orders* (7th edn) 775 at 776.
7 *Hamilton v Brewster* (1820) 2 Mol 407.
8 *Griffith v Griffith* (1751) 2 Ves Sen 400 at 401.
9 *O'Keeffe v Armstrong* (1852) 2 I Ch R 115.
10 (1852) 2 I Ch R 115.

recognisance. Such a declaration will negative the usual consequence that withdrawal by one party to a joint recognisance would discharge all parties to it.[11]

If a surety is discharged during the continuance of the receivership, the receiver will be required to find another surety to replace him.[12] If the surety has in fact become liable to pay he will not get his discharge on payment to someone other than the proper person to receive such payment, unless notice has been given to the person entitled to receive such payment then an order will be made for the discharge of the surety unless cause is shown to the contrary.[13]

Should a receiver die, abscond or become bankrupt his sureties may get an order for their discharge on paying into court the balances which may be certified due from the receiver. In *Shuff v Holdaway*[14] an order was made on the application of one of several sureties. It directed that the receiver's accounts down to that time be passed and that on payment into court by the receiver or the applicant of the certified balance (up to the limit of the guarantee) the applicant should be discharged as surety but that the applicant should be at liberty to attend the taking of the accounts and to apply to have the recognisance vacated as against him. The applicant was, for all that, ordered to pay the costs of the application.

A statement under the hand of the master, is conclusive evidence of the sum due from the surety.[15]

It is usual for the sureties to submit to the court by which the receiver was appointed to have the account against them as sureties taken by that court.[16]

---

11 (1852) 2 I Ch R 115.
12 *Vaughan v Vaughan* (1743) 1 Dick 90; *Blois v Betts* (1760) 1 Dick 336. In both these cases the time for enrolling the recognisances had expired but an order was made nunc pro tunc ie the recognisances were to take effect from the date when they ought to have been enrolled. Enrolment no longer obtains.
13 *Mann v Stennett* (1845) 8 Beav 189.
14 (1863) cited in 2 *Daniell's Chancery Practice* (8th edn) 1487n (Wood V-C).
15 *Smart v Flood & Co* (1883) 49 LT 467.
16 *Re Graham* [1895] 1 Ch 66; *Re British Power Traction and Lighting Co Ltd* [1910] 2 Ch 470 at 473.

CHAPTER 32

Remuneration and indemnity

REMUNERATION

General rules as to entitlement

A receiver, whether appointed to preserve property or by way of equitable execution, is allowed such proper remuneration, if any, as may be fixed by the court.[1] His right is limited to the assets and in case of a shortfall cannot be enforced against the plaintiff or other parties personally.[2]

A receiver may of course agree to act without a salary, or the court may specifically order that he shall not receive a salary. This latter eventuality occurs, generally, when an interested party or a trustee is appointed receiver. But in cases where the property to be received is small in value or amount and involves no difficulty in collection, the court has sometimes refused to allow remuneration.[3]

A legal mortgagee in possession who is himself appointed receiver by the court is not generally allowed remuneration.[4] Such a case will be rare, for legal mortgagees usually avoid going into possession and exercise their statutory right to appoint a receiver. But in a proper case no doubt he might be allowed the costs of employing an agent for the collection of rents.[5]

A trustee who is appointed receiver over the property of which he is trustee is not generally entitled to remuneration.[6] But there is no inflexible rule to this effect.[7] So a trustee receiver may be allowed remuneration where the

---

1 RSC Ord 30, r 3 applied to a receiver by way of equitable execution by Ord 51, r 3. See *Civil Procedure*, Vol 1, Spring 2000, Section A, Sch 1, sc 51.3.7.

2 *Boehm v Goodall* [1911] 1 Ch 155.

3 *Marr v Littlewood* (1837) 2 My & Cr 454 at 458 per Lord Cottenham LC.

4 *Re Prytherch* (1889) 42 Ch D 590 at 601. Prior to the repeal of the usury laws a mortgagee appointed out of court as a receiver could not be remunerated; but except in cases of inequality of bargaining power the parties could now specifically agree for payment of remuneration: *Chambers v Goldwin* (1804) 9 Ves 254 at 271.

5 *Bonithon v Hockmore* (1685) 1 Vern 316; *Davis v Dendy* (1818) 3 Madd 170; *Gilbert v Dyneley* (1841) 3 Man & G 12, 3 Scott NR 365; and see *Langstaffe v Fenwick* (1805) 10 Ves 405; *Sayers v Whitfield* (1829) 1 Knapp 133, PC at 142.

6 *Sykes v Hastings* (1805) 11 Ves 363; *Sutton v Jones* (1809) 15 Ves 584; *Pilkington v Baker, British Mutual Investment Co v Pilkington* (1876) 24 WR 234.

7 *Re Bignell* [1892] 1 Ch 59 at 63, CA; and see *Brodie v Barry* (1811) 3 Mer 695.

appointment of the trustee is made on the ground that no other person with equal qualifications for the task can be found.[8] The fact that the receivership order does not mention remuneration does not amount to a decision that there should not be any.

Remuneration may be given when the trustee would be entitled under the trust instrument to remuneration for his duties as a trustee. This happened in *Re Bignell*[9] where a testator who was the proprietor of a music hall called the Trocadero directed his trustees, of whom a Mrs Squiers was one, to allow Mrs Squiers to manage his business during her own life, subject to a power in the co-trustees to stop the carrying on of the business if carried on unsuccessfully for any period of eighteen months. The will specified a formula for calculating remuneration. Shortly after the testator's death, in an administration action Mrs Squiers was appointed receiver and manager without giving security, the judgment being silent as to remuneration. She resigned after 15 months through ill-health and shortly afterwards died. Her executors in passing her accounts claimed a remuneration which was resisted but the judge allowed the claim though reducing the amount claimed. The Court of Appeal disavowed the existence of an inflexible rule against remuneration of trustee-receivers and said that the judge had a discretion in the matter which had not been shown to have been improperly exercised. The object of the silence in the order as to remuneration was, it was held, to reserve the question of remuneration.[10]

The absence of any mention whatsoever of remuneration in the order appointing the receiver does not amount to a decision that there is to be no remuneration, and despite the absence of any such mention remuneration may still be allowed.[11] The circumstances of the case may nevertheless lead to the conclusion that the omission was intentional and that no remuneration is to be allowed.[12]

As a general rule an interested party who is appointed receiver is not allowed a salary.[13] The rule is, again, not inflexible. Apart from cases where the parties consent to the payment of a salary[14] a party to an action who is appointed receiver and manager is generally allowed remuneration in the absence of other reasons to the contrary. Thus a partner appointed receiver to wind up the partnership business has been held entitled to payment on a quantum meruit basis.[15] A receiver and manager in such a case who is contemplating doing additional personal work in the course of the winding up runs a risk in not asking for a suitable allowance at the time of his appointment, for if the order is

---

8 *Sykes v Hastings* (1805) 11 Ves 363.
9 [1892] 1 Ch 59, CA.
10 *Re Bignell* [1892] 1 Ch 59 at 63 per Lindley LJ.
11 *Re Bignell* [1892] 1 Ch 59, CA.
12 *Pilkington v Baker* (1876) 24 WR 234.
13 *A-G v Gee* (1813) 2 Ves & B 208; *Wilson v Greenwood* (1818) 1 Swan 471; *Gardner v Blane* (1842) 1 Hare 381; *Blakeney v Dufaur* (1851) 15 Beav 40; *Hoffman v Duncan* (1853) 18 Jur 69; *Powys v Blagrave* (1853) 18 Jur 462; *Rawson v Rawson* (1864) 11 LT 595; *Cookes v Cookes* (1865) 2 De GJ & Sm 526; *Sargant v Read* (1876) 1 Ch D 600; *Hyde v Warden* (1876) 1 Ex D 309, CA; *Beamish v Stephenson* (1886) 18 LR Ir 319, 20 ILT 45; *Re Golding* (1888) 21 LR Ir 194; *Taylor v Neate* (1888) 39 Ch D 538.
14 *Earl of Fingal v Blake* (1828) 2 Mol 50 at 60–61; *Davy v Scarth* [1906] 1 Ch 55.
15 *Davy v Scarth* [1906] 1 Ch 55.

silent on the point he will be paid for his additional services only as a matter of indulgence.[16]

Amount and scale

The amount and scale of the remuneration are, as has been said, in the discretion of the court.[17] Theoretically the amount may be fixed by the judge, at the time of the appointment of the receiver or afterwards. But more usually it is referred to a master or district judge to be determined when the accounts of the receiver are examined, since a receiver is not entitled to any remuneration until he has accounted for all his payments and receipts.[18] Another but less frequently taken course is for the court to direct that the amount be assessed by a court judge or district judge.[19]

As regards the scale of remuneration and the mode of calculating remuneration a distinction was formerly drawn between the methods adopted in the Chancery Division and the Queen's Bench Division. The distinction reflected the difference between the purpose of the receivership, for the Chancery Division is mainly concerned with appointments to preserve property while in the Queen's Bench Division applications are usually by way of equitable execution.

There are detailed guidelines as to the amount of remuneration to be allowed to a receiver appointed by way of equitable execution in the Queen's Bench Division. Otherwise there are no absolute rules.

It is convenient to consider first the case of a receivership to preserve property. As already mentioned the court may direct such remuneration to be fixed by reference to such scale or rates of professional charges as it thinks fit[1] or assessed by a cost judge or district judge.[2] In the Chancery Division in such a case remuneration was, under the old procedure, usually allowed on a quantum meruit basis according to the time, trouble and degree of responsibility involved.[3] It could be fixed as a percentage of gross receipts[4] an annual salary[5] or a lump sum.[6]

---

16 See *Harris v Sleep* [1897] 2 Ch 80, CA.
17 RSC Ord 30, r 3(2)(b).
18 *Re Ward* (1862) 31 Beav 1 at 12–13 per Sir John Romilly MR.
19 *Silkstone and Haigh Moor Coal Co v Edey* [1901] 2 Ch 652, CA.
 1 RSC Ord 30, r 3(2)(a).
 2 RSC Ord 30, r 3(2)(b).
 3 *Day v Croft* (1840) 2 Beav 488. There is no general and universal rule: ibid; *Prior v Bagster* (1887) 57 LT 760 (no fixed scale for a manager: each case must be decided on its merits); *Campbell v Arnot* (1915) 32 WLR 349, 24 DLR 699, Sask (receiver and manager). See also, most illuminatingly, *Mirror Group Newspapers plc v Maxwell (No 2)* [1998] 1 BCLC 638 summarised below.
 4 *Day v Croft* (1840) 2 Beav 488; *Prior v Bagster* (1887) 57 LT 760 (receiver and manager). A percentage may be applied to net profits if that appears to be a fairer scale: *Buckmaster v Buckmaster* (1859) 28 LJ Ch 564, 34 LTOS 36. For a Canadian discussion of a percentage basis, see *Ibar Developments Ltd v Marnt Citadel Ltd* (1978) 26 CBRNS 17.
 5 *Re Bignell* [1892] 1 Ch 59, CA.
 6 *Potts v Leighton* (1808) 15 Ves 273.

In appropriate cases a suitable professional scale was sometimes adopted as a guideline.[7] For example an estate agent appointed as a receiver in a case exclusively involving house property might be allowed his normal professional scale for collecting rents and managing the property, together with a quantum meruit allowance to cover any additional work involved in the preparation and examination of his accounts. It is the practice to call for a remuneration statement concisely summarising the work done during the period of the account and including a table showing the hours of work done by the receiver and his staff (separating each grade of work), the hourly rates claimed and the totals in each case.[8] The rates should be the usual professional rates or such rates as are reasonable having regard to the nature of the work done. The court may require to be satisfied by evidence that the rates are reasonable. If it does require such evidence, the production of professional fee rules or tables will normally be sufficient. Day sheets or other evidence to support the totals of hours worked may be required. It is usual to allow any expenses which the receiver has incurred and which can be directly related to the receivership[9] as, for example, the expenses of special journeys. A reasonable allowance for postage and telephone calls can be made but otherwise the receiver's normal office expenses cannot be included. Although there is no absolute rule, remuneration by reference to an hourly rate is a favoured approach. The criticism levelled against the receiver in *Walter E Heller (Canada) Ltd v Sea Queen of Canada Ltd*[10] was that he ought to have realised the property sooner and not to have carried on the business as long as he did. The court, in reviewing the receiver's remuneration decided that where a receiver carries on business for a number of months (in that case six months) a percentage of the rents and profits is not a fair calculation. The court continued:[11]

> 'The time spent on hourly rate is probably the fairest method, but even that cannot always be accurate . . . [The court] must look at the number of hours in relation to what was done and the length of time involved.'

The court's objective is to award a sum or devise a formula which will reasonably compensate the receiver for the time and trouble expended in the execution of his duties, and, to some extent, for the responsibility he has assumed.[12] While at the same time looking at the value of the services rendered by the receiver.[13] Time spent represents a measure not of the value of the service rendered but of the cost of rendering it. Remuneration should be fixed so as to reward value, not so as to indemnify against cost.[14]

---

7 See *Re Queensland Forests Ltd* [1966] Qd R 180; *Waldron v M G Securities (Australasia) Ltd* (1979) ACLC 32, 200. A scale fee is inappropriate to every single receivership: *Waldron v M G Securities (Australasia) Ltd* supra.

8 For an example see 33 *Court Forms* (1989 Issue) 238, Form 7.

9 *Potts v Leighton* (1808) 15 Ves 273.

10 (1975) 19 CBRNS 252; affd on rehearing 21 CBRNS 272n.

11 (1975) 19 CBRNS 252 at 260.

12 *Re Alexander McLean* (1912) 14 GLR 561 at 562 per Cooper J.

13 *Mirror Group Newspapers plc v Maxwell (No 2)* [1998] 1 BCLC 638.

14 [1998] 1 BCLC 638 at 652.

A leading modern case on the remuneration of court appointed receivers is *Mirror Group Newspapers plc v Maxwell (No 2)*[15] where court-appointed receivers produced five written reports and employed solicitors to assist in a complex investigation into the estate of Robert Maxwell. Costs of £1.628 million were claimed whereas the net assets amounted to about £1.672 million. Ferris J directed that the remuneration of the receivers should be fixed by the taxing officer and should be made on the standard basis rather than on the indemnity basis. However in reaching this conclusion he analysed in some detail the criteria to be adopted in considering the remuneration of court-appointed receivers.[16]

A firmer picture than can be found in the somewhat sketchy rules of court emerges if the matter is approached from the standpoint of general principle. Court appointed receivers are, as Ferris J pointed out, under a fiduciary duty to protect, get in and realise assets belonging to creditors or beneficiaries and pass it on to them. They are appointed because of their professional skills and experience.[17]

Accordingly they are expected to exercise proper commercial judgment in the carrying out of their duties and to account for both for the way in which they had exercised their powers and for the property dealt with. If they claim remuneration at a particular level they are required to justify their claim by giving full particulars as part of their obligation to account.[18] The test of whether they have acted properly in undertaking particular tasks at a particular cost in expenses or time spent is whether a reasonably prudent man faced with the same situation would have acted in the same way. They are expected to deploy commercial judgement not to act regardless of expense. High cost transactions may be allowable but they must be justified and will be subject to close scrutiny. So they must be prepared to show that what they have done was properly and effectively done, took the amount of time claimed and was of value to the estate.[19]

Again, their charging rate must be proved by reference to the broad average or general rate charged by persons of the relevant status and qualifications who carry out that kind of work and not that of the particular individual. They must keep proper records of what they have done and why they have done it otherwise they will find themselves having doubts resolved against them.[20]

In this connection it is important not to place too great an emphasis on time spent. Time spent is only one of a number of factors.[1] Also to be taken into account are (a) the complexity (or otherwise) of the case (b) any respects in which in connection with the affairs of the company estate or other property subject to the receivership there falls on the receiver any responsibility of an exceptional kind or degree (c) the effectiveness with which the receiver appears to be carrying out or to have carried out his duties as such and (d) the value and nature of the property with which he has to deal.[2] Moreover as already mentioned

15 [1998] 1 BCLC 638.
16 [1998] 1 BCLC 638 at 653i–657e.
17 [1998] 1 BCLC 638 at 648a–b.
18 [1998] 1 BCLC 638 at 648d–e.
19 [1998] 1 BCLC 638 at 649b–c.
20 [1998] 1 BCLC 649a.
 1 [1998] 1 BCLC 638 at 651f–652.
 2 [1998] 1 BCLC 638 at 650f–i.

it is the value of services rendered by the receiver which is to be rewarded and not the cost of rendering them.[3]

Where solicitors or other third parties are employed by receivers payments to them must be justified and their bills subjected to critical scrutiny since recovery out of the assets is only possible if they were properly instructed and monitored.[4] Obviously there are various factors to be taken into account: the difficulty involved in collecting and realising the assets; the volume of work; the complexity of work;[5] the time expended; the responsibilities undertaken; and the extent to which the company, its officers and employees have been able to provide assistance.[6]

While a commission basis may be appropriate, the simpler the task the lower the commission is likely to be. But the court will sometimes opt for a fixed salary instead.[7] Even then the court may still pare down the fixed salary when the circumstances justify that course, as for example in the case of a premature discharge of the receiver.[8]

In the end it comes down to this: the court will adopt whichever of the canons is fairest and make such adjustment as the circumstances of the case require to any particular yardstick that is adopted. As Lindley LJ put it in *Harris v Sleep*,[9] 'the court, when the circumstances are before it, will see that what is right is done'.

Variation

Variation upwards or downwards may become necessary. Thus a receiver who, without applying to the court for directions, performs extraordinary or extra services going beyond what it was his duty as receiver and manager to perform may be allowed remuneration in addition to his salary or commission if what he has done has benefited the receivership assets.[10] He will not, of course, be allowed to make an extra charge for work which is in fact within the ordinary scope of his duties as receiver,[11] or for personal attendance where that attendance was in fact unnecessary.[12]

Equally where the remuneration of a receiver is paid on a percentage of or commission on receipts the quantum may be reduced by allowing capital sums to be paid directly into court instead of going through the receiver's hands.[13]

---

3   [1998] 1 BCLC 638 at 652a–b.
4   [1998] 1 BCLC 638 at 661b–662a.
5   *Waldron v M G Securities (Australasia) Ltd* (1979) ACLC 32, 200.
6   See *Eastern Trust Co v Nova Scotia Steel and Coal Co Ltd* [1938] 4 DLR 808, NCCA.
7   *Re Bignell* [1892] 1 Ch 59, CA.
8   *Frost v Healy* (1866) 5 SCRNSW Eq 1 per Hargrave PJ in Eq.
9   [1897] 2 Ch 80 at 85, CA.
10 *Potts v Leighton* (1808) 15 Ves 273; *Malcolm v O'Callaghan* (1837) 3 My & Cr 52 at 58; *Bristowe v Needham* (1847) 2 Ph 190, 9 LTOS 69; *Harris v Sleep* [1897] 2 Ch 80 (wages for forgework and ironwork).
11 *Re Catlin* (1854) 18 Beav 508 at 511.
12 *Re Ormsby (a minor)* (1809) 1 Ball & B 189.
13 *Ex p Cranmer* (1808) 1 Russ 477n; *Haigh v Grattan* (1839) 1 Beav 201; *Weale v Ireland* (1841) 5 Jur 405; *Gardner v London Chatham and Dover Rly Co* (1867) 2 Ch App 201 at 219.

The amount of the remuneration may be varied from time to time. So the amount of the percentage may be increased in case of increased difficulty of collection.[14] Similarly, the form of the remuneration may be altered, as, for example, from a percentage of the gross receipts to a percentage of the net profits.[15] A failure on the part of the receiver to carry out particular duties may result in his remuneration being reduced.[16]

Priority

A receiver's right to payment of his remuneration is limited to the assets over which he is appointed.[17] But he is entitled to such payment even though the assets may be insufficient to meet *all* claims made upon them. As an officer of the court he 'has his remuneration provided for in front, as far as possible, of every other payment to be made out of the assets of which the court has assumed control'.[18] The payment of his remuneration is postponed to the costs of realisation: the costs of realisation must be paid first, and the balance due to the receiver or manager (including his remuneration) and his costs of the action must be paid next.[19] The costs of realisation, it should be noted, while including the costs of an abortive sale[20] do not include the costs of preservation of the property[1] nor the costs of taking any step in the action.[2]

A receiver appointed to preserve the assets of a company which is in truth a quasi-partnership will be remunerated out of these assets in the usual way. But any costs and expenses incurred on a s 459 petition may be ordered to be paid by a party whose dishonest actions precipitated the receivership and the petition.[3]

The receiver's remuneration may even take priority to advances made under a court order prescribing that repayment is to be a first charge on the assets. Thus in *Strapp v Bull Sons & Co*[4] receivers and managers who were appointed in the winding up of a company incurred expenses in completing the contracts of the company's business as builders. They were held entitled to be indemnified out of the assets of the business in priority to persons who had advanced money under a consent order providing that the advances were to be a first charge on the assets of the company. A similar rule was applied where the order authorising the advances did not itself create a charge, but simply gave liberty to the manager to

---

14 *Day v Croft* (1840) 2 Beav 488; *Neave v Douglas* (1857) 26 LJ Ch 756; *Buckmaster v Buckmaster* (1859) 28 LJ Ch 564, 34 LTOS 36; *Re Carton Ltd* (1923) 128 LT 629, 39 TLR 194.
15 *Buckmaster v Buckmaster* (1859) 28 LJ Ch 564, 34 LTOS 36.
16 *Thompson v Northern Trusts Co* [1924] 1 DLR 1135, 2 WWR 237; varied [1925] 4 DLR 184, Sask CA.
17 *Re Glasdir Coppers Mine Ltd* [1906] 1 Ch 365 at 378, CA.
18 *Re Beni-Felkai Mining Co Ltd* [1934] Ch 406 at 419 per Maugham J.
19 *Batten v Wedgwood Coal and Iron Co* (1884) 28 Ch D 317; *Re London United Breweries Ltd* [1907] 2 Ch 511; *Re Glyncorrwg Colliery Co* [1926] Ch 951.
20 *Batten v Wedgwood Coal and Iron Co* supra.
 1 *Re Oriental Hotels Co, Perry v Oriental Hotels Co* (1871) LR 12 Eq 126; *Lathom v Greenwich Ferry Co* (1895) 72 LT 790.
 2 *Re Callander's Paper Co* (18 January 1911, unreported) (Neville J in chambers).
 3 *Re Worldhams Park Golf Course Ltd* [1998] 1 BCLC 554.
 4 [1895] 2 Ch 1, CA.

borrow on the security of charges to be created by him.[5] The position is that a party who advances money to a receiver, knowing him to be a receiver, on the security of property subject to the receivership takes his security subject to the right of the receiver to his remuneration out of such property.[6] Probably the rule will not apply where the person making the advance is a stranger to the action in which the order has been made.

The receiver's right to payment of remuneration is also postponed to any over-riding charges outside the action.[7] But subject to that it takes priority over all other claims including the costs of the parties to the action.[8]

Forfeiture

Court receivers like privately appointed receivers may be deprived of their remuneration on the grounds of misconduct. Since such a receiver is not acting as an agent the agency principles which prompt automatic forfeiture of remuneration in the case of a breach of duty do not apply. He may get his reward even if he has acted irregularly particularly if his conduct has benefited the estate.[9] But he cannot look for remuneration for work done after his term of office has expired: his proper course is to apply for extension of his term of office so that the position does not arise.[10]

Failure on the part of a court receiver to render proper accounts in accordance with an order of the court may result in forfeiture of all rights to remuneration.[11] And failure to pay in a balance by a pre-ordained day may result in his being stripped of even that remuneration which he had had.[12]

Effect of terminating the receivership

It should be added that a receiver's costs and expenses do not form part of the costs 'of and incidental to' the action in which he is appointed and therefore cannot be recovered by a party successfully applying for discharge of the receivership order. The receiver's charges and remuneration are expenses of the receivership and once he has properly recouped his properly incurred costs from an asset which he has received, the costs of the receivership lie where they fall.[13]

---

5 *Re Glasdir Copper Mines* [1906] 1 Ch 365, 75 LJ Ch 109, CA.
6 *Re New Zealand Midland Rly Co* [1901] WN 105; *Re A Boynton Ltd* [1910] 1 Ch 519, 79 LJ Ch 247.
7 *Choudri v Palta* (1992) Times, 14 July, CA (receiver in partnership action: his costs and remuneration cannot be paid in priority to sums secured under prior or paramount charges).
8 *Re Johnson, ex p Royle* (1875) LR 20 Eq 780, 33 LT 39 (costs of debtor's solicitor); *Strapp v Bull Sons & Co* [1895] 2 Ch 1, CA.
9 *Harris v Sleep* [1897] 2 Ch 80, 66 LJ Ch 596, CA.
10 *Re Wood Green and Hornsey Steam Laundry Ltd* [1918] 1 Ch 423, 87 LJ Ch 171.
11 *Re St George's Estate* (1887) 19 LR Ir 566.
12 *Harrison v Boydell* (1833) 6 Sim 211.
13 *Re Andrews* [1999] 2 BCLC 442, CA.

REMUNERATION AND COSTS OF EQUITABLE EXECUTION

The costs and remuneration of a receiver appointed by way of equitable execution in the Queen's Bench Division are governed by the rules laid down for the appointment of receivers generally which provide[14] that a receiver shall be allowed such proper remuneration as the court authorises, and empowers the remuneration to be fixed by reference to a scale fee or rate of professional charges. They are also governed by particular guidelines. These guidelines are set out in a memorandum approved by the King's Bench Masters in June 1929. The memorandum provides as follows: 'Where a receiver is appointed by way of equitable execution, unless the Court or a judge otherwise orders, the total amount to be allowed for the costs of the receiver (including his remuneration, the costs of obtaining his appointment, of completing his security (if any) of passing his accounts, and of obtaining his discharge), should not exceed 10 per cent of the amount due under the judgment or the amount recovered by the receiver whichever may be the lesser sum; provided that not less than £5 be allowed unless otherwise ordered, and that where the amount due under the judgment does not exceed £50 the plaintiff or party applying shall be made answerable and the usual security be dispensed with. The amount allowed shall when required be apportioned by the Master as between costs and remuneration respectively'.[15]

In cases not falling within the ambit of the memorandum just cited the practice of the Queen's Bench Division is as follows:

(1) In the case of rent a percentage varying from, say 2 to 10 per cent, is allowed on the gross rents collected varying according to the amount of the rent and circumstances as follows:

   (a) If the rents are large, say over £100 per annum, and are payable yearly or half yearly and no undue trouble arises owing to the state of repair or otherwise 2 per cent, or slightly over would be allowed.

   (b) If the rents are collected monthly or quarterly, 3 to 5 per cent would be allowed.

   (c) If collected weekly, from 7 to 10 per cent would be allowed.

   In each of the above cases, the difficulties, trouble and labour involved would be taken into consideration, and although the percentage as above is taken as a guide, it is not slavishly followed, and is only used as means to arrive at a quantum meruit or proper remuneration. Moreover, the above figures and percentages would have to be adjusted to accord with modern financial conditions.

(2) In the case of dividends a percentage of 1 to 3 per cent on the gross sums collected would be allowed according to whether the dividends were numerous, or large or small, and in exceptional cases the percentage might

---

14 RSC Order 30, r 3.
15 See *Civil Procedure*, Vol 1, Spring 2000, Section A, Schedule 1, sc 51.3.10.

be reduced or increased—the percentage being only used to assist in arriving at the proper remuneration.

(3)   In other cases a quantum meruit allowance is made according to time and trouble involved.

INDEMNITY

Running in tandem with his personal answerability for liabilities incurred in the course of his receivership is the right of a court-appointed receiver and manager to be indemnified from the assets covered by his appointment.

The rule can be simply stated: in the absence of any express direction in the order itself a receiver and manager is entitled to be indemnified against all liabilities which he properly incurs,[16] in carrying on a business,[17] but the indemnity is limited to the assets.[18] Any expenses and liabilities bona fide incurred in the ordinary course of business would prima facie be treated as having been progressively incurred.[19] In the Australian case of *Price v Price*[20] the order allowed the receiver all costs properly incurred including the costs of settling his own remuneration. It was there held that the receiver was not confined to reimbursement simply on a common fund basis but could claim indemnity on a solicitor and client basis. In addition to his right of indemnity the receiver and manager has a lien over the receivership property as against all persons interested in it.[1]

It remains to be added by way of general introductory comment that a receiver can waive his right of indemnity although such waiver will not be implied from the circumstances.[2]

The right to indemnity also extends to all expenses incurred in carrying out, with the leave of the court, extraordinary services.[3] Sometimes in cases where prior leave could not be obtained in time or it was otherwise impracticable for the receiver and manager to seek leave in advance the expense may be allowed if it benefited the receivership.[4] A receiver *simpliciter* is entitled to be allowed all costs, charges and expenses and to be indemnified against all liabilities properly incurred in the protection and preservation of the property committed to his

---

16 *Re British Power Traction and Lighting Co* [1906] 1 Ch 497 at 505.
17 *Re Bushell, ex p Izard* (1883) 23 Ch D 75 at 79; *Re Brooke* [1894] 2 Ch 600; *Strapp v Bull Sons & Co* [1895] 2 Ch 1; *Re Glasdir Copper Mines Ltd* [1906] 1 Ch 365, CA; *Moss Steamship Co Ltd v Whinney* [1912] AC 254 at 270, HL.
18 *Boehm v Goodall* [1911] 1 Ch 155, 80 LJ Ch 86 followed in *Johnston v Courtney* [1920] 2 WWR 459, BCCA.
19 *Re Edinburgh Mortgage Ltd v Federal Business Development Bank* (1977) 24 CBRNS 187.
20 (1904) 29 VLR 719.
 1 *Bertrand v Davies* (1862) 31 Beav 429.
 2 *Re Glasdir Copper Mines Ltd* [1906] 1 Ch 365 at 378–379, CA.
 3 *Potts v Leighton* (1808) 15 Ves 273.
 4 *Re British Power Traction and Lighting Co Ltd* [1906] 1 Ch 497 at 506; and see *Walter E Heller (Canada) Ltd v Sea Queen of Canada Ltd* (1975) 19 CBRNS 252; affd on rehearing 21 CBRNS 272.

charge, or otherwise in the course of his duties even though they result in loss.[5] The indemnity for urgent necessary work (which benefits all interested creditors) may be given priority status over the claims of prior secured creditors.[6]

The receiver does not lose his right to indemnity simply because his office comes to an end.[7] But if he allows any costs to accrue which could have been prevented then he is liable to pay them out of his own pocket.[8] Thus in *Woodroffe v Green*[9] a receiver unnecessarily employed the services of a solicitor and was refused indemnity in respect of the fees which he was charged.

A receiver who has also been appointed manager of a business is allowed all the necessary expenses of carrying on the business with a view to an advantageous sale. He cannot manage the business without employing proper persons to assist him, and in the circumstances it may be that the best qualified helpers are the debtors. That at any rate was the conclusion on the facts in *Re Gomersall, ex p Gordon*[10] where Sir James Bacon CJ also held that the receiver and manager was justified in employing valuers to value the debtor's property and was therefore entitled to an indemnity for his expenditure. In the case of large business concerns arguments over the propriety of the receiver and manager incurring expenditure on employees and other assistance is precluded by express authority. The order of appointment often authorises the salaried engagement of sub-managers and agents for various purposes.[11]

All the same there can be no question, in the absence of some express provision to that effect, of a receiver being entitled to an indemnity from the company in respect of claims arising out of any neglect default breach of duty or breach of trust on his part whether the claim is made by the debenture holder or another party. As Somers J said in *RA Price Securities Ltd v Henderson*:[12]

> 'It is trite law that an agent is not entitled to be indemnified by his principal against losses or liabilities incurred in consequence of his own negligence or default.'

Accordingly a receiver will be left to carry the burden of any costs to the extent to which they relate to allegations of impropriety that are sustained.[13] If his entry into loss making contracts with third parties is attributable in any significant degree to his own negligence he cannot resort to an indemnity.[14]

---

5 *Morison v Morison* (1855) 7 De GM & G 214, 25 LTOS 110; *Re Gomersall, ex p Gordon* (1875) LR 20 Eq 291, 44 LJ Bcy 97; *Re Bushell, ex p Izard* (1883) 23 Ch D 75 at 80; *Re Brooke* [1894] 2 Ch 600 (where creditors had assented to carrying on of business). For a relatively recent Canadian case, see *Credit Foncier Franco-Canadian v Edmonton Airport Hotel Co Ltd* (1966) 55 WWR 734; affd 56 WWR 623n (reviewing the question of *speculative* outlays).

6 *Winnipeg Supply and Fuel Co Ltd v Genevieve Mortgage Corpn Ltd* [1972] 1 WWR 651 (Man CA); *Robert F Kowal Investments Ltd v Deeder Electric Ltd* (1975) 9 OR (2d) 84, Ont CA.

7 *Levy v Davis* [1900] WN 174.

8 *Cook v Sharman* (1844) 8 I Eq R 515.

9 (1852) 2 I Ch R 330.

10 (1875) LR 20 Eq 291.

11 1 *Seton's Judgments and Orders* (7th edn) 731, 732.

12 [1989] 2 NZLR 257 at 265.

13 *Expo International Pty Ltd v Chant (No 2)* (1980) 5 ACLR 193.

14 *RA Price Securities Ltd v Henderson* [1989] 2 NZLR 257 at 265 (where it had been argued that it was material that the loss was not wholly caused by but only contributed to by the receiver).

The court will look critically at any indemnity clause alleged to absolve the receiver from liability for neglects or defaults. This is illustrated by the case of *Re Just Juice Corpn Pty Ltd; James v Commonwealth of Australia*.[15] There a receiver was entitled to indemnity against losses or claims arising out of acceptance of his appointment as receiver and acts performed by him in that role. However the relevant indemnity expressly did not extend to losses or claims that were the result of 'personal default or neglect' of the receiver or his employees or agents. It was sought to argue that because there had been no personal default or neglect on the part of the receiver directly in incurring the relevant debt because the contracts which gave rise to the debts were appropriate for the business then being carried on. The court dismissed this argument: the 'personal default or neglect' with which the indemnity was concerned was the personal default or neglect of the receiver in the discharge of his office. On the assumed facts he had been guilty of default or neglect in the conduct of the receivership and the incurring of the debts being in an immediate sense the result of that personal default or neglect no indemnity could be claimed.[16] A further indemnity in the same case against liability for 'debts properly incurred by him in the course of the receivership' proved no more effective on the assumed facts. Whether the debts were properly incurred was likewise not to be determined by looking in isolation at the transactions between the receiver and each of the trade creditors. The overall picture had to be looked at and that involved inspecting the whole course of conduct of the receivership.

Any recovery by the debenture holder under any express provision or by virtue of being subrogated to the right of the receiver as against the company or a guarantor will be precluded where the payment made under the indemnity was for the costs of an action brought successfully against the receiver by the company.[17]

Occasionally a debenture holder sufficiently interferes in the conduct of a receivership, for example by giving directions to the receiver, so as to constitute himself a principal of the receiver.[18] Such interference may expose the debenture holder to a liability to indemnify the receiver against claims by the company arising out of those directions.[19] However, mere consultation between the receiver and debenture holder with no relevant instructions being given by the latter will not constitute the debenture holder as an exposed principal.[20] Similarly, the existence of a reserved but unexercised power to give instructions will not give rise to a right on the part of the receiver to an indemnity from the debenture holder.[1]

---

15 (1992) 8 ACSR 444.
16 Had he had a right of indemnity the court would in any event have allowed an equitable set off against it based on material misrepresentations assumed to have been made by the receiver.
17 *McCarty v ANZ Banking Group (New Zealand) Ltd* (1993) 6 NZCLC 68,382.
18 *Standard Chartered Bank v Walker* [1982] 1 WLR 1410; *American Express International Banking Corpn v Hurley* [1985] 3 All ER 564; *Edmonds v Westland Bank Ltd* [1991] 2 NZLR 655 at 661.
19 *Re B Johnson & Co (Builders) Ltd* [1955] Ch 634 at 647–648, CA.
20 *RA Price Securities Ltd v Henderson* [1989] 2 NZLR 257.
 1 *National Bank of Greece SA v Pinios Shipping Co* [1990] 1 AC 637.

A receiver may be ordered to pay the costs of any application to the court made necessary by his own default.[2] Thus a receiver who was brought before the court because of his very irregular handling of accounts and ordered to bring in proper accounts within a prescribed period was naturally ordered to pay the costs occasioned by his defaulting conduct.[3] A receiver who withholds information[4] or improperly retains a balance in his hands[5] or borrows in excess of his authorisation and more for the protection of his own business clients than for the purpose of discharging his duties as receiver and manager[6] brings down upon his own head a court application and the costs that go with it.

Nevertheless it seems that if a receiver who has been guilty of default is able to show that he acted on the prompting of parties interested in the property he may be allowed to charge those parties in account with any costs that have been thrown upon him personally as a result of the default.[7]

A receiver is allowed his costs of any action brought by direction of the court even though it is dismissed with costs. Moreover if the assets turn out to be insufficient to pay the costs of the successful defendant as well as those of the receiver priority will be given to the claim of the receiver.[8] While a receiver is not entitled to his costs, charges and expenses until his accounts have been examined, the costs of legal proceedings taken by the order of the court may be ordered to be paid to his solicitor out of funds in court, even though the receiver is in default.[9]

On the other hand the costs of bringing or defending legal proceedings without the leave of the court are not, in general, allowed.[10] The rule admits of exception where a receiver in the interest of the estate of which he is receiver defends an action successfully and the estate is thereby benefited; here the receiver is entitled to be indemnified against his costs despite the fact that he acted without leave.[11] The guiding principle in such cases is that the defence to the action was for the benefit of the estate. In *Re Dunn*[12] an action had been brought against a receiver and administrator pendente lite charging him with personal fraud and misconduct while acting as administrator and receiver but otherwise having no relation to the estate except so far that the acts complained of were acts done by him while acting as an officer of the court. It was held that the receiver was not entitled to be indemnified against the costs incurred in successfully defending the action. The receiver in the earlier case of *Courand v Hanmer*[13] was more fortunate. An application was there made by a party to the action against a receiver alleging neglect or default and the application was refused with costs.

2 *Walsh v Walsh* (1839) 1 I Eq R 209; *Saunderson v Stoney* (1839) 2 I Eq R 153.
3 *Bertie v Lord Abingdon* (1845) 8 Beav 53.
4 *Re Suffield and Watts, ex p Brown* (1888) 36 WR 303; revsd on another point 20 QBD 693, 58 LT 911, CA.
5 *Re St George's Estate* (1887) 19 LR Ir 566.
6 *Edinburgh Mortgage Ltd v Federal Business Development Bank* (1977) 24 CBRNS 187.
7 *Bertie v Lord Abingdon* (1845) 8 Beav 53 at 60.
8 *Ramsay v Simpson* [1899] 1 IR 194, Ir CA.
9 *McBride's Executors v Clarke* (1839) 1 I Eq R 203.
10 *Swaby v Dickon* (1833) 5 Sim 629; *Conyers v Crosbie* (1844) 6 I Eq R 657; *Re Dunn* [1904] 1 Ch 648.
11 *Courand v Hanmer* (1846) 9 Beav 3; *Bristowe v Needham* (1847) 2 Ph 190, 9 LTOS 69.
12 [1904] 1 Ch 648.
13 (1846) 9 Beav 3.

The applicant was in fact wholly unable to pay the costs. The court held that the receiver was entitled to be indemnified as between solicitor and client out of the fund in hand belonging to incumbrancers. The stricter rule that the action or defence must be for the benefit of the estate was applied in *Swaby v Dickon*[14] where a receiver was refused his costs of defending, without the leave of the court, an action arising out of a distress for rent made by him on the tenant. The action was in fact compromised, each party agreeing to pay its own costs. In the circumstances it was not necessary to defend the proceedings to protect the estate: it followed that the receiver's costs were not allowed.

In relation to his prospective disbursements a receiver and manager should only apply to the court if there is genuine doubt as to the propriety of a particular disbursement or liability. In such a case an application for leave is necessary because otherwise the receiver runs the risk of having the expenses disallowed and an indemnity against the liabilities refused.[15] On the other hand where it is clear that the relevant disbursement will be allowed the receiver is not justified in applying for belt-and-braces protection in the form of leave to expend the money; such an application is otiose and if made the cost of it will be laid at the door of the receiver who will have to pay the costs occasioned.[16]

A receiver is generally entitled to the costs of and incidental to the examination of his accounts. But if he is in default and has accounted only under the shadow of an order for attachment his costs will be disallowed.[17] Relevant objections to the receiver's right to his costs of the examination of his accounts should be taken at the time. Thus, for example, if no objection is raised at the time as to the lack of punctuality in accounting such costs are not afterwards disallowed save in very special circumstances.[18]

Formerly the expenses of funding securities and premiums paid by the receiver to a guarantee society as his surety were disallowed unless the receiver was acting with remuneration.[19] However nowadays such expenses are allowed in almost all cases.[20] As a rule a receiver who fails to complete his security will have to bear personally the costs of any proceedings to set his appointment aside and to replace him. But special circumstances may save the receiver from this fate. Thus in *Hunter v Pring*[1] the receiver, one Borgin, who was a very poor and struggling person in a small trade and it seems illiterate, was prevailed upon to accept the office of receiver by a person who misrepresented and concealed from him the nature of the office and the liabilities to which he would be subject. He was subsequently removed as receiver being unable to provide security but Blackburn MR declined to penalise him in costs. The receiver in *Lane v Townsend*[2] was in an exceptional predicament also. One of his sureties became

14 (1833) 5 Sim 629.
15 *Malcolm v O'Callaghan* (1837) 3 My & Cr 52; *Re British Power Traction and Lighting Co Ltd* [1906] 1 Ch 497; subsequent proceedings [1907] 1 Ch 528.
16 *Newtown v Obre* (1837) Sau & Sc 137; *Fitzgerald v Fitzgerald* (1843) 5 I Eq R 525.
17 *Traupaud v Cormick* (1825) 1 Hog 245.
18 *Ward v Swift* (1848) 8 Hare 139, 12 LTOS 190.
19 *Re Golding* (1888) 21 LR Ir 194; *Harris v Sleep* [1897] 2 Ch 80, CA.
20 See (1951) 101 L Jo 241.
 1 (1845) 8 I Eq R 102.
 2 (1852) 2 I Ch R 120.

insolvent and the other had gone to reside in America without leaving any property in the jurisdiction and the receiver was unable to find further recognisances. The receiver consented to be discharged but submitted that he ought not to be directed to pay the costs sought. Cusack Smith MR said that he had inquired into the practice, which he found to be not to charge a receiver who is unable to procure a new surety or other sureties, with the expense of the appointment of a new receiver but he should not give him the costs of appearing on the motion.

CHAPTER 33

Accounts

INTRODUCTION

The law relating to the accounts to be provided by a receiver has long been contained in Order 30 of the Rules of the Supreme Court.[1] That Order in its latest manifestation is designed to give greater flexibility in dealing with receivers' accounts and to bring receivers' accounts into line with judicial trustees' accounts.

The main features of the regime are as follows. First, the receiver has to be served with a copy of the order so that he knows what are his terms of reference. It will be for the parties in the first instance to audit and approve the accounts. The court only becomes involved if the parties cannot agree. The court 'examines' the accounts and does not any longer 'pass' them. It is only in exceptional cases that vouching and audit are used. After examination of the accounts the master certifies the accounts as before. An innovation is that the receiver has the right to apply to the court by letter for directions. This is a reflection of the similar right enjoyed by a judicial trustee.

FORM

There is no set form of account ordained by the Rules of the Supreme Court.

Application ought not to be made to the count in respect of disbursements which should be brought in as part of the receiver's bill when his accounts are examined. The receiver may be ordered to pay the costs of any unnecessary action of this kind.[2]

A receiver must submit such accounts to such parties at such intervals or on such dates as the court may direct.[3] It is most important that counsel should apply his mind to this question and ask the judge when the appointment is made to direct that accounts should be served on the required parties at six monthly or

---

1 *Civil Procedure*, Vol 1, Spring 2000, Section A, Sch 1, sc 30.5, and 30.5.1 which set out and comment on RSC Order 30, r 5.
2 *Newtown v Obre* (1837) Sau & Sc 137.
3 RSC Ord 30, r 5(1).

yearly intervals. If this is not done at the time of the hearing it will be necessary to apply to the master by summons to proceed when those directions will be given. To be driven to that case is a waste of time and money.

INSPECTION OF AND OBJECTION TO ACCOUNTS

Any party to whom a receiver is required to submit accounts may, on giving reasonable notice to the receiver, inspect, either personally or by an agent, the books and other papers relating to the accounts.[4]

Any party who is dissatisfied with the accounts of the receiver may give notice specifying the item or items to which objection is taken and requiring the receiver within a period of not less than 14 days to lodge his accounts with the court.[5] A copy of that notice must be lodged in the office of the Supreme Court having the conduct of the business of the division or court in which the cause or matter is proceeding, or if it is proceeding in a district registry in that registry.[6]

Where objection is taken to some item or items in the account and an examination by or on behalf of the court of such item or items ensues the court will give the parties an appointment before the relevant officer of the court, who is usually of course a Chancery master because Chancery receiverships are the most common.[7] At the conclusion of the court's examination the result of the examination must be certified by a master, the Admiralty registrar, a registrar of the Family Division or a district registrar as the case may be.[8] An order may then be made dealing with the costs and expenses incurred and in particular upon whom or where the burden should fall.[9]

Sometimes a receiver will need extra time in which to bring in his accounts. Where that is the case he should mention the matter to the Receivership Officer who will in a proper case ensure that the receiver has the time he needs referring it to a master if there is any undue delay. If necessary the question can be dealt with on a formal application by summons, but normally this should not be necessary.[10]

DEFAULT IN ACCOUNTING

If a receiver fails to attend for the examination of any account of his or fails to submit any account, provide access to any books or papers or do any other thing

---

4 RSC Ord 30, r 5(2).
5 RSC Ord 30, r 5(3).
6 RSC Ord 30.
7 RSC Ord 30, r 5(4).
8 RSC Ord 30.
9 RSC Ord 30.
10 RSC Ord 3, r 5. For a summons capable of adaptation for an application notice, see 33 *Court Forms* (1997 Issue) 137, Form 39.

which he is required to provide or do he and any or all of the other parties to the cause or matter in which he was appointed may be required to attend in chambers and show cause for his failure. At that stage the court may give such directions as may be appropriate either in chambers or after adjournment into court, including if necessary the discharge of the receiver and the appointment of another and payment of the costs.[11]

In addition if the receiver fails to attend for the examination of his accounts or fails to submit any account or fails to pay into court on the day fixed any sums required to be so paid, his remuneration may be disallowed. He may also be charged, where he has failed to pay any such sum into court, with interest at the rate currently payable in respect of judgment debts in the High Court on that sum while in his possession as receiver.[12] The receiver may be charged with interest whether he has made a profit for himself or not,[13] and that applies to a receiver of public funds[14] as to a receiver of private funds. And it is irrelevant that the parties have not objected to his balances on examination of his accounts.[15] The interest is calculated not on each sum from the time it comes into his hands but on yearly or half yearly rests in the accounts.[16]

Nor is the penalty of interest being charged the only sanction which a recalcitrant receiver faces. A receiver who fails to pay his balances into court after having been ordered by the court to do so is liable to committal for contempt[17] as a person acting in a fiduciary capacity within the meaning of the Debtors Act 1869.[18] He may also have a sequestration order made against him. And he will almost inevitably have to pay the costs of any application made to the court for committal or sequestration.[19]

A receiver who fails to comply with an order for payment to a particular person of a sum of money for costs or otherwise is also at risk as to committal.[20]

The delay of the parties may be a ground for not charging the receiver with interest.[1] For example a receiver may be excused for his delay if it is due to a desire to bring in a large sum receivable by him after the time fixed for an account at an earlier date then he would otherwise be liable to bring in the same.[2] But the fact that a receiver has failed to account for a sum owing to a mistake will not release him from the liability to pay interest in respect of that sum.[3]

---

11 RSC Ord 30, r 7(1). See also *Bertie v Lord Abingdon* (1845) 8 Beav 53 at 56; *Re St George's Estate* (1887) 19 LR Ir 566.
12 RSC Ord 30, r 7(1). See also *Anon v Jolland* (1802) 8 Ves 72; *Potts v Leighton* (1808) 15 Ves 273; *Bristowe v Needham* (1863) 8 LT 652.
13 *Dawson v Massey* (1809) 1 Ball & B 231.
14 *Lonsdale v Church* (1789) 3 Bro CC 41.
15 *Fletcher v Dodd* (1789) 1 Ves 85.
16 *Potts v Leighton* (1808) 15 Ves 273; 2 Ves Supp 406; *Daniell's Chancery Practice* (8th edn) 1494.
17 *Re Bell's Estate* (1870) LR 9 Eq 172, 21 LT 781; *Re Gent* (1888) 40 Ch D 190.
18 See Debtors Act 1869, s 4(3); *Re Gent* above.
19 *Macarty v Gibson* (1728) Mos 40; *Davies v Cracraft* (1807) 14 Ves 143; *Maunsell v Egan* (1846) 3 Jo & Lat 251, 9 I Eq R 283; *Sprunt v Pugh* (1878) 7 Ch D 567.
20 *Betagh v Concanon* (1836) L & G temp Plunk 355.
1 *Dawson v Raynes* (1826) 2 Russ 466; *Gurden v Badcock* (1842) 6 Beav 157.
2 *Flood v Lord Aldborough* (1845) 8 I Eq R 103.
3 *Braham v Bowes* (1836) Donnelly 84.

It is the duty of the parties, primarily of the plaintiff, to bring to the attention of the court any delay or other default on the part of the receiver and to apply for the appropriate remedy. In cases of delay the master himself may of his own motion restore the matter to his list for a report.

The procedure upon default by the receiver in his duty to bring in his account, or to lodge a balance in court is that any interested party[4] may apply on notice for a 'four-day' order, that is, an order that the defaulter do leave his account or pay in the balance within four days after service on him of the order to be made on the application notice. The four-day order will require the receiver to pay the price for his default by penalising him in costs.[5] A pre-condition of the making of such an order is that the receiver has been served with the application notice so that if he fails to appear the order will be made once an affidavit of service of the summons is produced.[6] Further formalities are required where the default consists of not paying a balance into court: the applicant must produce the order and the certificate under which the payment was required together with a certificate of default.[7]

ACCOUNTS IN THE COUNTY COURT

The provisions of the Rules of the Supreme Court with regard to receivers' accounts apply in relation to a receiver appointed by a county court as they apply in relation to a receiver appointed by the High Court.[8]

4 *Scott v Platel* (1847) 2 Ph 229 (application by joint receiver).
5 See 33 *Court Forms* (1997 Issue) 136–137, Form 37 (summons), Form 38 (order).
6 *Seton's Judgments and Orders* (7th edn) 771; *Daniell's Chancery Forms* (7th edn) Nos 1770, 1772.
7 *Daniell's Chancery Practice* (8th edn 1914) 1493.
8 *Civil Procedure*, Vol 1, Spring 2000, Section A, Sch 1, sc 30.A1.

CHAPTER 34

Discharge

INTRODUCTION

In most court receiverships the point will inevitably be reached where the receiver's task is done. But quite apart from those obvious cases where the receivership has run its course there will be cases when a particular receiver ought to be relieved of his duties. This chapter considers the grounds for discharging a receiver, the procedure by which his discharge is effected and the consequences of his discharge.

NECESSITY FOR ORDER OF DISCHARGE

Unless his appointment was for a limited time only[1] or the order appointing or continuing him contains a provision for his discharge[2] a receiver or receiver and manager appointed by the court can only be discharged by order, 'even though circumstances have rendered the appointment nugatory'.[3]

The necessity for an order for discharge is underlined in many of the cases.[4] In this connection the order need not expressly discharge the receiver: it will be sufficient if it has that effect. Thus an injunction to put a purchaser into possession amounts to a discharge of a receiver.[5] If the order does limit the term of office for a stated time the office terminates at the expiration of that time. Consequently when an application to continue the receivership has been refused there is no need for any other application to set aside the order or to discharge the receiver.[6]

---

1 *Brinsley v Lynton and Lynmouth Hotel and Property Co* as reported in [1895] WN 53 ('until judgment or further order'); *Canadian Permanent Mortgage Corpn v Dalgleish* [1928] 1 DLR 1113, BC CA; *Koffman v Filer* [1927] 4 DLR 604 at 606, Sask CA.

2 *Day v Sykes, Walker & Co Ltd* (1886) 55 LT 763.

3 *Canadian Permanent Mortgage Corpn v Dalgleish* [1928] 1 DLR 1113, BC CA per Macdonald JA.

4 *White v Lord Westmeath* (1828) Beat 174; *Kenny v Clarke* (1843) 5 I Eq R 280; *Johnston v Henderson* (1844) 8 I Eq R 521; *Burt, Boulton & Hayward v Bull* [1895] 1 QB 276; and see *Shankar Das v Behari Lal* (1925) 1 LR 6 Lah 442, Ind.

5 *Ponsonby v Ponsonby* (1825) 1 Hog 321; *Anon* (1839) 2 I Eq R 416.

6 *Koffman v Filer* [1927] 4 DLR 604 at 606, Sask CA.

DISCHARGE IN COMPANY'S LIQUIDATION

There is no general rule that on the winding up of a company by the court a court-appointed receiver is to be displaced in favour of a liquidator. It is a question of the balance of convenience and inconvenience in each case.[7]

The court will not without strong reason discharge in favour of a liquidator a receiver appointed by the court on the application of the mortgagees unless it is proposed to appoint the liquidator receiver in his place.[8] Expense alone is not a sufficiently strong reason.[9] But the court will, in order to avoid unnecessary expense and the possibility of conflict, discharge such a receiver and appoint the liquidator receiver in his place unless there are special circumstances which make such a course undesirable.[10] It will take a similar course in the case of a receiver and manager, and the fact that there is a business to be carried on would be a strong reason for the court to appoint the same person as liquidator and receiver and manager.[11]

The rule of convenience that the court will take care, in order to avoid trouble and expense, that the receiver and the liquidator shall be the same person in every case where that can properly be done[12] is not without its critics. To some it is undesirable that a person who is a receiver for debenture holders should act as a liquidator: their respective interests will necessarily be different and in many cases conflicting.[13] As Lawrence J pointed out in *Stead, Hazel & Co v Cooper*:[14] 'The liquidator acts for and in the interests of the company whereas the receiver and manager acts for and in the interests of the debenture holders and not for the company'. Nevertheless the rule of convenience is well established. And it may easily be displaced. It is only a prima facie rule of practice; if justice or convenience requires it, the rule will be displaced; and if there is any reasonable ground for supposing that the rights of the debenture holders or mortgagees will be in any way affected or diminished in fact that is quite sufficient to make the court depart from the prima facie rule.[15]

Cases where a receiver may remain

In the case of assets requiring special commercial knowledge the court may displace the receiver by a liquidator except in relation to those assets. Thus in

---

7 *Bartlett v Northumberland Avenue Hotel Co Ltd* (1885) 53 LT 611, CA.
8 *Strong v Carlyle Press* [1893] 1 Ch 268, CA; *British Linen Co v South American and Mexican Co* [1894] 1 Ch 108, CA.
9 *Strong v Carlyle Press* [1893] 1 Ch 268 at 273–274.
10 *Re Compagnie Générale de Bellegarde* (1876) 2 Ch D 181; *Tottenham v Swansea Zinc Ore Co Ltd* (1884) 53 LJ Ch 776, 51 LT 61; *Re Joshua Stubbs Ltd* [1891] 1 Ch 475; *British Linen Co v South American and Mexican Co* [1894] 1 Ch 108, CA.
11 *Re Joshua Stubbs Ltd* [1891] 1 Ch 475, CA.
12 Ibid at 482 per Kay LJ.
13 *Re Karamelli and Barnett Ltd* [1917] 1 Ch 203 at 205 per Neville J.
14 [1933] 1 KB 840 at 843.
15 *British Linen Co v South American and Mexican Co* [1894] 1 Ch 108 at 118 per Vaughan Williams J.

British Linen Co v South American and Mexican Co[16] the Official Receiver who was provisional liquidator moved the court for the discharge of the debenture holders' receiver and manager and for an order that the Official Receiver should be appointed in his place. The evidence before the judge at first instance did not indicate to him that the securities were of a kind with regard to which there was anything else to be done than to employ a broker to sell them. Accordingly the Official Receiver was a perfectly appropriate officer to be receiver and manager. Had the learned judge thought that there was something in the nature of the securities to be realised and the moneys to be collected which required negotiations and bargainings and compromises he would have considered that was a function much better performed by an accountant than by an officer of the court even with the assistance of a great government department. The evidence before the Court of Appeal established that the securities in question did require very special expertise for the purposes of realisation.[17] The Official Receiver was by far the best person to make calls and get in the general assets and in relation to those general assets he was left as receiver and manager. But the debenture holders' receiver was better qualified to realise the special securities which required bargainings, negotiations and compromise involving specialist expertise.[18] Accordingly the Court of Appeal varied the order of the court below and reinstated the debenture holders' receiver as receiver and manager of the special assets.

Another special circumstance rendering it undesirable that a liquidator should be appointed receiver is where he has assumed a position of hostility to the debenture holders.[19] So if there is a dispute between the receiver and the liquidator as to the validity of the debentures and the extent of the property comprised in the security an independent person may be appointed receiver pending determination of the dispute.[20] The fact that the liquidator in a voluntary liquidation is also receiver may be sufficient ground for removing him from his office of liquidator at the instance of unpaid creditors.[1]

Where a judge at first instance has in the exercise of his discretion refused to displace a receiver by a liquidator the Court of Appeal will not, in the absence of special circumstances to justify their so doing, interfere with the exercise of that discretion.[2] And if a judge at first instance has come to the conclusion that there are special circumstances rendering it undesirable that the liquidator should be appointed receiver the Court of Appeal will seldom overrule the exercise of his descretion.[3]

It remains to be noted that the court will not displace a receiver by the liquidator where such receiver has not been appointed by the court but by a debenture holder out of court under the powers given to him by his security.[4]

16 [1894] 1 Ch 108, CA.
17 The evidence is set out at [1894] 1 Ch 108 at 122–123.
18 [1894] 1 Ch 108 at 131 per A L Smith LJ.
19 *Giles v Nuttall* [1885] WN 51, CA.
20 [1885] WN 51.
 1 *Re Karamelli & Barnett Ltd* [1917] 1 Ch 203.
 2 *Re Joshua Stubbs Ltd* [1891] 1 Ch 475, CA.
 3 *Giles v Nuttall* [1885] WN 51, CA (where the matter is put even more dogmatically).
 4 *Re Henry Pound, Son & Hutchins* (1889) 42 Ch D 402; *Re Joshua Stubbs Ltd* [1891] 1 Ch 475, CA.

The fact that there is little for the receiver to do because there is no substantial amount of uncalled capital and similar assets outstanding[5] or that some of the assets are such as to require special commercial knowledge for their realisation[6] have been treated as special circumstances justifying the decision of the court not to discharge the existing receiver and appoint the liquidator as receiver. In *Strong v Carlyle Press*[7] there was an amply sufficient reason for departing from the rule, because there the assets, admittedly, were altogether insufficient to pay the debts due to the debenture holders, and the court was only following the well-established rule in taking care that the administration should be granted to those who had an exclusive interest in the realisation.[8]

FLAW IN THE APPOINTMENT

The most fundamental ground for the discharge of a receiver is that he ought never to have been appointed, and where that is the case he will be removed.[9] Thus if a receiver is appointed of property not capable of assignment at law[10] or of being charged[11] he will be discharged. The same applies if the property of a stranger is erroneously included in the order.[12] Thus in *Lavender v Lavender*[13] a receiver who had been wrongly appointed over property belonging to a person who was not a party to the action was discharged by order despite the abatement of the suit by the death of the sole defendant. Again if the sole purpose of the appointment is to carry into effect a scheme which falls outside the purview of a contract under which the receiver is appointed, the receiver will be discharged.[14] The court has no power to clothe a receiver with an authority which would wholly transcend the nature of the original arrangement between the parties and will strip the receiver of those clothes and his office.[15]

The court will likewise discharge a receiver who has been appointed for the purpose of preventing the exercise of a legal right such as an executor's right of retainer, for here again the appointment for such a purpose is improper.[16]

The appointment may be flawed because of the person appointed. The receiver in question may be a person who by reason of his position, interest, bias or

---

5   *Re Joshua Stubbs Ltd* [1891] 1 Ch 475 at 483, CA.

6   *British Linen Co v South American and Mexican Co* [1894] 1 Ch 108, CA.

7   [1893] 1 Ch 268, CA.

8   *British Linen Co v South American and Mexican Co* [1894] 1 Ch 108 at 118, CA per Vaughan Williams J.

9   *Graham v Graham* (1871) 2 VR (E) 145, 2 AJR 100.

10 *Lucas v Harris* (1886) 18 QBD 127, CA; *Brenan v Morrissey* (1890) 26 LR Ir 618; *Macdonald v O'Toole* [1908] 2 IR 386, 42 ILT 73.

11 *Beckett v Tasker* (1887) 19 QBD 7, 56 LT 636; *Walbrook & Co v Jones & Lewis* (1887) 3 TLR 609, CA (judgment debtor's salary).

12 *Fowler v Haynes* (1863) 2 New Rep 156 (goods).

13 (1875) IR 9 Eq 593.

14 *Niemann v Niemann* (1889) 43 Ch D 198, CA (partnership).

15 (1889) 43 Ch D 198 at 205 per Bowen LJ.

16 *Re Wells* (1890) 45 Ch D 569.

hostility[17] at the time ought not to have been appointed, in which case the court will discharge him.[18] Or he may be a person who has subsequently come under some disqualification[19] or has subsequently emerged as biased[20] or hostile.[1] In these cases too the receiver or the order appointing him will be discharged as the justice of the case may require. In *Parsons v Mather & Platt Ltd*[2] the receiver and manager appear to have been rather sinned against than sinning. Before Donaldson J the receiver and the manager asked to have their respective functions confined to a narrow compass or to be discharged because of the unco-operative behaviour of the parties. In the event the judge discharged them. The plaintiff appealed and the Court of Appeal reinstated the receiver to act on the very limited basis upon which he was prepared to act.

The court will discharge a receiver whose appointment is procured by means of misleading affidavit evidence as to his fitness, even though no discredit attaches to the receiver in question.[3] An appointment will also be vitiated and the receiver discharged if he fails to furnish the requisite security[4] or in the case of an extension of the scope of an existing receivership any additional security.[5]

MISCONDUCT AND OTHER BREACHES

A receiver may be discharged for any default or misconduct of such a degree as will forfeit the confidence of the court[6] or which is liable to prejudice the interests of the parties.[7] Thus a receiver may be discharged if he has been guilty of some gross dereliction of duty, for example in collecting rents[8] or in persistently refusing to perform any of the functions of a receiver.[9] He may be removed for committing waste[10] or for mismanagement or dishonesty.[11] In one case[12] a receiver appointed in a partnership action allowed the rent of the partnership premises to fall into arrear so that the landlord distrained, and he also tried to move the

---

17 As to these disqualifications see the discussion at pp 301–304.
18 *Taylor v Oldham* (1822) Jac 527 (son of next friend of infant); *Re Lloyd* (1879) 12 Ch D 447, 41 LT 171, CA (plaintiff's solicitor).
19 Such as becoming a party: *Barclay v O'Brien* (1825) unreported but noted (1846) 9 Ir Eq R 260 (receiver became executor of plaintiff); *Meara v Egan* (1846) 9 I Eq R 259.
20 *Mitchell v Condy* [1873] WN 232; and see *Graham v Graham* (1871) 2 VLR (E) 145, 2 AJR 100.
 1 *Giles v Nuttall* [1885] WN 51, CA. For a Canadian example see *Brant v Willoughby* (1870) 17 Gr 627.
 2 (9 December 1974, unreported), CA Court Judgment (Civil Division) No 392A (Lord Denning MR, Roskill LJ and Sir John Pennycuick).
 3 *Re Church Press Ltd* (1917) 116 LT 247 (receiver and manager was not an 'accountant' and had occupied his offices in the City of London for two months and not five years).
 4 *Re Sims & Woods Ltd* [1916] WN 223; *Rowley v Desborough* (1916) 60 Sol Jo 429.
 5 *Wise v Ashe* (1839) 1 I Eq R 210.
 6 *Mitchell v Condy* [1873] WN 232.
 7 *Re St George's Estate* (1887) 19 LR Ir 566.
 8 (1887) 19 LR Ir 566.
 9 *National Trust Co Ltd v Barcelona Traction Light and Power Co Ltd* [1951] OR 530, CA.
10 *Bell v Spereman* (1726) Sel Cas in Ch 169, Cas temp King 59.
11 *Chaytor v Maclean* (1848) 11 LTOS 2.
12 *Mitchell v Condy* [1873] WN 232.

business for the benefit of the plaintiff who was a personal friend. He was discharged from the receivership for impeding the impartial course of justice.

Where a receiver has been guilty of a breach of duty but has acted in good faith to the best of his judgment for the benefit of all parties he will not necessarily be removed for misconduct.[13]

A receiver appointed by the court is appointed for the benefit of all interested parties and so will not be discharged merely on the application of the party at whose interest he was appointed.[14] Accordingly the court will not accede to an application by one of several plaintiffs whose claim has been satisfied[15] or whose interest has matured[16] if the claims of other plaintiffs are still to be satisfied. In such a case the court may stay the action without prejudice to the receivership.[17]

REASON FOR APPOINTMENT CEASING

If the object for which the appointment was made is achieved or the reason for the appointment has in any way ceased the court will discharge the receiver.[18] Thus he will be discharged if having been appointed on the application of an annuitant whose annuity is in arrear the arrears are paid off[19] or the value of the annuity is paid to the annuitant,[20] notwithstanding the opposition of the annuitant[1] or of prior incumbrancers.[2] On the other hand a receiver will not be discharged so long as any relevant claim remains unsatisfied or unadjudicated[3] or any question of title to the property in receivership remains outstanding.[4]

Where a receiver is appointed because of the misconduct or incapacity of trustees of a will[5] or of directors of a company,[6] once suitable replacements are installed he will be functus officii and the court will discharge him.

Standing as he does in a fiduciary position a receiver owes particular fiduciary duties. If he allows his personal interests to conflict with those duties, he may be discharged.[7] And if a receiver has conflicting duties, as where he acts for two companies who are litigating with each other, the court may discharge him.[8]

13 *Simpson v Ottawa and Prescott Rly Co* (1865) 1 Chy Chrs 337, Can.
14 *Davis v Duke of Marlborough* (1818) 1 Swan 74, 2 Wils Ch 130; *Bainbrigge v Blair* (1841) 3 Beav 421 at 423, per Lord Langdale MR.
15 *Largan v Bowen* (1803) 1 Sch & Lef 296.
16 *Smith v Lyster* (1841) 4 Beav 227 (one of the two tenants in common coming of age).
17 *Murrough v French* (1827) 2 Mol 497; *Damer v Earl of Portarlington* (1846) 2 Ph 30; *Paynter v Carew* (1854) 23 LJ Ch 596, 23 LTOS 21.
18 *Tewart v Lawson* (1874) LR 18 Eq 490.
19 *Sankey v O'Maley* (1825) 2 Mol 491; *Braham v Strathmore* (1844) 3 LTOS 466, 8 Jur 567.
20 *Davis v Duke of Marlborough* (1819) 2 Swan 108, 2 Wils Ch 130.
 1 See cases cited in fn 19, above.
 2 *Davis v Duke of Marlborough* (1819) 2 Swan 108 at 167.
 3 *Largan v Bowen* (1803) 1 Sch & Lef 296 (claim of one creditor).
 4 *Reeves v Neville* (1862) 10 WR 335.
 5 *Bainbrigge v Blair* (1841) 3 Beav 421.
 6 *Lane v Phelan* (1871) 2 AJR 10, Vic.
 7 See *Re Erie Gas Co Ltd* [1938] 4 DLR 776.
 8 See *Re Nickel Mines Ltd* (1978) 3 ACLR 686 (provisional liquidator with two conflicting capacities).

In some cases the initiative for a discharge of the receiver comes from the receiver himself. A receiver wishing to take such an initiative should ask the solicitors having the conduct of the cause or matter to apply to the court (on his behalf). He will not as a general rule be discharged on his own initiative unless he can show reasonable cause why the parties to the action should be saddled with the expense of his removal.[9] Where co-operation is key to the success of the receivership a failure to co-operate even on the part of one of the parties to the litigation may be sufficient to justify discharge of the receiver.[10] Other examples of reasonable cause in this context include his own ill health or other incapacity.[11] And naturally if all the interested parties consent there is no bar to an application by a receiver to be discharged.[12]

A receiver will not be discharged on his own application unless he can show reasonable cause for his discharge[13] or all parties consent.[14] Naturally ill-health is reason enough for his discharge,[15] although if the illness is merely temporary the court may appoint an attorney on behalf of the receiver.[16] Service as receiver for a period of 30 years was held sufficient ground for removal in another case.[17] Where the co-operation of the parties is essential to the operation of the receivership and one of the parties is being totally non-cooperative the receiver may justifiably apply to be discharged from his predicament, or restricted to such activities as it is practicable for him to carry out.[18] On discharge for such reasonable ground the receiver will not be charged with the costs of his removal and the appointment of a new receiver,[19] though he may not be allowed his costs of the application.[20] But a receiver has been allowed the costs of his removal where he was in ill-health[1] where he had given 30 years' faithful service[2] and where he had been induced to accept the receivership by a misrepresentation.[3] The other parties may be allowed their costs out of the estate.[4]

A receiver ought not to apply for a discharge without also asking for further consideration of the action.[5] Accordingly if he fails to ask for further consideration and brings a separate application for discharge he will be refused the costs of the application.[6]

---

9 *Smith v Vaughan* (1744) Ridg temp H 251.
10 *Parsons v Mather & Platt Ltd* (9 December 1974, unreported) CA Court Judgments (Civil Division) No 392A.
11 *Richardson v Ward* (1822) 6 Madd 266.
12 *Cox v M'Namara* (1847) 11 I Eq R 356.
13 *Smith v Vaughan* (1744) Ridg temp H 251.
14 *Cox v M'Namara* above.
15 *Richardson v Ward* above.
16 *Constable v Constable* (1850) 2 Ir Jur 141.
17 *Cox v M'Namara* above.
18 *Parsons v Mather & Platt Ltd* above.
19 *Richardson v Ward*; *Constable v Constable* above.
20 *Constable v Constable* supra; *Hunter v Pring* (1845) 8 I Eq R 102; *Simpson v Simpson* (1856) 2 VLT 198.
1 *Richardson v Ward* above.
2 *Cox v M'Namara* (1847) 11 I Eq R 356.
3 *Hunter v Pring* (1845) 8 I Eq R 102.
4 *Simpson v Simpson* above.
5 *Stilwell v Mellersh* (1851) 20 LJ Ch 356.
6 (1851) 20 LJ Ch 356.

PROCEDURE

Any application for the discharge of a receiver was formerly made by summons in the action,[7] although on the footing that anything you could do by summons you can do by motion[8] such an application might be made by motion. The additional expense of a motion militated against that procedure and unless there were some particular or peculiar reason for bringing the matter before a judge an applicant by motion ran the risk of being penalised in relation to the additional costs by having to bear them himself.[9] Under the new rules an application notice replaces the summons. Sometimes it is unnecessary to issue any fresh application, for example an order for discharge might be made on the further consideration of the action. No special application is necessary where further consideration is looming and the costs of an unnecessary application for discharge in such a case may be disallowed.[10]

The application notice, if appropriate, must be addressed to and served upon the receiver and all parties who are before the court.[11] It should be supported by all necessary and relevant evidence giving the reason for discharge being sought.[12]

While the receiver should be served with the application notice[13] he should not be made a party to the application unless some allegation of impropriety or misconduct is made against him.[14] In those circumstances, and in those circumstances alone, he is *entitled* to appear. Otherwise he is not entitled to appear and if nevertheless he does he will be disallowed his costs of appearing.[15] When the application is prompted by the wilful default of the receiver he may be made to pay the costs of the application, of his own discharge and of the appointment of his successor.[16]

The order if conditional in form is produced to the master who once he is satisfied that its conditions have been complied with indorses a direction that the security be vacated. The order is then produced in the Queen's Bench Division to the Action Department at the Central Office and the guarantee is delivered to the solicitor on his receipt with a vacating note indorsed.[17] In the Chancery Division

---

7 For a form of summons to discharge, see 33 *Court Forms* (1997 Issue) 146, Form 44 (discharge and vacation of the security).

8 'Tomlin J a great master of Chancery procedure, used to say that anything you could do by summons you could do by motion. But the converse is not true' *Heywood v BDC Properties (No 2)* [1964] 1 WLR 971 at 974, CA.

9 Cf *Stilwell v Mellersh* (1851) 20 LJ Ch 356 at 362.

10 *Stilwell v Mellersh* (1851) 20 LJ Ch 356; *Tewart v Lawson* (1874) LR 18 Eq 490.

11 *A-G v Haberdashers' Co* (1838) 2 Jur 915.

12 For a form of affidavit, see 33 *Court Forms* (2nd edn 1997 Issue) 146, Form 45 (application by incapacitated receiver).

13 *A-G v Haberdashers' Co* (1838) 2 Jur 915; *Herman v Dunbar* (1857) 23 Beav 312. The suggestion that *service* is not necessary except in 'default' cases made by Jessel MR in *General Share and Trust Co v Wettey Brick and Pottery Co* (1882) 20 Ch D 260 at 267, CA perhaps goes too far.

14 *Lane v Townsend* (1852) 2 I Ch R 120; *Herman v Dunbar* above.

15 *Herman v Dunbar* above.

16 *Re St George's Estate* (1887) 19 LR Ir 566.

17 See 33 *Court Forms* (2nd edn 1997 Issue) 87 para 21.

the Receivership Officer has a similar procedure for endorsing a certificate as to discharge to enable the guarantee to be cancelled.[18]

Where a receiver applies for his discharge he is not allowed the costs of the application[19] unless there is very good reason for it. In *Stilwell v Mellersh*[20] the receiver presented a petition to be discharged to come on with the cause on further directions. The court would have made the order on further directions without any such petition so, not surprisingly, he was refused his costs. On the other hand in *Richardson v Ward*[1] the receiver was exceptionally allowed the costs of his application to be discharged having become medically unfit: his eyesight had been affected, he suffered from giddiness and impaired memory and his condition was becoming aggravated by his office.

Moreover as a general rule a receiver is not allowed the costs incidental to his own removal and the appointment of a new receiver. In *Cox v M'Namara*[2] the receiver had performed such sterling service that no one opposed his application to be discharged and for a reference to appoint a new receiver. The receiver had been acting for 30 years and had produced his final account and paid in the balance found due by him. In consideration of his long service he asked that he should not be charged with the costs consequent on his discharge. Cusack Smith MR said[3] that after having acted for so many years and paid in his balance, it would be hard to charge the receiver his costs. He was not prepared to give him the costs of the motion 'but would not charge him with the costs of his removal and of the appointment of the new receiver, *which in strictness he was bound to pay*'.[4]

The usual way for the application for discharge of a receiver to be made is by the parties to the action. The receiver will be served with notice of the application but being a mere officer of the court, as he was described by Sir John Romilly MR in *Herman v Dunbar*,[5] he ought not to appear and if he does his costs will be disallowed.

Where a receiver is discharged owing to gross dereliction of duty he may be ordered to pay the costs of the application to secure his discharge, and of his own discharge and of appointing his successor.[6]

CONSEQUENCES OF DISCHARGE

An order discharging a receiver puts an end to his right to receive but does not put an end to his liability to account.[7] If he has not submitted his final account and

---

18 See 33 *Court Forms* (2nd edn 1997 Issue) 87 para 21.
19 *Cox v M'Namara* (1847) 11 I Eq R 356; *Stilwell v Mellersh* (1851) 20 LJ Ch 356 at 362 per Lord Cranworth V-C.
20 (1851) 20 LJ Ch 356.
 1 (1822) 6 Madd 266.
 2 (1847) 11 I Eq R 356.
 3 (1847) 11 I Eq R 356 at 357.
 4 Emphasis added.
 5 (1857) 23 Beav 312 at 313.
 6 *Re St George's Estate* (1887) 19 LR Ir 566.
 7 *Ingham v Sutherland* (1890) 63 LT 614; *Wellesley v Mornington* (1863) 13 I Ch R 559.

paid over the balance shown on it or determined after examination to be due from him, the order discharging him directs him to follow that course. As noted earlier if the order is conditional on the performance of some act by the receiver or some other contingent event the master before indorsing a direction that the guarantee is to be cancelled will satisfy himself that the condition has been complied with.[8]

The discharge does not extinguish the receiver's right to indemnity in respect of his costs and remuneration from over the assets subject to the receivership and the consequent return of those assets to the legal owner is subject to the lien which the discharged receiver continues to have over those assets.[9] The lien exists independently of actual possession or a continuing right to possession of the assets. The court retains control over the question of the indemnity by virtue of its ability to disallow excessive claims or claims arising from improper or misguided actions.[10]

8 See at p 504, supra where the relevant steps are summarised.
9 *Mellor v Mellor* [1992] 1 WLR 517.
10 [1992] 1 WLR 517.

Part 3

Administrators

CHAPTER 35

Application for administrator

ADMINISTRATION PROCEDURE

The administration procedure was introduced to this country by the insolvency legislation following in the wake of the Cork Committee's Report.[1] It supplements existing insolvency procedures including receivership; and indeed it is largely based on insolvency procedures.

The procedure has a close parallel in the appointment of a 'judicial manager' in the company law of South Africa[2] and there are some similarities with the Australian procedure of 'official management',[3] which is not, however, a judicial remedy. Legislation has soon introduced a very similar administration procedure (there described as judicial management) to Singapore,[4] and the Republic of Ireland has also produced a home-grown (and home-honed) statutory equivalent.

It appears from the Cork Report itself that in a significant number of cases companies had been forced into liquidation and potentially viable businesses capable of being rescued had been closed down, for want of a floating charge under which a receiver and manager could have been approved. The choice in such a situation lay between an informal moratorium and a scheme of arrangement under the Companies Acts, neither of which was wholly satisfactory. The proposal was accordingly put forward that in all cases, whether or not there is a floating charge in existence, provision should be made to enable an 'administrator' to be appointed by the court with all the powers normally conferred upon

---

1 (1982) Cmnd 8558, Chapter 9.
2 See generally Cilliers and Benade *Company Law* (4th edn, 1982); David Schrand *Law and Practice of Insolvency Winding up of Companies and Judicial Management* (3rd edn, 1977) 325–346; *Henochsberg on the Companies Act* (4th edn, 1985), Vol 2, 753–782.
3 For an overview, see HAJ Ford *Principles of Corporations Law* (1995 with supplements). For detailed treatment see Paterson Ednie and Ford *Australian Company Law* (3rd edn, Vol 3, Part XI, 82,501–82,629 and *Ryan's Australian Company Practice* CA 20 (Receivers and Managers & Official Management).
4 Singapore Companies Amendment Act 1987 (13 of 1987), s 45 inserts a Part VIIA Judicial Management, ss 227A–227X in Singapore Companies Act (Chapter 185 of Revised Edition). And see Singapore Companies Regulations 1987 SI 38/87 Part V, regs 24–85 in Appendix 3. For discussion of these provisions, see Choong Thung Cheong 'Judicial Management in Corporate Insolvency' (1988) 30 Malaya LR 259–284; Walter Woon and A. Hicks 'The Companies Act of Singapore – An Annotation'; TC Choong and VK Rajah *Judicial Management in Singapore* (1990).

a receiver and manager appointed under a floating charge, including a power to carry on the business of the company.[5]

Under the administration procedure, directors and creditors are given the opportunity to apply for an administrator when a company or a partnership[6] is still solvent but is likely to become insolvent. Directors can thus limit the risks they might otherwise take, by applying for an administration order, and creditors can secure the displacement of the directors by an administrator.

The presentation of the petition freezes the company's position with regard to distress, execution and repossession by creditors.[7] Until an administration order is made on the petition presented or dismissal of the petition no resolution may be passed or order made for the winding up of the company;[8] and no other proceedings or legal process may be commenced or continued against the company or its property except with the leave of the court and subject to such terms as the court may impose.[9] Similarly, pending the making of an order on the petition or dismissal of the petition, no steps may be taken to enforce any security over the company's property or to repossess goods in the company's possession under any hire purchase agreement, except with the leave of the court and subject to such terms as the court may impose.[10]

POWER OF COURT TO MAKE ADMINISTRATION ORDER

Nature of an administration order

An administration order is an order directing that, during the period for which the order is in force, the affairs[11], business and property of the company[12] are to be managed by a person ('the administrator') appointed for the purpose by the court.[13] The court in this context means the court having jurisdiction to wind up the company.[14] It is usual to express a period of three months in the order but an application can be made for extension of the period by the company, though it would be better made by the administrator.[15]

Administration is intended to be a relatively short-term remedy in order to tide the company over a period until either the business run by the company can be sold or the assets can more advantageously be realised.[16]

5 (1982) Cmnd 8558, paras 496–497.
6 *Re Greek Taverna* [1999] BCC 153.
7 IA 1986, s 10.
8 IA 1986, s 10(1)(a).
9 IA 1986, s 10(1)(c). Both execution and the levying of distress are subject to this provision.
10 IA 1986, s 10(1)(b). 'Hire purchase agreement' is given an extended meaning for this purpose: see IA 1986, s 10(4).
11 See *Polly Peck International plc v Henry* [1999] 1 BCLC 407 (pension scheme and the trustee-ship of it were part of the 'affairs' of the company).
12 An administration order may also be made in relation to a partnership and its property: *Re Greek Taverna* [1999] BCC 153.
13 IA 1986, s 8(2).
14 IA 1986, s 251, applying CA 1985, s 744.
15 *Re Newport County Association Football Club Ltd* [1987] BCLC 582, 3 BCC 635.
16 *Re Arrows (No 3)* [1992] BCLC 555 at 560 c–d, per Hoffmann J.

The administration procedure can now be invoked in relation to banks[17] insolvent partnerships[18] and building societies.[19]

Grounds for making an administration order

The court may make an administration order in relation to a company, if it is satisfied that the company is or is likely to become unable to pay its debts,[20] and it considers that the making of such an order would be likely to achieve one or more of the following purposes:[1]

(1)   the survival of the company, and the whole or any part of its undertaking, as a going concern;

(2)   the approval of a voluntary arrangement;[2]

(3)   the sanctioning of a compromise or arrangement between the company and its creditors and members;[3]

(4)   a more advantageous realisation of the company's assets than would be effected on a winding up.[4]

Specifying the purpose

The order must specify the purpose or purposes for which it is made.[5] For that reason the court must consider separately in relation to each purpose relied upon whether the test of likelihood has been satisfied.[6] In *Re Consumer and Industrial Press Ltd*[7] it was said by Peter Gibson J that the court must be satisfied on the evidence before it that at least one of the specified purposes is likely to be achieved before it makes an administration order. Then he added:[8]

---

17 Banks (Administration Proceedings) Order 1989 (SI 1989 No 1276) which disapplies.
18 Insolvent Partnerships Order 1994 (SI 1994 No 2421) art 6 and Sch 2 (there must be actual inability to pay debts and not just likelihood of insolvency. See also *Re Greek Taverna* [1999] BCC 153.
19 See Building Society Act 1997, s 39 (with effect from 1 December 1997).
20 Ie within the meaning given to that expression by IA 1986, ss 123 and 8(1).
 1 IA 1986, s 8(1).
 2 Ie, under IA 1986, Pt I (ss 1–7). Once the moratorium provisions for company voluntary arrangements independent of any administration order contained in the Insolvency Bill 2000 come into force administration orders for the purpose of approving a voluntary arrangement will be likely to go into decline.
 3 Ie, under CA 1985, s 425.
 4 IA 1986, s 8(3). A breakdown of trust and confidence is not enough: *Re Business Properties* (1988) 4 BCC 684.
 5 IA 1986, s 8(3).
 6 *Re SCL Building Services Ltd* (1989) 5 BCC 746 at 747.
 7 [1988] BCLC 177 at 178.
 8 [1988] BCLC 177.

> 'That does not mean that it is merely possible that such purpose will be achieved; the evidence must go further than that to enable the court to hold that the purpose in question will more probably than not be achieved.'

The judge therefore required that on a scale of probability of 0 (impossibility) to 1 (absolute certainty) the likelihood of success should be more than 0.5.

In *Re Harris Simons Construction Ltd*[9] Hoffmann J said that this test set the standard of probability too high. He preferred to hold that the requirements of section 8(1)(b) of the Insolvency Act 1986 are satisfied if the court considers that there is a real prospect that one or more of the stated purposes may be achieved. It may be said, he conceded, that phrases like 'real prospect' lack precision compared with 0.5 on the scale of probability. But the courts are used to dealing in other contexts with such indications of the degree of persuasion they most feel. 'Prima facie case' and 'good arguable case' are well known examples. Such phrases are like tempo markings in music; although there is inevitably a degree of subjectivity in the way they are interpreted, they are nevertheless meaningful and useful.

Both Peter Gibson J[10] and Harman J[11] (who earlier[12] espoused the test laid down by Peter Gibson J in *Re Consumer and Industrial Press Ltd*[13] have expressed themselves content to follow the real prospects test enunciated by Hoffmann J[14] which may now be taken to have carried the day. It is therefore likely that the courts will now unhesitatingly apply the 'real prospects' test.

If in the course of the administration it becomes apparent that further purposes are likely to be achieved, an application may be made under section 18(1) to vary the order by the addition of a further specified purpose, or further specified purposes. Even if satisfied that one or more of the specified purposes is likely to be achieved, the court has a discretion whether or not to make an administration order. In exercising such discretion, the court will consider the benefit which would accrue to secured creditors, although their interests carry less weight than those of other creditors.

PETITION AND ORDER

Application by way of petition

An application to the court for an administration order must be by petition presented either by the company[15] or the directors, or by a creditor or creditors (including any contingent or prospective creditor or creditors), or by all or any of those parties, together or separately.[16] Where a company is or has been carrying

---

9 [1989] BCLC 202 at 203H–204G; followed by Vinelott J in *Re Primalaks UK Ltd* (1989) 5 BCC 710. Cf *Kotzé v Tolryk Bp* 1977 (3) SA 118 (7) at 122 (reasonable *probability*).
10 *Re SCL Building Services Ltd* (1989) 5 BCC 746.
11 *Re Rowbotham Boxter Ltd* [1990] BCC 113.
12 *Re Menlon Trading Ltd* (1988) 4 BCC 455.
13 (1988) 4 BCC 68.
14 *Re Harris Simons Construction Ltd* [1989] BCLC 202.
15 Ie the company acting in general meeting by shareholders' resolution.
16 IA 1986, s 9(1).

on investment business or purporting to do so there is a separate statutory provision outside the Insolvency Act 1986 which empowers a 'recognised self regulating organisation', a 'recognised professional body and the Secretary of State for Trade and Industry, in certain circumstances, to apply for an administration order against it.[17] Where there is an issue as to the standing of the petitioner, the court is not, as in a winding up, bound first just to resolve that debate.[18] A petition by the directors must be presented by all of them acting unanimously[19] unless a duly convened board has resolved to place the company into administration in which case any director may, and indeed is under a duty to, take the necessary steps to carry out the resolution. A petition for an administration order may also be presented by the supervisor of a voluntary arrangement.[20] Such a petition, and indeed a petition by the directors, is to be treated for all purposes as the petition of the company.[1] A supervisor should, it is considered petition in the name of the company.

The court has power to add an administrator to the one proposed by directors and may do so at the request of creditors who appear on the hearing of a directors' petition.[2] In the case of a disagreement between directors and creditors about the identity of the administrator, cost effectiveness and speed are crucial considerations[3]. An existing relationship between the creditor and a proposed appointee is not a bar to the latter accepting the appointment:[4] his prior information may give him an advantage. Joint appointments involving pension-free separate firms may incur expenses and joint appointments, though desirable as in many cases, ought probably to be avoided whenever possible.[5]

Form of petition

There is a prescribed form of petition for an administration order, and the Insolvency Rules 1986 make further provisions concerning the form of the petition.[6]

If presented by the company or by the directors, the petition must state the name of the company and its address for service, which, in the absence of special reasons to the contrary, is that of the company's registered office.[7] If presented by

---

17 Financial Services Act 1986, s 74.
18 *Re MTI Trading Systems Ltd* [1998] 2 BCLC 246, CA (leave to appeal refused).
19 *Re Instrumentation Electrical Services Ltd* (1988) 4 BCC 301; cf *Re Equiticorp International* [1989] BCLC 597 (board resolution). The directors could probably act informally for this purpose even when there is no enabling article as in Table A article 93: see *Charterhouse Investment Trust Ltd v Tempest Diesels Ltd* (1985) 1 BCC 99,554 at 99,551; *Runciman v Walter Runciman plc* [1993] BCC 223 at 240.
20 IA 1986, s 7(4).
1 IR 1986, SI 1986/1925, r 2.4(3).
2 *Re Maxwell Communications Corpn plc* [1992] BCLC 465.
3 [1992] BCLC 465 at 469B. And see *Re Strand Libraries Ltd* (20 May 1996, unreported), Knox J; *Re Structures & Computers Ltd* [1998] BCC 348.
4 *Re Strand Libraries Ltd, supra*.
5 *Re Strand Libraries Ltd, supra*.
6 See IR 1986, rr 2.1, 12.7, Sch 4, Form 2.1 (substituted by SI 1987/1915).
7 IR 1986, r 2.4(1). See 10(1) Court Forms (1999 Issue) 51–52, Form 19.

a single creditor, the petition must state his name and address for service.[8] If the petition is presented by the directors, it must state that it is so presented;[9] but from and after presentation it is to be treated for all purposes as the petition of the company.[10] If the petition is presented by two or more creditors, it must state that it is so presented, naming them; but from and after presentation it is to be treated for all purposes as the petition of one only of them, named in the petition as petitioning on behalf of himself and other creditors; and an address for service for that one must be specified.[11]

The petition must specify the name and address of the person proposed to be appointed as administrator; and it must be stated that, to the best of the petitioner's knowledge and belief, such person is qualified to act as an insolvency practitioner in relation to the company.[12]

Effect of presentation of petition

During the period beginning with the presentation of a petition for an administration order and ending with the making of such an order or the dismissal of the petition:

(1) no resolution may be passed or order made for the winding up of the company;

(2) no steps may be taken to enforce any security over the company's property, or to repossess goods in the company's possession under any hire purchase agreement,[13] conditional sale agreement,[13] chattel leasing agreement[14] or retention of title agreement,[15] except with the leave of the court and subject to such terms as the court may impose; and

(3) no other proceedings and no execution or other legal process may be commenced or continued, and no distress may be levied, against the company or its property except with the leave of the court and subject to such terms as the court may impose.[16]

---

8 IR 1986, r 2.4(2).
9 Ie, under IA 1986, s 9.
10 IR 1986, r 2.4(3).
11 IR 1986, r 2.4(4).
12 IR 1986, r 2.4(5). As to insolvency practitioners and their qualifications, see p 45 supra.
13 'Hire purchase agreement' and 'conditional sale agreement' have the same meanings as in the Consumer Credit Act 1974: IA 1986, s 436.
14 'Chattel leasing agreement' for the bailment (or, in Scotland, the hiring) of goods which is capable of subsisting for more than three months: IA 1986, s 251.
15 'Retention of title agreement' means an agreement for the sale of goods to a company, being an agreement (1) which does not constitute a charge on the goods, but (2) under which, if the seller is not paid and the company is wound up, the seller will have priority over all other creditors of the company as respects the goods or any property representing the goods: IA 1986, s 251.
16 IA 1986, s 10(1), (4). But a winding up petition may still be *presented*: IA 1986, s 10(2)(a). For the position in the case of market charges as defined in CA 1989, s 173 and money market charges as defined in the Financial Markets and Insolvency (Money Market) Regulations 1995, see CA 1989, s 175(1) and Financial Markets and Insolvency (Money Market) Regulations 1995, reg 21 (disapplying IA 1986, s 10(1)(b)).

Nothing in the above provisions requires the leave of the court:

(a)   for the presentation of a petition for the winding up of the company;

(b)   for the appointment of an administrative receiver of the company; or

(c)   for the carrying out by such a receiver, whenever appointed, of any of his functions.[17]

Where a petition for an administration order is presented at a time when there is an administrative receiver of the company, and the person by or on whose behalf the receiver was appointed has not consented to the making of the order, the period mentioned above is deemed not to begin unless and until that person so consents.[18]

A second petition for an administration order would appear to be caught by the provision that 'no other proceedings . . . may be commenced . . . except with the leave of the court'.[19] It has been suggested that directors could, without leave, present a second petition for an administration order specifying a different purpose, for example a more advantageous realisation of assets rather than the approval of a voluntary arrangement.[20] But the express wording already referred to is clear and unequivocal and must, it is submitted, override any possible implications which can otherwise be deduced from the immediately preceding section.[1]

Witness statement in support

Where it is proposed to apply to the court by petition for an administration order to be made in relation to a company, a witness statement must be prepared and signed by the relevant witness, with a view to its being filed in court[2] in support of the petition.[3] In other words, before the petition can be filed, a witness statement in support of the petition must be prepared and signed. An affidavit may be used in the alternative.[4]

Relevant deponents

If the petition is to be presented by the company or by the directors, the witness statement or affidavit must be made by one of the directors, or the secretary of the

---

17   IA 1986, s 10(2). Presumably a winding up petition may be *advertised*: see *Re Manlon Trading Ltd* (1988) 4 BCC 455 considering *Re a Company (No 001992 of 1988)* (1988) 4 BCC 451.

18   IA 1986, s 10(3).

19   IA 1986, s 10(1)(c).

20   Lingard *Corporate Rescues and Insolvencies* (2nd end, 1989) para 916; cf Gordon Stewart *Administrative Receivers and Administrators* (1987) 170 who puts the matter neutrally.

 1   IA 1986, s 9 is said to envisage multiple applications. But subsequent winding up petitions are the subject of express provisions: see IA 1986, ss 10(2)(a), 11(1)(a) and IR 1986, r 2.5(4).

 2   'File in court' means deliver to the court for filing: IR 1986, r 1.24(1).

 3   IR 1986, r 2.1(1). For a witness statement, see 10(1) Court Forms (1999 Issue) 56–58, Form 23.

 4   IR 1986, r 7.57 (as substituted by SI 1999 No 1022 r 3, Schedule).

company, stating himself to make it on behalf of the company or, as the case may be, on behalf of the directors.[5] If the petition is to be presented by creditors, the witness statement or affidavit must be made by a person acting under the authority of them all, whether or not himself one of their number; and in any case there must be stated in the witness statement or affidavit the nature of his authority and the means of his knowledge of the matters to which the witness statement or affidavit relates.[6] If the petition is to be presented by the supervisor of a voluntary arrangement,[7] it is to be treated as if it were a petition of the company.[8]

Contents

The witness statement must state (1) the deponent's belief that the company is, or is likely to become, unable to pay its debts and the grounds of that belief; and (2) which specified purposes[9] are expected to be achieved by the making of an administration order.[10]

In the witness statement or affidavit there must be provided a statement of the company's financial position, specifying, to the best of the deponent's knowledge and belief, assets and liabilities, including contingent and prospective liabilities.[11] Details must be given of any security known or believed to be held by the creditors of the company, and whether in any case the security is such as to confer power on the holder to appoint an administrative receiver; and if an administrative receiver has been appointed, the fact must be stated.[12] If any petition has been presented for the winding up of the company, details of it must be given in the witness statement or affidavit, so far as within the immediate knowledge of the deponent.[13] If there are other matters which, in the opinion of those intending to present the petition for an administration order, will assist the court in deciding whether to make such an order, those matters, so far as lying within the knowledge or belief of the deponent, must also be stated.[14] The necessary witness statement or affidavit calls for full and frank disclosure of those matters which are likely to be relevant at the hearing of the petition. For that reason deliberate concealment of the true position may fatally undermine the application.[15] If an independent report has been prepared for the

---

5 IR 1986, r 2.1(2).
6 IR 1986, r 2.1(3).
7 Ie under IA 1986, Pt I (ss 1–7).
8 IR 1986, r 2.1(4).
9 Those specified in IA 1986, s 8(3).
10 IR 1986, r 2.3(1). See 10(1) Court Forms (1999 Issue) 56, Form 23, para 4.
11 IR 1986, r 2.3(2).
12 IR 1986, r 2.3(3). Where any right to appoint an administrative receiver of a company is conferred by any debenture or floating charge created before 29 December 1986, the conditions precedent to the exercise of that right are deemed to include the presentation of a petition applying for an administration order to be made in relation to the company: IA 1986, s 437, which cross-refers to Sch 11, para 1(1).
13 IR 1986, r 2.3(4).
14 As to the independent report, see infra.
15 *Re West Park Golf & Country Club* [1997] 1 BCLC 20.

company,[16] that fact must be stated; if not, an explanation must be provided why not.[17]

There must be exhibited to the witness statement or affidavit in support of the petition (a) a copy of the petition; (b) a written consent[18] by the proposed administrator to accept appointment, if an administration order is made; and (c) if an independent report has been prepared, a copy of it.[19]

Independent report on company's affairs

There may be prepared, with a view to its being exhibited to the witness statement or affidavit in support of the petition, a report by an independent person[20] to the effect that the appointment of an administrator for the company is expedient.[1] Such a report is not obligatory[2] but its absence may be fatal[3] and for that reason, as already mentioned should be explained.[4] The significance of the independent report has been highlighted in the following judicial observations:[5]

'Such a report, which is of course an objective assessment by persons with no axe to grind (using that phrase non-pejoratively), that is to say by persons not having any reason to wish a particular result or to be optimistic about a particular outcome, is one which very much influences the court, because it is prepared by experienced people who are detached from the emotions raised by failure … and can make a serious and objective assessment of the chances.'

The report may be by the person proposed as administrator, or by any other person having adequate knowledge of the company's affairs, not being a director, secretary, manager, or employee of the company,[6] and it must specify the purposes[7] which, in the opinion of the person preparing it, may be achieved for the company by the making of an administration order.[8]

Filing and withdrawal of petition

The petition and witness statement must be filed in court, with a sufficient number of copies for service and use.[9] Each of the copies delivered to the court

---

16 IR 1986, r 2.3(5).
17 IR 1986, r 2.3(6).
18 For the prescribed form of written consent, see IR 1986, rr 2.4, 12.7, Sch 4, Form 2.2.
19 IR 1986, r 2.4(6). See the next section.
20 See IR 1986. For a form of report see 10(1) Court Forms (1999 Issue) 53–54, Form 21.
 1 IR 1986, r 2.2(1).
 2 IR 1986, r 2.2(1).
 3 *Re W F Fearman Ltd* (1988) 4 BCC 139.
 4 IR 1986, r 2.3(6).
 5 *Re Newport County Association Football Club Ltd* (1987) 3 BCC 635 at 635.
 6 IR 1986, r 2.2(2).
 7 Ie the purposes specified in IA 1986, s 8(3).
 8 IR 1986, r 2.2(3).
 9 IR 1986, SI 1986/1925 as amended by SI 1987/1919, r 2.5(1). As to the number of copies required for service and use, see IR 1986, r 2.6.

must have applied to it the seal of the court and be issued to the petitioner, and on each copy there must be indorsed the date and time of filing.[10] The court must fix a venue for the hearing of the petition and this also must be indorsed on each copy of the petition issued under the above provisions.[11] After the petition is filed, it is the duty of the petitioner to notify the court in writing of any winding up petition presented against the company, as soon as he becomes aware of it.[12]

Where a petition is presented to the court, the petition may not be withdrawn except with the leave of the court.[13] This restriction is designed to discourage irresponsible applications and the use of the procedure to put pressure on a debtor company.

Notice, service and proof of service of petition

Where a petition is presented to the court, notice of the petition must be given forthwith to any person who has appointed, or is or may be entitled to appoint, an administrative receiver of the company.[14] Notwithstanding this requirement that notice of his petition be given to a chargeholder, and the rules which contemplate that copies of the petition shall be served on specified persons[15] and that they and others may appear and be sequestered at the hearing of the petition, the court has, occasionally, been prepared to make an administration order ex parte and even, in cases of extreme urgency, before any petition has been issued.[16] Harman J in *Re Rowbotham Baxter Ltd*[17] described this somewhat helter-skelter procedure as 'an undesirable practice which should not continue':

> 'the danger is that the court hears one side only, the court has not the advantage of adversarial argument to draw its attention to parity which may weigh one way or the other; and this leads . . . to a serious risk of injustice being done.'

Subsequently the same judge, in *Re Cavco Floors Ltd*[18] toned down his criticism somewhat by saying that although it is undesirable for the court to act before presentation of the petition it is a procedure which may need to be adopted in some cases. A person with the power to appoint an administrative receiver should have or be afforded an adequate opportunity to consider whether he wishes to

---

10 IR 1986, r 2.5(2).

11 IR 1986, r 2.5(3).

12 IR 1986, r 2.5(4).

13 IA 1986, s 9(2)(b).

14 IA 1986, s 9(2)(a). The term 'forthwith' here probably means 'as soon as practicable': see *Sameen v Abeyewickrema* [1963] AC 597, [1963] 3 All ER 382, or 'as soon as reasonably practicable': see *Re Seagull Manufacturing Co Ltd (in liquidation)* [1993] Ch 345 at 359. On the term generally, see 45 *Halsbury's Laws* (4th edn) para 1148.

15 IR 1986, r 2.6, 2.9.

16 Against an undertaking by counsel that a petition will be presented in the immediate future.

17 [1990] BCC 113 at 114 expressly approved in *Cornhill Financial Services Ltd v Cornhill Insurance plc* [1992] BCC 818 per Dillon LJ.

18 [1990] BCC 589. For other examples, see *Re Shearing & Loader Ltd* [1991] BCLC 764; *Re Gallidoro Trawlers Ltd* [1991] BCLC 411 and *Re Chancery plc* [1991] BCLC 712 (where hearing was *in camera*).

exercise his power before it is extinguished by the appointment of an administrator.[19] The petitioner must also forthwith after filing the petition give notice of its presentation to any sheriff or other officer who, to his knowledge, is charged with an execution or other legal process against the company or its property, and any person who, to his knowledge, has distrained against the company or its property.[20]

The petition,[1] together with a copy of the evidence in support of it and the documents, other than the copy petition, exhibited to the witness statement or affidavit, must be served:

(1) on any person who has appointed, or is or may be entitled to appoint, an administrative receiver of the company;

(2) if an administrative receiver has been appointed, on him;

(3) if there is pending a petition for the winding up of the company, on the petitioner, and also on the provisional liquidator, if any;

(4) on the person proposed as administrator;[2] and

(5) if the petition for the making of an administration order is presented by creditors of the company, on the company.[3]

The purpose of this provision is to prevent executions and other legal process against the company or distraints being proceeded with in innocent contravention of the statutory prohibition.[4]

Service of the petition must be effected by the petitioner, or his solicitor, or by a person instructed by him or his solicitor, not less than five days before the date fixed for the hearing;[5] and must be effected: (a) on the company, by delivering the documents to its registered office; (b) on any other person, by delivering the documents to his proper address; (c) in either case, in such other manner as the court may direct.[6] For these purposes a person's proper address is any which he has previously notified as his address for service; but if he has not notified any such address, service may be effected by delivery to his usual or last known address.[7] In the case, however, of a person who (1) is an authorised institution or former authorised institution within the meaning of the Banking Act 1987, (2) has appointed, or is or may be entitled to appoint, an administrative receiver of the company, and (3) has not notified an address for service, the proper address is the address of an office of that person where, to the knowledge of the petitioner, the company maintains a bank account or, where no such office is

---

19 *Re a Company (No 00175 of 1987)* [1987] BCLC 467.

20 IR 1986, SI 1986/1925, r 2.6A (added by SI 1987/1919).

1 Ie a copy of the petition issued by the court under IR 1986, r 2.5(2).

2 IR 1986, r 2.6(1), (2) (amended by SI 1987/1919).

3 IR 1986, r 2.6(1), (3).

4 See IA 1986, s 11(3)(d).

5 IR 1986, r 2.7(1). The period of five days may be abridged under r 12.9: *Re a Company (No 00175 of 1987)* [1987] BCLC 467 and *Re Cavco Floors Ltd* [1990] BCLC 940.

6 IR 1986, r 2.7(2).

7 IR 1986, r 2.7(4) (amended by SI 1987/1919).

known to the petitioner, the registered office of that person, or, if there is no such office, his usual or last known address.[8]

If delivery to the company's registered office is not practicable, however, service may be effected by delivery to its last known principal place of business in England and Wales.[9] Delivery of documents to any place may be made by leaving them there, or sending them by first class post.[10]

Service of the petition must be verified by witness statement or affidavit, specifying the date on which, and the manner in which, service was effected.[11] The witness statement or affidavit, with a sealed copy of the petition exhibited to it, must be filed in court forthwith after service, and in any event not less than one day before the hearing of the petition.[12]

Dispensing with service and expedited hearings

The statutory procedure leading to the hearing of an administration petition lays down that notice of the petition must be given to any charge-holder with receiver appointing powers[13] and to such other persons as may be prescribed[14]. In addition the rules envisage that copies of the petition shall be served on specified persons[15]. Those persons and, with the leave or consent of the court, any other person who appears to have an interest justifying his appearance[16] is, under the rules, entitled to appear and be represented on the hearing of the petition[17]. As yet there has been no explicit consideration of what is meant by 'any other person who appears to have an interest justifying his appearance'. The category is defined in language admitting of a flexible meaning. Often there is no objection from the petitioner, though the court may give leave only on terms that the interested persons are to be 'on their own risk as to their own costs'[18]

Leave has been given in various cases to fixed charge receivers appointed before the issue of the petition; to holders of fixed charges; to a landlord owed arrears of rent where a right to forfeit has arisen; to court appointed receivers; to

---

8 Ibid, r 2.7(4) (amended by SI 1987/1919). This is is intended to ensure that notice is given to the company's bank at a place where its account can be most easily traced.

9 Ibid, r 2.7(3).

10 Ibid, r 2.7(5).

11 Ibid, r 2.8(1). For the prescribed form of witness statement of service see rr 1.8(1), 12.7, Sch 4, Form 2.3. See further 10(1) Court Forms (1999 Issue) 58–60, Form 24.

12 Ibid, r 2.8(2).

13 IA 1986 s 9(2) ('any person who has appointed or is entitled to appoint an administrative receiver of the company').

14 IA 1986, s 9(2).

15 IR 1986, r 2.6 (any charge-holders, administrative receiver, petitioner under a pending winding-up petition, any provisional liquidator and the proposed administrator; if the petition is a creditors petition the company has to be served).

16 IR 1986, r 2.9(1)(g).

17 IR 1986, r 2.9.

18 See *Re Rowbotham Baxter Ltd* [1990] BCC 113 at 114E per Harman J (ordinary unsecured creditors). According to the same judge during the hearing of the petition in *Re Land & Property Trust Co plc* in February 1991 this was becoming a settled practice. They will only have to contribute to the costs of other parties if they behave unreasonably.

third parties whose support and co-operation are essential for the proposed administration; and to unsecured creditors.

The mandatory provisions about notice and the entitlement to appear are suggestive of an inflexible rule that service is a pre-condition of any court hearing or order. Nevertheless, the court has, on occasions, been prepared to make an administration order *ex parte* (ie without notice). In cases of extreme urgency an order has even been granted before the petition has been issued or presented, on the undertaking of counsel that a petition will be presented forthwith.[19]

There has been some debate about the propriety of allowing such a helter skelter procedure. Originally Harman J expressed himself with unqualified dogmatism on this practice. In his view as expressed in *Re Rowbotham Baxter Ltd*[20] it was 'an undesirable practice which should not continue'. Then what, it may be asked, was the vice?

> 'The danger is that the court hears one side only, the court has not the advantage of adversarial argument to draw its attention to points which may weigh one way or the other; and this leads . . . to a serious risk of injustice being done.'[1]

On the other hand the same judge later toned down the unqualified nature of his original dictum by saying in *Re Cavco Floors Ltd*[2] that although it is undesirable for the court to act before presentation of the petition that procedure may need to be adopted in some cases. For example in *Re Chancery plc*[3] which involved an authorised institution under the Banking Act 1987 it was necessary to start insolvency proceedings very quickly to avoid a run on the bank. The court made an ex parte order appointing an administrator after a hearing in camera. Where the accelerated procedure is thought desirable the reasons for its adoption should be explained in the evidence put before the court and the petitioner should consider at least the desirability of allowing those parties with an interest to attend.[4]

Hearing of petition

At the hearing of the petition, any of the following may appear to be represented:

(1) the petitioner;

(2) the company;

---

19 See *Re Cavco Floors Ltd* [1990] BCC 589 at 590F-G; and for an earlier case where the undertaking was given, see *Re a Company* (No 001448 of 1989) [1989] BCLC 715 ; cf *Re SCL Building Services Ltd* (1989) 5 BCC 746 (manager appointed until issue of the petition, judge setting return date for hearing thereof).

20 [1990] BCC 113 at 114F.

1 For an example of the potential prejudice to creditors which may ensue from an administration order being granted when it should not have been granted, see *Cornhill Insurance plc v Cornhill Financial Services Ltd* [1992] BCC 818.

2 [1990] BCC 589.

3 [1991] BCC 171.

4 Goldring 'Administrations – Applications and Viability Reviewed in the Light of Recent Developments' [1990] 7 JIBL 284 at 284–285.

(3)   any person who has appointed, or is or may be entitled to appoint, an administrative receiver of the company;

(4)   if an administrative receiver has been appointed, he;

(5)   any person who has presented a petition for the winding up of the company;

(6)   the person proposed for appointment as administrator; and

(7)   with the leave of the court, any other person who appears to have an interest justifying his appearance.[5]

Various categories of person might appear to have an interest justifying their appearance. Secured and unsecured creditors and also contributories are regularly granted leave to be heard on administration petitions, sometimes at their own risk as to costs. As regards contributories, however, if it clear that the company is insolvent on a 'balance sheet' basis and that they would have no interest in an immediate liquidation, the court may decline to hear them at all.[6]

Where the court is satisfied that there is an administrative receiver of the company, the court must dismiss the petition unless it is also satisfied either:

(a)   that the person by whom or on whose behalf the receiver was appointed has consented to the making of the order; or

(b)   that, if an administration order were made, any security by virtue of which the receiver was appointed would be liable to be released or discharged as a transaction at an undervalue or a preference,[7] or be avoided under the provisions relating to the avoidance of floating charges,[8] or be challengeable[9] under any rule of law in Scotland.[10]

Subject to the above provisions, on hearing the petition the court may dismiss it, or adjourn the hearing conditionally or unconditionally, or make an interim order or any other order that it thinks fit.[11] The court has no power to appoint an interim administrator, but it may where appropriate (as where it is satisfied that the assets are in jeopardy) appoint a suitable person to take control of the company and to manage its affairs if the petition for an administration order is adjourned in order to enable the person entitled to appoint an administrative receiver to consider whether he wishes to do so. Once an administrative receiver has been appointed, subject to one proviso,[12] the court is required to dismiss the petition for an administration order. If a person has been appointed to preserve the property of a

---

5   Ibid, r 2.9(1) (amended by SI 1987/1919).

6   *Re Chelmsford City Football Club (1980) Ltd* [1991] BCC 133.

7   Ie under IA 1986, ss 238–240: see pp 214–218.

8   Ie under IA 1986, s 245: see p 218.

9   Ie under IA 1986, s 242 (gratuitous alienation) or s 243 (unfair preference) or any rule of law in Scotland.

10   IA 1986, s 9(3).

11   IA 1986, s 9(4). If the petition was presented reasonably on advice from an insolvency practitioner, the costs of the application may be costs in winding up: *Re Gosscott (Groundworks) Ltd* [1988] BCLC 363.

12   *Re a Company (No 00175 of 1987)* [1987] BCLC 467.

company, the administrative receiver may apply to the court to accelerate the hearing of the petition in order to dismiss it if he wishes to take immediate possession of the assets; alternatively, the order appointing the person to manage the affairs of the company may be framed to endure until the hearing of the adjourned petition, or the earlier appointment of an administrative receiver.[13]

Petitions for administration orders or applications for interim orders upon such a petition must be made direct to the judge and, unless otherwise ordered, must be heard in open court.[14]

Without prejudice to the generality of the court's powers on hearing the petition, an interim order may restrict the exercise of any powers of the directors or of the company, whether by reference to the consent of the court or of a person qualified to act as an insolvency practitioner in relation to the company or otherwise.[15] If the court makes an administration order, the costs of the practitioner, and of any person appearing whose costs are allowed by the court, are payable as an expense of the administrator.[16]

Notice of administration order

If the court makes an administration order, it must forthwith give notice[17] to the person appointed as administrator.[18] Two sealed copies of the order must be sent by the court to the administrator.[19] If the court makes any other order,[20] it must give directions as to the persons to whom, and how, notice of it is to be given.[1]

The administrator is also duty bound to advertise and give notice of the order to certain specified people once the order has been made.

Notification of administration order

Every invoice, order for goods or business letter which, at a time when an administration order is in force in relation to a company, is issued by or on behalf of the company or the administrator, being a document on or in which the company's name appears, must also contain the administrator's name and a statement that the affairs, business and property of the company are being managed by the administrator.[2] If default is made in complying with this

---

13 IA 1986, s 9(3).
14 *Practice Direction* [1987] 1 All ER 107, [1987] 1 WLR 53.
15 IA 1986, s 9(5).
16 IR 1986, r 2.9(2).
17 For the prescribed form of notice to the administrator of an administration order, see ibid, rr 2.10, 12.7, Sch 4, Form 2.4A (added by SI 1987/1919).
18 IR 1986, r 2.10(1).
19 Ibid, r 2.10(4). One of these copies must be sent by the administrator to the registrar of companies in accordance with IA 1986, s 21(2): IR 1986, r 2.10(4).
20 Ie under IA 1986, s 9(4).
 1 IR 1986, r 2.10(5).
 2 IA 1986, s 12(1).

provision, the company and any of the following persons who without reasonable excuse authorises or permits the default, namely the administrator and any officer[3] of the company, are liable on summary conviction to a fine not exceeding one-fifth of the statutory maximum.[4]

Effect of administration order

On the making of an administration order, any petition for the winding up of the company must be dismissed, and any administrative receiver of the company must vacate office;[5] and where an administration order has been made, any receiver of part of the company's property must vacate office on being required to do so by the administrator.[6]

Where at any time an administrative receiver of the company has vacated office under these provisions, or a receiver of part of the company's property has vacated office on the requirement of the administrator, (1) his remuneration and any expenses properly incurred by him, and (2) any indemnity to which he is entitled out of the assets of the company, constitute a charge on and, subject to certain limitations,[7] must be paid out of any property of the company which was in his custody or under his control at that time in priority to any security held by the person by or on whose behalf he was appointed.[8] Neither an administrative receiver nor a receiver who so vacates office is required on or after so vacating office to take any steps for the purpose of complying with any duty imposed on him[9] to pay preferential creditors.[10]

During the period for which an administration order is in force:

(1) no resolution may be passed or order made for the winding up of the company;

(2) no administrative receiver of the company may be appointed;

(3) no other steps may be taken to enforce any security[11] over the company's property, or to repossess goods in the company's possession under any hire purchase agreement,[12] conditional sale agreement,[12] chattel leasing agree-

---

3 For the meaning of 'officer', see CA 1985, s 744; IA 1986, s 251; and IR 1986, r 1.30(2).
4 IA 1986, ss 12(2), 430 and Sch 10.
5 IA 1986, s 11(1).
6 IA 1986, s 11(2).
7 See IA 1986, s 11(3). For the position in the case of market charges as defined in CA 1989, s 173 and money market charges as defined in the Financial Markets and Insolvency (Money Market) Regulations 1995, see CA 1989, s 175(1) and Financial Markets and Insolvency (Money Market) Regulations 1995, reg 21 (disapplying IA 1986, s 11(3)(c)).
8 IA 1986, s 11(4).
9 See IA 1986, ss 40 and 59.
10 IA 1986, s 11(5).
11 'Security' means, in relation to England and Wales, any mortgage, charge lien or other security: IA 1986, s 248.
12 For the meaning of 'hire purchase agreement' and 'conditional sale agreement' see IA 1986, s 436 referring in effect to definitions in Consumer Credit Act 1974, s 189(1).

ment[13] or retention of title agreement,[14] except with the consent of the administrator or the leave of the court and subject, where the court gives leave, to such terms as the court may impose; and

(4)   no other proceedings and no execution or other legal process may be commenced or continued, and no distress may be levied, against the company or its property except with the consent of the administrator or the leave of the court and subject, where the court gives leave, to such terms as the court may impose.[15]

Moratorium on enforcement, not destruction, or rights

The prohibition does not affect the substantive rights of the parties: it simply goes to procedure. It imposes a moratorium on the enforcement of creditors' rights but does not destroy those rights. The legal right of a person holding security to enforce his security, and the right of an owner of goods to possession of his goods, and the causes of action based on those rights remain vested in that party. Consent by the administrator or the leave of the court do not change the rights themselves. The consent or leave given simply releases the applicant's rights from baulk and grants him liberty to enforce them.[16]

A proceeding started without consent or leave is not a nullity and such a proceeding may therefore be stood over or adjourned while the relevant consent or leave is obtained.[17]

Taking steps

The prohibition on taking any other steps, either to enforce any security over the company's property or to repossess goods in the company's possession under any hire purchase agreement comprises several component parts.

The taking of steps does not necessarily involve some positive action. The expression is wide enough to include a refusal of a purely negative nature. Thus passive retention relying on a possessory lien is taking a step to enforce the security (namely the lien).[18]

---

13   For the meaning of 'chattel leasing agreement' see IA 1986, s 251 (agreement for bailment of goods capable of subsisting for more than three months).

14   For the meaning of 'retention of title agreement' see ibid.

15   IA 1986, ss 10(4), 11(3). Proceedings means creditors' proceedings to enforce their debts: *Air Ecosse Ltd v Civil Aviation Authority* (1987) 3 BCC 492, 1987 SLT 751 (application by competitor of airline subject to administration order to Civil Aviation Authority to revoke airline's licence held not to constitute 'other proceedings' or 'other legal process' against the company).

16   *Barclays Mercantile Business Finance Ltd v Sibec Developments Ltd* [1992] 1 WLR 1253, [1993] BCC 148.

17   *Carr v British International Helicopters Ltd* [1993] BCC 855.

18   *Re Paramount Airways Ltd* [1990] BCC 130 at 150–151; *Euro Commercial Leasing Ltd v Cartwright and Lewis* [1995] 2 BCLC 618 (solicitors' lien).

Enforcement

It has been said 'that there is no legal reason why the same act should not have a dual effect as being both the perfection of the security and a step taken to enforce it.'[19] This assertion, proceded without any reference to authority, was at the heart of the decision in *Re Paramount Airways Ltd*[20] where the exercise of the statutory power to detain aircraft for unpaid charges was held to constitute perfection of the charge and a step in its enforcement. Yet the assertion seems debateable. Until a security is created it cannot be enforced. But a reassertion of a right of detention a bare scintilla (or split second) of time after the first act of detention will amount to steps taken to enforce the security and as such will require the consent of the administrator or the leave of the court.

Security

The statutory definition of security in relation to England and Wales is curiously circular: it means 'any mortgage charge lien or other security'.[1] At the root of this definition is the notion of the creation of a proprietary right in assets belonging to the debtor in order to secure the discharge of the debtor's obligation to the creditor.[2] The owner's rights under a conditional sale, chattel leasing or retention of title agreement are included within this definition[3] which is certainly not exhaustive and so is a pledge. And the statutory right of an airport under the Civil Aviation Act 1982 to detain an aircraft for failure to pay outstanding aircraft charges is a 'lien or other security'.[4]

In *Re Exchange Travel Agency Ltd*[5] Harman J adopted a purposive construction of the words 'or other security' and held that a landlord's right of re-entry on non-payment of rent was 'security'.[6] In another case the Court of Appeal assumed obiter the same thing.[7] However Lightman J in *Razzaq v Pala*,[8] which involved a tenant in a bankruptcy case, also expressly commented on the cognate administrator provision[9] and said that the scheme of the Act confirmed that the word 'security' was used in its strict legal sense so that it could not include a right of re-entry. Neuberger J reached a similar conclusion in *Re Lomax Leisure Ltd*.[10]

---

19 *Re Paramount Airways Ltd* [1990] BCC 130 at 152A–B per Browne-Wilkinson V-C.
20 [1990] BCC 130.
 1 IA 1986, s 248(b).
 2 See *Bristol Airport plc v Powdrill* [1990] Ch 744 at 760D–E sub nom *Re Paramount Airways Ltd* [1990] BCC 130 at 149A–B. .
 3 IA 1986, s 10(4).
 4 Under IA 1986, s 248(b): see *Bristol Airport plc v Powdrill* [1990] Ch 744 sub nom *Re Paramount Airways Ltd* [1990] BCC 130.
 5 [1991] BCC 341.
 6 *Re Park Air Services plc* [1997] 3 All ER 193, CA.
 7 *Doorbar v Alltime Securities Ltd* [1996] 1 WLR 456, CA.
 8 [1998] BCC 66.
 9 IA 1986, s 11(3)(c).
10 [2000] BCC 352.

The enforcement of 'market charges'[11] is not subject to the prohibition because the insolvency legislation is disapplied to market charges and market contracts.[12]

The company's property

The relevant statutory definition of property for present purposes defined property as follows:

> 'property includes money, goods, things in action, land and every description of property wherever situated, and also obligations and every description of interest, whether present or future or vested or contingent, arising out of or incidental to property.'

One may readily agree with the judicial observation that 'it is hard to think of a wider definition of property.'[13]

Aircraft held under a seven-year lease has been held to be property of the lessee within this definition because the chattel lease was of a kind that was specifically enforceable and thus conferred on the lessee an equitable interest in the aircraft in favour of the company.[14]

Goods in the company's possession under a hire purchase agreement

The restriction on recovery of goods falling under this rubric raises questions as to whether there are goods in the company's possession and whether that possession is under a hire purchase agreement. The expression 'hire purchase agreement' is expressly enlarged to include a conditional sale chattel leasing or retention of title agreement.[15] Goods may remain in the company's possession for this purpose notwithstanding subleases of those goods.[16] Their physical location in such a case is irrelevant.[17] Nor is it necessary that the hire purchase agreement should still be in existence: it is enough that the relevant possession is attributable to or originated in a hire purchase agreement.[18]

---

11 As defined in CA 1989, s 173.

12 See CA 1989 s 175 and Financial Markets and Insolvency Regulations 1991, SI 1991/880.

13 *Bristol Airports plc v Powdrill* [1990] Ch 744 at 759D–E sub nom *Re Paramount Airways Ltd* [1990] BCC 130 at 148.

14 *Bristol Airways plc v Powdrill* [1990] Ch 744 sub nom *Re Paramount Airways Ltd* [1990] BCC 130. *Sed quaere*. See RM Goode *Proprietary Rights and Insolvency in Sale Transactions* (2nd edn, 1987) 7 and Swadling in Palmer and McKendrick *Interests in Goods* (504–508) 17–22.

15 IA 1986, s 10(4).

16 *Re Atlantic Computer Systems plc* [1992] Ch 505, [1990] BCC 859, CA.

17 *Re Atlantic Computer Systems plc* [1992] Ch 505 at 532B–C.

18 *Re David Meek Plant Ltd; Re David Meek Access Ltd* [1993] BCC 175.

Other proceedings, execution, other legal process and distress

(a) Proceedings

In their present context 'proceedings' means legal or quasi-legal proceedings such as arbitration[19] and not steps generally of a legal nature that may be taken against the company, or in relation to its contracts or property.[20] It is thought, however, that such proceedings should be proceedings pending in a court in Great Britain.[1] An application for extension of time for the registration of a charge granted by a company which has gone into administration cannot legitimately be described as 'proceedings *against* the company or its property'.[2]

A complaint or application to an industrial tribunal under employment protection legislation, as for example a complaint of unfair dismissal or unfair selection for redundancy, is within the ambit of the restriction and cannot be prosecuted without the consent of the administrator or the court.[3] It would however be a rare case where consent could justifiably be refused.[4]

Distress which has been held to be a continuing process[5] has also been to be a restrainable 'proceeding' in a voluntary winding up.[6] A distress commenced before the presentation of an administration petition or the making of an administration order would therefore probably rank as 'other proceedings' and likewise be caught by the restriction. A distress levied after the making of an administration order or the presentation of an administration petition is expressly covered by the statutory prohibition.

The prohibition is not confined to proceedings brought by creditors of the company: it applies to actions brought by competitors.[7]

(b) Execution

No execution may be commenced or proceeded with after the making of an administration order.

(c) Other legal process

In *Re Paramount Airways Ltd*[8,9] the Court of Appeal rejected the proposition that the service of a counter-notice claiming a new tenancy under the Landlord and Tenant Act 1954 making time of the essence of a contract or the acceptance of a

---

19 *Re Paramount Airways Ltd* [1990] BCC 130 at 139D. And see *A Straume (UK) Ltd v Bradlor Developments Ltd* [2000] BCC 333 (statutory adjudication scheme).
20 *Re Paramount Airways Ltd* [1990] BCC 130 at 153G–H rejecting the wider test enunciated by Harman J at 139D.
 1 In liquidation cases the term 'proceedings' is given that limited construction.
 2 *Re Barrow Borough Transport Ltd* [1990] Ch 227.
 3 *Carr v British International Helicopters Ltd* [1993] BCC 855.
 4 [1993] BCC 855.
 5 *Re Memco Engineering Ltd* [1985] BCLC 424.
 6 See *Re Herbert Berry Associates Ltd* (1977) 52 TC 113.
 7 *Biosource Technologies Inc v Axis Genetics plc* [2000] 1 BCLC 286.
 8 [1990] BCC 130 at 153G–H.
 9 [1990] BCC 130 at 153G–H.

repudiatory breach could be classified as a 'proceeding'. The question in *Re Olympia & York Canary Wharf Ltd*[10] was whether the service of a notice making time of the essence of a contract or the acceptance of a repudiatory breach, whether committed before or after the presentation of the petition or the making of the order, represented an 'other legal process'. Millett J answered this question in the negative. A legal process was one requiring the assistance of the court.[11]

(d) Levying distress

During the period for which an administration order is in force no distress may be levied against the property of the company without the relevant consent or leave. This is the express wording dealing with levying of distress after the making of an administration order.

Principles governing the granting of leave

The court has a discretion whether or not to grant leave in any particular case but the statutory provisions provide no express guidance on how that discretion is to be exercised.

Certainly it was early on established that an application for leave must be approached by balancing the interests of secured and unsecured creditors.[12] However in *Re Atlantic Computer Systems plc*[13] the Court of Appeal in the interests of administrators and holders of security and other proprietary rights laid down various more general guidelines, while retaining for the courts a flexibility of approach commensurate with the almost infinite variety of circumstances with which they may be faced.[14]

The main features of these guidelines (which may also give some help to the court in exercising its jurisdiction to grant leave to commence proceedings[15]) may be summarised as follows:[16]

(1) The applicant for leave must always make out a case: the burden of proof is on him to show that it is a proper case for leave to be given.

(2) If granting leave to an owner of land or goods to exercise his proprietary rights as lessor and repossess his land or goods is unlikely to impede the achievement of the purpose of the administration, leave should normally be given.

---

10 [1993] BCC 866.
11 And see *A Straume (UK) Ltd v Bradlor Developments Ltd* [2000] BCC 333.
12 *Re Meesan Investment Ltd* (1988) 4 BCC 788, *sub nom Royal Trust Bank v Buchler* [1989] BCLC 130.
13 [1992] Ch 505.
14 Ibid at 632 per Nicholls LJ. See, for example, *A Straume (UK) Ltd v Bradlor Developments Ltd* [2000] BCC 333.
15 *Re Polly Peck International plc (in administration) (No 4)* [1997] 2 BCLC 630.
16 For a more intersprinkled discussion see Gough *Company Charges* (2nd edn) 961–965 which details the various cases supporting each guideline.

(3)   In other cases where a lessor seeks possession, the court has to carry out a balancing exercise, weighing the legitimate interests of the lessor against those of the company's other creditors.

(4)   In carrying out this balancing exercise, great importance is normally to be given to the lessor's proprietary interests: an administration for the benefit of unsecured creditors should not be conducted at the expense of those who have proprietary rights.

(5)   It will normally be a sufficient ground for the grant of leave that significant loss would be caused to others by the grant of leave, that may outweigh the loss to the lessor caused by a refusal, the relevant losses being assessed in each case by reference to all the circumstances and in particular to the factors set out in (6)–(8) following.

(6)   In assessing relative losses the courts will have regard to matters such as the financial position of the company; rent arrears and the ability to pay continuing rents; the administrator's proposals; the period for which the administration order has been in force and is expected to remain in force; the effect on the administration if leave were given and on the applicant if leave were refused; the end result sought to be achieved by the administration; the prospects of that result being achieved; and the history of the administration to date.

(7)   In assessing relative losses the courts will have regard to the degree of probability of loss ranging from the virtually certain to the relatively remote.

(8)   Again in assessing relative losses the court will have regard to the conduct of the parties.

(9)   The preceding considerations may be relevant not only to the decision whether or not to grant leave, but also to a decision to impose terms if leave is granted.

(10)   The court may, in effect, impose conditions if leave is refused and the preceding considerations may be relevant to that decision.

(11)   A broadly similar approach will apply in many applications for leave to enforce a security where for example adequacy of the security may have a bearing on how prejudicial delay is thought to be.

(12)   It is not for the court on a leave application to seek to adjudicate on the existence, validity or nature of the security which the applicant is seeking leave to enforce: it is enough if the applicant has a seriously arguable case.

CHAPTER 36

Appointment and status, duties and powers

Appointment

The administrator of a company must be appointed by an administration order[1] or by a court order made to fill a vacancy in the office of administrator occurring by death, resignation or otherwise.[2] Where an administration order is made in relation to a company, the administrator must be a person who is qualified to act as an insolvency practitioner in relation to the company.[3]

The statute makes it plain that one or more persons may be appointed joint administrators. Where an appointment of a person to the office of administrator relates to more than one person or has the effect that the office is to be held by more than one person, the appointment must declare whether any act required or authorised under any enactment to be done by the administrator is to be done by all or any one of the persons for the time being holding the office of administrator.[4]

Status

In exercising his powers, the administrator is deemed to act as the company's agent,[5] and the acts of an individual as administrator of a company are valid notwithstanding any defect in his appointment, nomination or qualification.[6]

A third party dealing with an administrator would normally be protected by the rules of agency. But it is provided that persons dealing with an administrator in good faith and for value are not concerned to enquire whether the administrator is acting within his powers.[7]

---

1 IA 1986, s 13(1). For forms of order, see 10(1) Court Forms (1999 Issue) 65–67, Forms 29 and 30.
2 IA 1986, s 13(2).
3 IA 1986, s 230.
4 IA 1986, s 231.
5 IA 1986, s 14(5).
6 IA 1986, s 232.
7 IA 1986, s 14(6).

DUTIES

Notification duties following administration order

Where an administration order has been made, the administrator must forthwith send to the company a notice of the order and within 28 days after the making of the order, unless the court otherwise directs, send such a notice to all creditors of the company, so far as he is aware of their addresses.[8]

The administrator must also forthwith give notice of the making of the order:

(1) to any person who has appointed, or is or may be entitled to appoint, an administrative receiver of the company;

(2) if an administrative receiver has been appointed, to him;

(3) if there is pending a petition for the winding up of the company, to the petitioner, and also to the provisional liquidator, if any; and

(4) to the registrar of companies.[9]

Forthwith after the order is made, the administrator must also advertise its making once in the Gazette,[10] and once in such newspaper as he thinks most appropriate for ensuring that the order comes to the notice of the company's creditors.[11]

Where an administration order has been made, the administrator must also, within 14 days after the making of the order, send an office copy of the order to the registrar of companies and to such other persons as may be prescribed.[12]

If the administrator without reasonable excuse fails to comply with the above provisions, he is liable on summary conviction to a fine not exceeding one-fifth of the statutory maximum and, on conviction after continued contravention, to a daily default fine not exceeding one-fiftieth of the statutory maximum.[13]

General duties

The administrator of a company must on his appointment, take into his custody or under his control all the property to which the company is or appears to be

---

8 IA 1986, s 21(1).

9 IA 1986, s 21(2); IR 1986, SI 1986/1925, r 2.10(3) (amended by SI 1987/1919). For the prescribed form of notice of an administration order to be given to the registrar of companies, see rr 2.10, 12.7, Sch 4, Form 2.6.

10 In IR 1986 'the Gazette' means the London Gazette: IR 1986, rr 13.1, 13.13(4). In IA 1986 'the Gazette' means, except insofar as the context otherwise requires, the London Gazette, as respects companies registered in England and Wales; and the Edinburgh Gazette, as respects companies registered in Scotland: s 251, applying the Companies Act 1985, s 744.

11 IA 1986, s 21(1); IR 1986, r 2.10(2). For the prescribed form of notice of an administration order for newspapers, see rr 2.10, 12.7, Sch 4, Form 2.5 (substituted by SI 1987/1919). See further 10(1) Court Forms (1999 Issue) 267, Form 32.

12 IA 1986, s 21(2). For the prescribed form to be sent to the registrar of companies attaching the office copy of the administration order, see IR 1986, rr 2.10, 12.7, Sch 4, Form 2.7.

13 IA 1986, ss 21(3), 430, and Sch 10.

entitled;[14] and he must manage the affairs, business and property of the company at any time before proposals have been approved,[15] with or without modifications, in accordance with any directions[16] given by the court, and at any time after proposals have been so approved, in accordance with those proposals as from time to time revised, whether by him or a predecessor of his.[17]

The power to manage the affairs property and business of the company includes the power to sell the entire undertaking[18] of the company or a single asset[19] of the company in absence of any creditors' meeting if he considers that such a course is in the best interests of the company and its creditors and that he does not require the sanction of the court to do so. But since a premature disposal of the company's undertaking robs the creditors of their opportunity to consider the administrator's proposals and so frustrates the purpose of the Act,[20] it would be imprudent for an administrator to proceed with the sale of any substantial part of the assets without taking the precaution of seeking the permission of the court to do so.

The administrator must summon a meeting of the company's creditors if he is requested to do so[1] by one-tenth, in value, of the company's creditors, or if he is directed to do so by the court.[2]

Discharge or variation of administration order

The administrator of a company may at any time apply to the court for the administration order to be discharged or to be varied so as to specify an additional purpose;[3] and he must make such an application if it appears to him that the purpose or each of the purposes specified in the order either has been achieved or is incapable of achievement, or he is required to do so by a meeting of the company's creditors summoned for the purpose.[4] On the hearing of such an application, the court may by order discharge or vary the administration order

---

14 IA 1986, s 17(1). This includes property that is encumbered and property owned by another person but in the possession of the company under a hire purchase agreement or similar agreement: see IA 1986, ss 11 and 15.

15 Ie under IA 1986, s 24.

16 This means the directions if any: see *Re Charnley Davies Ltd* [1990] BCC 605 at 610G–611A.

17 IA 1986, s 17(2). The court has a residual jurisdiction under IA 1986, s 14(3) to authorise an administrator to depart from an approved scheme: *Re Smallman Construction Ltd* (1988) 4 BCC 784.

18 *Re Charnley Davies Ltd (No 2)* [1990] BCC 605 at 610G–611A (reciting Vinelott J's approval of counsel's opinion to that effect on an ex parte application by the administrator under IA 1986, s 14(3) on 21 January 1987); and see *Re P D Fuels Ltd* [1999] BCC 450 (sale of principal asset without sanction of creditors' meeting).

19 *Re N S Distribution Ltd* [1990] BCLC 169.

20 *Re Consumer & Industrial Press Ltd (No 2)* (1987) 4 BCC 72 at 73 per Peter Gibson J.

 1 As to the requisitioning of such a meeting, see p 568 below.

 2 IA 1986, s 17(3). As to meetings of the company's creditors, see p 567 post. As to the administrator's duty to keep creditors informed of what he is proposing, see p 555.

 3 IA 1986, s 18(1). The specified purposes are set out in ibid, s 8(3). The purpose must be an additional and not a *substituted* purpose.

 4 IA 1986, s 18(2). See *Re Charnley Davies Business Services Ltd* (1987) 3 BCC 408.

and make such consequential provision as it thinks fit, or adjourn the hearing conditionally or unconditionally, or make an interim order or any other order it thinks fit.[5] Applications under section 18(3) of the Insolvency Act 1986 must be made direct to the judge and, unless otherwise ordered, must be heard in open court.[6] The only person competent to apply for discharge or variation of the administration order is the administrator himself. However a creditor aggrieved by an administration order can apply to the court[7] to have the order rescinded on the ground that it ought not to have been made.[8]

An example of a variation of the administration order occurred in *Re St Ives Windings Ltd.*[9] The purposes for which the particular administrator had been appointed were (1) the survival of the company as a going concern, or (2) the more advantageous realisation of its assets. The administrator had made proposals for the realisation of the assets and a creditors' meeting had approved the general line of the proposals and also had approved proposals for distribution. The question for the court was whether there was any such power under an administrative order made for those purposes to support or sanction such a distribution in a binding way. Harman J formed the provisional view that there was no power in the court to sanction distributions made by an administrator appointed for the purposes of the order under consideration. But dealing with the matter under the provision concerning applications to *vary* the order, the judge was prepared to approve a variation adding as an additional purpose the approval of a voluntary arrangement. The administrator was thus able to produce a voluntary arrangement capable of sanction by the creditors in the usual way.

Where, on the other hand, the purposes of the administration orders have been achieved and it is desired that the companies involved should be wound up, the appropriate course for the administrators is to apply for the orders to be discharged.

It should be noted that the court has no jurisdiction to order a winding up of the company otherwise than on a petition lodged under the Insolvency Act.[10] It follows that it is not possible for a winding up order to be made on an application for the discharge of an administration order under the section dealing with the discharge of administration orders.[11]

There is no provision for a company to go into voluntary liquidation following the discharge of an administration order though the court could sanction such a course. Where a voluntary winding up is the reason for an application to discharge the administration order, the order for discharge can be made conditional on the passing of the winding up resolution or resolutions,[12] or alternatively by directing that the orders for discharge should not be drawn up until

5 IA 1986, s 18(3). See also *Re Charnley Davies Business Services Ltd* (1987) 3 BCC 408.
6 *Practice Direction* [1987] 1 All ER 107, [1987] 1 WLR 53.
7 Under IR 1986, r 7.47.
8 *Cornhill Insurance plc v Cornhill Finance Services Ltd* [1992] BCC 818 of *Re Sharps of Truro Ltd* [1990] BCC 94 at 95.
9 (1987) 3 BCC 634.
10 (1987) 3 BCC 634. *Re Brooke Marine Ltd* [1988] BCLC 546.
11 (1987) 3 BCC 634. But see now *Re Norditrack (UK) Ltd* [2000] BCC 441.
12 (1987) 3 BCC 634. *Re Powerstore (Trading) Ltd* [1998] 1 BCLC 90 at 94a–b; see further *Re Norditrack (UK) Ltd* [2000] BCC 441.

copies of the resolutions have been lodged in the court office.[13] Equally the court has no power to *direct* the liquidator in the future liquidation to make payments to the creditors in question as if they were preferential creditors.[14] Such a direction was to prevent creditors entitled to preferential payment being disenfranchised by virtue of a different 'relevant date' applying because of the winding up.[15] However, the court has power, derived from statute,[16] and its own inherent power to control an administrator as an officer of the court, to order an administrator to pay the preferential creditors on the same basis as if the winding up was a compulsory winding up or, alternatively, to set up a trust for the benefit of such creditors which will be binding on a future liquidator.[17]

If the administration order is discharged or varied, the administrator must, within fourteen days after the making of the order effecting the discharge or variation, send an office copy of that order to the registrar of companies;[18] and if the administrator without reasonable excuse fails to comply with this requirement, he is liable on summary conviction to a fine not exceeding one-fifth of the statutory maximum and, on conviction after continued contravention, to a daily default fine not exceeding one-fiftieth of the statutory maximum.[19]

Should the administrator intend to apply to the court under the above provisions for the administration order to be discharged at a time before he has sent a statement of his proposals to creditors,[20] he must, at least ten days before he makes such an application, send to all creditors of the company, so far as he is aware of their addresses, a report containing certain specified information.[1]

The court is understandably reluctant to grant a discharge before the creditors have had an opportunity to consider the proposals.[2]

POWERS

General powers

It is expressly provided in the Insolvency Act 1986 that the administrator of a company may do all such things as may be necessary for the management of the

---

13 *Re Powerstore (Trading) Ltd* [1998] 1 BCLC 90; *Re Mark One (Oxford Street) plc* [1998] BCC 984.
14 See IA 1986, s 387(3)(a) and (c).
15 IA 1986, ss 14(3) and 18(3).
16 *Re Mark One (Oxford Street) plc* [1998] BCC 984; and see, for another circumventory solution: *Re Philip Alexander Securities and Futures Ltd* [1998] BCC 819.
17 *Re Mark One (Oxford Street) plc* [1998] BCC 984.
18 IA 1986, s 18(4). For the prescribed forms of notice of discharge or variation of administration order, see IR 1986, r 12.7, Sch 4, Forms 2.19, 2.20 respectively.
19 IA 1986, ss 18(5), 430, and Sch 10.
20 Ie in accordance with ibid, s 23(1).
 1 IR 1986, r 2.16(2) (added by SI 1987/1919). Cf *Re Charnley Davies Business Services Ltd* (1987) 3 BCC 408. The specified information is that set out in IR 1986, r 2.16(1)(a)–(f)(i) (amended by SI 1987/1919).
 2 *Re Consumer & Industrial Press Ltd (No 2)* (1987) 4 BCC 72.

affairs, business and property of the company.[3] Moreover, without prejudice to the generality of that very widely expressed power, which is wide enough to cover the power which directors have, before an administration order is made, to appoint a trustee to an employees' pension scheme,[4] he has the following specified powers:[5]

(1)   power to take possession of, collect and get in the property of the company and, for that purpose, to take such proceedings as may seem to him expedient;

(2)   power to sell or otherwise dispose of the property of the company by public auction or private contract or, in Scotland, to sell, feu, hire out or otherwise dispose of the property of the company by public roup or private bargain;

(3)   power to raise or borrow money and grant security therefor over the property of the company;

(4)   power to appoint a solicitor or accountant or other professionally qualified person to assist him in the performance of his functions;

(5)   power to bring and defend any action or other legal proceedings in the name of and on behalf of the company;[6]

(6)   power to refer to arbitration any question affecting the company;

(7)   power to effect and maintain insurances in respect of the business and property of the company;

(8)   power to use the company's seal;

(9)   power to do all acts and to execute in the name and on behalf of the company any deed, receipt or other document;

(10)   power to draw, accept, make and indorse any bill of exchange or promissory note in the name and on behalf of the company;

(11)   power to appoint any agent to do any business which he is unable to do himself or which can more conveniently be done by an agent and power to employ and dismiss employees;[7]

---

3 IA 1986, s 14(1)(a).
4 *Denny v Yeldon* [1995] 1 BCLC 560; *Polly Peck International v Henry* [1999] 1 BCLC 407.
5 IA 1986, s 14(1)(b).
6 An administrator whose *only* claim to goods arises by virtue of non-registration of a security may not maintain an action for damages for conversion against a party no longer in possession of those goods under this power or under IA 1986, s 234: *Smith v Bridgend County Borough Council* [2000] 1 BCLC 775, CA.
7 There are statutory obligations laid on administrators to consult with representatives of a recognised trade union in the case of proposed dismissals: see Trade Union and Labour Relations (Consolidation) Act 1992, s 188. The existence of the administration is not in itself a special circumstance bringing the reduced consultation obligations into play: *Re Hartlebury Printers Ltd* [1992] BCC 428.

(12) power to do all such things, including the carrying out of works, as may be necessary for the realisation of the property of the company;

(13) power to make any payment which is necessary or incidental to the performance of his functions;

(14) power to carry on the business of the company;

(15) power to establish subsidiaries of the company;

(16) power to transfer to subsidiaries of the company the whole or any part of the business and property of the company;

(17) power to grant or accept a surrender of a lease or tenancy of any of the property of the company, and to take a lease or tenancy of any property required or convenient for the business of the company;

(18) power to make an arrangement or compromise on behalf of the company;

(19) power to call up any uncalled capital of the company;

(20) power to rank and claim in the bankruptcy, insolvency, sequestration or liquidation of any person indebted to the company and to receive dividends, and to accede to trust deeds for the creditors of any such person;

(21) power to present or defend a petition for the winding up of the company;

(22) power to change the situation of the company's registered office;

(23) power to do all things incidental to the exercise of the above powers.[8]

These powers are available to him from the moment of his appointment.[9] But they should not be abused by exercise for a purpose outside the statutory purpose or purposes contained in the order[10] and none of his powers extend to acts which the company itself is not competent to perform.[11]

The administrator also has a power to remove any director of the company[12] and to appoint any person to be a director of it, whether to fill a vacancy or otherwise, and to call any meeting of the members[13] or creditors of the company.[14]

A particularly important power at the disposal of an administrator is the power

---

8 IA 1986, s 14(1), Sch 1. In the application of Sch 1 to the administrator of a company, the words 'he' and 'him' in Sch 1 refer to the administrator: s 14(1). An administrative receiver has the like powers, except insofar as they are inconsistent with any of the provisions of the debentures by virtue of which he is appointed: see s 42(1), Sch 1.

9 See IA 1986, s 13.

10 *Denny v Yelden* [1995] 1 BCLC 560.

11 *Re Home Treat Ltd* [1991] BCC 165.

12 IA 1986, s 14(2)(a). If the removal constitutes a breach of contract the company will be exposed to liability: *Southern Foundries (1926) Ltd v Shirlaw* [1940] AC 701, [1940] 2 All ER 445; *Shindler v Northern Raincoat Co Ltd* [1960] 2 All ER 239, [1960] 1 WLR 1038.

13 For the purposes of any provisions in ibid, Pts I–VII (ss 1–251), a person who is not a member of a company but to whom shares in the company have been transferred, or transmitted by operation of law, is to be regarded as a member of the company; and references to a member or members are to be read accordingly: s 250.

14 IA 1986, s 14(2). As to creditors' meetings, see p 567 below; and as to meetings of members, see IR 1986, r 2.31.

he has to apply to the court[15] for directions in relation to any particular matter arising in connection with the carrying out of his functions.[16]

Pursuant to this power applications have been made for direction in order to obtain rulings on the effectiveness of debt subordination agreements[17] or of payments into a segregated trust account by concession-holders.[18]

Any power conferred on the company or its officers whether by the Insolvency Act 1986 or the Companies Act 1985 or by the memorandum or articles of association, which could be exercised in such a way as to interfere with the exercise by the administrator of his powers, is not exercisable except with the consent of the administrator, which may be given either generally or in relation to particular cases.[19]

In exercising his powers the administrator is deemed to act as the company's agent.[20] However, a person dealing with the administrator in good faith and for value is not concerned to inquire whether the administrator is acting within his powers.[1]

The administrator also has power to make a proposal for a voluntary arrangement in relation to the company[2] and to present a petition for the winding up of the company.[3] But he has no statutory power of disclaimer.[4]

Power to deal with charged property

Unique powers are conferred on an administrator to override the rights of the holder of a security over the company's property or the rights of the owner of property held by the company under a hire purchase or similar agreement, in each case without the consent of the chargee or owner of the property.

The administrator of a company may dispose of or otherwise exercise his powers in relation to any property of the company which is subject to a floating charge[5] as if the property were not subject to the security;[6] and where property is

15 The court having jurisdiction to wind up the company: IA 1986, s 251, applying CA 1985, s 744. The relevant courts are the High Court of Justice and certain county courts: see IA 1986, s 117(2)–(4).

16 IA 1986, s 14(3). As to the mode of application and the procedure see IR 1986, r 7.1–7.10. Applications under s 14(3) must be made direct to a judge and, unless otherwise ordered, must be heard in open court: *Practice Direction* [1987] 1 All ER 107, [1987] 1 WLR 53.

17 *Re British & Commonwealth Holdings plc (No 2)* [1992] 1 WLR 672, [1992] BCC 58 (created by trust deed); *Re Maxwell Communications Corpn plc (No 2)* [1993] 1 WLR 1402, [1993] BCC 369 (created by contract).

18 *Re Lewis's of Leicester Ltd* [1995] BCC 514 (trust, preference or transaction at undervalue was the question).

19 IA 1986, s 14(4).

20 IA 1986, s 14(5).

1 IA 1986, s 14(6).

2 See p 581.

3 See head (21) supra.

4 *Re P & C and R & T (Stockport) Ltd* [1991] BCC 98 at 104.

5 IA 1986, s 15(1) applies to any security which, as created, was a floating charge: s 15(3).

6 IA 1986, s 15(1). For the position in relation to market charges and money market charges as defined in CA 1989, respectively in CA 1989, s 173 and Financial Markets and Insolvency (Money Markets) Regulations 1995, see CA 1989, s 175 and Insolvency (Money Markets) Regulations 1995, reg 21 (disapplying IA 1986, s 15(1)). For an order notwithstanding the objection of a holder of a *fixed* charge: see *Re ARV Aviation Ltd* [1989] BCLC 664.

so disposed of, the holder of the security has the same priority in respect of any property of the company directly or indirectly representing the property disposed of as he would have had in respect of the property subject to the security.[7] Such a disposal may be effected without an order of the court if the security is (or was originally) a floating charge. In other cases the consent of the court is required. The court does not, however, have power to allow administrators to pay the sale proceeds of mortgaged property into a separate account until they have reached a decision whether or not to challenge the validity of the mortgage.[8]

Application by administrator

Where, on an application by the administrator, the court is satisfied that the disposal, with or without other assets, of any property of the company subject to any other security or any goods in the possession of the company under a hire purchase agreement,[9] conditional sale agreement,[9] chattel leasing agreement,[10] or retention of title agreement[11] would be likely to promote the purpose or one or more of the purposes specified in the administration order,[12] the court may by order authorise the administrator to dispose of the property as if it were not subject to the security or to dispose of the goods as if all rights of the owner under any such agreements were vested in the company.[13] Where the administrator so applies to the court for authority to dispose of such property, the court must fix a venue[14] for the hearing of the application, and the administrator must forthwith give notice[15] of the venue to the person who is the holder of the security or, as the case may be, the owner under the agreement.[16]

Conditions

It must be a condition of any such order that the net proceeds of the disposal, and, where those proceeds are less than such amount as may be determined by the court to be the net amount which would be realised on a sale of the property or

---

7   IA 1986, s 15(4).
8   *Re Newman Shop Fitters (Cleveland) Ltd* [1991] BCLC 407.
9   For the meaning of 'hire purchase agreement' and 'conditional sale agreement' see IA 1986, s 436 cross-referring to the Consumer Credit Act 1974.
10 'Chattel leasing agreement' means an agreement for the bailment of goods which is capable of subsisting for more than three months: see IA 1986, s 251.
11 For the meaning of 'retention of title agreement', see IA 1986.
12 IA 1986, s 8(1).
13 Ibid, s 15(2), (9). For the mode of making applications, see IR 1986, rr 7.1–7.10; and see 10(1) Court Forms (1999 Issue) 78–78, Form 39 (application), Form 40 (witness statement in support); disposal before the administrator's proposals have been considered by a creditors' meeting will only be authorised in quite exceptional circumstances: *Re Consumer and Industrial Press Ltd (No 2)* (1987) 4 BCC 72.
14 Date, time and place: IR 1986, rr 13.1, 13.6.
15 See IR 1986, rr 13.1, 13.3–13.5.
16 IR 1986, r 2.51(1), (2).

goods in the open market by a willing vendor, such sums as may be required to make good the deficiency, must be applied towards discharging the sums secured by the security or payable under the agreement.[17] Where a condition so imposed relates to two or more securities, such condition requires that the net proceeds of the disposal and, if applicable, the other sums referred to above, be applied towards discharging the sums secured by those securities in the order of their priorities.[18]

Notification

If such an order is made, the administrator must forthwith give notice of it to the holder of the security or, as the case may be, the owner under the agreement.[19] The court must send two sealed copies of the order to the administrator, who must send one of them to that person or owner.[20] An office copy of the order must, within 14 days after the making of the order, be sent by the administrator to the registrar of companies.[1] However, if the administrator without reasonable excuse fails to comply with this provision, he is liable on summary conviction to a fine not exceeding one-fifth of the statutory maximum and, on conviction after continued contravention, to a daily default fine not exceeding one-fiftieth of the statutory maximum.[2]

Power to ensure continuation of essential supplies by utilities

The administrator has the like powers as an administrative receiver to ensure continuation of supplies of gas, water, electricity and telecommunication services.[3] The effective date for the purposes of the relevant statutory provision is the date of the administration order.[4]

Duty to report on disqualifiable directors

Where it appears to the administrator that the conditions imposing a duty on the court to disqualify unfit directors of insolvent companies are satisfied,[5] the administrator is under a duty to report the matter to the Secretary of State.[6]

---

17 IA 1986, s 15(5).
18 IA 1986, s 15(6).
19 IR 1986, r 2.51(3). For a form of order, see 10(1) Court Forms (1999 Issue) 81–82, Form 41.
20 IR 1986, r 2.51(4).
 1 IA 1986, s 15(7). For the prescribed form of notice to the registrar of companies, see IR 1986, r 12.7, Sch 4, Form 2.18.
 2 IA 1986, ss 15(8), 430 and Sch 10.
 3 See the discussion at pp 108 and 122 above.
 4 IA 1986, s 233.
 5 Ie the conditions contained in the Company Directors Disqualification Act 1986, s 6(1).
 6 CDDA 1986, s 7(3).

Powers to get in the company's property and obtain information

The provision dealing with the getting in of the company's property,[7] the duty of certain persons to co-operate in giving information relating to the company's affairs[8] and the powers of the court to summon persons before it to give information about the company's affairs[9] which apply where the company has gone into liquidation or administrative receivership apply also where an administration order has been made in relation to the company.

Distributions by the administrator

An administrator has power to make any payment which is necessary and incidental to the performance of his functions[10].

He is also empowered to make payments to (among others) employees in order to secure their continued services and to suppliers to ensure continuing supplies in the course of an administration. Moreover he may be directed by the court to make payments to creditors of the company as expenses of the administration[11]. In determining whether or not to direct an administrator to make payments of administration expenses the court has a wide discretion. And it exercises this discretion by taking all the circumstances of the case into account. The words of Nicholls LJ in *Re Atlantic Computers plc*[12] provide useful guidance in this connection:

'Whether those whose land or goods are being used by the company during this interim period should be given leave to enforce their proprietary rights forthwith or should be paid ahead of everyone else must depend upon all the circumstances, which will vary from one case to the next. We do not think that Parliament intended, for example, that if a company's factory or offices are leasehold, and the administrator continues to carry on the business on those premises, the court as a matter of course would always give leave to re-enter, or to distrain in respect of rent accruing from the date of the administration order, or make a direction for the payment of the rent in full as an expense of the administration. Likewise in respect of vehicles or machinery which are in the company's possession under hire purchase agreements and which are being used by a company in the course of carrying on its business. Parliament must have intended, for instance, that in appropriate circumstances, and for a strictly limited period, such a lessor or owner of goods might not be given leave if giving leave would cause disruption and loss out of all proportion to the loss which the lessor or owner of goods would suffer if leave were refused. Indeed, Parliament must have intended that when exercising its discretion the court should have due regard to the property rights of those concerned. But Parliament must also have intended that the court should have regard to all other circumstances, such as the consequences which the grant

7 See IA 1986, s 234. See the discussion in relation to administrative receivers at 109.
8 See IA 1986, s 235.
9 See IA 1986, s 236.
10 IA 1986, s 14(1)(b), Sch 1, para 13.
11 *Re Atlantic Computer Systems plc* [1992] Ch 505, CA.
12 [1992] Ch 505 at 528C–G.

or refusal would have, the financial position of the company, the period for which the administration order is expected to remain in force, the end result sought to be achieved, and the prospects of that result being achieved.'

An administrator has been held entitled, if the assets of the company enable him to do so, to pay off pre-administration creditors in full in order to ensure the survival of the company as a going concernand as a prelude to their own discharge by the court and to the resumption of control by the directors[13]. It is otherwise where the liabilities exceed the value of realised assets: even a partial distribution to creditors against the wishes of dissentient creditors appears in those circumstances to be out of order[14], unless done by means of a voluntary arrangement or a scheme of arrangement under section 425 of the Companies Act 1985. An administrator has no power to distribute to members[15]. It appears that, subject to proper safeguards and undertakings, a payment on account to creditors could be proper if its purpose was to preserve the goodwill of the company's business pending further attempts to secure the survival of the company and its goodwill[16].

ADJUSTMENT OF ANTERIOR AND OTHER TRANSACTIONS

The provisions relating to the adjustment of anterior and other transactions[17] and, in particular, to transactions at an undervalue,[18] preferences,[18] extortionate credit transactions,[19] avoidance of certain floating charges[20] and unenforceability of liens on books[1] which apply when a company has gone into liquidation apply also where an administration order has been made in relation to a company. The administrator also has power to apply to the court for an order in relation to transactions defrauding creditors.[2]

All the foregoing provisions save those concerning the unenforceability of liens on books and transactions defrauding creditors are referred to in relation to the possible invalidation of charges under which receivers or administrative receivers have been appointed.[3]

The administrator will be concerned to see whether he is entitled to challenge any of the transactions entered into by the company prior to the administration order.

---

13 *Re John Slack Ltd* [1995] BCC 1116.
14 *Re St Ives Windings Ltd* (1987) 3 BCC 634 (provisional holding); followed by Vinelott J (who heard no argument to the contrary) in *Re British & Commonwealth Holdings plc (No 3)* [1992] 1 WLR 672 at 674E–G.
15 *Re Business Properties Ltd* (1988) 4 BCC 684 at 686, Harman J.
16 *Re Mount Banking plc* (25 January 1993, unreported) Ferris J.
17 See IA 1986, ss 238–246.
18 As to transactions at an undervalue and preferences, see IA 1986, ss 238–241.
19 IA 1986, s 244.
20 IA 1986, s 245.
 1 IA 1986, s 246.
 2 IA 1986, s 424(1)(a).
 3 See Chapter 7 at pp 87–88 supra, and Chapter 15 at pp 241–254 supra.

Unregistered charges

Any charge which has to be registered[4] but in respect of which the prescribed particulars and the relevant instrument of charge (if any) by which the charge is created or evidenced have not been delivered to or received by the registrar of companies for registration in the manner required by the Act within 21 days after the date of the charge's creation, is void against the administrator.[5]

Transactions at an undervalue

Transactions at an undervalue within the meaning attributed to that term[6] may be avoided or otherwise subjected to an order under section 241 of the Insolvency Act 1986[7] at the instance of an administrator[8] if they were carried out within the relevant time, namely within two years ending with the onset of insolvency.[9] In this context the onset of insolvency means the date of any administration order.[10]

Preferences under Insolvency Act 1986

It has already been pointed out that where a company has at a relevant time (as defined by the Act) given a preference to any person, the administrator may apply to the court for an order under section 239 of the Insolvency Act 1986 and the court must, on such application, make such order as it thinks fit for restoring the position to what it would have been if the company had not given that preference.[11] The terms 'preference'[12] and 'relevant time'[13] are both defined in the Insolvency Act 1986. The expression 'relevant time' is defined by references to the 'onset of insolvency', an expression which connotes in the context of an administration the date of the presentation of the petition on which the administration order was made.[14]

A preference is given to a person for the purposes of the avoidance section if he is a creditor or a surety or a guarantor for any of the company's debts or other liabilities and the company does or suffers anything to be done which has the effect of putting that person into a position in which, in the event of the company

---

4 For the list of charges required to be registered see CA 1985, s 396 discussed above.
5 CA 1985, s 395(1).
6 IA 1986, s 238(4).
7 An order may be made against a person whether or not resident within England and Wales or doing business there and whether or not within the jurisdiction at the time of the impugned transaction: *Re Paramount Airways Ltd (No 2)* [1993] Ch 223, [1992] 3 All ER 1, CA.
8 IA 1986, s 238(1). For the special position in relation to market contracts as defined in CA 1989, s 155 see ibid, at s 165.
9 IA 1986, s 240(1). See the discussion at p 246 supra.
10 IA 1986, s 240(3).
11 See the discussion at pp 241–246 supra. But see the special position of market contracts under CA 1989, s 165.
12 IA 1986, s 239(4). See at 242 supra; and see *Re M C Bacon Ltd* [1990] BCLC 324.
13 IA 1986, s 240. See at p 243 supra.
14 IA 1986, s 240(3).

going into insolvent liquidation will be better than the position he would have been in if that thing had not been done.[15] For the preference to be avoided the company must have been influenced in deciding to give it by a desire[16] to produce a preference for the person in fact preferred.[17] If there is no preference there is no need to consider the desire.[18]

Extortionate credit transactions

Undoing extortionate credit transactions

Where an administration order has been made in relation to a company and the company is or has been a party to a transaction for, or involving the provision of credit to the company, the administrator, as office holder, may be entitled to secure an order of the court with respect to the transaction if it is or was extortionate.[19]

Extortionate

A transaction is extortionate if, having regard to the risk accepted by the person providing the credit, the terms of it are or were such as to require grossly exorbitant payments to be made (whether unconditionally or in certain contingencies) in respect of the provision of credit or if it otherwise grossly contravened any principles of fair dealing.[20] Moreover it is to be presumed, unless the contrary is proved, that a transaction with respect to which an application is made under this head is, or was, extortionate.[1]

Ambit of permissible orders

On the application of the administrator,[2] the court may make an order with respect to the transaction if the transaction is or was extortionate[3] and was entered into in the period of three years ending with the day on which the administration order was made.[4] An order with respect to any such transaction may contain such one or more of the following provisions as the court thinks fit:

---

15 IA 1986, s 239(4).
16 The date at which the desire is considered is the date the preference is conferred: *Wills v Corfe Joinery Ltd* [1998] 2 BCLC 75.
17 See *Re M C Bacon Ltd* [1990] BCC 78 at 87.
18 *Lewis v Hyde* [1998] 1 WLR 94, PC.
19 IA 1986, s 244(1) and (2).
20 IA 1986, s 244(3). For the meaning of extortionate in this context see *Ketley Ltd v Scott* [1981] ICR 241, *Wills v Wood* (1984) 128 Sol Jo 222 and *Davies v Directloans Ltd* [1986] 2 All ER 783, [1986] 1 WLR 823; and see the discussion at p 253 above.
 1 IA 1986, s 244(3).
 2 See IA 1986, ss 238(1), 244(1).
 3 See above.
 4 IA 1986, s 244(2).

(1) provision setting aside the whole or part of any obligation created by the transaction;

(2) provision otherwise varying the terms of the transaction or varying the terms on which any security for the purposes of the transaction is held;

(3) provision requiring any person who is or was a party to the transaction to pay to the administrator any sums paid to that person, by virtue of the transaction, by the company;

(4) provision requiring any person to surrender to the administrator any property held by him as security for the purposes of the transaction; and

(5) provision directing accounts to be taken between any persons.[5]

Other remedies

The powers conferred with respect to extortionate credit transactions are exercisable in relation to any transaction concurrently with any powers exercisable in relation to that transaction as a transaction at an undervalue.[6]

Avoidance of certain floating charges

Introduction

There have for a long time been provisions in the Companies Acts avoiding certain floating charges in the event of liquidation. The history, rationale and details of the old law on this subject have been dealt with at length in the previous edition.[7] Moreover, by substantive provisions now in operation under the Insolvency Act 1986 they have likewise received treatment in the discussion of the effect of liquidation on a receivership. The chapter in which this discussion is to be found refers at various points to the applicability of the new provisions to the situation where an administration order has been made. For that reason it seems more suitable to single out some of the more important points for coverage here, leaving the reader to refer back to the previous discussion.

Invalidity of floating charge

The validity of floating charges created at 'a relevant time' prior to the administration is severely restricted.[8]

In this context a floating charge means a charge which as created was a floating charge.[9] A general point of importance is that if a floating charge would be avoided under the relevant statutory provision, the court may make an

---

5 IA 1986, s 244(4).
6 IA 1986, s 244(5).
7 See the 2nd edition at pp 197–214.
8 IA 1986, s 245.
9 IA 1986, s 257.

administration order notwithstanding the prior appointment of an administrative receiver under that security.[10]

Relevant time

The time at which a floating charge is created by a company is a relevant time for the purposes of the statutory provision[11] if the charge is created: (1) in the case of a charge which is created in favour of a person who is connected with the company,[12] at a time in the period of two years ending with the date of the presentation of the petition for an administration order;[13] (2) in the case of a charge created in favour of any other person, at any time in the period of 12 months ending with the date of the presentation of the petition; or (3) in either case, at a time between the presentation of a petition for the making of an administration order in relation to the company and the making of such an order on that petition.[14]

Where a company creates a floating charge in the period of 12 months ending with the onset of insolvency, and the person in favour of whom the charge is created is not connected with the company, that time is not a relevant time unless the company is at that time unable to pay its debts,[15] or becomes unable to pay its debts in consequence of the transaction under which the charge is created.[16]

Extent of invalidity

A floating charge on the company's undertaking or property created at a relevant time is invalid except to the extent of the aggregate of: (1) the value of so much of the consideration for the creation of the charge as consists of money paid, or goods or services supplied, to the company at the same time as, or after, the creation of the charge; (2) the value of so much of that consideration as consists of the discharge or reduction, at the same time as, or after, the creation of the charge, of any debt of the company; and (3) the amount of such interest, if any, as is payable on the amount falling within either of heads (1) and (2) above in pursuance of any agreement under which the money was so paid, the goods or services were so supplied or the debt was so discharged or reduced.[17]

Under the previous statutory provision and its predecessor it was held that despite the invalidation of the floating charge the covenant to pay the sum secured by it remained valid; and as the sum secured was paid before the winding up, the liquidator could not recover the sum so repaid[18] unless the repayment

---

10 IA 1986, s 9(3), (6).
11 Ie the IA 1986, s 245.
12 As to persons 'connected' with a company see 573 fn 16.
13 IA 1986, s 245(5).
14 IA 1986, s 245(3).
15 Ie within the meaning of ibid, s 123.
16 IA 1986, s 245(4).
17 IA 1986, s 245(2).
18 *Re Parkes Garage (Swadlincote) Ltd* [1929] 1 Ch 139; *Mace Builders (Glasgow) Ltd v Lunn* [1987] Ch 191, [1986] 3 WLR 921, CA.

could be set aside as a preference. A floating charge given within the relevant period pursuant to the terms of an agreement made outside the period providing for its execution on the happening of a certain event which happened within that period was held to be invalid.[19]

Payment at time of creation

The question whether or not the payment of money was effected at the time of the creation of the charge is one of fact; and a payment made shortly before and in anticipation of it, and in reliance on a promise to execute it, is made at the time of its creation.[20] However, where the creation of the charge is delayed after payment of the money with the acquiescence of the person advancing the money, the floating charge may be bad.[1]

Goods or services supplied

The value of any goods or services supplied by way of consideration for a floating charge is the amount in money which at the time they were supplied could reasonably have been expected to be obtained for supplying the goods or services in the ordinary course of business and on the same terms, apart from the consideration, as those on which they were supplied to the company.[2]

Transactions defrauding creditors

Introduction

When an administration order is in force an application to redress transactions defrauding creditors and to protect the interests of persons who are victims of the transaction[3] may be made by the administrator or, with the leave of the court,[4] by a person who is, or is capable of being, prejudiced by the transaction. In the case of such a transaction there is no such restriction as to the time during which a transaction at an undervalue may be subject to avoidance.[5] But the transaction in question must have been entered into with the requisite defined intention.

No matter who makes the application it is to be treated as made on behalf of every victim of the transaction.[6] Special provisions apply in relation to market contracts as defined by the Companies Act 1989. No order may be made unless

---

19 *Re Gregory Love & Co* [1916] 1 Ch 203.
20 *Re Columbian Fireproofing Co Ltd* [1910] 2 Ch 120, CA; *Re Olderfleet Shipbuilding and Engineering Co Ltd* [1922] 1 IR 26; *Re F & E Stanton Ltd* [1929] 1 Ch 180.
1 *Re F & E Stanton Ltd* [1929] 1 Ch 180 at 193.
2 IA 1986, s 245(6).
3 IA 1986, s 423(2). References in IA 1986, ss 423 and 424 to a victim of the transaction are to a person who is or is capable of being prejudiced by it: IA 1986, s 423(5).
4 The court means the High Court, or if the person entering into the transaction is a body capable of being wound up under the Insolvency Act 1986, Parts IV or V, any other court having jurisidiction to wind it up: IA 1986, s 423(4)(b).
5 IA 1986, ss 424 and 423(5).
6 IA 1986, s 424(2).

the court is satisfied that the person in favour of whom the contract was made knew at the time he entered into it that it was at an undervalue.[7]

Transaction at an undervalue

For present purposes a person[8] enters into such a transaction at an undervalue if: (1) he makes a gift to the other person or he otherwise enters into a transaction with the other on terms that provide for him to receive no consideration; or (2) he enters into a transaction with the other for a consideration the value of which, in money or money's worth, is significantly less than the value, in money or money's worth, of the consideration provided by himself.[9]

Requisite intention

However, in the case of a person entering into such a transaction, an order may only be made if the court is satisfied that it was entered into by him for the purpose: (a) of putting assets beyond the reach of a person who is making, or may at some time make, a claim against him; or (b) of otherwise prejudicing the interests of such a person in relation to the claim which he is making or may make.[10]

Ambit of permissible orders

Without prejudice to the generality of the above provisions,[11] an order made with respect to a transaction entered into at an undervalue may, subject to the following provisions:

(1)   require any property transferred as part of the transaction to be vested in any person, either absolutely or for the benefit of all the persons on whose behalf the application for the order is treated as made;

(2)   require any property to be so vested if it represents, in any person's hands, the application either of the proceeds of sale of property so transferred or of money so transferred;

(3)   release or discharge, in whole or in part, any security[12] given by the debtor;

(4)   require any person to pay to any other person in respect of benefits received from the debtor such sums as the court may direct;

(5)   provide for any surety or guarantor whose obligations to any person were

---

7 See CA 1989, s 165.

8 Unless the contrary intention appears, 'person' includes a body of persons corporate or unincorporate: Interpretation Act 1978, s 5, Sch 1.

9 IA 1986, s 423(1).

10 IA 1986, s 423(3).

11 Ie IA 1986, s 423.

12 For these purposes 'security' means any mortgage, charge lien or other security: IA 1986, s 425(4).

released or discharged, in whole or in part, under the transaction to be under such new or revived obligations as the court thinks appropriate;

(6) provide for security to be provided for the discharge of any obligation imposed by or arising under the order, for such an obligation to be charged on any property and for such security or charge to have the same priority as a security or charge released or discharged, in whole or in part, under the transaction.[13]

An order made under the above provisions may affect the property of, or impose any obligation on, any person whether or not he is the person with whom the debtor entered into the transaction; but such an order: (a) may not prejudice any interest in property which was acquired from a person other than the debtor and was acquired in good faith, for value and without notice of the relevant circumstances,[14] or prejudice any interest deriving from such an interest; and (b) may not require a person who received a benefit from the transaction in good faith, for value and without notice of the relevant circumstances, to pay any sum unless he was a party to the transaction.[15]

Unenforceability of liens on books and other records

Where an administration order has been made in relation to the company,[16] a lien or other right to retain possession of any of the books, papers or other records of the company is unenforceable to the extent that its enforcement would stop possession of any books, papers or other records by the administrator.[17] This provision does not apply where a lien is claimed on documents of title, that is documents which give a title to property and are held as such.[18] Examples would be title deeds, share certificates or shipping documents held as security for an advance. The meaning of the phrase 'held as such' is puzzling: it appears to refer to the case where the document of title is held by a third party as a specific incident of a particular transaction.[19]

---

13 IA 1986, s 425(1).
14 For these purposes the relevant circumstances in relation to a transaction are the circumstances by virtue of which an order under the main section may be made in respect of the transaction: s 425(3).
15 IA 1986, s 425(2).
16 IA 1986, s 245(1).
17 IA 1986, s 246(1) and (2).
18 IA 1986, s 246(3).
19 See Hamish Anderson *Administrators Part II of the Insolvency Act 1986* (1987) 123–4, para 7.8.

CHAPTER 37

Conduct of administration

INTRODUCTION

The conduct of the administration by the administrator discussed in this chapter embraces: (1) his duties in relation to the submission to him of a statement of affairs and the filing of a verified copy of it in court; (2) his duties in regard to the preparation and submission of his statement of proposals to the registrar of companies, all members and creditors of the company and to a meeting of the company's creditors; (3) the fixing of his remuneration; (4) his duties in relation to regular and terminal accounts and VAT bad debt relief; and (5) the termination of the office of administrator. Questions relating to meetings of creditors and members and the constitution and procedure of the creditors committee are dealt with in the next chapter.

STATEMENT OF AFFAIRS

Requirement for statement of affairs to be submitted to administrator

Where an administration order has been made, the administrator must forthwith require some or all of the following persons to make out and submit to him a statement in the prescribed form as to the affairs of the company.[1]

Such persons are:

(1) those who are or have been officers of the company;

(2) those who have taken part in the company's formation at any time within one year of the date of the administration order;

(3) those who are in the company's employment[2] or have been in its employ-

---

1 IA 1986, s 22(1). As to the notice requiring a statement of affairs and the prescribed form of statement of affairs itself, see the discussion at p 552. As to the meaning of 'forthwith', see *Sameen v Abeyewickrema* [1963] AC 597, [1963] 3 All ER 382 ('as soon as practicable').
2 IA 1986, s 22(3): 'employment' includes employment under a contract for services: s 22(3).

ment within that year, and are in the administrator's opinion capable of giving the information required;

(4)   those who are or have been within that year officers of or in the employment of a company which is, or within that year was, an officer of the company.[3]

The statement must be verified by affidavit by the person required to submit it and must show:

(a)   particulars of the company's assets, debts and liabilities;

(b)   the names and addresses of its creditors;

(c)   the securities held by them respectively;

(d)   the dates when the securities were respectively given; and

(e)   such further or other information as may be prescribed.[4]

Where any persons are so required to submit a statement of affairs to the administrator, they must do so before the end of the period of 21 days beginning with the day after that on which the prescribed notice of the requirement is given to them by the administrator.[5] However, the administrator, if he thinks fit, may at any time release a person from an obligation imposed on him under the above provisions, or, either when giving notice requiring a person to submit a statement of affairs or subsequently, extend the period within which the statement of affairs must be submitted; and where the administrator has refused to exercise such a power, the court, if it thinks fit, may exercise it.[6]

If a person without reasonable excuse fails to comply with any obligation imposed under the above provisions, he is liable on conviction on indictment to a fine or on summary conviction to a fine not exceeding the statutory maximum and, on conviction after continued contravention, to a daily default fine not exceeding one-tenth of the statutory maximum.[7]

Notice requiring statement of affairs

Where the administrator determines to require a statement of the company's affairs to be made out and submitted to him,[8] he must send notice to each of the persons whom he considers should be made responsible for submitting the statement, requiring them to prepare and submit the statement.[9]

---

3   IA 1986, s 22(3).
4   IA 1986, s 22(2).
5   IA 1986, s 22(4).
6   IA 1986, s 22(5).
7   IA 1986, ss 22(6), 430, and Sch 10.
8   Ie in accordance with IA 1986, s 22.
9   IR 1986, SI 1986/1925, r 2.11(1) (amended by SI 1987/1919). For the prescribed form of such notice, see rr 2.11, 12.7, and Sch 4, Form 2.8 (substituted by SI 1987/1919).

The notice must inform each of the deponents:[10]

(1) of the names and addresses of all others, if any, to whom the same notice has been sent;

(2) of the time within which the statement must be delivered;

(3) of the penalty for non-compliance;[11] and

(4) of the application to him, and to each of the other deponents, of their duty[12] to provide information, and to attend on the administrator if required.[13]

The administrator must, on request, furnish each deponent with the forms required for the preparation of the statement of affairs.[14]

Form of statement of affairs, verification and filing

The statement of affairs must be in the prescribed form,[15] must contain all the particulars required by the form and must be verified by affidavit by the deponents, using the same form,[16] and the administrator may require any of the persons who may be required to submit a statement of affairs[17] to submit an affidavit of concurrence, stating that he concurs in the statement of affairs.[18] An affidavit of concurrence may be qualified in respect of matters dealt with in the statement of affairs, where the maker of the affidavit is not in agreement with the deponents, or he considers the statement to be erroneous or misleading, or he is without the direct knowledge necessary for concurring with it.[19]

The statement of affairs must be delivered to the administrator by the deponent making the affidavit of verification, or by one of them, if more than one, together with a copy of the verified statement,[20] and every affidavit of concurrence must be delivered by the person who makes it, together with a copy.[1] The administrator must file the verified copy of the statement, and the affidavits of concurrence, if any, in court.[2]

---

10 The persons to whom notice under IR 1986, r 2.11(1) is sent are referred to in rr 2.11–2.17 as 'the deponents': r 2.11(2).
11 Ie the effect of IA 1986, s 22(6).
12 Ie under IA 1986, s 235.
13 IR 1986, r 2.11(3).
14 IR 1986, r 2.11(4) (amended by SI 1987/1919).
15 For the prescribed form of statement of affairs see IR 1986, rr 2.12, 12.7, Sch 4, Form 2.9.
16 IR 1986, r 2.12(1).
17 Ie those persons mentioned in IA 1986, s 22(3).
18 IR 1986, r 2.12(2).
19 IR 1986, r 2.12(3).
20 IR 1986, r 2.12(4).
 1 IR 1986, r 2.12(5).
 2 IR 1986, r 2.12(6).

Limited disclosure

Where the administrator thinks that it would prejudice the conduct of the administration for the whole or part of the statement of affairs to be disclosed, he may apply to the court for an order of limited disclosure in respect of the statement, or any specified part of it.[3] The court may, on the application, order that the statement or, as the case may be, the specified part of it, not be filed in court, or be filed separately and not be open to inspection otherwise than with leave of the court,[4] and the court's order may include directions as to the delivery of documents to the registrar of companies and the disclosure of relevant information to other persons.[5]

Release from duty to submit statement of affairs; extension of time

The power of the administrator[6] to give a release from the obligation to submit a statement of affairs, or to grant an extension of time, may be exercised at the administrator's own discretion, or at the request of any deponent,[7] and a deponent may, if he requests a release or extension of time and it is refused by the administrator, apply to the court for it.[8] The court may, if it thinks that no sufficient cause is shown for the application, dismiss it; but it must not do so unless the applicant has had an opportunity to attend the court for an ex parte hearing, of which he has been given at least seven days' notice; if, however, the application is not so dismissed, the court must fix a venue for it to be heard, and give notice to the deponent accordingly.[9]

The deponent must, at least 14 days before the hearing, send to the administrator a notice stating the venue and accompanied by a copy of the application, and of any evidence which he, the deponent, intends to adduce in support of it.[10] The administrator may appear and be heard on the application; and, whether or not he appears, he may file a written report of any matters which he considers ought to be drawn to the court's attention; and if such a report is filed, a copy of it must be sent by the administrator to the deponent, not later than five days before the hearing.[11]

Sealed copies of any order made on the application must be sent by the court to the deponent and the administrator.[12]

On any such application the applicant's costs must be paid in any event by him

3 IR 1986, r 2.13(1). As to the mode of making the application and the procedure see IR 1986, r 7.1–7.6.
4 IR 1986, r 2.13(2).
5 IR 1986, r 2.13(3).
6 Ie under IA 1986, s 22(5).
7 IR 1986, r 2.14(1).
8 IR 1986, r 2(14(2).
9 IR 1986, r 2.14(3).
10 IR 1986, r 2.14(4).
11 IR 1986, r 2.14(5).
12 IR 1986, r 2.14(6).

and, unless the court otherwise orders, no allowance towards them may be made out of the assets.[13]

Expenses of statement of affairs

A deponent making the statement of affairs and affidavit must be allowed, and paid by the administrator out of his receipts, any expenses incurred by the deponent in so doing which the administrator considers reasonable,[14] and any such decision by the administrator is subject to appeal to the court.[15] However, nothing in the above provisions relieves a deponent from any obligation with respect to the preparation, verification and submission of the statement of affairs, or to the provision of information to the administrator.[16]

ADMINISTRATOR'S PROPOSALS

Introduction

Because an administration order effects a suspension of the rights of creditors, the administrator should as a matter of principle keep those creditors informed of what he is proposing to do. For that reason he is put under the obligation of sending as soon as possible a statement of proposals to prescribed persons. The statement of proposals is required to be accompanied by a statement, again containing prescribed information, and statute requires the proposals and statement to be considered at a duly constituted meeting of creditors.

Statement of proposals

Where an administration order has been made, the administrator must, within three months,[17] or such longer period as the court may allow, after the making of that order:

(1)   send to the registrar of companies and, so far as he is aware of their address, to all creditors a statement of his proposals for achieving the purpose or purposes specified in the order;[18] and

---

13 IR 1986, r 2.14(7).
14 IR 1986, r 2.15(1).
15 IR 1986, r 2.15(2).
16 IR 1986, r 2.15(3).
17 The requirement is for the statement of proposals to be sent *within*, and not at the expiry of, three months: *Re Charnley Davies Business Services Ltd* (1987) 3 BCC 408. Although the company that is the subject of an administration order has standing to apply for an extension of the three-month period, it is preferable if the application is made by the administrator: *Re Newport County Association Football Club Ltd* [1987] BCLC 582. For such an application, a witness statement in support thereof and the order, see 10(1) Court Forms (1999 Issue) 82–85, Forms 42–44.
18 For the prescribed form of statement of the administrator's proposals to be sent to the registrar of companies, see IR 1986, r 12.7, Sch 4, Form 2.21.

(2) lay a copy of the statement before a meeting of the company's creditors summoned for the purpose on not less than 14 days' notice.[19]

The administrator must also, within three months, or such longer period as the court may allow, after the making of the order, either:

(a) send a copy of the statement, to all members of the company so far as he is aware of their addresses; or

(b) publish in the prescribed manner[20] a notice stating an address to which members of the company should write for copies of the statement to be sent to them free of charge.[1]

If the administrator without reasonable excuse fails to comply with these provisions, he is liable on summary conviction to a fine not exceeding one-fifth of the statutory maximum and, on conviction after continued contravention, to a daily default fine not exceeding one-fiftieth of the statutory maximum.[2]

Statement to be annexed to proposals

There must be annexed to the administrator's proposals, when sent to the registrar of companies[3] and laid before the creditors' meeting required to be summoned[3] to consider such proposals, a statement by him showing:

(1) details relating to his appointment as administrator, the purposes for which an administration order was applied for and made, and any subsequent variation of those purposes;

(2) the names of the directors and secretary of the company;

(3) an account of the circumstances giving rise to the application for an administration order;

(4) if a statement of affairs has been submitted, a copy or summary of it, with the administrator's comments, if any;

(5) if no statement of affairs has been submitted, details of the financial position of the company at the latest practicable date, which must, unless the court otherwise orders, be a date not earlier than that of the administration order;

---

19 IA 1986, s 23(1). A creditors' meeting under s 23(1) is not permissible simply to consider a report of what has happened on a proposal by the administrator that the company should petition for winding up; this is not one of the purposes in s 8: *Re Charnley Davies Business Services Ltd* (1987) 3 BCC 408.

20 The prescribed manner of publishing such notice is by gazetting; and the notice must also be advertised once in the newspaper in which the administration order was advertised: IR 1986, r 2.17(a).

1 IA 1986, s 23(2).

2 IA 1986, ss 23(3), 430, and Sch 10.

3 See IA 1986, s 23.

(6) the manner in which the affairs and business of the company have, since the date of the administrator's appointment, been managed and financed, and will, if the administrator's proposals are approved, continue to be managed and financed; and

(7) such other information, if any, as the administrator thinks necessary to enable creditors to decide whether or not to vote for the adoption of the proposals.[4]

Meeting to consider administrator's proposals

Notice of the creditors' meeting required to be summoned[5] to consider the administrator's proposals must be given to all the creditors of the company who are identified in the statement of affairs, or are known to the administrator and had claims against the company at the date of the administration order.[6] Unless the court otherwise directs, notice of the meeting must also be given by advertisement in the newspaper in which the administration order was advertised,[7] and notice to attend the meeting must be sent out at the same time to any directors or officers of the company, including persons who have been directors or officers in the past, whose presence at the meeting is, in the administrator's opinion, required.[8]

If at the meeting there is not the requisite majority for approval of the administrator's proposals, with modifications, if any, the chairman may, and must if a resolution is passed to that effect, adjourn the meeting for not more than 14 days.[9]

Consideration of proposals by creditors' meeting

A meeting of creditors summoned to consider the administrator's proposals[10] must decide whether to approve such proposals,[11] and the meeting may approve the proposals with modifications, but must not do so unless the administrator consents to each modification.[12] Subject to the above provisions, the meeting must be conducted in accordance with the rules.[13]

After the conclusion of the meeting in accordance with the rules, the administrator must report the result of the meeting to the court and must give notice of

---

4 IR 1986, r 2.16(1) (amended by SI 1987/1919).
5 See IA 1986, s 23(1).
6 IR 1986, r 2.18(1).
7 IR 1986, r 2.18(2).
8 IR 1986, r 2.18(3). For the prescribed form of notice to directors and others to attend the meeting of creditors, see rr 2.18, 12.7, Sch 4, Form 2.10.
9 IR 1986, r 2.18(4). As to the procedure generally at such meetings, see p 571 below.
10 See IA 1986, s 23.
11 IA 1986, s 24(1).
12 IA 1986, s 24(2). 'Modifications' includes additions, alterations and omissions and cognate expressions are to be construed accordingly: s 436.
13 IA 1986, s 24(3).

that result to the registrar of companies and to such persons as may be prescribed.[14] If a report is given to the court that the meeting has declined to approve the administrator's proposals, with or without modifications, the court may by order discharge the administration order and make such consequential provision as it thinks fit, or adjourn the hearing conditionally or unconditionally, or make an interim order or any other order that it thinks fit.[15]

Where the administration order is discharged, the administrator must, within fourteen days after the making of the order effecting the discharge, send an office copy of that order to the registrar of companies.[16] However, if the administrator without reasonable excuse fails to comply with this provision,[17] he is liable on summary conviction to a fine not exceeding one-fifth of the statutory maximum and, on conviction after continued contravention, to a daily default fine not exceeding one-fiftieth of the statutory maximum.[18]

Approval of substantial revisions

Where proposals have been approved, with or without modifications,[19] and the administrator proposes to make revisions of the proposals which appear to him substantial, the administrator must (1) send to all creditors of the company, so far as he is aware of their addresses, a statement in the prescribed form of his proposed revisions; and (2) lay a copy of the statement before a meeting of the company's creditors summoned for the purpose on not less than 14 days' notice,[20] and the administrator must not make the proposed revisions unless they are approved by the meeting.[1] Where, however, the administrator fears if there is a 14-day delay the sale may go off or result in a price reduction he may apply to the court for leave to proceed with the sale transaction.[2]

The administrator must also either (a) send a copy of the statement to all members of the company, so far as he is aware of their addresses; or (b) publish in the prescribed manner a notice stating an address to which members of the company should write for copies of the statement to be sent to them free of charge.[3]

---

14 IA 1986, s 24(4). Any report or notice by the administrator of the result of a creditors' meeting held under s 23 or s 25 must have annexed to it details of the proposals which were considered by the meeting and of the revisions and modifications to the proposals which were so considered: IR 1986, r 2.29 (substituted by SI 1987/1919). As to the prescribed form of notice to be given to the registrar of companies, see r 12.7, Sch 4, Form 2.23.
15 IA 1986, s 24(5).
16 IA 1986, s 24(6).
17 Ie IA 1986, s 24(6).
18 IA 1986, ss 24(7), 430, and Sch 10.
19 Under IA 1986, s 24.
20 IA 1986, s 25(2). For the prescribed form of statement of revised proposals and notice of meeting to consider them, see IR 1986, r 12.7, Sch 4, Form 2.22.
 1 IA 1986, s 25(1).
 2 *Re Dana (UK) Ltd* [1999] 2 BCLC 239 (leave granted: case urgent, sale shown to be desirable, administrators conduct unimpeachable); and see *Re Montin* [1999] 1 BCLC 663; *Re Osmosis Group Ltd* [1999] 2 BCLC 329.
 3 IA 1986, s 25(3). The prescribed manner of publishing such notice is by gazetting; and the notice must also be advertised once in the newspaper in which the administration order was advertised: IR 1986, r 2.17(b).

The meeting of creditors may approve the proposed revisions with modifications, but may not do so unless the administrator consents to each modification.[4] Subject to the above provisions, the meeting must be conducted in accordance with the rules.[5] After the conclusion of the meeting in accordance with the rules, the administrator must give notice of the result of the meeting to the registrar of companies and to such persons as may be prescribed.[6]

Notices to creditors

Within 14 days of the conclusion of a meeting of creditors to consider the administrator's proposals, the administrator must send notice of the result of the meeting, including, where appropriate, details of the proposals as approved, to every creditor who received notice of the meeting,[7] and to any other creditor of whom the administrator has since become aware.[8]

Within 14 days of the end of every period of six months beginning with the date of approval of the administrator's proposals or revised proposals, the administrator must send to all creditors of the company a report on the progress of the administration.[9]

On vacating office, the administrator must send to all creditors of the company a report on the administration up to that time.[10] This does not apply where the administration is immediately followed by the company going into liquidation, nor when the administrator is removed from office by the court or ceases to be qualified as an insolvency practitioner.

ADMINISTRATOR'S REMUNERATION

Fixing of remuneration

The administrator is entitled to receive remuneration for his services as such,[11] and the remuneration must be fixed either (1) as a percentage of the value of the property with which he has to deal; or (2) by reference to the time properly given by the insolvency practitioner, as administrator, and his staff in attending to matters arising in the administration.[12]

It is for the creditors' committee,[13] if there is one, to determine whether the

---

4 IA 1986, s 25(4).
5 IA 1986, s 25(5).
6 IA 1986, s 25(6). For the prescribed form of notice to be given to the registrar of companies, see r 12.7, Sch 4, Form 2.23.
7 Under IR 1986 (amended by SI 1987/1919).
8 IR 1986, r 2.30(1). For the prescribed form of the report of meeting of creditors, see rr 2.30, 12.7, Sch 4, Form 2.12 (substituted by SI 1987/1919).
9 IR 1986, r 2.30(2).
10 IR 1986, r 2.30(3).
11 IR 1986, r 2.47(1).
12 IR 1986, r 2.47(2).
13 As to the creditors' committee, see at p 570 below.

remuneration is to be fixed under heads (1) or (2) above and, if under head (1) above, to determine any percentage to be applied as there mentioned.[14] In arriving at that determination, the committee must have regard to the following matters:

(a) the complexity, or otherwise, of the case;

(b) any respects in which, in connection with the company's affairs, there falls on the administrator any responsibility of an exceptional kind or degree;

(c) the effectiveness with which the administrator appears to be carrying out, or to have carried out, his duties as such; and

(d) the value and nature of the property with which he has to deal.[15]

If, however, there is no creditors' committee, or the committee does not make the requisite determination, the administrator's remuneration may be fixed[16] by a resolution of a meeting of creditors.[17]

If not fixed as mentioned above, the administrator's remuneration must, on his application, be fixed by the court.[18]

Where there are joint administrators, it is for them to agree between themselves as to how the remuneration payable should be apportioned; and any dispute arising between them may be referred to the court, for settlement by order, or to the creditors' committee or a meeting of creditors, for settlement by resolution.[19] If the administrator is a solicitor and employs his own firm, or any partner in it, to act on behalf of the company, profit costs must not be paid unless this is authorised by the creditors' committee, the creditors or the court.[20]

Recourse to meeting of creditors and to the court

If the administrator's remuneration has been fixed by the creditors' committee, and he considers the rate or amount to be insufficient, he may request that it be increased by resolution of the creditors.[1]

If the administrator considers that the remuneration fixed for him by the creditors' committee, or by resolution of the creditors, is insufficient, he may apply to the court for an order increasing its amount or rate.[2] The administrator must give at least 14 days' notice of his application to the members of the

14 IR 1986, r 2.47(3).
15 IR 1986, r 2.47(4).
16 Ie in accordance with IR 1986, r 2.47(2).
17 IR 1986, r 2.47(5). In such a case r 2.47(4) applies to the creditors as it does to the creditors' committee: r 2.47(5).
18 IR 1986, r 2.47(6). See also *Re Charnley Davies Business Services Ltd* (1987) 3 BCC 408 (where it was held that remuneration should be determined in the way receivers and other court officers have remuneration fixed).
19 IR 1986, r 2.47(7) (substituted by SI 1987/1919).
20 IR 1986, r 2.47(8) (added by SI 1987/1919).
 1 IR 1986, r 2.48.
 2 IR 1986, r 2.49(1).

creditors' committee; and the committee may nominate one or more members to appear or be represented, and to be heard, on the application.[3] If there is no creditors' committee, the administrator's notice of his application must be sent to such one or more of the company's creditors as the court may direct, which creditors may nominate one or more of their number to appear or be represented.[4] The court may, if it appears to be a proper case, order the costs of the administrator's application, including the costs of any member of the creditors' committee appearing or being represented on it, or any creditor so appearing or being represented, to be paid as an expense of the administration.[5]

Creditors' claim that remuneration is excessive

Any creditor of the company may, with the concurrence of at least 25 per cent in value of the creditors, including himself, apply to the court for an order that the administrator's remuneration be reduced, on the grounds that it is, in all the circumstances, excessive.[6] The court may, if it thinks that no sufficient cause is shown for a reduction, dismiss the application; but it must not do so unless the applicant has had an opportunity to attend the court for an ex parte hearing, of which he has been given at least seven days' notice.[7] If the application is not so dismissed, the court must fix a venue[8] for it to be heard, and give notice to the applicant accordingly;[9] and the applicant must, at least 14 days before the hearing, send to the administrator a notice stating the venue and accompanied by a copy of the application, and of any evidence which the applicant intends to adduce in support of it.[10]

If the court considers the application to be well founded, it must make an order fixing the remuneration at a reduced amount or rate[11] and, unless the court orders otherwise, the costs of the application must be paid by the applicant, and are not payable as an expense of the administration.[12]

ACCOUNTS AND VAT BAD DEBT RELIEF

Abstract of receipts and payments

The administrator must (1) within two months after the end of six months from the date of his appointment, and every subsequent period of six months; and (2)

---

3 IR 1986, r 2.49(2).
4 IR 1986, r 2.49(3).
5 IR 1986, r 2.49(4) (amended by SI 1987/1919).
6 IR 1986, r 2.50(1).
7 IR 1986, r 2.50(2).
8 As to meaning of 'venue', see IR 1986, r 13.6 (time, date and place of the hearing).
9 IR 1986, r 2.50(2).
10 IR 1986, r 2.50(3).
11 IR 1986, r 2.50(4).
12 IR 1986, r 2.50(5).

within two months after he ceases to act as administrator, send to the court, and to the registrar of companies, and to each member of the creditors' committee, the requisite accounts of the receipts and payments of the company.[13] The court may, on the administrator's application, extend the period of two months mentioned above.[14] The accounts are to be in the form of an abstract showing (a) receipts and payments during the relevant period of six months, or (b) where the administrator has ceased to act, receipts and payments during the period from the end of the last six-month period to the time when he so ceased; alternatively, if there has been no previous abstract, receipts and payments in the period since his appointment as administrator.[15]

If the administrator makes default in complying with these provisions, he is liable on summary conviction to a fine not exceeding one-fifth of the statutory maximum and, on conviction after continued contravention, to a daily default fine not exceeding one-fiftieth of the statutory maximum.[16]

VAT bad debt relief and certificate of insolvency

It is the duty of the administrator to issue a certificate of insolvency[17] forthwith upon his forming the opinion that the relevant circumstances in which a company is deemed insolvent for the purposes of the provisions relating to value added tax bad debt relief are satisfied.[18] There must in the certificate be specified:

(1)   the name of the company and its registered number;

(2)   the name of the administrator and the date of his appointment;

(3)   the date on which the certificate is issued.[19]

Notice of the issue of the certificate must be given by the administrator within three months of his appointment or within two months of issuing the certificate, whichever is the later, to all the company's unsecured creditors of whose address he is then aware and who have, to his knowledge, made supplies to the company, with a charge to value added tax, at any time before his appointment.[20] Thereafter, he must give the notice to any creditor of whose address and supplies

---

13 IR 1986, r 2.52(1). For the prescribed form of the administrator's abstract of receipts and payments, see rr 2.52, 12.7, Sch 4, Form 2.15. As to the records to be kept by all insolvency practitioners, see Insolvency Practitioner Regulations 1986, reg 15, Sch 3.
14 IR 1986, r 2.52(2).
15 IR 1986, r 2.52(3).
16 IR 1986, rr 2.52(4), 12.21 and Sch 5.
17 Ie in the terms of the Value Added Tax Act 1983, s 22(3)(b) (substituted by the Finance Act 1985, s 32), which specifies the circumstances in which a company is deemed insolvent for the purposes of that section.
18 IR 1986, r 2.56(1).
19 IR 1986, r 2.56(2). The certificate must be entitled CERTIFICATE OF INSOLVENCY FOR THE PURPOSES OF SECTION 23(3)(B) OF THE VALUE ADDED TAX ACT 1983: IR 1986, r 2.56(3).
20 IR 1986, r 2.57(1).

to the company he becomes aware,[1] but he is not under obligation to provide any creditor with a copy of the certificate.[2]

The certificate must be retained with the company's accounting records, and the provisions relating to where and for how long records are to be kept[3] apply to the certificate as they apply to those records.[4] It is the duty of the administrator, on vacating office, to bring this provision[5] to the attention of the directors or, as the case may be, any successor of his as administrator.[6]

TERMINATION OF OFFICE OF ADMINISTRATOR

Vacation of office

The administrator of a company may at any time be removed from office by order of the court and may, in the prescribed circumstances, resign his office by giving notice of his resignation to the court.[7]

The administrator must vacate office if he ceases to be qualified as an insolvency practitioner in relation to the company,[8] or if the administration order is discharged.[9]

Liabilities ranking ahead of administrator's remuneration

Where at any time a person ceases to be administrator:

(1) his remuneration[10] and any expenses properly incurred by him are a charge on, and must be paid out of, any property of the company which is in his custody or under his control at that time in priority to any floating charge then existing over the property of the company;[11]

(2) any sums payable in respect of debts or liabilities incurred, while he was administrator, under contracts entered into by him or a predecessor of his in the carrying out of his or the predecessor's functions must be charged on

---

1 IR 1986, r 2.57(2).
2 IR 1986, r 2.57(3).
3 See Companies Act 1985, s 222.
4 IR 1986, r 2.58(1).
5 Namely IR 1986, r 2.58(1).
6 IR 1986, r 2.58(2).
7 IA 1986, s 19(1). As to the prescribed circumstances in which an administrator may resign his office, see IR 1986, r 2.53 discussed below.
8 As to insolvency practitioners and their qualifications, see pp 53–59 above.
9 IA 1986, s 19(2).
10 As to the administrator's remuneration see at p 559 above.
11 IA 1986, s 19(3), (4). But it is not payable out of trust property: *Tom Wise Ltd v Fillimore* [1999] BCC 129. The priority referred to is over any security to which s 15(1) applies. Where an administration order is discharged upon the making of a winding-up order, the company's property remains charged in the hands of the official receiver or liquidator: *Re Sheridan Securities Ltd* (1988) 4 BCC 200.

and paid out of any property as is mentioned in head (1) above in priority to any charge arising under head (1) above;[12]

(3)   any sums payable in respect of liabilities incurred, while he was administrator, under contracts of employment adopted[13] by him or a predecessor of his in the carrying out of his or her predecessor's function shall to the extent that the liabilities or qualifying liabilities, be charged on and paid out of any property such as is maintained in head (1) in priority to any charge arising under head (1) above.[14]

For this purpose, the administrator is not to be taken to have adopted a contract of employment by reason of anything done or omitted to be done within 14 days after his appointment.[15]

Qualifying liabilities

Qualifying liabilities were a concept introduced by the Insolvency Act 1994 and in connection with contracts of employment are restricted to wages, salaries and occupational pension contributions (wages and salary being given an enlarged meaning to cover holiday and sickness payments[16]) but only in respect of services rendered wholly or partly *after* the adoption of the contract.[17] In the case where services are rendered partly after the adoption of the contract, so much of the qualifying liability as respects payment in respect of services rendered *before* the adoption are to be disregarded.[18] For these purposes, wages or salary payable in respect of a period of holiday[19] or absence from work through sickness or other good cause are deemed to be wages or salary in respect of services rendered in that period[20] and a sum payable in lieu of holiday is deemed to be wages or (as the case may be) salary in respect of the period by reference to which the holiday entitlement arose.[1]

Resignation of administrator

The administrator may give notice of his resignation on the grounds of ill-health

12 IA 1986, s 19(3), (5).
13 Adoption is a matter not merely of words but of fact: see *Powdrill v Watson* [1994] 2 All ER 513 at 521 sub nom *Re Paramount Airways Ltd (No 3)* [1994] BCC 172 at 180. Earlier dicta on the meaning of 'adopted' are no longer authoritative. See the discussion at p 182 above.
14 IA 1986, s 19(6) (added with s 19(7)–(10) by IA 1994). Contracts of employment adopted by the administrator prior to 15 March 1994 are governed by the unamended law: see *Powdrill v Watson* [1995] 2 AC 394, HL.
15 IA 1986, s 19(6).
16 See IA 1986, s 19(9) and (10).
17 IA 1986, s 19(7)(a) and (b).
18 IA 1986, s 19(8).
19 This includes any sums which, if they had been paid, would have been treated for the purposes of the enactments relating to social security as earnings in respect of that period: IA 1986, s 19(10).
20 IA 1986, s 19(9)(a).
 1 IA 1986, s 19(9)(b).

or because he intends ceasing to practise as an insolvency practitioner,[2] or there is some conflict of interest, or change of personal circumstances, which precludes or makes impracticable the further discharge by him of the duties of administrator.[3] The administrator may, with the leave of the court, give notice of his resignation on grounds other than those specified above.[4]

The administrator must give to the persons specified below at least seven days' notice of his intention to resign, or to apply for the court's leave to do so:

(1)   if there is a continuing administrator of the company, to him;

(2)   if there is no such administrator, to the creditors' committee;[5] and

(3)   if there is no such administrator and no creditors' committee, to the company and its creditors.[6]

Death of administrator

Subject to the following provisions, where the administrator has died, it is the duty of his personal representatives to give notice[7] of the fact to the court, specifying the date of the death.[8]

If, however, the deceased administrator was a partner in a firm, notice may be given by a partner in the firm who is qualified to act as an insolvency practitioner, or is a member of any body recognised by the Secretary of State for the authorisation of insolvency practitioners;[9] and notice of the death may also be given by any person producing to the court the relevant death certificate or a copy of it.[10]

Appointment of administrator in event of vacancy

If a vacancy occurs by death, resignation or otherwise in the office of administrator, the court may by order fill the vacancy:[11]

(1)   by any continuing administrator of the company; or

---

2 As to insolvency practitioners and their qualifications, see the discussion at pp 53–59 above.
3 IR 1986, r 2.53(1). For the prescribed form of notice to the court of the resignation of the administrator, see rr 2.53, 12.7, Sch 4, Form 2.16 (substituted by SI 1987/1919). See also 10(1) Court Forms (1999 Issue) 89, Form 48.
4 IR 1986, r 2.53(2). For the prescribed form of notice of resignation of the administrator with leave of the court, see rr 2.53, 12.7, Sch 4, Form 2.17 (substituted by SI 1987/1919). See also 10(1) Court Forms (1999 Issue) 90, Form 50.
5 As to the creditors' committee, see at p 570 below.
6 IR 1986, r 2.53(3). As to the mode of giving notice, see r 13.3.
7 As to the giving of notice, see IR 1986, r 13.3.
8 IR 1986, r 2.54(1). Rule 2.54(1) does not apply if notice has been given under r 2.54(2) or (3).
9 IR 1986, r 2.54(2).
10 IR 1986, r 2.54(3).
11 IA 1986, s 13(2).

(2)   where there is no administrator, by the creditors' committee;[12] or

(3)   where there is no such administrator and no such committee, by the company or the directors or by any creditor or creditors of the company.[13]

Where the court makes an order filling a vacancy in the office of administrator, the same provisions apply in respect of giving notice of, and advertising, the order as in the case of the administration order.[14]

Release of administrator

A person who has ceased to be the administrator of a company has his release, in the case of a person who has died, with effect from the time at which notice is given to the court that he has ceased to hold office, and in any other case, with effect from such time as the court may determine.[15] Where an administration order was discharged upon the making of a winding up order and it appeared that the administrator had wrongly pursued purposes not specified in the administration order, the administrator's release was postponed in order to enable the official receiver and the liquidator to investigate the matter.

Where a person has his release under this provision, he is, with effect from the time specified above, discharged from all liability both in respect of acts or omissions of his in the administration and otherwise in relation to his conduct as administrator.[16] The court's powers under the provisions giving rise to a summary remedy against delinquent administrators[17] are not, however, affected in relation to a person who has had his release.[18]

---

12 As to the creditors' committee, see at p 570 below.
13 IA 1986, s 13(3).
14 IR 1986, r 2.55 (amended by SI 1987/1919).
15 IA 1986, s 20(1).
16 IA 1986, s 20(2).
17 Ie under IA 1986, s 212.
18 IA 1986, s 20(3).

CHAPTER 38

Meetings of creditors and members

CREDITORS' MEETINGS

Introduction

The following provisions apply to creditors' meetings (1) summoned by the administrator under the general power to summon meetings of creditors;[1] (2) requisitioned by creditors or directed to be held by the court;[2] (3) to consider the administrator's proposals;[3] or (4) to consider[4] substantial revisions.[5]

Venue and time

In fixing the venue[6] for the meeting, the administrator must have regard to the convenience of the creditors.[7] The meeting must be summoned for commencement between 10.00 and 16.00 hours on a business day,[8] unless the court otherwise directs.[9]

Notice

Notice of the meeting must be given to all creditors who are known to the administrator and had claims against the company at the date of the administration order; and the notice must specify the purpose of the meeting and contain

---

1 See IA 1986, s 14(2)(b).
2 See IA 1986, s 17(3).
3 See IA 1986, s 23(1) discussed at above.
4 See IA 1986, s 25(2)(b).
5 IR 1986, r 2.19(1).
6 Ie the time, date and place: IR 1986, rr 13.1 and 13.6.
7 IR 1986, r 2.19(2).
8 'Business day' means any day other than a Saturday or Sunday, Christmas Day, Good Friday or a day which is a bank holiday in any part of Great Britain: IA 1986, s 251; IR 1986, rr 13.1 and 13.13(1).
9 IR 1986, r 2.19(3).

a statement of the effect of the provision[10] dealing with the entitlement to vote.[11] Except in relation to a meeting summoned to consider the administrator's proposals[12] or to consider substantial revisions to such proposals,[13] at least 21 days' notice of the meeting must be given.[14] With the notice summoning the meeting there must be sent out forms of proxy.[15]

Adjournment

If within 30 minutes from the time fixed for commencement of the meeting there is no person present to act as chairman, the meeting stands adjourned to the same time and place in the following week or, if that is not a business day, to the business day immediately following.[16] The meeting may from time to time be adjourned, if the chairman thinks fit, but not for more than 14 days from the date on which it was fixed to commence.[17]

The chairman at meetings

At any meeting of creditors summoned by the administrator, either he must be chairman, or a person nominated by him in writing to act in his place.[18]

A person so nominated must be either one who is qualified to act as an insolvency practitioner in relation to the company,[19] or an employee of the administrator or his firm who is experienced in insolvency matters.[20]

Meeting requistioned by creditors

Any request by creditors to the administrator for a meeting of creditors to be summoned must be accompanied by:

(1)   a list of creditors concurring with the request, showing the amounts of their respective claims in the administration;

(2)   from each creditor concurring, written confirmation of his concurrence; and

---

10 IR 1986, r 2.22(1).
11 IR 1986, r 2.19(4) (amended by SI 1987/1919). As to the prescribed form of notice of creditors' meetings in administration proceedings, see rr 2.19, 12.7, Sch 4, Form 2.11 (substituted by SI 1987/1919).
12 See IA 1986, s 23(1).
13 IA 1986, s 25(2).
14 IR 1986, r 2.19(4A) (added by SI 1987/1919).
15 IR 1986, r 2.19(5). For the prescribed form of proxy, see rr 8.1, 12.7, Sch 4, Form 8.2.
16 IR 1986, r 2.19(6).
17 IR 1986, r 2.19(7).
18 IR 1986, r 2.20(1).
19 As to insolvency practitioners and their qualifications, see at pp 53–59 above.
20 IR 1986, r 2.20(2).

(3) a statement of the purpose of the proposed meeting.[1]

This does not apply if the requisitioning creditor's debt is alone sufficient without the concurrence of the other creditors.

The administrator must, if he considers the request to be properly made,[2] fix a venue[3] for the meeting, not more than 35 days from his receipt of the request, and give at least 21 days' notice of the meeting to creditors.[4]

The expenses of summoning and holding a meeting at the instance of any person other than the administrator must be paid by that person, who must deposit with the administrator security for their payment.[5] The sum to be deposited must be such as the administrator may determine, and he must not act without the deposit having been made.[6] The meeting may resolve that the expenses of summoning and holding it are to be payable out of the assets of the company, as an expense of the administration;[7] and to the extent that any such deposit is not required for the payment of expenses summoning and holding the meeting, it must be repaid to the person who made it.[8]

CREDITORS' COMMITTEE

Establishment of creditors' committee

Where a meeting of creditors summoned to consider the administrator's proposals[9] has approved such proposals, with or without modifications, the meeting may, if it thinks fit, establish a committee ('the creditors' committee') to exercise the functions conferred on it by or under the Insolvency Act 1986.[10] If such a committee is established, the committee may, on giving not less than seven days' notice, require the administrator to attend before it at any reasonable time and furnish it with such information relating to the carrying out of his functions as it may reasonably require.[11]

The acts of the creditors' committee established for any administration are valid notwithstanding any defect in the appointment, election or qualifications of any member of the committee or any committee-member's representative or in the formalities of its establishment.[12]

---

1 IR 1986, r 2.21(1).
2 Ie in accordance with IA 1986, s 17(3).
3 For the meaning of 'venue' see IR 1986, r 13.6 (time, date and place of the meeting).
4 IR 1986, r 2.21(2).
5 IR 1986, r 2.21(3).
6 IR 1986, r 2.21(4).
7 IR 1986, r 2.21(5).
8 IR 1986, r 2.21(6).
9 Under IA 1986, s 23.
10 IA 1986, s 26(1).
11 IA 1986, s 26(2).
12 IR 1986, r 2.46A (added by SI 1987/1919).

Constitution of creditors' committee

Where it is resolved by a creditors' meeting to establish a creditors' committee for the purposes of the administration, the committee must consist of at least three and not more than five creditors of the company elected at the meeting;[13] and any creditor of the company is eligible to be a member of the committee, so long as his claim has not been rejected for the purpose of his entitlement to vote.[14] A body corporate may be a member of the committee, but it cannot act as such otherwise than by a duly appointed representative.[15]

Formalities of establishment

The creditors' committee does not come into being, and accordingly cannot act, until the administrator has issued a certificate of its due constitution.[16]

Agreement to act

No person may act as a member of the committee unless and until he has agreed to do so and, unless the relevant proxy of authorisation contains a statement to the contrary, such agreement may be given by his proxy-holder or the representative of a corporation[17] present at the meeting establishing the committee.[18]

Certificate of due constitution

The administrator's certificate of the committee's due constitution must not be issued unless and until at least three of the persons who are to be members of the committee have agreed to act.[19] As and when the others, if any, agree to act, the administrator must issue an amended certificate.[20] The certificate, and any amended certificate, must be filed in court[1] by the administrator.[2]

Changes

If, after the first establishment of the committee, there is any change in its membership, the administrator must report the change to the court.[3]

---

13 IR 1986, r 2.32(1).
14 IR 1986, r 2.32(2).
15 IR 1986, r 2.32(3).
16 IR 1986, r 2.33(1). For the prescribed form of certificate of constitution of the creditors' committee, see rr 2.33, 12.7, Sch 4, Form 2.13.
17 Ie under the Companies Act 1985, s 375.
18 IR 1986, r 2.33(2) (substituted by SI 1987/1919).
19 IR 1986, r 2.33(2A) (added by SI 1987/1919).
20 IR 1986, r 2.33(3). For the prescribed form of amended certificate, see rr 2.33, 12.7, Sch 4, Form 2.13.
 1 Ie deliver to the court for filing: IR 1986, rr 13.1, 13.13(3).
 2 IR 1986, r 2.33(4).
 3 IR 1986, r 2.33(5). For the prescribed form of notice by the administrator of a change in committee membership, see rr 2.33, 12.7, Sch 4, Form 2.14.

Entitlement to vote: proxies

Subject to the following provisions, at a meeting of creditors in administration proceedings a person is entitled to vote only if:

(1)   he has given to the administrator, not later than 12.00 hours on the business day before the day[4] fixed for the meeting, details in writing of the debt,[5] which he claims to be due to him from the company, and the claim has been duly admitted under the ensuing provisions of the rule; and

(2)   there has been lodged with the administrator any proxy[6] which he intends to be used on his behalf.[7]

The chairman of the meeting may allow a creditor to vote, notwithstanding that he has failed to comply with head (1) above, if satisfied that the failure was due to circumstances beyond the creditor's control.[8]

The administrator or, if other, the chairman of the meeting may call for any document or other evidence to be produced to him, where he thinks it necessary for the purpose of substantiating the whole or any part of the claim.[9]

Votes are calculated according to the amount of a creditor's debt as at the date of the administration order, deducting any amounts paid in respect of the debt after that date.[10] In an appropriate case it is open to a creditor to split his vote by value.[11]

A creditor may not vote in respect of a debt for an unliquidated amount, or any debt whose value is not ascertained, except where the chairman agrees to put upon the debt an estimated minimum value for the purpose of entitlement to vote and admits the claim for that purpose.[12] The rule against double proof applies in this as in all insolvency situations.[13]

The chairman's decision in respect of any matter arising under the above provisions is subject to appeal to the court by any creditor.[14] In the event of such an appeal, the court is not limited to reviewing the material considered by the chairman and forming the basis of his decision: it may consider whatever admissible evidence the parties to the appeal put before it.[15]

---

4   For the meaning of 'business day', see p 567, note 8.

5   Details of the debt must include any calculation for the purposes of IR 1986, rr 2.24–2.27: r 2.22(1).

6   The provisions relating to proxies and company representation are the same as those which apply to meetings in a winding up. See IR 1986, rr 8.1–8.7.

7   IR 1986, r 2.22(1). There is no stipulation as to the time by which the proxy has to be lodged with the administrator; it can, accordingly, be lodged at the creditors' meeting, if necessary: *Re Philip Alexander Securities & Futures Ltd* [1998] BPIR 383.

8   IR 1986, r 2.22(2).

9   IR 1986, r 2.22(3).

10   IR 1986, r 2.22(4).

11   *Re Polly Peck International plc* [1991] BCC 503.

12   IR 1986, r 2.22(5).

13   *Re Polly Peck International plc* [1996] BCC 486.

14   IR 1986, r 2.23(2).

15   *Re Philip Alexander Securities & Futures Ltd* [1998] BPIR 383.

At a meeting of creditors a secured creditor[16] is entitled to vote only in respect of the balance, if any, of his debt after deducting the value of his security as estimated by him.[17]

A creditor may not vote in respect of a debt on, or secured by, a current bill of exchange or promissory note, unless he is willing:

(a)   to treat the liability to him on the bill or note of every person who is liable on it antecedently to the company, and against whom a bankruptcy order has not been made, or in the case of a company, which has not gone into liquidation, as a security in his hands; and

(b)   to estimate the value of the security and, for the purpose of his entitlement to vote, to deduct it from his claim.[18]

For this purpose of entitlement to vote at a creditors' meeting in administration proceedings, a seller of goods to the company under a retention of title agreement[19] must deduct from his claim the value, as estimated by him, of any rights arising under that agreement in respect of goods in the possession of the company.[20]

An owner of goods under a hire purchase[1] or chattel leasing agreement,[2] or a seller of goods under a conditional sale agreement,[3] is entitled to vote in respect of the amount of the debt due and payable to him by the company as at the date of the administration order.[4] However, in calculating the amount of any debt for this purpose, no account must be taken of any amount attributable to the exercise of any right under the relevant agreement, insofar as the right has become exercisable solely by virtue of the presentation of the petition for an administration order or any matter arising in consequence of that, or of the making of the order.[5]

Admission and rejection of claims

At any creditors' meeting the chairman has power to admit or reject a creditor's claim for the purpose of his entitlement to vote; and the power is exercisable with respect to the whole or any part of the claim.[6] If the chairman is in doubt as to whether a claim should be admitted or rejected, he must mark it as objected to and allow the creditor to vote, subject to his vote being subsequently declared

16 A 'secured creditor' is a creditor who holds in respect of his debt a security over property of the company: IA 1986, s 248.
17 IR 1986, r 2.24.
18 IR 1986, r 2.25.
19 For the meaning of 'retention of title agreement' see IA 1986, s 251.
20 IR 1986, r 2.26.
 1 For the meaning of 'hire-purchase agreement', see IA 1986, s 436.
 2 For the meaning of 'chattel leasing agreement', see IA 1986, s 251.
 3 For the meaning of 'conditional sale agreement', see IA 1986, s 436.
 4 IR 1986, r 2.27(1).
 5 IR 1986, r 2.27(2).
 6 IR 1986, r 2.23(1).

invalid if the objection to the claim is sustained.[7] The chairman's decision under these provisions is subject to appeal to the court by any creditor.[8] If on an appeal the chairman's decision is reversed or varied, or a creditor's vote is declared invalid, the court may order that another meeting be summoned, or make such order as it thinks just.[9] In the case of the meeting summoned to consider the administrator's proposals,[10] an application to the court by way of appeal under the above provisions against a decision of the chairman may not be made later than 28 days after the delivery[11] of the administrator's report.[12] Neither the administrator nor any person nominated by him to be chairman is personally liable for costs incurred by any person in respect of an appeal to the court under the above provisions, unless the court makes an order to that effect.[13]

Resolutions and minutes

At a creditors' meeting in administration proceedings, a resolution is passed when a majority, in value, of those present and voting, in person or by proxy, have voted in favour of it;[14] any resolution is, however, invalid if those voting against it include more than half in value of the creditors to whom notice of the meeting was sent and who are not, to the best of the chairman's belief, persons connected with the company.[15] A person is 'connected' with a company if he is a director or shadow director of the company or if he is an associate of the company.[16]

The chairman of the meeting must cause minutes of its proceedings to be entered in the company's minute book.[17] The minutes must include a list of the creditors who attended personally or by proxy and, if a creditors' committee has been established, the names and addresses of those elected to be members of the committee.[18]

Venue and conduct of company meetings

Where the administrator summons a meeting of members of the company, he must fix a venue[19] for it, having regard to their convenience.[20]

---

7 IR 1986, r 2.23(3).
8 IR 1986, r 2.23(2).
9 IR 1986, r 2.23(4).
10 See IA 1986, s 23.
11 Ie in accordance with IA 1986, s 24(4).
12 IR 1986, r 2.23(5).
13 IR 1986, r 2.23(6).
14 IR 1986, r 2.28(1) (amended by SI 1987/1919).
15 IR 1986, r 2.28(1A) (added by SI 1987/1919).
16 IA 1986, s 249. For shadow director, see IA 1986, s 251. As to associates, see IA 1986, s 435.
17 IR 1986, r 2.28(2).
18 IR 1986, r 2.28(3).
19 Ie the date, time and place.
20 IR 1986, r 2.31(1).

The chairman of the meeting must be the administrator or a person nominated by him in writing to act in his place.[1] A person so nominated must be either one who is qualified to act as an insolvency practitioner in relation to the company,[2] or an employee of the administrator or his firm who is experienced in insolvency matters.[3]

If within 30 minutes from the time fixed for commencement of the meeting there is no person present to act as chairman, the meeting stands adjourned to the same time and place in the following week or, if that is not a business day,[4] to the business day immediately following.[5]

Subject to the above provisions, the meeting must be summoned and conducted as if it were a general meeting of the company summoned under the company's articles of association, and in accordance with the applicable provisions of the Companies Act 1985.[6]

The chairman of the meeting must cause minutes of its proceedings to be entered in the company's minute book.[7]

Functions and meetings of the committee

The creditors' committee must assist the administrator in discharging his functions, and act in relation to him in such manner as may be agreed from time to time.[8]

Meetings of the committee must be held when and where determined by the administrator.[9] The administrator must, however, call a first meeting of the committee not later than three months after its establishment; and thereafter he must call a meeting (1) if so requested by a member of the committee or his representative, the meeting then to be held within 21 days of the request being received by the administrator; and (2) for a specified date, if the committee has previously resolved that a meeting be held on that date.[10]

The administrator must give seven days' written notice of the venue[11] of any meeting to every member of the committee, or his representative[12] designated for that purpose, unless in any case the requirement of notice has been waived by or on behalf of any member; and waiver may be signified either at or before the meeting.[13]

---

1 IR 1986, r 2.31(2).
2 As to insolvency practitioners and their qualification, see the discussion at pp 53–59 supra.
3 IR 1986, r 2.31(3).
4 For the meaning of 'business day', see p 567, note 8.
5 IR 1986, r 2.31(4).
6 IR 1986, r 2.31(5).
7 IR 1986, r 2.31(6).
8 IR 1986, r 2.34(1).
9 IR 1986, r 2.34(2).
10 IR 1986, r 2.34(3).
11 Ie the date, time and place.
12 For committee members' representatives see infra.
13 IR 1986, r 2.34(4).

The chairman and quorum at meetings

The chairman at any meeting of the creditors' committee must be the administrator or a person nominated by him in writing to act.[14] A person so nominated must be either one who is qualified to act as an insolvency practitioner in relation to the company,[15] or an employee of the administrator or his firm who is experienced in insolvency matters.[16]

A meeting of the committee is duly constituted if due notice of it has been given to all the members, and at least two members are present or represented.[17]

Committee members' representatives

A member of the committee may, in relation to the business of the committee, be represented by another person duly authorised by him for that purpose.[18] A person acting as a committee member's representative must, however, hold a letter of authority entitling him so to act, either generally or specially, and signed by or on behalf of the committee member.[19] For this purpose, any proxy or any authorisation[20] under the Companies Act 1985 in relation to any meeting of creditors of the company is, unless it contains a statement to the contrary, to be treated as such a letter of authority to act generally signed by or on behalf of the committee member.[1]

The chairman at any meeting of the committee may call on a person claiming to act as a committee member's representative to produce his letter of authority, and may exclude him if it appears that his authority is deficient.[2]

No member may be represented by a body corporate, or by a person who is an undischarged bankrupt, or is subject to a composition or arrangement with his creditors.[3]

No person may act on the same committee at one and the same time as representative of more than one committee member or may act both as member of the committee and as representative of another member.[4]

Where a member's representative signs any document on the member's behalf, the fact that he so signs must be stated below his signature.[5]

---

14 IR 1986, r 2.35(1). Rule 2.35(1) is subject to r 2.44(3) (administrator required to attend a meeting).
15 As to insolvency practitioners and their qualifications, see pp 53–59 above.
16 IR 1986, r 2.35(2).
17 IR 1986, r 2.36.
18 IR 1986, r 2.37(1).
19 IR 1986, r 2.37(2) (amended by SI 1987/1919).
20 See CA 1985, s 375.
 1 IR 1986, r 2.37(2) (as amended).
 2 IR 1986, r 2.37(4).
 3 IR 1986.
 4 IR 1986, r 2.37(5).
 5 IR 1986, r 2.37(6).

Termination of membership and removal

A member of the committee may resign by notice in writing delivered to the administrator.[6]

Membership of the creditors' committee is automatically terminated if the member:

(1) becomes bankrupt, or compounds or arranges with his creditors; or

(2) at three consecutive meetings of the committee is neither present nor represented, unless at the third of those meeting it is resolved that this provision is not to apply in his case; or

(3) ceases to be, or is found never to have been, a creditor.[7]

However, if the cause of termination is the member's bankruptcy, his trustee in bankruptcy replaces him as a member of the committee.[8]

A member of the committee may be removed by resolution at a meeting of creditors, at least fourteen days' notice having been given of the intention to move that resolution.[9]

Vacancies

If there is a vacancy in the membership of the creditors' committee, the vacancy need not be filled if the administrator and a majority of the remaining members of the committee so agree, provided that the total number of members does not fall below the minimum required.[10]

The administrator may appoint any creditor, being qualified to be a member of the committee, to fill the vacancy, if a majority of the other members of the committee agree to the appointment, and the creditor concerned consents to act.[11]

Procedure at meetings: resolutions by post

At any meeting of the creditors' committee, each member of it, whether present himself, or by his representative,[12] has one vote; and a resolution is passed when a majority of the members present or represented have voted in favour of it.[13] Every resolution passed must be recorded in writing, either separately or as part

---

6 IR 1986, r 2.38.
7 IR 1986, r 2.39(1).
8 IR 1986, r 2.39(2).
9 IR 1986, r 2.40.
10 IR 1986, r 2.41(1), (2). The minimum number of members required is at least three: IR 1986, r 2.32(1).
11 IR 1986, r 2.41(3).
12 As to committee members' representatives see p 570 above.
13 IR 1986, r 2.42(1).

of the minutes of the meeting,[14] and a record of each resolution must be signed by the chairman and placed in the company's minute book.[15]

The administrator may seek to obtain the agreement of members of the creditors' committee to a resolution by sending to every member, or his representative designated for the purpose, a copy of the proposed resolution.[16] Where the administrator makes use of such procedure, he must send out to members of the committee or their representatives, as the case may be, a copy of any proposed resolution on which a decision is sought which must be set out in such a way that agreement with or dissent from each separate resolution may be indicated by the recipient on the copy so sent.[17]

Any member of the committee may, within seven business days[18] from the date of the administrator sending out a resolution, require him to summon a meeting of the committee to consider the matters raised by the resolution.[19] In the absence of such a request, the resolution is deemed to have been passed by the committee if and when the administrator is notified in writing by a majority of the members that they concur with it.[20] A copy of every resolution passed under this procedure, and a note that the committee's concurrence was obtained, must be placed in the company's minute book.[1]

Information from administrator

Where the committee resolves to require the attendance of the administrator,[2] the notice to him must be in writing signed by the majority of the members of the committee for the time being; and a member's representative may sign for him.[3]

The meeting at which the administrator's attendance is required must be fixed by the committee for a business day;[4] and must be held at such time and place as he determines.[5]

Where the administrator so attends, the members of the committee may elect any one of their number to be chairman of the meeting, in place of the administrator or a nominee of his.[6]

Expenses of members

The administrator must defray out of the assets of the company any reasonable

14 IR 1986, r 2.42(2).
15 IR 1986, r 2.42(3).
16 IR 1986, r 2.43(1).
17 IR 1986, r 2.43(2) (amended by SI 1987/1919).
18 For the meaning of 'business day' see p 567, note 8.
19 IR 1986, r 2.43(3).
20 IR 1986, r 2.43(4).
 1 IR 1986, r 2.43(5).
 2 IA 1986, s 26(2).
 3 IR 1986, r 2.44(1).
 4 For the meaning of 'business day', see p 567, note 8.
 5 IR 1986, r 2.44(2).
 6 IR 1986, r 2.44(3).

travelling expenses directly incurred by members of the creditors' committee or their representatives in relation to their attendance at the committee's meetings, or otherwise on the committee's business, as an expense of the administration.[7] These provisions do not, however, apply to any meeting of the committee held within three months of a previous meeting, unless the meeting in question is summoned at the instance of the administrator.[8]

Members' dealing with the company

Membership of the committee does not prevent a person from dealing with the company while the administration order is in force, provided that any transactions in the course of such dealings are in good faith and for value.[9]

The court may, on the application of any person interested, set aside any transaction which appears to it to be contrary to these requirements, and may give such consequential directions as it thinks fit for compensating the company for any loss which it may have incurred in consequence of the transaction.[10]

Formal defects

The acts of the creditors' committee established for any administration are valid notwithstanding any defect in the appointment, election or qualifications of any member of the committee or any committee-members' representative or in the formalities of its establishment.[11]

PROTECTION OF INTERESTS OF CREDITORS AND MEMBERS

Petition on grounds of unfairly prejudicial conduct

At any time when an administration order is in force, a creditor or member of the company may apply to the court by petition on the ground:

(1) that the company's affairs, business and property are being or have been managed by the administrator in a manner which is unfairly prejudicial to the interests of its creditors or members generally, or of some part of its creditors or members, including at least himself; or

(2) that any actual or proposed act or omission of the administrator is or would be so prejudicial.[12]

---

7 IR 1986, r 2.45(1).
8 IR 1986, r 2.45(2).
9 IR 1986, r 2.46(1).
10 IR 1986, r 2.46(2).
11 IR 1986, r 2.46(A).
12 IA 1986, s 27(1).

Nothing in the provisions giving the administrator power to deal with charged property[13] is to be taken as prejudicing any such applications to the court.[14]

Orders which may be made

On a petition presented to the court on the grounds of unfairly prejudicial conduct (as discussed above) the court may, subject to the following provisions, make such order as it thinks fit for giving relief in respect of the matters complained of, or adjourn the hearing conditionally or unconditionally, or make an interim order or any other order that it thinks fit.[15]

Such an order must not prejudice or prevent:

(1) the implementation of a voluntary arrangement which has been approved,[16] or any compromise or arrangement which has been sanctioned;[17] or

(2) where the application for the order was made more than 28 days after the approval of any proposals or revised proposals,[18] the implementation of those proposals or revised proposals.[19]

Subject to the above provisions, such an order may in particular:

(a) regulate the future management by the administrator of the company's affairs, business and property;

(b) require the administrator to refrain from doing or continuing an act complained of by the petitioner, or to do an act which the petitioner has complained he has omitted to do;

(c) require the summoning of a meeting of creditors or members for the purpose of considering such matters as the court may direct;

(d) discharge the administration order and make such consequential provision as the court thinks fit.[20]

If the administration order ought not to have been made (as being unfairly prejudicial to the complaining creditor the court has jurisdiction to rescind it.[1]

---

13 Ie IA 1986, s 15 or 16.
14 IA 1986, s 27(5).
15 IA 1986, s 27(2). See *Re Charnley Davies Ltd* [1988] BCLC 243, 4 BCC 152 (trial of preliminary issues refused).
16 See IA 1986, s 4.
17 See Companies Act 1985, s 425 (amended by the IA 1985, s 109, Sch 6, para 11).
18 Ie under IA 1986, s 24 or 25.
19 IA 1986, s 27(3).
20 IA 1986, s 27(4).
 1 *Cornhill Insurance plc v Cornhill Financial Services Ltd* [1992] BCC 818, CA (invoking IR
1986, r 7.47).

Duty of administrator where administration order discharged

Where, on an application on the grounds of unfairly prejudicial conduct, the administration order is discharged, the administrator must, within 14 days after the making of the order effecting the discharge, send an office copy of that order to the registrar of companies. If, without reasonable excuse, he fails to comply with this provision, he is liable on summary conviction after continued contravention, to a daily default fine not exceeding one-fiftieth of the statutory maximum.[2]

---

2 IA 1986, ss 27(6), 430, and Sch 10.

CHAPTER 39

Voluntary arrangement under Insolvency Act 1986

INTRODUCTION

One of the specified purposes for which an administration order can be made is that it would be likely to achieve approval of a voluntary arrangement under Part I of the Insolvency Act 1986 or the sanctioning under section 425 of the Companies Act 1985 of a compromise or arrangement between the company and any such persons as are mentioned in section 425. For this reason where a company or its creditors see a voluntary arrangement as representing the best chance of the company's survival the administration procedure will be invoked first because the very presentation of the petition secures the necessary breathing space for the preparation of a voluntary arrangement.

The ensuing discussion refers exclusively to voluntary arrangements under the Insolvency Act 1986, and does not consider the section 425 procedure which it is expected to supplant.[1]

THE PROPOSAL

Definition of terms

A voluntary arrangement under the Insolvency Act 1986 is a composition in satisfaction of a company's debts or a scheme of arrangement of the company's affairs.[2] It involves a proposal to the company and its creditors for such a composition[3] or scheme of arrangement.[4] The word 'company' in this context and for the purposes of the provisions affecting administrators under the Insolvency Act 1986 is 'a company formed and registered under [the Companies Act 1985]' or the former Companies Acts excepting the Joint Stock Companies Acts, the Companies Act 1862, the Companies (Consolidation) Act 1908,[5] and

---

1 For discussion of the procedure under CA 1985, s 425, see *Palmer's Company Law* (24th edn) 1131–1150 (Chapter 79); and *Gore Browne on Companies* (44th edn) 30.10–30.14.
2 IA 1986, s 1(1).
3 See *Re Contal Radio Ltd* [1932] 2 Ch 66.
4 IA 1986, s 1(1).
5 See Companies Act 1985, s 735 referred to in IA 1986, s 251.

does not include a foreign corporation (except where a contrary intention appears).[6] The word 'arrangement' is one of wide import,[7] meaning more than a mere compromise, but it still involves some element of give and take.[8] It involves something less than the release or discharge of creditors' debts, eg a moratorium. But it does not necessarily involve a compromise or release and there is no such compromise or release in the case of a scheme which provides merely for a moratorium.[9] On the other hand the absence of any practical prospect of a dividend for unsound creditors does not permit a proposal being either a composition or a scheme of arrangement: the correct approach in the absence of authority suggesting an opposite conclusion is not to instruct the type of voluntary arrangement which could be opposed by creditors.[10] An express agreement in terms of such a proposal between the company and all the creditors being binding and enforceable[11] could properly be called both a composition in satisfaction of the company's debts and a scheme of arrangement of its affairs.[12]

A proposal, for this purpose, is one which provides for some person ('the nominee') to act in relation to the voluntary arrangement either as a trustee or otherwise for the purpose of supervising its implementation.[13] The nominee must be a person who is qualified to act as an insolvency practitioner in relation to the company.[14]

Once a voluntary arrangement is approved and takes effect the person supervising its implementation is known as the supervisor of the voluntary arrangement.[15] In the great majority of cases 'the supervisor' will be the same person as 'the nominee' unless the latter has been replaced.[16] The supervisor will of necessity be a person who is qualified to act as an insolvency practitioner in relation to the company.

Persons who may propose an arrangement

When there is no administration order in force in relation to a company and the company is not being wound up the directors may make the proposal.[17] If,

---

6 *Re International Bulk Commodities Ltd* [1992] BCC 463; and *Re Dallhold Estates Pty Ltd* [1992] BCC 394.

7 *Re Dorman Long & Co Ltd* [1934] Ch 635; *Re Savoy Hotel Ltd* [1981] Ch 351, [1981] 3 All ER 646.

8 *Mercantile Investment and General Trust Co v International Co of Mexico* [1893] 1 Ch 484n; *Re Guardian Assurance Co* [1917] 1 Ch 431; *Re National Bank Ltd* [1966] 1 All ER 1006, [1966] 1 WLR 819; *Re Re NFU Development Trust Ltd* [1973] 1 All ER 135, [1972] 1 WLR 1548; *Re Savoy Hotel Ltd* [1981] Ch 351, [1981] 3 All ER 646; see further *Re Suiderland Development Corpn Ltd, ex p Kaap-Kuene Beleggings Beperk* 1986 (2) SA 442 (C) and see Andre Coetzee 'More on companies' schemes of arrangement' (1986) 7 Co Lawyer 266–268.

9 *Marsh Estates plc v Gunmark Ltd* [1996] 2 BCLC 1 at 5; [1996] BPIR 439.

10 *IRC v Adams & Partners Ltd* [1999] 2 BCLC 730 (Nicholas Warren QC).

11 IA 1986, s 5(2).

12 *IRC v Adams & Partners Ltd* [1999] 2 BCLC 730.

13 IA 1986, s 1(1), (2).

14 IA 1986, s 1(2).

15 IA 1986, s 7(2).

16 See IA 1986, ss 2(4), 4(2).

17 IA 1986, s 1(1).

however, there is an administration order in force the administrator is the only person who can make the proposal.[18] Neither creditors nor members of a company have the standing to propose a voluntary arrangement.

The procedure differs according to whether the nominee is either the liquidator or the administrator of the company, or is another insolvency practitioner.

False representations

A person being a past or present officer[19] of a company commits an offence if he makes any false representation or commits any other fraud for the purpose of obtaining the approval of the company's members or creditors to a proposal for a voluntary arrangement.[20] A person guilty of such an offence is liable on indictment to imprisonment for a term not exceeding seven years or a fine, or to both, or on summary conviction to imprisonment for a term not exceeding six months or a fine not exceeding the statutory maximum or to both.[1]

PROCEDURE ON A PROPOSAL WHERE NOMINEE IS ANOTHER INSOLVENCY PRACTITIONER

Preparation and contents of the proposal

Where the intended nominee is not the liquidator or administrator of the company but rather some other insolvency practitioner the procedure is as set out in this section.

Preparation

An administrator intending to make the proposal must submit to the nominee a document setting out the terms of the proposed voluntary arrangement, and a statement of the company's affairs for the purposes of enabling the nominee to prepare his report to the court.[2]

He must prepare for the intended nominee a proposal on which, with or without amendments, to make his report to the court.[3] The directors' proposal must provide a short explanation of why, in their opinion, a voluntary arrangement is

---

18 IA 1986, s 1(3). If the company is being wound up the proposal must be made by the liquidator: ibid.
19 'Officer' includes a director, manager or secretary: IA 1986, s 251 applying CA 1985, s 744. In the context of the rule dealing with false representations officer includes a shadow director: IR 1986, r 1.30(2). 'Shadow director' in relation to a company means a person in accordance with whose directions or instructions the directors are accustomed to act; but so that a person is not deemed a shadow director by reason only that the directors act on advice given by him in a professional capacity: IA 1986, s 251.
20 IR 1986, r 1.30(1).
1 IR 1986, rr 1.30(1), (3), 12.21, Sch 5.
2 IA 1986, s 2(1), (3).
3 IR 1986, r 1.2.

desirable, and give reasons why the company's creditors may be expected to concur with such an arrangement.[4]

Contents of proposal

The following matters must be stated, or otherwise dealt with, in the administrator's proposal:

(1)   the following matters, so far as within the administrator's immediate knowledge:
  (a)   the company's assets, with an estimate of their respective values;
  (b)   the extent, if any, to which the assets are charged in favour of creditors;
  (c)   the extent, if any, to which particular assets are to be excluded from the voluntary arrangement;[5]

(2)   particulars of any property, other than assets of the company itself, which is proposed to be included in the arrangement, the source of such property and the terms on which it is to be made available for inclusion;[6]

(3)   the nature and amount of the company's liabilities, so far as within the administrator's immediate knowledge, the manner in which they are proposed to be met, modified, postponed or otherwise dealt with by means of the arrangement, and, in particular:
  (a)   how it is proposed to deal with preferential creditors and creditors who are, or claim to be, secured;[7]
  (b)   how persons connected with the company,[8] being creditors, are proposed to be treated under the arrangement; and
  (c)   whether there are, to the administrator's knowledge, any circumstances giving rise to the possibility, in the event that the company should go into liquidation, of claims under the provisions dealing with transactions at an undervalue,[9] preference,[10] extortionate credit transactions,[11] or invalidity of floating charges;[12] and, where any such circumstances are present, whether, and if so how, it is proposed under the voluntary arrangement to make provision for wholly or partly indemnifying the company in respect of such claims,[13]

---

4 IR 1986, r 1.3(2)(a).
5 IR 1986, r 1.3(2)(b).
6 'Secured creditor', in relation to a company, means a creditor of the company who holds in respect of his debt a security over property of the company; and 'unsecured creditor' is to be read accordingly: IA 1986, s 248. 'Security' means, in relation to England and Wales, any mortgage, charge, lien or other security: s 248.
7 For the meaning of 'connected' with a company see IA 1986, s 249.
8 Ie under the IA 1986, s 238.
9 Ie under IA 1986, s 239.
10 Ie under IA 1986, s 244.
11 Ie under IA 1986, s 245.
12 IR 1986, r 1.3(2)(c).
13 IR 1986, r 1.3(2)(d).

(4)   whether any, and if so what, guarantees have been given of the company's debts by other persons, specifying which, if any, of the guarantors are persons connected with the company;[14]

(5)   the proposed duration of the voluntary arrangement;[15]

(6)   the proposed dates of distributions to creditors, with estimates of their amounts;[16]

(7)   the amount proposed to be paid to the nominee, as such, by way of remuneration and expenses;[17]

(8)   the manner in which it is proposed that the supervisor of the arrangement should be remunerated, and his expenses defrayed;[18]

(9)   whether, for the purposes of the arrangement, any guarantees are to be offered by the administrator, or other persons, and whether, if so, any security is to be given or sought;[19]

(10)   the manner in which funds held for the purposes of the arrangement are to be banked, invested or otherwise dealt with pending distribution to creditors;[20]

(11)   the manner in which funds held for the purposes of payment to creditors, and not so paid on the termination of the arrangement, are to be dealt with;[1]

(12)   the manner in which the business of the company is proposed to be conducted during the course of the arrangement;[2]

(13)   details of any further credit facilities which it is intended to arrange for the company, and how the debts so arising are to be paid;[3]

(14)   the functions that are to be undertaken by the supervisor of the arrangement;[4] and

(15)   the name, address and qualification of the person proposed as supervisor of the voluntary arrangement, and confirmation that he is, so far as the administrator is aware, qualified to act as an insolvency practitioner in relation to the company.[5]

---

14 IR 1986, r 1.3(2)(c).
15 IR 1986, r 1.3(2)(d).
16 IR 1986, r 1.3(2)(f).
17 IR 1986, r 1.3(2)(g).
18 IR 1986, r 1.3(2)(h).
19 IR 1986, r 1.3(2)(j).
20 IR 1986, r 1.3(2)(k).
 1 IR 1986, r 1.3(2)(l).
 2 IR 1986, r 1.3(2)(m).
 3 IR 1986, r 1.3(2)(n).
 4 IR 1986, r 1.3(2)(o).
 5 IR 1986, r 1.3(2)(p). As to insolvency practitioners and their qualifications, see at pp 53–59 supra.

With the agreement in writing of the nominee, the administrator's proposal may be amended at any time up to the delivery of the nominee's report to the court.[6]

Notice to intended nominee

The administrator must give to the intended nominee written notice of his proposal.[7] The notice, accompanied by a copy of the proposal, must be delivered either to the nominee himself, or to a person authorised to take delivery of documents on his behalf.[8]

If the intended nominee agrees to act, he must cause a copy of the notice to be indorsed to the effect that it has been received by him on a specified date; and the period of 28 days in which he is under a duty to submit a report to the court[9] runs from that date.[10] The copy of the notice so indorsed must be returned by the nominee forthwith to the administrator at an address specified by him in the notice for that purpose.[11]

Statement of affairs

Where the proposal is made by the administrator, but he is not himself the nominee, he must provide to the nominee a copy of the company's statement of affairs with the proposal.[12]

Additional disclosure

If it appears to the administrator's nominee that he cannot properly prepare his report on the basis of information in the proposal and statement of affairs, he may call on the administrator to provide him with:

(1)   further and better particulars as to the circumstances in which, and the reasons why, the company is insolvent or, as the case may be, threatened with insolvency;

(2)   particulars of any previous proposals which have been made in respect of the company;[13]

---

6   IR 1986, r 1.3(3).
7   IR 1986, r 1.4(1), as applied to an administrator by r 1.12(1). For a form, see 10(1) Court Forms (1999 Issue) 249, Form 6.
8   IR 1986, r 1.4(2).
9   Ie under IA 1986, s 2(2).
10 IR 1986, r 1.4(3) as applied to the case where administrator makes proposal but is not the nominee by r 1.12(2).
11 IR 1986, r 1.4(4).
12 IR 1986, r 1.12(5). As to such statement of affairs see at p 551.
13 Ie under the Insolvency Act 1986, Pt 1 (ss 1–7).

(3)   any further information with respect to the company's affairs which the nominee thinks necessary for the purposes of his report.[14]

The nominee may call on the administrator to inform him, with respect to any person who is, or at any time in the two years preceding the notice to him[15] has been, a director or officer of the company, whether and in what circumstances, in those two years or previously, that person has been concerned in the affairs of any other company, whether or not incorporated in England and Wales, which has become insolvent, or has himself been adjudged bankrupt or entered into an arrangement with his creditors.[16]

For the purposes of enabling the nominee to consider the proposal and prepare his report, the administrator must give him access to the company's accounts and records.[17]

As the nominee will rely heavily on information provided by the company there is a need for complete candour on the part of the company.[18]

Nominee's report on the proposal

The nominee must, within 28 days, or such longer period as the court may allow, after he is given notice of the proposal for a voluntary arrangement, submit a report to the court stating whether, in his opinion, meetings of the company and of its creditors should be summoned to consider the proposal, and, if in his opinion such meetings should be summoned, the date on which, and the time and place at which, he proposes the meetings should be held.[19] With his report to the court the nominee must deliver a copy of the proposal[20] and a copy or summary of the company's statement of affairs.[1]

If the nominee makes known his opinion that meetings of the company and its creditors should be summoned,[2] his report must have annexed to it his comments on the proposal; and if his opinion is otherwise, he must give his reasons for that opinion.[3] The court must cause the nominee's report to be indorsed with the date on which it is filed in court; and any director, member or creditor of the company is entitled, at all reasonable times on any business day,[4] to inspect the

---

14   IR 1986, r 1.6(1), applied to cases where the administrator makes the proposal by r 1.12(4).
15   Ie under IR 1986, r 1.4.
16   IR 1986, r 1.6(2).
17   IR 1986, r 1.6(3).
18   See *Re Debtor (No 14010 of 1995)* [1996] 2 BCLC 429 (an individual voluntary arrangement). The principle would appear to apply to a company voluntary arrangement.
19   IA 1986, s 2(1), (2). For a form of report, see 10(1) Court Forms (1999 Issue) 39–41, Form 11.
20   Ie with amendments, if any, authorised under IR 1986, r 1.3(3).
 1   IR 1986, rr 1.7(1), 1.12(7).
 2   Ie under IA 1986, s 3.
 3   IR 1986, rr 1.7(2), 1.12(7).
 4   For these purposes, 'business day', if the court is the High Court, has the same meaning as is given in RSC Ord 65, r 5(4) and, in relation to a county court, it means any day on which the court is open in accordance with CCR 1981, Ord 2, r 2: IR 1986, rr 13.1, 13.13(1) (substituted by SI 1987/1919). 'Business day' has the same meaning in rr 4.10, 4.11 13.1, 13.13(1) (as so substituted). For the meaning of 'business day' elsewhere in the IR 1986 (amended by SI 1987/1919) and in the IA 1986, see p 567.

file.[5] The nominee must send a copy of his report, and of his comments if any, to the company.[6]

The ambit of the nominee's function in reviewing the proposal and reporting to the court on it was the subject of analysis by Lindsay J in *Re a Debtor (No 140 IO of 1995)*[7]. That case in fact involved an individual voluntary arrangement but similar principles apply *mutatis mutandis* in the case of company voluntary arrangements.

It was there held that it was no part of the nominee's duties to act as a postbox for the proposals without querying the information presented. It is not, of course, to be expected that in every case the nominee will have personally verified every figure and have tested every part of the proposal. Often, for example, the financial resources available to him to fund the inquiries that would be necessary to do that will be very limited or the figures will be plain and undoubted. But within the scheme of the 1986 Act, as discernible from the powers and duties given to the nominee, it is to be expected as a minimum of the nominee, at least in those cases where the fullness or candour of the debtor's information has properly come into question, that the nominee shall have taken such steps as are in all the circumstances reasonable to satisfy himself and shall have satisfied himself on three counts.

These three counts are (1) that the debtor's true position as to assets and liabilities does not appear to him in any material respect to differ substantially from that which it is represented to the creditors to be; (2) that it does appear to him that the debtor's proposal as put to the creditors' meeting has a real prospect of being implemented in the way it is represented it will be; (3) that the information that he has provides a basis such that (within the broad limits inescapably applicable to what have to be the speedy and robust functions of admitting or rejecting claims to vote and agreeing values for voting purposes) no already-manifest yet unavoidable prospective unfairness in relation to those functions is present[8].

Replacement of defaulting nominee

On an application made by the person intending to make the proposal, in a case where the nominee has failed to submit a report,[9] the court may direct that the nominee be replaced as such by another person qualified to act as an insolvency practitioner in relation to the company.[10] Where any person intends to make such an application to the court for the nominee to be replaced, he must give to the nominee at least seven days' notice of his application.[11]

5 IR 1986, rr 1.7(3), 1.12(7).
6 IR 1986, rr 1.7(4), 1.12(7).
7 [1996] 2 BCLC 429.
8 [1996] 2 BCLC 429 at 435c–e.
9 Ie as required by the IA 1986, s 2(2).
10 IA 1986, ss 2(1), (4).
11 IR 1986, rr 1.8, 1.12(7).

Summoning of meetings

Where the nominee is the administrator,[12] he must summon meetings of the company and of its creditors to consider the proposal for such a time, date and place as he thinks fit.[13] The persons to be summoned to a creditors' meeting are every creditor of the company of whose claim the person summoning the meeting is aware.[14]

The administrator must fix a venue[15] for the creditors' meetings and the company meeting and give at least 14 days' notice of the meetings, in the case of the creditors' meeting to all the creditors specified in the company's statement of affairs and to any other creditor of whom he is aware,[16] and in the case of the company meeting, to all persons who are, to the best of his belief, members of the company.[17]

Each such notice must state the effect of the provisions dealing with requisite majorities of creditors at the creditors' meeting,[18] and with each notice there must be sent a copy of the proposal, and a copy of the statement of affairs or, if the nominee thinks fit, a summary of it, the summary to include a list of creditors and the amount of their debts.[19]

CONSIDERATION OF THE PROPOSAL

Meetings of company's creditors and members

Calling of meetings

The rules for calling meetings of creditors and members in relation to a voluntary arrangement do not differ very greatly from those which apply in the case of an administration.

The first, overriding, point is that in fixing the venue for the creditors' meeting and the company meeting the person summoning the meeting must have regard to the convenience of the creditors.[20] Meetings must in each case be summoned for commencement between 10 am and 4 pm on a business day.[1] For these purposes, 'business day' means any day other than a Saturday, a Sunday, Christmas Day, Good Friday or a day which is a bank holiday in any part of Great Britain.[2] The meetings must be held on the same day and in the same place, but

---

12 The same rule applies to the liquidator who is the nominee.
13 IA 1986, s 3(2).
14 IA 1986, s 3(3).
15 References to the 'venue' for any proceedings or attendance before the court, or for a meeting, are to the time, date and place for the proceeding, attendance or meeting: IR 1986, rr 13.1, 13.6.
16 IA 1986, s 3(3).
17 IR 1986, r 1.11(1).
18 For the relevant provisions, see IR 1986, r 1.19(1), (3), (4).
19 IR 1986, r 1.11(2).
20 IR 1986, r 1.13(1).
 1 IR 1986, r 1.13(2).
 2 IA 1986, s 251; IR 1986, rr 13.1, 13.13(1).

the creditors' meeting must be fixed for a time in advance of the company meeting.[3] With every notice summoning either meeting there must be sent out forms of proxy.[4]

The chairman at meetings

Subject to the following provisions, at both the creditors' meeting and at the company meeting, and at any combined meeting, the person summoning the meeting must be chairman.[5] If, for any reason, he is unable to attend, he may nominate another person to act as chairman in his place; but a person so nominated must be either a person qualified to act as an insolvency practitioner in relation to the company, or an employee of the person summoning the meeting or his firm who is experienced in insolvency matters.[6]

The chairman may not, by virtue of any proxy held by him, vote to increase or reduce the amount of the remuneration or expenses of the nominee or the supervisor of the proposed arrangement, unless the proxy specifically directs him to vote in that way.[7]

Attendance by company officers

At least 14 days' notice to attend the meetings must be given by the person summoning the meetings to all directors of the company, and to any persons in the case of whom the person summoning the meeting thinks that their presence is required as being officers of the company, or as having been directors or officers of it at any time in the two years immediately preceding the date of the notice.[8]

The chairman may, if he thinks fit, exclude any present or former director or officer from attendance at a meeting, either completely or for any part of it; and this applies whether or not a notice to attend the meeting has been sent to the person excluded.[9]

Decisions of meetings and voting

Decisions of meetings

The meetings of creditors and the company summoned[10] to consider the proposal must decide whether to approve the proposed voluntary arrangement, with or

3 IR 1986, r 1.13(3).
4 IR 1986, r 1.13(4). For the prescribed form of proxy see IR 1986, rr 1.13(4), 12.7, Sch 4, Form 8.1.
5 IR 1986, r 1.14(1).
6 IR 1986, r 1.14(2).
7 IR 1986, r 1.15.
8 IR 1986, r 1.16(1).
9 IR 1986, r 1.16(2).
10 Ie the meeting summoned under the IA 1986, s 3.

without modifications.[11] The modifications may include one conferring the functions proposed to be conferred on the nominee on another person qualified to act as an insolvency practitioner in relation to the company, but they must not include any modification by virtue of which the proposal[12] ceases to be a proposal for a voluntary arrangement.[13]

A meeting so summoned may not approve any proposal or modification which affects the right of a secured creditor[14] of the company to enforce his security, except with the concurrence of the creditor concerned.[15] Nor may a meeting so summoned approve any proposal or modification under which any preferential debt[6] of the company is to be paid otherwise than in priority to such of its debts as are not preferential debts, or a preferential creditor[16] of the company is to be paid an amount in respect of a preferential debt that bears to that debt a smaller proportion than is borne to another preferential debt by the amount that is to be paid in respect of that other debt.[17] However, the meeting may approve such a proposal or modification with the concurrence of the preferential creditor concerned.[17]

Subject to the above provisions, each of the meetings must be conducted in accordance with the rules.[18] However, an approval given at a meeting is not invalidated by any irregularity at or in relation to the meeting.[19]

Creditors

It is convenient to separate first the voting rights and requisite majorities in respect of creditors.

Voting rights   Subject to the various other provisions set out below, every creditor who was given notice of the creditors' meeting is entitled to vote at the meeting or any adjournment of it.[20] And creditors who are deliberately not given notice of the meeting, but who obtain notice by another route may also attend and vote.[1] If a formal notice is put in the post but never arrives and the intended recipient hears of the meeting from another source but chooses not to attend he is bound by the voluntary arrangement on which he could have voted.[2] A voluntary arrangement does not bind a person who was not entitled to

---

11 IA 1986, s 4(1). 'Modifications' includes additions, alterations and omissions and cognate expressions are to be construed accordingly: s 436.
12 Ie a proposal such as is mentioned in IA 1986, s 1.
13 IA 1986, s 4(2).
14 For the meaning of 'secured creditor' see p 584 fn 6.
15 IA 1986, s 4(3).
16 For these purposes, references to preferential debts and preferential creditors are to be read in accordance with ibid, s 386: s 4(7). For the purposes of s 4 references to 'the relevant date' in relation to a company which is not being wound up are, where an administration order is in force in relation to the company, to the date of the making of that order: s 387(1), (2).
17 IA 1986, s 4(4).
18 IA 1986, s 4(5).
19 IA 1986, s 6(7). This is subject to the right to challenge decisions under s 6.
20 IR 1986, r 1.17(1).
 1 *Re Debtors (Nos 400 and 401 of 1996)* [1997] 1 WLR 1319 at 1327–1328.
 2 See *Beverley Group plc v McClue* [1995] 2 BCLC 407.

vote at the creditors' meeting: on a parity of reasoning such a person cannot take advantage of the arrangement.[3] It is otherwise if the creditor entitled to vote assigns the benefit of his contract with the company: the assignee is bound by the consequences and can sue on it.[4] Votes are calculated according to the amount of the creditor's debt as at the date of the meeting or, where the company is being wound up or is subject to an administration order, the date of its going into liquidation[5] or, as the case may be, of the administration order.[6] A creditor may not, however, vote in respect of a debt for an unliquidated amount, or any debt whose value is not ascertained, except where the chairman agrees[7] to put upon the debt an estimate minimum value for the purpose of entitlement to vote.[8] Moreover if a person declines to attend a creditors' meeting he cannot validly object that the chairman has failed to put an estimated reduction on his debt.[9]

At any creditors' meeting the chairman has power to admit or reject a creditor's claim for the purpose of his entitlement to vote, and the power is exercisable with respect to the whole or any part of the claim.[10] The chairman's decision on a creditor's entitlement to vote is subject to appeal to the court by any creditor or member of the company.[11] If the chairman is in doubt whether a claim should be admitted or rejected, he must mark it as objected to and allow the creditor to vote, subject to his vote being subsequently declared invalid if the objection to the claim is sustained.[12] If, on an appeal, the chairman's decision is reversed or varied, or a creditor's vote is declared invalid, the court may order another meeting to be summoned, or make such order as it thinks just; the court's power to make such an order is exercisable only if it considers that the matter is such as gives rise to unfair prejudice[13] or material irregularity.[14] A decision to reject a proof for voting purposes, if wrong, will be a material irregularity when it affected the outcome of the meeting.[15]

An application to the court by way of appeal against the chairman's decision may not be made after the end of the period of 28 days beginning with the first day on which each of the reports[16] of the results of the meetings has been made

3 *R A Securities Ltd v Mercantile Credit Co Ltd* [1994] BCC 598.
4 *Burford Midland Properties Ltd v Marley Extrusions Ltd* [1994] BCC 604.
5 For the meaning of 'go into liquidation' see IA 1986, s 247(2).
6 IR 1986, r 1.17(1).
7 This means 'expresses a willingness' to put a value on the debt: *Re Cancol Ltd* [1996] 1 BCLC 100 in which Knox J follows his earlier decision in *Doobar v Alltime Securities Ltd* [1995] 1 BCLC 316 (approved in [1996] 1 WLR 456, CA) and did not follow *Crawley Mansions Ltd* [1995] 1 BCLC 290 (Ferris J); *Re Sweatfield Ltd* [1997] BCC 744 (Judge Weeks).
8 IR 1986, r 1.17(2). See *Re Sweatfield Ltd* [1997] BCC 744.
9 *Beverley Group plc v McClue* [1995] 2 BCLC 407.
10 IR 1986, r 1.17(4).
11 IR 1986, r 1.17(5).
12 IR 1986, r 1.17(6). See *Re Debtor (No 222 of 1990), ex p Bank of Ireland* [1992] BCLC 137.
13 See *Sea Voyager Maritime Inc v Bielecki* [1999] 1 BCLC 133.
14 IR 1986, r 1.17(7). As to material irregularities see *Re Sweatfield Ltd* [1997] BCC 744; *Re Cardona* [1997] BCC 697 cf *National Westminster Bank plc v Scher* [1998] BPIR 224.
15 *Longford North Central plc v Brook* [1999] BPIR 701.
16 Ie the reports required by IA 1986, s 4(6).

to the court.[17] The chairman is not personally liable for any costs incurred by any person in respect of an appeal to the court under these provisions.[18]

Requisite majorities Subject to the following provisions, at the creditors' meeting for any resolution to pass approving any proposal or modification there must be a majority in excess of three-quarters in value of the creditors present in person or by proxy and voting on the resolution.[19] The same provision applies in respect of any other resolution proposed at the meeting, but substituting one-half for three-quarters.[20]

In the following cases there is to be left out of account a creditor's vote in respect of any claim or part of a claim:

(1) where written notice of the claim was not given, either at the meeting or before it, to the chairman or person summoning the meeting;

(2) where the claim or part is secured;[1]

(3) where the claim is in respect of a debt wholly or partly on, or secured by, a current bill of exchange or promissory note, unless the creditor is willing to treat the liability to him on the bill or note of every person who is liable on it antecedently to the company, and against whom a bankruptcy order has not been made or, in the case of a company, which has not gone into liquidation,[2] as a security in his hands, and to estimate the value of the security and, for the purpose of entitlement to vote, but not of any distribution under the arrangement, to deduct it from his claim.[3]

However where the debt is partly secured the creditor may put a value on the security and vote in respect of the unsecured balance.[4]

It is for the chairman of the meeting to decide whether a vote is to be left out of account in accordance with the above provisions.[5]

Any resolution is invalid if those voting against it include more than half in value of the creditors, counting in these latter only those:

(a) to whom notice of the meeting was sent;

(b) whose votes are not to be left out of account under the above provisions; and

(c) who are not, to the best of the chairman's belief, persons connected with the company.[6]

---

17 IR 1986, r 1.17(8). Semble, the court could nevertheless extend this time: *Tager v Westpac Banking Corpn* [1998] BCC 73 (corresponding provisions for *individual* voluntary arrangement).
18 IR 1986, r 1.17(9).
19 IR 1986, r 1.19(1).
20 IR 1986, r 1.19(2).
 1 For the meaning of 'secured creditor' see p 572 fn 16.
 2 For the meaning of 'go into liquidation' see IA 1986, s 247(2).
 3 IR 1986, r 1.19(3).
 4 *Calor Gas Ltd v Piercy* [1994] BCC 69.
 5 IR 1986, r 1.19(5)(a).
 6 IR 1986, r 1.19(4). For the meaning of 'connected' with a company see p 584 fn 7.

It is for the chairman of the meeting to decide whether a person is a connected person for these purposes; and in such a case the chairman is entitled to rely on the information provided by the company's statement of affairs or otherwise in accordance with the rules relating to company voluntary arrangements.[7]

If the chairman uses a proxy to vote for an increase or reduction in the amount of the remuneration or expenses of the nominee or supervisor where the proxy does not specifically direct him so to vote,[8] his vote with that proxy does not count towards any majority under the above provisions.[9]

An appeal against the decision of the chairman under the above provisions lies to the court.[10]

Members

Next, the voting rights and requisite majorities in the case of members require analysis.

Voting rights   Members of the company at their meeting vote according to the rights attaching to their shares respectively in accordance with the articles.[11] However, where no voting rights attach to a member's shares, he is nevertheless entitled to vote either for or against the proposal[12] or any modification of it.[13]

Requisite majorities   Subject to the following provisions, and to any express provision made in the articles, at a company meeting any resolution is to be regarded as passed if voted for by more than one-half in value of the members present in person or by proxy and voting on the resolution; and the value of members is determined by reference to the number of votes conferred on each member by the company's articles. In determining whether a majority for any resolution has been obtained, there is to be left out of account any vote cast in accordance with the provision entitling a member to vote notwithstanding that no voting rights attach to his shares.

If the chairman uses a proxy to vote for an increase or reduction in the amount of the remuneration or expenses of the nominee or supervisor where the proxy does not specifically direct him so to vote, his vote with that proxy does not count towards any majority under the above provisions.

Proceedings to obtain agreement on the proposal

On the day on which the meetings of creditors and the company are held, they may from time to time be adjourned; and if the chairman thinks fit for the

---

7 IR 1986, r 1.19(5).
8 Ie contrary to IR 1986, r 1.15.
9 IR 1986, r 1.19(6).
10 IR 1986, r 1.19(7). The applicable provisions regarding such an appeal are rr 1.17(5)–(9).
11 For these purposes, references to a person's shares include any other interest which he may have as a member of the company: IR 1986, r 1.18(3).
12 IR 1986, r 1.18(1).
13 IR 1986, r 1.18(2).

purpose of obtaining the simultaneous agreement of the meetings to the proposal, with the same modifications, if any, the meetings may be held together.[14]

If on that day the requisite majority for the approval of the voluntary arrangement, with the same modifications, if any, has not been obtained from both creditors and members of the company, the chairman may, and must if it is so resolved, adjourn the meetings for not more than 14 days.[15] If there are subsequently further adjournments, the final adjournment must not be to a day later than 14 days after the date on which the meetings were originally held.[16] There must, however, be no adjournment of either meeting unless the other is also adjourned to the same business day.[17] If, following any final adjournment of the meeting, the proposal, with the same modifications, if any, is not agreed by both meetings, it is deemed rejected.[18]

Report of meetings

After the conclusion of either meeting, the chairman of the meeting must report the result of the meeting to the court.[19] The report of the meetings must be prepared by the person who was chairman of them,[20] and the report must:

(1) state whether the proposal for a voluntary arrangement was approved or rejected and, if approved, with what, if any, modifications;

(2) set out the resolutions which were taken at each meeting, and the decisions on each one;

(3) list the creditors and members of the company, with their respective values, who were present or represented at the meetings, and how they voted on each resolution; and

(4) include such further information, if any, as the chairman thinks it appropriate to make known to the court.[1]

A copy of the chairman's report must, within four days of the meetings being held, be filed in court;[2] and the court must cause that copy to be indorsed with the date of filing.[3]

Immediately after reporting to the court, the chairman of each meeting must also give notice of its result to all those who were sent notice of the meeting.[4] If the voluntary arrangement has been approved by the meetings, whether or not in

---

14 IR 1986, r 1.21(1).
15 IR 1986, r 1.21(2).
16 IR 1986, r 1.21(3).
17 IR 1986, r 1.21(4). For the meaning of 'business day' see p 567 fn 8.
18 IR 1986, r 1.21(6).
19 IA 1986, s 4(6).
20 IR 1986, r 1.24(1).
 1 IR 1986, r 1.24(2).
 2 'File in court' means deliver to the court for filing: IR 1986, rr 13.1, 13.13(3).
 3 IR 1986, r 1.24(3).
 4 The notice must be sent immediately after a copy of the chairman's report is filed in court under IR 1986, r 1.24(3): r 1.24(4).

the form proposed, the supervisor must forthwith send a copy of the chairman's report[5] to the registrar of companies.[6]

EFFECT AND IMPLEMENTATION OF THE ARRANGEMENT

Effect of approval

Where each of the meetings of creditors and the company approves the proposed voluntary arrangement either with the same modifications or without modifications, the approved voluntary arrangement takes effect as if made by the company at the creditors' meeting, and binds every person who[7] had notice[8] of, and was entitled to vote at, that meeting, whether or not he was present or represented at the meeting, as if he were a party to the voluntary arrangement.[9]

A voluntary arrangement can be varied in accordance with the company's proposals put forward to the company's creditors, so long as that is an appropriate power of variation contained in the voluntary arrangement.[10] Such a power of variation should be so worded as to permit variations or modifications which could have been validly included in the original proposal.[11] The court should not, however, imply a term into a voluntary arrangement but it could be varied by the specified majority; even though such a term is not uncommon there is no justification, on grounds of business efficacy, for inferring such a term.[12]

If the company is being wound up or an administration order is in force, the court may do one or both of the following, namely: (1) by order stay all proceedings in the winding up or discharge the administration order; (2) give such directions with respect to the conduct of the winding up or the administration as it thinks appropriate for facilitating the implementation of the approved voluntary arrangement.[13]

The court may not make any such order or give such directions: (a) at any time before the end of the period of 28 days beginning with the first day on which each of the reports[14] of the result of the meetings has been made to the court; or (b) at

---

5 IA 1986, s 4(6); IR 1986, r 1.24(4). There exists a prescribed form in the Insolvency Rules 1986, rr 1.24, 12.7, Sch 4, Form 1.1 (substituted by SI 1987/1919) of a report by the chairman of the meeting to the registrar of companies, required under the IA 1986, s 4. However, the only person required by IA 1986 or IR 1986 (amended by SI 1987/1919) to send a copy of the chairman's report to the registrar of companies is the supervisor.

6 IR 1986, r 1.24(5).

7 Ie in accordance with IR 1986 (amended by SI 1987/1919).

8 Notice means *actual* notice: see *Re a Debtor (No 64 of 1992); Bradford & Bingley Building Society v a Debtor* [1994] BCC 55.

9 IA 1986, s 5(1), (2). See also the cases referred to an at pp 591–592 in footnotes 1–4; and see also *Re Millwall Football Club and Athletic Co (1985) plc* [1999] BCC 455.

10 *Horrocks v Broome* [1999] BPIR 66.

11 *Horrocks v Broome* [1999] BPIR 66.

12 *Raja v Rubin and Goodman* [1998] BPIR 647.

13 IA 1986, s 5(3). Applications pursuant to s 5(3) must be made direct to a judge and, unless otherwise ordered, must be heard in open court: *Practice Direction* [1987] 1 All ER 107, [1987] 1 WLR 53.

14 Ie the reports required by IA 1986, s 4(6).

any time when an application challenging the decisions of the meeting,[15] or an appeal in respect of such an application, is pending, or at any time in the period within which such an appeal may be brought.[16]

The supervisor

Where a voluntary arrangement approved by the meetings of creditors and the company[17] has taken effect, the person who is for the time being carrying out in relation to the voluntary arrangement the functions conferred by virtue of the approval on the nominee, or where the nominee has been replaced,[18] on a person other than the nominee, is to be known as the supervisor of the voluntary arrangement.[19] A supervisor though not formally constituted a trustee is in fact and in law in the position of a trustee and payments made to him by the company and not yet distributed to the creditors cease to be part of the company's assets and are held in trust for the creditors.[20]

Neither a supervisor nor a nominee owes a duty of care to post-CVA creditors except where such supervisor or nominee has made a negligent misrepresentation when under a duty not to do so which then resulted in loss.[1] Nor is a supervisor liable to a private right of action by a creditor for breach of duty by the supervisor in that capacity.[2] The creditors' right is to complain under the statute.[3]

The supervisor may apply to the court for directions in relation to any particular matter arising under the voluntary arrangement, and is included among the persons who may apply to the court for the winding up of the company or for an administration order to be made in relation to it.[4]

Control by the court

If any of the company's creditors or any other person is dissatisfied by any act, omission or decision of the supervisor, he may apply to the court.[5] On application the court may: (1) confirm, reverse or modify any act or decision of the supervisor; (2) give him directions; or (3) make such other order as it thinks fit.[6]

---

15 Ie under IA 1986, s 6.
16 IA 1986, s 5(4).
17 Ie the meetings summoned under IA 1986, s 3.
18 Ie by virtue of IA 1986, s 2(4) or s 4(2).
19 IA 1986, s 7(1), (2).
20 *Re Leisure Study Group Ltd* [1994] 2 BCLC 65.
 1 *Heritage Joinery (a firm) v Krasner* [1999] BPIR 683.
 2 *King v Anthony* [1999] BPIR 73, CA (individual voluntary arrangement).
 3 IA 1986, s 7(3), referred to below.
 4 IA 1986, s 7(4).
 5 IA 1986, s 7(3).
 6 IA 1986, s 7(3).

Appointment of supervisor by the court

Whenever it is expedient to appoint a person to carry out the functions of the supervisor, and it is inexpedient, difficult or impracticable for an appointment to be made without the assistance of the court, the court may make an order appointing a person who is qualified to act as an insolvency practitioner in relation to the company, either in substitution for the existing supervisor or to fill a vacancy.[7]

Such power conferred on the court is exercisable so as to increase the number of persons exercising the functions of supervisor or, where there is more than one person exercising those functions, so as to replace one or more of those persons.[8]

Hand-over of property to supervisor

After the approval of the voluntary arrangement, the directors or, where the company is subject to an administration order and a person other than the administrator is appointed as supervisor of the voluntary arrangement, the administrator, must forthwith do all that is required for putting the supervisor into possession of the assets included in the arrangement.[9]

Where the company is subject to an administration order, the supervisor must, on taking possession of the assets, discharge any balance due to the administrator by way of remuneration or on account of fees, costs, charges and expenses properly incurred and payable,[10] and any advances made in respect of the company, together with interest[11] on such advances.[12] Alternatively, the supervisor must, before taking possession, give the administrator a written undertaking to discharge any such balance out of the first realisation of assets.[13]

The administrator has a charge on the assets included in the voluntary arrangement in respect of any sums so due as above until they have been discharged, subject only to the deduction from realisations by the supervisor of the proper costs and expenses of such realisations.[14] The supervisor must from time to time out of the realisation of assets discharge all guarantees properly given by the administrator, for the benefit of the company, and must pay all the expenses of the administrator.[15]

The supervisor has power to apply to the court for an order under the provisions relating to transactions defrauding creditors where the victim of the

---

7 IA 1986, s 7(5).

8 IA 1986, s 7(6).

9 IR 1986, r 1.23(1). See *Re Leisure Study Group Ltd* [1994] 2 BCLC 65 for his position as trustee for creditors.

10 Ie under IA 1986 or IR 1986 (amended by SI 1987/1919).

11 Ie at the rate specified in the Judgments Act 1938, s 17 at the date on which the company became subject to the administration order.

12 IR 1986, r 1.23(2).

13 IR 1986, r 1.23(3).

14 IR 1986, r 1.23(4).

15 IR 1986, r 1.23(5).

transaction is bound by a voluntary arrangement.[16] He can also petition for a winding up and claim fees despite voluntary liquidation.[17]

Power to ensure continuation of essential supplies by utilities

Where a voluntary arrangement, approved by meetings of creditors and the company[18] takes effect[19] and, if a request is made by or with the concurrence of the supervisor for the giving after the effective date[20] of: (1) a public supply of gas;[1] (2) a supply of electricity by an electricity board;[2] (3) a supply of water by statutory water undertakers or in Scotland, a water authority;[3] or (4) a supply of telecommunication services[4] by a public telecommunications operator,[17] the supplier: (a) may make it a condition of the giving of the supply that the supervisor personally guarantees the payment of any charges in respect of that supply; but (b) must not make it a condition of the giving of the supply, or do anything which has the effect of making it a condition of the giving of the supply, that any outstanding charges in respect of a supply given to the company before the effective date are paid.[5]

Supervisor's accounts and reports

Where the voluntary arrangement authorises or requires the supervisor to carry on the business of the company or trade on its behalf or in its name, or to realise assets of the company, or otherwise to administer or dispose of any of its funds, he must keep accounts and records of his acts and dealings in and in connection with the arrangement including, in particular, records of all receipts and payments of money.[6]

---

16 IA 1986, s 424(1)(b).
17 *Re Arthur Rathbone Kitchens Ltd* [1998] BCC 450.
18 Ie the meeting summoned under IA 1986, s 3.
19 The provisions of IA 1986, s 233 apply also where an administration order is made in relation to the company, or an administrative receiver is appointed. In such cases references to 'the supervisor' should be read as references to the administrator or the administrative receiver.
20 The 'effective date' for these purposes is whichever is applicable of the following dates: (1) the date on which the voluntary arrangement was approved by the meetings summoned under IA 1986, s 3; (2) the date on which the administration order was made; (3) the date on which the administrative receiver was appointed or, if he was appointed in succession to another administrative receiver, the date on which the first of his predecessors was appointed.
 1 'Public supply of gas' means a supply of gas by the British Gas Corporation or a public gas supplier within the meaning of the Gas Act 1986, Pt 1 (ss 1–48): IA 1986, s 233(5)(a).
 2 'Electricity board' has the same meaning as in the Energy Act 1983: IA 1986, s 233(5)(b).
 3 'Water authority' means the same as in the Water (Scotland) Act 1980: IA 1986, s 233(5)(c).
 4 'Telecommunication services' and 'public telecommunications operator' mean the same as in the Telecommunications Act 1984, except that the former does not include services consisting in the conveyance of programme services within the meaning of the Cable and Broadcasting Act 1984: IA 1986, s 233(5)(d).
 5 IA 1986, s 233(1)–(3).
 6 IR 1986, r 1.26(1).

The supervisor must, not less often than once in every 12 months beginning with the date of his appointment, prepare an abstract of such receipts and payments, and send copies of it, accompanied by his comments on the progress and efficacy of the arrangement, to the court, the registrar of companies,[7] the company, all those of the company's creditors who are bound by the arrangement, the members of the company who are so bound,[8] and, if the company is not in liquidation, the company's auditors for the time being.[9] If in any period of 12 months the supervisor has made no payments and had no receipts, he must at the end of that period send a statement to that effect to all the persons specified above.[2] An abstract provided under the above provisions must relate to a period beginning with the date of the supervisor's appointment or, as the case may be, the day following the end of the last period for which an abstract was prepared under these provisions; and copies of the abstract must be sent out, as required by the above provisions, within the two months following the end of the period to which the abstract relates.[10]

If the supervisor is not authorised as mentioned above,[11] he must, not less often than once in every 12 months beginning with the date of his appointment, send to all those persons specified above a report on the progress and efficacy of the voluntary arrangement.[12]

The court may, on application by the supervisor, dispense with the sending under the above provisions of abstracts or reports to members of the company, either altogether or on the basis that the availability of the abstract or report to members is to be advertised by the supervisor in a specified manner, and vary the dates on which the obligation to send abstracts or reports arises.[13]

Production of accounts and records to Secretary of State

The Secretary of State may at any time during the course of the voluntary arrangement or after its completion require the supervisor to produce for inspection his records and accounts in respect of the arrangement, and copies of abstracts and reports.[14] The Secretary of State may require production either at the premises of the supervisor or elsewhere; and it is the duty of the supervisor to comply with any requirement imposed on him under these provisions.[15]

The Secretary of State may cause any accounts and records produced to him under the above provisions to be audited; and the supervisor must give to the

---

7 For the prescribed form to be sent to the registrar of companies, see IR 1986, rr 1.26, 12.7, Sch 4, Form 1.3.

8 This is subject to IR 1986, r 1.26(5).

9 IR 1986, r 1.26(2).

10 IR 1986, r 1.26(3).

11 Ie in IR 1986, r 1.26(1): see text to note 6 on p 599 above.

12 IR 1986, r 1.26(4).

13 IR 1986, r 1.26(5).

14 IR 1986, r 1.27(1). The copies of abstracts and reports referred to are those prepared in compliance with r 1.26.

15 IR 1986, r 1.27(2).

Secretary of State such further information and assistance as he needs for the purposes of his audit.[16]

Fees, costs, charges and expenses

The fees, costs, charges and expenses that may be incurred for any of the purposes of the voluntary arrangement are: (1) any disbursements made by the nominee prior to the approval of the arrangement, and any remuneration for his services as such agreed between himself and the company or, as the case may be, the administrator or liquidator; (2) any fees, costs, charges or expenses, which are sanctioned by the terms of the arrangement, or would be payable, or correspond to those which would be payable, in an administration or winding up.[17]

CHALLENGE OF DECISIONS: REVOCATION OR SUSPENSION OF THE ARRANGEMENT

Grounds of challenge

An application to the court[18] may be made, by any of certain specified persons, on one or both of the following grounds, namely that a voluntary arrangement approved at the meetings[19] unfairly prejudices the interests of a creditor, member or contributory of the company, or that there has been some material irregularity at or in relation to either of the meetings.[20]

Who may apply and when

The persons who may apply to the court are a person entitled[1] to vote at either of the meetings, the nominee or any person who has replaced him[2] and, if an administration order is in force, the administrator.[3]

Such an application may not be made after the end of the period of 28 days beginning with the first day on which each of the reports of the results of the meetings of creditors and members[4] has been made to the court.[5]

---

16 IR 1986, r 1.27(3).
17 IR 1986, r 1.28.
18 As to the mode of application and procedure see 10(1) Court Forms (1999 Issue) 44–48, Forms 14–16.
19 Ie the meetings summoned under the IA 1986, s 3.
20 IA 1986, s 6(1).
 1 Ie under IA 1986, s 6(1)–(3).
 2 Ie under IA 1986, s 2(4) or 4(2).
 3 IA 1986, s 6(2).
 4 Ie the reports required by IA 1986, s 4(6).
 5 IA 1986, s 6(3). The reason for these time limits appears from ibid, s 5(4).

Powers of the court

Where on such an application[6] the court is satisfied as to either of the specified grounds for making such an application,[7] it may do one or both of the following, namely:

(1) revoke or suspend the approvals given by the meetings or, where there has been some material irregularity at or in relation to either of the meetings, any approval given by the meeting in question;[8]

(2) give a direction to any person for the summoning of further meetings to consider any revised proposal the person who made the original proposal may make or, where there has been some material irregularity at or in relation to either of the meetings, a further company or, as the case may be, creditors' meeting to reconsider the original proposal.[9]

Where at any time after giving a direction for the summoning of meetings to consider a revised proposal[10] the court is satisfied that the person who made the original proposal does not intend to submit a revised proposal, the court must revoke the direction and revoke or suspend any approval given at the previous meetings.[11]

In a case where the court, on such an application with respect to any meeting, gives a direction,[12] or revokes or suspends an approval,[13] the court may give such supplemental directions as it thinks fit and, in particular, directions with respect to things done since the meeting under any voluntary arrangement approved by the meeting.[14]

Except in pursuance of the above provisions,[15] an approval given at a meeting of creditors or members[16] is not invalidated by any irregularity at or in relation to the meeting.[17]

Procedure following revocation or suspension

Where the court makes an order of revocation or suspension of the arrangement,[18] the person who applied for the order must serve sealed copies of it on the supervisor of the voluntary arrangement and on the directors of the company or

---

6 Ie under IA 1986, s 6(1)–(3).
7 Ie those specified in IA 1986, s 6(1).
8 As to the procedure where an order of revocation or suspension is made see pp 602–603.
9 IA 1986, s 6(4).
10 Ie under IA 1986, s 6(4)(b): see head (2) supra.
11 IA 1986, s 6(5).
12 Ie under IA 1986, s 6(4)(b).
13 Ie under IA 1986, s 6(4)(a) or (5).
14 IA 1986, s 6(6).
15 Ie IA 1986, s 6(1)–(6).
16 Ie the meetings summoned under IA 1986, s 3.
17 IA 1986, s 6(7).
18 Ie under IA 1986, s 6.

the administrator or liquidator, according to who made the proposal for the arrangement; and service on the directors may be effected by service of a single copy of the order on the company at its registered office.[19] If the order includes a direction by the court for any further meetings to be summoned,[20] notice must also be given, by the person who applied for the order, to whoever is, in accordance with the direction, required to summon the meetings.[1]

The directors or, as the case may be, the administrator or liquidator must: (1) forthwith after receiving a copy of the court's order, give notice of it to all persons who were sent notice of the creditors' and company meetings or who, not having been sent that notice, appear to be affected by the order; and (2) within seven days of their receiving a copy of the order, or within such longer period as the court may allow, give notice to the court whether it is intended to make a revised proposal to the company and its creditors, or to invite reconsideration of the original proposal.[2]

The person on whose application the order of revocation or suspension was made must, within seven days after the making of the order, deliver a copy of the order to the registrar of companies.[3]

COMPLETION OF THE ARRANGEMENT

Terminal formalities

Not more than 28 days after the final completion of the voluntary arrangement, the supervisor must send to all the creditors and members of the company who are bound by it[4] a notice that the voluntary arrangement has been fully implemented.[5] With the notice there must be sent to each creditor and member a copy of a report by the supervisor summarising all receipts and payments made by him in pursuance of the arrangement, and explaining any difference in the actual implementation of it as compared with the proposal as approved by the creditors' and company meetings.[6]

The supervisor must, within the 28 days mentioned above, send to the registrar of companies and to the court a copy of the notice to creditors and members, together with a copy of the report.[7]

The court may, on application by the supervisor, extend the period of 28 days referred to above.[8]

---

19 IR 1986, r 1.25(1), (2).
20 Ie under IA 1986, s 6(4).
 1 IR 1986, r 1.25(3).
 2 IR 1986, r 1.25(4).
 3 IR 1986, r 1.25(5). For the prescribed form of notice to be given to the registrar of companies see rr 1.25, 12.7, Sch 4, Form 1.2.
 4 As to those bound by the voluntary arrangement see pp 591–592 and 596.
 5 IR 1986, r 1.29(1).
 6 IR 1986, r 1.29(2).
 7 Ibid, r 1.29(3). For the prescribed form to be sent to the registrar of companies see ibid, rr 1.29, 12.7, Sch 4, Form 1.4.
 8 Ibid, r 1.29(4).

FAILURE

The courts have over the last five years been concerned with a number of cases where it has been said that the relevant company voluntary arrangement had failed or terminated.[9] If a company voluntary arrangement is followed by a liquidation then devolution of the funds held by the supervisor depends on whether the trust has come to an end.[10] If the petition is brought by the supervisor (who acts at the request of the bound creditors) it necessarily follows that the scheme has come to an end.[11] On the other hand if the petition is brought by someone else and there is no breach of the scheme, the scheme continues as the trust is not broken.[12] If the petition is brought by someone else and the scheme has broken so that the supervisor might have brought the petition, it depends on the circumstances, the trust of the scheme, the conduct of the trust creditors and the legislation to decide what indications are to be drawn as to the state of the trust.[13]

9 The cases on individual voluntary arrangements are also relevant: see *Re McKeen (a debtor)* [1995] BCC 412 (no termination); *Re Bradley-Hole (a bankrupt), ex p Knight* [1995] 1 WLR 1097 (no termination); *Davis v Martin-Sklan* [1995] BCC 1, 122 (bankruptcy petition by supervisor).

10 *Re Maple Environmental Services Ltd* [2000] BCC 93 at 96G–H (Judge Boggis).

11 [2000] BCC 93; and see *Re Arthur Rathbone Kitchens Ltd* [1998] BCC 450 (Roger Kaye QC); *Souster v Carman Construction Co Ltd* [2000] BPIR 371.

12 [2000] BCC 93; *Re Excalibur Airways Ltd (in liquidation)* [1998] 1 BCLC 436.

13 [2000] BCC 93, at 96H–97A. See *Kings v Cleghorn* [1998] BPIR 463 (individual voluntary arrangement).

Part IV

International aspects

CHAPTER 40

Conflict of laws

Finance and business are carried on on an increasingly international scale; and economic recession knows no boundaries. In consequence the position of the receiver and manager in private international law has become a matter of no little interest and importance[1] and the same is true of an administrator.

CO-OPERATION BETWEEN COURTS EXERCISING JURISDICTION IN RELATION TO INSOLVENCY

Enforcement of orders as between different parts of the United Kingdom

An order made by a court in any part of the United Kingdom in the exercise of jurisdiction in relation to insolvency law[2] must be enforced in any other part of the United Kingdom as if it were made by a court exercising the corresponding jurisdiction in that other part.[3] Subject however to what is provided under this rubric[4] this general rule about enforcement does not require a court in any part of the United Kingdom to enforce, in relation to property situated in that part, any order made by a court in any other part of the United Kingdom.[5]

In this context 'insolvency law' means in relation to England and Wales the provisions of the Insolvency Act 1986 and various sections[6] of Company Directors Disqualification Act 1986.[7] In relation to Scotland the provisions of the Insolvency Act 1986 extending to Scotland (together with the same provisions of the Company Directors Disqualification Act 1986 and in relation to Northern

---

1 The leading discussion in periodical literature is Lawrence Collins 'Floating Charges, Receivers and Managers and the Conflict of Laws' (1978) 27 ICLQ 691 reprinted (1979) 31 CBR (NS) 234 and Collins *Essays in International Litigation: The Conflict of Laws* (1994) 43 et seq.
2 IA 1986, s 426(10).
3 IA 1986, s 426(1).
4 Ie all the other provisions of IA 1986, s 426.
5 IA 1986, s 426(2).
6 IA 1986, ss 10, 12, 15, 19(c) and 20 with Sch 1.
7 IA 1986, s 426(10)(b). And see also Companies Act 1989, s 183(1) bringing Part VII of that Act (Financial Markets and Insolvency) within s 426.

Ireland provisions made by or under the Insolvency (Northern Ireland) Order 1989[8] constitute the relevant insolvency law.[9] This covers of course receiverships and administrations under the 1986 Act.

Assistance between courts in the United Kingdom and designated countries and territories: the 'judicial assistance' provision

It is further provided that courts having jurisdiction in relation to insolvency law[10] in any part of the United Kingdom shall assist the courts having corresponding jurisdiction in any other part of the United Kingdom or any relevant country or territory, which last expression includes any of the Channel Islands and the Isle of Man and any other designated country or territory.

Despite the use of the mandatory sounding 'shall' in this provision the Court of Appeal confirmed in *Hughes v Hannover Rückversicherungs AG*[11] that the court retained a discretion in the matter and might if it thought fit (as it did in that case) reject the request for assistance.

Designated countries and territories

Various countries and territories have been designated over the years for the purposes of this provision. So far three statutory instruments have been used. The main list dates back to 1986[12] and comprises Anguilla, Australia, The Bahamas, Bermuda, Botswana, Canada, Cayman Islands, Falkland Islands, Gibraltar, Hong Kong, Republic of Ireland, Montserrat, New Zealand, St Helena, Turks and Caicos Islands, Tuvalu, Virgin Islands. In 1996 two further countries joined the class namely Malaysia and the Republic of South Africa.[13] Finally and most recently Brunei was added.[14] The only other subordinate legislation worth mentioning is the Insolvency Act 1986 (Guernsey) Order 1989[15] which extends to the Bailiwick of Guernsey various provisions of section 426 of the Insolvency Act 1986.[16]

Source of the request

Fundamental to the exercise of the jurisdiction to give assistance under section 426 is the initiation of a request by a foreign court. The request must be an

---

8 SI 1989 No 2405.

9 IA 1986, s 426(10)(b) and (c).

10 See footnote 7 above. It includes procedural and substantive law: *Re Bank of Credit and Commerce International SA* [1993] BCC 787.

11 [1997] BCC 921, CA (material change of circumstances since request justified rejection of assistance).

12 Co-operation of Insolvency Courts (Designation of Countries and Territories) Order 1986, SI 1986 No 2123, art 2, Schedule.

13 Co-operation of Insolvency Courts (Designation of Countries and Territories) Order 1996, SI 1996 No 253, art 2, Schedule.

14 Co-operation of Insolvency Courts (Designation of Countries and Territories) Order 1998, SI 1998 No 2766.

15 SI 1989 No 2409.

16 IA 1986, s 426(4), (5), (10), (11) (as amended).

incoming request for assistance. The judicial assistance provision does not apply so as to enable the English court to request assistance from the relevant foreign court.[17] Whether the request must come from a foreign court recognised on English principles as having the power to appoint a liquidator or may emanate from any court having any type of insolvency jurisdiction is uncertain. It seems preferable simply to take such factors into account in the exercise of the court's discretion rather than treating the matter as going to the fundamental applicability of the judicial assistance provision.

Applicable law

The English court may apply either English insolvency law or the insolvency law of the requesting court in relation to comparable matters. By the law of the requesting court is meant so much of the law of the relevant country or territory as 'corresponds'[18] to the statutory provisions constituting insolvency law in England, Scotland and Northern Ireland as the case may be. This does not mean that the English court is restricted to applying just the statutory provisions mentioned in the judicial assistance provision. The English court can exercise its own general jurisdiction and powers.[19]

Assistance

Despite the mandatory language ('shall assist') the court has a discretion as to whether it will assist or not:[20] it can decide to reject the request.[1] It is inclined to lean in favour of the request and will co-operate with the foreign court unless there is some good[2] or compelling[3] reason for not doing so.[4] Moreover in exercising its discretion whether to apply a particular insolvency law the requested court is directed to have regard in particular to the rules of private international law. This means that it should consider the effect of those rules in the circumstances of the case, but 'having regard' to them does not prescribe the application of those rules in every situation. If acting pursuant to a request would result in an

---

17 As mistakenly assumed in *McIsaac and Wilson Petitioners* 1995 SLT 498.

18 It need not be the same: *Re Business City Express Ltd* [1997] 2 BCLC 510. Correspond should probably be given a broad meaning see Dicey and Morris *The Conflict of Laws* (13th edn, 2000) 1146–1147 paras 30-01–30-02 commenting on *Re Business City Express Ltd* [1997] 2 BCLC 510 where however there was no consideration of correspondence between English and Irish law.

19 *Hughes v Hannover Rückversicherungs AG* [1997] 1 BCLC 497, CA.

20 *Re Dallhold Estates (UK) Pty Ltd* [1992] BCLC 621; *Hughes v Hannover Rückversicherungs AG* [1997] 1 BCLC 497, CA.

 1 See for cases of rejection: *Re Focus Insurance Co Ltd* [1997] 1 BCLC 219 (undermining an insolvency procedure in England already initiated by the applicants); *Hughes v Hannover Rückversicherungs AG* [1997] 1 BCLC 497, CA (material change in circumstances since request made): *England v Purves* [1999] 2 BCLC 256 (order for examination would have been denied to English liquidator and though available under Australian law would be oppressive).

 2 *Re Bank of Credit and Commerce International SA (No 9)* [1994] 3 All ER 764 revsd in part but not on this point [1994] [1994] 1 WLR 708, CA.

 3 *Re Dallhold Estates (UK) Pty Ltd* [1992] BCLC 621 at 627.

 4 *Hughes v Hannover Rückversicherungs AG* [1997] 1 BCLC 497, CA.

English court enforcing a foreign revenue law[5] or infringing English public policy[6] the court may justifiably refuse to accede to the request.

Administration order may be made pursuant to a request even if no original jurisdiction to make such an order

An administration order may be made over a foreign or unregistered company at the request of a foreign company even though there may be no original jurisdiction to make such an order in this country independently of the judicial assistance provision.[7]

RECOGNITION OF RECEIVERS APPOINTED UNDER DEBENTURES

The position of a receiver in part depends upon the extent to which the floating charge under which he is appointed is recognised and enforced in the jurisdiction in which recovery is proposed. Accordingly it is necessary to consider a number of questions which go both to the validity and to the enforceability of the charge. Chief among these are: (1) What law governs the capacity to create a floating charge? (2) What is the proper law of the charge? (3) What is the scope of the charge? (4) To what extent will the charge be recognised abroad? (5) To what extent will the receiver and manager be recognised abroad and if appointed abroad recognised in this country?

Capacity to create a charge

There is at least one case which suggests that the capacity of a company to create a floating charge depends on the law of incorporation. The case in question *Carse v Coppen*[8] was a Scots case decided at a time when the concept of a floating charge was 'utterly repugnant' to the principles of Scots law. A company registered in Scotland with a place of business and assets in England executed a floating charge in Scotland but in the English form charging all its assets English and Scottish. It was conceded that the charge could not possibly take effect over the Scottish assets but the Court of Session, by a majority, held that the company had not created a valid charge over the English assets. The majority of the court viewed the floating charge as a type of universal assignment and on that footing it is not surprising that the governing law was considered to be the law of the place of incorporation. However, the classification of the floating charge as

---

5 *Re Bank of Credit and Commerce International (No 9)* [1994] 3 All ER 764 revsd in part but not on this point [1994] 1 WLR 708, CA.

6 *Hughes v Hannover Rückversicherungs AG* [1997] 1 BCLC 497, CA at 518; *England v Purves* [1999] 2 BCLC 256.

7 *Re Dallhold Estates (UK) Pty Ltd* [1992] BCLC 621. See the discussion at 624.

8 1951 SC 233. The case of *Re Anchor Line (Henderson Bros) Ltd* [1937] Ch 483, [1937] 2 All ER 823 was no support for the proposition: see 1951 SC 233 at 239–240.

equivalent to universal succession is difficult to accept.[9] Neither a receiver nor a debenture holder is in truth a successor. Until crystallisation the company is overlord of its own property and after crystallisation the company still retains its equity of redemption.

If a floating charge is viewed simply as a species of mortgage, idiosyncratic and sophisticated perhaps but a mortgage nevertheless, the importation of principles applicable to universal assignments seems quite inappropriate.

Scope of charge

The tendency today is to broaden the scope of floating charges. This tendency reflects not only a desire to maximise security in an unfavourable economic climate but also the increasing internationalism of trade and credit. For this reason, no doubt, mortgage debentures often create a charge over 'the whole of the company's undertaking, property and assets whatsoever and wheresoever'. Such a formulation plainly covers foreign assets. Indeed in *British South Africa Co v De Beers Consolidated Mines Ltd*[10] Swinfen Eady J said:

'An English debenture purporting to charge by way of floating security all the English company's property and assets does amount, where the English company possesses land abroad, to an agreement to charge that land, and is a valid equitable security according to English law.'

This passage was quoted with approval by Luxmoore J in *Re Anchor Line (Henderson Bros) Ltd*[11] who held that 'when an English company possesses land abroad and purports to charge it by way of floating charge, the charge, putting it at its lowest, amounts to an agreement to charge that land and is a valid equitable security according to English law.' The court in exercise of its equitable jurisdiction in personam enforces equities in regard to foreign land where the mortgagor company is within the jurisdiction.[12] The charge must however purport to charge all the assets of the company or 'all the assets whatsoever and wheresoever'.

The language of the floating charge may however be too narrow to extend to foreign assets and in that event the floating charge will not cover them.

Proper law

The proper law of the floating charge is dictated by the contract for the creation of the charge, and not by the situs of the propery charged.[13] If, as is frequently the

---

9 See the analysis in Lawrence Collins, op cit at 699–700 and 241–242.
10 [1910] 1 Ch 354 at 387.
11 [1937] Ch 483 at 488.
12 See *Penn v Lord Baltimore* (1750) 1 Ves Sen 444; *Mercantile Investment and General Trust Co v River Plate Trust, Loan and Agency Co* [1892] 2 Ch 303, 61 LJ Ch 473.
13 *British South Africa Co v De Beers Consolidated Mines Ltd* [1910] 1 Ch 354, 79 LJ Ch 345 (revsd on other grounds [1912] AC 52, 81 LJ Ch 137, HL); *Re Smith* [1916] 2 Ch 206, 85 LJ Ch 802.

case, the debenture contains an express choice of law that choice will generally be accepted.[14] In the absence of such an express choice the parties' intention may be inferred from the terms and nature of the contract and from the general circumstances of the case.[15] Failing a clearly implied intention the proper law will be the system of law with which the contract has its closest and most real connection.[16]

There was no express choice of law provision in the floating charge in issue in *Re Anchor Line (Henderson Bros) Ltd.*[17] A shipping company incorporated in England with a registered office in Liverpool had its head office in Glasgow, Scotland where a considerable part of its business was carried on. During the economic recession of the 1930s it got into financial difficulties and executed a charge in favour of the Union Bank of Scotland. The charge was executed in Glasgow but was in English form and was registered at the Companies Registry in London. The question raised was whether the charge operated as a valid and effective security over certain classes of assets so far as they were at the date of the commencement of the liquidation locally situate in Scotland. A preliminary question was: which law governed the construction of the charge? It was therefore necessary to identify the proper law, which governs such questions. Luxmoore J dealt with this point shortly:[18]

> 'In form the charge is substantially an English debenture with the usual floating charge. Such a charge is unknown to the law of Scotland. It was given by an English company and although it was executed in Scotland it must I think be construed according to English law.'

The form therefore prevailed over the place of execution.

Recognition of a floating charge in other jurisdictions

Difficult questions arise where a charge valid by its proper law is sought to be enforced in another jurisdiction where the *lex situs* of an asset included in the charge requires registration. In England a floating charge created by a company registered in England is void against the liquidator or any creditor of the company unless the prescribed particulars of the charge together with the instrument, if any, by which the charge is created or evidenced are returned to or received by the registrar of companies for registration within the prescribed period.[19] This registration procedure is mirrored in one way or another in many different jurisdictions. The counsel of caution is that floating charges on the assets of English companies with property abroad ought to comply with the relevant registration requirements of the foreign countries where the assets are

14 Dicey and Morris *Conflict of Laws* (13th edn) Vol 2, 1216–1232.
15 *Dicey and Morris*, 1223.
16 *Dicey and Morris*, 1234–1242.
17 [1937] Ch 483, [1937] 2 All ER 823.
18 [1937] Ch 483 at 487.
19 CA 1985, s 395(2)(f).

situated.[20] It has been stated judicially[1] that it 'is not unreasonable that a mortgagee, relying for his security on a floating charge over movables or over assets to be acquired by the mortgagor in the future, should ensure that whatever state in future those assets move to or be located in, his charge is there registered so that those who may deal with the mortgagor can ascertain its true position as to encumbrances over the assets'.

This counsel of prudence would in some cases give rise to multiple registration obligations where the movables are particularly mobile. In this connection the decision of the High Court of Australia in *Luckins v Highway Motel (Carnarvon) Pty Ltd*[2] is particularly interesting. A company incorporated and registered in Victoria carried on the business of a coach tour operator. Its coach tours never began or ended in Western Australia but they did sometimes pass through that state. In August 1973 the company created a floating charge over all its assets wherever situated. The charge was registered in Victoria but not in Western Australia. It crystallised in January 1974 when the debenture holder appointed a receiver and manager. Subsequently a creditor obtained a judgment in Western Australia and executed its judgment by directing the bailiff to seize a bus then in Western Australia. There was no evidence where the bus had been at the date of the creation of the charge or of its crystallisation. The receiver under the floating charge claimed the bus as subject to the receivership. The bailiff took out interpleader proceedings, in which the High Court, by a four to one majority, decided that the receiver's title under the charge was void against the judgment creditor because the charge was unregistered in Western Australia, notwithstanding that the company itself was not registered in that state.

Much of the argument was concerned with whether or not the company was 'carrying on business' in Western Australia. This was because the relevant legislation in that state applied to a foreign company which had a place of business or was carrying on business within the state. By a majority[3] the High Court held that the company was carrying on business in Western Australia: it incurred debts there for food, accommodation and camping fees in connection with the coach tours which it was conducting. Barwick CJ dissented: the main contractual obligations arose outside the state; and the incidental expenses relied upon by the majority were not such, in his view, as to amount to carrying on business in Western Australia.

One argument deployed on behalf of the receiver and manager was that if the charge over the bus was lawfully created in 1973 in the place where the bus was then situate the charge ought to be recognised in Western Australia. Gibbs J dealt with that argument as follows:[4]

'It may be accepted that, although there is not a great deal of authority on the point, that in general the validity of a charge on chattels is to be determined in accordance with the law of the place where the chattels are situated when the charge is created . . . although perhaps it could be suggested that the validity of

20 See Gower *Modern Company Law* (4th edn) 479–480 (not repeated in 6th edn).
1 See *Luckins v Highway Motel (Carnarvon) Pty Ltd* (1975) 133 CLR 164 at 186 per Stephen J.
2 (1975) 133 CLR 164.
3 Gibbs, Stephen, Mason and Jacobs JJ.
4 (1975) 133 CLR 164 at 174–175.

> a floating charge could be determined by the laws of the place where the assets were situated when the charge crystallises. It may also be accepted that if the bus had been validly subjected to a charge in Victoria the debenture holder in whose favour the charge was given would not lose his rights simply because the bus was moved from Victoria to Western Australia.'

The evidence of the relevant situs at the date of the creation of the charge was in fact unclear, but was in any case incapable of being decisive.

Registration of charges created by foreign companies

At one time there was some debate as to the course which a chargee under a floating charge created by an unregistered foreign company could take. One view was that if a foreign company created a registrable charge over its assets in England, then unless the charge was registered at the Companies Registry it was liable to be postponed to the claims of the liquidator and any secured creditors of the company.[5] This view assumed that the registrar would be prepared to register such a charge, which was not the case; and it also assumed that protection could not be obtained by delivery of particulars of the charge to the registrar.

In *Slavenburg's Bank NV v Intercontinental Natural Resources Ltd*[6] Lloyd LJ had to consider the case of an oil company incorporated in Bermuda and not registered in the United Kingdom which charged its entire business, including present and future trading stocks to the bank. The registrar of companies was not notified of the charges since it was not his practice to accept particulars of charges for registration from an overseas company with a place of business in England which was not registered in England under Part X of the Companies Act 1948. In subsequent proceedings after the company had been put into liquidation the question was raised whether the charges created in favour of the bank were void against the liquidators by virtue of sections 95 and 106 of the Companies Act 1948 (now sections 395 and 406 of the Companies Act 1985), there being also a question whether they were in addition void as unregistered bills of sale.

Although over 50 cases were cited to the court, *Luckins v Highway Motel (Caernavon) Pty Ltd*[7] was not among them. Lloyd J considered that the wording of section 106 was crystal clear: the provisions of what was then section 95(1) of the 1948 Act applied to charges on property in England created by a foreign company with a place of business in England and thus registration of a charge under section 95(1) was not dependent on registration of a foreign company under Part X of the Act. The learned judge further held that although it was the practice of the registrar *not* to register a charge where a foreign company had failed to comply with the requirements of Part X and register itself, the validity of a charge under section 95 did not depend on whether it had been registered but

---

5   See D Milman 'Foreign Companies: Compliance with Company Law' (1979) 123 Sol Jo 560 at 561.

6   [1980] 1 WLR 1076. See D Milman 'Registration of Charges Created by Overseas Companies' (1981) 125 Sol Jo 294–296.

7   (1975) 133 CLR 164.

on whether the particulars of the charge and the relevant documentary evidence had been delivered to the registrar within 21 days of its creation and therefore the bank to avoid the charges being held null and void should have delivered the necessary particulars within the time limit. He put the point in a forthright manner:[8]

> 'The fallacy in the argument lies in regarding registration of the charge under Part III as a condition precedent to its validity. It is clear both from the language of section 95 and from what was said in *National Provincial and Union Bank of England v Charnley* that it is delivery of particulars of the charge, together with the instrument (if any) by which it is created or evidenced that saves the charge and not its registration.'

Finally, he held that where a charge comes within section 106 then by virtue of section 95 it was to be treated as if it were a charge created by an English company even where the company ceased to have a place of business in England after the charge had been created, and similarly by virtue of section 95 floating charges and charges of future property came within the provisions of section 106. Accordingly since the parties before him had agreed to hold the proceeds of sale of the subject matter of the charge in a joint account, there could be no question of the charges being spent and, accordingly they were void against the liquidators for failure to deliver particulars to the registrar within 21 days. Section 95 of the 1948 is now section 395 of the Companies Act 1985 and section 106 of the 1948 is section 406 of the 1985 Act.

Position should Companies Act 1989 reforms come into force

A new code of registration of charges over the property of foreign companies was foreshadowed by the Companies Act 1989 which introduced a new Chapter III into Companies Act 1985 Part XXIII. This reform, however, has not, even now (and may never) come into force.[9] The most significant change, if and when the new code were ever to come into force, is a provision which will reverse the decision in *Slavenburgs Bank NV v Intercontinental Natural Resources Ltd*[10].

Cross border operation and recognition of private receiverships

(i) Recognition within the United Kingdom

A receiver[11] appointed in Scotland or in Northern Ireland in respect of the whole or any part of any property or undertaking of a company and in consequence of the company having created a charge which, as created, was a floating charge may exercise his powers in England and Wales so far as their exercise is not

---

8 [1980] 1 WLR 1076 at 1086.
9 For comments on this beached provision, see Dicey & Morris *Conflict of Laws* (13th edn) Vol 2 p 1153, 30–116.
10 [1980] 1 WLR 1076.
11 The term includes a manager and a person who is appointed both receiver and manager: IA 1986, s 72(2).

inconsistent with the law applicable in England and Wales.[12] The same applies to a receiver appointed in similar circumstances in England whose powers may equally be exercised in Scotland or Northern Ireland so long as that exercise is not inconsistent with the local law there.[13] The effect of the relevant provision in Scotland is that it gives the English receiver the same security over the assets that the appointment of a Scottish receiver could have given.[14] Furthermore the Courts of the United Kingdom are now bidden to assist each other in matters of insolvency law[15] and to recognise each other's orders[16] and this applies to receiverships in all three jurisdictions.[17]

(ii) Recognition of receivers otherwise than from the United Kingdom

There is some Commonwealth authority which underpins the proposition, implicitly supported by one English authority,[18] that a receiver appointed under a foreign floating charge may exercise his powers in a local jurisdiction if the powers are authorised by the law of the country of incorporation.[19] The point at issue in *Cretanor Maritime Co Ltd v Irish Marine Ltd*[20] was whether the assignee of a floating charge debenture executed after a time charter agreement was made but before the grant of a Mareva injunction, had the requisite standing to apply for a discharge of that injunction although not a party to the action. The Mareva injunction had been granted against the charterers of a ship called the *Cretan Harmony* at the instance of a Cypriot company. The charterers were an Irish company which executed a debenture in favour of the Ulster Bank Ltd. The debenture charged all the charterers' property present and future to the bank. This charge was duly registered in Dublin. One of the charterers' guarantors discharged the guarantee debt to the bank, took an assignment of the debenture and appointed a receiver.

One of the points decided by the English Court of Appeal was that the injunction did not prevail as against the debenture holder where the foreign floating charge crystallised after the injunction had been granted. The injunction was a relief in personam not a seizure. The rights of the debenture holder over a deposited fund with First National City Bank in England stemmed from the appointment of a receiver which merely crystallised the existing equitable charge and removed the right of the charterers to continue to deal with their assets in the

---

12 IA 1986, s 72(1) (Scotland); Administration of Justice Act 1977, s 7 (Northern Ireland).
13 See IA 1986, s 72(1) and Administration of Justice Act 1977, s 7.
14 *Gordon Anderson (Plant) Ltd v Campsie Construction Ltd and Anglo Scottish Plant Ltd* 1977 SLT 7 (on the statutory precursor of IA 1986, s 7); and see *Norfolk House plc (in receivership) v Repsol Petroleum Ltd* 1992 SLT 235n.
15 IA 1986, s 426(4), (10)(a), (b) and (c). For Northern Ireland, see Companies (Northern Ireland) Order 1986.
16 IA 1986, s 426(a), (2), 10(a), (b) and (c).
17 See footnotes 12 and 13.
18 *Cretanor Maritime Co Ltd v Irish Marine Management Ltd* [1978] 3 All ER 164, [1978] 1 WLR 966, CA.
19 See also O'Donovan *Company Receivers and Managers* (1981) 188 citing *Re CA Kennedy Co Ltd and Stibbe-Monk Ltd* (1976) 74 DLR (3d) 87 and *Re McKenzie Grant Ltd* (1899) 1 WALR 116.
20 [1978] 3 All ER 164, [1978] 1 WLR 966, CA.

course of their business. The receiver, as agent of the charterers, could not obtain discharge from the injunction but the debenture holder, as equitable assignee under Irish law of the deposited fund, became entitled to a fixed charge on the fund. So he was able to apply for such a discharge even though he was not a party to the action. It was implicit in this decision that had there been no Mareva injunction the receiver albeit agent in the usual way for the charterers could have exercised his rights under Irish law.[1]

The proposition that one looks to the authority of the law of the country of incorporation gains more direct support from a decision of the High Court of Ontario in *Re CA Kennedy & Co Ltd and Stibbe Monk Ltd*.[2] This involved a dispute in Canada between a Quebecois judgment creditor of an English company who had given a floating charge over all its assets to an English bank. The bank appointed a receiver and the contest was between the English receiver and the judgment creditor over a debt due from another Ontarian company to the English company. There was no registration difficulty: none was required. It all boiled down to priority. The court held that Ontario courts would recognise the appointment of a receiver in a foreign jurisdiction and accepted the argument that crystallisation assigned the benefit of the debt to the debenture holder. So the receiver's priority over the Ontarian debt prevailed as against the judgment creditor. In *Re McKenzie Grant & Co*[3] a company registered as a company in England carried on business in Coolgardie, Western Australia. It issued a number of debentures and at the same time a bill of sale over the assets of the company was given to a trustee for the debenture holders as collateral security. The bill of sale was registered but the debentures were not. The court held that under the terms of the bill of sale and debentures the debenture holders were entitled to all the assets of the company, present as well as future, including book debts. The inference sought to be drawn from this is, apparently, that a foreign receiver would stand in the same position so long at least as a collateral bill of sale was registered.[4]

A further colourful illustration occurs in *Banco de Bilbao v Sancha*,[5] a classic international law case arising out of the Spanish Civil War. The case concerned not receivership but what body of directors had the right to represent the Banco de Bilbao's branch in the City of London. That question, the Court of Appeal held, must depend on the articles under which the bank was constituted; moreover, the construction of those articles must be governed by the law from time to time prevailing at the place where the corporate home was set up. The relevant law reflected the fact that General Franco had captured Bilbao on 19 June 1937. The laws of the de jure recognised Government of the Republic were disregarded: the British Government recognised that General Franco's Government was the de facto government of the territory in which Bilbao, the *domicilio social* of the bank, was situate. Putting aside the international law question of recognition of governments, the case provides additional power to the argument that a

---

1 [1978] 1 WLR 966 at 975C–E per Buckley LJ.
2 (1976) 74 DLR (3d) 87 followed in *Re Abacus Cities Ltd* (1980) 34 CBRNS 244, Man QB.
3 (1899) 1 WALR 116.
4 O'Donovan op cit 188.
5 [1938] 2 KB 176, [1938] 2 All ER 253, CA.

foreign receiver (who largely supplants the directors) may exercise his powers if those powers are authorised by the law of the country of incorporation.

STATUS OF ADMINISTRATIVE RECEIVERS AND RECEIVERS OF FOREIGN COMPANIES

Administrative receivers within the meaning of the Insolvency Act 1986 enjoy certain statutory powers not available to contracted receivers whose powers are circumscribed by the terms of the debenture under which they are appointed. These statutory powers enable administrative receivers 'office-holders' to obtain information relating to a company from various persons pursuant to the provisions of the Insolvency Act 1986[6] 'but such powers are not available to contracted receivers, because they are not office-holders.[7]

The question which arose in *Re International Bulk Commodities Ltd*[8] was whether a person appointed receiver and manager of a foreign company could be an administrative receiver for the purposes of the Insolvency Act 1986 and thus exercise those statutory powers. Mummery J answered both questions affirmatively. The term administrative receiver is defined in the 1986 Act as 'a receiver or manager of the whole (or substantially the whole) of a company's property appointed by or on behalf of the holders of any debentures of the company secured by a charge which, as created, was a floating charge, or by such a charge and one or more other securities.'[9] 'Company' in this context means a company formed and registered under the Companies Act 1985 or under former Companies Acts[10] unless the contrary intention appears.[11] Mummery J identified such a contrary intention from the provisions relating to administrative receivers.[12] In the case before him the floating charge was in fact in the English form.[13] It is to be regarded that the correctness of this decision was doubted in *Re Devon and Somerset Farmers Ltd*[14] and distinguished on the ground that it was confined to the powers of receivers of foreign companies and did not extend to an English unregistered company.

Extra-territorial application of powers available to administrative receivers

A receiver of a company may wish to invoke particular provisions of the Insolvency Act 1986 to assist him in the discharge of his duties as against persons who are abroad and not within the jurisdiction of the English court. Two points

6   IA 1986, ss 234(1) 235(1) and 236(1).
7   *Re International Bulk Commodities Ltd* [1993] Ch 77 at 82.
8   [1993] Ch 77.
9   IA 1986, s 29(2).
10 Companies Act 1985, s 735(1) to which IA 1986, s 251 cross-refers.
11 Companies Act 1985, s 735(4).
12 [1993] Ch 77 at 85C–87C.
13 Ibid at 86D. If the foreign law governing the appointment had equivalent powers available to the receiver presumably the appointee could exercise total powers.
14 [1994] Ch 57.

arise. Does the provision have extra-territorial effect? And will it be possible to secure the co-operation either of the non-resident in question or of the relevant foreign court?

Enforceability by the foreign court is a separate question but the fact that it may be unlikely is relevant to any discretion vested in the court.

Extra-territoriality may be claimed for the power of an administrative receiver to obtain the company's property books papers or records;[15] for his power to secure that officers and certain other persons connected with the company co-operate with him;[16] and for his power to obtain an order for the examination on oath of an officer of the company, a person known or suspected to have in his possession any property of the company or supposed to be indebted to the company or a person thought to be capable of giving information concerning the promotion, formation, business dealings, affairs or property of the company.[17]

In each case the relevant statutory provision has to be construed both against the background of the well established rule of construction that English legislation is territorial in effect[18] and in the light of the policy of the legislature in enacting the section in question.[19]

(c) Getting possession of property books papers or records

It was held by the Court of Appeal in *Re Seagull Manufacturing Co Ltd*[20] affirming a decision in the court below, that the court had jurisdiction under the public examination provisions contained in section 133 of the Insolvency Act 1986 to direct public examination of any person within the statutory category whether or not they were British subjects or within the jurisdiction of the court at the time. Such persons were 'within the legislative grasp or intendment' of the section in question. Similar considerations would appear to apply to persons categorised in section 234 of the 1986 Act.

(b) Securing co-operation with an administrator or administrative receiver

A similar approach should be applied to the duty of co-operation covered by section 235.

(c) Private examination on oath

The position of the court in exercising its power under section 236 of the Insolvency Act 1986 is rather more complex.[1] It was formerly asserted[2] that

---

15 See IA 1986, s 234.
16 IA 1986, s 235.
17 IA 1986, s 236.
18 See *Re Sawers, ex p Blain* (1879) 12 Ch D 522, CA; *Clark (Inspector of Taxes) v Oceanic Construction Ltd* [1983] 2 AC 130 at 145, HL.
19 See *Re Seagull Manufacturing Co Ltd* [1993] BCLC 1139 at 1144–1145.
20 [1993] Ch 345, CA, [1993] BCLC 1139 affirming [1992] Ch 128.
 1 For a convenient summary of the case law on s 236 up to November 1998, see Sealey and Milman *Annotated Guide to the Insolvency Legislation* (1998) 272–276.
 2 See Fletcher Higham and Trower *The Law and Practice of Corporate Administration* (1994) 242–243.

under that section the court could not on the application of an administrator (and the position of an administrative receiver would be the same) summon before it a person beyond its territorial jurisdiction.[3] But it does, it seems, have the power to order the examination of such a person outside the jurisdiction[4] provided there is a real prospect that the foreign court will act so as to compel the examination.[5] The ambit of section 236 was not directly in issue in *Re Seagull Manufacturing Ltd*. Mummery J simply contrasted the provisions of section 133 with those of section 236 and said that the latter did not have extra-territorial effect. The Court of Appeal while affirming his decision on section 133 was more delphic on the position under section 236. The Court of Session on the other hand in *McIsaac Petitioners*[6] rejected a submission that a section 236 order could not be made against a person resident in New York. Lord Cameron of Lochbroom said

> 'The effectiveness of the court's powers to make an order, and hence the propriety of making an order ... will then depend on whether the court can effectively use the provisions of s 426[6A]

The assumption was wrongly made that New York was a relevant country or territory[7] from which it was deduced that the cooperation of the New York court could be expected.

An even more recent case is *Re Mid East Trading Ltd*[8] which involved a winding up of an unregistered company under Part V. In that case the Court of Appeal held that an order could be made in favour of the liquidator under section 236 in respect of documents situated abroad. But it was emphasised that the court's power extended only to documents relating to the particular company which was in liquidation. Presumably a similar principle would apply to an application by an administrator or administrative receiver.

RECOGNITION OF FOREIGN COURT-APPOINTED RECEIVERS

Before the English courts will recognise the title of a foreign court-appointed receiver to assets located in the United Kingdom or direct the setting up of an auxiliary receivership the court will need to be satisfied in three respects. The court will require it to be established (1) that any relevant charge given by the debtor is enforceable in the jurisdiction where the property is situated, that is in the United Kingdom, (2) that the foreign court was competent to make the appointment, and (3) that there is a sufficient connection between the defendant and the jurisdiction in which the foreign receiver was appointed to justify recognition of the foreign court's order as having effect outside the foreign

---

3   See *Re Tucker (a bankrupt)* [1990] Ch 148, CA; *Re Seagull Manufacturing Co Ltd* [1992] Ch 128 and [1993] Ch 345, CA.
4   IA 1986, s 237(3).
5   IA 1986, s 237(3).
6   [1994] BCC 410.
6A [1994] BCC 410 at 412C–D.
7   For the list of designated territories see at 608.
8   [1998] BCC 726, CA.

jurisdiction. The second and third conditions are two ways of saying the same thing because as will be seen competency is bound up with the sufficiency of the connection between the court and the defendant.

Enforceability of charge

It has already been noted in relation to privately appointed receivers that in private international law a floating charge created by a company domiciled in a country which does not recognise floating charges will be void both as to local and foreign assets.[9] That principle is applicable even if the floating charge would be recognised as valid had it been created in the jurisdiction where it is sought to be enforced. And it also applies to charges which are created by individuals.[10]

Competency of foreign court

A foreign receiver can only lay claim to be the receiver of local assets if the court which appointed him was one of competent jurisdiction.[11] This principle which is based on international comity[12] means in effect that there must be some sufficient connection between the company or person over whose assets the receiver is appointed and the country where the court is situated[13].

In *Schemmer v Property Resources Ltd*[14] Goulding J declined to attempt to define the cases where an English court will recognise directly the title of a foreign receiver to assets located in England or by its own order set up an auxiliary receivership in England. But he indicated that the principle of reciprocity or comity[15] was on its own not enough.[16]

Submission to the jurisdiction of the foreign court in the relevant proceedings is a clear case of sufficient connection.[17] But in the case of a company it is not enough that one of its subsidiaries with assets in the foreign jurisdiction has submitted to the foreign jurisdiction.[18]

---

9 See the discussion at p 610, above and the decision of the Scottish court in *Carse v Coppen* 1951 SC 233. Floating charges are now recognised in Scotland.

10 *Carse v Coppen* 1951 SC 233.

11 *Schemmer v Property Resources Ltd* [1975] Ch 273 at 287–288.

12 *Re CA Kennedy Co Ltd and Stibbe Monk Ltd* (1977) 74 DLR (3d) 87. See also *Weiler v Sigurdson* (1981) 40 CBRNS 221, Alta.

13 *Schemmer v Property Resources Ltd* [1975] Ch 273 at 287–288.

14 [1975] Ch 273 at 287.

15 See *Travers v Holley* [1953] P 246, CA.

16 See [1975] Ch 273 at 287D–E ('Travers v Holley must be followed only with caution outside its own subject matter of matrimonial status'). See also *Derby & Co Ltd v Weldon (No 6)* [1990] 1 WLR 1139 at 1150, CA.

17 *Schemmer v Property Resources Ltd* [1975] Ch 273 at 287; *White v Verkouille* [1990] 2 Qd R 191; see also *Canadian Imperial Bank of Commerce v Idanell Korner Ranch Ltd* [1990] 6 WWR 620, Sask; and *Houlditch v Marquess of Donegall* (1834) 2 Cl & Fin 470, 8 Bli NS 301, HL.

18 *Schemmer v Property Resources Ltd* [1975] Ch 273 at 287F–G.

As a rule an appointment by a court in the place of incorporation of a company will be recognised[19] but not if the receiver was appointed by way of equitable execution.[20] Although Goulding J in *Schemmer's*[1] case declined to express a view on the point an appointment in the jurisdiction where a company has established its central management and control would probably be recognised. It might even be the case that if the law of the company's place of incorporation would recognise the receivership order, an English court would do so.[2]

The rights of a person with powers analogous to those of a receiver appointed by a competent foreign court are also recognised by the court[3] and even given auxiliary status by it.[4]

An interlocutory receiver appointed by a foreign court may be refused final relief in a local jurisdiction. This was illustrated by the case of *Larkins v NUM*,[5] where a court-appointed receiver from England (appointed on an interlocutory basis) brought proceedings in the Republic of Ireland to recover union money taken out of the jurisdiction of the English court during the miners' strike of 1984. It was argued on behalf of the displaced union trustees and the union that (1) the receiver had been appointed in aid of the sequestrator, and (2) the receiver would have to account to the superior officer the sequestrator so that in either event the enforcement of the receiving rights would be an indirect enforcement of the penal judgment constituted by sequestration of the various assets. In the further alternative it was argued that no final judgment should be made in favour of a receiver who was only appointed on an interlocutory basis.[6] Barrington J, while accepting that sequestration was a penal order, found no evidence that the receivership was imposed by the court in aid of the sequestration; it was, rather, imposed because the trusteeship had to be in abeyance. He did not discuss the second allegation that the receiver could only account to the sequestrator, a point on which there was at the time no authority. He decided the case on the simple basis that the receiver being interlocutory it was inappropriate to make an order which in effect was final.[7]

Effect of recognition

At this point it is convenient to summarise the substantive effect of recognition of a receiver appointed by a foreign court.

---

19 *International Credit and Investment Co (Overseas) Ltd v Adham* [1994] 1 BCLC 66; affd [1999] Il Pr 302, CA; *Schemmer v Property Resources Ltd* [1975] Ch 273; and see *Macaulay v Guaranty Trust Co of New York* (1927) 44 TLR 99.
20 *Perry v Zissis* [1977] 1 Lloyd's Rep 607 at 615, CA.
 1 [1975] Ch 273 at 287–288.
 2 [1975] Ch 273 at 287H.
 3 *Lepage v San Paulo Coffee Estates Co* [1917] WN 216, 33 TLR 457; *Macaulay v Guaranty Trust Co of New York* (1927) 44 TLR 99.
 4 *Pélégrin v Coutts & Co* [1915] 1 Ch 696 (curateur of foreign bankrupt).
 5 [1985] IR 671.
 6 See [1985] IR 671 at 683.
 7 See [1985] IR 671 at 691–695.

An English court may recognise the receiver's title both directly and indirectly. It will do so directly by allowing him to sue for the assets in his own name. In *Macaulay v Guaranty Trust Co of New York*[8] there was evidence before Clauson J that in Delaware the plaintiffs could sue in their own name for assets of the company. Clauson J gave judgment in favour of the Delaware receiver plaintiffs for the balance standing to the credit of the company at its London bank.[9]

Again, the English court may recognise the receiver's title indirectly by constituting a subsidiary or auxiliary receivership within the jurisdiction. This alternative is mentioned by Goulding J in *Schemmer's* case.[10]

If the receiver's title is directly accepted he may collect the local property and give good discharge for it. This is what in effect happened in the Queensland case of *Re Young*.[11] Mansfield SPJ stated:[12]

'It would seem therefore that a receiver appointed by a Californian Court under the provisions of Californian law to the possession of Queensland property of a person over whom the Californian law had jurisdiction would be entitled to collect that property and give a good discharge for it'.

He accordingly confirmed that the auxiliary receiver appointed by the Queensland court had such a power. Similarly, the adminstrateur sequestre appointed according to the French expert evidence by a court of competent jurisdiction in *Lepage v San Paulo Copper Estates Ltd*[13] was able to give a receipt for dividends due to the alien enemy (a German widow) and give a good discharge to the company.

A further consequence of recognition is that those who wrongfully refuse to accept the receiver's authority to give valid receipts may be punished in costs. In *Pélégrin v Coutts & Co*[14] the bank, in an excess of caution, and despite a Court of Appeal decision demonstrating that excess of caution, insisted on a French provisional administrator's coming to the English court. Costs were not sought against the bank but the bank was disallowed its costs.

Where a foreign receiver does take proceedings in England he is liable to be ordered to give security for costs. 'The rule requiring security from a plaintiff being a foreigner resident abroad, is based on the ground that if a verdict be given against him, he is not within the reach of our law so as to have process served upon him for the costs.'[15]

---

8 (1927) 44 TLR 99.
9 See also *Alivon v Furnival* (1834) 1 Cr M & R 277 (where syndics of a French bankrupt were recognised as having title to sue).
10 [1975] Ch 273 at 287; see also *Re Young* [1955] St R Qd 254 at 261 (ancillary receivers appointed).
11 [1955] St R Qd 254.
12 [1955] St R Qd 254 at 263.
13 [1917] WN 216.
14 [1915] 1 Ch 696.
15 Per Hood J in *Bethune v Porteous* (1892) 18 VLR 493 at 494, citing *Raeburn v Andrews* (1874) LR 9 QB 118 at 120; see also *Lake Sulphite Pulp Co v Charles W Cox Ltd* [1938] 3 DLR 758.

RECOGNITION OF ADMINISTRATORS

Power of English court to appoint administrator over the property of a foreign company

In the previous edition of this book it was suggested that in the context of private international law 'an administrator cannot be appointed over the affairs business or property of an overseas company.'[16] As it happens, the suggestion coincided with a dictum of Hirst J in *Felixstowe Dock & Railway Co v United States Lines Inc*.[17] It was based on the fact that an administrator is a creature of statute and that the word 'company' in Part II of the Insolvency Act 1986 refers to a company formed and registered under the Companies Act because the definition of a company in the Companies Act 1985[18] to which the 1986 Act cross-refers does not on its face include unregistered companies here or abroad. Again in *Re Dallhold Estates (UK) Pty Ltd*[19] Chadwick J likewise assumed that there was no original jurisdiction to appoint an administrator over an Australian company though he acceded to the request of the Federal Court of Australia that an administration order should be made under the judicial assistance provision.[20] Mummery J in *Re International Bulk Commodities Ltd*[1] was concerned with the discreet question whether an administrative receiver (as opposed to an administrator) could be appointed over the affairs business or property) of an overseas company. There was some argument directed to the position of administrators and reference was made by the judge to the statement made in the previous edition of this book upon which he declined to express an opinion.[2] He was, he said, unable to derive any assistance from the provisions relating to administrators on the question whether administrative receivers could be appointed over the assets of a foreign company.

There has been considerable discussion of the issue among commentators.[3] One school lays stress on the provision in section 735(4) of the Companies Act 1985 which qualifies the definitions of the term company by saying that they apply 'unless the contrary appears', and on the decision of Mummery J in *Re International Bulk Commodities Ltd*.[4]

16 Picarda *Law Relating to Receivers Managers and Administrators* (2nd edn, 1990) 501.
17 [1989] QB 360 at 376.
18 See Companies Act 1985, s 735.
19 [1992] BCLC 621 at 623f–h. See also *Hughes v Hannover Rückversicherungs AG* [1997] 1 BCLC 497 at 511, per Morritt LJ apparently approving or not dissenting from Chadwick J's remarks.
20 IA 1986, s 426 discussed at 607 above.
 1 [1993] Ch 77.
 2 [1993] Ch 77 at 88D–F.
 3 See Lightman and Moss *The Law of Receivers of Companies* (2nd edn, 1994) 418–421; Fletcher Higham and Trower *The Law and Practice of Corporate Administrations* (1994) 251–254; Moss 'Insolvency Administration for Foreign Companies in England' (1993) 15 *Comparative Yearbook of International Business* 3–19; Moss and Segal 'Cross-Border Issues' in Oditah (ed) Insolvency of Banks: Managing the Risks (1996) 71–76; Smart *Cross-border Insolvency* (1998) 130–136; Dicey and Morris *The Conflict of Laws* (13th edn, 2000).
 4 [1993] Ch 77 which was doubted distinguished and not followed in *Re Devon and Somerset Farmers Ltd* [1994] Ch 57.

The existence of a sufficient contrary intention in the Insolvency Act 1986 is said[5] to be revealed in at least two of the purposes for which an administration order may be made. These are the making of an order to secure the survival of the company and the whole or any part of its undertaking as a going concern and to achieve a more advantageous realisation of the company's assets than would be effected on a winding up. Why it is asked somewhat rhetorically, should a foreign company all of whose business is carried on in England not be capable of being rescued by an administration order if its survival could be secured in that way? Equally why should a foreign company capable of being wound up here not be subjected to an administration order here so as to achieve a more advantageous realisation of the company's assets than would be effected on a winding up? And why, it is further asked, should an administration order be achieved indirectly through the judicial assistance provision[6] but not directly?

It is to be noted that aside from these rhetorical questions no provision is identified that gives a clear indication of a legislative intention to subject foreign companies to the administration procedure. Prima facie one would expect express words given the interventionist character of an administration order and the reluctance of the courts to interfere with internal management of foreign incorporated companies.[7]

On the other hand, the indications the other way are considerable. The suggestion that 'company' should be interpreted as including any company which may be wound up as an unregistered company pursuant to Part V of the Insolvency Act 1986 is inconsistent with the language of the provision of the 1986 Act which specifies that 'an unregistered company is not, except in the event of its being wound up, deemed to be a company under the Companies Act, and then only to the extent provided by this Part of this Act'. That provision is the statutory provision echoing *mutatis mutandis* the language of its statutory precursor in the Companies Act 1985 and carrying over the definition for the purposes of the Insolvency Act 1986 which consolidated the legislation about the winding up legislation as well as initiating the new administration procedure. Its function is to make clear that the word 'company' is only extended in the Insolvency Act 1986 for the purposes of the provisions about winding up of unregistered companies in Part V of the Insolvency Act 1986. Expression of this excludes extension of the definition in any other context. Had the legislators intended to extend the application of Part II of the Insolvency Act 1986 to companies to be wound up under Part V rather than to registered companies they could and should have used express language but they did not.

Moreover there are other instances in Part II where the language used in the

---

5 See Lightman and Moss *Law of Receivers of Companies* (2nd edn 1994) 419–420; and Dicey and Morris *The Conflict of Laws* (13th edn 2000) 1158. The relevant passage in each case was contributed by Professor C G Morse.

6 *Re Dallhold Estates (UK) Pty Ltd* [1992] BCLC 621.

7 See *Pergamon Press Ltd v Maxwell* [1970] 1 WLR 1167. An international convention or a request by a foreign court stand on a different footing.

substantive provisions hardly meshes with the notion that foreign companies are intended to be susceptible to administration orders.[8]

Again, the Insolvency Rules contain express reference to unregistered and overseas companies in the case of service of winding up petitions[9] but there is no such mention in the otherwise similarly drafted rule governing service of administration petitions.[10]

Lastly on the legislative front, to the extent that legislative intention can be deduced from subsequent subordinate legislation, it is apparent from The Banks (Administration Proceedings) Order 1989 and the Overseas Companies and Credit and Financial Institutions (Branch Disclosure) Regulations 1992 that the draftsman in each case took the view that foreign companies were not within the purview of Part II of the Insolvency Act 1986.[11]

The decision in *Re International Bulk Commodities Ltd* has not escaped criticism. In particular, it is weakened by the fact that it was not followed in *Re Devon and Somerset Farmers Ltd*[12] where the court held it had no jurisdiction to make an administration order in respect of an English unregistered company.

In conclusion it must be said that while it may be desirable that foreign companies be subjected to the possibility of the administration procedure it is necessary to distinguish between what should be and what is the law. In the light of the absence of any express words of contrary intent and given the presence of expressions elsewhere in the Insolvency Act and Rules and the subordinate legislation which demonstrate the willingness of the draftsman to be specific where needed the better view would appear to be that there is no original jurisdiction to make an administration order over a foreign company. Such an important inclusion in the framework of Part II would need express language and not come in by strained inference or ingenious deduction.[13]

An administrator is a creature of statute and is appointed over the affairs,[14] business and property of a company falling within the definition of company in section 735 of the Companies Act 1985.[15] This means that the company in question must be formed and registered under the Companies Act 1985 or under the former Companies Acts.[16] The 'former Companies Acts' means the Joint Stock

---

8 See IA 1986, s 10(1)(a) (because there can be no voluntary winding up of an unregistered company: see IA 1986, s 221(4)); IA 1986, s 81(1)(a) enabling the granting of an administration order where a company is unable to pay its debts within the meaning given to that expression by s 123. But for unregistered companies inability to pay debts is not determined by s 123 but by ss 222–224.

9 IR 1986, r 4.8.

10 IR 1986, r 2.7.

11 See for details of the argument on this point Smart *Cross-Border Insolvency* (1998) 134–135.

12 [1994] Ch 57.

13 See for further argument Smart *Cross-Border Insolvency* (1998) 130–136; and see also Fletcher Higham and Trower *Law and Practice of Corporate Administrations* (1994) 251–254.

14 Unlike an administrative receiver whose status is derived from contract. See *Re International Bulk Commodities Ltd* [1993] Ch 77 at 88H–89A.

15 IA 1986, s 251.

16 CA 1985, s 735(1).

Companies Acts,[17] the Companies Act 1862, the Companies (Consolidation) Act 1908, the Companies Act 1929 and the Companies Acts 1948 and 1981.[18] A company registered under the Joint Stock Companies Act, the Companies Act 1862 or the Companies (Consolidation) Act 1908 in what was at those times Ireland is not amenable to an administration order because it is not a company as defined.[19]

Recognition of an English administrator by a foreign court

An order made by a court in any part of the United Kingdom in the exercise of jurisdiction in relation to insolvency law[20] must be enforced in any other part of the United Kingdom as if it were made by a court exercising the corresponding jurisdiction in that other part.[1] Subject, however, to what is provided for in the Insolvency Act 1986, this does not require a court in any part of the United Kingdom to enforce in relation to property situated in that part any order made by a court in any other part of the United Kingdom.[2] All the same, the courts having jurisdiction in relation to insolvency law in any part of the United Kingdom must, on request,[3] assist the courts having the corresponding jurisdiction in any other part of the United Kingdom or any relevant country or territory.[4]

For this purpose a request made to a court in any part of the United Kingdom by a court in any other part of the United Kingdom or in a relevant country or territory is authority for the court to which the request is made to apply, in relation to any matters specified in the request, the insolvency law which is applicable by either court in relation to comparable matters falling within its jurisdiction.[5] A court in exercising its discretion in relation to such a request must have regard in particular to the rules of private international law.[6] The terms 'relevant country or territory' are defined as meaning any of the Channel Islands or the Isle of Man or any country or territory designated for that purpose by the Secretary of State by order made by statutory instrument.[7] The relevant countries or territories designated so far have been listed earlier.[8]

---

17 'The Joint Stock Companies Act' means the Joint Stock Companies Act 1856, the Joint Stock Companies Acts 1856, 1857, the Joint Stock Banking Companies Act 1857 or the Act to enable Joint Stock Banking Companies to be formed or the principle of limited liability, or any one or more of those principles of limited liability, or any one or more of those Acts (as the case may require) but does not include the Joint Stock Companies Act 1844: CA 1985, s 735(3).
18 CA 1985, s 735(1)(c). For other exceptions see IA 1986, s 8(4).
19 CA 1985, s 735(1)(b).
20 This includes provisions for the appointment of an administrator: see IA 1986, s 426(10). It also includes specific provisions added to insolvency law by virtue of the provisions of CA 1989.
 1 IA 1986, s 426(1).
 2 IA 1986, s 426(2).
 3 IA 1986, s 426(5).
 4 IA 1986, s 426(4).
 5 IA 1986, s 426(5).
 6 IA 1986, s 426(5). For detailed discussion of these and cognate provisions see at 608 above.
 7 IA 1986, s 426(11).
 8 See at 608 above.

Whether an English administrator would be recognised by a foreign court independently of designation under a statutory instrument in each jurisdiction is an open question on which there is no authority.[9]

Recognition of a foreign administrator in an English court

As has been seen, there are provisions for mutual recognition of administrators appointed in any jurisdiction having a corresponding jurisdiction to that of England and being either in the United Kingdom or in a relevant country or territory.[10] The extent to which a judicial manager appointed, for example, in Singapore[11] would be recognised in England in relation to a claim to assets in England must be debatable. On the one hand, comity would appear to justify recognition of a judicially appointed figure closely corresponding to an administrator, provided always that the court was competent to make the appointment and there was a sufficient connection between the defendant company and the jurisdiction in which the judicial manager was appointed.[15] On the other hand, the existence of a procedure enabling relevant countries and territories to be designated by statutory instrument might militate against mutual recognition in other cases.[12]

9 See the case of Singapore discussed below.
10 IA 1986, s 426(1)–(5), (10), (11).
11 Choong Thung Cheong 'Judicial Management in Corporate Insolvency' (1988) 30 Malaya LR 259–284.
12 Cf *Schemmer v Property Resources Ltd* [1975] Ch 273, [1974] 3 All ER 451 (foreign receiver) discussed at p 621 above.

Part V

Taxation

CHAPTER 41

Taxation

RECEIVERS

Introduction

The impact of tax liabilities upon the task of the receiver is clearly a matter of prime importance. A receiver will wish to know as soon as possible what outstanding tax liabilities there are. He will also wish to keep in view the accruing tax liabilities during his receivership. The ability of a receiver to trade efficiently will depend on what liabilities, both accrued and accruing, there are. Taxation liabilities will also need to be considered if a truly beneficial sale is to be achieved. The discussion which follows highlights the main taxing provisions which will concern a receiver.

Outstanding tax liabilities incurred prior to appointment

As a general rule a receiver will not incur any personal liability for tax liabilities which have accrued prior to his appointment. Such liabilities, whether in respect of taxes on income or on capital gains or in respect of value added tax (VAT) will rank as debts of the company and may be preferential debts so far as the new insolvency legislation allows them to be.

The extent to which accrued tax is a preferential debt is discussed elsewhere.[1] It has been suggested by one commentator that a receiver must take all the relevant administrative steps to deal with the company's liability to pay tax but he will not himself be personally answerable for such tax. Certainly a managing director of a company is not personally liable for the payment of the company's tax, although he may be the 'proper officer' of the company.[2] That is because a proper officer is responsible for administrative or ministerial action but is not personally liable.[3] But the proper officer is defined as the secretary, or the person

---

1 See at pp 264–266, above.
2 *Income Tax Comr v Chatani* [1983] STC 477, PC (on the wording of Jamaican Income Tax Act, s 52).
3 'Answerable' means 'responsible'. The language of TMA 1970, s 108 is the same as Jamaican Income Tax Act, s 52.

acting as secretary, of the company or, in the case of a winding up, the liquidator.[4] Where there is no proper officer the treasurer or person acting as treasurer is deemed to be the proper officer.[5] A receiver is not a treasurer or person acting as treasurer and is not therefore a proper officer. It follows that the person to make any relevant returns is the secretary. Only if the receiver can be viewed as the person acting as secretary of the company will he rank as the proper officer of the company with all that that entails.

Accruing tax liabilities

Income

Revenue profits earned after the commencement of the receivership are profits of the company. The receiver in the normal case will, at any rate until liquidation, be acting as the agent of the company, so that the company will remain liable for any relevant corporation tax chargeable on those profits. There is no provision imposing any liability on the receiver in respect of such income.

The position is no different, it would seem, when the receiver causes the company to continue to trade after his agency has determined. It is provided by the Taxes Act 1988 that, subject to any exceptions provided for by the Corporation Tax Acts, a company shall be chargeable to corporation tax on all its profits *wherever arising*.[6] The practice of the Revenue is to treat the liability as being that of the company and not of the receiver, and indeed the provision just cited does suggest that the liability is indeed one of the company itself.[7] Moreover, it is provided in the immediately following provision that the company is chargeable to corporation tax on profits accruing for its benefit.[8]

Income from land chargeable under Schedule A therefore remains properly assessable on the company notwithstanding the appointment of a receiver since the company is the person for whose benefit the income arises[9] and is also the person entitled to the income.[10] Income from any other investments remains income of the company for corporation tax purposes even though a receiver has been appointed, since the income likewise arises for the benefit of the company.[11]

Deduction of tax

A receiver is not usually liable for corporation tax on income and capital gains arising during the receivership. However he must account to the Revenue for tax

4 TMA 1970, s 108.
5 TMA 1970.
6 TA 1988, s 8(1).
7 The company *shall* be chargeable.
8 TA 1988, s 8(2).
9 TA 1988.
10 TA 1988, s 8(2).
11 TA 1988.

which he actually deducts from payments made by him. Some of the cases in which there is obligation to deduct tax from payments are of fairly general application, for example annual payments or interest or PAYE; others are referable to particular businesses or property rights. The following is a list of the main provisions requiring deduction of tax:

(i) rents paid to a non-resident landlord (TA 1988, s 43); (ii) rent payable in connection with mines and similar concerns (TA 1988, s 119); (iii) way leave rents (TA 1988, s 120); (iv) foreign dividends (TA 1988, s 123); (v) PAYE (TA 1988, s 203 and 203A–203L); (vi) annual payments (TA 1988, s 349(1)); (vii) annual interest (TA 1988, s 349(2)); (viii) patent royalties (TA 1988, s 524); (ix) copyright royalties (TA 1988, s 536); (x) payments to certain contractors in the construction industry (TA 1988, ss 559–560); (xi) National Insurance contributions (Social Security Contributions and Benefits Act 1992, Sch 1, paras 4 and 6); (xii) public lending rights income (TA 1988, Sch 29).

If the receiver fails to deduct and account for PAYE he will not, it is thought, be personally liable.[12]

Sums payable in respect of PAYE are a liability incurred by a receiver or administrator[13] and sums payable in respect of debts or liabilities incurred under new or adapted contracts are payable by way of wages or salary[14] with the result that they enjoy priority.[15]

As regards primary class I contributions of NIC (for which the earner is liable) if deducted from his wages they too enjoy priority: but standing contributions though incurred as a direct result of the employment are not deducted from the wages of the earner. That latter liability is that of the employer and is not derived from any liability of the employee it is outside the priority for liabilities incurred by the receiver or administrator.[16]

Capital gains

Where any chargeable gain arises on the sale of property by the receiver that gain will be treated as having been made by the company. Again the receiver is not personally liable for the tax on that gain. The case of *Re Mesco Properties Ltd*[17] is often cited in this context although it was in reality a case concerning a sale of properties by the liquidator, the mortgagee's receiver and the mortgagee. The receiver was appointed when the company was already in liquidation. The sale prices of the properties realised profits over the cost of the properties to the company. It was common ground between the liquidator and the receiver that

---

12 A receiver appointed by the court is an 'employer' for all purposes. An administrative receiver is not usually a contractual employer.

13 IA 1986, s 19(5).

14 IA 1986, s 19(6).

15 *IRC v Lawrence* (2000) NLD Revenue Law Com 125, 11 July, CA, upholding decision of Jules Sher QC sitting as a Deputy High Court Judge in *Re FJL* (2000) NLD Revenue Law Com 26, 24 March.

16 *IRC v Lawrence* (2000) supra.

17 [1980] 1 All ER 117, [1980] 1 WLR 96, CA. See also Capital Gains Tax Act 1979, s 23(2).

neither the liquidator nor any mortgagee or receiver was liable for any tax: the company alone was liable. The decision of Brightman J and of the Court of Appeal was that the corporation tax liability was not a fee or expense incurred in realising the assets[18] by the liquidator in the course of the winding up of the companies and that accordingly the tax was 'necessary disbursements'[19] in the course of the liquidation. The Court of Appeal also held that liability to tax constituted 'charges and expenses' within the meaning of the statutory predecessor[20] of section 156 of the Insolvency Act 1986. In consequence, in the event of the assets being insufficient to satisfy the liabilities, the court may make an order as to the payment out of the assets of the relevant tax liability in such order of priority as the court thinks just.[1]

Value added tax

The extent to which a receiver is responsible for the value added tax liabilities of a company was considered by Brightman J in *Re John Willment (Ashford) Ltd*,[2] which concerned the duly appointed receiver of a company which ran a garage business. The company continued to trade and the receiver charged value added tax on taxable supplies and services. At first he accounted to the Customs and Excise Commissioners for the tax collected, but then a doubt was raised as to the correctness of this and, at the invitation of the Commissioners, he took out a summons. It was held that the Commissioners had no right to demand the tax by virtue of section 109(8) of the Law of Property Act 1925: that section simply meant that if the receiver applied money received by him in discharge of taxes affecting the mortgaged property he could not be charged by the debenture holder (or by the person entitled to the property subject to the debenture) with having made an improper payment.[3] Nor was the money collected as value added tax impressed with any trust in favour of the Commissioners.[4] However, if the receiver does not make value added tax returns and pay the tax he will be causing the company to commit a criminal offence.[5] In the result the receiver who is entitled as between himself and the debenture holder to pay taxes has no option but to make value added tax returns and to pay the tax due.[6]

The decision in the *Willment* case was considered and distinguished by Vinelott J in *Re Liverpool Commercial Vehicles Ltd*[7] where goods sold subject to a title retention clause were repossessed by the supplier who issued credit notes

---

18 Under the Companies Winding Up Rules 1949, r 195(1), replaced by IR 1986, r 4.218(1)(a).
19 Under what is now IR 1986, r 4.218(1)(m), replacing the Companies Winding Up Rules 1949, r 195(1).
20 CA 1948, s 267, which uses the expression 'costs charges and expenses', a phrase which throughout IA 1986 is replaced by 'expenses'.
1 IA 1986, s 156.
2 [1979] 2 All ER 615, [1980] 1 WLR 73.
3 See *Liverpool Corpn v Hope* [1938] 1 KB 751, [1938] 1 All ER 492, CA.
4 *A-G v Antoine* [1949] 2 All ER 1000 (money retained as PAYE).
5 This is no longer the case: see at pp 635–636, below.
6 *Quaere* whether it is correct to describe the receiver as having any discretion under LPA 1925, s 109(8). For other unanswered questions, see [1980] 1 WLR 73 at 78e–g.
7 [1984] BCLC 587.

which included an amount of VAT. The claim of the Commissioners of Customs and Excise was to raise the claims for credit (by way of input tax deducted from output tax) by increasing the amount of the preferential debt by the amount shown in the credit notes. It was argued on their behalf that they could do so by treating the original supply as simply a provisional or contingent supply. That argument was rejected. Vinelott J went on to consider what the position would be on the assumption that there was a subsequent supply when the goods were returned to the original supplier. Even if this was the case he said:[8]

> 'The joint receivers cannot be required and indeed have no power to pay the VAT included in the credit notes in priority to the principal and interest payable under the banker's charge. The joint receivers have not received moneys representing VAT payable on a supply by them, and the principle explained by Brightman J in *Re John Willment (Ashford) Ltd* . . . can have no application. If output tax did become so payable it would be payable by the liquidator out of moneys, if any, coming into his hands, and the liquidator is not a party to this application.'

There has been some uncertainty as to whether it was strictly accurate to say that the receivers could not be required to pay the VAT included in the credit notes. It was common ground in the *Willment* case that the receiver had not, in fact, been 'required' by the Commissioners to comply with the provisions of the Value Added Tax (General) Regulations then in force. But there was also an oblique suggestion in the *Willment* decision that the requirement by the Commissioners to pay tax could not apply to a receiver appointed under a debenture, presumably on the footing that a company in receivership is hardly 'incapacitated'. An amendment has now been made to the Value Added Tax Regulations to make it clear by express language that:[9]

> 'In relation to a company which is a taxable person the reference . . . to the taxable person having become bankrupt or incapacitated shall be construed as a reference to its going into liquidation or receivership or to an administration order being in force in relation to it.'

Both the decisions so far referred to have to be viewed in the context of substantial amendments to VAT liabilities under the Finance Act 1985 and associated regulations.

The current position under the Value Added Tax Act 1994 as amended and the Value Added Tax (General) Regulations 1995 requires some rehearsal. It should first be noted that the registration of the company for the purposes of value added tax is in no way disturbed by the appointment of a receiver: the receiver as agent of the company does not have to register separately. On his appointment the current VAT accounting period is treated as having come to an end on the day immediately preceding his appointment[10] and a return made on behalf of the company must be furnished in respect of that period no later than the last day of the month next following the end of that period.[11] The next period will start on the

---

8 [1984] BCLC 587.
9 Value Added Tax Regulations 1995, reg 9(3).
10 VAT (General) Regulations 1995, regs 35(3)(a) and 30.
11 VAT (General) Regulations 1995, regs 25(3)(b) and 30.

following day and end (and all subsequent periods will begin and end) on the dates determined under regulation 25(1).[12] The Commissioners may treat the receiver as carrying on the business of the company and so as a taxable person and, if they do so, the Act and Regulations apply as if he were a taxable person.[13] Where any company subject to any requirements under the Part of the Regulations dealing with accounting and payment becomes incapacitated and control of its assets passes to a receiver such receiver must, if the Commissioners so require and so long as he has such control, comply with those requirements.[14] In relation to any requirement to pay tax that is only to apply to the receiver to the extent of the assets of the company over which he has control.[15]

Failure on the part of a receiver to make a return or the making of an incomplete or incorrect return will be treated as a failure on the part of the company.[16] Notification to a receiver will be treated as notification to the company.[17]

A receiver appointed by a mortgagee under the Law of Property Act 1925 in respect of a fixed charge over specific assets is not a taxable person under the regulations.[18] Going into receivership is to be construed as contemplating the general incapacity which would result from *administrative* receivership[19] or liquidation or administration and not from the partial incapacity which results from the appointment of a receiver of specific payments under the Law of Property Act 1925 or in equivalent power. Moreover and decisively the very words 'going into receivership', especially when associated with liquidation and administration connote a state of affairs when the management of the company's affairs is taken out of the hands of its directors and placed in the care of a third party.[20]

Hive down and tax liabilities

Introduction

The common practice of receivers in hiving down the business of the company to a subsidiary specially formed for that purpose is discussed in more detail in an earlier chapter.[1] The purpose of carrying out a hive down has been described judicially as being 'to segregate the saleable assets of the company into a clean package, free of obligations whether to staff or creditors, which will be more saleable and which if the transaction is correctly effected may bring to the purchaser certain fiscal advantage'.[2]

---

12 VAT (General) Regulations 1995, SI 1995 No 2518, regs 25(3)(c) and 30.
13 Ibid, reg 9.
14 Ibid, reg 30.
15 Ibid.
16 Value Added Tax Act 1994, s 73(1) and (5).
17 Ibid, s 73(1) and (5).
18 *Sargent v Customs and Excise Comrs* [1995] 2 BCLC 34, CA.
19 'Incapacitated' in relation to a company means incapable of carrying on its business: see at [1995] 2 BCLC 34 at 38a–b.
20 [1995] 2 BCLC 34 at 38b–c. It is not open to the receiver to exercise a discretion so as not to account to commissioners for any VAT collections.
 1 See at pp 174–176 below.
 2 *Pambakian v Brentford Nylons Ltd* [1978] ICR 665 at 669H–670 per Phillips J.

The practice has indeed achieved at any rate implicitly statutory recognition, because the statutory powers conferred upon an administrative receiver (and indeed upon an administrator) include:[3]

> '15. Power to establish subsidiaries of the company.
> 16. Power to transfer to subsidiaries of the company the whole or any part of the business and property of the company'.

The exercise of those statutory powers to effect a hive down as a preliminary to sale as a going concern is normally to ensure some measure of preservation of tax losses for the benefit of the purchaser.

Principle in Furniss v Dawson

Receivers who contemplate hiving down assets to a subsidiary of the company in receivership should be especially wary of Revenue attack under the *Furniss v Dawson*[4] principle. The principle is most likely to be invoked in relation to capital loss schemes which it is convenient to discuss in conjunction with capital gains tax liabilities in hive downs.

Normally, the effect of a sale of a capital asset by one group company to another is that the sale is treated as having taken place at such a price as would result in no gain and no loss to the vendor, whatever the actual consideration.[5] To counter avoidance schemes based on this rule section 278 of the Taxes Act 1970 provides that if the subsidiary leaves the group within six years of the date of the acquisition of the capital asset from its parent, the subsidiary is treated as having disposed of the asset immediately after acquiring it for a consideration equal to its market value at that time.[6] Section 278 of the Taxes Act 1970 applies whether or not there is a gain. If, therefore, there is an asset with an unrealised loss transferred down to a hive down subsidiary, on the sale of the shares in the subsidiary a loss would be produced which would be utilisable by the ultimate purchaser. The efficacy of such a scheme was raised with the Inland Revenue.[7] At a meeting on 6 January 1982 it was said by the Revenue that the decision in the *Ramsay* case would not generally be applied to 'the routing of assets through a company within the same Group which has allowable capital losses and had not been acquired after these had arisen'.[8] At a subsequent meeting on 10 June 1985 the Revenue indicated that this statement was still regarded as valid following *Furniss v Dawson*.[9] The Institute of Chartered Accountants in England and Wales while acknowledging that this guidance was of considerable help in a clear-cut case stated that some problems still remained. One example given was where a significant group might be acquired for demonstrably commercial reasons but

---

3 IA 1986, Sch 1.
4 [1984] AC 474.
5 TA 1970, s 273.
6 TA 1970, s 278.
7 TR 588: *Furniss v Dawson* 25 September 1985 (see Simon's Tax Intelligence 1985, Issue 39, 11 October).
8 TR 588, para 4.
9 TR 588.

one of the companies in that group has capital losses. It was said to be unclear whether the routing of assets from a member of the acquiring group to use that loss would be attacked.[10] The Institute indicated that they would have preferred the *Furniss v Dawson* doctrine to be identified as applicable under this heading only where a company with a capital loss was acquired with that loss being its sole or main asset and with a motive of acquisition to utilise the loss in question. Confirmation of this approach (they suggested) would do much to clarify the area of what constitutes 'straightforward transfers of assets between members of the same group'.[11]

The Revenue response was as follows:[12]

> 'I agree that this is an important area where, in our view, the *Ramsay* principles are likely to have considerable application. Let me say at once that the Board stands by the assurance given on 6 January 1982, about straightforward transfers of assets between members of the same group. By contrast, as you are no doubt aware, inspectors have advanced *Ramsay* contentions in a number of cases where the effect of a series of transactions has been to transfer the benefit of capital losses from one group to another. Whether the "new approach" is thought to be applicable will depend on the facts of particular cases bearing in mind, for example, the relationship between the amounts of the losses involved, the period for which the company with the losses has been within the group and on the circumstances in which the losses have arisen. On this approach it would seem unlikely that the judgment would be invoked where the losses were a relatively insubstantial element in the acquisition, as evidenced by the circumstances in which they were utilised and the commerciality of the circumstances surrounding the acquisition.'

Carrying forward of losses

A potential purchaser of a hived down business is likely to be particularly interested in the possibility of being able to set off accrued trading losses of the company in receivership against future earnings of the new trading company to which the business has been hived down. This factor has always been an important one in relation to hive downs although the opportunities for carrying forward losses have been substantially restricted by provisions which were contained in the Finance Act 1986 and which are now to be found in the Taxes Act 1988.

Continuation of ownership of the business

The first requirement for the carrying forward of losses is the continuation of ownership when the business is transferred to the subsidiary. This will be assured if the parent company owns not less than 75 per cent of the shares in the subsidiary.[13] The subsidiary will then, after the transfer of the business to it, inherit with that business the right to set off losses relevant for the tax purposes

10 TR 588, para 5.
11 TR 588, para 6.
12 TR 588.
13 See TA 1988, s 838.

of the parent company.[14] On a subsequent sale of the shares in the subsidiary there will be no change in ownership of the business: it will still be owned by the same company which in its turn will be owned by the purchaser of the shares in the hive down subsidiary.

Restrictions on passing on losses

The efficacy of a hive down for carrying forward the losses of a company in receivership against profits of the hive down subsidiary has been considerably affected by what is now section 768 of the Taxes Act 1988. This section provides that in two specified sets of circumstances no relief shall be given under section 343 of the Taxes Act by setting a loss incurred by the parent company in an accounting period beginning before the change of ownership against any income or other profits of an accounting period ending after the change of ownership.[15] The first is where within a period of three years, there is both a change in the ownership of the company, and (either earlier or later in the three-year period or at the same time) a major change in the nature or conduct of a trade carried on by the company.[16] The second set of circumstances is where, at any time after the scale of the activities in a trade carried on by a company has become small or negligible, and before any considerable revival of the trade there is a change in the ownership of the company.[17]

On the possible application of the doctrine of *Furniss v Dawson* as an alternative to the application of section 483 of the Taxes Act 1970 (now section 768 of the Taxes Act 1988), where the disposal of the business by the receiver is said to be governed by 'sound commercial reasons' the Inland Revenue were asked for an assurance that the *Furniss v Dawson* principle would not be applied. They replied as follows:[18]

> 'This is one of the topics on which it is particularly difficult to see at present where exactly the new approach might apply, if at all. On the face of it, the new approach might have some relevance in cases where little more than the tax losses are being hived down, though even then it would be necessary to demonstrate that there was a composite transaction and the insertion of a "non-commercial" step in that transaction. However, we would not normally expect the new approach to be relevant in cases where an entire trade, or part trade, together with its related assets and liabilities, are hived down with a view to its being carried on in other hands—although of course in those circumstances TA 1970, s 483 [now TA 1988, s 768] might apply.'

This statement should be considered with the other Revenue statement referred to above.

The ambit of carry forward relief is further curtailed by provisions requiring specified assets to be set off against specified liabilities.[19] Only if the latter exceed

---

14 TA 1988, ss 343 and 344.
15 TA 1988, s 768(1).
16 TA 1988, s 768(1)(a).
17 TA 1988, s 768(1)(b).
18 TR 588 (STI 1985, Issue 39) para 9.
19 TA 1988, s 343(3) and (4).

the former will there be a transferable loss. The wide-ranging specification of assets as opposed to the restricted list of liabilities will result in many cases in there being no transferable loss.

The specified liabilities[20] comprise: liabilities which were outstanding and vested in the predecessor immediately before it ceased to carry on the trade which were not transferred to the successor, but excluding any liability representing the predecessor's share capital, share premium account, reserves or relevant loan stock,[1] except where the creditor concerned carries on a trade of lending money.[2]

The relevant assets to be brought into the equation for the purpose of computing transferred losses are: all assets not transferred to the hive down company and the consideration given by the subsidiary to the parent company in respect of the change of the company carrying on the trade.[3] The assumption by the hive down subsidiary of any liabilities of the company in receivership is not to be treated as the giving of consideration to the parent company by the hive down subsidiary.[4]

Value added tax

For the purposes of value added tax the disposal of assets forming part of the business assets is a taxable supply regardless of what consideration is received.[5] However, if the subsidiary is included in a group registration[6] any supply from one member of the group to another is disregarded.[7] Alternatively, if the business is transferred as a going concern to another person and the assets are to be used by the transferee in carrying on the same kind of business, whether or not as part of the existing business, as that carried on by the transferor in relation to that part, the supply will be treated neither as a supply of goods nor of services but will be disregarded.[8] Either of these two provisions ought to be available as a means to escape value added tax liability on a normal hive down.

ADMINISTRATORS

Introduction

An administrator is as concerned as a receiver to know what outstanding tax liabilities there are affecting the company in relation to which the administration

---

20 In the case of a hive down after 18 March 1986: see TA 1988, s 343(4).
 1 TA 1988, s 344(6). For relevant loan stock: see TA 1988, s 344(11).
 2 TA 1988, s 344(12).
 3 TA 1988, s 344(5).
 4 TA 1988, s 344(5).
 5 Value Added Tax Act 1983, Sch 2, para 5(1).
 6 VATA 1983, s 29(4).
 7 VATA 1983, s 29(1)(a).
 8 Value Added Tax (Special Provisions) Order 1981, SI 1981/1741, para 12.

order has been made. He too will wish to keep in view the accruing tax liabilities during the administration. Again the discussion which follows looks to the main taxing provisions of concern, and inevitably refers back to the tax liabilities of receivers.

Existing tax liabilities

Here again, as a general rule, an administrator will not incur any personal liability for accrued tax. Such liabilities whether in respect of taxes on income or on capital gains or in respect of value added tax (VAT) will rank as debts of the company and may be preferential debts so far as the new insolvency legislation allows them to be.

Liability to make returns

Reference has already been made to the fact that corporation tax returns have to be made by 'the proper officer'[9]. Except in rare cases where the administrator can be accounted a person acting as secretary of the company[10] the administrator will not be liable to make tax returns.

Accruing tax liabilities

Income

Revenue profits earned after the making of an administration order are profits of the company. The administrator in exercising his powers is deemed to act as the company's agent,[11] so that the company will remain liable for any relevant corporation tax chargeable on those profits. There is no provision imposing any liability on the administrator in respect of such income. On the other hand, it is provided by the Taxes Act 1988 that, subject to any exception provided for by the Corporation Tax Acts, a company shall be chargeable to corporation tax on all its profits wherever arising.[12] This form of words certainly does suggest that the liability is indeed a liability of the company itself since it specifies that the company *shall* be chargeable. Moreover, it is provided in the immediately following provision that the company is chargeable to corporation tax on profits accruing for its benefit.[13] Income from land chargeable under Schedule A therefore remains properly assessable on the company notwithstanding the appointment of an administrator since the company is the person for whose benefit the income arises and is also the person entitled to the income.[14] Income

---

9 TMA 1970, s 108(3)(a).
10 TMA 1970, s 108(3)(b).
11 IA 1986, s 14(5). He is not deemed to *be* the agent of the company.
12 TA 1988, s 8(1).
13 TA 1988, s 8(2).
14 TA 1988.

from any other investments remains income for corporation tax purposes even though an administrator has been appointed since the income likewise arises for the benefit of the company.[15]

Deduction of tax

Notwithstanding the general rule that an administrator is not usually liable for corporation tax on income or capital gains arising during the administration, the administrator must account to the Revenue for tax which he actually deducts from payments made by him. A list of the main provisions requiring deduction of tax appears elsewhere in this book.[16]

Capital gains

Where any chargeable gain arises on the sale of property by the administrator, that gain will be treated as having been made by the company and the administrator will not be personally liable for the tax on that gain.[17]

Value added tax

The first point to note is that the registration of the company for the purposes of value added tax is in no way disturbed by the appointment of an administrator. The administrator who in exercising his powers is deemed to act as agent of the company does not have to register separately.

On his appointment the current VAT accounting period is treated as having come to an end on the day immediately preceding his appointment[18] and a return made on behalf of the company must be furnished in respect of that period not later than the last day of the month next following the end of that period.[19] The next period will start on the following day and end (and all subsequent periods will begin and end) on the dates determined under regulation 58(1).[20] The Commissioners may treat the administrator as carrying on the business of the company and so as a taxable person and, if they do so, the Act and Regulations apply as if he were a taxable person.[1] Where any company subject to any requirements under the Part of the Regulations dealing with accounting and payment becomes incapacitated and control of its assets passes to an administrator such administrator must, if the Commissioners so require and so long as he has such control, comply with those requirements.[2] In relation to any requirement to pay

---

15 TA 1988.
16 See at p 633 above.
17 See *Re Mesco Properties Ltd* [1980] 1 All ER 117, [1980] 1 WLR 96, CA discussed at p 507 supra.
18 VAT Regulations 1995, regs 25(3)(a) and 30.
19 VAT Regulations 1995, regs 25(3)(b) and 30.
20 VAT Regulations 1995, regs 25(3)(c) and 30.
 1 VAT Regulations 1995, reg 9.
 2 VAT Regulations 1995, reg 30.

tax, that is only to apply to the administrator to the extent of the assets of the company over which he has control.[3]

Failure on the part of an administrator to make a return or the making of an incomplete or incorrect return will be treated as a failure on the part of the company.[4] Notification to an administrator will be treated as notification to the company.[5]

Hive downs

The rules relating to hive downs by a receiver apply equally to hive downs by an administrator and reference should be made to the discussion of the receiver's tax liabilities on hive downs earlier in this chapter.[6]

3 VAT Regulations 1995.
4 Value Added Tax Act 1995, s 73(5).
5 VATA 1995, s 73(10).
6 See at p 636 above.

Bibliography

Anderson, H *Administrators: Part II of the Insolvency Act 1986* (1987)

Ashburner, W *Mortgages* (2nd edn, 1911)

Bennet, W H *A Practical Treatise on the Appointment, Office and Duties of a Receiver in the High Court of Chancery* (1849) (Lincoln's Inn)

Bennett, F *Receiverships* (1985) Carswell

Bertram, D *Tax Consequences of Receivership and Liquidation* (1982) Butterworths

Blackett Ord, M *Partnership* (1997)

Blanchard, P and Gedye M *The Law of Company Receiverships in Australia and New Zealand* (2nd edn, 1994) Butterworths Australia

Bowers, J *Transfers of Undertakings* (2000) looseleaf

Bramwell, H *Conveyancing in Hong Kong* (1981) Butterworths

Buckley *The Companies Act* (15th edn, 2000) Butterworths, looseleaf

Cababé, M *Attachment of Debts and Equitable Execution* (2nd edn, 1888)

Clark, R E *Treatise on the Law and Practice of Receivers* (3rd edn) 4 Vols, Cincinnati (Bodleian Library, Oxford)

Coote, R H *Mortgages* (9th edn, 1927)

Daniell, E R *Chancery Practice* (8th edn, 1914)

Daniell, E R *Chancery Forms* (7th edn, 1932)

Davies, P and Freedland, M *Transfers of Employment* (1982)

Doyle, L *Administrative Receivers* (1995)

Doyle, L *Insolvency Litigation* (1997)

Dunlop, C R B *Creditor-Debtor Law in Canada* (1981) (Carswell)

Edwards, C J *Law of Execution* (1888)

Fisher, W R and Lightwood, J M *Law of Mortgage* (10th edn, 1988), supplement (1994)

Fletcher, I *Insolvency in Private International Law* (1999) OUP

Fletcher, I M, Higham, J I and Trower, W *Law and Practice Corporate Administration* (1994)

Fletcher *Encyclopaedia on Corporations: Receivers* (Squire Law Library, Cambridge)

Francis, E A *Mortgages and Securities* (3rd edn, 1986)

Goode, R M *Legal Problems of Credit and Security* (2nd edn, 1988)

Goode, R M *Proprietary Rights and Insolvency in Sales Transactions* (2nd edn, 1989)

Goode, R M *Principles of Corporate Insolvency Law* (2nd edn, 1997)

Gore Brown, *Companies* (44th edn, 1986), looseleaf

Gough, W J *Company Charges* (2nd edn, 1996)

Gower, L C B *Modern Company Law* (6th edn, 1997)

Greene, J H and Fletcher, I M *Law and Practice of Receivership in Scotland* (1987) Butterworths

Heywood, N A and Massey, A S *Court of Protection Practice* (12 edn, 1991)

Higgins, P G P and Fletcher, K L *Law of Partnership* (4th edn, 1995)

High, J A *A Treatise on the Law of Receivers* (4th edn, 1910) Chicago (Bodleian Library, Oxford)

Hooper, A C *Receivers for Debenture-Holders appointed without the Aid of a Court* (1993)

Huston *The Enforcement of Decrees in Equity* (1915)

Keane, R Judge *Company Law in Ireland* (1988) Butterworths

Kerr, W W *Receivers and Administrators* (17th edn, 1989)

Lange, P and Hartwig, H J *Law and Practice of Administrative Receivership and Associated Remedies* (1989)

Lewin, T *Trusts* (16th edn, 1964)

Lightman, G and Moss, G *Law of Receivers of Companies* (2nd edn, 1994)

Lindley and Banks on *Partnerships* (17th edn, 1995)

Lingard, J R *Bank Security Documents* (3rd edn, 1993)

Lyle, J *A Handbook for Receivers* (1878)

McCormack, G *Proprietary Claims in Insolvency* (1996)

McCormack, G *Reservation of Title* (1995)

McMullen, J *Business Tranfers and Employee Rights* (1987) Butterworths

McPherson, B H *Law of Company Liquidation* (4th edn, 1999) Law Book Company of Australia

Meagher, R S, Gummow, W H C and Lehane, S R F *Equity: Doctrines and Remedies* (3rd edn, 1994)

Milman, D and Durrant, C *Corporate Insolvency Law and Practice* (2nd edn, 1994)

Milman, D and Rushworth, J *Receivers and Receiverships* (1987)

Molesworth, R *Receivers in Chancery in Ireland* (1838)

O'Donovan, J *Company Receivers and Managers* (2nd edn) Law Book Company of Australia, looseleaf.

Palmer, Sir F P *Company Law* (24th edn) looseleaf

Parris, J *Effective Retention of Title Clauses* (1986)

Pettit, P H *Equity and the Law of Trusts* (8th edn, 1997)

Reilly, J F *Practice and the High Court of Chancery in Ireland in Summary Petition Matters* (1855)

Riviere, E *Law Relating to Receivers and Managers* (1912)

Samwell, S *Corporate Receiverships – a practical approach* (2nd edn, 1988)

Sealy, L S and Milman, D *Annotated Guide to the 1986 Insolvency Legislation* (5th edn, 1999)

Seton, Sir H W *Judgements and Orders* (7th edn, 1912)

Smart, P *Cross-Border Insolvency* (2nd edn, 1998)

Smith, W *Treatise on the Duties and Office of a Receiver under the High Court of Chancery in Ireland* (1836) Dublin (Lincoln's Inn)

Stewart, G *Administrative Receivers and Administrators* (1987)

Suhendran S bin A, Lim, T H and Chew, E *Corporate Receivership, The Law and Practice in Malaysia and Singapore* (1996)

Totty, P and Moss, G *Insolvency Law* (looseleaf)

Woodroffe, J G *The Law Relating to Receivers and Managers in British India* (Tagore Law Lecture) Calcutta 1963 (Bodleian Library, Oxford)

Woon, W and Hicks, A *The Companies Act of Singapore. An Annotation*

Index